150 Careers
in the
Health Care Field
3rd Edition

150 Careers in the Health Care Field
3rd Edition

Compiled By
Janice Eldredge

Darrell Buono
Managing Editor

U.S. Directory Service™
Reed Reference Publishing

CONTENTS

PREFACE

This handbook is a concise, yet factual reference source for careers in allied health. It is written primarily as a counseling guide for high school students but may also be used by community college students, guidance counselors, health care recruiters, by persons who have been out of the work force for a period of time and wish to return, and for those who want to change careers. The discussion of each allied health career or occupational title in this handbook includes all or more of the following descriptions: job functions and responsibilities, work locations, training prerequisites and requirements, certification procedures, if applicable, recommended high school courses, financial aid information, potential salaries, and a list of community colleges, universities, vocational-technical schools, and other educational institutions that provide accredited training programs.

Compiled with reliable data obtained from medical and allied health associations and societies and from government publications, the information in this handbook is as current and as accurate as possible; however, because of the rapidly changing nature of scientific developments in medicine, the continued accreditation of new training programs, and the inflationary structure of wages, the publishers of the handbook cannot assume responsibility or liability for unintentional errors or omissions.

INTRODUCTION

This handbook describes the occupations and training of allied health personnel including administrators, assistants, auxiliary workers, technicians, technologists, and therapists. The handbook also includes- as its major feature- the listing of accredited training programs for most allied health occupations.

The student interested in a health-related career who finds it impossible or undesirable to meet the high costs and standards of education required by medical and dental schools should investigate a career in allied health. These careers represent excellent job opportunities in the ever-expanding fields of health care services and medical research and provide many of the same satisfactions, challenges, and benefits that are experienced by physicians, dentists, veterinarians, chiropractors, podiatrists, optometrists, pharmacists, and other professional medical practitioners- but with much less expensive, shorter, and less rigorous training requirements.

The reason for the present expansion in health services, which is causing a situation of demand exceeding supply in allied health personnel, is the increased demand for health care by the growing national population. People are living longer, and they have an increasing ability to pay for their health care, both because of higher personal incomes and because of the growth of public and private health insurance plans. Medical research is increasing the need for skilled allied health personnel, too, as it constantly develops new and specialized techniques and procedures for diagnosing, treating, and preventing diseases, illnesses, and injuries.

Though certain careers in allied health have been traditionally limited to either men or women in the past, the trend is now changing. Both men and women have equal opportunities for admittance into all training programs, for receiving financial aid, and for job placement.

There are certain personal qualifications all health workers must possess including good health, emotional stability, and an ability and desire to work with and help the sick and the injured. Health care personnel must also be accurate,thorough, responsible, sympathetic, versatile, and possess a willingness to keep abreast of new medical procedures and technical equipment. They must have an interest and aptitude for biological and physical sciences, and some, especially technologists and technicians, must be able to operate complicated electronic equipment and delicate instrumentation.

Many occupations in allied health, especially those of assistants or aides who work for physicians in their private practices, are excellent opportunities for persons who wish to work part-time in a health-related career.

According to the Bureau of Labor Statistics, more than eight million people work in health-related occupations in the United States, and projected employment in this industry is expected to reach over eleven million by the 2005. The majority of health care workers are employed in hospitals while the remainder are employed by clinics, laboratories, nursing homes, research institutes, public health services, mental health facilities, private medical practices, and pharmaceutical companies. Health related personnel are also employed by industry to administer basic health care and emergency first aid to workers,   to inspect equipment and assure that safety measures are followed and to act as technical advisors and representatives in the manufacturing and marketing of medical equipment and supplies.

For the person planning a career in allied health, the education and training he or she receives is of extreme significance when applying for good, well-paying jobs. Educational requirements vary as much as the range of careers in allied health, and the selection of an appropriate training program is a major decision that will later influence job placement opportunities.

Educational requirements in allied health vary from one-to-two-months of on-the-job training to graduation from a master's degree program. This handbook has limited its selection of health-related careers to those that require a maximum of a bachelor's degree as their educational requirement; that is, with practically all of the careers described herein a student can be in the work force earning a reasonably good salary within one-to-four years after graduation from high school. However, a few careers listed require further education.

Most allied health occupations at the professional level, such as those of dietitian, physical therapist, and medical record administrator, require bachelor's degrees to obtain employment in all but supervising, teaching, and research positions where a master's degree is needed. In most paraprofessional occupations, that is, those carried out by technologists, technicians, and assistants, graduation with an associate degree or certificate awarded by a community (junior) college or vocational-technical school is required. Aides and auxiliary workers who occupy entry-level positions are usually trained on-the-job in hospitals and in other health services facilities. It should be noted that the U.S. Armed Forces offer training in many health career occupations, and persons interested in combining a career in the military and in health care should contact their local recruiting office.

The lists of educational programs contained in this handbook are comprised, for the most part, solely of programs that are accredited by their respective professional associations or societies or by the Committee on Allied Health Education and Accreditation of the American Medical Association. Graduates from accredited programs have much better chances of being hired for the jobs they desire, especially as some employers will not hire graduates of non-accredited programs. Graduation from an accredited program is also often a major criterion for certification, or registration, with an occupation's respective professional health association.

In a few cases a school list will also include programs that are not accredited but have their accreditation pending.   Where there are no accreditation procedures available for an an occupation's respective professional health association.

In a few cases a school list will also include programs that are not accredited but have their accreditation pending. Where there are no accreditation procedures available for an occupation, all known schools offering programs are listed.

For some careers, such as for aides and auxiliary workers, there are training programs offered by hospitals, however the trend is for most allied health workers to obtain formal training in their respective occupation. It is beyond the scope of this handbook to list all hospital training programs. Employers often prefer graduates of universities, colleges, or vocational-technical schools because of their more well-rounded education that includes both classroom and clinical experience. Many hospital teaching programs are currently becoming associated with universities and colleges and thus providing their students with a more academic education. Hospital training programs, however, usually charge little or no tuition and in some cases even pay a minimal salary during training. For further information, persons interested in hospital training programs in a specific occupation, should contact their local hospital.

The reader is reminded that the listing of non-hospital educational programs are as current and accurate as possible. Omissions may occur, however, as new programs are constantly being accredited by their respective professional associations.

Persons interested in applying to a specific program should contact the school as early as possible. Considerable care should be taken in selecting a program, and information should be obtained on the following:

> . entrance prerequisites
> . length of program
> . accreditation qualifications
> . type of degree or certificate offered
> . tuition and other costs
> . types of employment obtained by recent graduates
> . length of time the program has been operating
> . types of scholarships and financial aid
> . instructional facilities
> . faculty qualifications

The potential student should apply to as many schools as reasonable to compare these data in different programs.

Where available, certification or registration by a professional health association is definitely beneficial to the allied health worker. Certification usually requires graduation from an accredited training program, successful completion of written or clinical examinations, and some work experience. The benefits of certification, however, include proof to future employers of the health worker's qualification, accessibility to a greater range of jobs, higher salaries, and greater potential for job advancement.

The data in the handbook on salaries are at best broad indicators of average incomes in recent years. The data are by no means completely accurate because salaries are affected by individual duties and responsibilities of each particular job, geographic location of employer, local hiring and salary policies, amount and quality of training and work experience, and fluctuating rates of inflation. In general, salaries are usually higher in industry than in government; they are usually higher in urban areas than in rural areas; and they are usually higher on the East and West coasts than in the rest of the country.

Finally, although training and experience are probably the most important factors in determining individual salaries, the exact amount of any salary is often negotiable.

Most hospital employees work a 36-40 hour week that often includes working on Saturdays and Sundays. Overtime is also sometimes required. Fringe benefits for hospital employees usually include paid vacations, health insurance, and sick leave. Some hospitals even provide free education courses, pension programs, uniforms, and salaries for-on-the-job training. Work surroundings in hospitals and in other health care facilities are usually bright, clean, and comfortable. But even though salaries, fringe benefits, and working conditions are favorable, the most satisfying reward for most health care workers is their own personal gratification of being able to provide humanitarian services to people and to relieve pain and suffering.

For the student interested in a career in allied health the handbook mentions recommended courses he or she should take while in high school. Good high school grades are important, especially in certain occupations where there is competition for the relatively few training facilities. In general, high school students should study biology, health, chemistry, physics, mathematics, and English. Being able to communicate effectively is also very important in health services, and the student should maximize his or her writing and speaking skills. A second language is often beneficial in applying for certain jobs in some areas of the country.

To develop an interest and prepare for a career in allied health, students should talk with their school guidance counselors and science teachers or with admissions counselors in schools of allied health. Students should also visit hospitals and other health facilities and talk with their respective personnel directors; or they should write to their state health departments to inquire about that state's particular health care needs and about career and training opportunities in their city or town. Students interested in locating hospitals in their area should refer to the Hospital Phone Book, published by Reed Reference Publishing, 121 Chanlon Road, New Providence, New Jersey 07974, in becoming a volunteer should contact their local Red Cross Officer; the American Health care Association 1201 "L" Street, N.W., Washington, D.C. 20005, the American Society of Directors of Volunteer Services, 840 North Lake Shore Drive, Chicago, Illinois 60611, or the Director of Volunteer Services of their local health care facility. Sometimes preference for admission into training programs is given to those who have been volunteers while in high school.

Another source of acquiring experience in the health field while still in high school is by enrolling in cooperative health occupations, a work-study program offered by many high schools in which students receive part-time, on-the-job training and salaries in a health facility as part of their regular high school education.

A chapter on nursing is included in this handbook, but because of its scope, specific information on nursing careers is condensed. Those students interested in a career in nursing, should contact the American Nurses Association, P.O. Box 2244 Waldorf, Maryland 20602, the National League for Nursing, 350 Hudson Street, 4th Fl., New York, New York 10014, or any of the above mentioned sources of health career information.

Membership in student health care organizations is also a valuable way to learn about health careers.

Secondary sources used in the compilation of this edition of 150 Careers in Health care are included in the Further Reading section at the end of the volume. Students wishing to explore further a given field of work may find these sources of value.

✚ AIDS COUNSELING

AIDS, which stands for Acquired Immunodeficiency Syndrome, is a disease caused by a virus that attacks the immune system and damages the body's ability to fight other diseases. Without a functioning immune system, the body becomes vulnerable to such life-threatening illnesses as cancer, pneumonia, and meningitis. There is presently no cure for AIDS, and no vaccine to prevent it. The spread of this life-threatening disease is rapidly growing in the United States. According to cumulative estimates by the Public Health Service, from 1981 to the end of 1994, 415,000 to 535,000 AIDS cases will have been diagnosed in the United States. By the end of 1994, 320,000 to 385,000 of these people are expected to have died from the disease. As AIDS impacts more strongly on our society, the need for responsible, caring, and sensitive AIDS-related healthcare workers is greater than ever. As a result, AIDS-related healthcare professions are rapidly growing and include such fields as health education (community health educators, school health educators, health educators in business and industry, and clinical health educators); homemaker-home health aide services (persons who provide homemaking and personal services, instructions, emotional support, and some minimal health care to clients in their own homes); medical laboratory (medical technologists, medical laboratory technicians, and specialists in blood bank technology); mental health (social workers and psychologists); nursing (community health nurses, public health nurses, nurse consultants, nurse practitioners, pediatric nurses, private duty nurses, respiratory therapy nurses, nursing aides, orderlies, RNs, and LPNs); as well as the vast field of public health. For more information on these careers, refer to their respective chapters elsewhere in this book. Two other AIDS-related careers are the *AIDS counselor* and the *AIDS information specialist*. Their job responsibilities may vary from state to state and amongst employers, but the *AIDS counselor* generally provides information, assistance, and support to AIDS sufferers, their family members, friends, and partners. The *AIDS Information Specialist* also provides information, as well as referrals.

1

AIDS Counselor

The *AIDS counselor* provides support to AIDS sufferers, their family, friends, and partners. He or she answers questions and provides information on the disease and its prevention. The AIDS counselor may also provide support through letters and phone calls, develop AIDS related workshops, and perform administrative duties. People suffering from AIDS may be depressed or under physical and emotional stress. They may also experience feelings of anger and guilt. The AIDS counselor must always show sensitivity, empathy, and objectivity, even though job responsibilities may seem emotionally draining and stressful at times.

AIDS counseling may be divided into a variety of specialties. The *grief counselor* counsels family, friends, and partners of AIDS victims through individual or family counseling sessions. He or she may set up and supervise support and discussion groups for those who have lost family members, friends and partners to AIDS. The grief counselor may also make referrals to other groups with similar objectives. The *safer sex counselor* and the *substance abuse counselor* may provide instruction and information to high-risk groups, make presentations at schools, and speak to specific groups and the general public. The *test counselor* who is employed at an HIV testing center, answers questions and explains test results. He or she may also provide advice and counseling, and make referrals to AIDS related organizations.

AIDS counselors are employed by hospitals, hospices, churches, HIV testing centers, public health clinics, mental health clinics, Planned Parenthood centers, American Red Cross offices, and numerous AIDS service organizations.

Educational requirements for the AIDS counselor vary depending upon the place of employment. On-the-job training with follow-up sessions is sometimes offered. While experience gained through volunteer work may also be helpful, a college degree in Mental Health or Social Work is the usual basic requirement and a Master's degree may be required in some instances. Educational preparation includes the study of counseling, sociology, psychology, human development, and mental health. Students may also participate in supervised internships outside of the classroom.

Recommended high school courses for the student interested in pursuing a career in AIDS counseling include health, sociology, psychology, and biology.

Salaries for the AIDS counselor vary widely depending upon experience, location, funding, and place of employment, but are generally comparable to those of social workers.

For more information on a career as an AIDS counselor, contact AIDS service organizations, hospitals, or the American Red Cross AIDS Coordinator in your area.

SOURCES:

American Counseling Association
Centers for Disease Control National AIDS Information Clearinghouse

---

AIDS Information Specialist

The position of *AIDS information specialist* is not a defined one. Job duties and responsibilities may vary from state to state and amongst employers. The AIDS information specialist primarily handles telephone calls and should therefore have good communications and listening skills. He or she may make local and national referrals for other AIDS service organizations or any other resources that a caller might need. The AIDS information specialist answers general questions and offers information on AIDS and HIV prevention and the disease process. He or she may explain the HIV testing process and the test results. Although the AIDS information specialist must be aware of the technical aspects of AIDS, he or she cannot answer specific medical or technical questions. The AIDS information specialist may also mail brochures and written information to callers.

AIDS information specialists are employed with state HIV and AIDS Prevention Coordinators, the American Red Cross, state and local health departments, and various AIDS service organizations.

Training requirements for the AIDS information specialist vary depending upon the place of employment. Some employers may require a two to four week training course with monthly in-service training to keep updated on new AIDS-related information. Some may require previous experience gained through volunteer work.

Recommended high school courses for students interested in becoming an AIDS information specialist include biology, health, and psychology.

As with the AIDS counselor, salaries for the AIDS information specialist vary widely depending upon experience, location, funding, and place of employment.

For more information on AIDS information specialists or other AIDS-related careers, interested individuals should contact AIDS-related organizations in their area. Information on these local organizations can be obtained from the following list of state HIV Prevention Program Coordinators.

SOURCE:

Centers for Disease Control National AIDS Information Clearinghouse

State HIV Prevention Program Coordinators

ALABAMA

Alabama Department of Public Health
Division of Disease Control
Sexually Transmitted Disease Branch
434 Monroe Street
Montgomery, Alabama 36130-1701

ALASKA

Alaska Department of Health & Social
  Services
Division of Public Health
Section of Epidemiology
AIDS/STD Program
3601 C Street, Suite 576
Anchorage, Alaska 99503-0249

ARIZONA

Arizona Department of Health Services
Division of Disease Prevention
Offie of HIV/AIDS Services
3008 North Third Street, Room 203
Phoenix, Arizona 85012

ARKANSAS

Arkansas Department of Health
Sexually Transmitted Diseases Division
AIDS Prevention Program
4815 West Markham
Little Rock, Arkansas 72205-3867

CALIFORNIA

Los Angeles County Department of
  Health Services
AIDS Programs
600 South Commonwealth
Los Angeles, California 90005

California Department of Health
  Services

Office of AIDS
830 S Street
Sacramento, California 94234

CONNECTICUT

Connecticut Department of Health
  Services
AIDS Program
150 Washington Street
Hartford, Connecticut 06106

DELAWARE

Delaware Department of Health and
  Social Services
Division of Public Health
Health Monitoring & Program
  Consultation
3000 Newport Gap Pike
Dover, Delaware 19901

DISTRICT OF COLUMBIA

District of Columbia Commission of
  Public Health
Office of AIDS Administration
1660 L Street NW
Washington, DC 20036

GEORGIA

Georgia Department of Human
  Resources
Division of Public Health
Communicable Disease Branch
AIDS Section
878 Peachtree Street NE
Atlanta, Georgia 30309

HAWAII

Hawaii Department of Health
Communicable Disease Division
AIDS and Sexually Transmitted Diseases
Control Branch
3627 Kilauea Avenue, Suite 305
Honolulu, Hawaii 96816

IDAHO

Idaho Department of Health and Welfare
Division of Health
Bureau of Preventive Medicine
AIDS Program
450 West State Street
Boise, Idaho 83720

ILLINOIS

Chicago Department of Health
50 West Washington
Chicago, Illinois 60602

Illinois Department of Public Health
Division of Infectious Diseases
AIDS Activity Section
111 North Canal Street
Chicago, Illinois 60601

KANSAS

Kansas Department of Health and
Environment
Bureau of Disease Control
AIDS Section
Mills Building, Suite 605
109 SW Ninth Street
Topeka, Kansas 66612-1271

LOUISIANA

Louisiana Department of Health and
Hospitals
Office of Public Health
Louisiana AIDS Prevention &
Surveillance Program
325 Loyola Avenue
New Orleans, Louisiana 70112

MAINE

Maine Department of Human Services
Division of Disease Control
AIDS Prevention Grant Project
State House Sta.
157 Capitol Street
Augusta, Maine 04333

MASSACHUSETTS

Massachusetts Department of Public
Health
150 Tremont Street
Boston, Massachusetts 02111

MICHIGAN

Michigan Department of Public Health
Bureau of Infectious Disease Control
HIV/AIDS Prevention and Intervention
Section
3423 North Logan
Lansing, Michigan 48909

MINNESOTA

Minnesota Department of Health
Division of Disease Prevention and
Control
AIDS/STD Prevention Services Section
717 SE Delaware Street
Minneapolis, Minnesota 55440

MISSISSIPPI

Mississippi Department of Public Health
AIDS/HIV Prevention Program
2423 North State Street
Jackson, Mississippi 39215-1700

MISSOURI

Missouri Department of Health
Bureau of AIDS Prevention
1730 East Elm
Jefferson City, Missouri 65102

MONTANA

Montana Department of Health &
  Environmental Sciences
Preventive Health Services Bureau
AIDS/STD Program
1400 Broadway
Helena, Montana 59620

NEVADA

Nevada Department of Human
  Resources
Health Program Section
Division of Sexually Transmitted
  Diseases/HIV
505 East King Street
Carson City, Nevada 89710

NEW HAMPSHIRE

New Hampshire Department of Health
  & Human Services
Division of Public Health Services
HIV/AIDS Program
Health and Welfare Building
Six Hazen Drive
Concord, New Hamshire 03301

NEW JERSEY

New Jersey Department of Health
Division of AIDS Prevention & Control
363 West State Street
Trenton, New Jersey 08625-0363

NEW MEXICO

New Mexico Health Department
Public Health Division
HIV/AIDS/STD Prevention & Services
  Bureau
1190 St. Francis Drive
Santa Fe, New Mexico 87502

NEW YORK

New York Department of Health
Office of Public Health
AIDS Institute
Empire State Plz.
Albany, New York 12237-0684

New York City Department of Health
Division of AIDS Program Services
AIDS Program Services Intervention
125 Worth Street
New York, New York 10013

NORTH CAROLINA

North Carolina Department of
  Environment
Health and Natural Resources
Communicable Disease Control Section
HIV/STD Control Branch
225 North McDowell Street
Raleigh, North Carolina 27611-7687

OHIO

Ohio Department of Health
Division of Preventive Medicine
AIDS Unit
246 North High Street
Columbus, Ohio 43266-0588

OKLAHOMA

Oklahoma Department of Health
AIDS Division
1000 NE Tenth Street
Oklahoma City, Oklahoma 73152

OREGON

Oregon Department of Human Resources
Health Division
HIV Program
800 NE Oregon Street, Suite 745
Portland, Oregon 97232-2109

PENNSYLVANIA

Pennsylvania Department of Health
Bureau of HIV/AIDS
Forester & Commonwealth Avenue
Harrisburg, Pennsylvania 17120

Philadelphia Department of Public
  Health
AIDS Program
500 South Broad Street
Philadelphia, Pennsylvania 19146

RHODE ISLAND

Rhode Island Department of Health
Division of Disease Control
Office of AIDS/STD
Three Capitol Hill
Providence, Rhode Island 02908-5097

SOUTH CAROLINA

South Carolina Dept. of Health &
  Environmental Control
Bureau of Preventive Health Services
HIV/AIDS Division
AIDS Prevention Program
2600 Bull Street
Columbia, South Carolina 29201

TENNESSEE

Tennessee Department of Health
AIDS Program
Cordell Hull Building
Nashville, Tennessee 37247-4947

TEXAS

Texas Department of Health
Bureau of HIV & Sexually Transmitted
  Disease Control
HIV Division
1100 West 49th Street
Austin, Texas 78756-3199

Houston Department of Health &
  Human Services
Bureau of HIV Prevention
8000 North Stadium Drive
Houston, Texas 77054

UTAH

Utah Department of Health
Division of Community Health Services
Bureau of HIV/AIDS Prevention &
  Control
288 North 1460 West
Salt Lake City, Utah 84116-0660

VERMONT

Vermont Department of Health
Division of Epidemiology
AIDS Program
108 Cherry Street
Burlington, Vermont 05401

VIRGINIA

Virginia Department of Health
Division of Communicable Disease
  Control
Sexually Transmitted Disease/AIDS
  Control Program
109 Governor Street
Richmond, Virginia 23219

WASHINGTON

Washington Department of Health
Division of HIV/AIDS & STDs
HIV/AIDS Program
Airdustrial Park, Building 9
Olympia, Washington 98504

WEST VIRGINIA

West Virginia Dept. of Health & Human
  Resources
Office of Epidemiology & Health
  Promotion
Division of Surveillance & Disease
  Control
AIDS Program
1422 Washington Street, E.
Charleston, West Virginia 25301

WISCONSIN

Wisconsin Dept. of Health & Social
  Services
Division of Health
AIDS/HIV Program
1414 East Washington
Madison, Wisconsin 53073-3044

WYOMING

Wyoming Dept. of Health & Social
  Services
Division of Health & Medical Services
Preventive Medicine Services
AIDS Prevention Program
Hathaway Building
Cheyenne, Wyoming 82002-0710

✚ ANIMAL TECHNOLOGY

Animal technology is the allied health profession concerned with providing qualified technical support to the care, use, production, and husbandry of animals - both in animal health and in research. In animal health the veterinarian, a doctor of veterinary medicine, treats sick and injured animals and protects human health by preventing and controlling the spread of diseases transmissible from animals to humans. The assistance given by the animal technology team provides the veterinarian with more time to spend with his or her patients and clients. In research, conducted in clinical and research laboratories located in pharmaceutical companies, public health organizations, universities, hospitals, research institutions, and zoos, animals are essential for training surgeons and for testing the efficiency of drugs and numerous diagnostic, surgical and medical procedures. Scientists or senior technologists in the laboratory rely on the animal technology staff to assist them in the care and feeding of laboratory animals and in performing routine laboratory tests. Two careers in animal technology are those of the *animal technician* and *animal caretaker*.

Animal Technician

Also known as an *animal health technician* or as a *veterinary technician*, the animal technician is knowledgeable in animal care and handling and in routine laboratory and clinical procedures. The technician acts primarily as an assistant to veterinarians, biological research workers, and other scientists.

In veterinary practices the animal technician is supervised by the veterinarian and performs most of the same duties except those involving diagnosis, prescription, and surgery. The animal technician records cases; performs laboratory tests; prepares patients, instruments, equipment and medication for surgery; collects specimens; assists in some medical procedures; dresses wounds; exposes and develops X-rays; and consults with animal owners.

In clinical and research laboratories the animal technician, often called a *laboratory animal technician*, is supervised by a scientist, or by a senior research or medical technologist, and may perform duties such as keeping records, performing laboratory procedures, maintaining equipment, and managing the business aspects of the animal laboratory. He or she may also be responsible for the caging, safety, basic health, sanitation and nutrition of the animals.

Most educational programs in animal technology are offered by community and junior colleges, are two years in length, and award associate degrees. There are a few four-year bachelor's degree programs also. Many veterinarians in private practice also conduct additional on-the-job training.

For animal technicians who are eligible and who have completed the academic and/or experience requirements, certification examinations are available from the Laboratory Animal Technician Certification Board, sponsored by the American Association for Laboratory Animal Science. Many states presently require that practicing animal technicians be registered or certified. Certification requirements for animal technicians include successfully passing the certification examination, recommendation by supervisors and (1) high school diploma or equivalent, plus three years full time work as an animal technician in a laboratory animal facility with experience in animal care and use; or (2) graduation from an accredited two year program in animal technology, plus one year full time work in a laboratory animal facility.

According to the 1989 American Veterinary Medical Association survey of veterinary programs, average starting salaries for animal technicians ranged from $10,372 to $15,784 per year. Average salaries for experienced graduates of accredited animal technology programs ranged from $11,992 to $24,339 per year.

For more information on a career in animal technology write to the American Veterinary Medical Association, 1931 North Meacham Road, Suite 100, Schaumburg, Illinois 60173-4360.

Following is a list of educational programs in animal technology, accredited by the American Veterinary Medical Association Committee on Veterinary Technician Education and Activities. Two year programs are listed as well as a few that offer a four-year bachelor's degree. Four year programs are marked by an asterisk (*). Refer to the key below for each program's accreditation status.

KEY:

(1) Full accreditation
(2) Provisional or probational accreditation

SOURCES:

American Veterinary Medical Association
Institute of Laboratory Animal Resources
Occupational Outlook Handbook

Animal Technician Programs

ALABAMA

Veterinary Technology Program (1)
Snead State Junior College
Boaz, Alabama 35957

CALIFORNIA

Animal Health Technology Program (1)
Cosumnes River College
8401 Center Parkway
Sacramento, California 95823

Animal Health Technology Program (1)
Foothill College
12345 El Monte Road
Los Altos Hills, California 94022

Animal Health Technology Program (1)
Hartnell College
156 Homestead Avenue
Salinas, California 93901

Animal Health Technology Program (1)
Mt. San Antonio College
1100 North Grand Avenue
Walnut, California 91789

Animal Health Technology Program (1)
San Diego Mesa College
7250 Mesa college Drive
San Diego, California 92111

Animal Health Technology Program (1)
Yuba College
2088 North Beale Road
Marysville, California 95901

COLORADO

Veterinary Technology Program (1)
Colorado Mountain College
Spring Valley Campus
3000 Colorado Road 114
Glenwood Springs, Colorado 81601

Animal Technology Program (1)
Bel-Rea Institute of Animal Technology
1681 South Dayton Street
Denver, Colorado 80231

CONNECTICUT

Veterinary Technology Program (1,*)
Quinnipiac College
Mt. Carmel Avenue
Hamden, Connecticut 06518

FLORIDA

Veterinary Technology Program (1)
St. Petersburg Junior College
Box 13489
St. Petersburg, Florida 33733

GEORGIA

Veterinary Technology Program (2)
Fort Valley State College
Fort Valley, Georgia 31030

ILLINOIS

Veterinary Technology Program (1)
Parkland College
2400 West Bradley Avenue
Champaign, Illinois 61821

INDIANA

Veterinary Technology Program (1)
Purdue University
School of Veterinary Medicine
West Lafayette, Indiana 47907

IOWA

Animal Technician Program (2)
Kirkwood Community College
6301 Kirkwood Boulevard SW
Cedar Rapids, Iowa 52406

KANSAS

Veterinary Technology Program (1)
Colby Community College
1255 South Range
Colby, Kansas 67701

KENTUCKY

Veterinary Technology Program (1)
Morehead State University
Box 995
Morehead, Kentucky 40351

Animal Health Technology
 Program   (1,*)
Murray State University
Department of Agriculture
Murray, Kentucky 42071

LOUISIANA

Veterinary Technology Program (1)
Northwestern State University of
 Louisiana
Department of Life Sciences
Natchitoches, Louisiana 71497

MAINE

Animal Medical Technology
 Program   (1)
University of Maine
Department of Animal & Veterinary
 Sciences
Orono, Maine 04473

MARYLAND

Veterinary Technology Program (1)
Essex Community College
7201 Rossville Boulevard
Baltimore, Maryland 21237

Veterinary Technology Program (2)
Essex Community College
Walter Reed Army Institute of Research
7201 Rossville Boulevard
Baltimore, Maryland 21237

MASSACHUSETTS

Veterinary Technician Program (1)
Becker College
3 Paxton Street
Leicester, Massachusetts 01524

Veterinary & Animal Science Career
 Program (2)
Holyoke Community College
303 Homestead Avenue
Holyoke, Massachusetts 01040-1099

Veterinary Technician Program (1,*)
Mount Ida College
777 Dedham Street
Newton Centre, Massachusetts 02192

MICHIGAN

Veterinary Technician Program (1)
Macomb Community College
Center Campus
44575 Garfield Road
Mt. Clemens, Michigan 48044

Veterinary Technology Program (1)
Michigan State University
College of Veterinary Medicine
East Lansing, Michigan 48823

Veterinary Technology Program (1)
Wayne County Community College
c/o Wayne State University
Dept. of Laboratory Animal Resources
540 East Canfield
Detroit, Michigan 48201

MINNESOTA

Veterinary Technician Program (1)
Medical Institute of Minnesota
5503 Green Valley Drive
Bloomington, Minnesota 55437

Veterinary Technology Program (1)
University of Minnesota
1000 University Drive SW
Waseca, Minnesota 56093

MISSISSIPPI

Veterinary Technology Program (2)
Hinds Community College
P.O. Box 10461
Raymond, Mississippi

MISSOURI

Veterinary Technology Program (2)
Jefferson College
Hillsboro, Missouri 63050

Veterinary Technology Program (1)
Maple Woods Community College
2601 NE Barry Road
Kansas City, Missouri 64156

NEBRASKA

Veterinary Technology Program (1)
Nebraska College of Technical
  Agriculture
Curtis, Nebraska 69025

Veterinary Technician Program (2)
Omaha College of Health Careers
1052 Park Avenue
Omaha, Nebraska 68105

NEW JERSEY

Animal Science Technology Program (1)
Camden County College
P.O. Box 200
Blackwood, New Jersey 08012

NEW YORK

Veterinary Technology Program (1)
La Guardia Community College
The City University of New York
31-10 Thomson Avenue
Long Island City, New York 11101

Veterinary Technology Program (1,*)
Mercy College
555 Broadway
Dobbs Ferry, New York 10522

Veterinary Science Technology
 Program (1)
State University of New York
Agricultural & Technical college
Agriculture & Life Sciences
Canton, New York 13617

Veterinary Science Technology
 Program (1)
State University of New York
College of Technology
Delhi, New York 13753

Veterinary Science Technology
 Program (1)
State University of New York
Agricultural & Technical College
Farmingdale, New York 11735

NORTH CAROLINA

Veterinary Medical Technology
 Program (1)
Central Carolina Community College
1105 Kelly Drive
Sanford, North Carolina 27330

NORTH DAKOTA

Veterinary Technology Program (1, *)
North Dakota State University
Department of Veterinary Science
Fargo, North Dakota 58105

OHIO

Veterinary Technology Program (1)
Columbus State Community College
550 East Spring Street
Columbus, Ohio 43216

Animal Health Technology Program (1)
Raymond Walters College
University of Cincinnati
Cincinnati, Ohio 45221

OKLAHOMA

Veterinary Technology Program (1)
Murray State College
Tishomingo, Oklahoma 73460

OREGON

Veterinary Technology Program (2)
Portland Community College
P.O. Box 19000
Portland, Oregon 97219

PENNSYLVANIA

Veterinary Technology Program (1)
Harcum Junior College
Bryn Mawr, Pennsylvania 19010

Veterinary Technology Program (2)
Manor Junior College
Fox Chase Road & Forest Avenue
Jenkintown, Pennsylvania 19046

Veterinary Medical Technology
 Program (1)
Wilson College
Chambersburg, Pennsylvania 17201

SOUTH CAROLINA

Veterinary Technology Program (1)
Tri-County Technical College
P.O. Box 587
Pendleton, South Carolina 29670

SOUTH DAKOTA

Veterinary Technology Program (1)
National College
Allied Health Division
321 Kansas City Street
Rapid City, South Dakota 57709

TENNESSEE

Veterinary Technology Program (1)
Columbia State Community College
Columbia, Tennessee 38401

Veterinary Technology Program (2)
Lincoln Memorial University
Harrogate, Tennessee 37752

TEXAS

Veterinary Technology Program (1)
Cedar Valley College
3030 North Dallas Avenue
Lancaster, Texas 75134

Veterinary Technology Program (2)
Midland College
3000 North Garland
Midland, Texas 79705

Veterinary Technology Program (1)
Sul Ross State University
Range Animal Science Department
Alpine, Texas 79830

Veterinary Technology Program (2)
Tomball College
30555 Tomball Parkway
Tomball, Texas 77375-4036

UTAH

Animal Health Technology
 Program   (1,*)
Brigham Young University
Provo, Utah 84602

VERMONT

Veterinary Technology Program (2)
Vermont Technical College
Randolph Center, Vermont 05061

VIRGINIA

Veterinary Technology Program (1)
Blue Ridge Community College
Box 80
Weyers Cave, Virginia 24486

Veterinary Technology Program (1)
Northern Virginia Community College
Loudoun Campus
1000 Harry Flood Byrd Highway
Sterling, Virginia 22170

WASHINGTON

Veterinary Technology Program (1)
Pierce College at Fort Steilacoom
9401 Farwest Drive SW
Tacoma, Washington 98498

WEST VIRGINIA

Veterinary Technology Program (1)
Fairmont State College
Fairmont, West Virginia 26554

WISCONSIN

Veterinary Technician Program (1)
Madison Area Technical College
3550 Anderson
Madison, Wisconsin 53704

WYOMING

Veterinary Technology Program (1)
Eastern Wyoming College
3200 West "C" Street
Torrington, Wyoming 82240

Animal Caretaker

Also known as an *animal health assistant, animal attendant* or *animal hospital attendant,* the animal caretaker works in a clinical or research laboratory, kennel, pound, or animal hospital, in an entry-level position. The caretaker cleans and sterilizes the animal's cages, pens, and the surrounding areas, prepares their meals and feeds them according to schedules and diet restrictions. The animal caretaker also keeps records on laboratory procedures, maintains prescribed temperature and humidity levels in the rooms, orders feed and supplies, and reports on any abnormal behavior in the animals. In general, the animal caretaker is responsible for the general health and well-being of animals.

A high school education, with courses in biology and chemistry, is the usual entrance prerequisite for admittance into an on-the-job training program, usually offered by laboratories and animal hospitals. Training may also be available in secondary schools, or in college level programs that are less than two years.

For career opportunities as an animal caretaker, contact area animal hospitals, clinics or research laboratories, or refer to the classified employment section in local newspapers.

SOURCES:

Dictionary of Occupational Titles
Institute of Laboratory Animal Resources

✚ ATHLETIC TRAINING

Athletic training is that part of the medical aspect of an athletic program that is concerned with the prevention and treatment of athletic injuries.

Athletic Trainer

The *athletic trainer* is a trained professional who implements prevention-of-injury programs and who, under the direction of the team physician, supervises the treatment and rehabilitation of the injured athlete. Working closely with the team physician, the coaches, and the administration, the athletic trainer is concerned with the athlete's fitness, performance, and overall physical and emotional well being. The athletic trainer must be a skilled individual with a thorough knowledge of anatomy, physiology, psychology, kinesiology (the study of human muscular movements), hygiene, nutrition, conditioning, prevention-of-injury methodology, taping, and protective equipment.

Responsibilities of an athletic trainer may include treating an injured athlete with ice and heat, treating cuts and abrasions, supervising strength and conditioning programs, inspecting athletic equipment to insure that it is working properly, purchasing and fitting equipment, taping knees and ankles to prevent or lessen injury, designing special equipment such as pads or braces, planning menus and supervising diets, and educating athletes on the prevention of injuries.

Athletic trainers are employed by high schools, school districts, colleges, universities, private or hospital based clinics, and by professional sports teams.

To become a certified athletic trainer, a student may follow one of two routes: (1) obtain a bachelor's degree or master's degree from a college sponsoring an athletic training education program and accredited by the National Athletic Trainers Association, or (2) obtain a bachelor's or master's degree in a related health field plus complete an 1800 hour internship under the direct supervision of an athletic trainer certified by the National Athletic Trainers Association. In both cases certification requirements also include (a) current certification in first aid and (b) current certification in CPR (cardiopulmonary resuscitation) and (c) successful completion of the National Athletic Trainers Association certification examination.

Recommended high school courses include health, biology, physiology, chemistry, physics, general science, and first aid. It is suggested that high school students interested in a career of athletic training should work as a student trainer or manager at the high school or college level.

Athletic trainers may be employed as a part of a facility's sports department, physical education department or as a member of a team's staff. An athletic trainer may be required to attend team activities, practices, and games, and may be expected to travel.

The following is a list of institutions that offer academic programs approved by the National Athletic Trainers Association. Most of the schools listed offer bachelor's degrees in athletic training, but some graduate degree programs are also included.

For more information on internships, certification requirements or athletic training education programs, contact either the individual schools or the National Athletic Trainers Association, 2952 Stemmons Freeway, Suite 200, Dallas, Texas 75247.

KEY:

(1)   Undergraduate Athletic Training Education Programs
(2)   Graduate Athletic Training Education Programs

SOURCE:

American Athletic Trainers Association & Certification Board
American Medical Association
National Athletic Trainers Association

Athletic Trainer Programs

ALABAMA

Exercise Science & Sports Medicine (1)
Samford University
Box 2448
Birmingham, Alabama 35229

Health & Human Performance
 Studies (1)
University of Alabama
Tuscaloosa, Alabama 35487-0312

ARIZONA

Department of Exercise & Sport
 Sciences (2)
University of Arizona
Tucson, Arizona 85721

CALIFORNIA

Department of Athletics (1)
California State University, Fresno
Fresno, California 93740-0027

Department of Health, P.E. &
 Recreation (1)
California State University, Fullerton
Fullerton, California 92634

Department of Physical Education (1)
California State University, Long Beach
Long Beach, California 90840

Department of Kinesiology (1)
California State University, Northridge
Northridge, California 91330

Department of Health & Physical
  Education (1)
California State University, Sacramento
Sacramento, California 95819-2694

Department of Human Performance (2)
San Jose State University
One Washington Square
San Jose, California 95192-0054

Department of Physical Education (1)
California Lutheran University
60 West Olsen Road
Thousand Oaks, California 91360

COLORADO

Department of Kinesiology & PE (1)
University of Northern Colorado
Greeley, Colorado 80639

CONNECTICUT

Physical Education Department (1)
Southern Connecticut State University
501 Crescent Street
New Haven, Connecticut 06515

DELAWARE

College of P.E., Athletics &
  Recreation (1)
University of Delaware
Newark, Delaware 19716

FLORIDA

Department of Exercise and Sport
  Sciences (2)
University of Florida
Gainesville, Florida 32611

GEORGIA

Department of Physical Education &
  Athletics (1)
Valdosta State College
Valdosta, Georgia 31698

IDAHO

Department of Physical Education,
  Health & Recreation (1)
Boise State University
Boise, Idaho 83725

ILLINOIS

Department of Physical Education &
  Athletics (1)
Eastern Illinois University
Charleston, Illinois 61920

Department of Health, P.E., Recreation
  & Dance (2)
Illinois State University
Normal, Illinois 61761

Department of Physical Education (1)
Southern Illinois University
Carbondale, Illinois 62901

Department of Kinesiology (1,2)
University of Illinois
Urbana, Illinois 61801

Physical Education & Athletics (1)
Western Illinois University
Macomb, Illinois 61455

INDIANA

Department of Physical Education (1)
Ball State University
Muncie, Indiana 47306

Department of Kinesiology (1, 2)
Indiana University
Bloomington, Indiana 47405

Department of Physical Education (1,2)
Indiana State University
Terre Haute, Indiana 47809

19

Department of P.E., Health &
  Recreational Studies (1)
Purdue University
West Lafayette, Indiana 47907

Athletic Department (1)
Anderson University
Anderson, Indiana 46012-1362

IOWA

Department of Exercise
  Science & P.E. (1)
University of Iowa
Iowa City, Iowa 52242

KANSAS

Department of Kinesiology (1)
Kansas State University
Manhattan, Kansas 66506-0302

KENTUCKY

Department of Physical Education (1)
Eastern Kentucky University
Richmond, Kentucky 40475-3103

MASSACHUSETTS

Department of Health, P.E. &
  Recreation (1)
Bridgewater State College
Bridgewater, Massachusetts 02324

Department of Health, Sport & Leisure
  Studies (1)
Northeastern University
Boston, Massachusetts 02115

Physical Education & Health Fitness (1)
Springfield College
Springfield, Massachusetts 01109

MICHIGAN

Department of Physical Education (1)
Central Michigan University
Mount Pleasant, Michigan 48859

Department of Physical Education &
  Athletics (1)
Grand Valley State College
Allendale, Michigan 49401

Department of Health, P.E., &
  Recreation (2)
Western Michigan University
Kalamazoo, Michigan 49008

MINNESOTA

Department of Physical Education (1)
Gustavus Adolphus College
St. Peter, Minnesota 56082

Department of Physical Education (1)
Mankato State University
Mankato, Minnesota 56002-8400

MISSISSIPPI

Department of Human Performance &
  Recreation (1)
University of Southern Mississippi
Hattiesburg, Mississippi 39406-5142

MISSOURI

Department of Health, P.E., &
  Recreation (1)
Southwest Missouri State University
Springfield, Missouri 65804-0094

MONTANA

Department of Health & Human
  Performance (1)
University of Montana
Missoula, Montana 59812

NEVADA

Health Education & Sports Injury
  Management (1)
University of Nevada, Las Vegas
Las Vegas, Nevada 89154-3032

NEW HAMPSHIRE

Physical Education Department (1)
University of New Hampshire
Durham, New Hampshire 03824

NEW JERSEY

Department of Physical Education (1)
Kean College of New Jersey
Union, New Jersey 07083

Department of Movement Science (1)
William Paterson College of New Jersey
Wayne, New Jersey 07470

NEW MEXICO

Department of P.E., Recreation, &
  Dance (1)
New Mexico State University
Las Cruces, New Mexico 88003-2215

Department of Health, P.E., &
  Recreation (1)
University of New Mexico
Albuquerque, New Mexico 87131

NEW YORK

Department of Physical Education (1)
Canisius College
Buffalo, New York 14208-1098

Department of Physical Education &
  Recreation (1)
State University of New York at
  Cortland
Cortland, New York 13045

Department of Exercise & Sports
  Science (1)
Ithaca College
Ithaca, New York 14850

Athletic Training Department (1)
Hofstra University
Hempstead, New York 11550

NORTH CAROLINA

Department of Health Education, P.E.,
  & Leisure Studies (1)
Appalachian State University
Boone, North Carolina 28608

Department of Health, P.E., Recreation
  & Safety (1)
East Carolina University
Greenville, North Carolina 27834-4353

Department of Physical Education (2)
University of North Carolina
Chapel Hill, North Carolina 27559-8700

NORTH DAKOTA

Department of Health, P.E., &
  Recreation (1)
North Dakota State University
Fargo, North Dakota 58105-5600

Department of Family Medicine (1)
University of North Dakota
Grand Forks, North Dakota 58202

OHIO

Department of Health, P.E., &
  Recreation (1)
Bowling Green State University
Bowling Green, Ohio 43403

Department of Sports Medicine (1)
Marietta College
Marietta, Ohio 45750-3058

Department of Health and Physical
Education (1)
Miami University of Ohio
Oxford, Ohio 45056

Department of Health & Sport
 Sciences (1)
Ohio University
Athens, Ohio 45701

Department of Health Promotion &
 Human Performance (1)
University of Toledo
Toledo, Ohio 43606

Department of Health & Sport
 Sciences (1)
Capital University
Columbus, Ohio 43209-6011

Department of Health, P.E., & Sports
 Management (1)
Mount Union College
Alliance, Ohio 44601

OKLAHOMA

Health, Physical Education &
 Recreation (1)
University of Tulsa
Tulsa, Oklahoma 74104-3189

OREGON

Exercise & Sport Science (1)
Oregon State University
Corvallis, Oregon 97331-3302

Department of Exercise & Movement
 Science (2)
University of Oregon
Eugene, Oregon 97403

PENNSYLVANIA

College of Education (1)
California University of Pennsylvania
California, Pennsylvania 15419

Department of Professional Physical
 Education (1)
East Stroudsburg University
East Stroudsburg, Pennsylvania 18301

Department of Health Science (1)
Lock Haven University
Lock Haven, Pennsylvania 17745

Department of Exercise Science (1)
Pennsylvania State University
University Park, Pennsylvania 16802

Instruction and Learning (1)
University of Pittsburgh
Pittsburgh, Pennsylvania 15261

Department of Health Sciences (1)
Slippery Rock University
Slippery Rock, Pennsylvania 16057

Department of Sports Medicine (1)
Westchester University
215 South Campus
Westchester, Pennsylvania 19383

College of Health, P.E., Recreation, &
 Dance (1)
Temple University
Philadelphia, Pennsylvania 19122

Department of Physical Education (2)
Temple University
Philadelphia, Pennsylvania 19122

Department of Health & Physical
 Education (1)
Messiah College
Grantham, Pennsylvania 17027

SOUTH CAROLINA

Department of Physical Education (1)
University of South Carolina
Blatt Physical Education Center
Columbia, South Carolina 29208

22

SOUTH DAKOTA

Department of Health, P.E. &
  Recreation (1)
South Dakota State University
Brookings, South Dakota 57007

TENNESSEE

Department of Physical Education &
  Athletics (1)
East Tennessee State University
Johnson City, Tennessee 37614-0634

TEXAS

Department of Health, P.E. &
  Recreation (1)
Southwest Texas State University
San Marcos, Texas 78666-4616

Athletic Trainer Program (1)
Texas Christian University
Fort Worth, Texas 76129-3292

UTAH

College of Physical Education Sports (1)
Brigham Young University
Provo, Utah 84602

VERMONT

Sports Therapy (1)
University of Vermont
Burlington, Vermont 05405

VIRGINIA

Department of Health Sciences (1)
James Madison University
Harrisonburg, Virginia 22807

Department of Human Services (2)
University of Virginia
Curry School of Education
Charlottesville, Virginia 22903

Department of Athletics (2)
Old Dominion University
Norfolk, Virginia 23529-0197

WASHINGTON

Department of P.E., Sport & Leisure
  Studies (1)
Washington State University
Pullman, Washington 99164-1610

WEST VIRGINIA

Department of Sports Medicine (1)
University of Charleston
2300 MacCorkle Avenue SE
Charleston, West Virginia 25304

Department of Health, P.E. &
  Recreation (1)
Marshall University
Huntington, West Virginia 25755

Department of Health Promotion (1)
West Virginia University
Morgantown, West Virginia 26506-6116

WISCONSIN

Department of Health, P.E. &
  Recreation (1)
University of Wisconsin, LaCrosse
LaCrosse, Wisconsin 54601

✚ BIOMEDICAL ENGINEERING

Biomedical engineering is the application of engineering principles and methods to biomedical research and healthcare. In this field of allied health, aspects of engineering, physics, and technology are combined to understand and solve problems in life science research, medical diagnosis, medical therapy, and prevention of human disease. It is a very diverse health field and involves career specializations in the following areas: healthcare delivery; hospital safety; rehabilitation; public health; data processing and systems analysis; biomechanics; artificial organs and assist devices; chemical and nuclear energy sources; and performance evaluation of drugs, surgery, and instrumentation. In these specializations there are two career occupations: the *biomedical engineer* and the *biomedical equipment technician*.

Biomedical Engineer

The *biomedical engineer* is primarily an engineer who has had specific training in various aspects of biology or medicine. There are three main specializations in which the biomedical engineer may work: bioengineering, medical engineering and clinical engineering.

In one area of bioengineering the biomedical engineer researches the engineering aspects of biological (often nonmedical) systems, including the structure, function, and pathology of man and animals. In another, he or she is engaged in what is known as *bioinstrumentation* in which the application of electronics and measurement techniques to develop devices, are used in diagnosis and treatment of disease. Computers, from microprocessors to those with extensive computing power, are becoming increasingly important in bioinstrumentation.

In *medical engineering* the biomedical engineer uses engineering concepts and technology to design and develop medical instrumentation, diagnostic and therapeutic devices, artificial organs, and other equipment including lasers for surgery and cardiac pacemakers. They may also design computer-assisted instrumentation to monitor a patient's heart rate, electrocardiogram, or blood pressure. As a member of the healthcare team this type of biomedical engineer works closely with physicians in surgical and intensive care units.

In *clinical engineering* the biomedical engineer uses engineering concepts and technology to improve health care delivery systems in hospitals and clinical settings. He or she may use computer-assisted systems in monitoring patients and evaluating diagnostic tests, investigate accidents involving medical devices, evaluate new patient-care technologies, and supervise and train the hospital staff in the proper use of instruments.

Career opportunities are varied and plentiful in this field with biomedical engineers working in universities, colleges, research institutions, hospitals, clinics, government programs, and industry.

The minimum educational requirement for a biomedical engineer is a four-year bachelor's degree from a biomedical engineering program or from an established program in electrical, mechanical, or chemical engineering with a specialty in biomedical engineering. Established engineering programs are available throughout the country at university and college schools of engineering. Many offer special courses in biomedical engineering as a minor, or option, for those students who are majoring in one of the more traditional engineering disciplines.

The bachelor's degree should not generally be regarded as a terminal degree, as many graduates go on to graduate or medical school. For students interested in research and university teaching, a doctorate is the prerequisite.

Courses in high school for interested students in biomedical engineering should emphasize mathematics, science, and communication skills.

Information on certification can be obtained through the Association for the Advancement of Medical Instrumentation at the address listed below.

For further career information in biomedical engineering, contact the Biomedical Engineering Society, P.O. Box 2399, Culver City, California 90231 or the Association for the Advancement of Medical Instrumentation, 3300 Washington Blvd., Arlington, Virginia 22201-4598.

Following is a list of programs in biomedical engineering accredited by the Accreditation Board for Engineering and Technology.

SOURCES:

Association for the Advancement of Medical Instrumentation
Biomedical Engineering Society
Junior Engineering Technical Society

Biomedical Engineering Programs

ARIZONA

Biomedical Engineering Program
Arizona State University
Tempe, Arizona 85287

CALIFORNIA

Biomedical Engineering Program
University of California-San Diego
La Jolla, California 92093

IOWA

Biomedical Engineering Program
University of Iowa
Iowa City, Iowa 52242

LOUISIANA

Biomedical Engineering Program
Tulane University
New Orleans, Louisiana 70118

MARYLAND

Biomedical Engineering Program
Johns Hopkins University
Baltimore, Maryland 21218

MASSACHUSETTS

Biomedical Engineering Program
Boston University
Boston, Massachusetts 02215

MISSISSIPPI

Biomedical Engineering Program
Mississippi State University
Mississippi State, Mississippi 39762

NEW YORK

Biomedical Engineering Program
Rensselaer Polytechnic Institute
Troy, New York 12181

Biomedical Engineering Program
Syracuse University
Syracuse, New York 13210

NORTH CAROLINA

Biomedical Engineering Program
North Carolina State University-Raleigh
Raleigh, North Carolina 27695

OHIO

Biomedical Engineering Program
Case Western Reserve University
Cleveland, Ohio 44106

Biomedical Engineering Program
Wright State University
Dayton, Ohio 45435

PENNSYLVANIA

Biomedical Engineering Program
University of Pennsylvania
Philadelphia, Pennsylvania 19104

WISCONSIN

Biomedical Engineering Program
Marquette University
Milwaukee, Wisconsin 53233

Biomedical Engineering Program
Milwaukee School of Engineering
Milwaukee, Wisconsin 53201

Biomedical Equipment Technician

The biomedical equipment technician is involved with all phases of biomedical engineering. They install, calibrate, inspect, maintain, and repair general biomedical and related technical equipment that is used to help diagnose and treat disease. Able to understand medical and biological terminology, the technician both assists physicians, nurses, and researchers in carrying out clinical procedures and experiments, and also instructs the medical staff in proper use and safety of the biomedical equipment.

Entry-level biomedical equipment technicians are supervised by biomedical engineers, but with experience they may advance to intermediate or senior levels where they work on a variety of medical instruments. Technicians who go on to get more education may become biomedical engineers.

Most biomedical equipment technicians are employed in hospitals. Others may work for medical research centers, biomedical equipment manufacturers, medical colleges, and medical supply firms.

The educational requirement for a biomedical equipment technician is an associate degree from a college or university in biomedical equipment technology, electronics, or a related engineering field.

Certification as a (CBET) certified biomedical equipment technician is granted by the International Certification Commission for Clinical Engineering and Biomedical Technology after successfully passing a national examination and meeting the education and experience requirements.

Recommended high school courses for students interested in a career in this field include electronics, mechanics, algebra, trigonometry, biology, physics, and physiology.

For further information on certification or a career as a biomedical equipment technician write to the Association for the Advancement of Medical Instrumentation, 3330 Washington Blvd., Suite 400, Arlington, Virginia 22201-4598.

Following is a list of educational institutions offering biomedical equipment technician programs.

SOURCES:

Association for the Advancement of Medical Instrumentation
Occupational Outlook Handbook

Biomedical Equipment Technician Programs

ALABAMA

Biomedical Equipment Technician
  Program
Alabama College of Technology
1900 28th Avenue South
Homewood, Alabama 35209

Biomedical Equipment Technician
  Program
Alexander City State Junior College
P.O. Box 699
Alexander City, Alabama 35010

Biomedical Equipment Technician
  Program
Brewer State Junior College
3621 Temple Avenue North
Fayette, Alabama 35555

Biomedical Equipment Technician
  Program
Chatahooche Valley State Community
  College
2602 Savage Drive
Phoenix City, Alabama 36867

Biomedical Equipment Technician
  Program
Community College of The Air Force
Maxwell AFB, Alabama 36112-6655

Biomedical Equipment Technician
  Program
John Patterson Technical College
3920 Troy Highway
Montgomery, Alabama 36116

Biomedical Equipment Technician
  Program
Muscle Shoals State Technical College
George Wallace Boulevard
P.O. Box 2545
Muscle Shoals, Alabama 35662

Biomedical Equipment Technician
  Program
University of Alabama
University Station
Birmingham, Alabama 35294

Biomedical Equipment Technician
  Program
Southwest State Technical College
925 Dauphin Island Parkway
Mobile, Alabama 36605

Biomedical Equipment Technician
  Program
University of Alabama
720 20th Street South
Birmingham, Alabama 35294

ALASKA

Biomedical Equipment Technician
  Program
Anchorage Community College
2533 Providence Avenue
Anchorage, Alaska 99508-4670

Biomedical Equipment Technician
  Program
Tanana Valley Community College
4280 Geist Road
Fairbanks, Alaska 99701

Biomedical Equipment Technician
  Program
University of Alaska
Fairbanks, Alaska 99701

ARIZONA

Biomedical Equipment Technician
  Program
Phoenix College
1202 West Thomas Road
Phoenix, Arizona 85013

Biomedical Equipment Technician
  Program
Pima County Community College
200 North Stone Avenue
P.O. Box 3010
Tucson, Arizona 85702

Biomedical Equipment Technician
  Program
University of Arizona
Tucson, Arizona 85721

ARKANSAS

Biomedical Equipment Technician
  Program
Texarkana Community College
2500 North Robinson Road
Texarkana, Arkansas 75501

Biomedical Equipment Technician
  Program
University of Arkansas
Engineering Training Center
VA Medical Center
North Little Rock Division
North Little Rock, Arkansas 72114

Biomedical Equipment Technician
  Program
University of Arkansas
4301 West Markham
Little Rock, Arkansas 72205

CALIFORNIA

Biomedical Equipment Technician
  Program
Bakersfield College
1801 Panorama Drive
Bakersfield, California 93305

Biomedical Equipment Technician
  Program
Cerritos College
11110 East Alondra Boulevard
Norwalk, California 90650

Biomedical Equipment Technician
  Program
College of the Desert
43-500 Montfrey Avenue
Palm Desert, California 92260

Biomedical Equipment Technician
  Program
College of the Redwoods
Eureka, California 95501

Biomedical Equipment Technician
  Program
Edison Technical College
4629 Van Nuys Boulevard
Sherman Oaks, California 91403

Biomedical Equipment Technician
  Program
Hartnell College
156 Homestead Avenue
Salinas, California 93901

Biomedical Equipment Technician
  Program
Los Angeles Valley College
5800 Fulton Avenue
Van Nuys, California 91401

Biomedical Equipment Technician
  Program
Napa Valley College
2277 Napa Vallejo Highway
Napa, California 94558

Biomedical Equipment Technician
  Program
Palomar Community College
1140 West Mission Road
San Marcos, California 92609

Biomedical Equipment Technician
  Program
San Bernardino Valley College
701 South Mt. Vernon Avenue
San Bernardino, California 92410

Biomedical Equipment Technician
  Program
San Diego Mesa College
3375 Camino Del Rio South
San Diego, California 92108

Biomedical Equipment Technician
  Program
Santa Ana College
1530 West 17th Street
Santa Ana, California 92706

Biomedical Equipment Technician
  Program
University of Southern California
Department of Biomedical Engineering
Los Angeles, California 90007

Biomedical Equipment Technician
  Program
Yuba College
2088 North Beale Road
Marysville, California 95901

COLORADO

Biomedical Equipment Technician
  Program
Colorado State University
Ft. Collins, Colorado 80523

Biomedical Equipment Technician
  Program
Colorado Technical College
4435 North Chestnut Street
Colorado Springs, Colorado 80907-3896

Biomedical Equipment Technician
  Program
Front Range Community College
3645 West 112th Avenue
Westminister, Colorado 80030

Biomedical Equipment Technician
  Program
Regis College
3539 West 50th Parkway
Denver, Colorado 80221

CONNECTICUT

Biomedical Equipment Technician
  Program
Greater New Haven State Technical
  College
88 Bassett Road
North Haven, Connecticut 06473

FLORIDA

Biomedical Equipment Technician
  Program
Brevard Community College
1519 Clear Lake Road
Cocoa, Florida 32922

Biomedical Equipment Technician
  Program
225 East Las Olas Boulevard
Ft. Lauderdale, Florida 33301

Biomedical Equipment Technician
  Program
Daytona Beach Community College
P.O. Box 1111
Daytona Beach, Florida 32015-1111

Biomedical Equipment Technician
  Program
Florida Junior College
21 Church Street
Jacksonville, Florida 32205

Biomedical Equipment Technician
  Program
Florida Junior College
Jacksonville Downtown Campus
101 West State Street
Jacksonville, Florida 32202

Biomedical Equipment Technician
  Program
Hillsborough Community College
P.O. Box 31127
Tampa, Florida 33631-3127

Biomedical Equipment Technician
  Program
Santa Fe Community College
3000 NW 83rd Street
Gainesville, Florida 32602

GEORGIA

Biomedical Equipment Technician
  Program
Augusta Area Technical College
Augusta, Georgia 30904

Biomedical Equipment Technician
  Program
Dekalb College
South Campus
3251 Pantherville Road
Decatur, Georgia 30034

Biomedical Equipment Technician
  Program
Devry Institute of Technology
250 North Arcadia Avenue
Decatur, Georgia 30030

Biomedical Equipment Technician
 Program
Macon Area Technical Vocational
3300 Macon Tech Drive
Macon, Georgia 31206

Biomedical Equipment Technician
 Program
North Georgia Technical Institute
Highway 197 North
Clarksville, Georgia 30523

Biomedical Equipment Technician
 Program
South Georgia Technical Institute
Southfield Road
P.O. Box 1088
Americus, Georgia 31709

HAWAII

Biomedical Equipment Technician
 Program
Honolulu Community College
874 Dillingham Boulevard
Honolulu, Hawaii 96817

ILLINOIS

Biomedical Equipment Technician
 Program
College of Lake County
Grayslake, Illinois 60030

Biomedical Equipment Technician
 Program
Devry Institute of Technology
3300 North Campbell Avenue
Chicago, Illinois 60618-5994

Biomedical Equipment Technician
 Program
Illinois Central College
Route 24
East Peoria, Illinois 61635

Biomedical Equipment Technician
 Program
Lincoln Land Community College
College Shepherd Road
Springfield, Illinois 62708

Biomedical Equipment Technician
 Program
Moraine Valley Community College
Palos Hills, Illinois 60465

Biomedical Equipment Technician
 Program
Morton College
3801 South Central
Cicero, Illinois 60650

Biomedical Equipment Technician
 Program
Parkland College
2400 West Bradley Street
Champaign, Illinois 61820

Biomedical Equipment Technician
 Program
Oakton Community College
1600 East Golf Road
Des Plains, Illinois 60016

Biomedical Equipment Technician
 Program
Richland Community College
2425 Federal Drive
Decatur, Illinois 62526

Biomedical Equipment Technician
 Program
Rock Valley College
3301 North Mulford Road
Rockford, Illinois 61111

Biomedical Equipment Technician
 Program
South Illinois University
School of Technical Careers
Carbondale, Illinois 62901

Biomedical Equipment Technician
  Program
Thornton Community College
15800 South State Street
South Holland, Illinois 60473

INDIANA

Biomedical Equipment Technician
  Program
Indiana University
1707 North Pennsylvania Street
Indianapolis, Indiana 46202

Biomedical Equipment Technician
  Program
Indiana Vocational Technical College
4100 Cowan Road
Muncie, Indiana 47302

Biomedical Equipment Technician
  Program
ITT Technical Institute
4919 Cold Water Road
Ft. Wayne, Indiana 46825

Biomedical Equipment Technician
  Program
ITT Technical Institute
9511 Angola Court
Indianapolis, Indiana 46268

Biomedical Equipment Technician
  Program
Ivy Technical Vocational College
1440 East 35th Avenue
Gary, Indiana 46409

Biomedical Equipment Technician
  Program
Purdue University
799 West Michigan Street
Indianapolis, Indiana 46202

IOWA

Biomedical Equipment Technician
  Program
Des Moines Area Community College
Ankemy, Iowa 50021

Biomedical Equipment Technician
  Program
Iowa Western Community College
2700 College Road
Box 4-C
Council Bluffs, Iowa 51501

Biomedical Equipment Technician
  Program
Northwest Iowa Technical College
Sheldon, Iowa 51201

Biomedical Equipment Technician
  Program
Western Iowa Technical Community
  College
P.O. Box 265
Sioux City, Iowa 51102

KANSAS

Biomedical Equipment Technician
  Program
Johnson County Community College
11th & Quivera Roads
Overland Park, Kansas 66506

Biomedical Equipment Technician
  Program
Kansas State University
Manhattan, Kansas 66502

Biomedical Equipment Technician
  Program
Kansas Technical Institute
2409 Scanlon
Salina, Kansas 67401

33

KENTUCKY

Biomedical Equipment Technician
    Program
Ashland State Vo-Tech
4818 Roberts Drive
Ashland, Kentucky 41101

Biomedical Equipment Technician
    Program
United Elec. Institute
3947 Park Drive
Louisville, Kentucky 40216

MAINE

Biomedical Equipment Technician
    Program
Eastern Maine Vocational Technical
    Institute
354 Hogan Road
Bangor, Maine 04401

Biomedical Equipment Technician
    Program
Southern Maine Vocational Technical
    Institute
Two Fort Road
South Portland, Maine 04106

MARYLAND

Biomedical Equipment Technician
    Program
Catonsville Community College
Catonsville, Maryland 21228

Biomedical Equipment Technician
    Program
Chesapeake College
P.O. Box 8
Wye Mills, Maryland 21679

Biomedical Equipment Technician
    Program
Howard Community College
Little Patuxent Parkway
Columbia, Maryland 21044

MASSACHUSETTS

Biomedical Equipment Technician
    Program
Berkshire Community College
West Street
Pittsfield, Massachusetts 01201

Biomedical Equipment Technician
    Program
Boston University
755 Commonwealth Avenue
Boston, Massachusetts 02116

Biomedical Equipment Technician
    Program
Franklin Institute of Boston
41 Berkeley Street
Boston, Massachusetts 02116

Biomedical Equipment Technician
    Program
Massachusetts Institute of Technology
77 Massachusetts Avenue
Cambridge, Massachusetts 02139

Biomedical Equipment Technician
    Program
Northeastern University
3460 Hunting Avenue
Boston, Massachusetts 02115

Biomedical Equipment Technician
    Program
Quincy Vocational Technical
107 Woodward Avenue
Quincy, Massachusetts 02167

Biomedical Equipment Technician
    Program
Springfield Technical Community
    College
One Armory Square
Springfield, Massachusetts 01105

Biomedical Equipment Technician
  Program
Wentworth Institute of Technology
Boston, Massachusetts 02115

Biomedical Equipment Technician
  Program
Worcester Polytech Institute
Biomedical Engineering Programs
Worcester, Massachusetts 01609

MICHIGAN

Biomedical Equipment Technician
  Program
Andrews University
Berrien Springs, Michigan 49104

Biomedical Equipment Technician
  Program
Detroit Institute of Technology
2727 Second
Detroit, Michigan 48201

Biomedical Equipment Technician
  Program
Grand Rapids Junior College
143 Bostwick Avenue NE
Grand Rapids, Michigan 49503

Biomedical Equipment Technician
  Program
Henry Ford Community College
5101 Evergreen
Dearborn, Michigan 48128

Biomedical Equipment Technician
  Program
Kalamazoo Valley Community College
6767 West O Avenue
Kalamazoo, Michigan 49009

Biomedical Equipment Technician
  Program
Lake Michigan College
2755 East Napier
Benton Harbor, Michigan 49022

Biomedical Equipment Technician
  Program
Lansing Community College
419 North Capitol Avenue
Lansing, Michigan 48901

Biomedical Equipment Technician
  Program
Lawrence Institute of Technology
21000 West Ten Mile Road
Southfield, Michigan 48075

Biomedical Equipment Technician
  Program
Macomb Community College
14500 Twelve Mile Road
Warren, Michigan 48093-3896

Biomedical Equipment Technician
  Program
Northwestern Michigan College
Traverse City, Michigan 49684

Biomedical Equipment Technician
  Program
Oakland Community College
2480 Updyke Road
P.O. Box 812
Bloomfield Hills, Michigan 48013

Biomedical Equipment Technician
  Program
Oakland University
Rochester, Michigan 48063

Biomedical Equipment Technician
  Program
Schoolcraft College
18600 Hagerty Road
Livonia, Michigan 48152

Biomedical Equipment Technician
  Program
Washtenau Community College
P.O. Box D-1
Ann Arbor, Michigan 48106

MINNESOTA

Biomedical Equipment Technician
  Program
Brown Institute
3123 East Lake Street
Minneapolis, Minnesota

Biomedical Equipment Technician
  Program
Hennepin Technical Center
9200 Flying Cloud Drive
Eden Prairie, Minnesota 55344

Biomedical Equipment Technician
  Program
Area Vocational Technical Institute
3300 Century Avenue
White Bear Lake, Minnesota 55110

MISSOURI

Biomedical Equipment Technician
  Program
Crowder College
Neosho, Missouri 64850

Biomedical Equipment Technician
  Program
Forest Park Community College
5600 Oakland
St. Louis, Missouri 63110

Biomedical Equipment Technician
  Program
Missouri Institute of Technology
1644 Wyandotte Street
Kansas City, Missouri 64108

Biomedical Equipment Technician
  Program
St. Louis Community College
5801 Wilson Avenue
St. Louis, Missouri 63110

NEVADA

Biomedical Equipment Technician
  Program
University of Nevada at Las Vegas
4505 South Maryland Parkway
Las Vegas, Nevada 89109

NEW JERSEY

Biomedical Equipment Technician
  Program
Atlantic Community College
Electronics Tech Program
Black Horse Pike
Mays Landing, New Jersey 08330

Biomedical Equipment Technician
  Program
Devry Technical Institute
479 Green Street
Woodbridge, New Jersey 07095

Biomedical Equipment Technician
  Program
Morris County College
Route 10 & Center Grove Road
Randolph, New Jersey 07869

Biomedical Equipment Technician
  Program
Salem Community College
460 Hollywood Avenue
Carney Point, New Jersey 08069

NEW MEXICO

Biomedical Equipment Technician
  Program
Eastern New Mexico University
417 Shepps Boulevard
Clovis, New Mexico 88101

NEW YORK

Biomedical Equipment Technician
  Program
Bramson Technical Institute
44 East 23rd Street
New York, NY 10010

Biomedical Equipment Technician
  Program
Cayuga County Community College
Franklin Street
Auburn, New York 13021

Biomedical Equipment Technician
  Program
Erie Community College
Main Street at Young Road
Williamsville, New York 14221

Biomedical Equipment Technician
  Program
Erie Community College
South Campus
4140 Southwestern Boulevard
Orchard Park, New York 14127

Biomedical Equipment Technician
  Program
Jamestown Community College
525 Falconer Street
Jamestown, New York 14701

Biomedical Equipment Technician
  Program
Monroe Community College
P.O. Box 9720
Rochester, New York 14623

Biomedical Equipment Technician
  Program
New York Institute of Technology
Wheatley Road
Old Westbury
Long Island, New York 11568

Biomedical Equipment Technician
  Program
State University of New York at
  Farmingdale
Farmingdale, New York 11735

Biomedical Equipment Technician
  Program
Suffolk County Community College
533 College Road
Selden, New York 11784

Biomedical Equipment Technician
  Program
SUNY Agricultural & Technical College
Melville Road
Farmingdale, New York 11735

NORTH CAROLINA

Biomedical Equipment Technician
  Program
Caldwell Community College
1000 Hickory Boulevard
Hudson, North Carolina 28638

Biomedical Equipment Technician
  Program
Coastal Carolina Community College
444 Western Boulevard
Jacksonville, North Carolina 28540

Biomedical Equipment Technician
  Program
Durham Technical Institute
1637 Lawson Street
Durham, North Carolina 27703

Biomedical Equipment Technician
  Program
McDowell Technical Institute
Route One Box 170
Marion, North Carolina 28752

Biomedical Equipment Technician
  Program
Rowan-Cabarrus Community College
P.O. Box 1595
Salisbury, North Carolina 28144

Biomedical Equipment Technician
  Program
Stanley Community College
Route 4, Box 55
Albermarle, North Carolina 28001

Biomedical Equipment Technician
  Program
Technical College of Almance
P.O. Box 623
Haw River, North Carolina 27258

OHIO

Biomedical Equipment Technician
  Program
Bowling Green State University
Bowling Green, Ohio 43403

Biomedical Equipment Technician
  Program
Cincinnati Technical College
3520 Central Parkway
Cincinnati, Ohio 45223

Biomedical Equipment Technician
  Program
Cleveland Institute of Electronics
1776 East 17th Street
Cleveland, Ohio 44114

Biomedical Equipment Technician
  Program
Columbus Technical Institute
P.O. Box 1609
550 East Spring Street
Columbus, Ohio 43216

Biomedical Equipment Technician
  Program
Franklin University
201 South Grant Avenue
Columbus, Ohio 43215

Biomedical Equipment Technician
  Program
ITT Technical Institute
4920 Northcutt Place
Dayton, Ohio 45414

Biomedical Equipment Technician
  Program
Kettering College of Medical Arts
3737 Southern Boulevard
Kettering, Ohio 45429

Biomedical Equipment Technician
  Program
Lake County Community College
Mentor, Ohio 44060

Biomedical Equipment Technician
  Program
Marion Technical College
1465 Mt. Vernon Avenue
Marion, Ohio 43302

Biomedical Equipment Technician
  Program
Ohio Institute of Technology
Columbus, Ohio 43209

Biomedical Equipment Technician
  Program
Owens Technical College
10,000 Oregon Road
Toledo, Ohio 43699

Biomedical Equipment Technician
  Program
Polaris Vocational Center
7285 Old Oak Boulevard
Middleburg Heights, Ohio 44130

Biomedical Equipment Technician
  Program
Terra Technical College
1220 Cedar Street
Fremont, Ohio 43420

Biomedical Equipment Technician
  Program
University of Akron
302 East Buchtel Avenue
Akron, Ohio 44325

Biomedical Equipment Technician
  Program
University of Dayton
300 College Park Avenue
Dayton, Ohio 45469

Biomedical Equipment Technician
  Program
University of Toledo
2801 Bancroft Street
Toledo, Ohio 43606

OKLAHOMA

Biomedical Equipment Technician
  Program
Oklahoma City Community College
7777 South May
Oklahoma City, Oklahoma 73159

Biomedical Equipment Technician
  Program
Rose State College
6420 SE 15th Street
Midwest City, Oklahoma 73110

Biomedical Equipment Technician
  Program
Tulsa Junior College
6111 East Skelley Drive
Tulsa, Oklahoma 74135

PENNSYLVANIA

Biomedical Equipment Technician
  Program
Bethlehem Area Vocational Technical
  College
3300 Chester Avenue
Bethlehem, Pennsylvania 18017

Biomedical Equipment Technician
  Program
Carnegie-Mellon University
5000 Forbes Avenue
Pittsburgh, Pennsylvania 15213

Biomedical Equipment Technician
  Program
Community College of Allegheny
  County
800 Allegheny Avenue
Pittsburgh, Pennsylvania 15233-1895

Biomedical Equipment Technician
  Program
Delaware County Community College
Media, Pennsylvania 19053

Biomedical Equipment Technician
  Program
Edinboro University of Pennsylvania
Edinboro, Pennsylvania 16444

Biomedical Equipment Technician
  Program
Erie Institute of Technology
2221 Peninsula Drive
Erie, Pennsylvania 16506

Biomedical Equipment Technician
  Program
Johnson School of Technology
3427 North Main Avenue
Scranton, Pennsylvania 18508

Biomedical Equipment Technician
  Program
Lincoln Technical Institute
5151 Tilghman Street
Allentown, Pennsylvania 18104

Biomedical Equipment Technician
  Program
Northampton County Area Community
  College
3835 Green Pond Road
Bethlehem, Pennsylvania 18017

Biomedical Equipment Technician
  Program
Pennsylvania State University
3550 Seventh Street Road
New Kensington, Pennsylvania 15068

Biomedical Equipment Technician
  Program
Pennsylvania State University
University Park, Pennsylvania 16802

Biomedical Equipment Technician
  Program
Pennsylvania State University
Wilkes-Barre Campus
P.O. Box PSU
Lehman, Pennsylvania 18627

Biomedical Equipment Technician
  Program
Pennsylvania State University
3550 Seventh St. Road
New Kensington, Pennsylvania 15068

Biomedical Equipment Technician
  Program
Pennsylvania Technical Institute
110 Ninth Street
Pittsburgh, Pennsylvania 15222

Biomedical Equipment Technician
  Program
Point Park College
201 Wood Street
Pittsburgh, Pennsylvania 15222

Biomedical Equipment Technician
  Program
Temple University
Broad at Montgomery Avenue
Philadelphia, Pennsylvania 19122

Biomedical Equipment Technician
  Program
University of Pennsylvania
3400 Spruce Street
Philadelphia, Pennsylvania 19104

RHODE ISLAND

Biomedical Equipment Technician
  Program
Rise Institute of Electr.
14 Third Street
Providence, Rhode Island 02906

SOUTH CAROLINA

Biomedical Equipment Technician
  Program
Sumter Area Technical College
506 North Guinard Drive
Sumter, South Carolina 29150

TENNESSEE

Biomedical Equipment Technician
  Program
East Tennessee State University
P.O. Box 2420-A
Johnson City, Tennessee 37614-0002

Biomedical Equipment Technician
  Program
State Technical Institute at Memphis
5983 Macon Cove at I-40
Memphis, Tennessee 38134-7694

TEXAS

Biomedical Equipment Technician
  Program
Amarillo College
P.O. Box 447
Amarillo, Texas 79178

Biomedical Equipment Technician
  Program
College of the Mainland
8001 Palmer Highway
Texas City, Texas 77591

Biomedical Equipment Technician
  Program
San Jacinto College
4624 Fairmont Parkway
Pasadena, Texas 77504

Biomedical Equipment Technician
  Program
St. Phillips College
2111 Nevada Street
San Antonio, Texas 78203

CARDIOVASCULAR TECHNOLOGY

Cardiovascular technology, also referred to as cardiology technology, is the allied health field that records and analyzes the functioning of the heart and blood vessels. Cardiovascular technology utilizes sophisticated testing procedures which assist the cardiologist (a physician who specializes in heart conditions) in the diagnosis and treatment of heart and circulatory problems.

Two careers in cardiovascular technology are those of the *cardiovascular technologist* and the *cardiographic (EKG) technician.*

Cardiovascular Technologist

The *cardiovascular technologist* provides supportive services to the cardiologist in the use of sophisticated diagnostic procedures in the diagnosis and treatment of diseases of the heart and blood vessels.

Cardiovascular technologists perform a variety of procedures, but generally specialize in invasive cardiology, noninvasive cardiology, or noninvasive peripheral vascular study. The cardiovascular technologist may perform these procedures in such settings as invasive cardiovascular laboratories, including cardiac catheterization, blood gas, and electrophysiology laboratories; noninvasive cardiovascular laboratories, including echocardiography, exercise stress test, and electrocardiography laboratories; and noninvasive peripheral vascular studies laboratories, including Doppler ultrasound, thermography, and plethysmography laboratories.

Cardiovascular technologists are employed in hospitals, clinics, cardiac rehabilitation centers, or health maintenance organizations.

Recommended high school courses include health, biology, anatomy, physiology, typing, and computer science.

Training for the cardiovascular technologist may be from one to four years in length, depending on student qualifications and number of areas of diagnostic evaluation selected, such as invasive cardiology, noninvasive cardiology, or non invasive peripheral vascular study. Prerequisites include a high school diploma or equivalent or qualification in a clinically related allied health profession.

Credentials are available with Cardiovascular Credentialing International (CCI). Applicants who meet the educational and/or experience requirements plus pass CCI's credentialing examination are eligible to apply for the status of Registered Cardiovascular Technologist (RCVT). For more information on registration, write to Cardiovascular Credentialing International, P.O. Box 611, Wright Brothers Station, Dayton, Ohio 45409-0611.

Career information in cardiovascular technology can be obtained from the Society of Vascular Technology, 1101 Connecticut Avenue NW, Suite 700, Washington, DC 20036-4303.

Following is a list of educational programs in cardiovascular technology.

SOURCES:

American College of Cardiology
Cardiovascular Credentialing International
Occupational Outlook Handbook

Cardiovascular Technology Programs

CALIFORNIA

Cardiovascular Technology Program
Grossmont College
8800 Grossmont College Drive
El Cajon, California 92020-1799

NEW YORK

Cardiovascular Technology Program
SUNY Health Science Center at Stony
 Brook
Health Science Center/School of Allied
 Health
Stony Brook, New York 11794-8203

VIRGINIA

Cardiovascular Technology Program
Sentara Norfolk General Hospital
600 Gresham Drive
Norfolk, Virginia 23507

WASHINGTON

Cardiovascular Technology Program
Spokane Community College
N 1810 Greene Street
Spokane, Washington 99207-5499

Cardiographic Technician
(EKG Technician)

The cardiographic technician, also referred to as an *EKG technician*, is trained in the operation of electrocardiograph (EKG) equipment. EKG equipment monitors variations in the electrical potential produced by the heart. Electrical changes that occur during a heartbeat are recorded as tracings on an electrocardiogram. The record is used by the cardiologist to diagnose irregularities in heart action.

In operating EKG equipment, the cardiographic technician records pulse rates by attaching electrodes to specified areas of the patient's body. The technician also moves chest electrodes in a specific pattern across the patient's chest to record variations in electrical potential in different parts of the heart. The technician is able to detect abnormalities or false readings in the electrocardiograms and to correct technical errors in the machine.

Most cardiographic technicians are employed in EKG departments of large hospitals, while others are employed in small hospitals, clinics, physicians' offices, cardiac rehabilitation centers, and health maintenance organizations.

Cardiographic technicians, in addition to performing electrocardiograms, may perform other diagnostic tests including Holter monitoring and cardiac stress testing.

Training for the cardiographic technician is usually performed on-the-job and generally lasts from four-to-six weeks. With additional training, the cardiographic technician may perform more complex cardiovascular procedures (see section on cardiovascular technologist). Some community and junior colleges, hospitals, and vocational-technical institutes offer formal training programs, lasting from 12-24 months, but to date only a few programs have received approval from the American Cardiology Technologists Association.

There are no licensing requirements for basic cardiographic technicians. For information on certification write to Cardiovascular Credentialing International (CCI) P.O. Box 611, Wright Brothers Station, Dayton, OH 45409-0611.

In 1991, cardiographic technicians employed full time in private hospitals averaged from $6.93 to $12.03 an hour. Cardiographic technicians who perform Holter monitoring and stress testing are paid the most.

Persons interested in a career as a cardiographic technician should contact the Society of Vascular Technology, 1101 Connecticut Ave. NW, Suite 700, Washington, DC 20036-4303.

SOURCES:

American College of Cardiology
Cardiovascular Credentialing International
Occupational Outlook Handbook
Society of Vascular Technology

CORRECTIVE KINESIOTHERAPY

Corrective kinesiotherapy, formerly called *corrective therapy*, uses exercise and movement in the prevention of muscular deterioration resulting from disease, injury, congenital defects or other disabilities that may limit mobility. Through medically prescribed exercise programs corrective kinesiotherapy strives to improve movement, increase self-confidence and independence, and promote social interaction.

Corrective Kinesiotherapist

Under the supervision of a physician, the certified corrective kinesiotherapist develops and executes therapeutic exercises, education and other physical activities adapted to each individual's needs.

Corrective kinesiotherapists work for Veterans Administration hospitals, in rehabilitation facilities, hospitals, clinics, nursing homes, schools for the handicapped and home healthcare programs. Corrective kinesiotherapists may work with a variety of individuals or may specialize in geriatric healthcare, psychiatric healthcare, long term care, care of physically handicapped children, developmentally disabled or in the rehabilitation of cardiac patients or amputees.

A bachelor's degree in physical education, with a specialization in corrective kinesiotherapy, plus clinical training experience, is the requirement for students pursuing a career in corrective kinesiotherapy. Graduate courses and an advanced degree are also available at some institutions. Recommended high school courses include health, biology, physics, math, and social science.

The credentials of certified kinesiotherapist are awarded to those individuals who meet academic and clinical requirements and have successfully passed the American Kinesiotherapy Association's certification examination.

For more information on a career as a corrective kinesiotherapist, write to the American Kinesiotherapy Association, P.O. Box 611, Wright Brothers Station, Dayton, Ohio 45409-0611.

Below is a list of bachelor degree programs in corrective kinesiotherapy.

SOURCE:

American Kinesiotherapy Association

Corrective Kinesiotherapy Programs

CALIFORNIA

Corrective Kinesiotherapy Program
California State University, Long Beach
Long Beach, California 90840

ILLINOIS

Corrective Kinesiotherapy Program
University of Illinois at Chicago
Chicago, Illinois 60680

MISSISSIPPI

Corrective Kinesiotherapy Program
University of Southern Mississippi
Hattiesburg, Mississippi 39406

OHIO

Corrective Kinesiotherapy Program
The University of Toledo, Ohio
Toledo, Ohio 43600

VIRGINIA

Corrective Kinesiotherapy Program
Norfolk State University
Norfolk, Virginia 23504

Corrective Kinesiotherapy Program
Virginia Commonwealth University
Richmond, Virginia 23284

MUSIC THERAPY, DANCE THERAPY, ART THERAPY

Music, dance, and art therapies involve the respective application of the principles and techniques of each art form in a prescribed and scientific manner to accomplish therapeutic rehabilitation; that is, the restoration, maintenance, and improvement of physical and mental health. By employing motivational and creative programs each of these therapies attempts to bring about positive changes in patients' behavior, such as extended attention span, improved coordination, increased verbalization, and increased socialization.

Creative arts therapists work with emotionally disturbed adolescents and adults, the disabled, the mentally retarded, children with learning problems, and geriatric patients.

Music, dance, and art goals play a secondary role to the social, communicational, and behavioral betterment goals of the therapies, which help the patient acquire self-confidence, self-awareness, and personal satisfaction and thereby adjust to an illness or disability. The therapy may serve as one integral part of a larger treatment program or actually act in some cases as the primary method of therapy.

As members of the therapeutic team, which may include physicians, psychiatrists, psychologists, teachers, nurses, families of patients, and others; music, dance, and art therapists help plan and perform treatment plans and analyze their effectiveness.

The careers of *music therapist, dance therapist,* and *art therapist* are discussed in this chapter. Persons interested in career opportunities and training in *drama* and *poetry therapy* should contact the National Association for Drama Therapy, 19 Edwards Street, New Haven, Connecticut 06511 and the National Association for Poetry Therapy, 225 Williams St., Huron, Ohio 44839, respectively.

Music Therapist

Able to sight-read music, play by ear, improvise, and accompany other performers, the *music therapist* organizes and conducts medically prescribed musical programs to assist in the rehabilitation of patients who suffer from mental or physical illness or disability. Music therapy programs involve vocal, rhythmic, instrumental, and listening activities and include individual and group sessions with orchestras, bands, and choruses; instrument instruction; music appreciation and theory; composition instruction; general music; and folk ensembles.

The music therapist arranges concerts, sometimes performed by members of the hospital staff or by talented and capable patients, for the other patients and also accompanies and conducts group singing and folk and square dancing, with the emphasis always on therapy and rehabilitation. The music therapist may use music along with other activities, including exercise, games, art and relaxation training, as a means of achieving therapeutic goals.

Music therapists may be employed in hospitals, clinics, nursing homes, day care facilities, public and private school systems, community mental health agencies, substance abuse facilities, hospices, rehabilitation centers, and correctional facilities.

The minimum educational requirement for a music therapist is a bachelor's degree with major emphasis on music including music theory, history, conducting, arranging, instrumental and vocal studies and group performance. Other college courses must be in biological sciences, sociology, anthropology, psychology, and human anatomy .

A student who completes specific academic and clinical requirements may obtain credentials from one of two professional music therapy associations.

' Registration as a Registered Music Therapist (RMT) is available with the National Association for Music Therapy, for individuals who have met rigorous educational and clinical requirements. Information on educational and registration requirements is available from the National Association for Music Therapy, 8455 Colesville Road, Silver Spring, Maryland 20910.

Certification as a Certified Music Therapist (CMT) is available with the American Association for Music Therapy, P.O. Box 80012, Valley Forge, Pennsylvania 19484.

For persons interested in entering this career, as much music as possible should be studied and performed while in high school. It is also recommended that volunteer work or summer employment in a rehabilitation setting would give a student experience in the music therapy field.

The average annual salary of a music therapist ranges from $24,500 to $31,000. Salaries may vary based on experience, amount of education, and geographic location.

Following is a list of bachelor's degree programs in music therapy that are approved by the National Association for Music Therapy. Those marked with an asterisk (*) offer graduate degrees. For specific information on programs, contact the Director of Music Therapy at the individual schools.

SOURCES:

American Association for Music Therapy
National Association for Music Therapy

Music Therapist Programs

ALABAMA

Music Therapy Program
University of Alabama
University, Alabama 35486

ARIZONA

Music Therapy Program
Arizona State University
Tempe, Arizona 85287

CALIFORNIA

Music Therapy Program
California State University
Long Beach, California 90840

Music Therapy Program
California State University
Northridge, California 91330

Music Therapy Program (*)
University of the Pacific
Stockton, California 95211

COLORADO

Music Therapy Program (*)
Colorado State University
Fort Collins, Colorado 80523

DISTRICT OF COLUMBIA

Music Therapy Program
Howard University
Washington, DC 20059

FLORIDA

Music Therapy Program (*)
Florida State University
Tallahassee, Florida 32306

Music Therapy Program (*)
University of Miami
Coral Gables, Florida 33124

GEORGIA

Music Therapy Program
Georgia College
Milledgeville, Georgia 31061

Music Therapy Program (*)
University of Georgia
Athens, Georgia 30602

ILLINOIS

Music Therapy Program
Illinois State University
Normal, Illinois 61761

Music Therapy Program
Western Illinois
Macomb, Illinois 61455

INDIANA

Music Therapy Program
Indiana University-Ft. Wayne
Ft. Wayne, Indiana 46805

Music Therapy Program
University of Evansville
Evansville, Indiana 47722

IOWA

Music Therapy Program
University of Iowa
Iowa City, Iowa 52242

Music Therapy Program
Wartburg College
Waverly, Iowa 50677

KANSAS

Music Therapy Program (*)
University of Kansas
Lawrence, Kansas 66045

LOUISIANA

Music Therapy Program (*)
Loyola University
New Orleans, Louisiana 70118

MASSACHUSETTS

Music Therapy Program
Anna Maria College
Paxton, Massachusetts 01612

MICHIGAN

Music Therapy Program
Eastern Michigan University
Ypsilanti, Michigan 48197

Music Therapy Program (*)
Michigan State University
East Lansing, Michigan 48824

Music Therapy Program
Wayne State University
Detroit, Michigan 48202

Music Therapy Program (*)
Western Michigan University
Kalamazoo, Michigan 49008

MINNESOTA

Music Therapy Program
Augsburg College
Minneapolis, Minnesota 55454

Music Therapy Program (*)
University of Minnesota
Minneapolis, Minnesota 55455

MISSISSIPPI

Music Therapy Program
William Carey College
Hattiesburg, Mississippi 39401

MISSOURI

Music Therapy Program
Maryville University
St. Louis, Missouri 63141

Music Therapy Program (*)
University of Missouri
Kansas City, Missouri 64110

NEW JERSEY

Music Therapy Program
Montclair State College
Upper Montclair, New Jersey 07043

NEW MEXICO

Music Therapy Program
Eastern New Mexico University
Portales, New Mexico 88130

52

NEW YORK

Music Therapy Program
Nazareth College
Rochester, New York 14610

Music Therapy Program
State University of New York
Fredonia, New York 14063

Music Therapy Program
State University of New York
New Paltz, New York 12561

NORTH CAROLINA

Music Therapy Program
Mars Hill College
Mars Hill, North Carolina 28754

Music Therapy Program (*)
East Carolina University
Greenville, North Carolina 27858

Music Therapy Program
Queens College
Charlotte, North Carolina 28274

OHIO

Music Therapy Program
Baldwin-Wallace College
Berea, Ohio 44017

Music Therapy Program
Cleveland State University
Cleveland, Ohio 44114

Music Therapy Program
College of Wooster
Wooster, Ohio 44691

Music Therapy Program
College of Mt. St. Joseph
Cincinnati, Ohio 45233

Music Therapy Program (*)
Ohio University
Athens, Ohio 45701

Music Therapy Program
University of Dayton
Dayton, Ohio 45469

OKLAHOMA

Music Therapy Program
Phillips University
Enid, Oklahoma 73702

Music Therapy Program
Southwestern Oklahoma State
Weatherford, Oklahoma 73096

OREGON

Music Therapy Program
Willamette University
Salem, Oregon 97301

PENNSYLVANIA

Music Therapy Program (*)
Duquesne University
Pittsburgh, Pennsylvania 15282

Music Therapy Program
Elizabethtown College
Elizabethtown, Pennsylvania 17022

Music Therapy Program (*)
Hahnemann University
Philadelphia, Pennsylvania 19102

Music Therapy Program
Mansfield University
Mansfield, Pennsylvania 16933

Music Therapy Program
Marywood College
Scranton, Pennsylvania 18509

Music Therapy Program
Slippery Rock University
Slippery Rock, Pennsylvania 16057

Music Therapy Program (*)
Temple University
Philadelphia, Pennsylvania 19122

SOUTH CAROLINA

Music Therapy Program
Charleston Southern University
Charleston, South Carolina 29411

TENNESSEE

Music Therapy Program
Tennessee Technological University
Cookeville, Tennessee 38505

TEXAS

Music Therapy Program
Sam Houston State University
Huntsville, Texas 77341

Music Therapy Program (*)
Southern Methodist University
Dallas, Texas 75275

Music Therapy Program (*)
Texas Woman's University
Denton, Texas 76204

Music Therapy Program
West Texas State University
Canyon, Texas 79016

UTAH

Music Therapy Program
Utah State University
Logan, Utah 84322

VIRGINIA

Music Therapy Program (*)
Radford University
Radford, Virginia 24142

Music Therapy Program
Shenandoah University
Winchester, Virginia 22601

WISCONSIN

Music Therapy Program
Alverno College
Milwaukee, Wisconsin 53215

Music Therapy Program
University of Wisconsin
Eau Claire, Wisconsin 54703

Music Therapy Program (*)
University of Wisconsin
Milwaukee, Wisconsin 53201

Music Therapy Program
University of Wisconsin
Oshkosh, Wisconsin 54901

Dance Therapist

With an extensive level of training and education in dance, dance theory, improvisation, choreography, and kinesiology (study of movement), the *dance therapist* also referred to as a *movement therapist*, incorporates dance and movement in the rehabilitation and treatment of physical, behavioral, and mental disorders.

Through the use of movement and dance, the dance therapist encourages patients to express themselves non-verbally. With therapeutic goals in mind, the dance therapist helps the patient improve coordination, acquire self-confidence, and increase socialization skills.

Dance therapists may be employed in psychiatric hospitals, clinics, community mental health centers, developmental centers, correctional facilities, special schools, and rehabilitation facilities.

The minimum educational requirement for a dance therapist is a master's degree in dance therapy. A bachelor's degree, with emphasis in psychology, liberal arts, and extensive training in a variety of dance forms with courses in theory, improvisation, choreography, and kinesiology, is required for preparedness for graduate study. Master degree curricula include courses in dance and movement therapy, theory and practice, psychopathology, and human development.

Registration as a Registered Dance Therapist (D.T.R.) is available from the American Dance Therapy Association after meeting specific academic and clinical requirements. Advance credential status, as a member of the Academy of Dance Therapists Registered (A.D.T.R.), is granted to those individuals who have met additional requirements.

For further information on registration and careers in dance therapy, write to the American Dance Therapy Association, 2000 Century Plaza, Suite 108, Columbia, Maryland 21044.

SOURCE:

American Dance Therapy Association

Art Therapist

Using drawings and other art forms, the *art therapist* works with patients, generally on a one-to-one basis, in the treatment and rehabilitation of mental and emotional disorders. Art therapy may also be incorporated in the rehabilitation of substance abuse, sexual and physical abuse and in marriage and family counseling.

Art therapy provides a means of non-verbal expression and communication. Often a patient can express feelings or thoughts through the creative process of art. The art therapist works with the patient towards reconciling emotional conflicts and acquiring self-confidence and self-awareness.

Art therapists are employed in hospitals, clinics, community mental health agencies, day care facilities, public and private school systems, special service agencies, and in some cases, in private practice.

The minimum educational requirement for the art therapist is a master's degree in art therapy. Preparation for the master's degree program is a bachelor's degree from an accredited university with a major in studio art and/or psychology.

Master's degree course curricula include courses in psychology, psychotherapy, counseling, plus the history, theory, and practice of art therapy.

Graduates of approved master's degree programs are eligible to apply for registration status of Registered Art Therapist (A.T.R.).

Students interested in a career in art therapy should develop a strong background in the fine arts through education and training. Volunteer work or summer employment in a rehabilitation setting would give a student experience in the art therapy field.

Following is a list of master's degree programs approved by the American Art Therapy Association, Inc.

For more information on a career as an art therapist, write to the American Art Therapy Association, Inc., 1202 Allanson Road, Mundelein, Illinois 60060.

SOURCE:

American Art Therapy Association

Art Therapist Programs

CALIFORNIA

Art Therapist Program
College of Notre Dame
1500 Ralston
Belmont, California 94002

Art Therapist Program
Loyola Marymount University
Campus Box 135
7101 West 80th Street
Los Angeles, California 90045

DISTRICT OF COLUMBIA

Art Therapist Program
George Washington University
2129 G Street NW, Building L
Washington, DC 20052

ILLINOIS

Art Therapist Program
School of the Art Institute of Chicago
Department of Art Education & Art
  Therapy
Columbus Drive
Chicago, Illinois 60603

Art Therapist Program
Southern Illinois University at
  Edwardsville
Department of Art and Design
Box 1764
Edwardsville, Illinois 62026

Art Therapist Program
University of Illinois at Chicago
School of Art and Design
Box 4348
Chicago, Illinois 60680

KANSAS

Art Therapist Program
Emporia State University
Division of Psychology & Special
  Education
1200 Commercial
Emporia, Kansas 66801

KENTUCKY

Art Therapist Program
University of Louisville
Louisville, Kentucky 40292

MASSACHUSETTS

Art Therapist Program
Lesley College
29 Everett Street
Cambridge, Massachusetts 02138

NEW MEXICO

Art Therapist Program
University of New Mexico
Department of Art Education
Albuquerque, New Mexico 87131

NEW YORK

Art Therapist Program
College of New Rochelle
New Rochelle, New York 10805

Art Therapist Program
Hofstra University
Hempstead, New York 11550

Art Therapist Program
New York University
34 Stuyvesant Street
New York, New York 10003

Art Therapist Program
Pratt Institute
East 3200 Willoughby Avenue
Brooklyn, New York 11205

OHIO

Art Therapist Program
Ursuline College
2550 Lander Road
Pepper Pike, Ohio 44124

OREGON

Art Therapist Program
Marylhurst College
P.O. Box 261
Marylhurst, Oregon 97036

PENNSYLVANIA

Art Therapist Program
Hahnemann University
905 Broad & Vine Streets
Philadelphia, Pennsylvania 19102

Art Therapist Program
Marywood College
2300 Adams Avenue
Scranton, Pennsylvania 18509

UTAH

Art Therapist Program
University of Utah
Department of Art
Salt Lake City, Utah 84112

VERMONT

Art Therapist Program
Vermont College of Norwich University
Montpelier, Vermont 05602

VIRGINIA

Art Therapist Program
Eastern Virginia Medical School
P.O. Box 1980
Norfolk, Virginia 23501

Dentistry is the health profession that maintains, improves, and corrects the health of the teeth and the supporting oral structures. Dentists are the major practitioners of dental care and have final responsibility for all dental services. Dentists are highly educated and often are very specialized professionals. Dental school curricula are generally four years in length, and admission to dental school requires a minimum of two-to-four years of undergraduate college. Dental students interested in going into a dental specialty will require at least two to three years of additional schooling.

There are eight dental specialties recognized by the American Dental Association: orthodontics (dentistry concerned with straightening teeth), periodontics (dentistry that treats diseases of the gums), prosthodontics (dentistry to make artificial teeth and dentures), pedodontics (dentistry of children), endodontics (dentistry dedicated to treating diseases of the dental pulp usually with root canal therapy), oral pathology (dentistry that involves performing tests to diagnose disease), public health dentistry (dentistry in community clinics or with the federal government), and dental surgery.

Persons employed in allied dental health are known as dental auxiliaries, and there are three kinds of dental auxiliary careers: *dental hygienist, dental assistant,* and *dental laboratory technician.* Each of the three undertakes specific functions that allow the dentist to devote more time to the specialized activities of the chairside operative and restorative dentistry they are trained and qualified to perform.

For more information on a career in dentistry, contact either the auxiliary dental associations listed in this chapter or the American Dental Association, Division of Educational Measurements, 211 East Chicago Avenue, Chicago, Illinois 60611.

Dental Hygienist

The *dental hygienist* is an oral health clinician and educator, whose goal is to improve the dental health of the patient. Under the dentist's supervision the dental hygienist may examine, clean and polish teeth, give fluoride treatments, take and process X-rays, place temporary fillings, educate the dental patient about proper oral hygiene, provide dietary recommendations for healthy teeth, take medical and dental histories, and work within the community to educate on dental health. In some states the dental hygienist may also give local anesthetics. Duties of the dental hygienist are governed by state law and may vary from state to state.

Most dental hygienists work in private dental offices while the remainder work in schools, clinics, hospitals, health maintenance organizations, public health agencies, and in private industry.

Training in dental hygiene can be obtained in a two year certificate or associate program offered at a community college or a vocational-technical school, or the prospective dental hygienist may complete a four year bachelor's degree program at a college or university. A high school degree is the minimum educational requirement for admission to dental hygiene schools. A two year degree would prepare a student for private practice office work, however, a student wishing to do research, teach or work in school health programs would require at a minimum, a bachelor's degree.

Dental hygienists are licensed by the state. All but one state require that hygienists be graduates of an accredited dental hygiene program and pass the Dental Hygienist National Board Exam before taking the state authorized licensure exam.

Following is a list of schools that offer dental hygiene programs accredited by the Commission on Dental Accreditation as part of the American Dental Association.

The ADHA (American Dental Hygienists' Association) Institute for Oral Health offers several scholarships to needy dental hygiene students enrolled in their second year of an accredited training program. For eligibility requirements and an application form, write to ADHA Institute for Oral Health, 444 North Michigan Avenue, Suite 3400, Chicago, Illinois 60611.

For other information on accredited programs and educational requirements, contact the American Dental Hygienists' Association, 444 North Michigan Avenue, Suite 3400, Chicago, Illinois 60611.

For information on licensing requirements, contact the State Board of Dental Examiners (located in the *state capital*) or the American Association of Dental Examiners, 211 East Chicago Avenue, Chicago, Illinois 60611.

SOURCES:

American Dental Association
American Dental Hygienists' Association
Occupational Outlook Handbook

Dental Hygienist Programs

ALABAMA

Dental Hygiene Program
University of Alabama
1919 Seventh Avenue South
Box 59
Birmingham, Alabama 35294

ALASKA

Dental Hygiene Program
University of Alaska
3211 Providence Drive
Anchorage, Alaska 99508

ARIZONA

Dental Hygiene Program
Northern Arizona University
Box 15065
Flagstaff, Arizona 86011-5065

Dental Hygiene Program
Phoenix College
1202 West Thomas Road
Phoenix, Arizona 85013

ARKANSAS

Dental Hygiene Program
University of Arkansas
4301 West Markham Street
Little Rock, Arkansas 72205

CALIFORNIA

Dental Hygiene Program
Cabrillo College
6500 Soquel Drive
Aptos, California 95003

Dental Hygiene Program
West Los Angeles College
4800 Freshman Drive
Culver City, California 90230

Dental Hygiene Program
Cypress College
9200 Valley View Street
Cypress, California 90630

Dental Hygiene Program
Fresno City College
1101 East University
Fresno, California 93741

Dental Hygiene Program
Chabot College
25555 Hesperian Boulevard
Hayward, California 94545

Dental Hygiene Program
Loma Linda University
School of Dentistry
Loma Linda, California 92350

Dental Hygiene Program
Foothill College
12345 El Monte Road
Los Altos Hills, California 94022

Dental Hygiene Program
University of Southern California
University Park
Los Angeles, California 90089-0641

Dental Hygiene Program
Cerritos College
11110 East Alondra Boulevard
Norwalk, California 90650

Dental Hygiene Program
Pasadena City College
1570 East Colorado Boulevard
Pasadena, California 91106

Dental Hygiene Program
Diablo Valley College
321 Golf Club Road
Pleasant Hill, California 94523

Dental Hygiene Program
Sacramento City College
3835 Freeport Boulevard
Sacramento, California 95822

Dental Hygiene Program
University of California School of
   Dentistry
San Francisco Medical Center
San Francisco, California 94143

COLORADO

Dental Hygiene Program
University of Colorado
4200 East Ninth Avenue
Denver, Colorado 80262

Dental Hygiene Program
Pueblo Community College
415 Harrison Avenue
Pueblo, Colorado 81004

Dental Hygiene Program
Colorado Northwestern Community
   College
500 Kennedy Drive
Rangely, Colorado 81648

CONNECTICUT

Dental Hygiene Program
University of Bridgeport
30 Hazel Street
Bridgeport, Connecticut 06601

Dental Hygiene Program
Tunxis Community College
Routes 6 & 177
Farmington, Connecticut 06032

DELAWARE

Dental Hygiene Program
Delaware Technical College
333 Shipley Street
Wilmington, Delaware 19801

DISTRICT OF COLUMBIA

Dental Hygiene Program
Howard University
College of Dentistry
600 "W" Street, NW
Washington, DC 20059

FLORIDA

Dental Hygiene Program
Brevard Community College
1519 Clearlake Road
Cocoa, Florida 32922

Dental Hygiene Program
Indian River Community College
3209 Virginia Avenue
Ft. Pierce, Florida 33454-9003

Dental Hygiene Program
Santa Fe Community College
3000 NW 83rd Street
Gainesville, Florida 32602

Dental Hygiene Program
Palm Beach Community College
4200 Congress Avenue
Lake Worth, Florida 33461

Dental Hygiene Program
Miami-Dade Community College
950 NW 20th Street
Miami, Florida 33127

Dental Hygiene Program
Valencia Community College
1800 South Kirkman Road
Orlando, Florida 32811

Dental Hygiene Program
Pensacola Junior College
5555 West Highway 98
Pensacola, Florida 32507

Dental Hygiene Program
St. Petersburg Junior College
P.O. Box 13489
St. Petersburg, Florida 33733

Dental Hygiene Program
Tallahassee Community College
444 Appleyard Drive
Tallahassee, Florida 32304

GEORGIA

Dental Hygiene Program
Darton College
2400 Gillionville Road
Albany, Georgia 31707

Dental Hygiene Program
Medical College of Georgia
1120 15th Street
Augusta, Georgia 30912

Dental Hygiene Program
Dekalb College
2101 Womack Road
Dunwoody, Georgia 30338

Dental Hygiene Program
Macon College
100 College Station Drive
Macon, Georgia 31297

Dental Hygiene Program
Clayton State College
5900 Lee Street
Morrow, Georgia 30260

Dental Hygiene Program
Lanier Technical/Gainesville College
P.O. Box 58
Oakwood, Georgia 30566

Dental Hygiene Program
Armstrong State College
11935 Abercorn Street
Savannah, Georgia 31406-1997

HAWAII

Dental Hygiene Program
University of Hawaii
2528 The Mall
Honolulu, Hawaii 96822

IDAHO

Dental Hygiene Program
Idaho State University
741 South Eighth Street
Pocatello, Idaho 83209

ILLINOIS

Dental Hygiene Program
Southern Illinois University
College of Technical Careers
Carbondale, Illinois 62901

Dental Hygiene Program
Parkland College
2400 West Bradley
Champaign, Illinois 61821

Dental Hygiene Program
Illinois Central College
One College Drive
East Peoria, Illinois 61635

Dental Hygiene Program
Lake Land College
South Route 45
Mattoon, Illinois 61938

Dental Hygiene Program
Loyola University School of Dentistry
2160 South First Avenue
Maywood, Illinois 60153

Dental Hygiene Program
William Rainey Harper College
1200 West Algonquin Road
Palatine, Illinois 60067

INDIANA

Dental Hygiene Program
University of Southern Indiana
8600 University Boulevard
Evansville, Indiana 47712

Dental Hygiene Program
Indiana University-Purdue University
2101 Coliseum Boulevard East
Ft. Wayne, Indiana 46805

Dental Hygiene Program
Indiana University Northwest
3223 Broadway
Gary, Indiana 46409

Dental Hygiene Program
Indiana University-Medical Center
1121 West Michigan Street
Indianapolis, Indiana 46202-5186

Dental Hygiene Program
Indiana University-South Bend
1700 Mishawaka Avenue
South Bend, Indiana 46634

IOWA

Dental Hygiene Program
Des Moines Area Community College
2006 Ankeny Boulevard
Ankeny, Iowa 50021

Dental Hygiene Program
University of Iowa
College of Dentistry
Iowa City, Iowa 52242

Dental Hygiene Program
Hawkeye Institute of Technology
1501 East Orange Road, Box 8015
Waterloo, Iowa 50704

KANSAS

Dental Hygiene Program
Johnson County Community College
12345 College at Quivira
Overland Park, Kansas 66210-1299

Dental Hygiene Program
Wichita State University
1854 Fairmount
Box 144
Wichita, Kansas 67208-1595

KENTUCKY

Dental Hygiene Program
Western Kentucky University
Academic Complex
Bowling Green, Kentucky 42101

Dental Hygiene Program
Hopkinsville Community College
P.O. Box 2100
Hopkinsville, Kentucky 42240-2697

Dental Hygiene Program
Lexington Community College
Cooper Drive
Lexington, Kentucky 40506

Dental Hygiene Program
University of Louisville
School of Dentistry
Louisville, Kentucky 40292

LOUISIANA

Dental Hygiene Program
Northeast Louisiana University
700 University Avenue
Monroe, Louisiana 71209

Dental Hygiene Program
Louisiana State University
1100 Florida Avenue
New Orleans, Louisiana 70119

MAINE

Dental Hygiene Program
University of Maine
29 Texas Avenue
Bangor, Maine 04401

Dental Hygiene Program
Westbrook College
716 Stevens Avenue
Portland, Maine 04103

MARYLAND

Dental Hygiene Program
University of Maryland
666 West Baltimore Street
Baltimore, Maryland 21201

Dental Hygiene Program
Community College of Baltimore
2901 Liberty Heights Avenue
Baltimore, Maryland 21218

Dental Hygiene Program
Allegany Community College
Willow Brook Road
Cumberland, Maryland 21502

MASSACHUSETTS

Dental Hygiene Program
Middlesex Community College
Springs Road
Bedford, Massachusetts 01730

Dental Hygiene Program
Forsyth School of Dental Hygiene
140 The Fenway
Boston, Massachusetts 02115

Dental Hygiene Program
Bristol Community College
777 Elsbree Street
Fall River, Massachusetts 02720

Dental Hygiene Program
Springfield Technical Community
  College
One Armory Square
Springfield, Massachusetts 01105

Dental Hygiene Program
Cape Cod Community College
Route 132
West Barnstable, Massachusetts 02668

Dental Hygiene Program
Quinsigamond Community College
670 West Boylston Street
Worcester, Massachusetts 01606

MICHIGAN

Dental Hygiene Program
University of Michigan
1011 North University
Ann Arbor, Michigan 48109

Dental Hygiene Program
Kellogg Community College
450 North Avenue
Battle Creek, Michigan 49016

Dental Hygiene Program
Ferris State University
901 South State Street
Big Rapids, Michigan 49307

Dental Hygiene Program
University of Detroit
2985 East Jefferson Avenue
Detroit, Michigan 48207

Dental Hygiene Program
Wayne County Community College
8551 Greenfield
Detroit, Michigan 48228

Dental Hygiene Program
C.S. Mott Community College
1401 East Court Street
Flint, Michigan 48503

Dental Hygiene Program
Grand Rapids Community College
143 Bostwick Avenue NE
Grand Rapids, Michigan 49503

Dental Hygiene Program
Kalamazoo Valley Community College
6767 West "O" Avenue
Kalamazoo, Michigan 49009

Dental Hygiene Program
Lansing Community College
P.O. Box 40010
Lansing, Michigan 48901-7210

Dental Hygiene Program
Oakland Community College
7350 Cooley Lake Road
Union Lake, Michigan 48387

Dental Hygiene Program
Delta College
University Center, Michigan 48710

MINNESOTA

Dental Hygiene Program
Normandale Community College
9700 France Avenue South
Bloomington, Minnesota 55431

Dental Hygiene Program
University of Minnesota
10 University Drive
Duluth, Minnesota 55812-2496

Dental Hygiene Program
Mankato State University
P.O. Box 81
Mankato, Minnesota 56002-8400

Dental Hygiene Program
University of Minnesota
9436 Moos Tower
Minneapolis, Minnesota 55455

MISSISSIPPI

Dental Hygiene Program
Northeast Mississippi Community
  College
Booneville, Mississippi 38829

Dental Hygiene Program
University of Mississippi
2500 North State Street
Jackson, Mississippi 39216-4505

Dental Hygiene Program
Meridian Community College
910 Highway 19 North
Meridian, Mississippi 39307

MISSOURI

Dental Hygiene Program
Missouri Southern State College
Newman & Duquesne Roads
Joplin, Missouri 64801

Dental Hygiene Program
University of Missouri
650 East 25th Street
Kansas City, Missouri 64108

Dental Hygiene Program
St. Louis Community College-Forest
  Park
5600 Oakland Avenue
St. Louis, Missouri 63110

NEBRASKA

Dental Hygiene Program
Central Technical Community College
P.O. Box 1024
Hastings, Nebraska 68902-1024

Dental Hygiene Program
University of Nebraska Medical Center
40th & Holdredge Streets
Lincoln, Nebraska 68583-0740

NEVADA

Dental Hygiene Program
Community College of Southern Nevada
6375 West Charleston Boulevard
Las Vegas, Nevada 89102

NEW HAMPSHIRE

Dental Hygiene Program
New Hampshire Technical Institute
P.O. Box 2039
Institute Drive
Concord, New Hampshire 03302-2039

NEW JERSEY

Dental Hygiene Program
Camden County College
P.O. Box 200
Blackwood, New Jersey 08012

Dental Hygiene Program
Unon County College
1033 Springfield Avenue
Cranford, New Jersey 07016

Dental Hygiene Program
University of Med-Dent of New Jersey
65 Bergen Street
Newark, New Jersey 07107-3006

NEW MEXICO

Dental Hygiene Program
University of New Mexico
Albuquerque, New Mexico 87131

NEW YORK

Dental Hygiene Program
Broome Community College
P.O. Box 1017
Binghamton, New York 13902

Dental Hygiene Program
Eugenio Maria De Hostos College
475 Grand Concourse
Bronx, New York 10451

Dental Hygiene Program
New York City Technical College
300 Jay Street
Brooklyn, New York 11201

Dental Hygiene Program
State University of New York
Melville Road
Farmingdale, New York 11735

Dental Hygiene Program
Orange County Community College
115 South Street
Middletown, New York 10940

Dental Hygiene Program
New York University Dental Center
345 East 24th Street
New York, NY 10010

Dental Hygiene Program
Monroe Community College
1000 East Henrietta Road
Rochester, New York 14623

Dental Hygiene Program
Onondaga Community College
Route 173
Syracuse, New York 13215

Dental Hygiene Program
Hudson Valley Community College
80 Vandenburgh Avenue
Troy, New York 12180

Dental Hygiene Program
Erie Community College-North Campus
6205 Main Street
Williamsville, New York 14221-7095

NORTH CAROLINA

Dental Hygiene Program
Asheville-Buncombe Tech.
340 Victoria Road
Asheville, North Carolina 28801

Dental Hygiene Program
University of North Carolina
367 Old Dental Building
Chapel Hill, North Carolina 27599-7450

Dental Hygiene Program
Central Piedmont Community College
1201 Elizabeth Avenue
Charlotte, North Carolina 28204

Dental Hygiene Program
Fayetteville Technical Community
  College
2201 Hull Road
P.O. Box 35236
Fayetteville, North Carolina 28303

Dental Hygiene Program
Wayne Community College
Caller Box 8002
Goldsboro, North Carolina 27530

Dental Hygiene Program
Coastal Carolina Community College
444 Western Boulevard
Jacksonville, North Carolina 28540

Dental Hygiene Program
Guilford Technical Community College
P.O. Box 309
Jamestown, North Carolina 27282

NORTH DAKOTA

Dental Hygiene Program
North Dakota State College of Science
Wahpeton, North Dakota 58075

OHIO

Dental Hygiene Program
University of Cincinnati
9555 Plainfield Road
Cincinnati, Ohio 45236

Dental Hygiene Program
Cuyahoga Community College
2900 Community College Avenue
Cleveland, Ohio 44115

Dental Hygiene Program
Ohio State University
305 West 12th Avenue
Columbus, Ohio 43210

Dental Hygiene Program
Sinclair Community College
444 West Third Street
Dayton, Ohio 45402

Dental Hygiene Program
Lima Technical College
4240 Campus Drive
Lima, Ohio 45804

Dental Hygiene Program
Lakeland Community College
7700 Clocktower Drive
Mentor, Ohio 44060

Dental Hygiene Program
Owens Technical College
P.O. Box 10,000
Toledo, Ohio 43699

Dental Hygiene Program
Youngstown State University
410 Wick Avenue
Youngstown, Ohio 44555

OKLAHOMA

Dental Hygiene Program
Rose State College
6420 Southeast 15th Street
Midwest City, Oklahoma 73110

Dental Hygiene Program
University of Oklahoma
Health Science Center
P.O. Box 26901
Oklahoma City, Oklahoma 73190

OREGON

Dental Hygiene Program
Lane Community College
4000 East 30th
Eugene, Oregon 97405

Dental Hygiene Program
Mt. Hood Community College
26000 Southeast Stark Street
Gresham, Oregon 97030

Dental Hygiene Program
Oregon Institute of Technology
3201 Campus Drive
Klamath Falls, Oregon 97601

Dental Hygiene Program
Oregon Health Sciences University
611 Southwest Campus Drive
Portland, Oregon 97201

Dental Hygiene Program
Portland Community College
P.O. Box 19000
Portland, Oregon 97219-0990

PENNSYLVANIA

Dental Hygiene Program
Northampton County Community
  College
3835 Green Pond Road
Bethlehem, Pennsylvania 18017

Dental Hygiene Program
Montgomery County Community
College
340 Dekalb Pike
P.O. Box 400
Blue Bell, Pennsylvania 19422-0758

Dental Hygiene Program
Harcum Junior College
Montgomery Avenue
Bryn Mawr, Pennsylvania 19010

Dental Hygiene Program
Harrisburg Area Community College
3300 Cameron State Road
Harrisburg, Pennsylvania 17110-2999

Dental Hygiene Program
Luzerne County Community College
13333 South Prospect Street
Nanticoke, Pennsylvania 18634-3899

Dental Hygiene Program
Community College of Philadelphia
1700 Spring Garden Street
Philadelphia, Pennsylvania 19130

Dental Hygiene Program
Thomas Jefferson University
130 South Ninth Street, 22nd Floor
Philadelphia, Pennsylvania 19107

Dental Hygiene Program
University of Pittsburgh
Pittsburgh, Pennsylvania 15261

Dental Hygiene Program
Pennsylvania College of Technology
One College Avenue
Williamsport, Pennsylvania 17701

RHODE ISLAND

Dental Hygiene Program
University of Rhode Island
Kingston, Rhode Island 02881-0817

Dental Hygiene Program
Community College of Rhode Island
Louisquisset Pike
Lincoln, Rhode Island 02865

SOUTH CAROLINA

Dental Hygiene Program
Midlands Technical College
P.O. Box 2408
Columbia, South Carolina 29202

Dental Hygiene Program
Florence-Darlington Technical College
P.O. Drawer F
Florence South Carolina 29501

Dental Hygiene Program
Greenville Technical College
P.O. Box 5616 Station B
Greenville, South Carolina 29606-5616

SOUTH DAKOTA

Dental Hygiene Program
University of South Dakota
414 East Clark Street
Vermillion, South Dakota 57069

TENNESSEE

Dental Hygiene Program
Chattanooga State Technical Community
  College
4501 Amnicola Highway
Chattanooga, Tennessee 37406-1097

Dental Hygiene Program
East Tennessee State University
P.O. Box 70690
Johnson City, Tennessee 37614-0690

Dental Hygiene Program
University of Tennessee
Memphis, Tennessee 38163

Dental Hygiene Program
Meharry Medical College
Tennessee State University
3500 John A. Merritt Boulevard
Nashville, Tennessee 37209-1561

Dental Hygiene Program
Roane State Community College
Oak Ridge, Tennessee 37748

TEXAS

Dental Hygiene Program
Amarillo College
Allied Health Division
P.O. Box 447
Amarillo, Texas 79178

Dental Hygiene Program
Lamar University
Box 10096
Beaumont, Texas 77710

Dental Hygiene Program
Bee County College
3800 Charco Road
Beeville, Texas 78102

Dental Hygiene Program
Howard College
1001 Birdwell Lane
Big Spring, Texas 79720

Dental Hygiene Program
Del Mar College
Baldwin & Ayers Streets
Corpus Christi, Texas 78404

Dental Hygiene Program
Baylor College of Dentistry
3302 Gaston Avenue
Dallas, Texas 75246

Dental Hygiene Program
Texas Woman's University
Box 22665
TWU Station
Denton, Texas 76204

Dental Hygiene Program
El Paso Community College
P.O. Box 20500
El Paso, Texas 79998

Dental Hygiene Program
University of Texas
Dental Branch
P.O. Box 20068
Houston, Texas 77225

Dental Hygiene Program
Tarrant County Junior College
828 Harwood Road
Hurst, Texas 76054

Dental Hygiene Program
University of Texas
7703 Floyd Curl Drive
San Antonio, Texas 78284-7904

Dental Hygiene Program
Tyler Junior College
P.O. Box 9020
Tyler, Texas 75711

Dental Hygiene Program
Wharton County Junior College
911 Boling Highway
Wharton, Texas 77488

Dental Hygiene Program
Midwestern State University
3400 Taft
Wichita Falls, Texas 76308

UTAH

Dental Hygiene Program
Weber State University
3750 Harrison Boulevard
Ogden, Utah 84408-1601

VIRGINIA

Dental Hygiene Program
Northern Virginia Community College
8333 Little River Turnpike
Annandale, Virginia 22003

Dental Hygiene Program
Old Dominion University
G.W. Hirschfeld School
Norfolk, Virginia 23529-0499

Dental Hygiene Program
Virginia Commonwealth University
Division of Dental Hygiene
Box 566
Richmond, Virginia 23298

Dental Hygiene Program
Virginia Western Community College
3095 Colonial Avenue SW
Roanoke, Virginia 24038

Dental Hygiene Program
Wytheville Community College
1000 East Main Street
Wytheville, Virginia 24382

WASHINGTON

Dental Hygiene Program
Shoreline Community College
16101 Greenwood Avenue
North Seattle, Washington 98133

Dental Hygiene Program
Eastern Washington University
Spokane, Washington 99201

Dental Hygiene Program
Pierce College
9401 Farwest Drive, SW
Tacoma, Washington 98498

Dental Hygiene Program
Clark College
1800 East McLoughlin Boulevard
Vancouver, Washington 98663

Dental Hygiene Program
Yakima Valley Community College
16th Avenue
Yakima, Washington 98907

WEST VIRGINIA

Dental Hygiene Program
West Virginia Institute of Technology
Montgomery, West Virginia 25136

Dental Hygiene Program
West Virginia University
Health Sciences Center North
Morgantown, West Virginia 26506

Dental Hygiene Program
West Liberty State College
West Liberty, West Virginia 26074

WISCONSIN

Dental Hygiene Program
Northeast Wisconsin Technical College
2740 West Mason Street
P.O. Box 19042
Green Bay, Wisconsin 54307-9042

Dental Hygiene Program
Madison Area Technical College
3550 Anderson Street
Madison, Wisconsin 53704

Dental Hygiene Program
Marquette University
604 North 16th Street
Milwaukee, Wisconsin 53233

Dental Hygiene Program
Milwaukee Area Technical College
700 West State Street
Milwaukee, Wisconsin 53233

Dental Hygiene Program
North Central Technical College
1000 Campus Drive
Wausau, Wisconsin 54401

WYOMING

Dental Hygiene Program
Sheridan College
3059 Coffeen Avenue
Sheridan, Wyoming 82801

Dental Assistant

Under supervision the *dental assistant* assists the dentist with direct care of the dental patient. The responsibilities of the dental assistant vary widely depending upon the requirements of the dentist-employer and the extent of the dental assistant's education and experience. Duties of the dental assistant are governed by state law and may vary from state to state. The dental assistant can perform four types of functions: chairside assistance, clinical support, laboratory support duties, and office duties.

In chairside assistance the dental assistant, if qualified, can assist in all aspects of general dentistry and dental specialties. In clinical support the dental assistant may process X-rays and take and record dental and medical histories from patients. Laboratory support duties include pouring molds and making preliminary impressions for study casts. Finally the dental assistant can perform business office procedures such as maintaining an appointment schedule, acting as office receptionist, receiving payment from patients, and controlling office inventory. In a larger dental office a receptionist or office manager may take on these business office responsibilities allowing the dental assistant to perform dental work.

The dental assistant can be trained by a dentist, as many are, or complete a one to two year postsecondary dental assisting program at a vocational technical school or community college and receive a certificate, diploma, or associate degree. Those who have completed an accredited dental assisting program are eligible to take the certification examination by the Dental Assisting National Board. Certification is required in some states. For information on certification in dental assisting, contact the Dental Assisting National Board, Inc., 216 East Ontario Street, Chicago, Illinois 60611.

Application for a limited number of educational scholarships may be obtained from the American Dental Assistants Association at the address listed below.

According to a 1991 survey by the National Association of Dental Assistants, the average weekly salary of dental assistants was approximately $370.

Following is a list of dental assisting programs accredited by the Commission on Dental Accreditation of the American Dental Association.

For more information on a career as a dental assistant, contact the American Dental Assistants Association, 919 North Michigan Avenue, Suite 3400, Chicago, Illinois 60611.

SOURCES:

American Dental Assistants Association
Occupational Outlook Handbook

Dental Assistant Programs

ALABAMA

Dental Assisting Program
James H. Faulkner State Community
  College
1900 Highway 31 South
Bay Minette, Alabama 36507-2619

Dental Assisting Program
Bessemer State Technical College
P.O. Box 308
Bessemer, Alabama 35021

Dental Assisting Program
University of Alabama
1919 Seventh Avenue South, Box 59
Birmingham, Alabama 35294

Dental Assisting Program
John Calhoun State Community College
P.O. Box 2216
Decatur, Alabama 35602

Dental Assisting Program
Wallace State Community College
801 Main Street NE
Hanceville, Alabama 35077-2090

Dental Assisting Program
Trehholm State Technical College
1225 Air Base Boulevard
Montgomery, Alabama 36108

ALASKA

Dental Assisting Program
University of Alaska
3211 Providence Drive
Anchorage, Alaska 99508

ARIZONA

Dental Assisting Program
Phoenix College
1202 West Thomas Road
Phoenix, Arizona 85013

Dental Assisting Program
Pima County Community College
2202 West Anklam Road
Tucson, Arizona 85709

ARKANSAS

Dental Assisting Program
Cotton Boll Technical Institute
Box 36
Burdette, Arkansas 72321

Dental Assisting Program
Pulaski Technical College
3000 West Scenic Road
North Little Rock, Arkansas 72118-3399

CALIFORNIA

Dental Assisting Program
College of Alameda
555 Atlantic Avenue
Alameda, California 94501

Dental Assisting Program
Chaffey Community College
5885 Haven Avenue
Alta Loma, California 91701

Dental Assisting Program
Orange Coast College
2701 Fairview Road
Costa Mesa, California 92628-0120

Dental Assisting Program
Cypress College
9200 Valley View Street
Cypress, California 90630

Dental Assisting Program
College of the Redwoods
Tompkins Hill Road
Eureka, California 95501

Dental Assisting Program
Citrus College
1000 West Foothill
Glendora, California 91740

Dental Assisting Program
Chabot College
25555 Hesperian Boulevard
Hayward, California 94545

Dental Assisting Program
College of Marin
College Avenue
Kentfield, California 94904

Dental Assisting Program
Foothill College
12345 El Monte Road
Los Altos Hills, California 94022

Dental Assisting Program
La Unified School District
3721 West Washington Boulevard
Los Angeles, California 90018

Dental Assisting Program
East Los Angeles Occ. Center
2100 Marengo Street
Los Angeles, California 90033

Dental Assisting Program
Merced College
3600 M Street
Merced, California 95348

Dental Assisting Program
North Valley Occ. Center
11450 Sharp Avenue
Mission Hills, California 91345

Dental Assisting Program
Modesto Junior College
435 College Avenue
Modesto, California 9535

Dental Assisting Program
Monterey Peninsula College
980 Fremont Avenue
Monterey, California 93940

Dental Assisting Program
Cerritos College
11110 East Alondra Boulevard
Norwalk, California 90650

Dental Assisting Program
Pasadena City College
1570 East Colorado Boulevard
Pasadena, California 91106

Dental Assisting Program
Diablo Valley College
321 Golf Club Road
Pleasant Hill, California 94523

Dental Assisting Program
Kings River Community College
995 North Reed Avenue
Reedley, California 93654

Dental Assisting Program
Sacramento City College
3835 Freeport Boulevard
Sacramento, California 95822

Dental Assisting Program
City College of San Francisco
50 Phelan Avenue
San Francisco, California 94112

Dental Assisting Program
San Jose City College
2100 Moorpark Avenue
San Jose, California 95128

Dental Assisting Program
Palomar Community College
1140 West Mission Road
San Marcos, California 92069

Dental Assisting Program
College of San Mateo
1700 West Hillsdale Boulevard
San Mateo, California 94402

Dental Assisting Program
Contra Costa College
2600 Mission Bell Drive
San Pablo, California 94806

Dental Assisting Program
Santa Barbara City College
721 Cliff Drive
Santa Barbara, California 93109-2394

Dental Assisting Program
Santa Rosa Junior College
1501 Mendocino Avenue
Santa Rosa, California 95401

COLORADO

Dental Assisting Program
T.H. Pickens Technical Center
500 Buckley Road
Aurora, Colorado 80011

Dental Assisting Program
Pikes Peak Community College
5765 South Academy Boulevard
Colorado Springs, Colorado 80906

Dental Assisting Program
Emily Griffith Oppor. School
1250 Welton Street
Denver, Colorado 80204

Dental Assisting Program
Front Range Community College
Larimer Campus
P.O. Box 2397
Ft. Collins, Colorado 80522

Dental Assisting Program
Front Range Community College
3645 West 112th Avenue
Westminister, Colorado 80030

CONNECTICUT

Dental Assisting Program
Tunxis Community College
Routes 6 & 177
Farmington, Connecticut 86032

Dental Assisting Program
Eli Whitney Reg. Vocational Technical
   School
71 Jones Road
Hamden, Connecticut 06514

Dental Assisting Program
Windham Reg. Vocational Technical
   School
210 Birch Street
Williamantic, Connecticut 06226

DISTRICT OF COLUMBIA

Dental Assisting Program
Margaret Murray Washington
27 "O" Street, NW
Washington, DC 20001

FLORIDA

Dental Assisting Program
Manatee Area Vocational Technical
   Center
5603 34th Street West
Bradenton, Florida 34210

Dental Assisting Program
Brevard Community College
1519 Clearlake Road
Cocoa, Florida 32922

Dental Assisting Program
Daytona Beach Community College
P.O. Box 2811
1200 Volusia Avenue
Daytona Beach, Florida 32115-2811

Dental Assisting Program
Broward Community College
3501 Southwest Davie Road
Ft. Lauderdale, Florida 33314

Dental Assisting Program
Indian River Community College
3209 Virginia Avenue
Ft. Pierce, Florida 33454-9003

Dental Assisting Program
Santa Fe Community College
3000 NW 83rd Street
Gainesville, Florida 32602

Dental Assisting Program
Lindsey Hopkins Tech-Ed Center
750 NW 20th Street
Miami, Florida 33127

Dental Assisting Program
Robert Morgan Vocational Technical
   Institute
18180 SW 122nd Avenue
Miami, Florida 33177

Dental Assisting Program
Orlando Vocational Technical Center
301 West Amelia Street
Orlando, Florida 32801

Dental Assisting Program
Southern College
5600 Lake Underhill Road
Orlando, Florida 32807

Dental Assisting Program
Gulf Coast Community College
5230 West Highway 98
Panama City, Florida 32401

Dental Assisting Program
Pensacola Junior College
5555 West Highway 98
Pensacola, Florida 32507

Dental Assisting Program
Charlotte Vocational Technical Center
18300 Toledo Blade Boulevard
Port Charlotte, Florida 33948-3399

Dental Assisting Program
Pinellas Technical Education Center
901 34th Street South
St. Petersburg, Florida 33711

GEORGIA

Dental Assisting Program
Albany Technical Institute
1021 Lowe Road
Albany, Georgia 31708

Dental Assisting Program
Augusta Technical Institute
3116 Deans Bridge Road
Augusta, Georgia 30906

Dental Assisting Program
Gwinnett Area Technical School
1250 Atkinson Road, Box 1505
Lawrenceville, Georgia 30246-1505

Dental Assisting Program
Lanier Tech/Gainesville College
P.O. Box 58
Oakwood, Georgia 30566

Dental Assisting Program
Savannah Technical Institute
5717 White Bluff Road
Savannah, Georgia 31499

ILLINOIS

Dental Assisting Program
John A. Logan College
Rural Route 2
Carterville, Illinois 62918

Dental Assisting Program
Kaskaskia College
Shattuc Road
Centralia, Illinois 62801

Dental Assisting Program
Parkland College
2400 West Bradley
Champaign, Illinois 61821

Dental Assisting Program
Morton College
3801 South Central Avenue
Cicero, Illinois 60650

Dental Assisting Program
Illinois Central College
One College Drive
East Peoria, Illinois 61635

Dental Assisting Program
Elgin Community College
1700 Spartan Drive
Elgin, Illinois 60123

Dental Assisting Program
Lewis & Clark Community College
5800 Godfrey Road
Godfrey, Illinois 62035

Dental Assisting Program
Black Hawk College
6600 34th Avenue
Moline, Illinois 61265

INDIANA

Dental Assisting Program
University of Southern Indiana
8600 University Boulevard
Evansville, Indiana 47712

Dental Assisting Program
Indiana University-Purdue University
2101 Coliseum Boulevard East
Ft. Wayne, Indiana 46805

Dental Assisting Program
Indiana University Northwest
3223 Broadway
Gary, Indiana 46409

Dental Assisting Program
Indiana University-Medical Center
1121 West Michigan Street
Indianapolis, Indiana 46202-5186

Dental Assisting Program
Professional Careers Institute
2611 Waterfront Parkway-East Drive
Indianapolis, Indiana 46214

Dental Assisting Program
Indiana Vocational Technical College
3208 Ross Road, Box 6299
Lafayette, Indiana 47903

Dental Assisting Program
Indiana University-South Bend
1700 Mishawaka Avenue
South Bend, Indiana 46634

IOWA

Dental Assisting Program
Des Moines Area Community College
2006 Ankeny Boulevard
Ankeny, Iowa 50021

Dental Assisting Program
Kirkwood Community College
6301 Kirkwood Boulevard SW
Box 2068
Cedar Rapids, Iowa 52406

Dental Assisting Program
Iowa Western Community College
2700 College Road, Box 4C
Council Bluffs, Iowa 51502

Dental Assisting Program
Marshall Community College
3700 South Center Street
Marshalltown, Iowa 50158

Dental Assisting Program
Northeast Iowa Community College
10250 Sundown road
Peosta, Iowa 52001

Dental Assisting Program
Western Iowa Tech Community College
P.O. Box 265
4647 Stone Avenue
Sioux City, Iowa 51102

Dental Assisting Program
Hawkeye Institute of Technology
1501 East Orange Road, Box 8015
Waterloo, Iowa 50704

KANSAS

Dental Assisting Program
Flint Hills Technical School
3301 West 18th Avenue
Emporia, Kansas 66801

Dental Assisting Program
Wichita Area Vocational Technical
  School
324 North Emporia
Wichita, Kansas 67202

KENTUCKY

Dental Assisting Program
Kentucky Tech-Central Campus
104 Vo-Tech Road
Lexington, Kentucky 40510-1020

Dental Assisting Program
Kentucky Tech-West Campus
Blandville Road-Highway 62 W. #7408
Paducah, Kentucky 42002-7408

MAINE

Dental Assisting Program
University of Maine
29 Texas Avenue
Bangor, Maine 04401

MARYLAND

Dental Assisting Program
Allegany Community College
Willow Brook Road
Cumberland, Maryland 21502

Dental Assisting Program
Montgomery College
Takoma & Fenton Street
Takoma Park, Maryland 20012

MASSACHUSETTS

Dental Assisting Program
Middlesex Community College
Springs Road
Bedford, Massachusetts 01730

Dental Assisting Program
Bunker Hill Community College
New Rutherford Avenue
Boston, Massachusetts 02129

Dental Assisting Program
Northern Essex Community College
Elliott Way
Haverhill, Massachusetts 01830-2399

Dental Assisting Program
Mount Ida College
777 Dedham Street
Newton Centre, Massachusetts 02159

Dental Assisting Program
Charles H. McCann Technical School
Hodges Crossroad
North Adams, Massachusetts 01247

Dental Assisting Program
Southeastern Technical Institute
250 Foundry Street
South Easton, Massachusetts 02375

Dental Assisting Program
Springfield Technical Community
 College
One Armory Square
Springfield, Massachusetts 01105

Dental Assisting Program
Worcester Technical Institute
251 Belmont Street
Worcester, Massachusetts 01605

MICHIGAN

Dental Assisting Program
Washtenaw Community College
4800 East Huron River Drive
Ann Arbor, Michigan 48106

Dental Assisting Program
Lake Michigan College
2755 East Napier
Benton Harbor, Michigan 49022

Dental Assisting Program
Wayne County Community College
8551 Greenfield
Detroit, Michigan 48228

Dental Assisting Program
C.S. Mott Community College
1401 East Court Street
Flint, Michigan 48503

Dental Assisting Program
Grand Rapids Community College
143 Bostwick Avenue NE
Grand Rapids, Michigan 49503

Dental Assisting Program
Lansing Community College
P.O. Box 40010
Lansing, Michigan 48901-7210

Dental Assisting Program
Northwestern Michigan College
1701 East Front Street
Traverse City, Michigan 49684

Dental Assisting Program
Delta College
University Center, Michigan 48710

MINNESOTA

Dental Assisting Program
Bemidji Technical College
905 Grant Avenue SE
Bemidji, Minnesota 56601

Dental Assisting Program
Normandale Community College
9700 France Avenue South
Bloomington, Minnesota 55431

Dental Assisting Program
Hennepin Technical College
9000 Brooklyn Boulevard
Brooklyn Park, Minnesota 55455

Dental Assisting Program
Southwestern Technical College
1011 First Street West
Canby, Minnesota 56220

Dental Assisting Program
Hibbing Technical College
2900 East Beltline
Hibbing, Minnesota 55746

Dental Assisting Program
Lakeland Medical Dental Academy
1402 West Lake Street
Minneapolis, Minnesota 55408

Dental Assisting Program
Concorde Career Institute
12 North 12th Street
Minneapolis, Minnesota 55403

Dental Assisting Program
Minneapolis Technical College
1415 Hennepin Avenue South
Room 446
Minneapolis, Minnesota 55403

Dental Assisting Program
Moorhead Technical College
1900 28th Avenue South
Moorhead, Minnesota 56560

Dental Assisting Program
Mankato Area Vocational Technical
   School
1920 Lee Boulevard
P.O. Box 1920
North Mankato, Minnesota 56003

Dental Assisting Program
Rochester CC/Riverland Tech.
1926 Collegeview Road SE
Rochester, Minnesota 55906

Dental Assisting Program
Northeast Metro Technical College
3300 Century Avenue North
White Bear Lake, Minnesota 55110

MISSISSIPPI

Dental Assisting Program
Hinds Community College
3925 Sunset Drive
Jackson, Mississippi 39213

MISSOURI

Dental Assisting Program
Nichols Career Center
609 Union Street
Jefferson City, Missouri 65101

Dental Assisting Program
Heart of the Ozarks Technical
   Community College
1417 North Jefferson
Springfield, Missouri 65802

Dental Assisting Program
East Central College
Box 529
Highway 50 & Prairie Dell
Union, Missouri 63084

MONTANA

Dental Assisting Program
Great Falls Vocational Technical Center
2100 16th Avenue South
Great Falls, Montana 59405

NEBRASKA

Dental Assisting Program
Central Technical Community College
P.O. Box 1024
Hastings, Nebraska 68902-1024

Dental Assisting Program
Southeast Community College
8800 "O" Street
Lincoln, Nebraska 68520

Dental Assisting Program
Mid-Plains Community College
Route 4, Box 1
North Platte, Nebraska 69101

Dental Assisting Program
Metropolitan Community College
P.O. Box 3777
Omaha, Nebraska 68103-0777

Dental Assisting Program
Omaha College of Health Careers
1052 Park Avenue
Omaha, Nebraska 68105

NEVADA

Dental Assisting Program
Truckee Meadows Community College
7000 Dandini Boulevard
Reno, Nevada 89512

NEW HAMPSHIRE

Dental Assisting Program
New Hampshire Technical Institute
P.O. Box 2039
Institute Drive
Concord, New Hampshire 03302-2039

NEW JERSEY

Dental Assisting Program
Camden County College
P.O. Box 200
Blackwood, New Jersey 08012

Dental Assisting Program
University of Med-Dent of New Jersey
65 Bergen Street
Newark, New Jersey 07107-3006

Dental Assisting Program
Technical Institute of Camden County
343 Berlin Cross Keys Road
Sicklerville, New Jersey 08081-9709

Dental Assisting Program
Berdan Institute
265 Route 46 West
Totowa, New Jersey 07512

NEW MEXICO

Dental Assisting Program
University of New Mexico
Albuquerque, New Mexico 87131

NEW YORK

Dental Assisting Program
SUNY Educational Opportunity Center
465 Washington Street
Buffalo, New York 14203

Dental Assisting Program
New York University Dental Center
345 East 24th Street
New York, New York 10010

NORTH CAROLINA

Dental Assisting Program
Asheville-Buncombe Tech
340 Victoria Road
Asheville, North Carolina 28801

Dental Assisting Program
University of North Carolina
367 Old Dental Building
Chapel Hill, North Carolina 27599-7450

Dental Assisting Program
Central Piedmont Community College
1201 Elizabeth Avenue-Kings Drive
Charlotte, North Carolina 28204

Dental Assisting Program
Fayetteville Technical Community
  College
2201 Hull Road
P.O. Box 35236
Fayetteville, North Carolina 28303

Dental Assisting Program
Wayne Community College
Caller Box 8002
Goldsboro, North Carolina 27530

Dental Assisting Program
Alamance Community College
P.O. Box 623
Haw River, North Carolina 27258

Dental Assisting Program
Coastal Carolina Community College
444 Western Boulevard
Jacksonville, North Carolina 28540

Dental Assisting Program
Guilford Technical Community College
P.O. Box 309
Jamestown, North Carolina 27282

Dental Assisting Program
Western Piedmont Community College
1001 Burkemont Avenue
Morganton, North Carolina 28655

Dental Assisting Program
Wake Technical Community College
9101 Fayetteville Road
Raleigh, North Carolina 27603-5696

Dental Assisting Program
Rowan-Cabarrus Community College
P.O. Box 1595
Salisbury, North Carolina 28144

Dental Assisting Program
Wilkes Community College
P.O. Box 120
Wilkesboro, North Carolina 28697-0120

NORTH DAKOTA

Dental Assisting Program
North Dakota State College of Science
Wahpeton, North Dakota 58075

OHIO

Dental Assisting Program
Cuyahoga Community College
2900 Community College Avenue
Cleveland, Ohio 44115

Dental Assisting Program
Jefferson Technical College
4000 Sunset Boulevard
Steubenville, Ohio 43952

OKLAHOMA

Dental Assisting Program
Rose State College
6420 Southeast 15th Street
Midwest City, Oklahoma 73110

OREGON

Dental Assisting Program
Linn-Benton Community College
6500 Southwest Pacific Boulevard
Albany, Oregon 97321

Dental Assisting Program
Lane Community College
4000 East 30th
Eugene, Oregon 97405

Dental Assisting Program
Blue Mountain Community College
2411 Northwest Carden
Pendleton, Oregon 97801

Dental Assisting Program
Bradford School
921 SW Washington
Portland, Oregon 97204

Dental Assisting Program
Portland Community College
P.O. Box 19000
Portland, Oregon 97219-0990

Dental Assisting Program
Chemeketa Community College
4000 Lancaster Drive NE
Salem, Oregon 97309

PENNSYLVANIA

Dental Assisting Program
Harcum Junior College
Montgomery Avenue
Bryn Mawr, Pennsylvania 19010

Dental Assisting Program
Manor Junior College
700 Fox Chase Road
Jenkintown, Pennsylvania 19046-3399

Dental Assisting Program
Harrisburg Area Community College
3300 Cameron State Road
Harrisburg, Pennsylvania 17110-2999

Dental Assisting Program
Community College of Philadelphia
1700 Spring Garden Street
Philadelphia, Pennsylvania 19130

Dental Assisting Program
Murrell Dobbins Vocational Technical
   School
22nd Street & Lehigh Avenue
Philadelphia, Pennsylvania 19132

Dental Assisting Program
Median School of Allied Health
125 Seventh Street
Pittsburgh, Pennsylvania 15222-3400

RHODE ISLAND

Dental Assisting Program
Community College of Rhode Island
Louisquisset Pike
Lincoln, Rhode Island 02865

SOUTH CAROLINA

Dental Assisting Program
Trident Technical College
P.O. Box 10367
Charleston, South Carolina 29411

Dental Assisting Program
Midlands Technical College
P.O. Box 2408
Columbia, South Carolina 29202

Dental Assisting Program
Florence-Darlington Technical College
P.O. Drawer F
Florence, South Carolina 29501

Dental Assisting Program
Greenville Technical College
P.O. Box 5616 Station B
Greenville, South Carolina 29606-5616

Dental Assisting Program
Tri-County Technical College
P.O. Box 587
Pendleton, South Carolina 29670

Dental Assisting Program
York Technical College
452 South Anderson Road
Rock Hill, South Carolina 29730

Dental Assisting Program
Spartanburg Technical College
P.O. Drawer 4386
Highway I-85
Spartanburg, South Carolina 29305-4386

SOUTH DAKOTA

Dental Assisting Program
Lake Area Vocational Technical Institute
230 Eleventh Street NE
Watertown, South Dakota 57201

TENNESSEE

Dental Assisting Program
Chattanooga State Technical Community
  College
4501 Amnicola Highway
Chattanooga, Tennessee 37406-1097

Dental Assisting Program
East Tennessee State University
1000 West E Street
Elizabethton, Tennessee 37643

Dental Assisting Program
Volunteer State Community College
Nashville Pike
Gallatin, Tennessee 37066

Dental Assisting Program
Knoxville Area Vocational Technical
1100 Liberty Street
Knoxville, Tennessee 37919

Dental Assisting Program
Memphis Area Vocational Technical
  School
620 Mosby Street
Memphis, Tennessee 38105

TEXAS

Dental Assisting Program
Del Mar College
Baldwin & Ayers Streets
Corpus Christi, Texas 78404

Dental Assisting Program
Grayson County College
6101 Grayson Drive
Denison, Texas 75020

Dental Assisting Program
El Paso Community College
P.O. Box 20500
El Paso, Texas 79998

Dental Assisting Program
Houston Community College
3100 Shenandoah
Houston, Texas 77021

Dental Assisting Program
North Harris County College
2700 NW Thorne Drive
Houston, Texas 77073

Dental Assisting Program
San Antonio College
1300 San Pedro Avenue
San Antonio, Texas 78212-4299

Dental Assisting Program
School of Health Care Sciences
3790 Medical Service Training Wing
Sheppard AFB, Texas 76311-5465

Dental Assisting Program
Texas State Technical College
3801 Campus Drive
Waco, Texas 76705

UTAH

Dental Assisting Program
Provo College
1275 North University Avenue
Provo, Utah 84604

Dental Assisting Program
American Institute of Med-Dent Tech
1675 North Freedom Boulevard
Bldg. 9A
Provo, Utah 84604

VIRGINIA

Dental Assisting Program
Old Dominion University
G.W. Hirschfeld School
Norfolk, Virginia 23529-0499

Dental Assisting Program
J. Sargeant Reynolds College
Eighth & Jackson
P.O. Box C32040
Richmond, Virginia 23261-2040

Dental Assisting Program
Wytheville Community College
1000 East Main Street
Wytheville, Virginia 24382

WASHINGTON

Dental Assisting Program
Bellingham Vocational Technical
    Institute
3028 Lindbergh Avenue
Bellingham, Washington 98225

Dental Assisting Program
Highline Community College
P.O. Box 98000
Des Moines, Washington 98198-9800

Dental Assisting Program
Lake Washington Vocational Technical
11605 132nd Avenue NE
Kirkland, Washington 98034

Dental Assisting Program
South Puget Sound Community College
2011 Mottman Road
Olympia, Washington 98502

Dental Assisting Program
Renton Vocational Technical Institute
3000 Northeast Fourth Street
Renton, Washington 98056

Dental Assisting Program
Trend College Spokane
North 214 Wall Street
Spokane, Washington 99201

Dental Assisting Program
Spokane Community College
North 1810 Greene Street
Spokane, Washington 99207

Dental Assisting Program
Clover Park Technical College
4500 Steilacoom Boulevard SW
Tacoma, Washington 98498-4098

Dental Assisting Program
L.H. Bates Vocational Technical
    Institute
1101 South Yakima Avenue
Tacoma, Washington 98405

WISCONSIN

Dental Assisting Program
Fox Valley Technical College
1825 Bluemound Drive
Appleton, Wisconsin 54913

Dental Assisting Program
Lakeshore Technical College
1290 North Avenue
Cleveland, Wisconsin 53015

Dental Assisting Program
Northeast Wisconsin Technical College
2740 West Mason Street
P.O. Box 19042
Green Bay, Wisconsin 54307-9042

Dental Assisting Program
Blackhawk Technical College
6004 Prairie Road
Janesville, Wisconsin 53547

Dental Assisting Program
Gateway Technical College
3520 30th Avenue
Kenosha, Wisconsin 53144-1690

Dental Assisting Program
Western Wisconsin Technical College
Sixth and Vine Streets
La Crosse, Wisconsin 54601

Dental Assisting Program
Madison Area Technical College
3550 Anderson Street
Madison, Wisconsin 53704

Dental Assisting Program
Milwaukee Area Technical College
700 West State Street
Milwaukee, Wisconsin 53233

WYOMING

Dental Assisting Program
Sheridan College
3059 Coffeen Avenue
Sheridan, Wyoming 82801

Dental Laboratory Technician

The *dental laboratory technician* works in the field of dental laboratory technology. The dental laboratory technician constructs or repairs artificial teeth, fixed bridges, removable partial dentures, crowns, inlays, and orthodontic appliances, according to dentists' prescriptions. Using precision instruments and specialized equipment, the dental laboratory technician works with a range of material including gold, silver, stainless steel, porcelain, and plastics.

Most dental laboratory technicians work in commercial dental laboratories while the remainder are employed by private dental practices or by federal and state agencies. There are also career opportunities available in education, research, and sales. Some technicians own their own commercial dental laboratories while others may work after hours in home dental labs.

There are two ways of becoming a dental laboratory technician, and both require a high school diploma. The apprenticeship program involves on-the-job training in a commercial dental laboratory and usually lasts for three-to-four years, depending upon the trainee's ability and previous experience. The trainee receives a salary during this apprenticeship. The academic program involves completion of a two-year certificate or associate degree program in a community or junior college, vocational-technical school, or trade school. The academic programs provide both classroom instruction and "hands on" practical experience. Training is also available through the Armed Forces.

The National Association of Dental Laboratories states that high school students interested in a career in dental laboratory technology would be more qualified for apprenticeship or admission into a dental laboratory technician program if they have taken courses in ceramics, sculpture, chemistry, physiology, blue print reading, plastics, and metal working. Also, employers and school admission officers more readily accept trainees or students who have a high degree of manual dexterity and a good sense of color perception as well as an affinity for accurate and detailed work.

A number of scholarships are available for study at accredited dental laboratory technician schools. For more information, contact The American Fund for Dental Health, 211 East Chicago Avenue, Chicago, Illinois 60611.

According to the National Association of Dental Laboratories, the average starting salary for trainee technicians is $155 for a forty hour work week. Experienced technicians earn up to $400 per week, depending upon their skill and experience. Master technicians in managerial positions often earn much more.

For additional information on educational programs or requirements for certification, contact the National Association of Dental Laboratories, 3801 Mt. Vernon Avenue, Alexandria, Virginia 22305.

Following is a list of schools that offer programs in dental laboratory technology accredited by the Commission on Dental Accreditation.

SOURCES:

National Association of Dental Laboratories
Occupational Outlook Handbook

Dental Laboratory Technician Programs

ALABAMA

Dental Laboratory Technology Program
Trenholm State Technical College
1225 Air Force Boulevard
P.O. Box 9000
Montgomery, Alabama 36108

ARIZONA

Dental Laboratory Technology Program
Pima Community College
2202 West Anklam Road
Tucson, Arizona 85709

CALIFORNIA

Dental Laboratory Technology Program
City College of San Francisco
50 Phelan Avenue
San Francisco, California 94112

Dental Laboratory Technology Program
Diablo Valley College
231 Golf Club Road
Pleasant Hill, California 94523

Dental Laboratory Technology Program
Los Angeles City College
855 North Vermont Avenue
Los Angeles, California 90029

Dental Laboratory Technology Program
Merced College
3600 M Street
Merced, California 95340

Dental Laboratory Technology Program
Orange Coast College
2701 Fairview Road, Box 5005
Costa Mesa, California 92628-0120

Dental Laboratory Technology Program
Pasadena City College
1570 East Colorado Boulevard
Pasadena, California 91101

FLORIDA

Dental Laboratory Technology Program
Indian River Community College
3209 Virginia Avenue
Ft. Pierce, Florida 33450

Dental Laboratory Technology Program
Lindsey Hopkins Education Center
750 NW 20th Street
Miami, Florida 33127

Dental Laboratory Technology Program
Palm Beach Community College
4200 Congress Avenue
Lake Worth, Florida 33460

Dental Laboratory Technology Program
Pensacola Junior College
Warrenton Campus
5555 Highway 98 West
Pensacola, Florida 32507

Dental Laboratory Technology Program
Southern College
5600 Lake Underhill Road
Orlando, Florida 32807

Dental Laboratory Technology Program
McFatter Vocational Technical Center
6500 Nova Drive
Davie, Florida 33317

GEORGIA

Dental Laboratory Technology Program
Atlanta Area Technical School
1560 Stewart Avenue SW
Atlanta, Georgia 30310

Dental Laboratory Technology Program
Augusta Area Technical School
Medical College of Georgia
Augusta, Georgia 30902

Dental Laboratory Technology Program
Gwinnett Area Technical School
1250 Atkinson Road, Box 1505
Lawrenceville, Georgia 30246

IDAHO

Dental Laboratory Technology Program
Idaho State University
741 South Eighth Street
Pocatello, Idaho 83209

ILLINOIS

Dental Laboratory Technology Program
Southern Illinois University
School of Technical Careers
Carbondale, Illinois 62901

Dental Laboratory Technology Program
Triton College
2000 North Fifth Avenue
River Grove, Illinois 60171

INDIANA

Dental Laboratory Technology Program
Indiana University at Ft. Wayne
2102 Coliseum Boulevard, East
Ft. Wayne, Indiana 46805

IOWA

Dental Laboratory Technology Program
Kirkwood Community College
P.O. Box 2068
Cedar Rapids, Iowa 52406

KENTUCKY

Dental Laboratory Technology Program
Lexington Community College
Cooper Drive
Lexington, Kentucky 40506

Dental Laboratory Technology Program
Phillips College
1615 Crums Lane
Louisville, Kentucky 40216

LOUISIANA

Dental Laboratory Technology Program
Louisiana State University School of
Dentistry
1100 Florida Avenue
New Orleans, Louisiana 70199

MASSACHUSETTS

Dental Laboratory Technology Program
Middlesex Community College
Springs Road
Bedford, Massachusetts 01730

MICHIGAN

Dental Laboratory Technology Program
Ferris State College
Big Rapids, Michigan 49307

MINNESOTA

Dental Laboratory Technology Program
Northeast Metro Technical Institute
3300 Century Avenue, North
White Bear Lake, Minnesota 55110

MISSOURI

Dental Laboratory Technology Program
St. Louis Community College
11333 Big Bend Boulevard
St. Louis, Missouri 63122

NEBRASKA

Dental Laboratory Technology Program
Central Technical Community College
P.O. Box 1024
Hastings, Nebraska 68901

NEW JERSEY

Dental Laboratory Technology Program
Union County College
1776 Raritan Road
Scotch Plains, New Jersey 07076

NEW YORK

Dental Laboratory Technology Program
Erie Community College South
4140 Southwestern Boulevard
Orchard Park, New York 14127

Dental Laboratory Technology Program
New York City Technical College
300 Jay Street
Brooklyn, New York 11201

NORTH CAROLINA

Dental Laboratory Technology Program
Durham Technical Institute
1637 Lawson Street
Durham, North Carolina 27703

OHIO

Dental Laboratory Technology Program
Columbus State Community College
P.O. Box 1609
Columbus, Ohio 43215

Dental Laboratory Technology Program
Cuyahoga Community College
Metro Campus
2900 Community College Avenue
Cleveland, Ohio 44115

OREGON

Dental Laboratory Technology Program
Portland Community College
1200 SE 49th Avenue
Portland, Oregon 97219

PENNSYLVANIA

Dental Laboratory Technology Program
Mastbaum Area Vocational-Technical
School
Frankford & Clementine Street
Philadelphia, Pennsylvania 19134

TENNESSEE

Dental Laboratory Technology Program
East Tennessee State University
1000 West "E:" Street
Elizabethton, Tennessee 37643

TEXAS

Dental Laboratory Technology Program
School of Health Care Sciences
Sheppard AFB, Texas 76311

Dental Laboratory Technology Program
Texas State Technical Institute
James Connally Campus
Waco, Texas 76705

Dental Laboratory Technology Program
University of Texas, HSC
7703 Floyd Curl Drive
San Antonio, Texas 78284

Dental Laboratory Technology Program
U.S. Army Academy of Health Sciences
Ft. Sam Houston, Texas 78234

VIRGINIA

Dental Laboratory Technology Program
J. Sargeant Reynolds Community
College
P.O. Box C-32040
Richmond, Virginia 23261

WASHINGTON

Dental Laboratory Technology Program
LH Bates Vocational Technical Institute
1101 South Yakima Avenue
Tacoma, Washington 98405

WISCONSIN

Dental Laboratory Technology Program
Milwaukee Area Technical College
700 West State Street
Milwaukee, Wisconsin 53203

DIETETICS AND NUTRITIONAL CARE

Dietetics and nutritional care is the health profession concerned with human nutrition, that is, the study of the relationships between components of food and the body's needs. Quality nutritious food is essential in maintaining good health, in preventing or treating illness, and in aiding rehabilitation. Dietetics and nutritional care is one of the larger allied healthcare professions. It incorporates several career occupations including *dietitian, nutritionist, dietetic technician, dietetic manager, dietetic aide,* and *dietetic clerk.*

Dietitian

The *dietitian* is a food specialist responsible for nutritional care and food service. Generally speaking, the dietitian applies the principles of nutrition and management to the administration of institutional food service. He or she may also plan special diets for hospital patients and teach groups and individuals nutritional health, especially in food selection and eating habits. There are five specialized careers for dietitians; administrative, clinical, community work, education, and research.

The *administrative dietitian* supervises food service systems in large institutions by managing the large-scale planning, preparation and service of quality nutritious food. He or she establishes and maintains standards for food production, food service, sanitation, safety, and security and also budgets for and purchases food, equipment, and supplies. Large institutions where administrative dietitians are employed include hospitals; universities; schools; and government, commercial, and industrial establishments.

The *clinical dietitian*, who is also known as a *therapeutic dietitian*, assures that nutrition is incorporated as an integral part of a patient's recovery program from illness or injury. As a member of the hospital health team the clinical dietitian assesses the nutritional needs of patients, plans their diets, and provides dietary counseling to them and to their families so that special diets may be maintained after patients leave the hospital, clinic, or nursing home. Some clinical dietitians specialize in the management of obese patients, care of the critically ill, or care of renal and diabetic patients.

The *community dietitian* is the member of the community health team who plans and coordinates the nutritional component of improved health and preventive health in a community. Concerned with problems such as inadequate nutrients or overconsumption, the community dietitian assesses nutritional needs of the population or portions of it, such as the elderly or adolescents, and then counsels individuals or families on nutrition, food selection, and economics in food purchasing. The community dietitian is usually employed by community or government agencies, such as day-care centers and public health facilities.

Working in a university, college, medical school, or vocational-technical institute, the *dietetic educator* plans and implements the educational curricula of dietetic students on the one hand and the teaching of nutrition to medical, dental, nursing, and other allied health students on the other.

The *research dietitian* conducts research for universities, medical centers, government agencies, and food and pharmaceutical companies. They research alternative foods and dietary recommendations for the public.

With experience a dietitian may also serve as a consultant on nutrition, nutritional care, or food service to hospitals, clinics, nursing homes, daycare centers, or restaurants. Dietitians may also be employed in food manufacturing, advertising, and marketing, where they analyze foods, prepare literature for distribution, or report on issues such as dietary fiber or vitamin supplements.

The minimum educational requirement for a dietitian is a bachelor's degree, preferably with a major in dietetics, nutrition, or institution or food systems management. These programs are primarily offered by departments of home economics or of nutritional sciences in colleges and universities. A graduate degree is usually required for teaching, research, and public or community health nutrition.

The American Dietetic Association's Commission on Dietetic Registration awards the Registered Dietitian credential to those who pass a certification exam after completing their academic education and supervised experience. Supervised experience can be acquired through (1) coordinated programs that combine academic and supervised practice experience in a four year program, (2) an accredited internship lasting 9-12 months, or (3) in an approved preprofessional practice program lasting 6 months to 2 years.

Recommended high school courses for students interested in dietetics are home economics, biology, health, mathematics, chemistry, and communications.

According to a national survey conducted by the University of Texas Medical Branch, the median salary for hospital dietitians was about $27,200 annually in 1990.

A list supplied by the American Dietetic Association lists institutions throughout the United States that offer educational programs in dietetics. Most of these programs offer the traditional bachelor's degree in dietetics. (On completion of the bachelor's degree program, students must complete an approved preprofessional practice program, or an accredited dietetic internship. For a list of these programs write to the American Dietetic Association, 216 West Jackson Boulevard, Chicago, Illinois 60606-6995.) Other programs, which are also listed below, offer the coordinated program. (The coordinated program consists of supervised practical experience plus an accredited bachelor or master's degree program meeting the American Dietetic Association's academic requirements.) Persons interested in attending a specific university or college should contact that school's registrar for complete information on its curriculum in dietetics.

Further information on dietetic careers and registration requirements can also be obtained from the American Dietetic Association at the above listed address.

The following is a list of coordinated programs accredited by the American Dietetic Association.

SOURCES:

American Dietetic Association
Occupational Outlook Handbook

Dietitian Programs

ALABAMA

Program in Dietetics
The University of Alabama
Tuscaloosa, Alabama 35487-1488

CALIFORNIA

Program in Dietetics
Loma Linda University
Loma Linda, California 92350

Program in Dietetics
California State University, Los Angeles
Los Angeles, California 90032

Program in Dietetics
Charles R. Drew University
Los Angeles, California 90059

CONNECTICUT

Program in Dietetics
The University of Connecticut
Storrs, Connecticut 06268

Program in Dietetics
St. Joseph College
West Hartford, Connecticut 06117

DELAWARE

Program in Dietetics
University of Delaware
Newark, Delaware 19716

DISTRICT OF COLUMBIA

Program in Dietetics
Howard University
Washington, DC 20059

FLORIDA

Program in Dietetics
Florida International University
Miami, Florida 33199

GEORGIA

Program in Dietetics
Georgia State University
Atlanta, Georgia 30303-3083

IDAHO

Program in Dietetics
University of Idaho
Moscow, Idaho

ILLINOIS

Program in Dietetics
University of Illinois at Chicago
Chicago, Illinois 60612

INDIANA

Program in Dietetics
Indiana State University
Terre Haute, Indiana 47809

Program in Dietetics
Purdue University
West Lafayette, Indiana 47907

IOWA

Program in Dietetics
Iowa State University
Ames, Iowa 50011

KANSAS

Program in Dietetics
Kansas State University
Manhattan, Kansas 66506

KENTUCKY

Program in Dietetics
University of Kentucky
Lexington, Kentucky 40506-0054

MASSACHUSETTS

Program in Dietetics
Framingham State College
Framingham, Massachusetts 01701

MICHIGAN

Program in Dietetics
Wayne State University
Detroit, Michigan 48202

Program in Dietetics
Eastern Michigan University
Ypsilanti, Michigan 48197

MINNESOTA

Program in Dietetics
College of St. Benedict
St. Joseph, Minnesota 56374

Program in Dietetics
University of Minnesota
St. Paul, Minnesota 55108

MISSISSIPPI

Program in Dietetics
University of Southern Mississippi
Hattiesburg, Mississippi 39406

MISSOURI

Program in Dietetics
University of Missouri-Columbia
Columbia, Missouri 65211

NEW YORK

Program in Dietetics
D'Youville College
Buffalo, New York 14201

Program in Dietetics
State University College at Buffalo
Buffalo, New York 14222-1095

Program in Dietetics
Rochester Institute of Technology
Rochester, New York 14623

Program in Dietetics
Syracuse University
Syracuse, New York 13244-1250

NORTH CAROLINA

Program in Dietetics
University of North Carolina
Chapel Hill, North Carolina 27514

NORTH DAKOTA

Program in Dietetics
North Dakota State University
Fargo, North Dakota 58102

Program in Dietetics
University of North Dakota
Grand Forks, North Dakota 58202

OHIO

Program in Dietetics
University of Akron
Akron, Ohio 44325

Program in Dietetics
Ohio State University
Columbus, Ohio 43210

Program in Dietetics
Youngstown State University
Youngstown, Ohio 44555-0001

OKLAHOMA

Program in Dietetics
University of Oklahoma Health Sciences
  Center
Oklahoma City, Oklahoma 73190

PENNSYLVANIA

Program in Dietetics
Edinboro University of Pennsylvania
Edinboro, Pennsylvania 16444

Program in Dietetics
Gannon University
Erie, Pennsylvania 16541

Program in Dietetics
Mercyhurst College
Erie, Pennsylvania 16546

Program in Dietetics
Seton Hill College
Greensburg, Pennsylvania

Program in Dietetics
University of Pittsburgh
Pittsburgh, Pennsylvania 15261

Program in Dietetics
Marywood College
Scranton, Pennsylvania 18509-1598

TEXAS

Program in Dietetics
University of Texas at Austin
Austin, Texas 78712

Program in Dietetics
University of Texas
Dallas, Texas 75235

Program in Dietetics
University of Texas-Pan American
Edinburg, Texas 78539-2999

Program in Dietetics
Texas Christian University
Ft. Worth, Texas 76129

Program in Dietetics
University of Texas Health Science
  Center at Houston
Houston, Texas 77225

UTAH

Program in Dietetics
Utah State University
Logan, Utah 84322-8700

Program in Dietetics
Brigham Young University
Provo, Utah 84602

Program in Dietetics
University of Utah
Salt Lake City, Utah 84132

WASHINGTON

Program in Dietetics
Washington State University
Pullman, Washington 99164-2032

WISCONSIN

Program in Dietetics
Viterbo College
La Crosse, Wisconsin 54601-4797

Program in Dietetics
University of Wisconsin-Madison
Madison, Wisconsin 53706

Program in Dietetics
Mount Mary College
Milwaukee, Wisconsin 53222

Nutritionist

Although sometimes regarded as a general title for all food service science and nutrition occupations, including dietitians, home economists, and food technologists, the *nutritionist* is more specifically an educator of human nutrition. As a specialist, the nutritionist attempts to solve food problems, control disease, and maintain and promote health, all through education.

Although some may conduct research or teach nutrition to medical personnel while others act as consultants on health teams or in industry, most nutritionists work in the field of public health. Employed in government and voluntary health agencies, public health nutritionists are responsible for the nutritional aspects of community health care and preventive health services. They counsel and instruct the elderly, the poor, adolescents, and mothers with babies and young children, among other groups, on sound nutrition practices including special diets, meal planning and preparation, and food budgeting.

The nutritionist may also work for the media, conveying nutrition information on radio, television, or in newspapers. She or he may even help provide technical assistance in underdeveloped countries that are trying to improve their nutritional standards in food production.

Similar to a dietitian, the minimum educational requirement for nutritionists employed in healthcare facilities, business and industry is generally a bachelor's degree in dietetics, nutrition, or institution or food systems management. A graduate degree is required for nutritionists employed in public or community health.

Consult the previous section on Dietitians for information on the similar wage scales, educational programs and opportunities for nutritionists.

SOURCE:

Occupational Outlook Handbook

Dietetic Technician

The *dietetic technician* works on a healthcare team assisting the dietitian and specializing in either food service management or nutritional care services. In food service management the dietetic technician assists in the assessment, planning, implementation, and evaluation of food programs. In a large hospital he or she works under the supervision of an administrative dietitian. In a small hospital or extended care facility where he or she may be responsible for the daily food service operation, the dietetic technician is usually supervised by a consultant dietitian.

Other responsibilities of the dietetic technician might include providing patient education, developing recipes and menus, purchasing food, and monitoring inventory.

Training to become a dietetic technician involves completion of a two-year associate degree program that combines classroom and supervised practical experience. These programs are offered by universities, colleges, community colleges, and vocational-technical schools.

Dietetic technicians are employed in the same facilities that employ dietitians, such as hospitals, clinics, community or government agencies, day-care programs, nutrition programs for the elderly, and in school systems.

Registration as a Registered Dietetic Technician (D.T.R.) is awarded after completion of an American Dietetic Association-approved program and after successfully passing the Registration Examination for Dietetic Technicians

Following is a list of education programs for dietetic technicians approved by the American Dietetic Association. Contact the American Dietetic Association, 216 West Jackson, Chicago, Illinois 60606-6995, for registration and career information.

SOURCE:

American Dietetic Association

Dietetic Technician Programs

ARIZONA

Dietetic Technician Program
Central Arizona College
Coolidge, Arizona 85228

CALIFORNIA

Dietetic Technician Program
Orange Coast College
Costa Mesa, California 92628-0120

Dietetic Technician Program
Grossmont College
El Cajon, California 92020

Dietetic Technician Program
Loma Linda University
Loma Linda, California 92350

Dietetic Technician Program
Long Beach City College
Long Beach, California 90808

Dietetic Technician Program
Los Angeles City College
Los Angeles, California 90029

Dietetic Technician Program
San Bernardino Valley College
San Bernardino, California 92410

COLORADO

Dietetic Technician Program
Front Range Community College
Westminister, Colorado 80030

CONNECTICUT

Dietetic Technician Program
South Central Community College
New Haven, Connecticut 06511

Dietetic Technician Program
Briarwood College
Southington, Connecticut 06489

FLORIDA

Dietetic Technician Program
Florida Community College at
  Jacksonville-North Campus
Jacksonville, Florida 32205

Dietetic Technician Program
Palm Beach Community College
Lake Worth, Florida 33461

Dietetic Technician Program
Miami-Dade Community College
Miami, Florida 33132

Dietetic Technician Program
Orlando Vocational Technical Center
Orlando, Florida 32801

Dietetic Technician Program
Pensacola Junior College
Pensacola, Florida 32504

IDAHO

Dietetic Technician Program
Ricks College
Rexburg, Idaho 83460

ILLINOIS

Dietetic Technician Program
Malcolm X College
City Colleges of Chicago
Chicago, Illinois 60612

Dietetic Technician Program
Olivet Nazarene University
Kankakee, Illinois 60901

Dietetic Technician Program
William Rainey Harper College
Palatine, Illinois 60067

INDIANA

Dietetic Technician Program
Purdue University-Calumet
Hammond, Indiana 46323

Dietetic Technician Program
Ball State University
Muncie, Indiana 47306

MAINE

Dietetic Technician Program
Southern Maine Technical College
South Portland, Maine 04106

MARYLAND

Dietetic Technician Program
New Community College of Baltimore
Baltimore, Maryland 21215

MASSACHUSETTS

Dietetic Technician Program
Laboure College
Boston, Massachusetts 02124-5698

MICHIGAN

Dietetic Technician Program
Wayne County Community College
Detroit, Michigan 48226

MINNESOTA

Dietetic Technician Program
Normandale Community College
Bloomington, Minnesota 55431

Dietetic Technician Program
University of Minnesota-Crookston
Crookston, Minnesota 56716

Dietetic Technician Program
Lakewood Community College
White Bear Lake, Minnesota 55110

MISSOURI

Dietetic Technician Program
St. Louis Community College at
  Florissant Valley
St. Louis, Missouri 63135

NEBRASKA

Dietetic Technician Program
Central Community College
Hastings, Nebraska 68901-1024

Dietetic Technician Program
Southeast Community College
Lincoln, Nebraska 68520

NEW JERSEY

Dietetic Technician Program
Camden County College
Blackwood, New Jersey 08012

Dietetic Technician Program
Middlesex County College
Edison, New Jersey 08818-3050

NEW YORK

Dietetic Technician Program
Erie Community College
North Campus
Buffalo, New York 14221

Dietetic Technician Program
LaGuardia Community College
Long Island City, New York 11101

Dietetic Technician Program
State University of New York
Agricultural and Technical College
Morrisville, New York 13408

Dietetic Technician Program
Dutchess Community College
Poughkeepsie, New York 12601

Dietetic Technician Program
Suffolk County Community College
Riverhead, New York 11901

Dietetic Technician Program
Rockland Community College
Suffern, New York 10901

OHIO

Dietetic Technician Program
Cincinnati Technical College
Cincinnati, Ohio 45223

Dietetic Technician Program
Cuyahoga Community College
Cleveland, Ohio 44115

Dietetic Technician Program
Columbus State Community College
Columbus, Ohio 43215-9965

Dietetic Technician Program
Sinclair Community College
Dayton, Ohio 45402

Dietetic Technician Program
Lima Technical College
Lima, Ohio 45804

Dietetic Technician Program
Hocking Technical College
Nelsonville, Ohio 45764-9704

Dietetic Technician Program
Owens Technical College
Toledo, Ohio 43699

Dietetic Technician Program
Youngstown State University
Youngstown, Ohio 44555

OKLAHOMA

Dietetic Technician Program
University of Central Oklahoma
Edmond, Oklahoma

Dietetic Technician Program
Oklahoma State University
Okmulgee, Oklahoma 74447

OREGON

Dietetic Technician Program
Portland Community College
Portland, Oregon 97219

PENNSYLVANIA

Dietetic Technician Program
Bucks County Community College
Newtown, Pennsylvania 18940

Dietetic Technician Program
Community College of Philadelphia
Philadelphia, Pennsylvania 19130

Dietetic Technician Program
Community College of Allegheny
  County
Allegheny Campus
Pittsburgh, Pennsylvania 15212-6097

Dietetic Technician Program
Pennsylvania State University
University Park, Pennsylvania 16802

Dietetic Technician Program
Westmoreland County Community
  College
Youngwood, Pennsylvania 15697

TENNESSEE

Dietetic Technician Program
Shelby State Community College
Memphis, Tennessee 38174-0568

TEXAS

Dietetic Technician Program
El Paso Community College
El Paso, Texas 79998

Dietetic Technician Program
Tarrant County Junior College
Ft. Worth, Texas 76119

Dietetic Technician Program
San Jacinto College Central
Pasadena, Texas 77505

Dietetic Technician Program
St. Philip's College
San Antonio, Texas 78203

VIRGINIA

Dietetic Technician Program
Northern Virginia Community College
Annandale, Virginia 22003

Dietetic Technician Program
J. Sargeant Reynolds Community
  College
Richmond, Virginia 23261-2040

Dietetic Technician Program
Tidewater Community College
Virginia Beach, Virginia 23456

WASHINGTON

Dietetic Technician Program
Shoreline Community College
Seattle, Washington 98133

Dietetic Technician Program
Spokane Community College
Spokane, Washington 99207

Dietetic Technician Program
Yakima Valley Community College
Yakima, Washington 98907

Dietetic Technician Program
Milwaukee Area Technical College
Milwaukee, Wisconsin 53205

WISCONSIN

Dietetic Technician Program
Madison Area Technical College
Madison, Wisconsin 53704

Dietary Manager

Working together with registered dietitians, the *dietary manager* provides food service supervision and nutritional care. She or he processes dietary orders by writing food menus following dietetic specifications, interviews patients for diet history, instructs patients on dietary restrictions, calculates nutrients intake, coordinates food service to patients, orders supplies, maintains sanitation, develops the annual budget, and supervises the work of food service employees.

Dietary managers work in schools, correctional institutions, hospitals and other healthcare facilities where food is served to patients.

Training to become a dietary manager requires high school graduation or the equivalent and completion of a 12 to 18 month program offered at community colleges, and vocational-technical schools, or on-the-job training in a hospital food service program. A certificate of completion is generally awarded to training program graduates.

To become a certified dietary manager (CDM), students must pass a competency exam and apply for certification through the Certifying Board for Dietary Managers. Certified dietary managers are required to earn 45 hours of continuing education every three years to maintain their certification.

For more information on certification or careers in dietary management, write to the Dietary Managers Association, One Pierce Place, Suite 1220W, Itasca, Illinois 60143-3111.

Following is a list of dietary manager programs.

SOURCES:

American Dietetic Association
Dietary Managers Association

Dietary Manager Programs

ALABAMA

Dietary Manager Program
Auburn University
Auburn University, Alabama 36849-
5611

ALASKA

Dietary Manager Program
University of Alaska
3211 Providence Avenue
Anchorage, Alaska 99508

ARIZONA

Dietary Manager Program
Arizona Western College
P.O. Box 929
Yuma, Arizona 85364

Dietary Manager Program
Central Arizona College
Woodruff & Overfield Roads
Coolidge, Arizona 85228

CALIFORNIA

Dietary Manager Program
American River College
4700 College Oak Drive
Sacramento, California 95841

Merritt College
12500 Campus Drive
Oakland, California 94602

Modesto Junior College
435 College Avenue
Modesto, California 95350

FLORIDA

Dietary Manager Program
Clearwater Evening Adult Center
540 South Hercules Avenue
Clearwater, Florida 34627

Dietary Manager Program
Erwin Technical Center
5410 North 20th Street
Tampa, Florida 33610-8299

Dietary Manager Program
Florida Community College
North Campus
4501 Capper Road
Jacksonville, Florida 32218

Dietary Manager Program
Lindsey Hopkins Education Center
750 NW 20th Street
Miami, Florida 33127

Dietary Manager Program
North Technical Ed Center
7061 Garden Road
Riviera Beach, Florida 33404

Dietary Manager Program
Northeast Community School
1717 54th Avenue North
St. Petersburg, Florida 33714

Dietary Manager Program
Orlando Voc-Tech Center
301 West Amelia Street
Orlando, Florida 32901

Dietary Manager Program
Pensacola Junior College
1000 College Boulevard
Pensacola, Florida 32504

Dietary Manager Program
Sarasota Cty Technical Inst.
4748 Beneva Road
Sarasota, Florida 34233-1758

Dietary Manager Program
University of Florida
1223 Northwest 22nd Avenue
Gainesville, Florida 32609

GEORGIA

Dietary Manager Program
University of Georgia
Georgia Center for Cont Ed
Athens, Georgia 30602

IDAHO

Dietary Manager Program
Lewis Clark State College
Eighth Avenue & Sixth Street
Lewiston, Idaho 83501-2698

INDIANA

Dietary Manager Program
Ball State University
School of Continuing Education
Muncie, Indiana 47306

Dietary Manager Program
Indiana Voc-Tech College
3800 North Anthony Boulevard
Ft. Wayne, Indiana 46805

Dietary Manager Program
Indiana Voc-Tech College
3208 Ross Road
P.O. Box 6299
Lafayette, Indiana 47903

Dietary Manager Program
Indiana Voc-Tech College
2325 Chester Boulevard
Richmond, Indiana 47374

Dietary Manager Program
J. Everett Light Career Center
1901 East 86th Street
Indianapolis, Indiana 46240

Dietary Manager Program
University of Southern Indiana
8600 University Boulevard
Evansville, Indiana 47712

Dietary Manager Program
Vincennes University
1002 North First Street
Vincennes, Indiana 47591

IOWA

Dietary Manager Program
Des Moines Area Community College
2006 South Ankeny Boulevard
Ankeny, Iowa 50021

Dietary Manager Program
Eastern Iowa Community College
  District
306 West Second Street
Davenport, Iowa 52801

KANSAS

Dietary Manager Program
Southeast Kansas Area Vo-Tech School
Sixth & Roosevelt
Coffeyville, Kansas 67337

Dietary Manager Program
Washburn University
1700 College
Topeka, Kansas 66621

Dietary Manager Program
Wichita Area Vo-Tech School
324 North Emporia
Wichita, Kansas 67202

Dietary Manager Program
Barton Cty Community College
Route 3, Box 136Z
Great Bend, Kansas 67530-9283

KENTUCKY

Dietary Manager Program
Spaulding University
851 South Fourth Street
Louisville, Kentucky 40203

Dietary Manager Program
University of Kentucky
College of Allied Health
Lexington, Kentucky 40536-0218

MAINE

Dietary Manager Program
Southern Maine Vo-Tech Institute
Fort Road
South Portland, Maine 04106

MARYLAND

Dietary Manager Program
Baltimore City Community College
2901 Liberty Heights Avenue
Baltimore, Maryland 21215

MASSACHUSETTS

Dietary Manager Program
Bunker Hill Community College
New Rutherford Avenue
Charleston, Massachusetts 02129

MICHIGAN

Dietary Manager Program
Lansing Community College
P.O. Box 40010
Lansing, Michigan 48901-7210

MINNESOTA

Dietary Manager Program
Alexandria Vo-Tech Institute
1601 Jefferson Street
Alexandria, Minnesota 56308

Dietary Manager Program
St. Paul Vo-Tech Institute
235 Marshall Avenue
St. Paul, Minnesota 55102

Dietary Manager Program
Mankato Technical College
1920 Lee Boulevard
North Mankato, Minnesota 56002-1920

MISSOURI

Dietary Manager Program
Northwest Missouri Area Tech
1515 South Munn
Maryville, Missouri 64468

Dietary Manager Program
St. Louis Community College
3400 Pershall Road
St. Louis, Missouri 63135

Dietary Manager Program
Columbia Public Schools
4203 South Providence Road
Columbia, Missouri 65203

Dietary Manager Program
Penn Valley Community College
3201 SW Trafficway
Kansas City, Missouri 64111

NEW JERSEY

Dietary Manager Program
Essex Cty Voc School
68 South Harrison Street
East Orange, New Jersey 07018

Dietary Manager Program
Passaic Cty Voc School
45 Reinhardt Road
Wayne, New Jersey 07470

NEW YORK

Dietary Manager Program
Erie Community College
6205 Main Street
Williamsville, New York 14221

Dietary Manager Program
Dutchess Community College
53 Pendell Road
Poughkeepsie, New York 12601

Dietary Manager Program
Broome Community College
P.O. Box 1017
Binghampton, New York 13902

Dietary Manager Program
Adelphi University
School of Nursing
P.O. Box 516
Garden City, New York 11530

Dietary Manager Program
Westchester Community College
75 Grasslands Road
Valhalla, New York 10595

Dietary Manager Program
Suffolk County Community College
533 College Road
Seldon, New York 11784

Dietary Manager Program
LaGuardia Community College
31-10 Thomson Avenue
Long Island City, New York 11101

Dietary Manager Program
New York University
35 West Fourth Street
New York, New York 10003

OHIO

Dietary Manager Program
Cincinnati Technical College
3520 Central Parkway
Cincinnati, Ohio 45223

Dietary Manager Program
Columbus State Community College
Box 1609
550 East Spring Street
Columbus, Ohio 43125

Dietary Manager Program
Hocking Technical College
3301 Hocking Parkway
Nelsonville, Ohio 45764

Dietary Manager Program
Kent State University
Kent, Ohio 44242

Dietary Manager Program
Notre Dame College of Ohio
4545 College Road
South Euclid, Ohio 44112

Dietary Manager Program
Nursing Home Area Training Center
27100 Cedar Road
Beachwood, Ohio 44122

Dietary Manager Program
Owens Technical College
Caller No. 10,000 Oregon Road
Toledo, Ohio 43699

Dietary Manager Program
Sinclair Community College
444 West Third Street
Dayton, Ohio 45402-9932

OKLAHOMA

Dietary Manager Program
Kiamichi Area Vo-Tech School
P.O. Box 220
Atoka, Oklahoma 74525

Dietary Manager Program
Tulsa Cty Area Vo-Tech School
4600 South Olive
Broken Arrow, Oklahoma 74011-1706

Dietary Manager Program
Great Plains Area Vo-Tech
4500 West Lee Boulevard
Lawton, Oklahoma 73505

Dietary Manager Program
Moore-Norman Area Vo-Tech
4701 12th Avenue NW
Norman, Oklahoma 73069

Dietary Manager Program
High Plains Area Vo-Tech School at
  Woodward
3921 34th Street
Woodward, Oklahoma 73801

Dietary Manager Program
Francis Tuttle Area Voc
12777 North Rockwell Avenue
Oklahoma City, Oklahoma 73142

Dietary Manager Program
High Plains Area Vo-Tech at Guymon
3421 34th Street
Guymon, Oklahoma 73942

OREGON

Dietary Manager Program
Chemeketa Community College
4000 Lancaster Drive
P.O. Box 14007
Salem, Oregon 97309

Dietary Manager Program
Portland Community College
P.O. Box 19000
Portland, Oregon 97280-0990

PENNSYLVANIA

Dietary Manager Program
Luzerne Cty Community College
Prospect Street & Middle Road
Naticoke, Pennsylvania 18634

Dietary Manager Program
Pennsylvania State University
School of Hotel, Rest. & Institutional
  Mgmt.
University Park, Pennsylvania 16802

Dietary Manager Program
Community College of Philadelphia
1700 Spring Garden Street
Philadelphia, Pennsylvania 19130

Dietary Manager Program
North Hampton County Area Comm.
  College
3835 Green Pond Road
Bethlehem, Pennsylvania 18017

Dietary Manager Program
Harrisburg Area Community College
3300 Cameron Street Road
Harrisburg, Pennsylvania 17110

RHODE ISLAND

Dietary Manager Program
University of Rhode Island
530 Liberty Lane
Dept. of Food Science & Nutrition
West Kingston, Rhode Island 02892

SOUTH CAROLINA

Dietary Manager Program
Greenville Technical College
P.O. Box 5616
Greenville, South Carolina 29606-5616

SOUTH DAKOTA

Dietary Manager Program
South Dakota State University
Nutritional & Food Science Dept.
c/o SDSU Box 2275A
Brookings, South Dakota 57007-0497

TEXAS

Dietary Manager Program
Lamar University-Baptist Hospital
P.O. Box 10035
Beaumont, Texas 77710

Dietary Manager Program
North Harris College
2700 NW Thorne Drive
Houston, Texas 77073-9988

Dietary Manager Program
San Jacinto College
8060 Spencer Highway
P.O. Box 2007
Pasadena, Texas 77505

Dietary Manager Program
South Plains College
1302 Main
Lubbock, Texas 79401

Dietary Manager Program
Tarrant Cty Junior College
5301 Campus Drive
Ft. Worth, Texas 76119

Dietary Manager Program
Texas State Technical College
Continuing Ed Center
Waco, Texas 76705

UTAH

Dietary Manager Program
Brigham Young University
Center for Continuing Ed
1521 East 3900 S.
Salt Lake City, Utah 84124-1501

VIRGINIA

Dietary Manager Program
J. Sargeant Reynolds Comm College
700 East Jackson Street
Richmond, Virginia 23219

WASHINGTON

Dietary Manager Program
Yakima Valley College
P.O. Box 1647
16th and Nob Hill
Yakima, Washington 98802

Dietary Manager Program
Bellingham Technical College
3028 Lindbergh Avenue
Bellingham, Washington 98225

Dietary Manager Program
Clover Park Vo-Tech Institute
4500 Steliacoom Boulevard SW
Tacoma, Washington 98499

WISCONSIN

Dietary Manager Program
Moraine Park Tech College
235 North National Avenue
P.O. Box 1940
Fond du Lac, Wisconsin 54936-1940

Dietary Manager Program
Northeast Wisconsin Vocational
2740 West Mason Street
P.O. Box 19042
Green Bay, Wisconsin 54307-9042

Dietary Manager Program
Gateway Tech Institutes of Elkhorn,
  Kenosha, & Racine
1001 South Main Street
Racine, Wisconsin 53403

Dietary Manager Program
Western WI Technical Institute
Sixth & Vine Streets
LaCrosse, Wisconsin 54602

Dietary Manager Program
Wisconsin Indianhead Tech College
1900 College Drive
Rice Lake, Wisconsin 54868

Dietary Manager Program
Waukesha Cty Tech College
800 Main Street
Pewaukee, Wisconsin 53072

Dietary Manager Program
Madison Area Tech College
3550 Anderson Street
Madison, Wisconsin 53704

Dietary Manager Program
Southwest Wisconsin Tech College
Highway 18 East
Fennimore, Wisconsin 53809

Dietary Manager Program
Chippewa Valley Tech College
620 West Clairemont Avenue
Eau Clair, Wisconsin 54701

Dietary Manager Program
Milwaukee Area Tech College
700 West State Street
Milwaukee, Wisconsin 53233

Dietetic Aide

The *dietetic aide* works in the food service departments of hospitals or extended care facilities. Dietetic aides may deliver and read menus to patients and assist in the preparation and serving of food to patients. Educational and training requirements may vary amongst hospitals, but generally high school graduation or the equivalent is the prerequisite for admittance into a three to six month on-the-job hospital training program. Those persons interested in becoming a dietetic aide should contact the Personnel Director or the Chief Dietitian of their local hospital.

SOURCE:

American Dietetic Association

Dietetic Clerk

Supervised by an administrative or a clinical dietitian, the *dietetic clerk* assists with the paperwork and inventory duties in the operation of the dietetic department. He or she examines diet orders, processes new diets, and informs kitchen personnel of food requirements. The clerk also keeps an inventory of food and equipment purchases and a record of costs and of total number of meals served. The dietetic clerk may also enter diet changes into patients' medical records.

Educational and training requirements may vary amongst hospitals, but generally high school graduation or the equivalent is the prerequisite for admittance into an on-the-job training program.

For further information on career opportunities, salaries, and training, interested persons should contact the Personnel Director or the Chief Dietitian of their local hospital.

SOURCE:

American Dietetic Association

ELECTROENCEPHALOGRAPHIC TECHNOLOGY

Electroencephalographic (EEG) technology records and studies the electrical activity of the brain. As the brain controls breathing, heart rate, body temperature, and other essential bodily functions, it continually produces electrical impulses that can be amplified and measured by an EEG machine called the electroencephalograph. The written tracings of these electrical impulses are called electroencephalograms. By measuring impulse amplitude and frequency, EEG technology is used by neurologists and other physicians to diagnose brain diseases such as epilepsy, brain tumor, and stroke. It is also used to evaluate the effects of head trauma and infectious disease, as well as to indicate abnormal brain functions and pinpoint areas of the brain involved in disease processes.

EEG technology assists in determining the exact time that the body functions cease in a patient who is undergoing a vital organ transplantation. It is also used to diagnose any organic bases for serious adjustment problems or learning disabilities in children. Allied health personnel trained in EEG technology are referred to as EEG technologists or technicians. In some cases the terms EEG technologist and EEG technician refer to a similar skill level. In other cases, an EEG technologist refers to an individual with greater experience and possible supervisory responsibilities, while an EEG technician may denote an entry level position. The following chapter will refer to the EEG *technologist* position.

Electroencephalographic Technologist

Usually under the supervision of a department head or chief EEG technologist, the *EEG technologist* is responsible for the actual recording of a patient's EEG activity. With a thorough understanding of the EEG equipment and of common mental disorders, the EEG technologist selects the most appropriate combination of electrodes and instrument controls to produce the necessary electroencephalogram for interpretation by the neurologist (a physician with special training in the structure and diseases of the nervous system). The

111

procedure involves placing small electrodes on the patient's scalp in standard locations and connecting them to the recording instruments. As the recording proceeds, the technologist, who is capable of distinguishing between normal brain activity and abnormal EEG characteristics, observes and keeps a careful record of the patient's behavior. The technologist must also be capable of handling basic medical emergencies in the laboratory; for example, he or she should be able to respond swiftly and wisely if a patient suffers an epileptic seizure.

Other duties of the EEG technologist may include taking medical histories, putting the patient at ease during the EEG recording, writing descriptive reports to accompany the EEG for use by the neurologist or other physicians, keeping accurate records, scheduling appointments, and ordering supplies.

Besides working in a hospital or clinic neurology department laboratory, EEG technologists may also work in neurologists' and neurosurgeons' offices, large medical centers, psychiatric facilities, or health maintenance organizations, or with enough experience, they may conduct research or become members of a highly specialized neurosurgical team.

Training to become an EEG technologist involves the completion of a one to two year certificate or associate degree program offered by community and junior colleges, colleges and universities, vocational-technical institutes, or hospitals. Many EEG technologists learn their skill through on-the-job training in large hospitals and clinics.

Following training and experience, EEG technologists are eligible to voluntarily apply for examination in subsections of technology. After meeting all requirements, the title of Registered EEG Technologist (R.EEG.T.) is granted by the American Board of Registration of EEG Technicians.

At present, registration is not mandatory, but is advantageous for job placement, advancement, and higher salaries. For further information on registration requirements, write to the American Board of Registration for Electroencephalographic Technologists, P.O. Box 11434, Norfolk, Virginia 23517.

Recommended high school courses for students interested in a career in EEG technology include health, biology, human anatomy, and mathematics.

Salaries for electroencephalographic technologists vary depending on educational background, experience, level of responsibility, type of employment, and geographic area of location. Average annual salaries range from $15,000 to $38,000 per year. According to the 1991 Committee on Allied Health Education and Accreditation's annual survey, entry level salaries averaged $21, 400.

For more information on a career as an electroencephalographic technologist or for further information on other electroneurodiagnostic careers, contact the American Society of Electroneurodiagnostic Technologists, 204 West Seventh, Carroll, Iowa 51401. For information about on-the-job training possibilities in EEG technology, students should contact the Personnel Director at large hospitals or clinics in their area. Following is a list of education programs in Electroneurodiagnostic Technology, accredited by the Committee on Allied Health Education and Accreditation of the American Medical Association.

SOURCES:

American Medical Association
American Society of Electroneurodiagnostic Technologists
Occupational Outlook Handbook

Electroneurodiagnostic Technology Programs

ARIZONA

EEG Technology Program
Barrow Neurological Institute of St.
  Joseph's Hospital & Medical Center
P.O. Box 2071
Phoenix, Arizona 85001

CALIFORNIA

Neurodiagnostic Technologist Program
Orange Coast College
2701 Fairview Road
P.O. Box 5005
Costa Mesa, California 92628-0120

FLORIDA

EEG Technology Program
St. Joseph's Hospital
P.O. Box 4227
3001 Dr. Martin Luther King Jr.
  Boulevard
Tampa, Florida 33677

ILLINOIS

EEG Technology Program
St. John's Hospital
800 East Carpenter Street
Springfield, Illinois 62769

IOWA

EEG Technology Program
Kirkwood Community College
University of Iowa Hospital
1084 Carver Pavilion
Iowa City, Iowa 52242

MARYLAND

EEG Technology Program
Naval School of Health Science
8901 Wisconsin Avenue
Bethesda, Maryland 20889-5033

MASSACHUSETTS

EEG Technology Program
Children's Hospital Medical Center
300 Longwood Avenue
Boston, Massachusetts 02115

Clinical Neurophysiology Technology
Catherine Laboure' College
2120 Dorchester Avenue
Boston, Massachusetts 02124

MINNESOTA

EEG Technology Program
Anoka-Hennepin Vocational Technical
  School
1355 West Highway 10
Anoka, Minnesota 55303

NEW YORK

EEG Technology Program
Niagara County Community College
3111 Saunders Settlement Road
Sandborn, New York 14132

PENNSYLVANIA

EEG Technology Program
Crozier-Chester Medical Center
School of EEG
15th & Upland Avenue
Chester, Pennsylvania 19013

VIRGINIA

EEG Technology Program
Sentara Norfolk General Hospital
School of EEG Technology
600 Gresham Avenue
Norfolk, Virginia 23507

WISCONSIN

EEG Technology Program
Western Wisconsin Technical Institute
304 North Sixth Street
P.O. Box 908
LaCrosse, Wisconsin 54602

When an accident or other medical emergency occurs, emergency medical services are employed to initially treat and transport the victims to the hospital. These services are regarded as an extension of a hospital's emergency department. A person employed in these services is known as an *emergency medical technician* (EMT). The career of dispatcher is summarized at the end of this chapter.

Emergency Medical Technician (EMT): EMT-Ambulance EMT-Intermediate EMT-Paramedic

Formerly referred to as ambulance attendants, *emergency medical Technicians* are often the first qualified medical personnel to arrive at the scene of an emergency. Upon arrival they evaluate the nature and extent of the victims' illnesses or injuries and then administer specified diagnostic and emergency treatment procedures under standing orders or specific instructions of a physician. Emergency medical care may involve administering cardiac resuscitation, restoring breathing, controlling bleeding, treating for shock, immobilizing fractures, assisting in childbirth, or giving initial treatment to poison and burn victims. Using special equipment and techniques, EMT's may also have to extricate trapped victims.

The EMT is responsible for operating the emergency vehicle safely and efficiently and for maintaining continued medical care to the victims while in radio communication with the emergency departments in route to the hospital. The EMT must also transmit medical records and reports of each emergency to the hospital staff for their diagnostic purposes. The EMT must be alert and quick thinking, especially in crucial situations. Finally, the EMT must maintain a clean, well-equipped ambulance in good operating condition.

There are three classifications of the emergency medical technician (EMT): the EMT-*Ambulance*, the EMT-*Intermediate* and the EMT-*Paramedic*.

The EMT-*Ambulance* is trained in basic life support and is certified to perform specific pre-hospital duties in emergency situations, including treating shock and poison victims, dressing and bandaging wounds, controlling bleeding, resuscitating heart attack victims, restoring breathing, maintaining a patient's airway, immobilizing fractures, and providing obstetrical assistance.

The certified EMT-*Intermediate* provides the same care as the EMT-Ambulance, but because of additional training may also assess trauma patients, administer intravenous therapy, use antishock trousers, defibrillators, and airway maintenance equipment.

The certified EMT-*Paramedic* is the more highly trained technician who is qualified (subject to state law) to administer drugs, both orally and intravenously, and to operate more complicated equipment in an advanced life-support ambulance (intensive care vehicle), such as a defibrillator to shock a stopped heart into action. The EMT-Paramedic may also be required to assist in hospital emergency departments and intensive care units.

Training courses are available for all three levels of EMT. The basic national standard EMT training course is 80-120 hours of classroom work and 10 hours of internship in a hospital emergency room. Applicants must be at least eighteen years of age, high school graduates or the equivalent, possess a valid driver's license, and be physically and emotionally capable to meet the rigors of the profession.

The training course for the EMT-Intermediate includes the same basic training course as the EMT-Ambulance, but includes 35-55 hours of further instruction including some of the EMT-Paramedic Courses which cover patient assessment and use of the Esophageal Obturator Airway, intravenous fluids, and antishock garments.

Training courses for the EMT-Paramedic include 750 to 2,000 hours of intensive classroom and clinical training. Some EMT-Paramedic programs are accredited by the American Medical Association's Committee on Allied Health Education and Accreditation.

Graduates of approved EMT-training programs, with the required amount of work experience, are qualified to take the written and practical certification examinations sponsored by the National Registry of Emergency Medical Technicians. All states have some form of certification requirement. Recertification is required every two to three years and refresher training in the latest techniques and equipment is available. Certification information can be obtained from the National Registry of Emergency Medical Technicians, P.O. Box 29233, Columbus, Ohio 43229.

A large percentage of basic EMT's (EMT-Ambulance) are non paid volunteers for rescue squads that work closely with fire departments. Volunteer EMT's must be certified and successfully complete the basic training course. Employed EMT's work for police and fire departments, private ambulance companies and hospital-based ambulance teams.

The average salary of the EMT varies depending upon training, experience, employment setting, and geographic location. Average starting salaries in 1991 were $19,200 for EMT-Ambulance, $20,600 for EMT-Intermediate, and $23,300 for EMT-Paramedic, according to a survey conducted by the *Journal of Emergency Medical Services*.

Students interested in a career in emergency medical services may find it helpful to talk with faculty at area EMT training sites or to arrange for an appointment at a local fire/rescue station for an observational meeting.

For further information on the location of training programs contact the State Emergency

Medical Services Offices listed at the end of this chapter.

For more information on a career as an emergency medical technician, write to the National Association of Emergency Medical Technicians, 9140 Ward Parkway, Kansas City, Missouri 64114.

SOURCES:

American Medical Association
National Registry of Emergency Medical Technicians
Occupational Outlook Handbook

Dispatcher

Although not directly involved with emergency patients, the *dispatcher* provides a channel for communication among all aspects of emergency medical services. He or she receives calls for emergency medical help, dispatches the appropriate medical resources, and then acts as the communication link between the medical facility and the ambulance team. Besides working in emergency medical services, the dispatcher may also handle communication for public safety agencies such as police and fire departments. Interested persons should contact their municipal fire-rescue departments or State Emergency Medical Services Offices for more information on requirements and job opportunities.

SOURCE:

Occupational Outlook Handbook

State Emergency Medical Services Offices

ALABAMA

Emergency Medical Services Director
Bureau of EMS
Department of Health
Division of EMS
746 Adams Avenue
Montgomery, Alabama 36104

ALASKA

Emergency Medical Services Director
Emergency Medical Services Section
Division of Public Health
Pouch H-06C
Juneau, Alaska 99811

Emergency Medical Services Director
Interior Region EMS Council, Inc.
P.O. Box 2120
Fairbanks, Alaska 99707

Emergency Medical Services Director
Southern Region EMS Council, Inc.
1135 West Eighth Avenue, Suite 7
Anchorage, Alaska 99501

Emergency Medical Services Director
Southeast Region EMS Council, Inc.
1135 West Eighth Street, Suite 7
Anchorage, Alaska 99504

ARIZONA

Emergency Medical Services Director
Office of Emergency Medical Services
Department of Health Services
1740 West Adams Street, Room 101
Phoenix, Arizona 85007

ARKANSAS

Emergency Medical Services Director
Office of Emergency Medical Services
Department of Health
4815 West Markham
Little Rock, Arkansas 72201

CALIFORNIA

Emergency Medical Services Director
Emergency Medical Services Authority
1600 Ninth Street, Room 400
Sacramento, California 95814

COLORADO

Emergency Medical Services Director
Emergency Medical Services Division
Department of Health
4210 East 11th Avenue
Denver, Colorado 80220

CONNECTICUT

Emergency Medical Services Director
Office of Emergency Medical Services
Department of Health Services
79 Elm Street
Hartford, Connecticut 06106

DELAWARE

Emergency Medical Services Director
Division of Public Health
Jesse Cooper Memorial Building
William Penn & Federal Streets
Dover, Delaware 19901

DISTRICT OF COLUMBIA

Emergency Medical Services Director
Office of Emergency Medical Services
1875 Connecticut Avenue, NW
Room 833D
Washington, DC 20009

FLORIDA

Emergency Medical Services Director
Emergency Medical Services Section
Department of Health & Rehabilitative
  Services
1317 Winewood Boulevard, Room 267,
  Bldg.6
Tallahassee, Florida 32301

GEORGIA

Emergency Medical Services Director
Emergency Health Section
State Department of Human Resources
618 Ponce de Leon Avenue, NE
Atlanta, Georgia 30308

GUAM

Emergency Medical Services Director
Criminal Justice Academy
P.O. Box 23069
Main Postal Facility
Guam Mariana Islands 96921

HAWAII

Emergency Medical Services Director
Department of Health
P.O. Box 3378
Honolulu, Hawaii 96801

IDAHO

Emergency Medical Services Director
Emergency Medical Services Bureau
Department of Health and Welfare
450 West State
Boise, Idaho 83720

ILLINOIS

Emergency Medical Services Director
Department of Public Health
Division of EMS and Health Services
525 West Jefferson Street
Springfield, Illinois 62761

INDIANA

Emergency Medical Services Director
Emergency Medical Services
  Commission
State Office Building, Room 315
100 North Senate Avenue
Indianapolis, Indiana 46204

IOWA

Emergency Medical Service Director
Department of Health
Lucas State Office Building
Des Moines, Iowa 50319

KANSAS

Emergency Medical Service Director
Emergency Medical Training Program
University of Kansas Medical Center
39th Rainbow Boulevard, Building 45
Kansas City, Kansas 66103

KENTUCKY

Emergency Medical Service Director
Emergency Medical Services
Department of Human Resources
275 East Main Street
Frankfort, Kentucky 40601

LOUISIANA

Emergency Medical Service Director
Bureau of Emergency Medical Services
Department of Health & Human
  Resources
200 Lafayette Street, Suite 600
Baton Rouge, Louisiana 70801

MAINE

Emergency Medical Service Director
Department of Human Services
295 Water Street
Augusta, Maine 04330

MARYLAND

Emergency Medical Service Director
Testing and Certifications
Maryland Institute for EMS
22 South Greene Street
Baltimore, Maryland 21201

MASSACHUSETTS

Emergency Medical Service Director
Office of Emergency Medical Services
Department of Public Health
80 Boylston Street, Room 1230
Boston, Massachusetts 02116

MICHIGAN

Emergency Medical Service Director
Division of Emergency Medical Services
Department of Public Health
P.O. Box 30035
3500 North Logan
Lansing, Michigan 48909

MINNESOTA

Emergency Medical Service Director
Emergency Medical Services Training
Minnesota Department of Health
717 Delaware Street, SE
Minneapolis, Minnesota 55440

MISSISSIPPI

Emergency Medical Service Director
Department of Health
P.O. Box 1700
Jackson, Mississippi 39205

MISSOURI

Emergency Medical Service Director
Bureau of Emergency Medical Services
Division of Health
P.O. Box 570
Jefferson City, Missouri 65102

MONTANA

Emergency Medical Service Director
Emergency Medical Services Bureau
Department of Health
Cogswell Building
Helena, Montana 59620

NEBRASKA

Emergency Medical Service Director
Emergency Medical Services Division
Department of Health
301 Centennial Mall, South
Box 95007
Lincoln, Nebraska 68509

NEVADA

Emergency Medical Service Director
Department of Health
505 East King Street
Kinkead Building
Capital Complex
Carson City, Nevada 89710

NEW HAMPSHIRE

Emergency Medical Service Director
Division of Public Health
Health & Welfare Building
Hazen Drive
Concord, New Hampshire 03301

NEW JERSEY

Emergency Medical Service Director
Department of Health
CN 363
Trenton, New Jersey 08625

NEW MEXICO

Emergency Medical Service Director
Health & Environmental Department
P.O. Box 968
Santa Fe, New Mexico 87503

NEW YORK

Emergency Medical Service Director
Bureau of Emergency Health Services
Department of Health
Tower Building, 7th Floor
Empire State Plaza
Albany, New York 12237

NORTH CAROLINA

Emergency Medical Service Director
Office of Emergency Medical Services
Department of Human Resources
P.O. Box 12200
Raleigh, North Carolina 27605

NORTH DAKOTA

Emergency Medical Service Director
Division of Emergency Health Services
Department of Health
State Capitol Building, Judicial Wing
Bismarck, North Dakota 58505

OHIO

Emergency Medical Service Director
Department of Education
65 South Front Street, Room 918
Columbus, Ohio 43215

OKLAHOMA

Emergency Medical Service Director
Department of Health
1000 NE Tenth Street, Room 211
Box 53551
Oklahoma City, Oklahoma 73152

OREGON

Emergency Medical Service Director
Department of Human Resources
P.O. Box 231
Portland, Oregon 97207

PENNSYLVANIA

Emergency Medical Service Director
Division of Emergency Health Services
Department of Health
Box 90
1033 Health & Welfare Building
Harrisburg, Pennsylvania 17120

PUERTO RICO

Emergency Medical Service Director
Emergency Health Services
Department of Health
Ponce de Leon Avenue
San Juan, Puerto Rico 00908

RHODE ISLAND

Emergency Medical Service Director
Emergency Medical Services Division
Department of Health
75 Davis Street, Room 301
Providence, Rhode Island 02908

SOUTH CAROLINA

Emergency Medical Service Director
Division of Emergency Medical Services
Department of Health & Environmental
  Control
2600 Bull Street
Columbia, South Carolina 29201

SOUTH DAKOTA

Emergency Medical Service Director
Department of Health
523 East Capitol
Pierre, South Dakota 57501

TENNESSEE

Emergency Medical Service Director
Emergency Medical Services Division
Department of Health
RS Gass Office Building
Ben Allen Road
Nashville, Tennessee 37216

TEXAS

Emergency Medical Service Director
Bureau of Emergency Medical
  Management
Department of Health
1100 West 49th Street
Austin, Texas 78756

UTAH

Emergency Medical Service Director
Department of Health
P.O. Box 2500
Salt Lake City, Utah 84110

VERMONT

Emergency Medical Service Director
Department of Health
Montpelier, Vermont 05602

VIRGIN ISLANDS

Emergency Medical Service Director
Department of Health
Govt of Virgin Islands of the U.S.
P.O. Box 7309
St. Thomas, Virgin Islands 00801

VIRGINIA

Emergency Medical Service Director
Division of Emergency Medical Services
Department of Health
1102 James Madison Building
109 Governor Street
Richmond, Virginia 23219

WASHINGTON

Emergency Medical Service Director
Department of Social & Health Services
DSHS Mail Stop ET-34
Olympia, Washington 98504

WEST VIRGINIA

Emergency Medical Service Director
Office of Emergency Medical Services
Department of Health
1800 Washington Street, East
Building 3, Room 426
Charleston, West Virginia 25305

WISCONSIN

Emergency Medical Service Director
Division of Health
P.O. Box 309
Madison, Wisconsin 53701

WYOMING

Emergency Medical Service Director
Emergency Medical Services Program
Department of Health & Social Services
Hathaway Building, Room 478
Cheyenne, Wyoming 82002

ENVIRONMENTAL HEALTH

As one of the many specialized professions in the field of public health, environmental health is concerned with the protection, maintenance, and improvement of the human environment. Environmental health occupations discussed below are those of the *sanitarian*, the *environmental health technician*, and the *executive housekeeper*.

Sanitarian

Also referred to as an *environmentalist, environmental specialist*, or *environmental health inspector*, the sanitarian applies the principles of the physical, biological, and social sciences to a broad range of environmental management functions. The sanitarian plans, develops, directs, interprets, controls, and enforces comprehensive environmental health standards and programs in the following areas: air, water, land, and noise pollution; solid and hazardous waste management; food supply sanitation; consumer protection; epidemiology; and community sanitation. Other areas of concern to the sanitarian are occupational safety and health, health education, and radiologic health. Careers in these allied fields are discussed elsewhere in this handbook in their respective sections.

A sanitarian's specific duties might include the health inspection of food supplies; the sanitary inspection of restaurants, food processing plants, hospitals, nursing homes, recreation areas, and housing projects; the supervision of collection, treatment, and disposal of community wastes; or the monitoring of toxicant levels in public water supplies. Each location and process that the sanitarian inspects must comply with local, state, and federal public health regulations.

The range of job locations and types of employers for the sanitarian is almost as varied as the job responsibilities themselves. Sanitarians work for local, state and federal departments of health and of environmental protection. They are also employed in healthcare facilities, food processing plants, chemical industries, and in the military.

A bachelor's degree in environmental health or in the physical or biological sciences is the minimum educational requirement for the professional sanitarian. Supervisory, research, and teaching positions require graduate degrees.

Credentials as a Registered Sanitarian are awarded by the National Environmental Health Association to applicants who meet all educational and experience requirements and satisfactorily pass the registration examination. Registration information is available from the National Environmental Health Association, 720 South Colorado Blvd., Suite 970, South Tower, Denver, Colorado 80222.

Following is a list provided by the National Environmental Health Association of bachelor degree programs in environmental health.

SOURCES:

National Environmental Health Association
Occupational Outlook Handbook

Environmental Health Programs

CALIFORNIA

Environmental Health Program
California State University-Fresno
Health Science Department
Fresno, California 93740-0030

Environmental Health Program
California State University-Northridge
Department of Health Science
18111 Nordhoff Street
Northridge, California 91330

COLORADO

Environmental Health Program
Colorado State University
Environmental Health Sciences
Ft. Collins, Colorado 80523

GEORGIA

Environmental Health Program
University of Georgia
Environmental Health Science
Athens, Georgia 30602

IDAHO

Environmental Health Program
Boise State University
College of Health Science
1910 University Drive
Boise, Idaho 83725

ILLINOIS

Environmental Health Program
Illinois State University
Dept. of Health Sciences
Normal, Illinois 61761

INDIANA

Environmental Health Program
Indiana State University
Terre Haute, Indiana 47809

KENTUCKY

Environmental Health Program
Eastern Kentucky University
Richmond, Kentucky 40477

MICHIGAN

Environmental Health Program
Ferris State University
School of Allied Health
Big Rapids, Michigan 49307

MISSISSIPPI

Environmental Health Program
Mississippi Valley State University
P.O. Box 1240
Itta Bena, Mississippi 38941

MONTANA

Environmental Health Program
Montana State University
Department of Microbiology
Bozeman, Montana 59717

NORTH CAROLINA

Environmental Health Program
East Carolina University
School of Allied Health Sciences
Greenville, North Carolina 27858

Environmental Health Program
Western Carolina University
School of Nursing and Health Sciences
Cullowhee, North Carolina 28723

OHIO

Environmental Health Program
Bowling Green State University
College of Health and Human Service
Bowling Green, Ohio 43403

Environmental Health Program
Ohio University
School of Health and Sport Sciences
Athens, Ohio 45701-2979

Environmental Health Program
Wright State University
Dept. of Biological Sciences
Dayton, Ohio 45435

OKLAHOMA

Environmental Health Program
East Central University
School of Mathematics and Science
Ada, Oklahoma 74820

OREGON

Environmental Health Program
Oregon State University
Dept. of Public Health
Corvallis, Oregon 97331

TENNESSEE

Environmental Health Program
East Tennessee State University
Johnson City, Tennessee 37614

VIRGINIA

Environmental Health Program
Old Dominion University
College of Health Sciences
Norfolk, Virginia 23529

WASHINGTON

Environmental Health Program
University of Washington
Public Health and Community Medicine
Seattle, Washington 98195

WISCONSIN

Environmental Health Program
University of Wisconsin
Division of Allied Health Professions
Eau Claire, Wisconsin 54702

Environmental Health Technician

The *environmental health technician* is a para-professional who assists and is supervised by a registered sanitarian or other environmental professional. Employed primarily in community sanitation, in such locations as solid waste collection and disposal facilities or water purification and waste water treatment plants, the environmental health technician obtains samples of air and water and tests their quality in relation to health standards. The technician also assists the sanitarian in the inspection and evaluation of procedures involved with most other public health programs.

Formal training programs for the environmental health technician are generally two year associate degree programs in either environmental health, environmental science, or a related field. These programs are usually entitled environmental health technology or sanitation technology and are offered by community colleges, universities, and vocational-technical schools. Students interested in such programs should contact postsecondary institutions in their area.

For further information on the certification of environmental health technicians, interested persons should contact the National Environmental Health Association at 720 South Colorado Boulevard, Suite 970, South Tower, Denver, Colorado 80222.

SOURCE:

National Environmental Health Association

Executive Housekeeper

In hospitals and many other healthcare facilities the *executive housekeeper* is responsible for all environmental services, including cleaning, bacteriologic testing, and interior decorating. In some facilities the executive housekeeper is also responsible for the operation of the laundry and for security. His or her primary function is to maintain clean, antiseptic conditions in all the areas of the health facility that require a high degree of sanitation and sterilization especially patient wards, operating rooms, treatment rooms, and intensive care units.

Familiar with labor relations and safety/health regulations, the executive housekeeper also manages the housekeeping staff. He or she establishes work schedules and supervises the activities of the housekeeping department, so that its staff does not impede or interfere with the administration of healthcare by physicians, nurses, and other medical personnel. The housekeeper purchases cleaning supplies and equipment, forecasts future needs for the department, and prepares departmental budgets. He or she conducts continual research into new housekeeping products and into new healthcare facilities that will require housekeeping services.

In interior decorating the executive housekeeper selects furnishings, carpets, and wall coverings that provide pleasant yet utilitarian surroundings. If the housekeeping department supervises the facility's laundry, it is the executive housekeeper who maintains established sanitary standards and supervises the selection, laundering, and distribution of linens.

Because executive housekeepers already hold the top position in their profession, further advancement may be limited. Housekeepers in hospitals may advance by taking similar jobs at higher pay in larger hospitals or some housekeeping department heads may become hospital administrators. Executive housekeepers are employed by hospitals, nursing homes, healthcare centers, hotels, colleges, universities, and in private industry.

On-the-job training is provided for the lower level jobs in hospital housekeeping. However, for those individuals interested in management positions there are certificate, associate, and bachelor degree programs available in institutional housekeeping management.

The credential of Certified Executive Housekeeper (C.E.H.) is awarded to those members of the National Executive Housekeeper Association who have fulfilled the educational requirements through a certificate program, a collegiate degree program, or a home study program. The Registered Executive Housekeeper (R.E.H.) title is the highest level recognition awarded to those who have met the educational requirements and maintained their certified membership for one year.

Recommended high school courses for students interested in a career in housekeeping include general science, textiles, chemistry, and business.

Salaries for executive housekeepers vary depending upon the size of the establishment where they are employed and years of experience. Executive housekeepers who work in healthcare institutions may earn over $40,000. Salaries for those employed by hotels and motels range from $15,000 to $32,000 a year.

Following is a list, supplied by the National Executive Housekeepers Association, of approved schools offering certified membership programs in Executive Housekeeping.

For additional information on a career as an executive housekeeper, write to the National Executive Housekeepers Association, 1001 Eastwind Drive, Suite 301, Westerville, Ohio 43081-3361.

SOURCES:

National Executive Housekeepers Association

Executive Housekeeper Programs

ALABAMA

Executive Housekeeper Program
University of Alabama
1919 University Boulevard
Birmingham, Alabama 35294

ARIZONA

Executive Housekeeper Program
Pima County College
P.O. Box 5027
Tucson, Arizona 85703

Executive Housekeeper Program
Rio Salado Community College
640 North First Avenue
Phoenix, Arizona 85003

CALIFORNIA

Executive Housekeeper Program
Fresno City College
1101 North University Avenue
Fresno, California 93741

Executive Housekeeper Program
Palomar College
San Marcos, California 92069

Executive Housekeeper Program
Rancho Santiago Community College
541 North Lemon Street
Orange, California 92667

Executive Housekeeper Program
San Diego Community College
3375 Camino Del Rio South
San Diego, California 92108

Executive Housekeeper Program
Skyline College
3300 College Drive
San Bruno, California 94066

Executive Housekeeper Program
University of California
740 Front Street
Santa Cruz, California 95060

COLORADO

Executive Housekeeper Program
T.H. Pickens Tech
500 Buckley Road
Aurora, Colorado 80011

CONNECTICUT

Executive Housekeeper Program
Briarwood College
2279 Mt. Vernon Road
Southington, Connecticut 06489

FLORIDA

Executive Housekeeper Program
Collier County Vo-Tech
3702 Estey Avenue
Naples, Florida 33942

Executive Housekeeper Program
Daytona Beach Community College
P.O. Box 1111
Daytona Beach, Florida 32015

Executive Housekeeper Program
Indian River Community College
3209 Virginia Avenue
Ft. Pierce, Florida 33901

Executive Housekeeper Program
Lee Vo-Tech
3800 Michigan Avenue
Ft. Myers, Florida 33901

Executive Housekeeper Program
McFatter Vo-Tech
6500 Nova Drive
Davie, Florida 33317

Executive Housekeeper Program
Mid-Florida Tech
2900 West Oak Ridge
Orlando, Florida 32809

Executive Housekeeper Program
Palm Beach Junior College
4200 Congress Avenue
Lake Worth, Florida 33461

Executive Housekeeper Program
Pasco Hernando Community College
7025 Moon Lake Road
New Port Richey, Florida 34654

Executive Housekeeper Program
Ridge Vo-Tech Center
7700 State Road 544 North
Winter Haven, Florida 33881

Executive Housekeeper Program
Sarasota County Vocational Center
4748 Beneva Road
Sarasota, Florida 33583

Executive Housekeeper Program
Tampa Bay Vocational
6410 Orient Road
Tampa, Florida 33610

Executive Housekeeper Program
University of Florida
SW 13th and Museum
Gainesville, Florida 32611

GEORGIA

Executive Housekeeper Program
Macon Technical Institute
P.O. Box 1009
Milledgeville, Georgia

Executive Housekeeper Program
Savannah Area Vocational
107 Gignilliat Street
Savannah, Georgia 31408

HAWAII

Executive Housekeeper Program
Kapiolani Community College
4303 Diamond Head Road
Honolulu, Hawaii 96816

ILLINOIS

Executive Housekeeper Program
Black Hawk College
6600 34th Avenue
Moline, Illinois 61265

Executive Housekeeper Program
Chicago City Wide
226 West Jackson Boulevard
Chicago, Illinois 60606

Executive Housekeeper Program
College of Lake County
19351 West Washington
Grayslake, Illinois 60030

Executive Housekeeper Program
DePaul University
243 South Wabash
Chicago, Illinois 60604

Executive Housekeeper Program
Illinois Central
One College Drive
East Peoria, Illinois 61635

Executive Housekeeper Program
Lincoln Land Community College
Shepherd Road
Springfield, Illinois 62708

Executive Housekeeper Program
Oakton Community College
1600 East Golf Road
Des Plaines, Illinois 60016

Executive Housekeeper Program
Parkland College
2400 West Bradley Avenue
Champaign, Illinois 61821

INDIANA

Executive Housekeeper Program
Indiana Vo-Tech
P.O. Box 1763
Indianapolis, Indiana 46206

Executive Housekeeper Program
Ivy Tech-Evansville
3501 First Avenue
Evansville, Indiana 47710

IOWA

Executive Housekeeper Program
Eastern Iowa Community College
306 West River Road
Davenport, Iowa 52801

Executive Housekeeper Program
Hawkeye Institute of Technology
Box 8015
Waterloo, Iowa 50704

KENTUCKY

Executive Housekeeper Program
Hopkinsville Community College
P.O. Box 2100
Hopkinsville, Kentucky 42240

Executive Housekeeper Program
Jefferson Community College
109 East Broadway
Louisville, Kentucky 40202

Executive Housekeeper Program
Paducah Community College
P.O. Box 7380
Paducah, Kentucky 42002

Executive Housekeeper Program
Somerset Community College
808 Monticello Road
Somerset, Kentucky 42501

LOUISIANA

Executive Housekeeper Program
Delgado Community College
615 City Park Avenue
New Orleans, Louisiana 70119

Executive Housekeeper Program
Jefferson Parish Vo-Tech
5200 Blair Drive
Metairie, Louisiana 70001

Executive Housekeeper Program
LSU-Eunice
P.O. Box 1129
Eunice, Louisiana 70535

Executive Housekeeper Program
New Orleans Regional Tech
980 Navarre Avenue
New Orleans, Louisiana 70124

MAINE

Executive Housekeeper Program
University of South Maine
96 Falmouth Street
Portland, Maine 04103

MARYLAND

Executive Housekeeper Program
Catonsville Community College
880 South Rolling Road
Baltimore, Maryland 21228

Executive Housekeeper Program
Montgomery College
235 Human Building
Germantown, Maryland

Executive Housekeeper Program
Wor-Wic Technical College
Route 3, Box 79
Berlin, Maryland 21811

MASSACHUSETTS

Executive Housekeeper Program
Massachusetts Bay Community College
50 Oakland Street
Wellsley, Massachusetts

MICHIGAN

Executive Housekeeper Program
Lansing Community College
P.O. Box 40010
Lansing, Michigan 48901

Executive Housekeeper Program
Mary Grove College
8425 West McNichols
Detroit, Michigan 48221

MINNESOTA

Executive Housekeeper Program
Normandale Community College
9700 Frances South
Bloomington, Minnesota 55431

Executive Housekeeper Program
Rochester Vo-Tech
1926 Second Street SE
Rochester, Minnesota 55904

MISSISSIPPI

Executive Housekeeper Program
Hinds Community College
3805 Highway 80 East
Pearl, Mississippi 39208

Executive Housekeeper Program
Meridian Junior College
5500 Highway 19 North
Meridian, Mississippi 39305

MISSOURI

Executive Housekeeper Program
Maple Woods Community College
2601 NE Barry Road
Kansas City, Missouri 64156

Executive Housekeeper Program
South West Missouri State
901 South National
Springfield, Missouri 65804

Executive Housekeeper Program
University of Missouri
8001 Natural Bridge
St. Louis, Missouri 63121

NEVADA

Executive Housekeeper Program
Clark County Community College
3200 East Cheyenne
Las Vegas, Nevada 89030

NEW JERSEY

Executive Housekeeper Program
Burlington County College
Pemberton-Brown Mill Road
Pemberton, New Jersey 08068

Executive Housekeeper Program
Montclair State College
Center for Continuing Education
Montclair, New Jersey 07043

NEW MEXICO

Executive Housekeeper Program
National College
8005 Hendrix Road
Albuquerque, New Mexico 87109

NEW YORK

Executive Housekeeper Program
NYC Technical College
300 Jay Street
Brooklyn, New York 11201

Executive Housekeeper Program
Orange County Community College
115 South Street
Middletown, New York 10940

Executive Housekeeper Program
SUNY Agricultural & Technical College
Cobleskill, New York 12043

NORTH CAROLINA

Executive Housekeeper Program
Catawba Valley Community College
Route 3, Box 283
Hickory, North Carolina 28602

Executive Housekeeper Program
Forsyth Technical College
2100 Silas Creek
Winston-Salem, North Carolina 27103

Executive Housekeeper Program
Wake Technical College
9101 Fayetteville
Raleigh, North Carolina 27603

OHIO

Executive Housekeeper Program
Bowling Green State
300 McFall Center
Bowling Green, Ohio 43403

Executive Housekeeper Program
Clark Technical College
P.O. Box 570
Springfield, Ohio 45501

Executive Housekeeper Program
Columbus State Community College
550 East Spring Street
Columbus, Ohio 43215

Executive Housekeeper Program
Cuyahoga Community College
2900 Community College
Cleveland, Ohio 44115

Executive Housekeeper Program
University of Akron
Akron, Ohio 44325

OKLAHOMA

Executive Housekeeper Program
Oklahoma State University
Stillwater, Oklahoma 74078

OREGON

Executive Housekeeper Program
Lane Community College
1059 Willamette Street
Eugene, Oregon 97401

Executive Housekeeper Program
Portland Community College
12000 SW 49th Avenue
Portland, Oregon 97219

PENNSYLVANIA

Executive Housekeeper Program
Marywood College
2300 Adams Avenue
Scranton, Pennsylvania 18509

SOUTH CAROLINA

Executive Housekeeper Program
Horry Georgetown Technical College
Box 1966
Conway, South Carolina 29526

Executive Housekeeper Program
Trident Technical College
P.O. Box 10367
Charleston, South Carolina 29411

Executive Housekeeper Program
University of South Carolina
Columbia, South Carolina 29201

TENNESSEE

Executive Housekeeper Program
Shelby State Technical
P.O. Box 40568
Memphis, Tennessee 38174

Executive Housekeeper Program
Technical Education Center
Fulton High School
Knoxville, Tennessee 37917

TEXAS

Executive Housekeeper Program
Amarillo College
Box 447
Amarillo, Texas 79178

Executive Housekeeper Program
Del Mar College
Baldwin and Ayers
Corpus Christi, Texas 78404

Executive Housekeeper Program
El Centro College
Main and Lamar Streets
Dallas, Texas 75202

Executive Housekeeper Program
El Paso Community College
P.O. Box 20500
El Paso, Texas 79998

Executive Housekeeper Program
Grayson County College
6101 Grayson Drive
Denison, Texas 75020

Executive Housekeeper Program
Odessa College
201 West University
Odessa, Texas 79764

Executive Housekeeper Program
San Antonio College
1300 San Pedro
San Antonio, Texas 78284

Executive Housekeeper Program
South Plains College
2579 South Loop 289
Lubbock, Texas 79423

Executive Housekeeper Program
Texarkana College
2500 North Robison Road
Texarkana, Texas 75501

Executive Housekeeper Program
Texas State Technical Institute -
 Harlingen
P.O. Box 2628
Harlingen, Texas 78551

Executive Housekeeper Program
UT & Arlington
Box 91997
Arlington, Texas

Executive Housekeeper Program
Tyler Junior College
1530 SSW Loop 323
Tyler, Texas 75701

Executive Housekeeper Program
Vernon Regional Junior College
4400 College Drive
Vernon, Texas 76384

UTAH

Executive Housekeeper Program
Utah Valley Community College
800 West, 1200 South
Orem, Utah 84058

VERMONT

Executive Housekeeper Program
Norwich University
Vermont College Campus
Montpelier, Vermont 05602

VIRGINIA

Executive Housekeeper Program
Arlington Public Schools
2700 South Lang Street
Arlington, Virginia 22206

Executive Housekeeper Program
Piedmont Virginia Community College
Route 6, Box 1-A
Charlottesville, Virginia 22901

Executive Housekeeper Program
Thomas Nelson Community College
P.O. Box 9407
Hampton, Virginia 23670

Executive Housekeeper Program
William Fleming
3649 Ferncliff
Roanoke, Virginia 24017

WEST VIRGINIA

Executive Housekeeper Program
West Liberty State College
West Liberty, West Virginia 26074

WISCONSIN

Executive Housekeeper Program
Milwaukee Area Technical College
1200 South 71st Street West
West Allis, Wisconsin 53214

Executive Housekeeper Program
Northeast Wisconsin Technical Institute
2740 West Mason Street
Green Bay, Wisconsin 54307

Executive Housekeeper Program
Chippewa Valley
620 West Clairemont
Eau Claire, Wisconsin 54701

✚ FOOD TECHNOLOGY

Food technology, also known as food science, is the application of chemistry, microbiology, and engineering to the production, processing, packaging, distribution, preparation, utilization, and evaluation of foods. Food technology is of vital importance in less developed countries where it attempts to alleviate problems of malnutrition and lack of food. It is also of importance in developed countries where it investigates food-processing methods and ingredients and attempts to provide greater varieties of nutritious foods that are easier to preserve and prepare. There are two career occupations in food technology, the *food technologist* and the *food science technician.*

Food Technologist

Also known as a *food scientist* or *food scientist technologist*, the food technologist is a trained professional in the food industry who is concerned with the processing, preserving, sanitation, storage, and marketing of nutritious, wholesome, and economic foods. By researching the physical, chemical and biological nature of food, the technologist studies the changes that occur in the nutritional value and suitability of industrially prepared foods throughout their processing and storage.

In the research and development of new products, processes, and equipment, the food technologist may develop new foods or new factors that will improve the flavor, texture or appearance of existing foods.

In the assurance of quality control, the technologist tests new ingredients for freshness and suitability for processing, and tests finished products for purity and safety in storage.

In production, the technologist prepares production specifications and schedules processing operations, maintains the proper temperature and humidity in storage areas, and supervises economic and sanitary disposal of wastes.

The food technologist may also teach or be involved with market research, advertising, or technical sales.

The majority of all food technologists are employed in the food processing industry, while the remainder teach in universities and colleges or work in various government departments such as the Department of Agriculture or the Food and Drug Administration. At the international level, food technologists are employed by the World Health Organization and the United Nations.

The usual minimum educational requirement for employment as a food technologist is a bachelor's degree with a major in food science, food engineering, or food technology. A master's degree is usually required for research and management positions.

Recommended high school courses for students preparing for a career in food science include biology, chemistry, mathematics, physics, English, social science, and a foreign language.

Starting pay for food scientists with a bachelor's degree who worked for the federal government in 1990, averaged from $16,300 to $21,200. Food technologists with graduate degrees earned considerably more.

Fellowships and scholarships for students entering universities in this field and students already enrolled in food science programs are administered by the Institute of Food Technologists. Information on the fellowship/scholarship program is available from the Institute of Food Technologists, 221 North LaSalle Street, Chicago, Illinois 60601.

Following the Food Science Technician chapter is a list of educational programs in Food Science which have been approved by the Institute of Food Technologists Education Committee.

SOURCES:

Institute of Food Technologists
Occupational Outlook Handbook

Food Science Technician

Employed in the same locations as the food technologist, the food science technician assists the technologist in quality control and in laboratory research and development. The food science technician also assists in supervising the processing and packaging of food and in the maintenance of sanitary conditions.

Junior colleges, technician training schools, and community vocational schools offer two year programs for people wishing to enter food careers at the technician level.

Salaries for food science technicians are lower than those for food technologists.

Following is a list of educational programs in Food Science which have been approved by the institute of Food Technologists Education Committee. Other programs in food science may exist throughout the country and it is recommended that interested students contact the educational institutions in their area for information.

SOURCE:

Institute of Food Technologists

Food Science Programs

ALABAMA

Food Science Program
Alabama A&M University
Dept of Food Science & Animal
Industries
Normal, Alabama 35762

Food Science Program
Auburn University
Dept of Nutrition & Food Science
Auburn, Alabama 36849-5605

ARKANSAS

Food Science Program
University of Arkansas
Dept of Food Science
272 Young Avenue
Fayetteville, Arkansas 72703

CALIFORNIA

Food Science Program
University of California-Davis
Dept of Food Science & Technology
Davis, California 95616-8598

Food Science Program
California Polytechnic State University
Food Science & Nutrition Dept
San Luis Obispo, California 93407

Food Science Program
San Jose State University
Dept of Nutrition & Food Science
San Jose, California 95192-0058

COLORADO

Food Science Program
Colorado State University
Dept of Food Science & Nutrition
Ft. Collins, Colorado 80523

DELAWARE

Food Science Program
University of Delaware
Dept of Food Science
Newark, Delaware 19716

FLORIDA

Food Science Program
University of Florida
Food Science & Human Nutrition Dept
P.O. Box 110370
Gainesville, Florida 32611-0370

GEORGIA

Food Science Program
University of Georgia
Dept of Food Science Engineering &
Technology
Athens, Georgia 30602

ILLINOIS

Food Science Program
University of Illinois
Department of Food Science
1302 Pennsylvania Avenue
Urbana, Illinois 61801

INDIANA

Food Science Program
Purdue University
Department of Food Science
West Lafayette, Indiana 47907-1160

IOWA

Food Science Program
Iowa State University
Dept of Food Science & Human
Nutrition
Ames, Iowa 50011-1060

KANSAS

Food Science Program
Kansas State University
Manhattan, Kansas 66506-0201

Food Science Program
Kansas State University
Dept of Foods & Nutrition
Manhattan, Kansas 66506

KENTUCKY

Food Science Program
University of Kentucky
Lexington, Kentucky 40546-0215

MAINE

Food Science Program
University of Maine
Department of Food Science
Orono, Maine 04469

MARYLAND

Food Science Program
University of Maryland
Food Science Program
College Park, Maryland 20742

MASSACHUSETTS

Food Science Program
University of Massachusetts
Department of Food Science
Amherst, Massachusetts 01003

MICHIGAN

Food Science Program
Michigan State University
Dept of Food Science & Human
Nutrition
East Lansing, Michigan 48824-1224

MINNESOTA

Food Science Program
University of Minnesota
Dept of Food Science & Nutrition
1334 Eckles Avenue
St. Paul, Minnesota 55108-6099

MISSISSIPPI

Food Science Program
Mississippi State University
Dept of Food Science & Technology
P.O. Box NH
Mississippi State, Mississippi 39762

MISSOURI

Food Science Program
University of Missouri
Dept of Food Science & Human
Nutrition
Columbia, Missouri 65211

NEBRASKA

Food Science Program
University of Nebraska
Dept of Food Science & Technology
Lincoln, Nebraska 68583-0919

NEW JERSEY

Food Science Program
Rutgers State University
Department of Food Science
P.O. Box 231
New Brunswick, New Jersey 08903

NEW YORK

Food Science Program
Cornell University
Department of Food Science
Ithaca, New York 14853-7201

NORTH CAROLINA

Food Science Program
North Carolina State University
Department of Food Science
Box 7624
Raleigh, North Carolina 27695-7624

NORTH DAKOTA

Food Science Program
North Dakota State University
Cereal Science & Food Technology Dept
P.O. Box 5728
Fargo, North Dakota 58105

OHIO

Food Science Program
Ohio State University
Dept of Food Science & Technology
2121 Fyffe Road
Columbus, Ohio 43210-1097

OKLAHOMA

Food Science Program
Oklahoma State University
Stillwater, Oklahoma 74078

OREGON

Food Science Program
Oregon State University
Dept of Food Science & Technology
Corvallis, Oregon 97331-6602

PENNSYLVANIA

Food Science Program
Delaware Valley College
Dept of Food Science & Management
700 East Butler Avenue
Doylestown, Pennsylvania 18901

Food Science Program
Pennsylvania State University
Department of Food Science
University Park, Pennsylvania 16802

RHODE ISLAND

Food Science Program
University of Rhode Island
Dept of Food Science & Nutrition
Kingston, Rhode Island 02881

SOUTH CAROLINA

Food Science Program
Clemson University
Department of Food Science
Clemson, South Carolina 29634-0371

TENNESSEE

Food Science Program
University of Tennessee
Dept of Food Science & Technology
P.O. Box 1071
Knoxville, Tennessee 37901

TEXAS

Food Science Program
Texas A&M University
College Station, Texas 77843

UTAH

Food Science Program
Brigham Young University
Dept of Food Science & Nutrition
Provo, Utah 84602

Food Science Program
Utah State University
Dept of Nutrition & Food Science
Logan, Utah 84322-8700

VIRGINIA

Food Science Program
Virginia Polytechnic Institute & State
University
Dept of Food Science & Technology
Blacksburg, Virginia 24061

WASHINGTON

Food Science Program
Washington State University
Dept of Food Science & Human
Nutrition
Pullman, Washington 99164-6376

Food Science Program
University of Washington
Institute for Food Science & Technology
School of Fisheries
Seattle, Washington 98195

WISCONSIN

Food Science Program
University of Wisconsin-Madison
1605 Linden Drive
Department of Food Science
Madison, Wisconsin 53706

Food Science Program
University of Wisconsin-River Falls
Dept of Animal & Food Science
River Falls, Wisconsin 54022

CANADA

Food Science Program
Acadia University
Department of Food Science
Wolfville, N.S., Canada B0P 1X0

Food Science Program
University of Alberta
Department of Food Science
Edmonton, Alberta, Canada T6G 2P5

Food Science Program
University of British Columbia
Department of Food Science
6650 NW Marine Drive
Vancouver, B.C., Canada V6T 1Z4

Food Science Program
University of Guelph
Department of Food Science
Guelph, Ontario, Canada N1G 2W1

Food Science Program
Universite Laval
Dept of Food Science & Technology
1312 Comtois
Ste Foy, P.Q., Canada G1K 7P4

Food Science Program
McGill University
Macdonald Campus
Dept of Food Science & Agri Chemistry
21111 Lakeshore Road
Ste. Anne de Bellevue, P.Q., Canada
H9X 1C0

✚ HEALTH EDUCATION

Health education teaches individuals and communities the methods of and the necessity for improving and maintaining optimum health practices. Health education is taught to the general public by *community health educators*, to students by *school health educators*, to the work force by *business* and *industry health educators* and to healthcare patients by *clinical health educators*. These four career classifications are listed below.

Community Health Educator

The *community health educator* works as a specialist on a community health team in the teaching and promoting of quality health. When people in a community, or the community as a whole, do not practice good health habits, the community health educator diagnoses why health information is lacking or why the information that is available is not utilized. She or he then implements appropriate educational programs that are designed to stimulate people to recognize and to rectify their own and the community's health inadequacies. Community health problems today include, among others, environmental pollution, drug and alcohol abuse, poor nutrition, and AIDS.

The Community Health Educator works for voluntary and private health organizations, as well as local, state, and federal government agencies.

Positions in public or community health education usually require a bachelor or master's degree in community or public health education, and participation in a community health education internship.

For more information on a career as a community or public health educator contact the Association for Advancement of Health Education, 1900 Association Drive, Reston, Virginia 22091.

Following is a list of graduate degree programs in community health education accredited by the Council on Education for Public Health.

A list of additional bachelor and master degree programs in community/public health education, supplied by the Association for the Advancement of Health Education, is included with those of school health education, medical care/patient health education, and worksite health education listed at the end of this chapter.

SOURCES:

Association for the Advancement of Health Education
Council on Education for Public Health

Community Health Education Programs

CALIFORNIA

Community Health Education Program
California State University-Long Beach
College of Health & Human Services
1250 Bellflower Boulevard
Long Beach, California 90840

Community Health Education Program
California State University-Northridge
School of Communication, Health &
  Human Services
18111 Nordhoff Street
Northridge, California 91330

Community Health Education Program
San Jose State University
School of Applied Sciences and Arts
San Jose, California 95192

COLORADO

Community Health Education Program
University of Northern Colorado
College of Health & Human Sciences
Greeley, Colorado 80639

ILLINOIS

Community Health Education Program
University of Illinois
Department of Community Health
1206 South Fourth Street
Champaign, Illinois 61820

NEW YORK

Community Health Education Program
Hunter College
School of Health Sciences
425 East 25th Street
New York, New York 10010

Community Health Education Program
New York University
Department of Health Education
35 West Fourth Street, Suite 1200
New York, New York 10003

PENNSYLVANIA

Community Health Education Program
East Stroudsburg State University
Health Department
East Stroudsburg, Pennsylvania 18201

Community Health Education Program
Temple University
Department of Health Education
Philadelphia, Pennsylvania 19122

WISCONSIN

Community Health Education Program
University of Wisconsin at LaCrosse
Health Education Department
LaCrosse, Wisconsin 54601

School Health Educator

The *school health educator* teaches elementary, secondary, and college students the principles and methods of developing proper attitudes and skills toward the maintenance of optimal good health. In the classroom the school health educator teaches courses on family life, nutrition, safety education, first aid, personal hygiene, drug and alcohol abuse, mental health, human relations, disease prevention and control, community health, environmental pollution, and the use of health services and products. In addition to classroom instruction the school health educator actively cooperates with the rest of the school staff, including the school physician and nurse, other teachers, athletic coaches, and service personnel, in attempting to influence and instill the students with a sense of good healthcare judgment. They also represent the school in community health activities and use the latter's resources to supplement the school's health education program.

The school health educator is employed in elementary schools, junior and senior high schools and colleges, voluntary agencies, professional organizations, public health departments, and other government agencies.

Four years of college leading to a bachelor's degree with a major in health education is the minimum training criteria for the school health educator. A period of internship may also be required.

For more information on a career as a school health educator, contact the Association for the Advancement of Health Education, 1900 Association Drive, Reston, Virginia 22091.

A list of bachelor and master degree programs in school health education, supplied by the Association for the Advancement of Health Education, is included with those of community/public health education, medical care/patient health education, and worksite health education listed at the end of this chapter.

SOURCES:

American School Health Association
Association for the Advancement of Health Education

Health Educator In Business and Industry

The *health educator in business and industry* plans and conducts health maintenance programs for employees and executives in the work place. Utilizing numerous educational tools, including videotapes, slide presentations and informational brochures, the health educator directs workshops and group discussions on topics including nutrition, exercise, weight control, smoking cessation and stress management. The health educator may also make recommendations to executives on health policies.

As a health promoter, the health educator is aware of the advantages to employees of beginning and maintaining healthy lifestyles: advantages such as improved appearance, emotional and physical well being, and physiological improvements. The company benefits as well, through positive employee moral, reduced absenteeism, and increased productivity.

Educational requirements for a career in Health Education in Business and Industry are either a bachelor's or master's degree in health education with course emphasis on business and industry programs.

A list of bachelor and master degree programs in worksite health education, supplied by the Association for the Advancement of Health Education, is included with those of community/public health education, school health education, and medical care/patient health education listed at the end of this chapter.

SOURCE:

Association for the Advancement of Health Education

Clinical Health Educator

The *clinical health educator* develops and administers health maintenance and wellness programs in a healthcare setting. Clinical health educators mainly work in hospitals, but are also employed by clinics, health maintenance organizations, and with private physicians.

The clinical health educator can work one-on-one in a hospital setting, or may direct programs to groups of patients in an out-patient facility. On an individual basis, the clinical health educator deals with the patient, family and friends, and helps them better understand the patient's health condition. He or she explains the necessity of following the physicians' instructions and provides recommendations for avoiding recurrence of health problems in the future.

The clinical health educator also conducts educational programs on an out-patient basis for groups of patients with similar health conditions. Through the use of slide presentations, reading material and group discussions, the clinical health educator helps the patients develop ways to control their health situation.

The educational requirement for a clinical health educator is a degree in community health education plus an internship in a clinical setting. Some clinical health educators may also have experience or degrees in health services administration. Some clinical health educators have prior experience as registered nurses or related health professionals.

A list of bachelor and master degree programs in medical care/patient health education, supplied by the Association for the Advancement of Health Education, is included with those of community/public health education, school health education, and worksite health education listed at the end of this chapter.

For further information on a career as a clinical health educator write to the Association for the Advancement of Health Education, 1900 Association Drive, Reston, Virginia 22091.

144

SOURCE:

Association for the Advancement of Health Education

KEY:

(B)	Bachelor's degree
(M)	Master's degree

(1)	Community/Public Health Education
(2)	School Health Education
(3)	Medical Care Setting/Patient Health Education
(4)	Worksite Health Education

Health Education Programs

ALABAMA

Health Education Program (B4)
Auburn University
Auburn, Alabama 36849-5323

Health Education Program (B2)
Samford University
Birmingham, Alabama 35229

Health Education Program (B2, M2)
Troy State University
Troy, Alabama 36082

Health Education Program
 (B1, B2, M1, M2)
University of Alabama at Birmingham
Birmingham, Alabama 35294

Health Education Program
 (B1, M1, M2, M4)
University of Alabama
Tuscaloosa, Alabama 35487

Health Education Program (B2, M2)
University of South Alabama
Mobile, Alabama 36688

ARIZONA

Health Education Program (B1, B2)
Northern Arizona University
Flagstaff, Arizona 86011

Health Education
 Program (B1, B2, M1, M2)
University of Arizona
Tucson, Arizona 85719

ARKANSAS

Health Education Program (B1, B2, M1,
 M2, M3, M4)
University of Arkansas
Fayetteville, Arkansas 72701

Health Education Program (B1)
University of Arkansas at Little Rock
Little Rock, Arkansas 72204

Health Education Program
 (B1, B2, M1, M2)
University of Central Arkansas
Conway, Arkansas 72032

CALIFORNIA

Health Education Program (B1, M1)
California State University
Fresno, California 93740-0030

Health Education Program
 (B1, B2, M1, M2)
California State University
Long Beach, California 90840-4906

Health Education Program
 (B1, B2, M1, M2)
California State University
Los Angeles, California 90032-8172

Health Education Program (B1, M1)
California State University
Northridge, California 91330

Health Education Program
 (B1, B2, M1, M2)
California State University
San Bernardino, California 92407-2397

Health Education Program (M1, M2)
Loma Linda University
Loma Linda, California 92399

Health Education Program (B1, B2, M1)
San Diego State University
San Diego, California 92182-0252

Health Education Program (B1, B2)
San Francisco State University
San Francisco, California 94132

Health Education Program (B1, M2)
San Jose State University
San Jose, California 95192-0052

Health Education Program (M1)
University of California
Berkeley, California 90024

Health Education Program (M1)
University of California
Los Angeles, California 90024

COLORADO

Health Education Program (B1, M1)
University of Northern Colorado
Greenley, Colorado 80639

CONNECTICUT

Health Education Program (M1)
Southern Connecticut State University
New Haven, Connecticut 06515

Health Education Program (B1, B2)
Western Connecticut State University
Danbury, Connecticut 06810

FLORIDA

Health Education Program (B1, M1)
Florida State University
Tallahassee, Florida 32306-3001

Health Education Program (B1, B2, B4,
 M1, M2, M4)
University of Florida
Gainesville, Florida 32611-2034

Health Education Program (B1, M1)
University of North Florida
Jacksonville, Florida 32216-6699

Health Education Program (M1)
University of South Florida
Tampa, Florida 33612-3899

Health Education Program (B1, B2, M1)
University of West Florida
Pensacola, Florida 32514

GEORGIA

Health Education Program (B1, B5)
Columbus College
Columbus, Georgia 31993

Health Education Program (M1)
Emory University
Atlanta, Georgia 30322

146

Health Education Program
(B1, B2, B4, M2, M4)
Georgia College
Milledgeville, Georgia 31061

Health Education Program
(B2, M1, M2, M4)
University of Georgia
Athens, Georgia 30602

IDAHO

Health Education Program
(B1, B2, M1, M2)
Idaho State University
Pocatello, Idaho 83209

ILLINOIS

Health Education Program (B1, B2)
Eastern Illinois University
Charleston, Illinois 61920

Health Education Program (M1)
Illinois Benedictine College
Lisle, Illinois 60532

Health Education Program (B1, B2)
Illinois State University
Normal Illinois 61761

Health Education Program (B2)
Northern Illinois University
DeKalb, Illinois 60115

Health Education Program
(B1, B2, M1, M2)
Southern Illinois University
Carbondale, Illinois 62901-6618

Health Education Program (B1, B2)
Southern Illinois University
Edwardsville, Illinois 62026

Health Education Program
(B1, M1, M2)
University of Illinois
Champaign, Illinois 61820

Health Education Program
(B1, B2, B3, B4)
Western Illinois University
Macomb, Illinois 61455

INDIANA

Health Education Program
(B1, B2, M1, M2)
Ball State University
Muncie, Indiana 47306

Health Education Program (B1, B2, M2)
Indiana State University
Terre Haute, Indiana 47809

Health Education Program (B1, B2, M1, M2)
Indiana University
Bloomington, Indiana 47405

Health Education Program (B1, B2, M1)
Purdue University
West Lafayette, Indiana 47907

IOWA

Health Education Program (B1)
Iowa State University
Ames, Iowa 50010

Health Education Program (B1, B2)
Luther College
Decorah, Iowa 52101

Health Education Program
(B1, B2, M1, M2, M4)
University of Northern Iowa
Cedar Falls, Iowa 50614-0241

Health Education Program (B2)
Emporia State University
Emporia, Iowa 66801

KANSAS

Health Education Program
 (B1, B2, M1, M2)
University of Kansas
Lawrence, Kansas 60045

KENTUCKY

Health Education Program (B1, B2)
Cumberland College
Williamsburg, Kentucky 40769

Health Education Program
 (B1, B2, M1, M2)
Eastern Kentucky University
Richmond, Kentucky 40475-3103

Health Education Program (B1, B2)
Morehead State University
Morehead, Kentucky 40351

Health Education Program (B2, M2)
Murray State University
Murray, Kentucky 42071

Health Education Program (B2, M2)
University of Kentucky
Lexington, Kentucky 40506-0219

Health Education Program
 (B1, B2, M3, M4)
Western Kentucky University
Bowling Green, Kentucky 42101

LOUISIANA

Health Education Program (M4)
Southeastern Louisiana University
Hammond, Louisiana 70402

Health Education Program (M1)
Tulane University
New Orleans, Louisiana 70112

MAINE

Health Education Program (B1, B2)
University of Maine at Farmington
Farmington, Maine 04938

Health Education Program (B2)
University of Maine at Presque Isle
Presque Isle, Maine 04769

MARYLAND

Health Education Program
 (B1, B2, M1, M2, M3)
Towson State University
Towson, Maryland 21204-7097

Health Education Program
 (B1, B2, M1, M4)
University of Maryland
College Park, Maryland 20742-2611

MASSACHUSETTS

Health Education Program
 (M1, M2, M3)
Boston University
Boston, Massachusetts 02215

Health Education Program (M1)
Boston University School of Public
 Health
Boston, Massachusetts 02118-2389

Health Education Program (B1, B2)
Northeastern University
Boston, Massachusetts 02115

Health Education Program (B1, B2, M4)
Springfield College
Springfield, Massachusetts 01109

Health Education Program (B1)
University of Lowell
Lowell, Massachusetts 01854

148

Health Education Program (M1)
University of Massachusetts
Amherst, Massachusetts 01003

Health Education Program
 (B2, B4, M2, M3, M4)
Worcester State College
Worcester, Massachusetts 01602

MICHIGAN

Health Education Program (B1, B2, B4)
Central Michigan University
Mt. Pleasant, Michigan 48859

Health Education Program (B2)
Concordia College
Moorhead, Michigan 56560

Health Education Program (B2, B4)
Northern Michigan University
Marquette, Michigan 49855

Health Education Program (M5)
University of Michigan
Ann Arbor, Michigan 48109-2029

Health Education Program
 (M1, M2, M4)
Wayne State University
Detroit, Michigan 48202

Health Education Program (B1, B2)
Western Michigan University
Kalamazoo, Michigan 49079

MINNESOTA

Health Education Program (B1)
Bemidji State University
Bemidji, Minnesota 56601

Health Education Program (B1, B2)
Bethel College
St. Paul, Minnesota 55112

Health Education Program (B2)
Gustavus Adolphus College St. Peter,
Minnesota 56082

Health Education Program
 (B1, B2, M1, M2)
Mankato State University
Mankato, Minnesota 56002-8400

Health Education Program (B1, B2)
Moorhead State University
Moorhead, Minnesota 56560

Health Education Program (B1, B2, M2)
St. Cloud State University
St. Cloud, Minnesota 56301

Health Education Program (B1)
Southwest State University
Marshall, Minnesota 56258

Health Education Program (B1, B2)
University of Minnesota
Duluth, Minnesota 55812-2495

Health Education Program (M1)
University of Minnesota
Minneapolis, Minnesota 55455

Health Education Program (B1, B3, M2)
Winona State University
Winona, Minnesota 55987-0838

MISSISSIPPI

Health Education Program (B2)
Jackson State University
Jackson, Mississippi 39217

Health Education Program (B1, B2, M1)
University of Southern Mississippi
Hattiesburg, Mississippi 39406-5122

MISSOURI

Health Education Program (B1, M2)
Northeast Missouri State University
Kirksville, Missouri 63501

Health Education Program (M2)
Northwest Missouri State University
Maryville, Missouri 64468

Health Education Program (M1)
St. Louis University
St. Louis, Missouri 63104

Health Education Program
(B1, B2, M1, M2, M4)
University of Missouri
Columbia, Missouri 65211

MONTANA

Health Education Program (B2)
Eastern Montana College
Billings, Montana 59101-0298

Health Education Program (B5)
University of Montana
Missoula, Montana 59812

NEBRASKA

Health Education Program (B2)
Chadron State College
Chadron, Nebraska 65337

Health Education Program (B1, B2)
University of Nebraska
Kearney, Nebraska 68849

Health Education Program (B1, B2, M2)
University of Nebraska
Lincoln, Nebraska 68588

Health Education Program (B1, B2)
University of Nebraska
Omaha, Nebraska 68182-0216

NEVADA

Health Education Program (B1, B2)
University of Nevada
Las Vegas, Nevada 89154

Health Education Program (B1, B2)
University of Nevada
Reno, Nevada 89557-0068

NEW HAMPSHIRE

Health Education Program (B2)
Keene State College
Keene, New Hampshire 03431

Health Education Program (B1, B2, M1)
Plymouth State College
Plymouth, New Hampshire 03264

NEW JERSEY

Health Education Program (B1)
Kean College of New Jersey
Union, New Jersey 07083

Health Education Program (B1)
Montclair State College
Upper Montclair, New Jersey 07043

Health Education Program (B1, B2)
Seton Hall University
South Orange, New Jersey 07079

Health Education Program (B1)
William Paterson College of New Jersey
Wayne, New Jersey 07470

NEW MEXICO

Health Education Program (B1)
Eastern New Mexico University
Portales, New Mexico 88130

Health Education Program (B1, B4)
New Mexico State University
Las Cruces, New Mexico 88003

Health Education Program
(B1, B2, M1, M2)
University of New Mexico
Albuquerque, New Mexico 87131

NEW YORK

Health Education Program (M1, M2)
Adelphi University
Garden City, New York 11530

Health Education Program (B1, B2)
College of Mount St. Vincent
Riverdale, New York 10471

Health Education Program (B1, B2)
Long Island University
Greenvale, New York 11548

Health Education Program
 (B1, B2, M1, M2)
Lehman College
Bronx, New York 10468

Health Education Program
 (B1, B2, M1, M2)
Hofstra University
Hempstead, New York 11550

Health Education Program (B2)
City University of New York
New York, New York 10021

Health Education Program
 (B2, M1, M2)
New York University
New York, New York 10003

Health Education Program (B1, B2, B4)
Queens College
Flushing, New York 11367

Health Education Program (B1, B2, M1,
 M2)
Russell Sage College
Troy, New York 12180

Health Education Program (B1)
St. Francis College
Brooklyn, New York 11201

Health Education Program (M1, M2)
State University of New York
Brockport, New York 14420

Health Education Program (B2)
State University of New York
Plattsburgh, New York 12901

Health Education Program (B1, B2, M2)
State University of New York
Cortland, New York 13045

Health Education Program
 (B1, B2, B4, M1, M4)
Syracuse University
Syracuse, New York 13244-5040

NORTH CAROLINA

Health Education Program (B2)
Appalachian State University
Boone, North Carolina 28608

Health Education Program (B1, B2, B4,
 M1, M2, M4)
East Carolina University
Greenville, North Carolina 27858-4353

Health Education Program (B2, M2)
Gardner Webb College
Boiling Springs, North Carolina 28017

Health Education Program (B1, B2)
North Carolina Central University
Durham, North Carolina 27707

Health Education Program (B1, M1)
University of North Carolina
Chapel Hill, North Carolina 27599-7400

Health Education Program (M2, M4)
University of North Carolina
Charlotte, North Carolina 28223

Health Education Program
 (B1, B2, M1, M2)
University of North Carolina
Greensboro, North Carolina 27412

151

Health Education Program (B2)
University of North Carolina
Wilmington, North Carolina 28403

Health Education Program (B2)
Mayville State University
Mayville, North Carolina 58257

OHIO

Health Education Program (B2)
Ashland University
Ashland, Ohio 44805

Health Education Program (B1, B2)
Baldwin Wallace College
Berea, Ohio 44017

Health Education Program (B2)
Capital University
Columbus, Ohio 43209

Health Education Program (B1, B2)
Central State University
Wilberforce, Ohio 45384

Health Education Program
 (B1, B2, B3, B4)
Heidelberg College
Tiffin, Ohio 44883

Health Education Program
 (B1, B2, M1, M2, M4)
Kent State University
Kent, Ohio 44242

Health Education Program (B2, M2)
Miami University
Oxford, Ohio 45056

Health Education Program (B1, B2)
Ohio Northern University
Ada, Ohio 45810

Health Education Program (B1, B2, M1,
 M2)
Ohio State University
Columbus, Ohio 43210

Health Education Program
 (B1, B2, M3, M4)
Ohio University
Athens, Ohio 45701

Health Education Program (B2, B4)
Otterbein College
Westerville, Ohio 43081

Health Education Program (B2)
University of Akron
Akron, Ohio 44325

Health Education Program
 (B1, B2, M1, M4)
University of Cincinnati
Cincinnati, Ohio 45221-0022

Health Education Program (B1, B2)
University of Dayton
Dayton, Ohio 45469-1210

Health Education Program
 (B1, B2, M1, M2)
University of Toledo
Toledo, Ohio 43606

Health Education Program (B2)
Wilmington College
Wilmington, Ohio 45177

Health Education Program (B1, B2)
Wittenberg University
Springfield, Ohio 45501

Health Education Program (B2, M2)
Xavier University
Cincinnati, Ohio 45207

Health Education Program (B1, B2, M2)
Youngstown State University
Youngstown, Ohio 44555

OKLAHOMA

Health Education Program (B1, B2)
University of Central Oklahoma
Edmond, Oklahoma 73034-0189

Health Education Program (B1, M1)
Oklahoma State University
Stillwater, Oklahoma 74078

Health Education Program (M1)
University of Oklahoma
Oklahoma City, Oklahoma 73190

OREGON

Health Education Program
 (B1, B4, M1, M2, M4)
Oregon State University
Corvallis, Oregon 97331-6406

Health Education Program (B1)
Portland State University
Portland, Oregon 97207

Health Education Program
 (B1, B2, B3, B4)
Western Oregon State College
Monmouth, Oregon 97361

PENNSYLVANIA

Health Education Program
 (B1, B2, M1, M2)
East Stroudsburg University
East Stroudsburg, Pennsylvania 18301-2999

Health Education Program (B2)
Gettysburg College
Gettysburg, Pennsylvania 17325

Health Education Program (B1)
Indiana University of Pennsylvania
Indiana, Pennsylvania 15705

Health Education Program (B1, B2, B4,
 M1, M2, M4)
Penn State University
University Park, Pennsylvania 16802

Health Education Program (B1, B2)
Slippery Rock University
Slippery Rock, Pennsylvania 16057

Health Education Program
 (B1, B2, M1, M2)
Temple University
Philadelphia, Pennsylvania 19122

Health Education Program (B1, B2, B3,
 B4, M1, M2, M3, M4)
Westchester University
West Chester, Pennsylvania 19383

RHODE ISLAND

Health Education Program (B1, B2, M1)
Rhode Island College
Providence, Rhode Island 01908

SOUTH CAROLINA

Health Education Program
 (M1, M2, M3, M4)
University of South Carolina
Columbia, South Carolina 29208

TENNESSEE

Health Education Program
 (B1, B2, B4, M1)
Austin Peay State University
Clarksville, Tennessee 37044

Health Education Program
 (B1, B2, B3, B4)
East Tennessee State University
Johnson City, Tennessee 37614

Health Education Program
 (B1, B2, M1, M2)
Memphis State University
Memphis, Tennessee 38152

Health Education Program
 (B1, B2, M1, M2)
Middle Tennessee State University
Murfreesboro, Tennessee 37132

Health Education Program (B2, M2)
Tennessee State University
Nashville, Tennessee 37209-1561

153

Health Education Program (B2, M2)
University of Tennessee
Chattanooga, Tennessee 37403

Health Education Program
 (B1, B3, M1, M2)
University of Tennessee
Knoxville, Tennessee 37996-2700

TEXAS

Health Education Program (B1, B2)
Abilene Christian University
Abilene, Texas 79699

Health Education Program (B2, M2)
Baylor University
Waco, Texas 76798-7313

Health Education Program (B4, M4)
East Texas State University
Commerce, Texas 75429

Health Education Program (B1, B2)
Lamar University
Beaumont, Texas 77710

Health Education Program (B1, M1)
Prairie View A&M University
Prairie View, Texas 77446

Health Education Program (B1, B2, B4,
 M1, M2)
Sam Houston State University
Huntsville, Texas 77341

Health Education Program (B1, B2)
Southwest Texas State University
San Marcos, Texas 78666-4616

Health Education Program
 (B1, B2, M1, M2)
Texas A&M University
College Station, Texas 77843

Health Education Program (B1, M1, M2,
 M4)
Texas Woman's University
Denton, Texas 76201

Health Education Program (B1, B2, M1,
 M2, M4)
University of North Texas
Denton, Texas 76203

Health Education Program (B4, M4)
University of Texas
Austin, Texas 78712

Health Education Program (B2)
University of Texas-Pan American
Edinburg, Texas 78539

Health Education Program (B1, B2)
University of Texas
San Antonio, Texas 78249-0616

UTAH

Health Education Program (B1, B2, B3,
 M1, M2, M3)
Brigham Young University
Provo, Utah 84602

Health Education Program
 (B1, B2, M1, M2)
University of Utah
Salt Lake City, Utah 84112

Health Education Program (B1)
Utah State University
Logan, Utah 84322

Health Education Program (B4, M2)
Weber State University
Ogden, Utah 84408-2801

VIRGINIA

Health Education Program (B2)
Averett College
Danville, Virginia 24541

Health Education Program (B1, B2, M1)
George Mason University
Fairfax, Virginia 22030-4444

Health Education Program
 (B1, B2, M1, M2)
James Madison University
Harrisonburg, Virginia 22807

Health Education Program
 (B1, B2, B3, B4)
Liberty University
Lynchburg, Virginia 24506

Health Education Program (B2, M1)
Old Dominion University
Norfolk, Virginia 23529-0196

Health Education Program (B1, B2)
Radford University
Radford, Virginia 24142

Health Education Program (B1, B2)
Virginia Commonwealth University
Richmond, Virginia 25284-2037

Health Education Program (B1, M1)
Virginia Polytechnic Institute & State
 University
Blacksburg, Virginia 24016

WASHINGTON

Health Education Program (B1, B2)
Central Washington University
Ellensburg, Washington 98926

Health Education Program (B1, B2, M2)
Eastern Washington University
Cheney, Washington 99004

Health Education Program (B1, B2)
Western Washington University
Bellingham, Washington 98225

WEST VIRGINIA

Health Education Program (B2)
Marshall University
Huntington, West Virginia 25755-2420

Health Education Program (B2)
Shepherd College
Shepherdstown, West Virginia 25443

Health Education Program (B2)
West Virginia State College
Institute, West Virginia 25112

Health Education Program (M1)
West Virginia University
Morgantown, West Virginia 26505

WISCONSIN

Health Education Program
 (B1, B2, M1, M2)
University of Wisconsin
La Crosse, Wisconsin 54601

Health Education Program (B2, M2)
University of Wisconsin
Madison, Wisconsin 53706

Healthcare professionals, students and the general public rely on accurate and up-to-date healthcare information in their jobs, education and everyday life. It is the field of *health sciences communications,* also referred to as *biocommunications,* that disseminates scientific, medical and healthcare information.

The *health sciences communicator* communicates healthcare data using a variety of educational media including photographs; medical books, texts and journals; information data bases; medical illustrations; films, video and television.

Seven major careers in health sciences communications are discussed in this chapter: the *biophotographer, medical writer/editor, health sciences librarian* and *health sciences library technician, medical illustrator, medical television producer,* and the *biocommunications manager.*

Biophotographer

The biophotographer utilizes photography and other visual media, such as prints, transparencies, films, computer-generated graphics, television, and still video techniques to aid in the biological and medical teaching and research of living and non-living things.

The *biophotographer* is a trained specialist in optics, light theory, and the use of photosensitive materials. In the course of their work, biophotographers may utilize infra-red light sources, high speed cinematography, X-ray photography, and slow motion/stop motion photography.

The biophotographer must possess a reasonable understanding of the subject matter being photographed. Techniques unique to the biophotography field include photomicrography (taking photographs through a microscope) and the video taping of surgical procedures. Among other subjects, the photographer records anatomy, evidence of diseases, diagnostic and therapeutic procedures, plant and animal tissues, and pathological specimens.

The biophotographer may be found working in hospitals; medical, veterinary and dental schools; laboratories and research institutes; museums; and zoos. Some biophotographers work on a freelance basis.

Two and four year degree programs in biophotography are offered at a limited number of universities and colleges and are listed below. Individual courses in biological and medical photography are offered at universities, colleges, community and junior colleges, and vocational-technical schools throughout the country. The photo departments of teaching hospitals may also offer a brief course or on-the-job training. Through membership in the Biological Photographic Association, many professionals attend seminars and workshops to enhance their photographic skills.

Certification as a Registered Biological Photographer, (R.B.P.), is granted after successfully passing an intensive three-part examination sponsored by the Board of Registry of the Biological Photographic Association. For further information on certification or a career in biophotography, direct inquiries to the Biological Photographic Association, 115 Stoneridge Drive, Chapel Hill, North Carolina 27514.

Following is a list provided by the Health Sciences Communications Association of accredited institutions with programs in biophotography. Some programs in biophotography may require past experience or aptitude in science and/or in visual media. Prospective students may be asked to present a portfolio of photographs to show proficiency in photography. Contact the program directly for specific admission requirements, length of program, financial aid, and degree awarded.

SOURCE:

Biological Photographic Association
Health Sciences Communication Association

Biophotography Programs

INDIANA

Biophotography Program
Purdue University
Medical Illustration and Communications
School of Veterinary Medicine
West Lafayette, Indiana 47907

NEW YORK

Biophotography Program
Rochester Institute of Technology
School of Photographic Arts and
   Sciences

Department of Biomedical Photographic
   Communications
One Lomb Memorial Drive
P.O. Box 9887
Rochester, New York 14623-0887

NORTH CAROLINA

Biophotography Program
Randolph Technical College
629 Industrial Park Avenue
P.O. Box 1009
Asheboro, North Carolina 27203

158

OHIO

Biophotography Program
Ohio Institute of Photography
2025 Edgefield Road
Dayton, Ohio 45439

WASHINGTON

Biophotography Program
Bellevue Community College
3000 Landerholm Circle
Bellevue, Washington 98009-2037

Medical Writer And Editor

The medical writer or editor uses the written word to communicate scientific or technical information into language that is easily understood by the reader. The *medical writer* gathers information through research, interviews, or personal experience. *Editors* usually rewrite or revise material, choose and arrange articles for publication, and supervise writers.

Medical writers or editors are usually divided into two categories-those that provide health information to the public and those that make technical, medical, and scientific information available to healthcare professionals. Medical writers who provide information to the public on the latest, scientific developments are called *scientific writers*, and commonly work for newspapers, magazines, television, and radio stations. *Health information specialists* are employed by health organizations, such as the American Heart Association, to inform the public of their achievements and activities. Medical writers who provide technical information to healthcare professionals are called *technical writers*, and may be employed by pharmaceutical companies, research institutes, federal healthcare agencies, and universities. Medical writers or editors may also write for professional journals, newsletters, and health related books. Medical writers or editors may work on a freelance basis, or may be employed as part of an organization's writing staff.

A bachelor's degree in journalism, liberal arts, science or engineering, with several years writing experience is the usual prerequisite to entry level positions in medical writing. Relatively few medical writers enter the occupation directly from college. Many often start as assistants, trainees, or come from medical, technical, or scientific backgrounds. Medical writers should have a solid background in the sciences and a working knowledge of medical and technical terminology. Continuing education programs in medical writing and editing are available through membership in the American Medical Writer's Association.

Employers of medical writers and editors usually request printed samples of an individual's writing that demonstrates the ability to communicate scientific and technical information. Interested students could gain writing experience by volunteering for high school and college newspapers or submitting articles to community or local newspapers. Recommended high school and college courses should include the physical and biological sciences, English composition, humanities, and computer science. It may also be helpful to learn to use basic office equipment, including typewriters, word processors, and computers.

For more information on a career as a medical writer or editor, contact the American Medical Writer's Association, 9650 Rockville Pike, Bethesda, Maryland 20814.

Following is a list provided by the Health Sciences Communications Association of accredited institutions offering programs in medical writing and editing. Degrees in the biological or physical sciences, writing, or journalism are available at numerous colleges and universities throughout the United States.

SOURCES:

American Medical Writer's Association
Health Sciences Communication Association

Medical Writing and Editing Programs

MASSACHUSETTS

Medical Writing and Editing Program
Northeastern University
Department of English
Boston, Massachusetts 02115

MICHIGAN

Medical Writing and Editing Program
Ferris State University
Department of Language and Literature
Big Rapids, Michigan 49307

OHIO

Medical Writing and Editing Program
Ohio State University
Division of Biomedical Communications
School of Allied Medical Professions
College of Medicine
1583 Perry Street
Columbus, Ohio 43210

TEXAS

Medical Writing and Editing Program
Texas A&M University
College Station, Texas 77843

Health Sciences Librarian
Health Sciences Library Technician

The *health sciences librarian*, also known as a *medical librarian*, is a highly trained specialist who manages the professional and technical services of a medical library. Healthcare facilities, departments of public health, medical schools, medical research institutions, and most pharmaceutical companies have libraries, and it is the responsibility of the health sciences librarian to assist physicians, researchers, and medical students to search for, and find, the information they require. Having a thorough knowledge of the kinds of medical books, journals, reports, films, microfiche, microfilm, computerized data-bases and other information resources that are available, the health sciences librarian selects publications to be purchased; classifies and catalogs new materials; issues materials to borrowers; prepares

160

library material, such as bibliographies, abstracts, and reviews for teaching and research; teaches students and professionals how to use library resources; and manages the daily operations of the medical library.

In large institutions the duties of the health sciences librarian may be highly specialized, but in a small hospital library the health sciences librarian provides personalized services in all library functions.

High school courses should include biology, chemistry, computer science, oral and written communications, foreign languages, and mathematics.

The health sciences librarian must have a master's degree in library science from a program accredited by the American Library Association. A bachelor's degree with coursework in library science, the physical and life sciences, and management, is the usual prerequisite for admission to graduate level health sciences librarian programs. For specific graduate school prerequisites, contact the program director at the individual schools. Since many library functions are computerized, it is recommended that a student take courses in information and computer science.

The position of *health sciences library technician*, on the other hand, is an entry-level position in the health sciences library. They receive much of their training on-the-job and often attend continuing education workshops and courses. Many states offer two year educational programs for library technicians through community or junior colleges. Because the duties performed by library technicians vary according to size and type of library, the education required for the duties will also vary. Computer literacy is often required. Primarily responsible for carrying out routine library procedures under the supervision of a medical librarian, the technician catalogs books and periodicals, maintains records and files, prepares volumes for binding, prepares invoices, issues and receives books, supervises book shelvers, assists users with audiovisuals or computer software packages, and answers basic information questions.

The Medical Library Association recommends that health science librarians be certified through membership in the Academy of Health Information Professionals. A master's degree from a library school accredited by the American Library Association, two years of experience, and evidence of knowledge in ten core areas of health information science fulfill requirements for certification.

For additional information on training and career opportunities in the health sciences library field, interested persons should contact the Medical Library Association, Six North Michigan Avenue, Suite 300, Chicago, Illinois 60602-4805, or the American Library Association, 50 East Huron Street, Chicago, Illinois 60611.

Following is a list provided by the Health Sciences Communications Association of accredited institutions offering programs in Health Sciences Librarianship.

SOURCES:

Health Sciences Communication Association
Medical Library Association

Health Sciences Librarianship Programs

ALABAMA

Library Science Program
University of Alabama
Graduate School of Library Service
Box 870252
Tuscaloosa, Alabama 35487-0252

CALIFORNIA

Library Science Program
University of California, Los Angeles
Graduate School of Library and
  Information Science
Los Angeles, California 90024

DISTRICT OF COLUMBIA

Library Science Program
Catholic University of America
School of Library and Information
  Science
Washington, DC 20064

ILLINOIS

Library Science Program
Rosary College
Graduate School of Library and
  Information Science
7900 West Division Street
River Forest, Illinois 60305

Library Science Program
University of Illinois at Urbana-
Champaign
Graduate School of Library and
  Information Science
1407 West Gregory Drive
Urbana, Illinois 61801

INDIANA

Library Science Program
Indiana University
School of library and Information
  Science
Bloomington, Indiana 47405

IOWA

Library Science Program
University of Iowa
School of Library and Information
  Science
Iowa City, Iowa 52242

KENTUCKY

Library Science Program
University of Kentucky
College of Library and Information
  Science
Lexington, Kentucky 40506-0039

LOUISIANA

Library Science Program
Louisiana State University
School of Library and Information
  Science
Baton Rouge, Louisiana 70803

MARYLAND

Library Science Program
University of Maryland
College of Library and Information
  Services
College Park, Maryland 20742

162

MASSACHUSETTS

Library Science Program
Simmons College
Graduate School of Library and
  Information Science
300 The Fenway
Boston, Massachusetts 02115

MICHIGAN

Library Science Program
University of Michigan
School of Information & Library Studies
550 E. University
Ann Arbor, Michigan 48109-1092

Library Science Program
Wayne State University
Detroit, Michigan 48202

MISSOURI

Library Science Program
University of Missouri-Columbia
School of Library and Informational
  Science
Columbia, Missouri 65211

NEW YORK

Library Science Program
Long Island University
Palmer School of Library and
  Information Science
C.W. Post Campus
Brookville, New York 11548

Library Science Program
State University of New York at Buffalo
School of Information and Library
  Studies
Buffalo, New York 14260

OKLAHOMA

Library Science Program
University of Oklahoma
School of Library and Information
  Studies
Norman, Oklahoma 73019

PENNSYLVANIA

Library Science Program
Drexel University
College of Information Studies
Philadelphia, Pennsylvania 19104

SOUTH CAROLINA

Library Science Program
University of South Carolina
College of Library and Information
  Science
Columbia, South Carolina 29208

TEXAS

Library Science Program
Texas Woman's University
School of Library and Information
  Studies
P.O. Box 22905
TWU Station
Denton, Texas 76204

Library Science Program
University of Texas at Austin
Graduate School of Library and
  Information Science
Austin, Texas 78712-1276

WASHINGTON

Library Science Program
University of Washington
Graduate School of Library Science
Seattle, Washington 98195

Medical Illustrator

The *medical illustrator* produces a variety of artwork, including paintings, drawings, sketches and model designs, to visually communicate and teach complex medical and scientific data. Art mediums used by the medical illustrator may include watercolors, pen and ink, plaster, wax, plastics, airbrush, and computer graphics. The medical illustrator has extensive training in both art and science. This knowledge is utilized through a variety of assignments such as painting or drawing the human anatomy for medical textbooks, sketching multi-dimensional models to illustrate a surgical procedure, sculpturing a three-dimensional model for medical students, or perhaps designing projects such as "moving" illustrations for television documentaries or films through the use of computer graphics.

The medical illustrator may be found working in a variety of settings, including hospitals; clinics; medical, dental and veterinary schools; large medical centers; as well as the private sector in medical publishing companies, advertising agencies, or in freelance work providing services to many facilities.

Degree programs in medical illustration are usually at the graduate level, with a bachelor's degree as a prerequisite.

Recommended course work at the bachelor's level should include the fine arts, pre-med biology, and the humanities. High school courses should also emphasize the arts and sciences. Graduate programs in medical illustration are usually two to three years in length. There are a limited number of programs in medical illustration, with limited enrollment in each. When applying to medical illustration schools, a prospective student may be asked to present a portfolio of art work and participate in a personal interview.

Salary information for medical illustrators will vary, based on quality of work, geographic location, type of employer, and years of experience. Medical illustrators who freelance their work may not be guaranteed a steady income until they develop a reputation. They may hold other jobs to supplement their earnings.

In medical illustration, demonstrated ability and appropriate training are needed for success. Medical illustrators perform detail work and are relied upon to submit illustrations that are on time and precise. Medical illustrators may have to meet tight deadlines and sometimes work long or irregular hours.

Following is a list of programs in medical illustration that are accredited by the American Medical Association's Committee on Allied Health Education and Accreditation. There are a limited number of scholarships available to students enrolled in accredited medical illustration programs. For more information on financial aid or a career as a medical illustrator, contact the Association of Medical Illustrators, 1819 Peachtree Street NE, Suite 560, Atlanta, Georgia 30309.

SOURCES:

Association of Medical Illustrators
Health Sciences Communications Association
Occupational Outlook Handbook

Medical Illustration Programs

COLORADO

Medical Illustration Program
Colorado State University
Department of Anatomy and
  Neurobiology
Fort Collins, Colorado 80523

GEORGIA

Medical Illustration Program
Medical College of Georgia
School of Graduate Studies
Augusta, Georgia 30912-0300

ILLINOIS

Medical Illustration Program
University of Illinois at Chicago
Department of Biomedical Visualization
College of Associated Health Professions
1919 West Taylor Street
Chicago, Illinois 60612

MARYLAND

Medical Illustration Program
Johns Hopkins School of Medicine
Department of Art as Applied to
  Medicine
1830 East Monument Street
Baltimore, Maryland 21205

MICHIGAN

Medical Illustration Program
University of Michigan
Northern Brewery
1327 Jones Drive
Ann Arbor, Michigan 48109-1897

TEXAS

Medical Illustration Program
University of Texas Southwestern
  Medical Center at Dallas
Department of Biomedical
  Communications
P.O. Box 45668, Exchange Park
Dallas, Texas 75245

Medical Television Producer

A *medical television producer* produces video programs to teach patients about their medical problems. They also produce highly technical programs to train physicians, nurses, and other healthcare staff. Hospitals, private healthcare companies, and medical schools may employ a medical television team, including producers, directors, and camera personnel.

Most medical television producers receive their academic training in radio, television, broadcasting or educational media. For a list of schools offering programs in television and radio broadcasting, contact the Broadcast Education Association, 1771 "N" Street, NW, Washington, DC 20036.

Following is a list provided by the Health Sciences Communications Association of accredited institutions offering programs in Medical Television/Instructional Media.

SOURCE:

Health Sciences Communications Association

Medical Television/Instructional Media Programs

OHIO

Medical Television/Instructional Media
Program
Ohio State University
Division of Biomedical Communications
School of Allied Medical Professions
College of Medicine
1583 Perry Street
Columbus, Ohio 43210

TEXAS

Medical Television/Instructional Media
Program
University of Texas Southwestern
Medical Center at Dallas
5323 Harry Hines Boulevard
Dallas, Texas 75235-9065

Biocommunications Manager

The *biocommunications manager* supervises biocommunications professionals in a communications department and coordinates their activities. Biocommunications managers assure that the department runs smoothly and that high quality communications services are provided. They must be knowledgeable in a variety of biocommunications fields, including medical illustration, biophotography, medical writing, and medical television/instructional media. Many managers start out in one of these biocommunications specialty areas.

Following is a list of programs accredited by the Health Sciences Communications Association in Biocommunications Management.

For more information on a career as a biocommunications manager, contact the Health Sciences Communications Association, 6728 Old McLean Village Drive, McLean, Virginia 22101.

SOURCE:

Health Sciences Communications Association

Biocommunications Management Programs

NEBRASKA

Biocommunications Management
Program
University of Nebraska Medical Center
42nd and Dewey Avenue
Omaha, Nebraska 68105

NEW YORK

Biocommunications Management
Program
Ithaca College
Graduate Program in Communications
Ithaca, New York 14850

OHIO

Biocommunications Management
Program
Ohio State University
Division of Biomedical Communications
School of Allied Medical Professions
College of Medicine
1583 Perry Street
Columbus, Ohio 43210

TEXAS

Biocommunications Management
Program
University of Texas Health Science
Center-Houston
School of Allied Health
P.O. Box 20708
Houston, Texas 77225

HEALTH SERVICES ADMINISTRATION

In general terms health services administration is that field responsible for the management of all aspects of healthcare including patient care, health education, and health research. Specifically, the planning, organization, and operation of all healthcare facilities, from large hospitals to small walk-in clinics, is the concern of each healthcare facility's office of administration. Administrators of health services work in every organization or institution that is connected to the health field, including general hospitals, extended care facilities, health maintenance organizations, nursing homes, psychiatric hospitals, rehabilitation institutes, group practice plans, outpatient clinics, private insurance programs, federal and state health departments, hospital associations, health education programs, and research institutes. Opportunities for upper level management and administrative positions in health services administration are most often granted to individuals with specialized graduate degrees in health services or hospital administration.

Below is general information on the careers involved with the overall administration of health services, including those of the *health services administrator*, the *associate administrator*, and the *administrative assistant.*

Health Services Administrator
Associate Administrator
Administrative Assistant

The *health services administrator* occupies the senior-most executive position in the organization of the many complex components of a healthcare system. The primary responsibilities of the administrator lie in policy development, activity coordination, and procedural planning. Skilled in management decision making, the administrator decides on such matters as budget, personnel, equipment, and space allocations as well as taking an active role in labor relations and acting as a liaison between the governing bodies of the organization and its medical, health, and support staffs.

In a small health organization the administrator coordinates and administers all of its various functions and activities; while in a large organization or institution the administrator directs a staff of associated administrators in the operation of individual departments. Besides overseeing the actual daily operation of the various departments, the *associate administrator* (also referred to as an *assistant administrator*) acts as an advisor to the administrator interpreting hospital policies; assisting in budgeting and planning; resolving problems concerning staffing, equipment, and facilities; acting as a fund raiser and as a public relations officer; and finally recommending when and how changes in policy, physical plant, personnel, and equipment should be made.

The third administrative position, that of the *administrative assistant,* is considered an entry-level trainee position in health services administration. A hospital may employ several administrative assistants who work in specific projects that investigate, analyze, and evaluate the various services and functions carried out within the hospital. Examples of these projects include the studying of the inter-relationships between specific hospital services; the recommending of alternatives for more efficient and less costly operating procedures; the comparing of cost structures of different institutions; and the determining of personnel work schedules, salaries and fringe benefits. All studies of these kinds are reported directly to the administrator.

Educational requirements for health services administrators vary according to the size of the health organization and the individual level of responsibility. Larger health institutions usually require their administrative personnel to have a higher degree of education than do smaller institutions. A graduate degree in health services administration is required for the senior-level positions of administrator, associate administrator, and department head while a bachelor's degree usually qualifies a candidate for the mid-level positions of hospital administrative assistant, assistant department head, unit manager, or nursing home associate administrator.

Salaries in hospital administration vary considerably depending upon job responsibility, the size of the particular administration department, and the size and location of the health facility. Chief administrators averaged between $58,000 and $122,000 or more a year in 1990-1991, according to the Medical Group Management Association and the American Hospital Association. Average salaries for mid-level administrative positions ranged from $42,000 to $60,000 a year, according to a 1991 survey by *Modern Healthcare Magazine.* Average annual salaries for beginning master's degree graduates ranged from low to mid thirties, according to the American College of Healthcare Executives.

Following is a list supplied by the Association of University Programs in Health Administration of schools that offer either bachelor's or master's degrees in health services administration. Interested students should contact the schools of their choice for specific information on particular programs.

For further information on a career in health services administration, write to the Association of University Programs in Health Administration, 1911 North Fort Myer Drive, Suite 503, Arlington, Virginia 22209 and American College of Healthcare Executives, 840 North Lake Shore Drive, Chicago, Illinois 60611.

SOURCES:

American College of Healthcare Executives
Association of University Programs in Health Administration
Occupational Outlook Handbook

Health Services Administration Graduate Programs

ALABAMA

Health Services Administration Graduate
  Program
University of Alabama at Birmingham
School of Health Related Professions
1675 University Boulevard
Birmingham, Alabama 35124-3361

ARIZONA

Health Services Administration Graduate
  Program
Arizona State University
School of Health Administration &
  Policy
College of Business
Tempe, Arizona 85287-4506

ARKANSAS

Health Services Administration Graduate
  Program
University of Arkansas-Little Rock
2801 South University Avenue
Little Rock, Arkansas 72204

CALIFORNIA

Health Services Administration Graduate
  Program
University of California-Berkeley
School of Business Administration
Berkeley, California 94720

Health Services Administration Graduate
  Program
University of California-Los Angeles
School of Public Health
10833 Le Conte Avenue
Los Angeles, California 90024-1772

Health Services Administration Graduate
  Program
University of Southern California
School of Public Administration
University Park
Los Angeles, California 90089-0041

Health Services Administration Graduate
  Program
San Diego State University
Graduate School of Public Health
San Diego, California 92182-0405

COLORADO

Health Services Administration Graduate
  Program
University of Colorado
Graduate School of Business
  Administration
P.O. Box 173364
Denver, Colorado 80217-3364

CONNECTICUT

Health Services Administration Graduate
  Program
Hartford Graduate Center
275 Windsor Street
Hartford, Connecticut 06120-2991

Health Services Administration Graduate
  Program
Yale University
Dept. of Epidemiology & Public Health
60 College Street
New Haven, Connecticut 06510

DISTRICT OF COLUMBIA

Health Services Administration Graduate
  Program
George Washington University
Department of Health Services
600 21st Street NW
Washington, DC 20052

Health Services Administration Graduate
  Program
Howard University
School of Business & Public
  Administration
2600 Sixth Street NW
Washington, DC 20059

FLORIDA

Health Services Administration Graduate
  Program
University of Miami
School of Business Administration
P.O. Box 248505
Coral Gables, Florida 33124-6524

Health Services Administration Graduate
  Program
University of Florida
Colleges of Business & Health Related
  Professions
Gainesville, Florida 32610

Health Services Administration Graduate
  Program
Florida International University
North Miami Campus
151st Street and Biscayne Boulevard
North Miami, Florida 33181

Health Services Administration Graduate
  Program
University of South Florida
Dept. of Health Policy & Management
College of Public Health
13301 North Bruce B. Downs Boulevard
Tampa, Florida 33612-3899

GEORGIA

Health Services Administration Graduate
  Program
Georgia State University
Institute of Health Administration
University Plaza
1060 Lawyer's Title Building
Atlanta, Georgia 30303

ILLINOIS

Health Services Administration Graduate
  Program
Rush University
Rush-Presbyterian-St. Luke's Medical
  Center
1653 West Congress Parkway
Chicago, Illinois 60612

Health Services Administration Graduate
  Program
University of Chicago
969 East 60th Street
Chicago, Illinois 60637

Health Services Administration Graduate
  Program
Northwestern University
Kellogg Graduate School of
  Management
2001 Sheridan Road
Evanston, Illinois 60208-2007

172

Health Services Administration Graduate
  Program
Governors State University
College of Health Professions
University Park, Illinois 60466

INDIANA

Health Services Administration Graduate
  Program
Indiana University
School of Public & Environmental
  Affairs
801 West Michigan Street
Indianapolis, Indiana 46202-5152

IOWA

Health Services Administration Graduate
  Program
University of Iowa
College of Medicine & Graduate College
Iowa City, Iowa 52242

KANSAS

Health Services Administration Graduate
  Program
University of Kansas
School of Pharmacy
Lawrence, Kansas 66045-2503

KENTUCKY

Health Services Administration Graduate
  Program
University of Kentucky
103 Medical Center
Lexington, Kentucky 40536-0080

LOUISIANA

Health Services Administration Graduate
  Program
Tulane University
School of Public Health & Tropical
  Medicine
1430 Tulane Avenue
New Orleans, Louisiana 70112

MASSACHUSETTS

Health Services Administration Graduate
  Program
Boston University
School of Management
685 Commonwealth Avenue
Boston, Massachusetts 02215

Health Services Administration Graduate
  Program
Simmons College
300 The Fenway
Boston, Massachusetts 02115

Health Services Administration Graduate
  Program
Clark University/University of
  Massachusetts Medical School
Graduate School of Management
950 Main Street
Worcester, Massachusetts 01610

MICHIGAN

Health Services Administration Graduate
  Program
University of Michigan
School of Public Health II
1420 Washington Heights
Ann Arbor, Michigan 48109-2029

MINNESOTA

Health Services Administration Graduate
  Program
University of Minnesota
School of Public Health
Minneapolis, Minnesota 55455

MISSOURI

Health Services Administration Graduate
  Program
University of Missouri-Columbia
Columbia, Missouri 65211

Health Services Administration Graduate
  Program
St. Louis University
School of Public Health
3663 Lindell Boulevard
St. Louis, Missouri 63108

Health Services Administration Graduate
  Program
Washington University
School of Medicine
4547 Clayton Avenue
St. Louis, Missouri 63110-1593

NEW HAMPSHIRE

Health Services Administration Graduate
  Program
University of New Hampshire
Durham, New Hampshire 03824-3563

NEW YORK

Health Services Administration Graduate
  Program
Cornell University
Dept. of Human Services Studies
College of Human Ecology
Ithaca, New York 14853

Health Services Administration Graduate
  Program
City University of New York
Baruch College/Mt. Sinai School of
  Medicine
17 Lexington Avenue, Box 313
New York, New York 10010

Health Services Administration Graduate
  Program
New York University
Wagner Graduate School of Public
  Service
40 West Fourth Street
New York, New York 10012

Health Services Administration Graduate
  Program
Union College
Union Avenue
Schenectady, New York 12308

NORTH CAROLINA

Health Services Administration Graduate
  Program
University of North Carolina-Chapel Hill
School of Public Health
Chapel Hill, North Carolina 27599-7400

Health Services Administration Graduate
  Program
Duke University
Fuqua School of Business
Durham, North Carolina 27706

OHIO

Health Services Administration Graduate
  Program
Xavier University
3800 Victory Parkway
Cincinnati, Ohio 45207

Health Services Administration Graduate
  Program
Cleveland State University
Nance College of Business
  Administration
Cleveland, Ohio 44115

Health Services Administration Graduate
  Program
Ohio State University
1583 Perry Street
Columbus, Ohio 43210

OKLAHOMA

Health Services Administration Graduate
  Program
University of Oklahoma
P.O. Box 26901
Oklahoma City, Oklahoma 73190

PENNSYLVANIA

Health Services Administration Graduate
  Program
Widener University
School of Management
Chester, Pennsylvania 19013

Health Services Administration Graduate
  Program
Temple University
School of Business Administration &
  Management
Philadelphia, Pennsylvania 19122

Health Services Administration Graduate
  Program
University of Pennsylvania
The Wharton School
3641 Locust Walk
Colonial Penn Center
Philadelphia, Pennsylvania 19104

Health Services Administration Graduate
  Program
University of Pittsburgh
Graduate School of Business & Public
  Health
130 DeSoto Street
Pittsburgh, Pennsylvania 15261

Health Services Administration Graduate
  Program
Pennsylvania State University
College of Health and Human
  Development
University Park, Pennsylvania 16802

PUERTO RICO

Health Services Administration Graduate
  Program
University of Puerto Rico
Graduate School of Public Health
Medical Sciences Campus Building
San Juan, Puerto Rico 00936

SOUTH CAROLINA

Health Services Administration Graduate
  Program
Medical University of South Carolina
171 Ashley Avenue
Charleston, South Carolina 29425

Health Services Administration Graduate
  Program
University of South Carolina
School of Public Health
Columbia, South Carolina 29208

TENNESSEE

Health Services Administration Graduate
  Program
Memphis State University
Memphis, Tennessee 38152

Health Services Administration Graduate
  Program
Meharry Medical College/Tennessee
  State University
1005 Todd Boulevard
Nashville, Tennessee 37208

TEXAS

Health Services Administration Graduate
  Program
Texas Women's University
1810 Inwood Road
Dallas, Texas 75236

Health Services Administration Graduate
  Program
U.S. Army-Baylor University
Academy of Health Sciences
Ft. Sam Houston, Texas 78234-6100

Health Services Administration Graduate
  Program
University of Houston-Clear Lake
School of Business and Public
  Administration
2700 Bay Area Boulevard
Houston, Texas 77058-1098

Health Services Administration Graduate
  Program
Texas Tech University
College of Business Administration
Lubbock, Texas 79409

Health Services Administration Graduate
  Program
Trinity University
715 Stadium Drive
San Antonio, Texas 78212

Health Services Administration Graduate
  Program
Southwest Texas State University
School of Health Professions
San Marcos, Texas 78666-4616

VIRGINIA

Health Services Administration Graduate
  Program
Medical College of Virginia/Virginia
  Commonwealth University
School of Allied Health Professions
Richmond, Virginia 23298-0203

WASHINGTON

Health Services Administration Graduate
  Program
University of Washington-Seattle
Dept. of Health Services
Seattle, Washington 98195

WISCONSIN

Health Services Administration Graduate
  Program
University of Wisconsin-Madison
210 Bradley Memorial Hospital
1300 University Avenue
Madison, Wisconsin 53706

CANADA

Health Services Administration Graduate
  Program
University of Alberta
83rd Avenue & 112th Street
Edmonton, Alberta T6G 2G3

Health Services Administration Graduate
  Program
Dalhousie University
Faculty of Health Professions
1234 Seymour Street
Halifax, Nova Scotia B3H 3M3

Health Services Administration Graduate
  Program
Universite de Montreal
Faculte de medecine
P.O. Box 6128-A
Montreal, Quebec H3C 3J7

Health Services Administration Graduate
  Program
University of Ottawa
136 Jean-Jacques Lussier Private
Ottawa, Ontario K1N 6N5

Health Services Administration Graduate
  Program
University of Toronto
Faculty of Medicine
12 Queens Park Crescent West
Toronto, Ontario M5S 1A8

Health Services Administration Graduate
  Program
University of British Columbia
Dept. of Health Care & Epidemiology
5804 Fairview Crescent
Vancouver, British Columbia V6T 1W5

Health Services Administration Bachelor Degree Programs

CALIFORNIA

Health Services Administration Bachelor
  Degree Program
California State University-Long Beach
Department of Health Science
1250 Bellflower Boulevard
Long Beach, California 90840-4604

Health Services Administration Bachelor
  Degree Program
California State University-Northridge
School of Comm., Health & Human
  Services
Health Science Dept.
18111 Nordhoff Street
Northridge, California 91330

COLORADO

Health Services Administration Bachelor
  Degree Program
Metropolitan State College of Denver
1006 11th Street
Denver, Colorado 80204

CONNECTICUT

Health Services Administration Bachelor
  Degree Program
Quinnipiac College
Mount Carmel Avenue
Hamden, Connecticut 06518

Health Services Administration Bachelor
  Degree Program
University of Connecticut
Center for Health Systems Management
Storrs, Connecticut 06269-2041

FLORIDA

Health Services Administration Bachelor
  Degree Program
Florida A&M University
Tallahassee, Florida 32307

IDAHO

Health Services Administration Bachelor
  Degree Program
Idaho State University
Box 8002
Pocatello, Idaho 83209-0009

ILLINOIS

Health Services Administration Bachelor
  Degree Program
Sangamon State University
School of Public Affairs & Admin.
Public Affairs Center
Springfield, Illinois 62794-9243

Health Services Administration Bachelor
  Degree Program
Governors State University
College of Health Professions
University Park, Illinois 60466

KANSAS

Health Services Administration Bachelor
  Degree Program
Wichita State University
College of Health Professions
Wichita, Kansas 67208

KENTUCKY

Health Services Administration Bachelor
  Degree Program
Western Kentucky University
Department of Health & Safety
Bowling Green, Kentucky 42101

Health Services Administration Bachelor
  Degree Program
University of Kentucky
Department of Health Services
College of Allied Health Professions
Lexington, Kentucky 40536-0080

MASSACHUSETTS

Health Services Administration Bachelor
  Degree Program
Stonehill College
Washington Street
North Easton, Massachusetts 02357

MICHIGAN

Health Services Administration Bachelor
  Degree Program
Eastern Michigan University
Ypsilanti, Michigan 48197

NEVADA

Health Services Administration Bachelor
  Degree Program
University of Nevada-Las Vegas
College of Health Sciences
4505 Maryland Parkway
Las Vegas, Nevada 89154-3023

NEW HAMPSHIRE

Health Services Administration Bachelor
  Degree Program
University of New Hampshire
School of Health Studies
Durham, New Hampshire 03824-3563

NEW JERSEY

Health Services Administration Bachelor
  Degree Program
Rutgers University
Dept. of Urban Studies & Comm. Health
  Planning
New Brunswick, New Jersey 08903-
5070

NEW YORK

Health Services Administration Bachelor
  Degree Program
Alfred University
P.O. Box 515
Alfred, New York 14802

Health Services Administration Bachelor
  Degree Program
Herbert H. Lehman College
City University of New York
Bedford Park Boulevard West
Bronx, New York 10468

Health Services Administration Bachelor
  Degree Program
Ithaca College
School of Health Sciences & Human
  Performance
Ithaca, New York 14850

NORTH CAROLINA

Health Services Administration Bachelor
  Degree Program
University of North Carolina-Asheville
Department of Management
One University Heights
Asheville, North Carolina 28804-3299

Health Services Administration Bachelor
  Degree Program
Appalachian State University
Walker College of Business
Boone, North Carolina 28608

Health Services Administration Bachelor
  Degree Program
University of North Carolina-Chapel Hill
Department of Health Policy &
  Administration
School of Public Health
Chapel Hill, North Carolina 27599-7400

OHIO

Health Services Administration Bachelor
  Degree Program
University of Cincinnati
School of Planning
College of Design, Architecture, Art &
  Planning
Cincinnati, Ohio 45221

OREGON

Health Services Administration Bachelor
  Degree Program
Oregon State University
Corvallis, Oregon 97331-6406

PENNSYLVANIA

Health Services Administration Bachelor
  Degree Program
Pennsylvania State University
College of Health & Human
  Development
University Park, Pennsylvania 16802

SOUTH CAROLINA

Health Services Administration Bachelor
  Degree Program
Winthrop College
School of Business Administration
Rock Hill, South Carolina 29733

SOUTH DAKOTA

Health Services Administration Bachelor
  Degree Program
University of South Dakota
School of Business
Vermillion, South Dakota 57069

TENNESSEE

Health Services Administration Bachelor
  Degree Program
Meharry Medical College/Tennessee
  State University
1005 Todd Boulevard
P.O. Box 63-A
Nashville, Tennessee 37208

TEXAS

Health Services Administration Bachelor
  Degree Program
Southwest Texas State University
Health Science Center
San Marcos, Texas 78666-4616

UTAH

Health Services Administration Bachelor
  Degree Program
Weber State College
School of Allied Health Sciences
3750 Harrison Boulevard
Ogden, Utah 84408-3911

HEALTHCARE SECURITY AND SAFETY

Healthcare security and safety personnel are responsible for the security of a healthcare facility and the safety of its patients and staff. The healthcare security and safety worker may be responsible for handling and investigating crimes that can occur in a healthcare facility such as thefts and assaults. He or she may also be responsible for electrical, radiation, and fire safety; construction and renovation safety; and the safe handling and disposal of hazardous materials. The field of healthcare security and safety is generally divided into the four positions of, *security and safety officer, supervisor of security and safety, assistant director of security and safety,* and *director of security and safety.* The job titles and responsibilities of each of these professions may vary depending upon place of employment.

Security and Safety Officer

The *healthcare security and safety officer*, also known as the *hospital security officer* or *hospital safety officer*, is under the supervision of the healthcare security and safety supervisor and is directly involved with the security and safety of the healthcare facility. Within the security segment of the job, he or she is responsible for handling disturbed visitors, patients, or employees. The security and safety officer investigates thefts or assaults which may occur in patient rooms, employee workplaces, patient care areas, and emergency rooms. He or she must be skilled in self-defense and in the handling and use of weapons. The security and safety officer should have a thorough knowledge of patrol procedures; the laws of arrest, search, and seizure; and emergency first aid and life saving techniques. He or she should also have a thorough understanding of the facility's alarm system as well as the lock and key systems.

Within the safety segment of the job, the security and safety officer must know the facility's correct fire response procedures and must be familiar with the use of such protective equipment as smoke detectors, sprinklers, fire extinguishers, and hoses. He or she should be capable of investigating, reporting, and responding to injuries and accidents such as slips and falls and vehicle accidents. The security and safety officer may also be responsible for the proper storage, handling, and disposal of hazardous waste materials.

Healthcare security and safety officers are employed in hospitals, armed forces healthcare facilities, nursing homes, VA hospitals, clinics, and doctors' offices.

A certificate in Safety Training for the healthcare security and safety officer is available from the International Association for Healthcare Security and Safety (IAHSS). The twenty hour training program may be completed by either of two methods. The first method is a Senior Membership process in which the student makes arrangements with a Senior Member of the IAHSS to provide, monitor, and certify the training activity. Upon completion of the program, the student must successfully pass an exam issued by the IAHSS Training and Education Committee. The second method is self directed learning using the IAHSS Safety Training Manual and Study Guide. The student must complete the work contained in the manual and then successfully pass an exam issued by the IAHSS Training and Education Committee.

IAHSS Security Officer Basic Training Certification is a forty hour program consisting of instruction and/or study. Thirty-four of the forty hours are mandatory, but six additional hours are allowed to the student to fit his or her needs, or the needs of the institution, while still maintaining a training standard. Security Officer Basic Training Certification is accomplished by the same methods used when earning a certificate in Safety Training. The first method is a Senior Member Sponsorship in which the student makes arrangements with a Senior Member of IAHSS to provide, monitor, and certify the training activity. Upon completion of the program, the student must successfully pass an exam issued by the IAHSS Education and Training Committee. The second method of certification requires the student to complete the course of study contained in the IAHSS Basic Training Manual and Study Guide and then successfully pass the IAHSS exam.

According to a 1991 survey taken by the International Association for Healthcare Security and Safety, annual salaries for the healthcare security and safety officer averaged $15,000 to $19,000.

For more information on becoming a healthcare security and safety officer, contact the International Association for Healthcare Security and Safety, P.O. Box 637, Lombard, Illinois 60148.

SOURCE:

International Association for Healthcare Security and Safety

Supervisor of Security and Safety

The *supervisor of security and safety* , also known as the *supervisor of security* or the *supervisor of safety,* may work under the supervision of a Director of Security and Safety. The supervisor of security and safety is experienced in and knowledgeable of the duties of the security and safety officer. Supervisory responsibilities include handling complaints and grievances, customer relations and employee relations. He or she may also be involved in employee appraisals, budgeting, and cost control. The supervisor of security and safety must be aware of the appropriate procedures to follow in the event of a bomb threat, fire, mass casualty incident, civil disturbance, or natural disaster. He or she must display authority, control, and effective leadership skills. The supervisor of security and safety should also possess effective communications and management skills and a knowledge of contemporary healthcare issues.

Security and Safety supervisors are employed in such healthcare facilities as hospitals, armed forces healthcare facilities, nursing homes, VA hospitals, clinics, and doctors' offices.

The International Association for Healthcare Security and Safety offers a twenty hour supervisory training course. To receive a certificate, the training program must be accomplished by either of two methods. The first method is a Senior Member Sponsorship in which the individual makes arrangements with a Senior Member of the IAHSS to provide, monitor, and certify the training activity. Upon completion of the program, the individual must successfully pass an exam issued by the Education and Training Committee of IAHSS. The second method is self-directed learning. The individual must complete a course of study contained in the IAHSS Supervisory Training Manual and Study Guide. Upon completion of the course, the individual must pass a written exam administered by the IAHSS.

According to a 1991 survey taken by the International Association of Healthcare Security and Safety, annual salaries for first line healthcare security and safety supervisors averaged $20,000 to $29,000.

For more information on becoming a supervisor of security and safety, contact the International Association for Healthcare Security and Safety, P.O. Box 637, Lombard, Illinois 60148.

SOURCE:

International Association for Healthcare Security and Safety

Assistant Director of Security and Safety

The *assistant director of security and safety* works under the supervision of the director of security and safety. The assistant director should have a thorough knowledge of the responsibilities of the department supervisor and the security and safety officers. The duties of the assistant director may vary amongst healthcare facilities, but he or she generally assists the security and safety director and may be involved in supervising the entire security and safety department. He or she may also assist with hiring, budgeting, and cost control.

The assistant director of security and safety may be employed in hospitals, armed forces healthcare facilities, nursing homes, VA hospitals, clinics, and doctors' offices.

The educational requirements of the assistant director of security and safety may also vary amongst healthcare facilities. Many employers require a college degree in business administration or criminal justice. Individual courses in business administration and criminal justice are offered at universities and colleges throughout the country. Other employers may only require thorough experience in the healthcare security and safety field.

According to a 1991 survey taken by the International Association for Healthcare Security and Safety, annual salaries for assistant directors of security and safety averaged $25,000 to

$29,000.

For more information on a career in healthcare security and safety, contact the International Association for Healthcare Security and Safety, P.O. Box 637, Lombard, Illinois 60148.

SOURCE:

International Association for Healthcare Security and Safety

Director of Security and Safety

The *director of security and safety,* also called *director of security* or *director of safety,* oversees the entire security and/or safety program. He or she may be in charge of radiation safety, hazardous waste disposal, infection control, fire safety, accident prevention, environmental safety, construction or renovation safety, and the handling of emergencies such as mass casualties or natural disasters. The director of security and safety may participate in environmental and safety surveys and inspections. Depending upon the particular healthcare facility, he or she may also be in charge of hiring, scheduling, and budgeting for the security and safety department. The director of security and safety should have a thorough knowledge of the job responsibilities of the security/safety supervisor and officers. He or she should also have a thorough knowledge of patrol procedures, the laws of arrest, and courtroom procedures.

Employment opportunities for the director of security and safety include hospitals, armed forces healthcare facilities, nursing homes, VA hospitals, clinics, and doctor's offices.

The educational requirements for the director of security and safety vary. Many healthcare institutions require a college degree in business administration or criminal justice while others may only require a background of thorough healthcare security and safety experience. Individual courses in business administration and criminal justice are offered at universities and colleges throughout the country.

The International Healthcare Security and Safety Foundation administers an IAHSS credentialing program for members of healthcare security and safety administration. Qualified candidates are accepted into the credentialing program at the Nominee level by meeting the educational, experience, membership, and special training qualifications. After successful completion of a written exam covering management, security, safety/life safety, and risk management, nominees progress to the graduate level. Upon successful completion of the graduate exam, an applicant then becomes a Certified Healthcare Protection Administrator (C.H.P.A.).

According to a 1991 survey taken by the International Association for Healthcare Security and Safety, annual salaries for Directors of Healthcare Security and Safety averaged $30,000 to $49,000.

For more information on a career in healthcare security and safety, contact the International Association for Healthcare Security and Safety, P.O. Box 637, Lombard, Illinois 60148.

SOURCES:

International Association for Healthcare Security and Safety
International Healthcare Security and Safety Foundation

HOMEMAKER - HOME HEALTH AIDE SERVICES

Based on the principle that family solidarity is essential to family and community life, homemaker-home health aide services involve domestic and social services and healthcare. They are provided by public, private, and voluntary health or welfare agencies and offer a variety of "in-home" services for families or individuals who are experiencing disruptions in normal living habits because of illness, disability, or social disadvantage. The primary concern of homemaker-home health aide services is the maintenance and improvement of the health and well-being of those who must, or choose to, live at home instead of remaining in, or entering a hospital or institution. The advantage of these services is that they allow the ill or disabled individual to benefit from the familiar surroundings of home and community in relative independence. Examples of when these services are needed include situations when the mother of a family is ill or incapacitated, when discharged surgery patients are permitted to recuperate at home, or when handicapped or elderly persons require personal care and domestic assistance. The individual who performs these services in the home is the *homemaker-home health aide,* also called *home care aide* or *personal care attendant.*

Homemaker - Home Health Aide

As the recruited, trained, and supervised staff member of a health or welfare agency, the *homemaker-home health aide* may provide homemaking and personal services, instructions, emotional support, and some minimal healthcare to clients in their own homes. Although also caring for children and the disabled, most of the aide's clients are elderly persons with medical problems, decreased mobility, and/or little or no family to care for them.

Job titles and duties for the homemaker-home health aide often differ between agencies and states. Often, homemaker and home-health aide are separate positions with varied job responsibilities. Generally, the position of homemaker refers to an individual who performs light homemaking duties that include cleaning, laundering, planning and preparing nutritious meals, and shopping for food. Homemakers may also provide instruction to individuals or families on home management skills, including budgeting, basic child care techniques and safety.

A home-health aide often performs personal care duties such as bathing, feeding, and helping the client move about the home. With training and supervision from a registered nurse, the home-health aide performs basic nursing tasks which may include changing bandages, reminding clients to take medications, and assisting with prescribed exercises or with special therapies. The aide also offers instruction in how to adapt both physically and mentally to illness or disability, and how to cope with daily tasks that are difficult for the client to perform, such as caring for children or cooking meals. Finally, the aide provides emotional support and understanding when the client is depressed, frustrated, or lonely.

Homemaker-home health aide services may be used on an "as needed" basis or may be one part of a longer term home healthcare plan that may include a physician, nurse, social worker, therapist and dietitian. If complex medical treatments are required, a client may employ a home healthcare nurse or visiting nurse service. Registered nurses (RN's) can provide hospital-type care in the comfort of home. Licensed practical nurses (LPN's) usually provide more routine treatment and care. For more details on a career as a registered nurse or licensed practical nurse, refer to the chapter in this book titled, "Nursing".

The homemaker-home health aide is expected to be responsible, dependable, and resourceful. The aide is generally supervised by a registered nurse, social worker, or a professional with a four year degree in a related field, who visits the client's home on a regular basis. During these meetings with the supervisor, the homemaker-home health aide can report on the client's condition and make recommendations for a change in services.

The Federal law requires that home health aides, whose employers receive reimbursement from Medicare, pass a competency test and complete at least 75 hours of classroom and practical training supervised by a registered nurse. Training may be administered at the home healthcare agency and should include basic home nursing, personal care, safety, food and nutrition.

One way to gain a better understanding of the home healthcare field is through volunteering. Some social service organizations provide supplementary home health services and need volunteers to provide companionship to homebound individuals, to deliver nutritious meals, and to assist with transportation. For more information on volunteering, contact The United Way, American Red Cross, or other social service organizations (generally listed under "Social Service Organizations", in the local telephone directory).

Salaries for homemaker-home health aides vary considerably depending upon the type and location of the health or welfare agency. Earnings range from minimum wage to $10 an hour for aides in large cities. Benefits such as guaranteed hours, sick leave, health insurance, and pension plans also vary greatly between agencies. Persons interested in becoming aides should compare these factors when considering various salaries.

Those interested in additional information on a career as a homemaker-home health aide should contact the secondary public schools, vocational-technical institutes, and community colleges in their area, or refer to telephone listings under "Home Health Aide Agencies", "Home Health Care", or "Social Service Organization". Potential employment opportunities may also be found in the classified advertising section of local newspapers under the heading "Medical" or "Domestic".

Additional reading material on homemaker-home health aide services can be obtained from the Foundation for Hospice and Homecare/National Home Caring Council, 519 "C" Street NE, Washington, DC 20002.

SOURCES:

Foundation for Hospice and Homecare
Occupational Outlook Handbook

✚ LABOR AND BIRTH SUPPORT

Labor and birth support services for the expectant mother consist of prenatal visits, early labor support at home, relaxation and visualization skills used during labor, postpartum home help, information on the newborn, and information on parenting. The women working in labor and birth support services may be trained volunteers or employed professionals. They may be known as *labor companions, trained labor coaches, birth assistants,* and *labor support persons.* The *doula* and the *monitrice* are also birth support providers. A *doula* may aid during labor by providing support to both mother and father, but she primarily provides postpartum help at home. She assists the new mother in caring for herself, assists with household chores, and cares for any other children within the home. A *monitrice* is a registered nurse (RN) who provides support and comfort measures for labor and birth. She can also provide such labor and delivery nursing skills as examining the mother at home and monitoring the fetal heartbeat. For information on nurse mid-wives, see the *nurse mid-wife* chapter in the *Nursing* section of this book. For information on obstetric nurses, see the *obstetric nurse* chapter also in the *Nursing* section of this book. Two other careers within the field of labor and birth support are the *childbirth assistant* and the *perinatal counselor*.

Childbirth Assistant
Perinatal Counselor

The *childbirth assistant* provides a series of prenatal home visits in which she assists the client in defining her own personal birth philosophy. She provides birth pain counseling and discusses the resources that will help the expectant mother achieve the planned for birth experience. She also discusses postpartum planning, introduces social support systems, and provides other services particular to the client's needs. During early labor support at home, and later at the birth facility, the childbirth assistant provides non-medical emotional and physical comfort measures such as verbal support, massage, and position changes. She may also teach the client methods of relaxation, visualization, breathing patterns, and other methods that provide comfort. In a series of postnatal home visits that coincide with the three phases of postpartum, the childbirth assistant provides information and guidance on issues determined by the client's individual needs. She may discuss newborn care, infant feeding methods, parenting concerns, postpartum healing, changes in the family, and social support systems.

The majority of childbirth assistants are self-employed, developing their own client base. Others may be employed in special positions in hospitals, public health departments, and care-providers offices. Some childbirth assistants may establish non-profit labor and birth support services in their communities to meet the needs of such women as pregnant teens and pregnant women on Medicaid.

The childbirth assistant should have an interest in working with birthing women and their families. Any previous education, regardless of specialty, will enhance her work. The National Association of Childbirth Assistants offers training for childbirth assistants. For more information on training procedures contact the National Association of Childbirth Assistants, P.O. Box 12037, Santa Rosa, California 95043.

To achieve certification as a childbirth assistant, candidates must complete a Level 1 training program in which labor support and educational counseling skills are taught. Level 2 and Level 3 training and certification are also available. Level 2 training teaches such skills as visualization, body work, rapport building and counseling. Level 3 teaches skills used in teaching family classes. Upon completion of Level 3, the status of Perinatal Counselor is achieved.

In addition to her role as a childbirth assistant, the *perinatal counselor* teaches parenting and family classes. Most perinatal counselors are self-employed, but some may teach in clinics.

Recommended high school courses for students interested in pursuing a career as a childbirth assistant or perinatal counselor include health, anatomy and physiology, and psychology.

According to the National Association of Childbirth Assistants, starting salaries for the childbirth assistant average $6,000 to $8,000 a year. Childbirth assistants with advanced degrees average $8,000 to $15,000 a year. Annual salaries for the perinatal counselor average $15,000 to $30,000.

For more information on the professions of childbirth assistant or perinatal counselor, contact the National Association of Childbirth Assistants, P.O. Box 12037, Santa Rosa, California 95043.

SOURCES:

Birth Support Providers International
National Association of Childbirth Assistants

✚ MEDICAL ASSISTING

Medical assisting is the allied health profession that provides administrative and clinical support for physicians in the efficient operation of their office practices as well as in hospitals, clinics and other healthcare facilities. In a small, one-employee office the *medical assistant* performs all the necessary supportive duties for the physician, but in a large office or medical practice these duties are differentiated among two or more medical assistants.

The various job functions of medical assisting are discussed under the heading of medical assistant. The occupations of medical assisting in dentistry, optometry, and ophthalmology are discussed in their respective chapters elsewhere in this handbook.

Medical Assistant

Most often employed in a physician's office, the *medical assistant* serves as the direct link between the physician and his or her patients, professional associates, and suppliers of medical drugs and equipment. Nearly every practicing physician requires at least one medical assistant.

Depending on degree of training and working conditions the medical assistant may perform either administrative and/or clinical duties.

The responsibilities of a medical assistant who performs administrative duties include scheduling appointments; receiving patients; answering the telephone; operating office machinery; handling correspondence; taking medical dictation; transcribing shorthand; typing medical reports; maintaining patients' files and medical records; receiving representatives of pharmaceutical companies and medical equipment suppliers; arranging hospital admissions and laboratory tests; processing the paperwork involved with health insurance data and claims; and finally handling the office's financial records including patients' fees. If responsibilities are limited to secretarial and receptionist functions, the medical assistant may often be referred to as a *medical secretary*. If the assistant is employed solely as an office receptionist and not as an overall secretary, a high degree of training and knowledge in medical terminology is not required.

In a small office, advancement opportunities may be limited. However, in a large office or clinic, medical assistants may be promoted to office manager after several years experience plus demonstrated leadership ability.

With sufficient formal or on-the-job training, the medical assistant can go beyond office management and perform clinical duties that include preparing patients for examination; taking blood pressures and temperatures; recording medical histories; performing diagnostic and routine laboratory procedures; and assisting the physician with examinations and treatment.

Training in medical assisting varies with specific job responsibilities. For medical secretaries, general secretarial programs of one-to-two years are offered by most community colleges and vocational-technical schools. More comprehensive training is available from formal medical assistant educational programs offered by community colleges and vocational-technical schools. Training is also available from specialized schools of medical assisting, which include practical experience in physicians' offices or hospitals.

Certification as a Certified Medical Assistant (CMA) is available from the American Association of Medical Assistants for candidates who successfully complete the association's examination and satisfy the educational and/or experience requirements. Credentials are also granted by the American Medical Technologists for the Registered Medical Assistant (RMA) status. For information on certification or registration awards write to the American Association of Medical Assistants, 20 North Wacker Drive, Suite 1575, Chicago, Illinois 60606 or the American Medical Technologists, 710 Higgins Road, Park Ridge, Illinois 60068, respectively.

Recommended high school courses include typing, business, mathematics, secretarial skills, biology, chemistry, psychology, health, bookkeeping, and computers.

The American Association of Medical Assistants' Endowment awards scholarships semi-annually. Interested students should contact the American Association of Medical Assistants' Endowment, 20 North Wacker Drive, Suite 1575, Chicago, Illinois 60606.

A medical assistant with experience of two years or less averages $14,000 a year. Medical assistants with eleven or more years average $21,000 a year. Some medical assistants who become office managers can earn significantly more.

For more information on careers as a medical assistant, contact the American Association of Medical Assistants, 20 North Wacker Drive, Suite 1575, Chicago, Illinois 60606, or the American Medical Technologists, 710 Higgins Road, Park Ridge, Illinois 60068.

Two agencies are recognized by the U.S. Department of Education to accredit medical assisting programs. They are the Committee on Allied Health Education and Accreditation (CAHEA) of the American Medical Association and the Accrediting Bureau of Health Education Schools (ABHES)

Following is a list of medical assisting programs accredited by the Committee on Allied Health Education and Accreditation.

SOURCES:

American Association of Medical Assistants
Occupational Outlook Handbook

194

Medical Assistant Programs

ALABAMA

Medical Assistant Program
University of Alabama at Birmingham
School of Health Related Professions
UAB Station
Birmingham, Alabama 35294

Medical Assistant Program
G.C. Wallace State Community College
Napier Field Road
Dothan, Alabama 36303

Medical Assistant Program
Draughons Junior College
122 Commerce Street
Montgomery, Alabama 36104-0122

Medical Assistant Program
Trenholm State Technical College
1225 Air Base Boulevard
P.O. Box 9000
Montgomery, Alabama 36108

ALASKA

Medical Assistant Program
University of Alaska Anchorage
3211 Providence Drive
Anchorage, Alaska 99508

ARIZONA

Medical Assistant Program
Phoenix College
1202 West Thomas Road
Phoenix, Arizona 85013

Medical Assistant Program
The Bryman School
4343 North 16th Street
Phoenix, Arizona 85016

ARKANSAS

Medical Assistant Program
Capital City Junior College
7723 Asher Avenue
Little Rock, Arkansas 72204

Medical Assistant Program
Arkansas Technical University
Russellville, Arkansas 72801

CALIFORNIA

Medical Assistant Program
Concorde Career Institute
1717 South Brookhurst Street
Anaheim, California 92804

Medical Assistant Program
National Education Center-Bryman
 Campus
1120 North Brookhurst Street
Anaheim, California 92801

Medical Assistant Program
Orange Coast College
2701 Fairview Road
Costa Mesa, California 92628

Medical Assistant Program
De Anza College
21250 Stevens Creek Boulevard
Cupertino, California 95014

Medical Assistant Program
Chabot College
25555 Hesperian Boulevard
Hayward, California 94545-5001

Medical Assistant Program
National Education Center-Bryman
 Campus
5350 Atlantic Avenue
Long Beach, California 90805

Medical Assistant Program
Modesto Junior College
435 College Avenue
Modesto, California 95350-9977

Medical Assistant Program
Pasadena City College
1570 East Colorado Boulevard
Pasadena, California 91106

Medical Assistant Program
National Education Center-Bryman
  Campus
3505 North Hart Avenue
Rosemead, California 91770

Medical Assistant Program
Cosumnes River College
8401 Center Parkway
Sacramento, California 95823

Medical Assistant Program
Concorde Career
600 North Sierra Way
San Bernardino, California 92401

Medical Assistant Program
San Diego Mesa College
7250 Mesa College Drive
San Diego, California 92111

Medical Assistant Program
City College of San Francisco
50 Phelan Avenue
San Francisco, California 94112

Medical Assistant Program
National Education Center-Bryman
  Campus
731 Market Street
San Francisco, California 94103

Medical Assistant Program
National Education Center-Bryman
  Campus
2015 Naglee Avenue
San Jose, California 95128

Medical Assistant Program
West Valley Community College District
14000 Fruitvale Avenue
Saratoga, California 95070

Medical Assistant Program
National Education Center-Bryman
  Campus
4212 West Artesia Boulevard
Torrance, California 90504

COLORADO

Medical Assistant Program
T.H. Pickens Technical Center
500 Buckley Road
Aurora, Colorado 80011

Medical Assistant Program
Boulder Valley Area Vocational
  Technical Center
805 Gillaspie Drive
Boulder, Colorado 80303

Medical Assistant Program
Blair Junior College
828 Wooten Road
Colorado Springs, Colorado 80915

Medical Assistant Program
Emily Griffith Opportunity School
1250 Welton Street
Denver, Colorado 80204

Medical Assistant Program
Parks Junior College
9065 Grant Street
Denver, Colorado 80229

CONNECTICUT

Medical Assistant Program
Stone Academy
1315 Dixwell Avenue
Hamden, Connecticut 06514

Medical Assistant Program
Morse School of Business
275 Asylum Street
Hartford, Connecticut 06103

Medical Assistant Program
Northwestern Connecticut Community
  College
Park Place East
Winsted, Connecticut 06098-1798

FLORIDA

Medical Assistant Program
Broward Community College
3501 SW Davie Road
Ft. Lauderdale, Florida 33301

Medical Assistant Program
Phillips Junior College
2401 North Harbour City Boulevard
Melbourne, Florida 32935

Medical Assistant Program
Pensacola Junior College
Warrington Campus
5555 West Highway 98
Pensacola, Florida 32507

Medical Assistant Program
Sarasota County Technical Institute
4748 Beneva Road
Sarasota, Florida 34233

Medical Assistant Program
Pinellas Tech Education Center-St.
  Petersburg
901 34th Street South
St. Petersburg, Florida 33711

Medical Assistant Program
David G. Erwin Technical Center
2010 East Hillborough Avenue
Tampa, Florida 33610-8299

Medical Assistant Program
South College
1760 North Congress Avenue
West Palm Beach, Florida 33409

Medical Assistant Program
Winter Park Adult Vocational Center
901 Webster Avenue
Winter Park, Florida 32789

GEORGIA

Medical Assistant Program
Atlanta Area Technical School
1560 Stewart Avenue SW
Atlanta, Georgia 30310

Medical Assistant Program
Atlanta College of Medical & Dental
  Careers
1240 West Peachtree Street NW
Atlanta, Georgia 30309

Medical Assistant Program
National Education Center-Bryman
  Campus
40 Marietta Street
Atlanta, Georgia 30303

Medical Assistant Program
Augusta Technical Institute
3116 Deans Bridge Road
Augusta, Georgia 30906

Medical Assistant Program
Columbus Technical Institute
928 Fifth Street
Columbus, Georgia 31995

Medical Assistant Program
Medix School
2480 Windy Hill Road
Marietta, Georgia 30067

Medical Assistant Program
Savannah Technical Institute
5717 White Bluff Road
Savannah, Georgia 31499

Medical Assistant Program
South College
709 Mall Boulevard
Savannah, Georgia 31406

Medical Assistant Program
Thomas Technical Institute
U.S. Highway 19 at 319
P.O. Box 1578
Thomasville, Georgia 31799

Medical Assistant Program
Valdosta Technical Institute
Route 12, Box 1273
Valdosta, Georgia 31602

HAWAII

Medical Assistant Program
Kapiolani Community College
4303 Diamond Head Road
Honolulu, Hawaii 96816

IDAHO

Medical Assistant Program
College of Southern Idaho
P.O. Box 1238
Twin Falls, Idaho 83303-1238

ILLINOIS

Medical Assistant Program
Belleville Area College
2500 Carlyle Road
Belleville, Illinois 62221

Medical Assistant Program
Northwestern Business College
4829 North Lipps Avenue
Chicago, Illinois 60630

Medical Assistant Program
Robert Morris College
180 North LaSalle Street
Chicago, Illinois 60601

Medical Assistant Program
William Rainey Harper College
1200 West Algonquin Road
Palatine, Illinois 60067

Medical Assistant Program
Midstate College
224 SW Jefferson Street
Peoria, Illinois 61602

INDIANA

Medical Assistant Program
Indiana Vocational Technical College
 - Columbia
4475 Central Avenue
Columbus, Indiana 47203

Medical Assistant Program
Indiana Vocational Technical College
 SW-Evansville
3501 First Avenue
Evansville, Indiana 47710

Medical Assistant Program
Indiana Vocational Technical College
 NE-Ft. Wayne
3800 North Anthony Boulevard
Ft. Wayne, Indiana 46305

Medical Assistant Program
International Business College-Ft.
 Wayne
3811 Old Illinois Road
Ft. Wayne, Indiana 46804-1298

Medical Assistant Program
Indiana Vocational Technical College-
Indianapolis
One West 26th Street
P.O. Box 1763
Indianapolis, Indiana 46206

Medical Assistant Program
International Business College-
Indianapolis
7205 Shadeland Station
Indianapolis, Indiana 46256

198

Medical Assistant Program
Professional Careers Institute
2611 Waterfront Parkway, East Drive
Indianapolis, Indiana 46214

Medical Assistant Program
Indiana Vocational Technical College-
Kokomo
1815 East Morgan Street
Kokomo, Indiana 46901

Medical Assistant Program
Indiana Vocational Technical College-
Lafayette
3208 Ross Road
P.O. Box 6299
Lafayette, Indiana 47903

Medical Assistant Program
Indiana Vocational Technical College
  SE-Madison
590 Ivy Tech Drive
Madison, Indiana 47250

Medical Assistant Program
Indiana Vocational Technical College
  EC-Muncie
4100 Cowan Road
Muncie, Indiana 47302

Medical Assistant Program
Indiana Vocational Technical College
  SC-Sellersburg
8204 Highway 311
Stillersburg, Indiana 47172

Medical Assistant Program
Indiana Vocational Technical College
  NC-South Bend
1534 West Sample Street
South Bend, Indiana 46619

Medical Assistant Program
Michiana College
1030 East Jefferson Boulevard
South Bend, Indiana 46617

Medical Assistant Program
Indiana Vocational Technical College-
Terre Haute
7377 South Dixie Bee Road
Terre Haute, Indiana 47802-4898

Medical Assistant Program
Indiana Vocational Technical College
  NW-Valparaiso
2401 Valley Drive
Valparaiso, Indiana 46383

IOWA

Medical Assistant Program
Des Moines Area Community college
2006 Ankeny Boulevard
Ankeny, Iowa 50021

Medical Assistant Program
Kirkwood Community College
6301 Kirkwood Boulevard SW
Cedar Rapids, Iowa 52406

Medical Assistant Program
Iowa Western Community College
2700 College Road
Box 4-C
Council Bluffs, Iowa 51501

Medical Assistant Program
American Institute of Commerce
1801 East Kimberly Road
Davenport, Iowa 52807

Medical Assistant Program
Iowa Central Community College
330 Avenue "M"
Ft. Dodge, Iowa 50501

Medical Assistant Program
Marshalttown Community College
3700 South Center Street
Marshalttown, Iowa 50158

Medical Assistant Program
Spencer School of Business
217 West Fifth Street
Spencer, Iowa 51301

Medical Assistant Program
Southeastern Community College
1015 South Gear Avenue
West Burlington, Iowa 52655

KENTUCKY

Medical Assistant Program
Fugazzi College
406 Lafayette Avenue
Lexington, Kentucky 40502

Medical Assistant Program
Kentucky Tech-Jefferson State Campus
800 West Chestnut Street
Louisville, Kentucky 40203-2071

Medical Assistant Program
Spencerian College
914 East Broadway
Louisville, Kentucky 40204

Medical Assistant Program
Watterson College
4400 Breckenridge Lane
Louisville, Kentucky 40218

Medical Assistant Program
West Kentucky State Vocational
  Technical
P.O. Box 7408
Blandville Road
Paducah, Kentucky 42002-7408

Medical Assistant Program
Eastern Kentucky University
Richmond, Kentucky 40475-3135

LOUISIANA

Medical Assistant Program
Phillips Junior College
5001 Westbank Expressway
Marrero, Louisiana 70072

Medical Assistant Program
Phillips Junior College
822 South Clearview Parkway
New Orleans, Louisiana 70123

MAINE

Medical Assistant Program
Beal College
629 Main Street
Bangor, Maine 04401

MARYLAND

Medical Assistant Program
Medix School
1017 York Road
Towson, Maryland 21204

MASSACHUSETTS

Medical Assistant Program
Middlesex Community College
Springs Road
Bedford, Massachusetts 01730

Medical Assistant Program
Aquinas Junior College
303 Adams Street
Milton, Massachusetts 02186

Medical Assistant Program
Southeastern Technical Institute
250 Foundry Street
South Easton, Massachusetts 02375

Medical Assistant Program
Springfield Tech Community College
One Amory Square
Springfield, Massachusetts 01105

MICHIGAN

Medical Assistant Program
Henry Ford Community College
22586 Ann Arbor Trail
Dearborn Heights, Michigan 48128

Medical Assistant Program
Baker College
G 1050 West Bristol
Flint, Michigan 48507

Medical Assistant Program
Davenport College
415 East Fulton Street
Grand Rapids, Michigan 49503

Medical Assistant Program
Kalamazoo Valley Community College
6767 West "O" Street Avenue
Kalamazoo, Michigan 49009

Medical Assistant Program
Macomb Community College
4475 Garfield Road
Mt. Clemens, Michigan 48044

Medical Assistant Program
Baker College of Muskegon
141 Hartford
Muskegon, Michigan 49442

Medical Assistant Program
Baker College of Owosso
Owosso Campus
120 South Washington Street
Owosso, Michigan 48867

Medical Assistant Program
Carnegie Institute
550 Stephenson Highway
Troy, Michigan 48083

Medical Assistant Program
Oakland Community College
7350 Cooley Lake Road
Union Lake, Michigan 48085-2198

MINNESOTA

Medical Assistant Program
Anoka Technical College
1355 West Highway 10
Anoka, Minnesota 55303

Medical Assistant Program
Medical Institute of Minnesota
5503 Green Valley Drive
Bloomington, Minnesota 55437

Medical Assistant Program
East Grand Forks Technical College
Highway 220 North
East Grand Forks, Minnesota 56721

Medical Assistant Program
Lakeland Medical Dental Academy
1402 West Lake Street
Minneapolis, Minnesota 55408

Medical Assistant Program
Rochester Community College
851 30th Avenue SE
Highway 14 E
Rochester, Minnesota 55904-4999

Medical Assistant Program
Minneapolis Business College
1711 West County Road B
Roseville, Minnesota 55113

Medical Assistant Program
Northeast Metro Technical College
3300 Century Avenue North
White Bear Lake, Minnesota 55110

Medical Assistant Program
Willmar Technical College
P.O. Box 1097
Willmar, Minnesota 56201

MISSISSIPPI

Medical Assistant Program
Northeast Mississippi Community
 College
Cunningham Boulevard
Booneville, Mississippi 38829

Medical Assistant Program
Phillips Junior College
2680 Insurance Center Drive
Jackson, Mississippi 39216

MISSOURI

Medical Assistant Program
Phillips Colleges Inc.
625 North Benton
Springfield, Missouri 65806

Medical Assistant Program
The Hickey School
6710 Clayton Road
St. Louis, Missouri 63117

NEBRASKA

Medical Assistant Program
Central Community College
Hastings Campus
P.O. Box 1024
Hastings, Nebraska 68902-1024

Medical Assistant Program
Southeast Community College
8800 "O" Street
Lincoln, Nebraska 68520

Medical Assistant Program
Omaha College of Health Careers
1052 Park Avenue
Omaha, Nebraska 68105

NEW HAMPSHIRE

Medical Assistant Program
New Hampshire Technical College
One College Drive
Claremont, New Hampshire 03743

NEW JERSEY

Medical Assistant Program
Barclay Career School
28 South Harrison Street
East Orange, New Jersey 07017

Medical Assistant Program
Hudson County Community College
2039 Kennedy Boulevard
Jersey City, New Jersey 07305

Medical Assistant Program
Bergen County Community College
400 Paramus Road
Paramus, New Jersey 07652

Medical Assistant Program
Technical Institute of Camden County
Cross Keys Road
P.O. Box 566
Sicklerville, New Jersey 08081

Medical Assistant Program
Berdan Institute
265 Route 46 West
Totowa, New Jersey 07512

NEW YORK

Medical Assistant Program
Broome Community College
Business Building
P.O. Box 1017
Binghamton, New York 13902

Medical Assistant Program
Bryant & Stratton Business Institute
1028 Main Street
Buffalo, New York 14202

Medical Assistant Program
Erie Community College
North Campus
Main Street & Youngs Road
Buffalo, New York 14221

Medical Assistant Program
Bryant & Stratton Business Institute
82 St. Paul Street
Rochester, New York 14604

Medical Assistant Program
Bryant & Stratton Business Institute
400 Montgomery Street
Syracuse, New York 13202

NORTH CAROLINA

Medical Assistant Program
Central Piedmont Community College
P.O. Box 35009
Charlotte, North Carolina 28235

Medical Assistant Program
Kings College
322 Lamar Avenue
Charlotte, North Carolina 28204

Medical Assistant Program
Haywood Community College
Freelander Drive
Clyde, North Carolina 28721-9454

Medical Assistant Program
Gaston College
201 Highway 321 South
Dallas, North Carolina 28034-1499

Medical Assistant Program
Pitt Community College
Highway 11 South
P.O. Drawer 7007
Greenville, North Carolina 27835-7007

Medical Assistant Program
Guilford Technical Community College
P.O. Box 309
Jamestown, North Carolina 27282

Medical Assistant Program
Carteret Community College
3505 Arendell Street
Morehead City, North Carolina 28557

Medical Assistant Program
Western Piedmont Community College
1001 Burkemont Avenue
Morganton, North Carolina 28655

Medical Assistant Program
Wake Technical Community College
9101 Fayetteville Road
Raleigh, North Carolina 27603-5676

Medical Assistant Program
Wingate College
P.O. Box 3024
Wingate, North Carolina 28174

OHIO

Medical Assistant Program
Akron Medical-Dental Institute
733 West Market Street
Akron, Ohio 44303

Medical Assistant Program
Southern Ohio College NE
2791 Mogadore Road
Akron, Ohio 44312

Medical Assistant Program
University of Akron
Akron, Ohio 44325-3702

Medical Assistant Program
Mansfield Business College
3011 Mahoning Road NE
Canton, Ohio 44705

Medical Assistant Program
Stark Technical College
6200 Frank Avenue NW
Canton, Ohio 44720

Medical Assistant Program
Cincinnati Technical College
3520 Central Parkway
Cincinnati, Ohio 45223

Medical Assistant Program
Southern Ohio College
1055 Laidlaw Avenue
Cincinnati, Ohio 45237

Medical Assistant Program
Cuyahoga Community College
Metro Campus
700 Carnegie Avenue
Cleveland, Ohio 44115

Medical Assistant Program
MTI Business College
1901 East 13th Street, Suite 310
Cleveland, Ohio 44114

Medical Assistant Program
Wooster Business College
11610 Euclid Avenue
Cleveland, Ohio 44106

Medical Assistant Program
Bradford School
6170 Busch Boulevard
Columbus, Ohio 43229

Medical Assistant Program
Ohio Valley Business College
500 Maryland Street
P.O. Box 7000
East Liverpool, Ohio 43920

Medical Assistant Program
Southern Ohio College
4641 Bach Lane
Fairfield, Ohio 45014

Medical Assistant Program
Medina County Career Center
1101 West Liberty Street
Medina, Ohio 44256-9969

Medical Assistant Program
Knox County Career
306 Martinsburg Road
Mt. Vernon, Ohio 43050

Medical Assistant Program
Hocking Technical College
Route One
Nelsonville, Ohio 45764

Medical Assistant Program
Jefferson Technical College
4000 Sunset Boulevard
Steubenville, Ohio 43952

Medical Assistant Program
Davis Junior College of Business
4747 Monroe Street
Toledo, Ohio 43623

Medical Assistant Program
University of Toledo Community &
 Technical College
2801 West Bancroft Street
Toledo, Ohio 43606

Medical Assistant Program
Muskingum Area Technical College
1555 Newark Road
Zanesville, Ohio 43701

OKLAHOMA

Medical Assistant Program
Tulsa Junior College
909 South Boston Avenue
Tulsa, Oklahoma 74119

OREGON

Medical Assistant Program
Mt. Hood Community College
26000 SE Stark Street
Gresham, Oregon 97030

Medical Assistant Program
Bradford School
921 SW Washington, Suite 200
Portland, Oregon 97205

Medical Assistant Program
Portland Community College
12000 SW 49th Avenue
Portland, Oregon 97219

Medical Assistant Program
Chemeketa Community College
P.O. Box 14007
Salem, Oregon 97309

PENNSYLVANIA

Medical Assistant Program
Harcum Junior College
Montgomery & Morris Avenues
Bryn Mawr, Pennsylvania 19010

Medical Assistant Program
Gannon University
University Square
Erie, Pennsylvania 16541

Medical Assistant Program
Delaware County Community College
Route 252 & Media Line Road
Media, Pennsylvania 19063

Medical Assistant Program
Career Training Academy, Inc.
703 Fifth Avenue
New Kensington, Pennsylvania 15068

Medical Assistant Program
Community College of Philadelphia
1700 Spring Garden Street
Philadelphia, Pennsylvania 19130

Medical Assistant Program
Bradford School-Pittsburgh
The Park Building
355 Fifth Avenue
Pittsburgh, Pennsylvania 15222

Medical Assistant Program
Community College of Allegheny
  County
Allegheny Campus
808 Ridge Avenue
Pittsburgh, Pennsylvania 15212

Medical Assistant Program
Duffs Business Institute
110 Ninth Street
Pittsburgh, Pennsylvania 15222

Medical Assistant Program
ICM School of Business
10 Wood Street
Pittsburgh, Pennsylvania 15222

Medical Assistant Program
Median School of Allied Health Careers
125 Seventh Street
Pittsburgh, Pennsylvania 15222

Medical Assistant Program
Sawyer School
717 Liberty Avenue
Pittsburgh, Pennsylvania 15222

Medical Assistant Program
Lehigh County Community College
2370 Main Street
Schnecksville, Pennsylvania 18078

Medical Assistant Program
Central Pennsylvania Business School
Campus on College Hill
Summerdale, Pennsylvania 17093

Medical Assistant Program
Berks Technical Institute
833 North Park Road
Wyomissing, Pennsylvania 19610

SOUTH CAROLINA

Medical Assistant Program
Trident Technical College
P.O. Box 10367
Charleston, South Carolina 29411

SOUTH DAKOTA

Medical Assistant Program
National College
321 Kansas City Street
Rapid City, South Dakota 57709

TENNESSEE

Medical Assistant Program
Edmondson Junior College
3635 Brainerd Road
Chattanooga, Tennessee 37411

Medical Assistant Program
East Tennessee State University
1000 West "E" Street
Box 19 690A
Elizabethton, Tennessee 37643

Medical Assistant Program
Knoxville College
901 College Street
Knoxville, Tennessee 37921

Medical Assistant Program
Trevecca Nazarene College
333 Murfreesboro Road
Nashville, Tennessee 37210

TEXAS

Medical Assistant Program
El Paso Community College
P.O. Box 20500
El Paso, Texas 79998

Medical Assistant Program
Western Technical Institute
4710 Alabama Street
El Paso, Texas 79930

Medical Assistant Program
San Antonio College
1300 San Pedro Avenue
San Antonio, Texas 78284

Medical Assistant Program
National Education Center-Bryman
 Center
National Institute of Technology Campus
10945 Estate Lane
Dallas, Texas 75238

UTAH

Medical Assistant Program
American Institute of Med & Dental
 Tech
1675 North Freedom Boulevard,
 Building 9A
Provo, Utah 84604

Medical Assistant Program
Bryman School
1144 W 3300 S
Salt Lake City, Utah 84119

Medical Assistant Program
Latter Day Saints Business College
411 E South Temple
Salt Lake City, Utah 84111

Medical Assistant Program
Salt Lake Community College
4600 South Redwood Road
P.O. Box 30808
Salt Lake City, Utah 84130

VIRGINIA

Medical Assistant Program
National Business College
P.O. Box 6400
Roanoke, Virginia 24017-0400

WASHINGTON

Medical Assistant Program
Highline Community College
P.O. Box 98000
Des Moines, Washington 98198-9800

Medical Assistant Program
Edmonds Community College
20000 68th Avenue West
Lynnwood, Washington 98036

Medical Assistant Program
North Seattle Community College
9600 College Way North
Seattle, Washington 98103

Medical Assistant Program
Trend College
N 214 Wall Street
Spokane, Washington 99201-0865

WISCONSIN

Medical Assistant Program
Lakeshore Technical College
1290 North Avenue
Cleveland, Wisconsin 53015

Medical Assistant Program
Northeast Wisconsin Technical College
2740 West Mason Street
P.O. Box 19042
Green Bay, Wisconsin 54307-9042

Medical Assistant Program
Blackhawk Technical College
6004 Prairie Road
P.O. Box 53547
Janesville, Wisconsin 53547

Medical Assistant Program
Western Wisconsin Technical College
304 North Sixth Street
P.O. Box 908
La Crosse, Wisconsin 54602-0908

Medical Assistant Program
Madison Area Technical College
3550 Anderson Street
Madison, Wisconsin 53791-9674

Medical Assistant Program
Mid-State Technical College
2600 West Fifth Street
Marshfield, Wisconsin 54449

Medical Assistant Program
Milwaukee Area Technical College
700 West State Street
Milwaukee, Wisconsin 53233

Medical Assistant Program
Stratton College
1300 North Jackson Street
Milwaukee, Wisconsin 53202

Medical Assistant Program
Wisconsin Indianhead Technical College
1019 South Knowles Avenue
New Richmond, Wisconsin 54017

Medical Assistant Program
Waukesha County Technical College
800 Main Street
Pewaukee, Wisconsin 53072

Medical Assistant Program
Gateway Technical College
1001 South Main Street
Racine, Wisconsin 53403

✚ MEDICAL LABORATORY

The medical or clinical laboratory is essential to the modern practice of medicine. Tests and studies are carried out in the medical laboratory with the use of precision instruments and automated and electronic equipment to determine causes and patterns of disease, to develop better diagnostic procedures, and to innovate new methodologies in preventive medicine. The tests are specifically designed to both assist medical staff in making or confirming diagnoses and also to evaluate the effectiveness of medical treatment.

Laboratories are located in hospitals of all sizes; clinics; physicians' offices; independent laboratory companies; public health agencies; pharmaceutical and industrial companies; medical, dental, and veterinary schools; and research institutions.

In medical laboratories tests are generally performed in *bacteriology* (the study of microorganisms in the human body), *cytology* (the study of human cells), *histology* (the study of human tissue), *biochemistry* (the study of chemical processes within the human body and of the effects of chemical compounds upon the body's physiological and biochemical functions), *immunology* (the study of the mechanisms that fight infection), and *hematology* (the testing of blood specimens). These tests are all oriented to provide data on the cause, cure, and prevention of disease.

Career opportunities are found at every level in the medical laboratory. The pathologist (a physician who specializes in the causes and nature of disease) is the director of the medical laboratory, and he or she directly supervises laboratory specialists, or scientists, including the biochemist (a scientist who studies the chemical components of living things) and the microbiologist (a scientist who studies the relationship between bacteria and disease or the effect that antibodies have on bacteria), both of whom have earned advanced degrees in their respective fields.

Discussed below are the other careers in the medical laboratory, all of which fall under the general occupational heading of medical technology. Medical technology personnel include *medical technologists* and *medical technicians*. Personnel in these occupations may work in a small laboratory and perform a wide range of clinical tests, or they may work in a large laboratory and specialize in one of the six previously discussed scientific fields. Certain positions in *blood banking technology, cytotechnology,* and *histologic technology* are discussed in detail below.

In addition to all these laboratory personnel, there are two occupations that provide essential services to the laboratory but require only minimal training. They are the *laboratory aide* and the *morgue attendant*.

Medical Technologist

As a top-level laboratory worker the *medical technologist* is supervised by, and works in conjunction with, the pathologist and also with other physicians and scientists. The medical technologist exercises independent judgment in carrying out a broad range of complex chemical, microscopic, and bacteriological laboratory procedures that help to identify and control disease. The technologist supervises laboratory technicians and assists in their training. She or he may also calibrate equipment and evaluate the accuracy and utility of new laboratory tests.

In a small laboratory the worker performs many types of tests and is known as a medical technologist. In a larger laboratory setting, where the technologist usually specializes in a field and has had more specialized training, he or she is referred to as a *microbiology technologist, histologic technologist, chemistry technologist, immunology technologist, hematology technologist, blood bank technologist,* or *cytotechnologist*.

The educational requirement for the medical technologist is completion of two to four years of formal college study. The bachelor's degree program consists of three to four years of college study and nine to twelve months of clinical practice in a hospital or other medical setting affiliated with an accredited program. Persons interested in becoming a medical technologist may also attend a vocational school, receive training in the military, or acquire a combination of formal study and on-the-job training.

After graduation from an accredited bachelor's degree program which includes the twelve-month hospital course in medical technology, the candidate may take the registry examinations and become certified as a Medical Technologist, MT(ASCP), by the Board of Registry of the American Society of Clinical Pathologists; or as a Medical Technologist, MT(AMT), by the American Medical Technologists; or as a Registered Medical Technologist, RMT, by the International Society for Clinical Laboratory Technology or as a Clinical Laboratory Scientist, CLS, by the National Certification Agency for Medical Laboratory Personnel.

To date, a license to practice as a medical technologist is required in the following states: California, Florida, Georgia, Hawaii, North Dakota, Nevada, Tennessee, and West Virginia. New York City and Puerto Rico also require licenses. Write to the state Board of Occupational Licensing for specifics on state requirements.

According to a 1990 salary survey by the College Placement Council, Inc., graduates with a bachelor's degree averaged $24,000 a year. Experienced medical technologists averaged $31,000 a year. Salaries for beginning technologists in the federal government ranged from about $14,500 to $17,800 a year.

For more details on a career in medical technology, write to the American Medical Technologists, 710 Higgins Road, Park Ridge, Illinois 60068, and the American Society of Clinical Pathologists, 2100 W. Harrison Street, Chicago, Illinois 60612.

Certification information can be obtained from any of the following agencies: American Society of Clinical Pathologists, Board of Registry, P.O. Box 12270, Chicago, Illinois 60612; American Medical Technologists, 710 Higgins Road, Park Ridge, Illinois 60068; or

International Society for Clinical Laboratory Technology, 818 Olive Street, St. Louis, Missouri 63101.

Following is a list of educational programs in medical technology accredited by the American Medical Association's Committee on Allied Health Education and Accreditation.

SOURCES:

American Society of Clinical Pathologists
International Society for Clinical Laboratory Technology
Occupational Outlook Handbook

Medical Technologist Programs

ALABAMA

Medical Technologist Program
Baptist Medical Centers
800 Montclair Road
Birmingham, Alabama 35213

Medical Technologist Program
University of Alabama at Birmingham
School of Health Related Professions
UAB Station
Birmingham, Alabama 35294

Medical Technologist Program
University of South Alabama
Mobile, Alabama 36688-0001

Medical Technologist Program
Alabama Reference Laboratories, Inc.
543 South Hull Street
P.O. Box 4600
Montgomery, Alabama 36103-4600

Medical Technologist Program
Auburn University at Montgomery
School of Science
Department of Biology
Montgomery, Alabama 36193

Medical Technologist Program
Baptist Medical Center
2105 East South Boulevard
Montgomery, Alabama 36198

Medical Technologist Program
Tuskegee University
Tuskegee, Alabama 36088

ARIZONA

Medical Technologist Program
Arizona State University
Clinical Lab Sciences
Department of Microbiology
Tempe, Arizona 85287

Medical Technologist Program
University of Arizona
School of Health Related Professions
1435 North Fremont
Tucson, Arizona 85719

ARKANSAS

Medical Technologist Program
Baptist Medical System
11900 Colonel Glenn Road, Suite 1000
Little Rock, Arkansas 72210-2820

Medical Technologist Program
University of Arkansas for Med Sciences
4301 West Markham
Little Rock, Arkansas 72205

Medical Technologist Program
Arkansas State University
P.O. Box 69
State University, Arkansas 72467

CALIFORNIA

Medical Technologist Program
California State University
9001 Stockdale Highway
Bakersfield, California 93311

Medical Technologist Program
California State University-Dominguez
  Hills
1000 East Victoria Street
Carson, California 90747

Medical Technologist Program
Fresno Community Hospital & Medical
  Center
P.O. Box 1232
Fresno, California 93715

Medical Technologist Program
Valley Children's Hospital
3151 North Milbrook Avenue
Fresno, California 93703

Medical Technologist Program
Scripps Clinic & Research Foundation
10666 North Torrey Pines Road
La Jolla, California 92037-1093

Medical Technologist Program
Scripps Memorial Hospital
Pathology Med Lab Dept 8970
9888 Genesee Avenue
La Jolla, California 92037

Medical Technologist Program
Grossmont District Hospital Lab
5555 Grossmont Center Drive
La Mesa, California 92042

Medical Technologist Program
Loma Linda University
Loma Linda, California 92350

Medical Technologist Program
St. Mary Medical Center Bauer Hospital
1050 Linden Avenue
Long Beach, California 90813

Medical Technologist Program
VA Medical Center
5901 East Seventh Street
Long Beach, California 90822

Medical Technologist Program
Cedars Sinai Medical Center
8700 Beverly Boulevard
Los Angeles, California 90048

Medical Technologist Program
Charles R. Drew University of Medicine
  & Science
King/Drew Medical Center
12021 South Wilmington Avenue
Los Angeles, California 90059

Medical Technologist Program
Children's Hospital of Los Angeles
4650 Sunset Boulevard
Los Angeles, California 90027

Medical Technologist Program
Los Angeles County-USC Medical
  Center
1200 North State Street
Los Angeles, California 90033

Medical Technologist Program
UCLA Center for Health Sciences
10833 Le Conte Avenue
Los Angeles, California 90024

Medical Technologist Program
VA Med Center W Los Angeles-
Wadsworth Div
Wilshire & Sawtelle Boulevards
Los Angeles, California 90073

Medical Technologist Program
VA Medical Center
150 Muir Road
Martinez, California 94553

Medical Technologist Program
El Camino Hospital
2500 Grant Road
Mountain View, California 94040

Medical Technologist Program
St. Joseph Hospital
1100 Stewart Drive
P.O. Box 5600
Orange, California 92268

Medical Technologist Program
University of California Irvine Medical
   Center
101 City Drive South
Orange, California 92668

Medical Technologist Program
Huntington Memorial Hospital
100 Congress Street
Pasadena, California 91105

Medical Technologist Program
Eisenhower Medical Center
39000 Bob Hope Drive
Rancho Mirage, California 92270

Medical Technologist Program
U of California Davis Medical Center
2315 Stockton Boulevard
Sacramento, California 95817

Medical Technologist Program
San Bernardino County Medical Center
780 East Gilbert Street
San Bernardino, California 92404

Medical Technologist Program
Sharp Memorial Hospital
7901 Frost Street
San Diego, California 92123

Medical Technologist Program
California Pacific Medical Center
3700 California Street
San Francisco, California 94118

Medical Technologist Program
San Francisco State University
Center for Advanced Med Tech
San Francisco, California 94132

Medical Technologist Program
San Jose Medical Center
675 East Santa Clara Street
San Jose, California 95112

Medical Technologist Program
Santa Clara Valley Medical Center
751 South Bascom Avenue
San Jose, California 95128

Medical Technologist Program
Santa Barbara Cottage Hospital
P.O. Box 689
Pueblo at Bath Streets
Santa Barbara, California 93102

Medical Technologist Program
St. John's Hospital & Health Center
1328 Twenty Second Street
Santa Monica, California 90404

Medical Technologist Program
Sepulveda VA Medical Center
16111 Plummer Street
Sepulveda, California 91343

Medical Technologist Program
LA County Harbor UCLA Medical
   Center
1000 West Carson Street
Box 22
Torrance, California 90509

COLORADO

Medical Technologist Program
Penrose Hospitals
2215 North Cascade Avenue
P.O. Box 7021
Colorado Springs, Colorado 80933

Medical Technologist Program
Presbyterian/St. Luke Center for Health
  Science Education
1955 Pennsylvania
Denver, Colorado 80203

Medical Technologist Program
University of Colorado Health Science
  Center
4200 East Ninth Avenue
Denver, Colorado 80262

Medical Technologist Program
North Colorado Medical Center
1801 16th Street
Greeley, Colorado 80631

Medical Technologist Program
Parkview Episcopal Medical Center
400 West 16th Street
Pueblo, Colorado 81003

CONNECTICUT

Medical Technologist Program
Bridgeport Hospital
267 Grant Street
Bridgeport, Connecticut 06602

Medical Technologist Program
St. Vincent's Medical Center
2800 Main Street
Bridgeport, Connecticut 06606

Medical Technologist Program
Danbury Hospital
24 Hospital Avenue
Danbury, Connecticut 06810

Medical Technologist Program
Quinnipiac College
Mt. Carmel Avenue
Hamden, Connecticut 06518

Medical Technologist Program
Hartford Hospital
School of Allied Health
80 Seymour Street
Hartford, Connecticut 06115

Medical Technologist Program
St. Mary's Hospital
56 Franklin Street
Waterbury, Connecticut 06702

Medical Technologist Program
Waterbury Hospital Health Center
64 Robbins Street
Waterbury, Connecticut 06721

Medical Technologist Program
University of Hartford
200 Bloomfield Avenue
West Hartford, Connecticut 06117-1599

Medical Technologist Program
University of Delaware
Newark, Delaware 19716

DISTRICT OF COLUMBIA

Medical Technologist Program
Catholic University of America
620 Michigan Avenue NE
Washington, DC 20064

Medical Technologist Program
George Washington University Medical
  Center
901 23rd Street NW
Washington, DC 20037

Medical Technologist Program
Howard University
Sixth & Bryant Streets NW
Washington, DC 20059

Medical Technologist Program
Walter Reed Army Medical Center
Clinical Lab Officer Course
6825 16th Street NW
Washington, DC 20307-5001

Medical Technologist Program
Washington Hospital Center
110 Irving Street NW
Washington, DC 20010

FLORIDA

Medical Technologist Program
Florida Atlantic University
NW 20th Street
Boca Raton, Florida 33431

Medical Technologist Program
Bethune-Cookman College
640 Second Avenue
Daytona Beach, Florida 32115

Medical Technologist Program
University of Florida
Health Science Center
Box J-194
Gainesville, Florida 32610

Medical Technologist Program
Baptist Medical Center
800 Prudential Drive
Jacksonville, Florida 32207

Medical Technologist Program
St. Vincent's Medical Center
1800 Barrs Street
P.O. Box 2982
Jacksonville, Florida 32203

Medical Technologist Program
University Medical Center
655 West Eighth Street
Jacksonville, Florida 32209

Medical Technologist Program
Florida International University
University Park Campus
Miami, Florida 33199

Medical Technologist Program
Mt. Sinai Medical Center of Greater
 Miami
4300 Alton Road
Miami Beach, Florida 33140

Medical Technologist Program
Florida Hospital Medical Center
601 East Rollins
Orlando, Florida 32803

Medical Technologist Program
University of Central Florida
P.O. Box 25000
Orlando, Florida 32816

Medical Technologist Program
University of West Florida
Dept of Nursing and Medical
 Technology
11000 University Parkway
Pensacola, Florida 32514-5751

Medical Technologist Program
Bayfront Medical Center
701 Sixth Street South
St. Petersburg, Florida 33701

Medical Technologist Program
Tallahassee Memorial Regional Med
 Center
Magnolia & Miccousukee Roads
Tallahassee, Florida 32308

Medical Technologist Program
Tampa General Hospital
P.O. Box 1289
Tampa, Florida 33601

GEORGIA

Medical Technologist Program
Crawford Long Hospital of Emory
  University
550 Peachtree Street NE
Atlanta, Georgia 30365

Medical Technologist Program
Emory University Hospital
1364 Clifton Road NE
Atlanta, Georgia 30322

Medical Technologist Program
Georgia Baptist Medical Center
300 Boulevard NE
Atlanta, Georgia 30312

Medical Technologist Program
Georgia State University
University Plaza
Atlanta, Georgia 30303-3090

Medical Technologist Program
Grady Memorial Hospital
80 Butler Street SE
Atlanta, Georgia 30335-3801

Medical Technologist Program
Medical College of Georgia
Augusta, Georgia 30912-1650

Medical Technologist Program
Columbus College
Algonquin Drive
Columbus, Georgia 31993-2399

Medical Technologist Program
Armstrong State College
11935 Abercorn Street
Savannah, Georgia 31419-1997

HAWAII

Medical Technologist Program
University of Hawaii at Manoa
2538 The Mall
Honolulu, Hawaii 96822

IDAHO

Medical Technologist Program
St. Alphonsus Regional Medical Center
1055 North Curtis Road
Boise, Idaho 83706

ILLINOIS

Medical Technologist Program
St. Elizabeth Hospital
211 South Third Street
Belleville, Illinois 62222

Medical Technologist Program
Louis A. Weiss Memorial Hospital
4646 North Marine Drive
Chicago, Illinois 60640

Medical Technologist Program
Rush Presbyterian St. Luke's Medical
  Center
1753 West Congress Parkway
Chicago, Illinois 60612

Medical Technologist Program
University of Illinois at Chicago
P.O. Box 6998
Chicago, Illinois 60680

Medical Technologist Program
Decatur Memorial Hospital
2300 North Edward Street
Decatur, Illinois 62526

Medical Technologist Program
National-Louis University
2840 Sheridan Road
Evanston, Illinois 60201

Medical Technologist Program
Edward Hines Jr., VA Hospital
Fifth Avenue & Roosevelt Road
Hines, Illinois 60141

Medical Technologist Program
Hinsdale Hospital
120 North Oak Street
Hinsdale, Illinois 60521

Medical Technologist Program
Foster G. McGaw Hospital of Loyola
    University
2160 South First Avenue
Maywood, Illinois 60153

Medical Technologist Program
U of Health Science/Chicago Medical
    School
3333 Greenbay Road
North Chicago, Illinois 60064

Medical Technologist Program
Christ Hospital
4440 West 95th Street
Oak Lawn, Illinois 60453

Medical Technologist Program
Methodist Medical Center of Illinois
221 NE Glen Oak Avenue
Peoria, Illinois 61636

Medical Technologist Program
St. Francis Medical Center
530 NE Glen Oak Avenue
Peoria, Illinois 61637

Medical Technologist Program
Rockford Memorial Hospital
2400 North Rockton Avenue
Rockford, Illinois 61103

Medical Technologist Program
St. Anthony Medical Center
Medical Technologist Program
5666 East State Street
Rockford, Illinois 61108

Medical Technologist Program
Swedish American Hospital
1400 Charles Street
Rockford, Illinois 61104

Medical Technologist Program
Sangamon State University
Shepherd Road
Springfield, Illinois 62794

Medical Technologist Program
St. John's Hospital
800 East Carpenter
Springfield, Illinois 62769

Medical Technologist Program
Governors State University
Route 54 & Stuenkel Road
University Park, Illinois 60466

INDIANA

Medical Technologist Program
St. Francis Hospital Center
1600 Albany Street
Beech Grove, Indiana 46107

Medical Technologist Program
St. Mary's Medical Center
3700 Washington Avenue
Evansville, Indiana 47750

Medical Technologist Program
Lutheran Hospital of Indiana, Inc.
3024 Fairfield Avenue
Ft. Wayne, Indiana 46807

Medical Technologist Program
Parkview Memorial Hospital
2200 Randallia
Ft. Wayne, Indiana 46805

Medical Technologist Program
St. Margaret Hospital & Health Centers
5454 Hohman Avenue
Hammond, Indiana 46320

Medical Technologist Program
St. Mary Medical Center
1500 South Lake Park Avenue
Hobart, Indiana 46342

Medical Technologist Program
Indiana University School of Medicine
1120 S Drive
Indianapolis, Indiana 46202-5113

Medical Technologist Program
Methodist Hospital of Indiana
1701 North Senate Boulevard
P.O. Box 1367
Indianapolis, Indiana 46206

Medical Technologist Program
St. Vincent Hospital & Health Care
  Center, Inc.
2001 West 86th Street
Indianapolis, Indiana 46264

Medical Technologist Program
St. Joseph Hospital & Health Center
1907 West Sycamore Street
Kokomo, Indiana 46901

Medical Technologist Program
Ball Memorial Hospital
2401 University Avenue
Muncie, Indiana 47303

Medical Technologist Program
Indiana State University
217 North Sixth Street
Terre Haute, Indiana 47809

Medical Technologist Program
Good Samaritan Hospital
520 South Seventh Street
Vincennes, Indiana 47591

IOWA

Medical Technologist Program
St. Luke's Hospital
1026 "A" Avenue NE
Cedar Rapids, Iowa 52402

Medical Technologist Program
Iowa Methodist Medical Center
1200 Pleasant Street
Des Moines, Iowa 50309

Medical Technologist Program
Mercy Hospital Medical Center
Mercy Ct., 921 Sixth Avenue
Des Moines, Iowa 50314

Medical Technologist Program
University of Iowa
U IA Hosps & Clins-Pathology
150A Medical Laboratories
Iowa City, Iowa 52242

Medical Technologist Program
Marian Health Center
801 Fifth Street
Sioux City, Iowa 51101

Medical Technologist Program
St. Luke's Medical Center
2720 Stone Park Boulevard
Sioux City, Iowa 51104

Medical Technologist Program
Covenant Medical Center
3421 West Ninth Street
Waterloo, Iowa 50702

KANSAS

Medical Technologist Program
University of Kansas Medical Center
39th Street & Rainbow Boulevard
Kansas City, Kansas 66103

Medical Technologist Program
Topeka School of Medical Technology
1915 SW Sixth Street
Topeka, Kansas 66606

Medical Technologist Program
Wichita State University
Dept of Clinical Sciences
Campus Box 43
Wichita, Kansas 67208

KENTUCKY

Medical Technologist Program
St. Elizabeth Medical Center
One Medical Village Drive
Edgewood, Kentucky 41017

Medical Technologist Program
University of Kentucky
Division of Clinical Lab Sciences
Lexington, Kentucky 40536-0080

Medical Technologist Program
University of Louisville
Health Sciences Center
Louisville, Kentucky 40292

Medical Technologist Program
Owensboro Davies County Hospital
811 East Parrish Avenue
P.O. Box 2799
Owensboro, Kentucky 42302

Medical Technologist Program
Lourdes Hospital
1530 Lone Oak Road
Paducah, Kentucky 42001

Medical Technologist Program
Methodist Hospital of Kentucky
911 South ByPass
Pikeville, Kentucky 41501

Medical Technologist Program
Eastern Kentucky University
Richmond, Kentucky 40475

LOUISIANA

Medical Technologist Program
Rapides Regional Medical Center
211 Fourth Street
P.O. Box 30101
Alexandria, Louisiana 71301

Medical Technologist Program
Our Lady of the Lake Regional Medical
  Center
5000 Hennessy Boulevard
Baton Rouge, Louisiana 70808

Medical Technologist Program
University Medical Center
2390 West Congress
P.O. Box 4016-C
Lafayette, Louisiana 70502

Medical Technologist Program
Lake Charles Memorial Hospital School
  of MT
1701 Oak Park Boulevard
Lake Charles, Louisiana 70601

Medical Technologist Program
St. Patrick Hospital
524 South Ryan Street
P.O. Box 3401
Lake Charles, Louisiana 70602-3401

Medical Technologist Program
St. Francis Medical Center
309 Jackson Street
Monroe, Louisiana 71201

Medical Technologist Program
Alton Ochsner Medical Foundation
1516 Jefferson Highway
New Orleans, Louisiana 70121

Medical Technologist Program
Louisiana State U Medical Center
1900 Gravier Street
New Orleans, Louisiana 70112

Medical Technologist Program
Touro Infirmary School of Med Tech
1401 Foucher Street
New Orleans, Louisiana 70115

Medical Technologist Program
Overton Brooks VA Medical Center
510 East Stoner Avenue
Shreveport, Louisiana 71101-4295

Medical Technologist Program
Schumpert Medical Center
P.O. Box 21976
Shreveport, Louisiana 71120-1976

MAINE

Medical Technologist Program
Eastern Maine Medical Center
489 State Street
Bangor, Maine 04401

Medical Technologist Program
Maine Medical Center
22 Bramhall Street
Portland, Maine 04102-3175

MARYLAND

Medical Technologist Program
Morgan State University
Coldspring Land & Hillen Road
Baltimore, Maryland 21239

Medical Technologist Program
University of Maryland School of
  Medicine
32 South Green Street
Baltimore, Maryland 21201

Medical Technologist Program
Oscar B. Hunter Memorial Laboratory
8218 Wisconsin Avenue
Bethesda, Maryland 20814

Medical Technologist Program
Malcolm Grow USAF Medical Center
Andrews AFB, DC
Camp Springs, Maryland 20331-5300

Medical Technologist Program
Salisbury State University
Camden Avenue
Salisbury, Maryland 21801

Medical Technologist Program
Columbia Union College
7600 Flower Avenue
Takoma Park, Maryland 20912

MASSACHUSETTS

Medical Technologist Program
New England Deaconess Hospital
185 Pilgrim
Boston, Massachusetts 02215

Medical Technologist Program
Northeastern University
360 Huntington Avenue
Boston, Massachusetts 02215

Medical Technologist Program
Veterans Administration Medical Center
150 South Huntington Avenue
Boston, Massachusetts 02130

Medical Technologist Program
Cambridge Hospital
1493 Cambridge Street
Cambridge, Massachusetts 02139

Medical Technologist Program
Fitchburg State College
160 Pearl Street
Fitchburg, Massachusetts 01420

Medical Technologist Program
Lawrence General Hospital
One General Street
Lawrence, Massachusetts 01842

Medical Technologist Program
University of Lowell
One University Avenue
Lowell, Massachusetts 01854

Medical Technologist Program
University of Massachusetts Dartmouth
Dept of Med Lab Science
Old Westport Road
North Dartmouth, Massachusetts 02747

Medical Technologist Program
Newton Wellesley Hospital
2014 Washington Street
Newton Lower Falls, Massachusetts
  02162

Medical Technologist Program
Berkshire Medical Center
725 North Street
Pittsfield, Massachusetts 01201

Medical Technologist Program
Baystate Medical Center
759 Chestnut Street
Springfield, Massachusetts 01199

Medical Technologist Program
Life Laboratories
299 Carew Street
Springfield, Massachusetts 01104

MICHIGAN

Medical Technologist Program
Andrews University
Berrien Springs, Michigan 49104

Medical Technologist Program
Ferris State University
S State Street
Big Rapids, Michigan 49307

Medical Technologist Program
Damon Clinical Labs at Detroit Med
  Center
4201 St. Antoine
Detroit, Michigan 48201

Medical Technologist Program
St. John Hospital and Medical Center
22101 Moross Road
Detroit, Michigan 48236

Medical Technologist Program
Wayne State University
Detroit, Michigan 48202

Medical Technologist Program
Michigan State University
East Lansing, Michigan 48825

Medical Technologist Program
Hurley Medical Center
Number One Hurley Plaza
Flint, Michigan 48502

Medical Technologist Program
St. Joseph Hospital
302 Kensington Avenue
Flint, Michigan 48503-2000

Medical Technologist Program
Garden City Hospital, Osteopathic
6245 North Inkster Road
Garden City, Michigan 48135

Medical Technologist Program
Butterworth Hospital
100 Michigan Street NE
Grand Rapids, Michigan 49503

Medical Technologist Program
W.A. Foote Memorial Hospital
205 N. East Avenue
Jackson, Michigan 49201

Medical Technologist Program
Northern Michigan University
Learning Resources Building
Marquette, Michigan 49855-5346

Medical Technologist Program
Pontiac General Hospital
Dept of Laboratories
Pontiac, Michigan 48053

Medical Technologist Program
William Beaumont Hospital
3601 West 13 Mile Road
Royal Oak, Michigan 48073-6769

Medical Technologist Program
St. Mary's Medical Center
830 South Jefferson Avenue
Saginaw, Michigan 48601

221

Medical Technologist Program
Providence Hospital
School of Medical Technology
16001 West 9 Mile Road
P.O. Box 2043
Southfield, Michigan 48037

Medical Technologist Program
Munson Medical Center
1105 Sixth Street
Traverse City, Michigan 49684

Medical Technologist Program
Eastern Michigan University
Ypsilanti, Michigan 48197

MINNESOTA

Medical Technologist Program
College of St. Scholastica
Clinical Laboratory Science Dept.
1200 Kenwood Avenue
Duluth, Minnesota 55811

Medical Technologist Program
Hennepin County Medical Center
701 Park Avenue South
Minneapolis, Minnesota 55415

Medical Technologist Program
U of Minnesota Health Science Center
420 Delaware Street SE
Box 198
Minneapolis, Minnesota 55455

Medical Technologist Program
St. Cloud Hospital
1406 Sixth Avenue North
St. Cloud, Minnesota 56303

Medical Technologist Program
St. Paul Ramsey Medical Center
640 Jackson Street
St. Paul, Minnesota 55101

Medical Technologist Program
United Hospital
333 North Smith Avenue
St. Paul, Minnesota 55102

MISSISSIPPI

Medical Technologist Program
University of Southern Mississippi
Southern Station
P.O. Box 5134
Hattiesburg, Mississippi 39406

Medical Technologist Program
William Carey College
Tuscan Avenue
Hattiesburg, Mississippi 39401-9913

Medical Technologist Program
Mississippi Baptist Medical Center
1225 North State Street
Jackson, Mississippi 39202

Medical Technologist Program
University of Mississippi Medical Center
2500 North State Street
Jackson, Mississippi 39216

Medical Technologist Program
North Mississippi Medical Center
830 South Gloster
Tupelo, Mississippi 38801

MISSOURI

Medical Technologist Program
St. John's Regional Medical Center
2727 McClelland Boulevard
Joplin, Missouri 64804-7170

Medical Technologist Program
Avila College
11901 Wornall Road
Kansas City, Missouri 64145

Medical Technologist Program
Menorah Medical Center
4949 Rockhill Road
Kansas City, Missouri 64110

Medical Technologist Program
Research Medical Center
2316 East Meyer Boulevard
Kansas City, Missouri 64132

Medical Technologist Program
St. Luke's Hospital of Kansas City
4400 Wornall Road
Kansas City, Missouri 64111

Medical Technologist Program
Trinity Lutheran Hospital
31st & Wyandotte Streets
Kansas City, Missouri 64108

Medical Technologist Program
North Kansas City Hospital
2800 Clay Edwards Drive
North Kansas City, Missouri 64116

Medical Technologist Program
Cox Medical Centers
3801 South National Avenue
Springfield, Missouri 65807

Medical Technologist Program
St. John's Regional Health Center
1235 East Cherokee
Springfield, Missouri 65804

Medical Technologist Program
Jewish Hospital of St. Louis
216 South Kingshighway Boulevard
St. Louis, Missouri 63110

Medical Technologist Program
St. John's Mercy Medical Center
615 South New Ballas Road
St. Louis, Missouri 63141

Medical Technologist Program
St. Louis University
1504 South Grand Boulevard
St. Louis, Missouri 63104

MONTANA

Medical Technologist Program
St. James Community Hospital
400 South Clark Street
Butte, Montana 59701

Medical Technologist Program
Columbus Hospital
500 15th Avenue South
Great Falls, Montana 59403

NEBRASKA

Medical Technologist Program
Bishop Clarkson Memorial Hospital
44th & Dewey Avenue
Omaha, Nebraska 68105

Medical Technologist Program
Nebraska Methodist Hospital
8303 Dodge Street
Omaha, Nebraska 68114

Medical Technologist Program
University of Nebraska Medical Center
600 South 42nd Street
Omaha, Nebraska 68198-3135

NEVADA

Medical Technologist Program
University of Nevada-Reno
Reno, Nevada 89557

NEW HAMPSHIRE

Medical Technologist Program
University of New Hampshire
Durham, New Hampshire 03824

NEW JERSEY

Medical Technologist Program
Cooper Hospital/University Medical
  Center
One Cooper Plaza
Camden, New Jersey 08103

Medical Technologist Program
Mountainside Hospital
Bay & Highland Avenues
Glen Ridge/Montclair, New Jersey
  07042-4898

Medical Technologist Program
Monmouth Medical Center
One Centennial Way
Long Branch, New Jersey 07740

Medical Technologist Program
Morristown Memorial Hospital
100 Madison Avenue
Morristown, New Jersey 07960

Medical Technologist Program
Jersey Shore Medical Center
1945 Corlies Avenue
Neptune, New Jersey 07753

Medical Technologist Program
St. Peter's Medical Center
254 Easton Avenue
New Brunswick, New Jersey 08903

Medical Technologist Program
U of Medicine & Dentistry of New
  Jersey
School of Health Related Professions
65 Bergen street
Newark, New Jersey 07107-3006

Medical Technologist Program
St. Joseph's Hospital Medical Center
703 Main Street
Paterson, New Jersey 07503

Medical Technologist Program
Valley Hospital
223 North Van Dien Avenue
Ridgewood, New Jersey 07450

Medical Technologist Program
Somerset Medical Center
Rehill Avenue
Somerville, New Jersey 08876

NEW MEXICO

Medical Technologist Program
U of New Mexico School of Medicine
Health Sciences & Svc Building
Albuquerque, New Mexico 87131

Medical Technologist Program
Memorial Medical Center
2450 Telshor Boulevard
Las Cruces, New Mexico 88001

NEW YORK

Medical Technologist Program
Albany Medical Center Hospital
New Scotland Avenue
Albany, New York 12208

Medical Technologist Program
College of St. Rose
432 Western Avenue
Albany, New York 12203

Medical Technologist Program
Daemen College
4380 Main Street
Amherst, New York 14226

Medical Technologist Program
Methodist Hospital of Brooklyn
506 Sixth Street
Brooklyn, New York 11215

Medical Technologist Program
Long Island University
C.W. Post Campus
Northern Boulevard
Brookville, New York 11548

Medical Technologist Program
Millard Fillmore Hospital
Three Gates Circle
Buffalo, New York 14209

Medical Technologist Program
SUNY at Buffalo
462 Grider Street
Buffalo, New York 14215

Medical Technologist Program
Women's Christian Association Hospital
207 Foote Avenue
Jamestown, New York 14701-7077

Medical Technologist Program
Northern Westchester Hospital Center
East Main Street
Mt. Kisco, New York 10549

Medical Technologist Program
St. Vincent's Hospital & Med Ctr of
  New York
153 West 11th Street
New York, New York 10011

Medical Technologist Program
New York Institute of Technology
Wheatley Road
Old Westbury, New York 11568

Medical Technologist Program
Marist College
North Road
Poughkeepsie, New York 12601

Medical Technologist Program
Rochester General Hospital
1425 Portland Avenue
Rochester, New York 14621

Medical Technologist Program
St. Mary's Hospital
89 Genesee Street
Rochester, New York 14611

Medical Technologist Program
SUNY Health Science Ctr at Stony
  Brook
Allied Health
Stony Brook, New York 11794

Medical Technologist Program
SUNY Health Science Center at
  Syracuse
750 Adams Street
Syracuse, New York 13210

Medical Technologist Program
Utica College of Syracuse University
1600 Burrstone Road
Utica, New York 13502

Medical Technologist Program
Catholic Medical Center
88-15 Woodhaven Avenue
Woodhaven, New York 11421

NORTH CAROLINA

Medical Technologist Program
University of North Carolina
Medical Allied Health Profs
Chapel Hill, North Carolina 27599-7145

Medical Technologist Program
Carolinas Medical Center
P.O. Box 32861
Charlotte, North Carolina 28232

Medical Technologist Program
Presbyterian Hospital
200 Hawthorne Land
P.O. Box 33549
Charlotte, North Carolina 28233-3549

Medical Technologist Program
Western Carolina University
Clinical Laboratory Sciences Program
Cullowhee, North Carolina 28723

Medical Technologist Program
Duke University Medical Center
Box 2929
Hospital Labs
Durham, North Carolina 27710

Medical Technologist Program
Moses H. Cone Memorial Hospital
1200 North Elm Street
Greensboro, North Carolina 27401

Medical Technologist Program
East Carolina University
Dept Clinical Lab Science
School of Allied Health Sciences
Greenville, North Carolina 27858

Medical Technologist Program
New Hanover Memorial Hospital
2131 South 17th Street
P.O. Box 9000
Wilmington, North Carolina 28402-7407

Medical Technologist Program
Bowman Gray School of Medicine
Medical Center Boulevard
Winston-Salem, North Carolina 27157

Medical Technologist Program
Forsyth Memorial Hospital
3333 Silas Creek Parkway
Winston-Salem, North Carolina 27103

Medical Technologist Program
Winston-Salem State University
P O. Box 13156
Winston-Salem, North Carolina 27110

NORTH DAKOTA

Medical Technologist Program
St. Alexius Medical Center
900 East Broadway
P.O. Box 1658
Bismarck, North Dakota 58501

Medical Technologist Program
Fargo Clinic/St. Lukes Hospital
  Meritcare
737 Broadway
P.O. Box 2067
Fargo, North Dakota 58123

Medical Technologist Program
University of North Dakota
Department of Pathology
Grand Forks, North Dakota 58201

Medical Technologist Program
St. Joseph's Hospital
Third Street SE & Burdick Expressway
Minot, North Dakota 58701

Medical Technologist Program
Trinity Medical Center
Main Street & Burdick Expressway
Minot, North Dakota 58701

OHIO

Medical Technologist Program
Children's Hospital Medical Center of
  Akron
281 Locust Street
Akron, Ohio 44308

Medical Technologist Program
St. Thomas Medical Center
444 North Main Street
Akron, Ohio 44310

Medical Technologist Program
Bowling Green State University
Bowling Green, Ohio 43403

Medical Technologist Program
Christ Hospital
2139 Auburn Avenue
Cincinnati, Ohio 45219

Medical Technologist Program
University of Cincinnati Medical Center
231 Bethesda Avenue
Cincinnati, Ohio 45267

Medical Technologist Program
Cleveland Clinic Foundation
One Clinic Center
9500 Euclid Avenue
Cleveland, Ohio 44195-5130

Medical Technologist Program
MetroHealth Medical Center
3395 Scranton Road
Cleveland, Ohio 44109

Medical Technologist Program
University Hospitals of Cleveland
2074 Abington Road
Cleveland, Ohio 44106

Medical Technologist Program
Ohio State University
1583 Perry Street
Columbus, Ohio 43210

Medical Technologist Program
University of Dayton
300 College Park
Dayton, Ohio 45469

Medical Technologist Program
Wright State University
Dayton, Ohio 45435

Medical Technologist Program
Southwest General Hospital
18697 East Bagley Road
Middleburg Heights, Ohio 44130

Medical Technologist Program
St. Charles Hospital
2600 Navarre Avenue
Oregon, Ohio 43616-3297

Medical Technologist Program
Ohio Valley Hospital
One Ross Park Boulevard
Steubenville, Ohio 43952

Medical Technologist Program
Mercy Hospital
2200 Jefferson Avenue
Toledo, Ohio 43624

Medical Technologist Program
Riverside Hospital
1600 North Superior Street
Toledo, Ohio 43604

Medical Technologist Program
Trumbull Memorial Hospital
1350 East Market Street
Warren, Ohio 44482

Medical Technologist Program
St. Elizabeth Hospital Medical Center
1044 Belmont Avenue
Youngstown, Ohio 44501-1790

Medical Technologist Program
Western Reserve Care System
500 Gypsy Lane
Youngstown, Ohio 44501

OKLAHOMA

Medical Technologist Program
Valley View Regional Hospital
430 North Monte Vista
Ada, Oklahoma 74820

Medical Technologist Program
St. Mary's Hospital
305 South Fifth Street
Enid, Oklahoma 73702-0232

Medical Technologist Program
Comanche County Memorial Hospital
P.O. Box 129
Lawton, Oklahoma 73502

Medical Technologist Program
Muskogee Regional Medical Center
300 Rockefeller Drive
Muskogee, Oklahoma 74401

Medical Technologist Program
Mercy Health Center
4300 West Memorial Road
Oklahoma City, Oklahoma 73120

Medical Technologist Program
St. Anthony Hospital
1000 North Lee Street
P.O. Box 205
Oklahoma City, Oklahoma 73101

Medical Technologist Program
University of Oklahoma at Oklahoma
  City
P.O. Box 26901
Oklahoma City, Oklahoma 73190

Medical Technologist Program
St. Francis Hospital
6161 South Yale Avenue
Tulsa, Oklahoma 74136

OREGON

Medical Technologist Program
Oregon Institute of Technology
Clinical Laboratory Sciences
3201 Campus Drive
Klamath Falls, Oregon 97601-8801

Medical Technologist Program
Oregon Health Sciences University
3181 SW Sam Jackson Park
Portland, Oregon 97201

PENNSYLVANIA

Medical Technologist Program
Abington Memorial Hospital
1200 Old York Road
Abington, Pennsylvania 19001

Medical Technologist Program
Sacred Heart Hospital
421 Chew Street
Allentown, Pennsylvania 18201

Medical Technologist Program
Altoona Hospital
620 Howard Avenue
Altoona, Pennsylvania 16601-4899

Medical Technologist Program
Neumann College
Convent Road
Aston, Pennsylvania 19014

Medical Technologist Program
The Bryn Mawr Hospital
130 South Bryn Mawr Avenue
Bryn Mawr, Pennsylvania 19010

Medical Technologist Program
Geisinger Medical Center
North Academy Avenue
Danville, Pennsylvania 17822

Medical Technologist Program
Rolling Hill Hospital
60 East Township Line Road
Elkins Park, Pennsylvania 19117

Medical Technologist Program
St. Vincent Health Center
232 West 25th Street
Erie, Pennsylvania 16544

Medical Technologist Program
Harrisburg Hospital
South Front Street
Harrisburg, Pennsylvania 17101

Medical Technologist Program
Polyclinic Medical Center
2601 North Third Street
Harrisburg, Pennsylvania 17110

Medical Technologist Program
Conemaugh Valley Memorial Hospital
1086 Franklin Street
Johnstown, Pennsylvania 15905-4398

Medical Technologist Program
Lancaster General Hospital
555 North Duke Street
Lancaster, Pennsylvania 17603

Medical Technologist Program
Latrobe Area Hospital
West Second Avenue
Latrobe, Pennsylvania 15650

Medical Technologist Program
Hahnemann University
Broad & Vine Streets
Philadelphia, Pennsylvania 19102

Medical Technologist Program
Lankenau Hospital
Lancaster & City Line Avenue
Philadelphia, Pennsylvania 19151

Medical Technologist Program
Nazareth Hospital
2601 Holme Avenue
Philadelphia, Pennsylvania 19152

Medical Technologist Program
Pennsylvania Hospital
Eighth & Spruce Streets
Philadelphia, Pennsylvania 19107

Medical Technologist Program
Thomas Jefferson University
130 South North Street
Philadelphia, Pennsylvania 19107

Medical Technologist Program
Allegheny General Hospital
320 East North Avenue
Pittsburgh, Pennsylvania 15212-9986

Medical Technologist Program
University of Pittsburgh
Department of Medical Technology
Pittsburgh, Pennsylvania 15261

Medical Technologist Program
Western Pennsylvania Hospital
4900 Friendship Avenue
Pittsburgh, Pennsylvania 15224

Medical Technologist Program
Reading Hospital and Medical Center
P.O. Box 16052
Reading, Pennsylvania 19612-6052

Medical Technologist Program
St. Joseph Hospital
12th & Walnut Street
P.O. Box 316
Reading, Pennsylvania 19603

Medical Technologist Program
Robert Packer Hospital
Guthrie Square
Sayre, Pennsylvania 18840

Medical Technologist Program
Scranton Medical Technology
  Consortium
700 Quincy Avenue
Scranton, Pennsylvania 18510

Medical Technologist Program
Washington Hospital
155 Wilson Avenue
Washington, Pennsylvania 15301

Medical Technologist Program
Chester County Hospital
701 East Marshall Street
West Chester, Pennsylvania 19380

Medical Technologist Program
Wilkes Barre General Hospital
North River & Auburn Streets
Wilkes-Barre, Pennsylvania 18764

Medical Technologist Program
Divine Providence Hospital
1100 Grampian Boulevard
Williamsport, Pennsylvania 17701

Medical Technologist Program
York Hospital
1001 South George Street
York, Pennsylvania 17405

PUERTO RICO

Medical Technologist Program
Interamerican University-Metro Campus
P.O. Box 1293
Hato Rey, Puerto Rico 00919-1293

Medical Technologist Program
Catholic University of Puerto Rico
P.O. Station No. 6
Ponce, Puerto Rico 00732

Medical Technologist Program
Interamerican University-San German
Call Box 5100
San German, Puerto Rico 00753

Medical Technologist Program
University of Puerto Rico
P.O. Box 365067
San Juan, Puerto Rico 00936-5067

Medical Technologist Program
University of the Sacred Heart
P.O. Box 1283
Loiza Station
Santurce, Puerto Rico 00914

RHODE ISLAND

Medical Technologist Program
General Hospital, Rhode Island Med Ctr
P.O. Box 8269
Cranston, Rhode Island 02920

Medical Technologist Program
St. Joseph Hospital OLF Unit
200 High Service Avenue
North Providence, Rhode Island 02904

Medical Technologist Program
Memorial Hospital of Rhode Island
111 West Brewster Street
Pawtucket, Rhode Island 02860

Medical Technologist Program
Rhode Island Hospital
593 Eddy Street
Providence, Rhode Island 02902

SOUTH CAROLINA

Medical Technologist Program
Anderson Memorial Hospital
800 North Fant Street
Anderson, South Carolina 29621

Medical Technologist Program
Medical University of South Carolina
Coll Hlth Related Prof-Med Lab Sci
 Dept
171 Ashley Avenue
Charleston, South Carolina 29425

Medical Technologist Program
Baptist Medical Center at Columbia
Taylor at Marion
Columbia, South Carolina 29220

Medical Technologist Program
McLeod Regional Medical Center
555 East Cheves Street
Florence, South Carolina 29501

SOUTH DAKOTA

Medical Technologist Program
St. Luke's Midland Regional Medical
  Center
305 South State Street
Aberdeen, South Dakota 57401

Medical Technologist Program
Rapid City Regional Hospital
353 Fairmont Boulevard
Rapid City, South Dakota 57701

Medical Technologist Program
Sioux Valley Hospital
1100 South Euclid Avenue
Sioux Falls, South Dakota 57117-5039

TENNESSEE

Medical Technologist Program
Austin Peay State University
Clarksville, Tennessee 37044

Medical Technologist Program
Lincoln Memorial University
Harrogate, Tennessee 37752-0901

Medical Technologist Program
Holston Valley Hospital & Med Center
West Ravine Road
Kingsport, Tennessee 37662

Medical Technologist Program
U of Tennessee Medical Ctr at
  Knoxville
1924 Alcoa Highway
Knoxville, Tennessee 37920

Medical Technologist Program
St. Francis Hospital
5959 Park Avenue
Memphis, Tennessee 38119-5150

Medical Technologist Program
University of Tennessee Memphis
822 Beale Avenue
Memphis, Tennessee 38163

Medical Technologist Program
St. Thomas Hospital
4220 Harding
P.O. Box 380
Nashville, Tennessee 37202

Medical Technologist Program
Tennessee State University
Tenn State U-Meharry Med Coll
3500 John A. Merritt Boulevard
Nashville, Tennessee 37203

Medical Technologist Program
Vanderbilt University Medical Center
4605D The Vanderbilt Clinic
21st Avenue South
Nashville, Tennessee 37232-5310

TEXAS

Medical Technologist Program
Hendrick Medical Center
1242 North 19th
Abilene, Texas 79601-2316

Medical Technologist Program
Amarillo Affiliated School of Med Tech
P.O. Box 1110
Amarillo, Texas 79175

Medical Technologist Program
Austin State Hospital
4110 Guadalupe Street
Austin, Texas 78751

Medical Technologist Program
St. Elizabeth Hospital
2830 Calder Street
P.O. Box 5405
Beaumont, Texas 77726-5405

Medical Technologist Program
Robert L. Thompson Strategic Hospital
School of Med Tech
Carswell AFB, Texas 76127-5300

231

Medical Technologist Program
Corpus Christi State University
6300 Ocean Drive
Corpus Christi, Texas 78412

Medical Technologist Program
U of TX Southwestern Med Ctr at
  Dallas
5323 Harry Hines Boulevard
Dallas, Texas 75235-8878

Medical Technologist Program
Univ of Texas-Pan American
1201 West University Drive
Edinburg, Texas 78539

Medical Technologist Program
University of Texas at El Paso
1101 North Campbell
El Paso, Texas 79968

Medical Technologist Program
Harris Methodist Fort Worth
1301 Pennsylvania
Ft. Worth, Texas 76104

Medical Technologist Program
Tarleton State University
1625 West Myrtle Street
Ft. Worth, Texas 76104

Medical Technologist Program
University of Texas Medical Branch
School of Allied Health Scis
Galveston, Texas 77550

Medical Technologist Program
Harris County Hosp Dist/Ben Taub Hosp
1502 Taub Loop
Houston, Texas 77030

Medical Technologist Program
Methodist Hospital
6565 Fannin Mail St 205
Houston, Texas 77030

Medical Technologist Program
Texas Southern University
3100 Cleburne
Houston, Texas 77004

Medical Technologist Program
U of Texas Hlth Sciences Ctr at Houston
P.O. Box 20708
Houston, Texas 77225

Medical Technologist Program
Texas Tech U Health Sciences Center
School of Allied Hlth
Lubbock, Texas 79430

Medical Technologist Program
Midland Memorial Hospital
2200 West Illinois Street
Midland, Texas 79701

Medical Technologist Program
Shannon West Texas Memorial Hospital
120 East Harris
P.O. Box 1879
San Angelo, Texas 76902

Medical Technologist Program
Baptist Memorial Hospital System
111 Dallas Street
San Antonio, Texas 78286

Medical Technologist Program
U of Texas Hlth Sci Ctr at San Antonio
Dept of Clinical Laboratory Sciences
7703 Floyd Curl Drive
San Antonio, Texas 78284

Medical Technologist Program
Southwest Texas State University
Prgm in Clinical Lab Sciences
San Marcos, Texas 78666-4616

Medical Technologist Program
Scott & White Memorial Hosp and
  Clinic
2401 South 31st Street
Temple, Texas 76508

Medical Technologist Program
Wadley Regional Medical Center
1000 Pine Street
Texarkana, Texas 75501

Medical Technologist Program
University of Texas at Tyler
3900 University Boulevard
Tyler, Texas 75701

Medical Technologist Program
Wichita General Hospital
1600 Eighth Street
Wichita Falls, Texas 76301

UTAH

Medical Technologist Program
McKay Dee Hospital Center
3939 Harrison Boulevard
Ogden, Utah 84409

Medical Technologist Program
Weber State University
3750 Harrison Boulevard
Ogden, Utah 84408-3905

Medical Technologist Program
Brigham Young University
Provo, Utah 84602

Medical Technologist Program
Univ of Utah Health Sciences Center
Department of Pathology
15 North Medical Drive
Salt Lake City, Utah 84132

VERMONT

Medical Technologist Program
University of Vermont
Burlington, Vermont 05405

VIRGINIA

Medical Technologist Program
University of Virginia Health Sci Center
Box 268-Medical Center
Charlottesville, Virginia 22908

Medical Technologist Program
Memorial Hospital
142 South Main Street
Danville, Virginia 24541

Medical Technologist Program
Fairfax Hospital
3300 Gallows Road
Falls Church, Virginia 22046

Medical Technologist Program
Rockingham Memorial Hospital
235 Cantrell Avenue
Harrisonburg, Virginia 22801

Medical Technologist Program
Norfolk State University
2401 Corprew Avenue
Norfolk, Virginia 23504

Medical Technologist Program
Old Dominion University
School of Med Lab Sciences
Norfolk, Virginia 23529

Medical Technologist Program
Med Coll of VA/Virginia
 Commonwealth U
MVC Station-Box 583
Richmond, Virginia 23298

Medical Technologist Program
Carilion Health Systems
Roanoke Memorial Hospital
Belleview at Jefferson
Roanoke, Virginia 24033

Medical Technologist Program
King's Daughters' Hospital
1410 North Augusta Street
P.O. Box 3000
Staunton, Virginia 24401

WASHINGTON

Medical Technologist Program
St. John's Medical Center
1614 East Kessler Boulevard
Longview, Washington 98632

Medical Technologist Program
Children's Hospital & Medical Center
4800 Sand Pt Way NE
Seattle, Washington 98105

Medical Technologist Program
Laboratory of Pathology of Seattle
1229 Madison 500
P.O. Box 14950
Seattle, Washington 98114-0950

Medical Technologist Program
University of Washington
Dept of Lab Medicine
Seattle, Washington 98195

Medical Technologist Program
Deaconess Medical Center
800 West Fifth Avenue
Spokane, Washington 99210

Medical Technologist Program
Sacred Heart Medical Center
W 101 Eighth Avenue
Spokane, Washington 99220-4045

Medical Technologist Program
Central Washington University
1114 West Spruce
Yakima, Washington 98902

WEST VIRGINIA

Medical Technologist Program
Marshall University
Fourth Street at Hal Green Boulevard
Huntington, West Virginia 25701

Medical Technologist Program
West Virginia University
Morgantown, West Virginia 26506

Medical Technologist Program
West Liberty State College
Dept of Med Tech
West Liberty, West Virginia 26074

WISCONSIN

Medical Technologist Program
St. Elizabeth Hospital
1506 South Oneida Street
Appleton, Wisconsin 54915

Medical Technologist Program
Sacred Heart Hospital
900 West Clairemont Avenue
Eau Claire, Wisconsin 54701

Medical Technologist Program
St. Vincent Hospital
P.O. Box 13508
Green Bay, Wisconsin 54307

Medical Technologist Program
University of Wisconsin-Madison
1300 University Avenue
Madison, Wisconsin 53706

Medical Technologist Program
St. Joseph's Hospital
611 St. Joseph Avenue
Marshfield, Wisconsin 54449

Medical Technologist Program
Aurora Health Care, Inc.
Aura, Sinai Samaritan and St. Luke's
22900 West Oklahoma Avenue
Box 2901
Milwaukee, Wisconsin 53201-2901

Medical Technologist Program
Clement J. Zablocki VA Medical Center
5000 West National Avenue
Milwaukee, Wisconsin 53295

Medical Technologist Program
Milwaukee County Medical Complex
8700 West Wisconsin Avenue
Milwaukee, Wisconsin 53226

Medical Technologist Program
St. Mary's Hospital
2323 North Lake Drive
P.O. Box 503
Milwaukee, Wisconsin 53201

Medical Technologist Program
University of Wisconsin Milwaukee
School of Allied Health Professions
P.O. Box 413
Milwaukee, Wisconsin 53201

Medical Technologist Program
St. Luke's Memorial Hospital
1320 South Wisconsin Avenue
Racine, Wisconsin 53403

Medical Technologist Program
Wausau Hospital Center
333 Pine Ridge Boulevard
Wausau, Wisconsin 54401

Medical Technologist Program
Franciscan Shared Laboratory, Inc.
11020 West Plank Court, Suite 100
Wauwatosa, Wisconsin 53226

WYOMING

Medical Technologist Program
University of Wyoming
Univ Station
P.O. Box 3837
Laramie, Wyoming 82071

Medical Laboratory Technician

The *medical laboratory technician* is an intermediate-level worker on the laboratory career ladder. Requiring only a limited amount of supervision by the pathologist or the medical technologist, the medical laboratory technician does not possess the same level of knowledge as the medical technologist and performs less complicated tests. However, the technician still uses a high degree of skill and some independent judgment in carrying out a wide range of tests and procedures that provides data for diagnosis and treatment of disease.

Like the medical technologist, the technician may work in all fields of laboratory testing or specialize in one, such as immunology, hematology, cytology, and so on. The position of histologic technician is described in detail later in this section.

Medical laboratory technicians may receive training in hospitals, vocational and technical schools, community and junior colleges, in the armed forces, or through on-the-job training. Two year programs lead to an associate degree while shorter programs lead to a certificate in medical laboratory technology.

The societies that certify medical technologists also certify medical laboratory technicians and the same states require licensure to practice.

Recommended high school courses are chemistry, biology, and mathematics.

Medical laboratory technicians employed in the federal government averaged $22, 000 a year in 1991.

Following is a list of schools accredited by the American Medical Association's Committee on Allied Health Education & Accreditation that offer accredited associate degree programs for the medical laboratory technician.

KEY:

(1)   Associate Degree Programs
(2)   Certificate Programs

SOURCES:

American Society of Clinical Pathologists
Occupational Outlook Handbook

Medical Laboratory Technician Programs

ALABAMA

Medical Laboratory Technician
 Program (1)
Jefferson State Community College
2601 Carson Road
Birmingham, Alabama 35215

Medical Laboratory Technician
 Program (1)
University of Alabama at Birmingham
School of Health Related Professions
UAB Station
Birmingham, Alabama 35294

Medical Laboratory Technician
 Program (1)
G.C. Wallace State Community College
Napier Field
Dothan, Alabama 36303

Medical Laboratory Technician
 Program (1)
Gadsden State Community College
P.O. Box 227
Gadsden, Alabama 35999-0227

Medical Laboratory Technician
 Program (1)
Wallace State Community College
P.O. Box 250
Hanceville, Alabama 35077

ALASKA

Medical Laboratory Technician
 Program (1)
University of Alaska Anchorage
2533 Providence Drive
Anchorage, Alaska 99508

ARIZONA

Medical Laboratory Technician
 Program (1,2)
Phoenix College
1202 West Thomas Road
Phoenix, Arizona 85013

ARKANSAS

Medical Laboratory Technician
 Program (1)
S Arkansas University Eldorado
 Branch
300 South West Avenue
El Dorado, Arkansas 71730

Medical Laboratory Technician
 Program (1)
Phillips County Community College
P.O. Box 785
Helena, Arkansas 72342

Medical Laboratory Technician
 Program (1)
Garland County Community College
#1 College Drive
Hot Springs, Arkansas 71913

Medical Laboratory Technician
 Program (1)
Arkansas State University
P.O. Box 69
State University, Arkansas 72467

CALIFORNIA

Medical Laboratory Technician
 Program (2)
Naval School of Hlth Sciences-San
 Diego
San Diego, California 92134-6000

COLORADO

Medical Laboratory Technician
 Program (2)
T.H. Pickens Technical Center
500 Buckley Road
Aurora, Colorado 80011

Medical Laboratory Technician
 Program (1)
Arapahoe Community College
2500 West College Drive
P.O. Box 9002
Littleton, Colorado 80160-9002

CONNECTICUT

Medical Laboratory Technician
 Program (1)
Housatonic Community College
510 Barnum Avenue
Bridgeport, Connecticut 06608

Medical Laboratory Technician
 Program (1)
Manchester Community College
60 Bidwell Street
Manchester, Connecticut 06040

DELAWARE

Medical Laboratory Technician
 Program (1)
Del Tech-Comm Coll-Southern Campus
P.O. Box 610
Georgetown, Delaware 19947

FLORIDA

Medical Laboratory Technician
 Program (1)
Brevard Community College
1519 Clearlake Road
Cocoa, Florida 32922

237

Medical Laboratory Technician
Program (1)
Broward Community College
3501 SW Davie Road
Ft. Lauderdale, Florida 33314

Medical Laboratory Technician
Program (1)
Indian River Community College
3209 Virginia Avenue
Ft. Pierce, Florida 34981-9003

Medical Laboratory Technician
Program (2)
Sheridan Vocational Technical Center
5400 Sheridan Street
Hollywood, Florida 33021

Medical Laboratory Technician
Program (1)
Florida Community•College-Jacksonville
North Campus
4501 Capper Road
Jacksonville, Florida 32218

Medical Laboratory Technician
Program (1)
Lake City Community College
Route 3 Box 7
Lake City, Florida 32055

Medical Laboratory Technician
Program (1)
Miami-Dade Community College
950 NW 20th Street
Miami, Florida 33127

Medical Laboratory Technician
Program (1)
Valencia Community College
P.O. Box 3028
Orlando, Florida 32802-9961

Medical Laboratory Technician
Program (1)
St. Petersburg Junior College
P.O. Box 13489
St. Petersburg, Florida 33733-3489

Medical Laboratory Technician
Program (2)
David G. Erwin Technical Center
2010 East Hillsborough Avenue
Tampa, Florida 33610-8299

GEORGIA

Medical Laboratory Technician
Program (1)
Darton College
2400 Gillionville Road
Albany, Georgia 31707

Medical Laboratory Technician
Program (2)
Atlanta Area Technical School
1560 Stewart Avenue SW
Atlanta, Georgia 30310

Medical Laboratory Technician
Program (2)
Augusta Technical Institute
3166 Deans Bridge Road
Augusta, Georgia 30906

Medical Laboratory Technician
Program (1)
Brunswick College
Altama at Fourth Street
Brunswick, Georgia 31523

Medical Laboratory Technician
Program (2)
North Georgia Technical Institute
Highway 197 North
P.O. Box 65
Clarkesville, Georgia 30523

Medical Laboratory Technician
Program (2)
De Kalb Technical Institute
495 North Indian Creek Drive
Clarkston, Georgia 30021-2397

Medical Laboratory Technician
  Program (1)
Columbus College
Algonquin Drive
Columbus, Georgia 31993-2399

Medical Laboratory Technician
  Program (1)
Dalton College
213 North College Drive
Dalton, Georgia 30720

Medical Laboratory Technician
  Program (2)
Macon Technical Institute
3300 Macon Tech Drive
Macon, Georgia 31206

Medical Laboratory Technician
  Program (2)
Lanier Technical Institute
P.O. Box 58
Oakwood, Georgia 30566-0058

Medical Laboratory Technician
  Program (2)
Okefenokee Technical Institute
1701 Carswell Avenue
Waycross, Georgia 31501

HAWAII

Medical Laboratory Technician
  Program (1)
Kapiolani Community College
4303 Diamond Head Road
Honolulu, Hawaii 96816

ILLINOIS

Medical Laboratory Technician
  Program (1)
Belleville Area College
2500 Carlyle Road
Belleville, Illinois 62221

Medical Laboratory Technician
  Program (1)
Malcolm X College
1900 West Van Buren Street
Chicago, Illinois 60612

Medical Laboratory Technician
  Program (1)
Oakton Community College
1600 East Golf Road
Des Plaines, Illinois 60016

Medical Laboratory Technician
  Program (1)
Sauk Valley Community College
173 IL Route #2
Dixon, Illinois 61021-9110

Medical Laboratory Technician
  Program (1)
Illinois Central College
Clinical HO Dept.
One College Drive
East Peoria, Illinois 61635

Medical Laboratory Technician
  Program (1)
Lewis & Clark Community College
5800 Godfrey Road
Godfrey, Illinois 62035-2466

Medical Laboratory Technician
  Program (1)
College of Lake County
19351 West Washington Street
Grayslake, Illinois 60030-1198

Medical Laboratory Technician
  Program (1)
Kankakee Community College
Box 888, River Road
Kankakee, Illinois 60901

Medical Laboratory Technician
  Program (1)
Moraine Valley Community College
Ridgeland Center Campus
10900 South 88th Avenue
Palos Hills, Illinois 60465

Medical Laboratory Technician
  Program (2)
Blessing Hospital
1005 Broadway Street
Quincy, Illinois 62301

Medical Laboratory Technician
  Program (1)
Triton College
2000 Fifth Avenue
River Grove, Illinois 60171

INDIANA

Medical Laboratory Technician
  Program (1)
Indiana University Northwest
3400 Broadway
Gary, Indiana 46408

Medical Laboratory Technician
  Program (1)
Indiana Wesleyan University
4201 South Washington Street
Marion, Indiana 46953

Medical Laboratory Technician
  Program (2)
Lakeshore Medical Lab Training
Program
402 Franklin Street
P.O. Box 25
Michigan City, Indiana 46360-0025

Medical Laboratory Technician
  Program (1)
Indiana Voc Tech College NC-South
  Bend
1534 West Sample Street
South Bend, Indiana 46619

Medical Laboratory Technician
  Program (1)
Indiana State University
217 North Sixth Street
Terre Haute, Indiana 47809

Medical Laboratory Technician
  Program (1)
Indiana Voc Tech College-Terre Haute
7377 South Dixie Bee Road
Terre Haute, Indiana 47802

Medical Laboratory Technician
  Program (1)
Vincennes University
1002 North First Street
Vincennes, Indiana 47591

IOWA

Medical Laboratory Technician
  Program (1)
Des Moines Area Community College
2006 Ankeny Boulevard
Ankeny, Iowa 50021

Medical Laboratory Technician
  Program (1)
Scott Community College
500 Belmont Road
Bettendorf, Iowa 52722

Medical Laboratory Technician
  Program (1)
Hawkeye Institute of Technology
P.O. Box 8015
Waterloo, Iowa 50704

KANSAS

Medical Laboratory Technician
  Program (1)
Barton County Community College
RR #3
Great Bend, Kansas 67530

Medical Laboratory Technician
  Program (1)
Seward County Community College
P.O. Box 1137
Liberal, Kansas 67901

Medical Laboratory Technician
  Program (2)
Wichita Area Vocational Technical
  School
324 North Emporia Street
Wichita, Kansas 67202

KENTUCKY

Medical Laboratory Technician
  Program (1)
Henderson Community College
2660 South Green Street
Henderson, Kentucky 42420

Medical Laboratory Technician
  Program (1)
Jefferson Community College
University of Kentucky
109 East Broadway
Louisville, Kentucky 40202

Medical Laboratory Technician
  Program (1)
Phillips College
1517 Crums Lane
Louisville, Kentucky 40216

Medical Laboratory Technician
  Program (2)
Health Occupations School
701 North Laffoon Street
Madisonville, Kentucky 42431

Medical Laboratory Technician
  Program (1)
Eastern Kentucky University
Richmond, Kentucky 40475

Medical Laboratory Technician
  Program (1)
Somerset Community College
Monticello Road
Somerset, Kentucky 42501

LOUISIANA

Medical Laboratory Technician
  Program (2)
Lafayette Reg Technical Institute
P.O. Box 4909
Lafayette, Louisiana 70502

Medical Laboratory Technician
  Program (1)
Southern University
3050 Martin Luther King Jr. Drive
Shreveport, Louisiana 71107

MAINE

Medical Laboratory Technician
  Program (1)
University of Maine at Augusta
University Height's
Augusta, Maine 04330

Medical Laboratory Technician
  Program (1)
Eastern Maine Technical College
354 Hogan Road
Bangor, Maine 04401

Medical Laboratory Technician
  Program (1)
University of Maine at Presque Isle
181 Main
Presque Isle, Maine 04769

MARYLAND

Medical Laboratory Technician
  Program (1)
Essex Community College
7201 Rossville Boulevard
Baltimore, Maryland 21237

Medical Laboratory Technician
  Program (2)
Naval School of Health Sciences-MD
Technical Training Department
Bethesda, Maryland 20889-5033

Medical Laboratory Technician
  Program (1)
Allegany Community College
Willow Brook Road
Cumberland, Maryland 21502

Medical Laboratory Technician
  Program (1)
Villa Julie College
Green Spring Valley Road
Stevenson, Maryland 21153

Medical Laboratory Technician
  Program (1)
Columbia Union College
7600 Flower Avenue
Takoma Park, Maryland 20912

Medical Laboratory Technician
  Program (1)
Montgomery College
7600 Takoma Avenue
Takoma Park, Maryland 20912

MASSACHUSETTS

Medical Laboratory Technician
  Program (1)
Middlesex Community College
Springs Road
Bedford, Massachusetts 01730

Medical Laboratory Technician
  Program (1)
Northeastern University
360 Huntington Avenue
Boston, Massachusetts 02115

Medical Laboratory Technician
  Program (1)
Massasoit Community College
Blue Hills Campus
900 Randolph Street
Canton, Massachusetts 02021-1399

Medical Laboratory Technician
  Program (1)
Bristol Community College
777 Elsbree Street
Fall River, Massachusetts 02720

Medical Laboratory Technician
  Program (1)
Mt. Wachusett Community College
444 Green Street
Gardner, Massachusetts 01440

Medical Laboratory Technician
  Program (1)
Anna Maria College
Sunset Lane
P.O. Box 34
Paxton, Massachusetts 01612

Medical Laboratory Technician
  Program (1)
Springfield Tech Community College
One Amory Square
Springfield, Massachusetts 01105-1204

Medical Laboratory Technician
  Program (2)
Southeastern Technical Institute
250 Foundry Street
South Easton, Massachusetts 02375

MICHIGAN

Medical Laboratory Technician
  Program (1)
Kellogg Community College
450 North Avenue
Battle Creek, Michigan 49016

Medical Laboratory Technician
  Program (1)
Ferris State University
901 South State Street
Big Rapids, Michigan 49307

Medical Laboratory Technician
  Program (1)
Highland Park Community College
Glendale at Third
Highland Park, Michigan 48203

Medical Laboratory Technician
  Program (1)
Northern Michigan University
Marquette, Michigan 49855

Medical Laboratory Technician
  Program (1)
Oakland Community College
7350 Cooley Lake Road
Union Lake, Michigan 48085-2198

MINNESOTA

Medical Laboratory Technician
  Program (1)
Alexandria Technical College
1601 Jefferson Street
Alexandria, Minnesota 56308

Medical Laboratory Technician
  Program (2)
Medical Institute of Minnesota
5503 Green Valley Drive
Bloomington, Minnesota 55437

Medical Laboratory Technician
  Program (1)
Duluth Technical College
2101 Trinity Road
Duluth, Minnesota 55811

Medical Laboratory Technician
  Program (1)
East Grand Forks Technical College
Highway 220 North
East Grand Forks, Minnesota 56721

Medical Laboratory Technician
  Program (2)
Minnesota Riverland Tech Coll-Faribault
1225 SW Third Street
Faribault, Minnesota 55021

Medical Laboratory Technician
  Program (1)
Fergus Falls Community College
1414 College Way
Fergus Falls, Minnesota 56537

Medical Laboratory Technician
  Program (1)
Hibbing Technical College
2900 East Beltline
Hibbing, Minnesota 55746

Medical Laboratory Technician
  Program (2)
Lakeland Medical Dental Academy
1402 West Lake Street
Minneapolis, Minnesota 55408

Medical Laboratory Technician
  Program (2)
Mayo Foundation
School/Hlth Related Sciences
200 First Street SW
Rochester, Minnesota 55905

Medical Laboratory Technician
  Program (1)
St. Paul Technical College
235 Marshall Avenue
St. Paul, Minnesota 55102

MISSISSIPPI

Medical Laboratory Technician
  Program (1)
Northeast Mississippi Community
  College
Cunningham Boulevard
Booneville, Mississippi 38829

Medical Laboratory Technician
  Program (1)
Mississippi Gulf Coast Community
  College
Highway 90
P.O. Box 100
Gautier, Mississippi 39553

Medical Laboratory Technician
  Program (1)
Hinds Community College District
Nursing/Allied Health Center
1750 Chadwick Drive
Jackson, Mississippi 39204-3402

Medical Laboratory Technician
  Program (1)
Meridian Community College
910 Highway 19 North
Meridian, Mississippi 39307

Medical Laboratory Technician
  Program (1)
Mississippi Delta Community College
P.O. Box 668
Moorhead, Mississippi 38761

Medical Laboratory Technician
  Program (1)
Copiah-Lincoln Community College
P.O. Box 457
Wesson, Mississippi 39191

MISSOURI

Medical Laboratory Technician
  Program (1)
Three Rivers Community College
Three Rivers Boulevard
Poplar Bluff, Missouri 63901

Medical Laboratory Technician
  Program (1)
St. Louis Community College at Forest
  Park
5600 Oakland Avenue
St. Louis, Missouri 63110

NEBRASKA

Medical Laboratory Technician
  Program (1)
Southeast Community College
8800 "O" Street
Lincoln, Nebraska 68520

Medical Laboratory Technician
  Program (1)
Mid Plains Community College
Route 4 Box 1
North Platte, Nebraska 69101

NEVADA

Medical Laboratory Technician
  Program (1)
Community College of Southern Nevada
3200 East Cheyenne
North Las Vegas, Nevada 89030

Medical Laboratory Technician
  Program (2)
University of Nevada-Reno
School of Medicine
Reno, Nevada 89557-0046

NEW HAMPSHIRE

Medical Laboratory Technician
  Program (1)
New Hampshire Tech College
Claremont, New Hampshire 03743

NEW JERSEY

Medical Laboratory Technician
  Program (1)
Camden County College
P.O. Box 200
Blackwood, New Jersey 08012

Medical Laboratory Technician
  Program (1)
Union County College
1033 Springfield Avenue
Cranford, New Jersey 07016

244

Medical Laboratory Technician
  Program (1)
Middlesex County College
155 Mill Road
Edison, New Jersey 08818-3050

Medical Laboratory Technician
  Program (1)
Brookdale Community College
765 Newman Springs Road
Lincroft, New Jersey 07738

Medical Laboratory Technician
  Program (1)
Felician College
260 South Main Street
Lodi, New Jersey 07644

Medical Laboratory Technician
  Program (1)
Bergen County Community College
400 Paramus Road
Paramus, New Jersey 07652

Medical Laboratory Technician
  Program (1)
Burlington County College
Pemberton-Brown's Mill Road
Pemberton, New Jersey 08068

Medical Laboratory Technician
  Program (1)
County College of Morris
Route 10 & Center Grove Road
Randolph, New Jersey 07869

Medical Laboratory Technician
  Program (2)
Ocean County College
Department of Nursing & Hlth Tech
Ocean County College Drive
Toms River, New Jersey 08754

Medical Laboratory Technician
  Program (1)
Mercer County Community College
1200 Old Trenton Road
P.O. Box B
Trenton,, New Jersey 08690

NEW MEXICO

Medical Laboratory Technician
  Program (1)
New Mexico State U at Alamogordo
Box 477
Alamogordo, New Mexico 88310

Medical Laboratory Technician
  Program (1)
Albuquerque Tech Voc Institute
525 Buena Vista, SE
Albuquerque, New Mexico 87106

Medical Laboratory Technician
  Program (1)
University of New Mexico Gallup
  Branch
Gallup Indian Medical Center
P.O. Box 1337
Gallup, New Mexico 87305-1337

Medical Laboratory Technician
  Program (1)
New Mexico Junior College
5317 Lovington Highway
Hobbs, New Mexico 88240

NEW YORK

Medical Laboratory Technician
  Program (1)
SUNY College of Technology at Alfred
Alfred State College
Alfred, New York 14802

Medical Laboratory Technician
  Program (1)
Broome Community College
P.O. Box 1017
Binghampton, New York 13902

Medical Laboratory Technician
  Program (1)
Erie Community College
Youngs Road & Main Street (Amherst)
Buffalo, New York 14221

Medical Laboratory Technician
  Program (1)
Trocaire College
110 Red Jacket Parkway
Buffalo, New York 14220

Medical Laboratory Technician
  Program (1)
SUNY College of Technology at Canton
Cornell Drive
Canton, New York 13617

Medical Laboratory Technician
  Program (1)
State University of New York in
  Farmingdale
Farmingdale, New York 11735

Medical Laboratory Technician
  Program (1)
Orange County Community College
115 South Street
Middletown, New York 10940

Medical Laboratory Technician
  Program (1)
Rockland Community College
94 Main Street
Nyack, New York 10960

Medical Laboratory Technician
  Program (1)
Clinton Community College
Bluff Point
Plattsburgh, New York 12901

Medical Laboratory Technician
  Program (1)
Dutchess Community College
Pendell Road
Poughkeepsie, New York 12601

Medical Laboratory Technician
  Program (1)
CUNY College of Staten Island
715 Ocean Terrace
Staten Island, New York 10301

Medical Laboratory Technician
  Program (1)
Hudson Valley Community College
80 Vanderburgh Avenue
Troy, New York 12180

Medical Laboratory Technician
  Program (1)
Jefferson Community College
Outer Coffeen Street
Watertown, New York 13601

NORTH CAROLINA

Medical Laboratory Technician
  Program (1)
Asheville Buncombe Technical
  Community College
340 Victoria Road
Asheville, North Carolina 28801

Medical Laboratory Technician
  Program (1)
Alamance Community College
P.O. Box 623
Haw River, North Carolina 27258

Medical Laboratory Technician
  Program (1)
Coastal Carolina Community College
444 Western Boulevard
Jacksonville, North Carolina 28546-6877

Medical Laboratory Technician
  Program (1)
Western Piedmont Community College
P.O. Box 680
Morganton, North Carolina 28655-0680

Medical Laboratory Technician
Program (1)
Sandhills Community College
2200 Airport Road
Pinehurst, North Carolina 28374

Medical Laboratory Technician
Program (1)
Wake Technical Community College
9101 Fayetteville Road
Raleigh, North Carolina 27603

Medical Laboratory Technician
Program (1)
Southwestern Community College
P.O. Box 67
275 Webster Road
Sylva, North Carolina 28779

Medical Laboratory Technician
Program (1)
Beaufort County Community College
P.O. Box 1069
Washington, North Carolina 27889

Medical Laboratory Technician
Program (1)
Halifax Community College
P.O. Box 809
Weldon, North Carolina 27890

NORTH DAKOTA

Medical Laboratory Technician
Program (1)
Bismarck State College
1500 Edwards Avenue
Bismarck, North Dakota 58501

OHIO

Medical Laboratory Technician
Program (1)
Stark Technical College
6200 Frank Avenue NW
Canton, Ohio 44720

Medical Laboratory Technician
Program (1)
Cincinnati Technical College
3520 Central Parkway
Cincinnati, Ohio 45223

Medical Laboratory Technician
Program (1)
Cuyahoga Community College
Metro Campus Sci & Tech
2900 Community College Avenue
Cleveland, Ohio 44115-3196

Medical Laboratory Technician
Program (1)
Columbus State Community College
550 East Spring Street
Columbus, Ohio 43215

Medical Laboratory Technician
Program (1)
Lorain County Community College
1005 North Abbe Road
Elyria, Ohio 44035

Medical Laboratory Technician
Program (1)
Washington State Community College
710 Colegate Drive
Marietta, Ohio 45750

Medical Laboratory Technician
Program (1)
Marion Technical College
1467 Mt. Vernon Avenue
Marion, Ohio 43302

Medical Laboratory Technician
Program (1)
Lakeland Community College
7700 Clocktower Drive
Mentor, Ohio 44060-7495

Medical Laboratory Technician
Program (2)
Middletown Regional Hospital
105 McKnight Drive
Middletown, Ohio 45044-8787

Medical Laboratory Technician
  Program (1)
Shawnee State University
940 Second Street
Portsmouth, Ohio 45662

Medical Laboratory Technician
  Program (1)
University of Rio Grande
First & Cedar
Rio Grande, Ohio 45674

Medical Laboratory Technician
  Program (1)
Clark State Community College
570 East Leffel Lane
Springfield, Ohio 45505

Medical Laboratory Technician
  Program (1)
Jefferson Technical College
4000 Sunset Boulevard
Steubenville, Ohio 43952

Medical Laboratory Technician
  Program (1)
Youngstown State University
Allied Health Department
410 Wick Avenue
Youngstown, Ohio 44555

Medical Laboratory Technician
  Program (1)
Muskingum Area Technical College
1555 Newark Road
Zanesville, Ohio 43701

OKLAHOMA

Medical Laboratory Technician
  Program (1)
Northeastern Oklahoma A&M College
Second & "I" Streets NE
Miami, Oklahoma 74354

Medical Laboratory Technician
  Program (1)
Rose State College
6420 SE 15th Street
Midwest City, Oklahoma 73110

Medical Laboratory Technician
  Program (1)
Seminole Junior College
P.O. Box 351
Seminole, Oklahoma 74868

Medical Laboratory Technician
  Program (1)
Tulsa Junior College
909 South Boston Avenue
Tulsa, Oklahoma 74119

OREGON

Medical Laboratory Technician
  Program (1)
Portland Community College
12000 SW 49th Avenue
Portland, Oregon 97219

PENNSYLVANIA

Medical Laboratory Technician
  Program (2)
Ashland State General Hospital
101 Broad Street
Ashland, Pennsylvania 17921

Medical Laboratory Technician
  Program (1)
Northampton Community College
3835 Green Pond Road
Bethlehem, Pennsylvania 18017

Medical Laboratory Technician
  Program (1)
Montgomery County Community
  College
340 DeKalb Pike
Blue Bell, Pennsylvania 19422-1412

Medical Laboratory Technician
    Program (1)
Harcum Junior College
Montgomery & Morris Avenues
Bryn Mawr, Pennsylvania 19010

Medical Laboratory Technician
    Program (2)
Chambersburg Hospital
112 North Seventh Street
Chambersburg, Pennsylvania 17201

Medical Laboratory Technician
    Program (1)
Mt. Aloysius Junior College
William Penn Highway
Cresson, Pennsylvania 16630

Medical Laboratory Technician
    Program (2)
Hamot Medical Center
201 State Street
Erie, Pennsylvania 16550

Medical Laboratory Technician
    Program (2)
Westmoreland Hospital Association
532 West Pittsburgh Street
Greensburg, Pennsylvania 15601

Medical Laboratory Technician
    Program (1)
Harrisburg Area Community College
3300 Cameron St Road
Harrisburg, Pennsylvania 17110-2999

Medical Laboratory Technician
    Program (1)
Penn State University-Hazleton
Hazleton, Pennsylvania 18201

Medical Laboratory Technician
    Program (1)
Manor Junior College
Fox Chase Road
Jenkintown, Pennsylvania 19046

Medical Laboratory Technician
    Program (2)
Conemaugh Valley Memorial Hospital
1086 Franklin Street
Johnstown, Pennsylvania 15905

Medical Laboratory Technician
    Program (1)
Community College of Beaver County
College Drive
Monaca, Pennsylvania 15061

Medical Laboratory Technician
    Program (1)
Penn State U-New Kensington Campus
3550 Seventh St Road
New Kensington, Pennsylvania 15068

Medical Laboratory Technician
    Program (1)
Community College of Philadelphia
1700 Spring Garden Street
Philadelphia, Pennsylvania 19130

Medical Laboratory Technician
    Program (1)
Hahnemann University
Broad & Vine Streets
Philadelphia, Pennsylvania 19102

Medical Laboratory Technician
    Program (1)
Comm Coll of Allegheny Cty-Alleg
    Campus
808 Ridge Avenue
Pittsburgh, Pennsylvania 15212

Medical Laboratory Technician
    Program (1)
Reading Area Community College
10 South Second Street
P.O. Box 1706
Reading, Pennsylvania 19603

Medical Laboratory Technician
  Program (1)
Comm Coll of Allegheny Cty-South
  Campus
1750 Clairton Road
Route 885
West Mifflin, Pennsylvania 15122

RHODE ISLAND

Medical Laboratory Technician
  Program (1)
Community College of Rhode Island
1762 Louisquiest Pike
Lincoln, Rhode Island 02865

SOUTH CAROLINA

Medical Laboratory Technician
  Program (1)
Trident Technical College
P.O. Box 10367
Charleston, South Carolina 29411

Medical Laboratory Technician
  Program (1)
Midlands Technical College
P.O. Box 2408
Columbia, South Carolina 29202

Medical Laboratory Technician
  Program (1)
Florence Darlington Technical College
P.O. Box 100548
Florence, South Carolina 29501-0548

Medical Laboratory Technician
  Program (1)
Greenville Technical College
P.O. Box 5616-Station B
Greenville, South Carolina 29606

Medical Laboratory Technician
  Program (1)
Orangeburg Calhoun Technical College
3250 St. Matthews Road
Orangeburg, South Carolina 29115

Medical Laboratory Technician
  Program (1)
Tri-County Technical College
P.O. Box 587
Pendleton, South Carolina 29670

Medical Laboratory Technician
  Program (1)
York Technical College
452 South Anderson Road
Rock Hill, South Carolina 29730

Medical Laboratory Technician
  Program (1)
Spartanburg Technical College
P.O. Drawer 4386
Spartanburg, South Carolina 29305

SOUTH DAKOTA

Medical Laboratory Technician
  Program (1)
Presentation College
1500 North Main Street
Aberdeen, South Dakota 57401

Medical Laboratory Technician
  Program (2)
Mitchell Vocational Technical School
821 North Capital Street
Mitchell, South Dakota 57301

Medical Laboratory Technician
  Program (2)
Lake Area Vocational Technical School
200 NE Ninth Street
Watertown, South Dakota 57201

TENNESSEE

Medical Laboratory Technician
  Program (1)
Cleveland State Community College
One Adkisson Road
P.O. Box 3750
Cleveland, Tennessee 37320

Medical Laboratory Technician
  Program (1)
Columbia State Community College
Highway 99 West
P.O. Box 1315
Columbia, Tennessee 38401-1315

Medical Laboratory Technician
  Program (2)
Cumberland School of Technology
1065 East Tenth Street
Cookeville, Tennessee 38501

Medical Laboratory Technician
  Program (1)
East Tennessee State University
Marshall T. Nave Center
1000 West E Street
Elizabethton, Tennessee 37643

Medical Laboratory Technician
  Program (1)
Jackson State Community College
2046 North Parkway Street
Jackson, Tennessee 38301-3797

Medical Laboratory Technician
  Program (1)
Roane State Community College
8373 Kingston Pike
Knoxville, Tennessee 37919

Medical Laboratory Technician
  Program (2)
Memphis Area Vocational Technical
  School
620 Mosby Avenue
Memphis, Tennessee 38105-3799

Medical Laboratory Technician
  Program (1)
Shelby State Community College
P.O. Box 40568
Memphis, Tennessee 38174-0568

TEXAS

Medical Laboratory Technician
  Program (1)
Alvin Community College
3110 Mustang Road
Alvin, Texas 77511

Medical Laboratory Technician
  Program (1)
Amarillo College
P.O. Box 447
Amarillo, Texas 79178

Medical Laboratory Technician
  Program (1)
Austin Community College
1020 Grove Boulevard
Austin, Texas 78741

Medical Laboratory Technician
  Program (1)
Texas Southmost College
83 Ft. Brown
Brownsville, Texas 78520

Medical Laboratory Technician
  Program (1)
Del Mar College
Baldwin & Ayers
Corpus Christi, Texas 78404

Medical Laboratory Technician
  Program (1)
El Centro College
Main & Lamar Streets
Dallas, Texas 75202-3604

Medical Laboratory Technician
  Program (1)
Grayson County College
6101 Grayson Drive
Denison, Texas 75020

Medical Laboratory Technician
  Program (1)
El Paso Community College
P.O. Box 20500
El Paso, Texas 79998

Medical Laboratory Technician
  Program (1)
Houston Community College System
5514 Clara
Houston, Texas 77041

Medical Laboratory Technician
  Program (1)
Tarrant County Junior College
828 Harwood Road
Hurst, Texas 76054

Medical Laboratory Technician
  Program (1)
Kilgore College
1100 Broadway
Kilgore, Texas 75662

Medical Laboratory Technician
  Program (1)
Central Texas College
US Highway 190 West
P.O. Box 1800
Killeen, Texas 76541-9990

Medical Laboratory Technician
  Program (1)
Laredo Junior College
West End Washington Street
Laredo, Texas 78040

Medical Laboratory Technician
  Program (1)
Odessa College
201 West University
Odessa, Texas 79764-8299

Medical Laboratory Technician
  Program (2)
Baptist Hospital, Orange
608 Strickland
P.O. Box 37
Orange, Texas 77630

Medical Laboratory Technician
  Program (1)
San Jacinto College Central Campus
8060 Spencer Highway
Pasadena, Texas 77505

Medical Laboratory Technician
  Program (1)
St. Phillip's College
P.O. Box 3800
San Antonio, Texas 78284

Medical Laboratory Technician
  Program (1)
Temple Junior College
2600 South First Street
Temple, Texas 76504

Medical Laboratory Technician
  Program (1)
Tyler Junior College
P.O. Box 9020
Tyler, Texas 75711-9020

Medical Laboratory Technician
  Program (1)
Victoria College
2200 East Red River
Victoria, Texas 77901

Medical Laboratory Technician
  Program (1)
McLennan Community College
1400 College Drive
Waco, Texas 76708

Medical Laboratory Technician
  Program (1)
Wharton County Junior College
911 Boling Highway
Wharton, Texas 77488

Medical Laboratory Technician
  Program (2)
School of Health Sciences
3790th MSTG
Sheppard Air Force Base
Wichita Falls, Texas 76311

UTAH

Medical Laboratory Technician
  Program (1)
Weber State University
Ogden, Utah 84408-3905

VIRGINIA

Medical Laboratory Technician
  Program (1)
Northern Virginia Community College
8333 Little River Turnpike
Annandale, Virginia 22003

Medical Laboratory Technician
  Program (1)
Thomas Nelson Community College
P.O. Box 9407
Hampton, Virginia 23670

Medical Laboratory Technician
  Program (1)
Central Virginia Community College
3506 Wards Road
Lynchburg, Virginia 24502

Medical Laboratory Technician
  Program (2)
Riverside Regional Med Ctr-Newport
  News
1300 Old Denbigh Boulevard
Newport News, Virginia 23602

Medical Laboratory Technician
  Program (2)
Sentara Norfolk General Hospital
600 Gresham Drive
Norfolk, Virginia 23507

Medical Laboratory Technician
  Program (1)
Sargeant Reynolds Community College
P.O. Box C-32040
Richmond, Virginia 23261

Medical Laboratory Technician
  Program (1)
Wytheville Community College
1000 East Main Street
Wytheville, Virginia 24382

WASHINGTON

Medical Laboratory Technician
  Program (1)
Shoreline Community College
16101 Greenwood Avenue North
Seattle, Washington 98133

Medical Laboratory Technician
  Program (2)
Clover Park Technical College
4500 Steilacoom Boulevard, SW
Tacoma, Washington 98499-4098

Medical Laboratory Technician
  Program (1)
Wenatchee Valley College
1300 Fifth Street
Wenatchee, Washington 98801

WEST VIRGINIA

Medical Laboratory Technician
  Program (2)
Dept of Veterans Affairs Medical Center
200 Veterans Avenue
Beckley, West Virginia 25801

Medical Laboratory Technician
  Program (2)
Bluefield Regional Medical Center
500 Cherry Street
Bluefield, West Virginia 24701

Medical Laboratory Technician
  Program (1)
Fairmont State College
Locust Avenue
Fairmont, West Virginia 26554

Medical Laboratory Technician
  Program (1)
Marshall University
Clinical Lab Science Dept
Huntington, West Virginia 25701

Medical Laboratory Technician
  Program (1)
West Virginia Northern Community
  College
15th & Jacob Streets
Wheeling, West Virginia 26003

WISCONSIN

Medical Laboratory Technician
  Program (1)
Chippewa Valley Technical College
620 West Clairemont Avenue
Eau Claire, Wisconsin 54701

Medical Laboratory Technician
  Program (1)
Western Wisconsin Technical College
304 North Sixth Street
La Crosse, Wisconsin 54602-0908

Medical Laboratory Technician
  Program (1)
Madison Area Technical College
2550 Anderson Street
Madison, Wisconsin 53704-2599

Medical Laboratory Technician
  Program (1)
Milwaukee Area Technical College
700 West State Street
Milwaukee, Wisconsin 53233

Specialist in Blood Bank Technology

Under the direction of a pathologist or other physician, the *specialist in blood bank technology* specializes in typing, cross matching, and testing of blood for life-giving transfusions. In collecting, classifying, storing, and processing blood, the specialist detects and identifies antibodies in patient and donor bloods and selects suitable blood for transfusion.

Although medical technologists and medical laboratory technicians may all perform various tests in blood bank technology, the specialist is a more highly trained individual who interprets technical work and who performs specialized tests such as *immunohematology* (the study of blood and its immunities). The specialist may also be a blood bank supervisor, and educator, a consultant, or a researcher.

Certification in medical technology by the Board of Registry and a bachelor's degree from a regionally accredited college or university, or a bachelor's degree from a regionally accredited college or university with a major in any of the biological or physical sciences, are prerequisites for entrance into an accredited twelve-month training program in blood bank technology.

254

After completion of this program, certification as a specialist in blood bank technology, SBB(ASCP), is available from the Board of Registry of the American Society of Clinical Pathologists.

For further career information, write to the American Association of Blood Banks, 8101 Glenbrook Road, Bethesda, Maryland 20814-2749.

Following is a list of educational programs for the specialist in blood bank technology, accredited by the American Association of Blood Banks in collaboration with the Committee on Allied Health Education and Accreditation of the American Medical Association.

SOURCES:

American Association of Blood Banks
American Medical Association
American Society of Clinical Pathologists

Specialist in Blood Bank Technology Programs

ALABAMA

Specialist in Blood Bank Technology
  Program
University of Alabama Hospital Blood
  Bank and American Red Cross Blood
  Services
Alabama Region
University of Alabama Hospital
619 South 19th Street
Birmingham, Alabama 35233

ARIZONA

Specialist in Blood Bank Technology
  Program
Blood Systems, Inc.
6220 East Oak Street
Scottsdale, Arizona 85257

CALIFORNIA

Specialist in Blood Bank Technology
  Program
Sacramento Medical Foundation Blood
  Bank
1625 Stockton Boulevard
Sacramento, California 95816-7089

CONNECTICUT

Specialist in Blood Bank Technology
  Program
American Red Cross Blood Services
Connecticut Region
209 Farmington Avenue
Farmington, Connecticut 06032

DISTRICT OF COLUMBIA

Specialist in Blood Bank Technology
  Program
U.S. Army Blood Bank Fellowship
Dept of Pathology, ALS
Walter Reed Army Medical Center
Washington, DC 20307-5001

FLORIDA

Specialist in Blood Bank Technology
  Program
Jackson Memorial Hospital
1611 NW 12th Avenue
Miami, Florida 33136-1094

Specialist in Blood Bank Technology
  Program
Central Florida Blood Bank, Inc.
32 West Gore Street
Orlando, Florida 32806

Specialist in Blood Bank Technology
  Program
Transfusion Medicine Academic Center
  of the Southwest Florida Blood Bank
P.O. Box 2125
Tampa, Florida 33601-2125

GEORGIA

Specialist in Blood Bank Technology
  Program
The Atlanta Specialist in Blood Bank
  Technology Program
1925 Monroe Drive NE
Atlanta, Georgia 30324

ILLINOIS

Specialist in Blood Bank Technology
  Program
University of Illinois/Life Source
Dept of Medical Laboratory Sciences
P.O. Box 6998
Chicago, Illinois 60680

LOUISIANA

Specialist in Blood Bank Technology
  Program
Alton Ochsner Foundation Hospital
  Blood Bank
1516 Jefferson Highway
New Orleans, Louisiana 70121

Specialist in Blood Bank Technology
  Program
Medical Center of Louisiana at New
  Orleans
1532 Tulane Avenue
New Orleans, Louisiana 70140

MARYLAND

Specialist in Blood Bank Technology
  Program
Johns Hopkins Hospital Blood Bank
600 North Wolfe Street
Baltimore, Maryland 21205

Specialist in Blood Bank Technology
  Program
National Institutes of Health
9000 Rockville Pike
Bethesda, Maryland 20892

MASSACHUSETTS

Specialist in Blood Bank Technology
  Program
New England Deaconess Hospital Blood
  Bank
185 Pilgrim Road
Boston, Massachusetts 02215-5399

MINNESOTA

Specialist in Blood Bank Technology
  Program
Memorial Blood Center of Minneapolis
2304 Park Avenue South
Minneapolis, Minnesota 55404

MISSOURI

Specialist in Blood Bank Technology
  Program
Barnes School of Blood Banking
One Barnes Hospital Plaza
St. Louis, Missouri 63110

NORTH CAROLINA

Specialist in Blood Bank Technology
  Program
Duke University Medical Center
Transfusion Service
P.O. Box 2928
Durham, North Carolina 27710

OHIO

Specialist in Blood Bank Technology
  Program
American Red Cross Blood Services
Northern Ohio Region
3747 Euclid Avenue
Cleveland, Ohio 44115-2501

Specialist in Blood Bank Technology
  Program
Hoxworth Blood Center
3231 Burnet Avenue
Cincinnati, Ohio 45267-0055

Specialist in Blood Bank Technology
  Program
The Ohio State University Hospitals
  Blood Bank and American Red Cross
  Blood Services
Central Ohio Region
995 East Broad Street
Columbus, Ohio 43205

OREGON

Specialist in Blood Bank Technology
  Program
Pacific Northwest Regional Red Cross
  Blood Services
3131 North Vancouver
P.O. Box 3200
Portland, Oregon 97208-3200

TEXAS

Specialist in Blood Bank Technology
  Program
Gulf Coast School of Blood Bank
  Technology
1400 La Concha Lane
Houston, Texas 77054-1802

Specialist in Blood Bank Technology
  Program
The University of Texas
Southwestern Medical Center
Southwestern Allied Health Sciences
  School
5323 Harry Hines Boulevard
Dallas, Texas 75235-8878

Specialist in Blood Bank Technology
  Program
University of Texas Health Science
  Center
Department of Pathology
7703 Floyd Curl Drive
San Antonio, Texas 78284-7750

Specialist in Blood Bank Technology
  Program
University of Texas Medical Branch
  Blood Bank
Eighth & Mechanic Streets
Galveston, Texas 77550

UTAH

Specialist in Blood Bank Technology
  Program
IHC Blood Services at LDS Hospital
Eighth Avenue and "C" Streets
Salt Lake City, Utah 84143

WISCONSIN

Specialist in Blood Bank Technology
  Program
The Blood Center of SE Wisconsin
1701 West Wisconsin Avenue
Milwaukee, Wisconsin 53233

Cytotechnologist

The *cytotechnologist* is a medical technologist who specializes in cytology, the medical science that detects early evidence of cancerous cells and usually allows for effective treatment of lung, stomach, mouth, cervical, and other cancers. With minimal supervision from the pathologist, the cytotechnologist screens specially stained slides of human cells under the microscope. In the delicate patterns of the cell's cytoplasm and nucleus, the technologist looks for minute abnormalities in cell structure that might be the first warning signs of cancer. The most familiar cytologic test is the Pap smear, which tests cervical cancer in the female reproductive tract.

Most cytotechnologists do their work in hospitals and private laboratories. They also work in clinics, university medical centers, nursing homes, and public health facilities. Cytotechnologists may advance to a specialist level serving as senior cytotechnologists, supervisors, or educators.

The usual educational requirement for the cytotechnologist is a bachelor's degree plus clinical education in a cytotechnology program accredited by the Committee on Allied Health Education and Accreditation.

Recommended high school courses include biology, chemistry, math, and computer science.

Certification as a cytotechnologist, CT(ASCP), is available and recommended upon successful completion of academic and laboratory education requirements and the American Society of Clinical Pathologist's certification examination.

According to the 1991 Committee on Allied Health Education and Accreditation's annual survey, entry level salaries for cytotechnologists averaged $31,000 a year.

Following is a list of educational programs in cytotechnology that are accredited by the Committee on Allied Health Education and Accreditation of the American Medical Association in collaboration with the American Society of Cytology. For more information on a career as a cytotechnologist, write to the American Society of Cytology, 1015 Chestnut Street, Suite 1518, Philadelphia, Pennsylvania 19107.

SOURCES:

American Society of Clinical Pathologists
American Society of Cytology

Cytotechnologist Programs

ALABAMA

Cytotechnologist Program
University of Alabama at Birmingham
School of Health Related Professions
UAB Station
Birmingham, Alabama 35294-1270

ARKANSAS

Cytotechnologist Program
University of Arkansas for Medical
  Sciences
College of Health Related Professions
Department of Cytotechnology
4301 West Markham
Little Rock, Arkansas 72205-7199

CALIFORNIA

Cytotechnologist Program
Loma Linda University
School of Allied Health Professions
Dept. of Clinical Laboratory Science
Loma Linda, California 92350

Cytotechnologist Program
Los Angeles County Univ. of Southern
  California
School of Cytotechnology
1200 North State Street
Los Angeles, California 90033

Cytotechnologist Program
Sharp Memorial Hospital
Hippen School of Cytotechnology
7901 Frost Street
San Diego, California 92123

CONNECTICUT

Cytotechnologist Program
University of Connecticut Health Center
Department of Pathology
263 Farmington Avenue
Farmington, Connecticut 06030

FLORIDA

Cytotechnologist Program
University of Miami School of Medicine
School of Cytotechnology
1611 NW 12th Avenue
Miami, Florida 33136

GEORGIA

Cytotechnologist Program
Grady Memorial Hospital
School of Cytotechnology
80 Butler Street SE, Box 056
Atlanta, Georgia 30335

ILLINOIS

Cytotechnologist Program
Humana Hospital-Michael Reese
School of Cytotechnology
2929 South Ellis
Chicago, Illinois 60616-3390

INDIANA

Cytotechnologist Program
Indiana University School of Medicine
635 Barnhill Drive
Indianapolis, Indiana 46202-5120

Cytotechnologist Program
Lakeshore Medical Laboratory Training
  Programs
School of Cytotechnology
422 Franklin Street
P.O. Box 25
Michigan City, Indiana 46360

KANSAS

Cytotechnologist Program
University of Kansas Medical Center
1600 Bell, Cytology Laboratory
3901 Rainbow Boulevard
Kansas City, Kansas 66160-7281

KENTUCKY

Cytotechnologist Program
Pathology & Cytology Laboratory
School of Cytotechnology
290 Big Run Road
Lexington, Kentucky 40503-2903

Cytotechnologist Program
University of Louisville
College of Health & Social Services
School of Allied Health Sciences
Louisville, Kentucky 40292

MARYLAND

Cytotechnologist Program
The Johns Hopkins Hospital
Program in Clinical Cellular Sciences
Dept. of Pathology
600 North Wolfe Street
Baltimore, Maryland 21205

Cytotechnologist Program
Naval School of Health Sciences
Bethesda, Maryland 20889-5033

MICHIGAN

Cytotechnologist Program
Henry Ford Hospital
School of Cytotechnology
2799 West Grand Boulevard
Detroit, Michigan 48202-2689

Cytotechnologist Program
Wayne State University
Program in Cytotechnology
Harper Hospital-Cytopathology Dept.
3990 John R. Boulevard
Detroit, Michigan 48201

MINNESOTA

Cytotechnologist Program
Mayo School of Health Related Sciences
200 First Street SW
Rochester, Minnesota 55905

MISSISSIPPI

Cytotechnologist Program
University of Mississippi Medical Center
School of Health Related Professions
Dept. of Cytotechnology
2500 North State Street
Jackson, Mississippi 39216

MISSOURI

Cytotechnologist Program
Truman Medical Center
School of Cytotechnology
2301 Holmes Street
Kansas City, Missouri 64108

NEVADA

Cytotechnologist Program
APL School of Cytotechnology
Associated Pathologists' Laboratories
4230 South Burnham, Suite 250
Las Vegas, Nevada 89119

NEW JERSEY

Cytotechnologist Program
University of Medicine & Dentistry of
  New Jersey
School of Health Related Professions
65 Bergen Street
Newark, New Jersey 07107-3001

NEW YORK

Cytotechnologist Program
Albany Medical College
School of Cytotechnology
47 New Scotland Avenue
Albany, New York 12208

Cytotechnologist Program
Memorial Sloan-Kettering Cancer Center
School of Cytotechnology
1275 York Avenue
New York, New York 10021

Cytotechnologist Program
New York University Medical Center
Cytotechnology Training Program
Bellevue Hospital, Cytology Dept.
27th Street & First Avenue
New York, New York 10016

Cytotechnologist Program
The Papanicolaou Cytology Laboratory
  School of Cytotechnology
The New York Hospital/Cornell Med
  Center
Pathology Dept.
525 East 68th Street
New York, New York 10021

Cytotechnologist Program
State University of New York (SUNY)
Health Science Center at Syracuse
Program in Cytotechnology
750 East Adams Street
Syracuse, New York 13210

NORTH CAROLINA

Cytotechnologist Program
University of North Carolina at Chapel
  Hill
Dept of Med Allied Health Professions
Chapel Hill, North Carolina 27599-7120

Cytotechnologist Program
East Carolina University
School of Allied Health Sciences
Greenville, North Carolina 27858

NORTH DAKOTA

Cytotechnologist Program
University of North Dakota
School of Medicine, Dept. of Pathology
College Station
Grand Forks, North Dakota 58203

OHIO

Cytotechnologist Program
Akron General Medical Center
School of Cytotechnology
400 Wabash Avenue
Akron, Ohio 44307

Cytotechnologist Program
MetroHealth St. Luke's Medical Center
School of Cytotechnology
11311 Shaker Boulevard
Cleveland, Ohio 44104-3850

Cytotechnologist Program
St. Elizabeth Hospital Medical Center
School of Cytotechnology
1044 Belmont Avenue
Youngstown, Ohio 44501

OKLAHOMA

Cytotechnologist Program
University of Oklahoma
College of Allied Health
Dept. of Clinical Laboratory Sciences
P.O. Box 26901
Oklahoma City, Oklahoma 73190

PENNSYLVANIA

Cytotechnologist Program
Thomas Jefferson University
College of Allied Health Sciences
Dept. of Laboratory Sciences
130 South Ninth Street
Philadelphia, Pennsylvania 19107-5233

Cytotechnologist Program
University Health Center of Pittsburgh
School of Cytotechnology
Magee Women's Hospital
300 Halket Street
Pittsburgh, Pennsylvania 15213-3180

RHODE ISLAND

Cytotechnologist Program
St. Joseph Hospital
200 High Service Avenue
North Providence, Rhode Island 02904

SOUTH CAROLINA

Cytotechnologist Program
Medical University of South Carolina
College of Health Related Professions
171 Ashley Avenue
Charleston, South Carolina 29425

SOUTH DAKOTA

Cytotechnologist Program
LCM School of Cytotechnology
Laboratory of Clinical Medicine
1212 South Euclid Avenue
Sioux Falls, South Dakota 57105

TENNESSEE

Cytotechnologist Program
The University of Tennessee
Medical Center Hospital at Knoxville
1924 Alcoa Highway
Knoxville, Tennessee 37920-6999

Cytotechnologist Program
The University of Tennessee-Memphis
College of Allied Health Sciences
Dept of Clinical Laboratory Sciences
800 Madison Avenue
Memphis, Tennessee 38163

TEXAS

Cytotechnologist Program
DPA Laboratories
School of Cytotechnology
Dallas Pathology Associates
4350 Alpha Road
Dallas, Texas 75244-4494

Cytotechnologist Program
Brooke Army Medical Center
U.S. Army School of Cytotechnology
Dept of Pathology
Fort Sam Houston, Texas 78234-6200

Cytotechnologist Program
University of Texas
M.D. Anderson Cancer Center
Dept of Pathology-Box 053
1515 Holcombe Boulevard
Houston, Texas 77030

Cytotechnologist Program
Medical Center Hospital at San Antonio
School of Cytotechnology
Pathology Department
Univ. of Texas Health Science Center
7703 Floyd Curl Drive
San Antonio, Texas 78284-7750

UTAH

Cytotechnologist Program
University of Utah
School of Medicine, Dept. of Pathology
Medical Laboratory Sciences
50 North Medical Drive
Salt Lake City, Utah 84132

VERMONT

Cytotechnologist Program
Medical Center Hospital of Vermont
School of Cytotechnology
111 Colchester Avenue
Burlington, Vermont 05401

VIRGINIA

Cytotechnologist Program
Old Dominion University
Norfolk, Virginia 23529-0286

WASHINGTON

Cytotechnologist Program
Harborview Medical Center
University of Washington
School of Cytotechnology
325 Ninth Avenue
Seattle, Washington 98104-2499

WEST VIRGINIA

Cytotechnologist Program
Charleston Area Medical Center
School of Cytotechnology
3200 MacCorkle Avenue SE
Charleston, West Virginia 25304

Cytotechnologist Program
Cabell Huntington Hospital
School of Cytotechnology
1340 Hal Greer Boulevard
Huntington, West Virginia 25701-0195

WISCONSIN

Cytotechnologist Program
University of Wisconsin-Madison
Center for Health Sciences
State Laboratory of Hygiene
Madison, Wisconsin 53706-1578

Cytotechnologist Program
Marshfield Clinic
Cytotechnology Program
1000 North Oak Avenue
Marshfield, Wisconsin 54449-5795

Cytotechnologist Program
Milwaukee County Medical Complex
Cytotechnology Training Program
8700 West Wisconsin Avenue
Milwaukee, Wisconsin 53226

Histologic Technician

The *histologic technician* is a medical laboratory technician who specializes in preparing sections of body tissues for microscopic examination by the pathologist. Often while the patient lies in the operating room, the histologic technician, under supervision of the pathologist, freezes and sections tissue samples taken from the patient, mounts them on slides, and stains them with special dyes to make details visible under the microscope. The pathologist then looks for malignant or questionable cells and makes his final diagnosis, allowing the surgeons to proceed with the operation in the appropriate manner.

High school graduation or the equivalent is the prerequisite for entrance into an accredited clinical pathology program in histologic techniques. Community college programs that offer associate degrees in histologic techniques are recommended after they have received accreditation. Certificate programs are also offered in hospitals. A histologic technician who earns a bachelor's degree and has one year experience or attends a CAHEA accredited histotechnology program, can become a *histotechnologist*. The histotechnologist performs more complex techniques, teaches, and can become a supervisor in the laboratory or the director of a school for histologic technology.

Recommended high school courses include biology, chemistry, math, and computer science.

Certification as a histologic technician, HT(ASCP), is available after students have met their academic and laboratory education requirements and after passing the American Society of Clinical Pathologists' examination.

The national average beginning salary for histologic technicians is $19,000, although salaries vary by area of the country.

Following is a list of educational programs accredited by the American Medical Association's Committee on Allied Health Education and Accreditation for the histologic technician. Contact the program directly for details on entrance prerequisites and length of program.

SOURCE:

American Society of Clinical Pathologists

Histologic Technician Programs

ALABAMA

Histologic Technician Program
Baptist Medical Centers
800 Montclair Road
Birmingham, Alabama 35213

Histologic Technician Program
University of Alabama at Birmingham
School of Health Related Professions
Birmingham, Alabama 35294

ARKANSAS

Histologic Technician Program
Baptist Medical System
11900 Colonel Glenn Road
Little Rock, Arkansas 72210-2820

COLORADO

Histologic Technician Program
Penrose Hospitals
2215 North Cascade Avenue
P.O. Box 7021
Colorado Springs, Colorado 80933

CONNECTICUT

Histologic Technician Program
Hartford Hospital
80 Seymour Street
Hartford, Connecticut 06115

FLORIDA

Histologic Technician Program
U of Miami-Jackson Memorial Med
Center
1611 NW 12th Avenue
Miami, Florida 33136

GEORGIA

Histologic Technician Program
Georgia Baptist Medical Center
300 Boulevard NE
Atlanta, Georgia 30312

Histologic Technician Program
St. Joseph Hospital
5665 Peachtree-Dunwoody Road
Atlanta, Georgia 30342

ILLINOIS

Histologic Technician Program
University of Chicago Hospital
Dept of Pathology
5841 South Maryland Avenue
Chicago, Illinois 60617

Histologic Technician Program
Methodist Medical Center of Illinois
221 NE Glen Oak Avenue
Peoria, Illinois 61636

Histologic Technician Program
St. Francis Medical Center
530 NE Glen Oak Avenue
Peoria, Illinois 61637

MARYLAND

Histologic Technician Program
Harford Community College
401 Thomas Run Road
Bel Air, Maryland 21014

MICHIGAN

Histologic Technician Program
Hurley Medical Center
Number One Hurley Plaza
Flint, Michigan 48502

Histologic Technician Program
Blodgett Memorial Medical Center
1840 Wealthy Street SE
Grand Rapids, Michigan 49506

Histologic Technician Program
St. Mary's Medical Center
830 South Jefferson
Saginaw, Michigan 48601

MINNESOTA

Histologic Technician Program
Fergus Falls Community College
1414 College Way
Fergus Falls, Minnesota 56537

MISSOURI

Histologic Technician Program
Trinity Lutheran Hospital
3030 Baltimore Avenue
Kansas City, Missouri 64108

Histologic Technician Program
Truman Medical Center
2301 Holmes
Kansas City, Missouri 64108

NEW JERSEY

Histologic Technician Program
Mountainside Hospital
Bay & Highland Avenues
Glen Ridge/Montclair, New Jersey
07042

NEW YORK

Histologic Technician Program
SUNY College of Agric & Tech at
Cobleskill
Route 7
Cobleskill, New York 12043

NORTH DAKOTA

Histologic Technician Program
University of North Dakota
University Station
Grand Forks, North Dakota 58201

OHIO

Histologic Technician Program
Columbus State Community College
550 East Spring Street
Columbus, Ohio 43215

Histologic Technician Program
St. Elizabeth Hospital Medical Center
1044 Belmont Avenue
Youngstown, Ohio 44501-1790

PENNSYLVANIA

Histologic Technician Program
Geisinger Medical Center
North Academy Avenue
Danville, Pennsylvania 17822

Histologic Technician Program
Conemaugh Valley Memorial Hospital
1086 Franklin Street
Johnstown, Pennsylvania 15905

Histologic Technician Program
Western School of Health & Business
Careers
Chamber of Commerce Building
411 Seventh Avenue
Pittsburgh, Pennsylvania 15219

SOUTH CAROLINA

Histologic Technician Program
Medical University of South Carolina
Coll Hlth Related Prof-Med Lab Sci
Dept
171 Ashley Avenue
Charleston, South Carolina 29425

TEXAS

Histologic Technician Program
Seton Medical Center
1201 West 38th Street
Austin, Texas 78705

Histologic Technician Program
St. Luke's Episcopal Hospital
6720 Bertner Avenue
P.O. Box 20269
Houston, Texas 77030

Histologic Technician Program
U Texas M D Anderson Cancer Center
1515 Holcombe Boulevard, Box 85
Houston, Texas 77030

Histologic Technician Program
Medical Center Hospital at San Antonio
Dept of Pathology
7703 Floyd Curl Drive
San Antonio, Texas 78284

WASHINGTON

Histologic Technician Program
Shoreline Community College
16101 Greenwood Avenue North
Seattle, Washington 98133

WISCONSIN

Histologic Technician Program
Chippewa Valley Technical College
620 West Clairemont Avenue
Eau Claire, Wisconsin 54701

Histologic Technician Program
St. Joseph's Hospital
611 St. Joseph Avenue
Marshfield, Wisconsin 54449

Laboratory Aide

Under direct supervision of the medical technologist, the *laboratory aide* requires minimal training to carry out routine responsibilities in the laboratory. The aide cleans and sterilizes instruments and equipment, maintains records of specimens, keeps an inventory of supplies, and assembles and repairs laboratory equipment. He or she may also perform simple tests such as preparing simple stains, solutions, and culture media. The laboratory aide is also responsible for keeping the laboratory clean, which means scrubbing walls, floors, tables, sinks, and shelves.

In a small hospital the laboratory aide may also be in charge of caring for the animals kept in the laboratory for research purposes. (Refer to the section on Animal Technology).

A high school education, including courses in biology and chemistry, is the usual prerequisite for on-the-job training in a hospital laboratory. Training usually lasts about two months. Educational prerequisites and training periods may vary amongst hospitals.

Individuals interested in career opportunities and salaries for this job, should contact the Personnel Director of their local hospital.

Morgue Attendant

Directly responsible to, and supervised by the pathologist, the *morgue attendant* maintains the hospital morgue room and equipment in a clean, well stocked, and orderly condition. Besides performing janitorial duties, the morgue attendant also assists the pathologist in autopsy procedures. Before the autopsy, the attendant prepares the body for examination. During the autopsy, the attendant hands the pathologist surgical instruments, prepares specimens for microscopic examination, and may sometimes performs minor prosections. Afterwards the morgue attendant closes the incisions in the body cavities and prepares the body for the undertaker.

Educational requirements vary from three months on-the-job training to graduation from a two year college program.

For persons interested in this position, information on job opportunities and salaries may be obtained from the Personnel Director of their local hospital.

A medical record is a complete and permanent documentation of a patient's history of illnesses and injuries, and of all related medical treatments. Among other data, the record includes all medical observations and findings, laboratory and X-ray reports, diets, and medications. Compiled from the records of each healthcare facility the patient has attended, the comprehensive medical record is used by a physician to aid in the diagnosis and treatment of illness, and to ensure continuity of care in the future. The record may also be used by healthcare researchers, hospital administrators and planners, community public health officials, insurance companies, and legal professionals in their planning and research. There are three levels of careers for medical record personnel: *medical record administrator, medical record technician,* and *medical record clerk.*

Medical Record Administrator

The *medical record administrator* is a professional member of a medical health team, and is responsible for the innovation and management of health information systems. In administering the medical record department of a hospital, clinic, or other healthcare facility, the medical record administrator plans and directs a system of medical record retention and retrieval systems, and compiles statistical data from medical records. Medical record administrators often manage the medical record department and train and supervise medical record technicians and clerks. Although the medical record administrator interacts with other members of the facility staff, the position does not provide any patient contact.

As a specialist in information management, the medical record administrator is often relied upon to provide information to members of the facility staff for research projects utilizing healthcare information, and for cost-saving studies. The medical record administrator may also assist administrative staff in evaluating the performance of the healthcare facility, provide consultant services to other healthcare facilities and health data systems, and provide statistical facts to government agencies. Although most work in a healthcare facility, the medical record administrator may also find employment with state and federal health agencies, long-term care facilities, and private industry.

Training for high school graduates involves completion of an accredited four year bachelor's degree program in medical record administration. Individuals who have already earned a bachelor's degree in a related field may also be trained by completing a one to two year postgraduate certificate program in medical record administration. The student completes courses in medical terminology, fundamentals of medical science, administrative management, healthcare statistics, and computerized health information systems. Recommended high school subjects include math, biology, and data processing.

The graduate of an accredited program is eligible to complete a national registration examination, sponsored by the American Medical Record Association. Upon successful completion of the exam, the graduate is then designated as a professional Registered Record Administrator (RRA).

Salaries vary as a result of degree earned, credentials awarded, experience level, size of facility, and geographic location. According to a 1991 survey by the Committee on Allied Health Education and Accreditation, entry level salaries for medical record administrators averaged $23,000.

For more information on a career as a medical record administrator, contact the American Medical Record Association, 919 North Michigan Avenue, Suite 1400, Chicago, Illinois 60611.

Following is a list of university and college educational programs accredited by the Committee on Allied Health Education and Accreditation of the American Medical Association, in collaboration with the Council on Education of the American Health Information Management Association.

Medical Record Administration Programs

ALABAMA

Medical Record Administration Program
University of Alabama at Birmingham
Medical Record Division
1679 University Boulevard
Birmingham, Alabama 35294

ARKANSAS

Medical Record Administration Program
Arkansas Tech University
Health Information Management
Russelville, Arkansas 72801

CALIFORNIA

Medical Record Administration Program
Loma Linda University
Loma Linda, California 92350

COLORADO

Medical Record Administration Program
Regis University
3333 Regis Boulevard
Denver, Colorado 80221-1099

DISTRICT OF COLUMBIA

Medical Record Administration Program
George Washington University
School of Medicine and Health Sciences
Health Information Management
2300 "I" Street NW
Washington, DC 20037

FLORIDA

Medical Record Administration Program
Florida International University
North Miami, Florida 33181

Medical Record Administration Program
University of Central Florida
Box 25000
Orlando, Florida 32816

Medical Record Administration Program
Florida A&M University
Tallahassee, Florida 32307

GEORGIA

Medical Record Administration Program
Clark Atlanta University
James P. Brawley Drive at Fair Street SW
Atlanta, Georgia 30314

Medical Record Administration Program
Medical College of Georgia
Dept. of Health Info. Management
School of Allied Health Sciences
Augusta, Georgia 30912-0400

ILLINOIS

Medical Record Administration Program
Chicago State University
College of Allied Health
95th at King Drive
Chicago, Illinois 60628-1598

Medical Record Administration Program
University of Illinois at Chicago
Dept of Health Info Management
College of Associated Health Professions
1919 West Taylor
Chicago, Illinois 60612

Medical Record Administration Program
Illinois State University
Department of Health Sciences
Normal, Illinois 61761

INDIANA

Medical Record Administration Program
Indiana University School of Medicine
1140 West Michigan Street
Indianapolis, Indiana 46202-5119

KANSAS

Medical Record Administration Program
University of Kansas Medical Center
Dept of Medical Record Administration
School of Allied Health
39th & Rainbow Boulevard
Kansas City, Kansas 66103

KENTUCKY

Medical Record Administration Program
Eastern Kentucky University
Department of Medical Record Science
Richmond, Kentucky 40475

LOUISIANA

Medical Record Administration Program
University of Southwestern Louisiana
P.O. Box 41007, USL Station
Lafayette, Louisiana 70504

Medical Record Administration Program
Louisiana Tech University
Department of Medical Record Science
P.O. Box 3171
Ruston, Louisiana 71272

MASSACHUSETTS

Medical Record Administration Program
Northeastern University
Health Record Administration Program
Boston, Massachusetts 02115

MICHIGAN

Medical Record Administration Program
Ferris State University
919 North State Street
Big Rapids, Michigan 49307

Medical Record Administration Program
University of Detroit-Mercy
8200 West Outer Drive, Box 8
Detroit, Michigan 48219

MINNESOTA

Medical Record Administration Program
College of St. Scholastica
Department of Health Information
  Administration
1200 Kenwood Avenue
Duluth, Minnesota 55811

MISSISSIPPI

Medical Record Administration Program
University of Mississippi Medical Center
Dept. of Medical Record Administration
School of Health Related Professions
2500 North State Street
Jackson, Mississippi 39216-4505

MISSOURI

Medical Record Administration Program
St. Louis University
Dept. of Health Information Management
School of Allied Health Professions
1504 South Grand Boulevard
St. Louis, Missouri 63104

Medical Record Administration Program
Stephens College
Health Information Management Program
Campus Box 2083
Columbia, Missouri 65215

MONTANA

Medical Record Administration Program
Carroll College
Health Information Management Program
Faculty Box 90
Helena, Montana 59625

NEBRASKA

Medical Record Administration Program
College of St. Mary
Health Information Management Program
1901 South 72nd Street
Omaha, Nebraska 68124

NEW JERSEY

Medical Record Administration Program
Kean College of New Jersey
Morris Avenue
Union, New Jersey 07083

Medical Record Administration Program
Hudson County Community College
Jersey City State College
900 Bergen Avenue
Jersey City, New Jersey 07306

Medical Record Administration Program
Burlington County Community College
Pemberton-Browns Mills Road
Pemberton, New Jersey 08068

NEW YORK

Medical Record Administration Program
State University of New York
Health Science Center at Brooklyn
College of Health Related Professions
450 Clarkson Avenue, Box 105
Brooklyn, New York 11203

Medical Record Administration Program
Long Island University
C.W. Post Campus
Brookville, New York 11548

Medical Record Administration Program
Ithaca College
933 Danby Road
Ithaca, New York 14850

Medical Record Administration Program
Touro College
Health Information Mgmt. Program
844 Avenue of the Americas
New York, New York 10001-4103

Medical Record Administration Program
SUNY Institute of Technology at
  Utica/Rome
P.O. Box 3050
Utica, New York 13504-3050

NORTH CAROLINA

Medical Record Administration Program
Western Carolina University
School of Nursing & Health Sciences
Cullowhee, North Carolina 28723

Medical Record Administration Program
East Carolina University
Dept. of Medical Record Administration
School of Allied Health Sciences
Greenville, North Carolina 27858

OHIO

Medical Record Administration Program
Ohio State University
Medical Record Administration Division
School of Allied Medical Professions
1583 Perry Street
Columbus, Ohio 43210

OKLAHOMA

Medical Record Administration Program
East Central University
Dept. of Medical Record Administration
Ada, Oklahoma 74820

Medical Record Administration Program
Southwestern Oklahoma State University
100 Campus Drive
Weatherford, Oklahoma 73096

PENNSYLVANIA

Medical Record Administration Program
Temple University
Dept. of Health Information Management
College of Allied Health Professions
3307 North Broad Street
Philadelphia, Pennsylvania 19140

Medical Record Administration Program
University of Pittsburgh
Dept. of Health Records Administration
School of Health Related Professions
Pittsburgh, Pennsylvania 15261

Medical Record Administration Program
York College of Pennsylvania
Health Record Administration Program
Country Club Road
York, Pennsylvania 17403-3426

PUERTO RICO

Medical Record Administration Program
University of Puerto Rico
College of Health Related Professions
Medical Science Campus
GPO Box 5067
San Juan, Puerto Rico 00936

SOUTH CAROLINA

Medical Record Administration Program
Medical University of South Carolina
Dept. of Health Information
 Administration
College of Health Related Professions
171 Ashley Avenue
Charleston, South Carolina 29425

SOUTH DAKOTA

Medical Record Administration Program
Dakota State University
Madison, South Dakota 57042-1799

TENNESSEE

Medical Record Administration Program
University of Tennessee, Memphis
Dept. of Medical Record Administration
The Health Science Center
822 Beale Street
Memphis, Tennessee 38163

Medical Record Administration Program
Tennessee State University
Dept. of Medical Record Administration
3500 John A. Merrit Boulevard, Box 654
Nashville, Tennessee 37209-1561

TEXAS

Medical Record Administration Program
University of Texas Medical Branch
Dept. of Health Information Management
School for Allied Health Science
Galveston, Texas 77550-2782

Medical Record Administration Program
Texas Southern University
3100 Cleburne
Houston, Texas 77004

Medical Record Administration Program
Southwest Texas State University
Health Information Management Program
San Marcos, Texas 78666

VIRGINIA

Medical Record Administration Program
Norfolk State University
Health Related Professions & Natural
 Sciences
2401 Corprew Avenue
Norfolk, Virginia 23504

Medical Record Administration Program
Medical College of Virginia
Health Information Management
Department of Health Administration
MCV Station-Box 205
Richmond, Virginia 23298-0205

WASHINGTON

Medical Record Administration Program
University of Washington
Health Information Administration
 Program
1107 NE 45th
Mail Stop JD-02
Seattle, Washington 98105

WISCONSIN

Medical Record Administration Program
University of Wisconsin-Milwaukee
Health Information Administration
 Program
School of Allied Health Professions
Box 413
Milwaukee, Wisconsin 53201

Medical Record Technician

As a specially trained and skilled assistant to the medical record administrator, the *medical record technician* performs the many technical activities in a medical record department. In general, the technician compiles codes and analyzes, prepares, and maintains health information. Specifically, the technician reviews medical records for completeness and accuracy; codes symptoms, diseases, operations and therapies; indexes and classifies diagnoses and treatments; and supervises medical records clerks. The medical record technician has no direct patient contact.

In addition to being employed in a large hospital, the medical record technician may be employed in ambulatory healthcare facilities, industrial clinics, state and federal health agencies, and long-term care facilities.

Those interested in becoming a medical record technician should enroll in an accredited two year community college, junior college, or vocational/technical institute associate degree program.

For those individuals interested in entering the medical record field, or for medical record clerks who wish to advance to the technician level, the American Medical Record Association offers a home-study, independent study program in medical record technology. For additional information on the home study program write to the American Medical Record Association, 919 North Michigan Avenue, Suite 1400, Chicago, Illinois 60611.

Upon completion of an approved academic program, the graduate is qualified to take the accreditation examination sponsored by the American Medical Record Association, and if successful, can apply to become an Accredited Record Technician (ART). Graduates of the independent study program who also have completed 30 semester credits of approved college work, may also apply to take the accreditation examination.

Recommended high school subjects include science, English, typing, mathematics, office procedures, and computer science.

According to surveys by the Committee on Allied Health Education and Accreditation and the American Medical Record Association, entry level salaries for medical record technicians averaged $18,500 annually. Medical record technicians employed by the Federal Government averaged $19,600 and accredited medical record technicians averaged over $22,000 annually. For further career information in medical record technology, contact the American Medical Record Association, 919 North Michigan Avenue, Suite 1400, Chicago, Illinois 60611.

Following is a list of academic programs accredited by the Committee on Allied Health Education and Accreditation of the American Medical Association in collaboration with the Council on Education of the American Health Information Management Association.

SOURCES:

American Health Information Management Association
Occupational Outlook Handbook

Medical Record Technician Programs

ALABAMA

Medical Record Technician Program
University of Alabama at Birmingham
1679 University Boulevard
Birmingham, Alabama 35294

Medical Record Technician Program
Wallace State Community College
801 Main Street NW
Hanceville, Alabama 35077-9080

ARIZONA

Medical Record Technician Program
Phoenix College
1202 West Thomas Road
Phoenix, Arizona 85013

ARKANSAS

Medical Record Technician Program
Garland County Community College
One College Drive-Mid America Park
Hot Springs National park, Arkansas
71913-9120

CALIFORNIA

Medical Record Technician Program
Cosumnes River College
8401 Center Parkway
Sacramento, California 95823

Medical Record Technician Program
Cypress College
9200 Valley View
Cypress, California 90630

Medical Record Technician Program
Chabot College
Health Information Technology Program
25555 Hesperian Boulevard
Hayward, California 94545

Medical Record Technician Program
East Los Angeles College
1301 Brooklyn Avenue
Monterey Park, California 91754

Medical Record Technician Program
San Diego Mesa College
7250 Mesa College Drive
San Diego, California 92111

Medical Record Technician Program
Charles R. Drew University of Medicine
and Science
1621 East 120th Street
Los Angeles, California 90059

COLORADO

Medical Record Technician Program
Arapahoe Community College
5900 South Santa Fe Drive
Littleton, Colorado 80120-9988

CONNECTICUT

Medical Record Technician Program
Briarwood College
2279 Mount Vernon Road
Southington, Connecticut 06489

FLORIDA

Medical Record Technician Program
Daytona Beach Community College
P.O. Box 2811
Daytona Beach, Florida 32115-2811

Medical Record Technician Program
Broward Community College
3501 SW Davie Road
Davie, Florida 33314

Medical Record Technician Program
Miami-Dade Community College
Medical Center Campus
950 NW 20th Street
Miami, Florida 33127

Medical Record Technician Program
Pensacola Junior College
5555 West Highway 98
Warrington Campus
Pensacola, Florida 32507

Medical Record Technician Program
St. Petersburg Junior College
Health Education Center
P.O. Box 13489
St. Petersburg, Florida 33733

GEORGIA

Medical Record Technician Program
Medical College of Georgia
Dept. of Health Information
Management
School of Allied Health Sciences
Augusta, Georgia 30912-0400

IDAHO

Medical Record Technician Program
Boise State University
Dept. of Medical Record Science
1910 University Drive
Boise, Idaho 83725

ILLINOIS

Medical Record Technician Program
Belleville Area College
2500 Carlyle Road
Belleville, Illinois 62221

Medical Record Technician Program
Southern Illinois Collegiate Common
    Market
Route #3, Box 112
Carterville, Illinois 62918

Medical Record Technician Program
Truman College
1145 West Wilson Avenue
Chicago, Illinois 60640

Medical Record Technician Program
Oakton Community College
1600 East Golf Road
Des Plaines, Illinois 60016

Medical Record Technician Program
College of DuPage
22nd & Lambert Roads
Glen Ellyn, Illinois 60137

Medical Record Technician Program
College of Lake County
19351 West Washington Street
Grayslake, Illinois 60030

Medical Record Technician Program
Moraine Valley Community College
10900 South 88th Avenue
Palos Hills, Illinois 60465

INDIANA

Medical Record Technician Program
Indiana University-Northwest
3400 Broadway
Gary, Indiana 46408

Medical Record Technician Program
Vincennes University
1002 North First Street
Vincennes, Indiana 47591

IOWA

Medical Record Technician Program
Northeast Iowa Community College
Box 400
Calmar, Iowa 52132

Medical Record Technician Program
Kirkwood Community College
6301 Kirkwood Boulevard SW
P.O. Box 2068
Cedar Rapid, Iowa 52406

Medical Record Technician Program
Indian Hills Community College
525 Grandview Avenue
Ottumwa, Iowa 52501

KANSAS

Medical Record Technician Program
Dodge City Community College
2501 North 14th Street
Dodge City, Kansas 67801

Medical Record Technician Program
Hutchinson Community College
815 North Walnut Street
Hutchinson, Kansas 67501

Medical Record Technician Program
Washburn University of Topeka
1700 SW College Avenue
Topeka, Kansas 66621

KENTUCKY

Medical Record Technician Program
Western Kentucky University
Healthcare Information Systems
Bowling Green, Kentucky 42101

Medical Record Technician Program
Eastern Kentucky University
Department of Medical Record Science
Richmond, Kentucky 40475

LOUISIANA

Medical Record Technician Program
Louisiana Tech University
P.O. Box 3171 T.S.
Ruston, Louisiana 71272-0001

MAINE

Medical Record Technician Program
University of Maine
Health Information Tech. Program
128 Texas Avenue
Bangor, Maine 04401

MARYLAND

Medical Record Technician Program
Baltimore City Community College
2901 Liberty Heights Avenue
Baltimore, Maryland 21215

Medical Record Technician Program
Essex Community College
7201 Rossville Boulevard
Baltimore, Maryland 21237

Medical Record Technician Program
Prince George's Community College
301 Largo Road
Largo, Maryland 20772

Medical Record Technician Program
Montgomery College
Takoma & Fenton Streets
Takoma Park, Maryland 20912

MASSACHUSETTS

Medical Record Technician Program
Catherine Laboure College
2120 Dorchester Avenue
Boston, Massachusetts 02124

Medical Record Technician Program
Northern Essex Community College
Elliott Way
Haverhill, Massachusetts 01830

278

Medical Record Technician Program
Holyoke Community College
303 Homestead Avenue
Holyoke, Massachusetts 01040

MICHIGAN

Medical Record Technician Program
Ferris State University
919 North State Street
Big Rapids, Michigan 49307

Medical Record Technician Program
Henry Ford Community College
Dearborn Heights Center
22586 Ann Arbor Trail
Dearborn Heights, Michigan 48127

University of Detroit-Mercy
8200 West Outer Drive, Box 8
Detroit, Michigan 48219

Medical Record Technician Program
Baker College of Flint
G-1050 West Bristol Road
Flint, Michigan 48507

Medical Record Technician Program
Baker College of Muskegon
141 Hartford
Muskegon, Michigan 49442

Medical Record Technician Program
Schoolcraft College
1751 Radcliff Street
Garden City, Michigan 48135-1197

MINNESOTA

Medical Record Technician Program
Anoka Technical College
1355 West Highway 10
Anoka, Minnesota 55303

Medical Record Technician Program
College of St. Catherine
St. Mary's Campus
2500 South Sixth Street
Minneapolis, Minnesota 55454

Medical Record Technician Program
Moorhead Technical College
1900 28th Avenue South
Moorhead, Minnesota 56560

MISSISSIPPI

Medical Record Technician Program
Meridian Community College
910 Highway 19 North
Meridian, Mississippi 39307

Medical Record Technician Program
Hinds Community College
P.O. Box 10428
Raymond, Mississippi 39154-0999

MISSOURI

Medical Record Technician Program
Penn Valley Community College
3201 Southwest Trafficway
Kansas City, Missouri 64111

Medical Record Technician Program
St. Charles County Community College
4601 Mid Rivers Mall Drive
St. Peters, Missouri 63376

NEBRASKA

Medical Record Technician Program
College of St. Mary
1901 South 72nd Street
Omaha, Nebraska 68124

NEVADA

Medical Record Technician Program
Community College of Southern Nevada
3200 East Cheyenne Avenue
North Las Vegas, Nevada 89030

NEW YORK

Medical Record Technician Program
SUNY College of Technology at Alfred
Alfred, New York 14802

Medical Record Technician Program
Broome Community College
P.O. Box 1017
Binghamton, New York 13902

Medical Record Technician Program
Borough of Manhattan Community
College
199 Chambers Street
New York, New York 10007

Medical Record Technician Program
Monroe Community College
1000 East Henrietta Road
Rochester, New York 14623

Medical Record Technician Program
National Technical Institute for the Deaf
at Rochester Institute of Technology
One Lomb Memorial Drive
P.O. Box 9887
Rochester, New York 14623-0887

Medical Record Technician Program
Rockland Community College
145 College Road
Suffern, New York 10901

Medical Record Technician Program
Onondaga Community College
Syracuse, New York 13215

Medical Record Technician Program
Mohawk Valley Community College
1101 Sherman Drive
Utica, New York 13501

NORTH CAROLINA

Medical Record Technician Program
Central Piedmont Community College
P.O. Box 35009
Charlotte, North Carolina 28235-5009

Medical Record Technician Program
Davidson County Community College
P.O. Box 1287
Highway 29-70
Lexington, North Carolina 27293-1287

Medical Record Technician Program
Pitt Community College
P.O. Drawer 7007
Highway 11 South
Greenville, North Carolina 27835-7007

NORTH DAKOTA

Medical Record Technician Program
North Dakota State College of Science
801 North Sixth Street
Wahpeton, North Dakota 58075

OHIO

Medical Record Technician Program
Stark Technical College
Health Information Technology
6200 Frank Avenue, NW
Canton, Ohio 44720

Medical Record Technician Program
Cincinnati Technical College
3520 Central Parkway
Cincinnati, Ohio 45223

Medical Record Technician Program
Cuyahoga Community College
2900 Community College Avenue
Cleveland, Ohio 44115

Medical Record Technician Program
Sinclair Community College
444 West Third Street
Dayton, Ohio 45402

Medical Record Technician Program
Bowling Green State University-
Firelands College
901 Rye Beach Road
Huron, Ohio 44839

Medical Record Technician Program
Hocking College
3301 Hocking Parkway
Nelsonville, Ohio 45764

OREGON

Medical Record Technician Program
Central Oregon Community College
2600 NW College Way
Bend, Oregon 97701

Medical Record Technician Program
Portland Community College
P.O. Box 19000
Portland, Oregon 97219-0990

PENNSYLVANIA

Medical Record Technician Program
Gwynedd Mercy College
Sumneytown Pike
Gwynedd Valley, Pennsylvania 19437

Medical Record Technician Program
Community College of Allegheny
  County
Allegheny Campus
808 Ridge Avenue
Pittsburgh, Pennsylvania 15212

Medical Record Technician Program
Lehigh County Community College
2370 Main Street
Schnecksville, Pennsylvania 18078

Medical Record Technician Program
South Hills Business School
480 Waupelanie Drive
State College, Pennsylvania 16801

PUERTO RICO

Medical Record Technician Program
Puerto Rico Junior College
Box 21373
Rio Piedras, Puerto Rico 00928

SOUTH CAROLINA

Medical Record Technician Program
Midlands Technical College
Airport Campus
P.O. Box 2408
Columbia, South Carolina 29202

Medical Record Technician Program
Florence-Darlington Technical College
P.O. Box 100548
Florence, South Carolina 29501-0548

SOUTH DAKOTA

Medical Record Technician Program
Dakota State University
Madison, South Dakota 57042-1799

Medical Record Technician Program
National College
Box 1780
Rapid City, South Dakota 57709-1780

TENNESSEE

Medical Record Technician Program
Chattanooga State Technical Community
  College
4501 Amnicola Highway
Chattanooga, Tennessee 37406-1097

Medical Record Technician Program
Volunteer State Community College
Nashville Pike
Gallatin, Tennessee 37066

Medical Record Technician Program
Roane State Community College
Patton Lane
Harriman, Tennessee 37748

TEXAS

Medical Record Technician Program
El Paso Community College
P.O. Box 20500
El Paso, Texas 79998

Medical Record Technician Program
Lee College
511 South Whiting Street
Baytown, Texas 77520-4703

Medical Record Technician Program
Texas State Technical College
2424 Boxwood
Harlingen, Texas 78550-3697

Medical Record Technician Program
Tarrant County Junior College
Northeast Campus
828 Harwood Road
Hurst, Texas 76054

Medical Record Technician Program
South Plains College
1302 Main Street
Lubbock, Texas 79401

Medical Record Technician Program
Houston Community College System
3100 Shenandoah
Houston, Texas 77021

Medical Record Technician Program
St. Philip's College
2111 Nevada Street
San Antonio, Texas 78205

Medical Record Technician Program
Wharton County Junior College
911 Boling Highway
Wharton, Texas 77488

UTAH

Medical Record Technician Program
Weber State College
School of Allied Health Sciences
Ogden, Utah 84408-3908

VIRGINIA

Medical Record Technician Program
Northern Virginia Community College
8333 Little River Turnpike
Annandale, Virginia 22003

Medical Record Technician Program
Tidewater Community College
1700 College Crescent
Virginia Beach, Virginia 23456

WASHINGTON

Medical Record Technician Program
Shoreline Community College
16101 Greenwood Avenue North
Seattle, Washington 98133

Medical Record Technician Program
Spokane Community College
North 1810 Green Street
Spokane, Washington 99207

Medical Record Technician Program
Tacoma Community College
5900 South 12th Street
Tacoma, Washington 98465

WEST VIRGINIA

Medical Record Technician Program
Fairmont State College
Locust Avenue
Fairmont, West Virginia 26554

Medical Record Technician Program
Marshall University Community College
Huntington, West Virginia 25755-2700

WISCONSIN

Medical Record Technician Program
Chippewa Valley Technical College
620 West Clairemont Avenue
Eau Claire, Wisconsin 54701

Medical Record Technician Program
Western Wisconsin Technical College
304 North Sixth Street
LaCrosse, Wisconsin 54601

Medical Record Technician Program
Moraine Park Technical College
2151 North Main Street
West Bend, Wisconsin 53095-1598

Medical Record Clerk

The duties and responsibilities of a *medical record clerk* vary greatly from employer to employer. Under supervision of a medical record technician, the medical record clerk generally performs routine clerical tasks in the maintenance of medical information systems. The clerk may assemble, verify, and provide to the hospital staff the non-technical data in medical records. Other duties of a medical record clerk may include data entry, typing, filing, and related clerical duties.

Besides working in a hospital, the medical record clerk may also be employed in a smaller health care facility such as a nursing home. The medical record clerk may be solely responsible for the medical records. He or she may work under the supervision of a medical record consultant who is credentialed as a Registered Record Administrator (RRA) or as an Accredited Record Technician (ART). The medical record clerk should enjoy working in an office setting since there is no direct patient contact.

Educational and training requirements for the medical record clerk vary. Some employers may require a high school education, or the equivalent, and on-the-job training while others may require formal training.

Salaries for medical record clerks are similar to full-time clerical and data entry positions in other service industries. Annual salaries vary depending upon geographic location, experience level, and size of facility.

SOURCES:

American Health Information Management Association
Occupational Outlook Handbook

Medical Transcriptionist

The *medical transcriptionist* is the allied health professional who transcribes, edits, and types physicians' dictated notes of patients' medical procedures and treatments. The medical transcriptionist must have sharp listening skills to translate the physicians' oral comments into well-organized and accurate typewritten statements. The physician records patients' cases onto tape-recording devices and submits the cassettes to the medical transcriptionist for transcription. As a medical terminology specialist, the medical transcriptionist transcribes each report accurately, ensuring that the meaning does not change. The medical terminologist correctly translates complex medical terms, being sure to use correct usage, spelling and punctuation. The medical transcriptionist is able to detect discrepancies in dictation and edit them accordingly. The medical transcriptionist is a proficient typist, familiar with a variety of medical documents, including medical histories, physicals, consultations, and operative reports.

Medical transcriptionists must be organized, prompt, able to type quickly and accurately, and not easily distracted.

Medical transcriptionists work independently, with little supervision. They work in office settings in hospitals, clinics, laboratories, physicians' offices, insurance companies, emergency and outpatient diagnostic centers, extended-care facilities, with medical transcribing services, and sometimes out of their own homes. Some medical transcriptionists concentrate in one particular area of the medical profession such as radiology, pathology, or emergency room medicine. The medical transcriptionist may transcribe for one or a few physicians in a small medical practice, or for several hundred in a large healthcare facility.

Salaries for medical transcriptionists vary throughout the country. Some are paid by salary, some by the hour, some by incentive, and some by a combination of the above.

Formal training programs for medical transcription are offered through universities, colleges, community and junior colleges, vocational-technical institutes, and adult education programs. Graduates of these programs develop an extensive knowledge of medical terminology, and demonstrate an understanding of anatomy and physiology, medical supplies, equipment, drugs, surgical procedures, medicolegal issues, and laboratory procedures and results.

The American Association for Medical Transcription recommends that interested individuals contact educational institutions in their community to determine where such programs exist.

For further information on a career as a medical transcriptionist, write to the American Association for Medical Transcription, P.O. Box 576187, Modesto, California 95355.

SOURCES:

American Association for Medical Transcription

Mental health is the medical profession concerned with the diagnosis, prevention, treatment, and rehabilitation of human mental disorders.

The *psychiatrist*, a physician trained in the specialized field of psychiatry, diagnoses and treats disorders of the mind. The psychiatrist must graduate from an accredited medical school and complete extensive additional training in psychiatry.

The *psychologist* is a highly trained professional with doctorate degree training who studies and assesses human behavior and works in the prevention and treatment of emotional and mental disorders. The majority of psychologists specialize in clinical psychology, helping those with emotional or mental disorders adjust to everyday life. Others specialize in counseling, research, or education.

Counselors help individuals deal with personal or social problems. The *mental health counselor* helps individuals resolve marriage and family conflicts, deal with substance abuse problems, and improve interpersonal relationships. The *rehabilitation counselor* helps physically, mentally, emotionally, or socially impaired individuals become self sufficient. A master's degree in rehabilitation counseling or psychology is generally the minimum educational requirement for a career as a counselor.

Social workers in mental health help individuals and families find ways to deal with their mental health problems. They provide individual and group therapy, social rehabilitation, crises intervention, and training in skills of everyday living. A master's degree in social work is generally the minimum requirement for a career in social work.

The psychiatrist, psychologist, counselor, and social worker work as part of a mental health team along with other healthcare professionals including psychiatric nurses, therapeutic recreation specialists and occupational specialists, whose career descriptions are listed elsewhere in this handbook.

In the practice of mental health there are also several allied health careers. Because the occupational titles and training requirements for the allied mental health careers may vary among the different mental health programs of each state, careers in allied mental health will be discussed collectively in the following section.

Described below are the careers of the *mental health technician*, the *human services technician*, and the *psychiatric aide*. These positions are available in mental healthcare programs managed by hospitals and/or by federal, state, and

285

local agencies. The reader should remember that the following descriptions are general in nature and that individual job classifications and responsibilities may vary among the different state mental health programs.

For further information on careers in psychiatry write to the American Psychiatric Association, 1400 K Street NW, Washington, DC 20005. For information on careers in psychology write to the American Psychological Association, 1200 17th Street NW, Washington, DC 20036. For information on mental health or rehabilitation counseling careers write to the American Association for Counseling and Development, 5999 Stevenson Avenue, Alexandria, Virginia 22304 or the National Rehabilitation Counseling Association, 633 South Washington Street, Alexandria Virginia 22314. For information on careers in social work contact the National Association of Social Workers, 750 First Street NE, Suite 700, Washington, DC 20002-4241.

Mental Health Technician
Human Services Technician
Psychiatric Aide

The *mental health technician* works with mentally retarded, emotionally disturbed, or psychiatric patients. Some of these technicians work under close supervision while others have little or no direct supervision. Trained as a generalist in a number of mental health fields and employed in a variety of health institutions, the mental health technician provides physical and mental rehabilitation for patients through recreational, occupational, and readjustment activities. The technician participates in group therapy with patients and their families, refers patients to community agencies, and visits patients after their release from an institution.

Working with the mentally retarded, the mental health technician attends to patients' physical needs and well being. The technician also assists in the rehabilitation of patients through teaching and recreation activities, helps patients communicate more effectively, and helps patients master everyday living skills. Mental health technicians are also employed in private and public mental hospitals or on the psychiatric wards of general hospitals, mental health clinics, and human services programs.

The mental health technician also may work as a community health worker in a variety of agencies that rehabilitate and resocialize people, and may be referred to as a *human services technician*. The human services technician is trained as a generalist, but with emphasis in community mental health as opposed to institutional mental health. He or she uses the noncustodial approach in an attempt to rehabilitate those who have problems responding to their social environment. Under supervision of a healthcare professional, the human services technician interviews and counsels clients, administers psychological tests, and participates in group activities. He or she may be primarily concerned with drug and alcohol abuse, parental effectiveness, the elderly, and/or interpersonal relationships. Human services technicians work in social welfare departments, child care centers, preschool nurseries, vocational rehabilitation workshops, and schools for the learning disabled, emotionally

286

disturbed, and mentally handicapped.

The *psychiatric aide* works as a type of nursing aide/orderly performing routine nursing tasks and caring for the patients' eating, sleeping, and personal hygiene habits. He or she also takes temperatures, blood pressure, pulse and respiration counts in addition to providing rehabilitation assistance in the patient's development of social relationships and vocational responsibilities. The psychiatric aide also spends time talking with patients and accompanying them to activities and games.

The psychiatric aide works in state and county mental hospitals, psychiatric departments of general hospitals, private psychiatric facilities, community mental health and substance abuse treatment programs.

Education for a career as a mental health or human services technician usually involves some college preparation in human services, social work, or one of the social or behavioral sciences. Some employers prefer those with a four year college degree.

Training programs for the psychiatric aide are usually held on-the-job. Formal nursing aide training programs are offered through community colleges, vocational-technical schools, and post-secondary educational institutions. For more information on the career of nursing aide refer to the chapter titled Nursing Aide/Orderly.

For further information on the careers of mental health technician, human services technician or psychiatric aide, interested persons should contact the National Mental Health Association, 1021 Prince Street, Alexandria, Virginia 22314; their local Mental Health Association or community mental health program; or state, community, or local mental health facilities.

SOURCES:

American Psychiatric Association
Occupational Outlook Handbook

✚ NURSING

Nursing is the healthcare profession concerned with patient care. The professional nurse handles a variety of tasks relating to both health and illness. Providing direct patient care is the most common job responsibility.

Nursing is a growing field and nurses with appropriate education and experience may find expanding opportunities in the clinical, managerial, academic, and entrepreneurial fields.

Nurses are employed in a variety of settings, including hospitals, clinics, nursing homes, community agencies, public and private schools, health maintenance organizations, outpatient care facilities, colleges and universities, overseas, and in the Armed Forces.

Training requirements vary depending upon the type of nursing career desired. Training for the nursing aide generally involves six-to-eight weeks on-the-job training with formal training programs available through community or junior colleges, vocational-technical institutes, hospitals, and other post-secondary institutions. Licensed practical nurses must graduate from a state approved nursing training program which generally lasts one year and is offered in post-secondary institutes around the country. Registered nurse training programs last from two-to-five years beyond high school and award an associates degree for a two year program to a bachelor's degree for four to five year programs. Master's degree programs are available in numerous colleges and universities for nurses who want advanced education.

All nurses must be licensed and licensure requirements include graduating from an approved school of nursing and passing a national examination administered by each state. Certification in addition to licensure is required for some nursing specialties. Each state's Board of Licensing can provide further details on licensure requirements for nurses.

Salaries for nurses vary by geographic location, amount of education, employer, and years of experience. Experienced nurses earn more than those in starting positions and Registered Nurses earn more than Licensed Practical Nurses.

This chapter provides a summary of the varied opportunities in the nursing field. For information on educational programs, financial aid, career opportunities, and licensure requirements, write to either of the respective nursing associations listed in this chapter, the National League for Nursing, 350 Hudson Street, New York, New York 10014, or the American Nurses' Association, 9 Jay Gould Court, P.O. Box 2244, Waldorf, Maryland 20602.

The Registered Nurse

The *registered nurse* (RN) is a person who has received training in techniques for delivering nursing services to patients found in hospitals, clinics, health agencies, physicians' offices, private homes, and many other places where people need medical attention.

These nurses take temperatures, pulse rates, blood pressure readings, and check other vital signs to evaluate the patient's progress. They record data from these observations on the patient's chart and notify the supervisor or physician of any change indicating the need for special attention.

The nurse prepares the patient for examination and assists the physician during examination and treatment. Registered nurses administer medications and treatments under the direction of the physician.

The nurse's duties vary according to the size and staffing of the place of employment. In a large, well-staffed hospital with many nursing aides (assistants), the nurse's duties may be almost exclusively patient treatment, but in a smaller institution with less support staff, the nurse may also sterilize instruments, make beds, feed and bathe patients, and prepare rooms for occupancy. The experienced nurse may have some supervisory duties over the nursing aides (assistants).

Registered nurses may be assigned to work in a special section in the hospital, such as surgery, pediatrics, obstetrics, psychiatry, or the admitting office. The nurse who works in several of the special sections of the hospital gets a good overview of the scope of nursing specialties and is able to make a more informed decision regarding further study and specialization.

For more information on a career as a registered nurse, write to the National League for Nursing, 350 Hudson Street, New York, New York 10014.

The Air Force Nurse

The *Air Force nurse* works in hospitals, medical centers, and clinics to deliver nursing and health services to Air Force personnel and their families.

Air Force nurses perform the same duties as a civilian registered nurse. Working under the direction of a licensed physician, they administer prescribed medication and treatment; check vital signs such as pulse, respiration, and blood pressure; and perform other nursing duties to aid the patient's comfort and recovery. As in civilian nursing, Air Force nurses may specialize in such areas as surgery, intensive care, anesthesia, mental health, pediatrics, coronary care, and flight nursing aboard an aircraft.

Further information regarding a nursing career in the Air Force is available from the nearest Air Force recruiter, listed in the telephone directory under U.S. Government, Air Force.

The Army Nurse

Army Nurses work in Army hospitals, health centers, clinics, and physicians' offices to deliver nursing services to army personnel and their dependents.

Army nurses perform the same duties as civilian registered nurses. Working under the direction of a licensed physician, they administer prescribed medication and treatment; check such vital signs as pulse, respiration, and blood pressure; and perform other nursing duties to aid the patient's comfort and recovery. Army nurses may specialize in surgical nursing, midwifery, pediatrics, community health, anesthesiology, psychiatric nursing, intensive care, and obstetric and gynecologic nursing.

For details regarding a career in the Army Nurse Corps, contact the nearest Army Recruiting Office, listed in the telephone directory under U.S. Government, Army.

The Community Health Nurse

Community health nurses, sometimes called *public health nurses,* are registered nurses (RNs) who visit homes to provide nursing services and health education to patients and their families. These nurses are stationed in public health departments, visiting nurse associations, voluntary health agencies, school health programs, and occupational health programs.

Community health nurses work with the patient in the home to develop a plan of treatment and rehabilitation and involve the family in assisting in the patient's recovery, as well as providing education in the prevention of disease and the maintenance of good health for the entire family. These nurses work under the instruction of the physician to administer needed medication and treatment. In the case of a patient who is attended by a licensed practical nurse (LPN), the community health nurse instructs and supervises the treatment to be given by the LPN. Part of the duties of the community health nurse include instruction in home nursing and child care.

The community health nurse must be able to assess the needs of the patient who may need referral for professional help with emotional problems, and must maintain a good relationship with other community agencies where ancillary services may be available.

This nurse works with the physician, the family, the patient, and other community health personnel to find accommodations in nursing homes or other rehabilitative facilities when the patient must be cared for outside the home.

The community health nurse is very involved in the entire health services delivery system for the community, working with other agencies in assessing community health needs and planning for meeting those needs. This nurse also participates actively in programs to improve the health of the children of the community, often working with the school system to assist in immunization campaigns and educating school students about good health habits. He or she may also conduct group instruction for parents regarding community health programs. By virtue of experience and continuing education, these nurses may specialize in one phase of nursing, such as, pediatrics or geriatrics.

The Diabetes Nurse

The *diabetes nurse* is a registered nurse (RN) who has received special training to work with the diabetic patient. This nurse must be able to assist in treatment from the admission to the hospital in which the patient may be in a diabetic coma, to the time of discharge after the patient has been taught how to care for the diabetes at home.

The diabetes nurse must have a thorough knowledge of nutrition and its relation to diabetes and must educate the patient and family to care for the condition at home. This involves teaching the patient how to administer insulin, the importance of exercise and weight control, side effects of medications, care of the feet, and how to recognize and react to complications. The patient must be taught the importance of taking care to avoid acidosis and coma, which are life threatening.

The Emergency Room Nurse

The *emergency room nurse* is a registered nurse (RN) who works in the emergency room in hospitals, clinics, or other healthcare agencies.

The emergency room nurse works with persons who are victims of automobile accidents, drowning, drug overdoses, assaults, burns, heart attacks, strokes, diabetic comas, and many other conditions. In these cases, the speed and competence of the emergency room staff may make the difference between life and death.

Emergency room nurses clean wounds or cuts; stop minor bleeding; take temperatures, pulse rates, and blood pressure; and record this information on patient charts. They apply bandages, splints, tape, slings, and cervical collars; insert tubes into tracheotomy openings, perform electrocardiograms, defibrillate cardiac patients; remove stitches; and may suture minor cuts. In some hospitals, under the physician's supervision, more complicated procedures such as nitroglycerin IV therapy and pacemaker therapy may be performed.

For further details on a career as an emergency room nurse, write to the Emergency Nurses Association, 230 East Ohio Street, Suite 600, Chicago, Illinois 60611-3297.

The Geriatric Nurse

The *geriatric nurse* has been trained in the aging process and how it affects the healthcare needs of the older person. Geriatric nurses deliver nursing care in hospitals, nursing homes, clinics, and physicians' offices, and some are visiting nurses taking nursing services to the homes of the patients.

Geriatric nurses work with physicians and other medical staff to assess the condition of the patient and to devise an individual healthcare plan, then seeing that the plan is implemented. They also keep records showing the patient's condition, amount and times of medication, and other treatments such as physical therapy or radiation treatment.

Nursing care for the elderly has a large counseling component. Nurses must help patients understand the aging process and how it affects their health and life-styles. The nurse helps the patient find ways of adjusting to these changes in a manner that will allow for a life-style as comfortable as the situation will permit. Great care must be taken to recognize and take care of the psychological needs of the patient.

Patience is one of the greatest assets a geriatric nurse can have. Assisting patients with such basic needs as dressing, eating, and bathing calls for infinite amounts of patience and tact. Because of age and ill health, elderly patients may be very slow in performing routine tasks, but the help of understanding nurses enables these patients to do things for themselves and retain some feelings of independence and self esteem.

The visiting geriatric nurse works under the supervision of the physician, but since the physician is not always readily available, some independent action is necessary. These nurses work without the technical equipment in a hospital and must improvise to provide treatment in whatever setting the patient resides. Obviously, the visiting geriatric nurse must be resourceful and able to work with all types of people. Some nurses derive great job satisfaction from working as a visiting nurse because of the close involvement with patients and their families.

The Gynecologic Nurse

The *gynecologic nurse* is a registered nurse (RN) especially trained to work with women with problems relating to their reproductive and sexual lives and the relationship of those systems to the complete health of the women.

This nurse may work in hospitals, physicians' offices, public health departments, clinics, and community agencies.

The gynecologic nurse takes medical histories of patients, performs pregnancy tests and Pap smears, participates in the family planning program by counseling women in the use of contraceptives, and may fit diaphragms. In the hospital, the gynecologic nurse administers medications, dresses surgical wounds, and removes sutures. They assist with patients who have had mastectomies, hysterectomies, sterilizations, or abortions.

This nurse has been very instrumental in programs promoting the early detection of breast cancer and may perform breast examinations and instruct women in the technique of self examination. They also play an important part in the education of the general public in campaigns for the control of venereal disease and may participate in programs for the testing of venereal disease.

The gynecologic nurse needs to have good command of counseling skills in order to help rape victims, women who are considering abortion or giving their babies up for adoption, and women who are having difficulty adjusting to sexual problems. This nurse must be very aware of the psychological problems that can attend some gynecologic procedures and be able to give counseling to those patients. The gynecologic nurse must also be aware of referral sources to which the patient can be referred to at the level of counseling or psychiatric care indicated.

For more information, write to the Nurses Association of the American College of Obstetrics and Gynecologists, 409 Twelfth Street SW, Washington, DC 20024-2191.

The Head Nurse

The *head nurse* is an experienced registered nurse in charge of the nursing activities in a hospital unit, instructing the nurses, and coordinating the work of the unit to secure the best care for its patients.

The head nurse observes the work of the staff nurses and assistants to see that care is being given to patients as directed and that the physicians' instructions are being followed. This nurse makes assignments to duties, evaluates the performance of the nursing staff, plans needed changes to upgrade the service, and makes sure that rooms and wards are kept clean and comfortable. The head nurse also directs staff in keeping patient records and makes rounds with physicians to keep abreast of any special instructions for patients. Drugs and supplies are either ordered by or at the direction of the head nurse who also is responsible for keeping records of the supply and distribution of narcotics in the unit. This nurse takes care of such problems as conflicts between staff members and resolves these differences or refers to higher authority in order to maintain smooth personnel relations.

The Infection Control Nurse

The *infection control nurse* is a registered nurse (RN) who organizes and directs the health care facility's infection control program. He or she is knowledgeable of communicable diseases and their modes of transmission. The infection control nurse investigates possible infection control problems and may compare lab reports with a list of known communicable diseases to identify situations that would require infection control procedures to be enacted. He or she discusses the situation with the healthcare facility's staff, physicians, and nurses. He or she may then recommend which safety precautions should be taken to protect patients and staff from infection or contamination. The infection control nurse instructs the staff in specific and universal infection control precautions. He or she may also arrange for follow-up care for patients or staff exposed to infection or contamination.

The Intensive Care Nurse

The *intensive care nurse* is a registered nurse who provides nursing services to patients admitted to the hospital in such a critical state that specific, immediate, and expert care will make the difference in whether the patient lives or dies.

In the intensive care unit, staffed by nurse-physician teams, constant monitoring and assessment of the patient is coupled with treatment administered by trained staff experts. In this unit treatment is available constantly and immediately when needed. The nurse in the intensive care unit is trained in the use of the newest, most sophisticated medical life-support equipment.

The nursing service is under the direction of the physician. The nurse has the responsibility of determining the nursing needs of the patient, devising a nursing plan for each individual, making sure that such plans are carried out, and coordinating tests and other diagnostic procedures. The nurse communicates to the family appropriate information on the patient's condition. Preparation of the family is very important; studies have shown that family anxiety transfers to the patient.

The intensive care nurse is trained to recognize danger signals calling for initiation of emergency procedures and the techniques of administering that treatment. The nurse observes the behavior of patients to determine their psychological state and provides the support and reassurance necessary to enable patients to participate in their own recovery.

Nurses receive special preparation for work in the particular unit in which they will be stationed. There are intensive care units for heart failure, stroke, kidney failure, diabetic coma, shock, pediatric problems, respiratory failure, newborns, burns, surgical complications, and others. Each type of unit has its own particular lifesaving equipment and procedures. Nurse preparation includes understanding the function of the machines, being able to operate them, and knowing the techniques of administration of lifesaving procedures.

Perhaps the best known of the intensive care units is the coronary care unit, where patients are placed to recover from heart attacks. These attacks are a major cause of deaths in the United States. As soon as patients arrive in the unit, they are in the hands of professionals, well trained in the use of the life-support systems and the most important methods of communication, emotional support, and reassurance to allay the panic of the patients. As patients improve, the nurse becomes both counselor and teacher, helping patients to understand their conditions and learn what must be done to adjust to a new life-style compatible with their new state of health.

There is probably no specialty in nursing that has as strong an emotional impact on the nurse as intensive care nursing. In any such unit, there is an atmosphere of crisis much of the time. The nurses must be strong and stable emotionally and need constantly to reexamine their own feelings toward events that arise in life and death situations. The patient, often fearing that death is imminent, depends on the nurse for reassurance. The intensive care nurses must be very emotionally involved with their patients, understanding their need to be angry, fearful, and uncooperative because of the threatening situation in which they are involved. The patient is often connected to strange machines on which life depends and the nurse is the means of conveying to the patient that there is a human, caring presence.

The Legal Nurse Consultant

The *legal nurse consultant* is a registered nurse (RN) who has extensive experience and academic preparation in the nursing field. Employed by a law firm, he or she may work in a consulting role and perform paralegal functions. The legal nurse consultant that works independently may both consult and/or testify. Job functions include evaluation of physician and nurse performances, reviewing of medical records for evidence of medical malpractice and documentation of injury, and identification and development of medical and nursing consultants as expert witnesses. While legal nurse consulting is a growing field, registration procedures are not yet available. The American Association of Legal Nurse Consultants is currently in the process of developing certification procedures. Many legal nurse consultants are obtaining certification as legal assistants. Recommended high school courses for students interested in pursuing a career as a legal nurse consultant include biology, chemistry, psychology, and anatomy and physiology. Salaries for the legal nurse consultant are comparable to those of nurses practicing within hospital settings. For more information on the profession of legal nurse consultant, contact the American Association of Legal Nurse Consultants, P.O. Box 3616, Phoenix, Arizona 85030-3616.

Licensed Practical Nurses

Licensed practical nurses (LPNs), also known as *licensed vocational nurses*, work under the supervision of physicians and registered nurses in hospitals, convalescent and nursing homes, clinics, schools, public health agencies, and private homes to deliver nursing services to the ill and injured. The LPN performs many of the same nursing tasks as the registered nurse (RN), but does not receive the same level of academic and clinical preparation. The length of the training period for LPNs is twelve to eighteen months, compared to two to four years for the RN. Upward mobility for the LPN is considerably less than that for the RN.

Licensed practical nurses employ the techniques and principles of nursing to perform such duties as dressing wounds, taking temperatures and pulse and respiration rates, giving prescribed medication, and recording the results of these activities on the patients' records. They administer enemas and douches, carry out catheterization, and may perform routine laboratory procedures such as urinalysis. They answer patients' calls, observe patients, and report any changes of condition to supervisory staff on duty. They supply patients with ice bags and hot water bottles and give massages or alcohol rubs as directed. They sometimes make beds and clean rooms. They may be assigned to special duty stations such as the geriatric unit of the hospital. Licensed practical nurses may assist in the supervision of nurse's aides, orderlies, and attendants. For more information on a career as a licensed practical nurse, write to the National Federation of Licensed Practical Nurses, P.O. Box 18088, Raleigh, North Carolina 27619.

The Navy Nurse

Navy nurses work in naval hospitals, clinics, and dispensaries delivering nursing services to Navy personnel and their families. Navy nurses perform the same duties as civilian registered nurses. Working under the direction of a licensed physician, they administer prescribed medication and treatment; check such vital signs as pulse, respiration, and blood pressure; and perform other nursing duties for the patient's comfort and recovery. In the Navy, the nurse may also specialize in such areas as pediatrics, anesthesia, family practice, and obstetrics.

For details regarding a career in the Navy Nurse Corps, contact the nearest Navy Recruiting Office, listed in the telephone directory under U.S. Government, Navy.

The Neonatal Nurse

The *neonatal nurse* works in the hospital nursery and has the responsibility of constantly monitoring the newborns to make sure that they are making normal progress. This nurse evaluates the condition of the patients; keeps records of vital signs; and if a change should develop warranting it, alerts the physician.

An important duty of the neonatal nurse is the care of premature infants and those born with defects that may endanger their normal developmental progress. Some neonatal nurses may specialize in these problems and be assigned to the high-risk nursery. Neonatal nurses are responsible for initiating lifesaving procedures and administering complicated medical treatment under the supervision of the physician.

Another function of the neonatal nurse is the education and counseling of parents in the care of the infant and the awareness of the developmental progress to be expected in the normal growth of the infant. The neonatal nurse usually works with the obstetric nurse assigned to postpartum care in the counseling and education of the parents and other members of the family.

For more information on a career as a neonatal nurse, write to the Nurses Association of the American College of Obstetricians & Gynecologists, 409 Twelfth Street SW, Washington, DC 20024-2191.

The Nephrology Nurse

The *nephrology nurse* is a registered nurse who works in a renal dialysis center, a community health agency, or in the home to provide nursing services to patients with kidney diseases, kidney transplants, or abnormalities producing kidney dysfunction. The nephrology nurse is part of a team that includes the physician, other health services personnel, and the patients and their families.

The nephrology nurse participates in setting up individualized plans of care for each patient. The patient is examined and evaluated so that appropriated treatment and other services can be arranged. Counseling and emotional support are provided to lessen the patient's anxiety over a condition that often poses a real threat to life and requires long-term care.

The nephrology nurse working with kidney transplant patients will be involved in preparing both the donor and the recipient physically and emotionally for the surgery and the postoperative recovery period. The nurse, as well as the other members of the team, will be trained to recognize and handle the psychological problems that arise in kidney transplant cases.

The nephrology nurse checks the dialysis equipment and ensures that it is operating properly, making adjustments or having them made by maintenance personnel. During the dialysis, the patient and the equipment are monitored carefully and the patient is taught to monitor his or her own dialysis equipment. This nurse teaches the patient proper care between dialysis to avoid infections, and instructs the patient on matters of diet. The nephrology nurse also receives training in the management of acute renal failure and other emergency conditions such as massive blood loss, shock, or equipment failure.

The nephrology nurse will need some teaching skills in order to instruct the patient and members of the family in the patient's home care. The patient may need to adopt a new life-style compatible to his or her altered physical state and will need the nurse's instruction and support. This nurse will also keep comprehensive records of the schedule and type of treatment and changes in the condition of the patient.

Persons interested in entering this specialty may get further information by contacting the American Nephrology Nurses Association, North Woodbury Road, Box 56, Pitman, New Jersey 08071.

The Neurosurgical/Neurological Nurse

The *neurosurgical/neurological nurse* is a registered nurse who has been specifically trained to furnish nursing services to persons who, by injury or disease, are suffering physical or mental disorders due to dysfunction of the nervous system.

The progress of the neurological patient is best assessed by close monitoring at periodic intervals of vital signs, responsiveness, and motor ability; as well as subtle changes in the physiological, behavioral, and emotional conditions of the patient. Pain and hyperactivity must be controlled with minimum sedation so as not to suppress the responses necessary in evaluation of the patient's state. The nurse must be able to interpret the significance of these changes in light of treatment and prognosis. Using reports, records, interviews, and physical examinations, the nurse assesses the condition and nursing needs of the patient, then implements, under the physician's direction, emergency or other measures designed to work toward the rehabilitation of the patient.

The aim of the neurosurgical nurse is to return the patient to a condition that is as nearly normal as possible, given the extent of injury or deterioration of the nervous system. This nurse must have knowledge of rehabilitation nursing skills. The problems of the neurosurgical patient range from disturbance of the most basic bodily functions to the most complicated functions of the human mind. This requires a thorough understanding of the physiological and neurological functions of the mind and body on the part of the nurse.

The Nurse Anesthetist

The *nurse anesthetist* is an important part of the surgical team and must offer psychological assurance and support to the patient as well as perform the highly technical and scientific part of the operation. Since all situations in which anesthesia is required have a certain amount of stress, the person who enters this specialty must be able to work under pressure and to maintain control of his or her mind and emotions at all times.

Most anesthetists are employed by hospitals, but some work in group practices and surgical clinics and there are those who independently contract their services where needed. Some anesthetists are employed by dentists who perform dental surgery.

Nurse anesthetists administer intravenous, spinal, and other anesthetics as needed for surgical operations, deliveries, and other medical and dental procedures. They control the flow of the gases or injected fluids to maintain the needed anesthetic state of the patient.

Anesthetists monitor such vital signs as blood pressure, pulse, and color to assess the condition of the patient and administer emergency measures when indicated to prevent the patient from going into shock. They keep the physician apprised of the patient's condition and keep records of the preoperative and postoperative condition of the patient and all anesthesia and medication administered. Nurse anesthesiologists may, under the direction of the physician, give postoperative care.

For more information on this career, write to the American Association of Nurse Anesthetists, 216 West Higgins Road, Park Ridge, Illinois 60068.

The Nurse Clinical Specialist

The *nurse clinical specialist* is a registered nurse who is considered to be an expert in the care of patients and in a specific area of specialization. These areas of specialization include pediatrics, geriatrics, surgery, psychiatry and mental health, neurology, oncology, and community health.

Clinical specialists manage and improve patient care by identifying nursing problems and assisting the staff in dealing with specific patient needs. They are involved in education, research, consultation, supervision, and in the coordination of patient care.

Clinical specialists may asses the health of patients by physical examination and taking medical histories. They may counsel and teach patients and their family members in order to promote health maintenance and disease prevention. They may also evaluate the service being provided to patients and make recommendations and implement changes needed to improve the service.

Nurse clinical specialists are employed in hospitals, clinics, nursing homes, schools, health maintenance organizations, health centers, and physicians' offices.

The Nurse Consultant

Nurse consultants are registered nurses who have extensive experience in the nursing field and work in a consulting role to solve problems in nursing and other health services. They're employed with schools of nursing, industrial organizations, hospitals, attorneys, public health agencies, and more depending upon the area of specialization.

These nurses assist nursing education programs by reviewing curricula and making suggestions for changes to be made to improve the programs. They also assist in preparation of manuals and procedures and the setting up of staff development programs for hospitals, schools, and agencies. Nurse consultants review nursing programs in hospitals, nursing homes, and clinics and make recommendations for changes in nursing techniques, administration, and procedures to increase efficiency in the delivery of nursing services. They also work with industrial and community groups by preparing educational materials, participating in setting up educational programs, and advising these organizations about community resources in the nursing and healthcare field. Some consulting may be with nursing associations and organizations regarding nursing education and professional development programs.

The Nurse Instructor

The *nurse instructor* is a registered nurse who may work in a college, university, or hospital nursing school. The employment may be part time while the nurse is employed in a nursing capacity or it may be full time as a member of a college or university faculty.

The nurse instructor conducts classroom instruction in such nursing-related subjects as physiology, anatomy, and psychology and supervises nursing students in the performance of laboratory work. The instructor prepares and administers examinations to evaluate the progress of the students and monitors students' progress in the clinical work experience part of the training.

Nurse instructors work with the medical and nursing staff to plan curricula and to evaluate and improve training programs. They may assist in setting up seminars and workshops or the continuing education of the hospital staff. These nurses work under the supervision of the medical and nursing staff in a hospital and under the department head in a college or university. They may specialize in a particular subject in the nursing curriculum such as nutrition, physiology or anatomy, or they may specialize in a special field of nursing such as surgical nursing or gynecologic nursing.

The Nurse-Midwife

The *nurse-midwife* works as a part of a medical team in the prenatal, delivery, and postnatal care of women with normal pregnancies.

The nurse-midwife participates in the initial examination of the pregnant woman and works in collaboration with the physician to determine responsibilities during the period of the pregnancy, labor, and delivery. The nurse-midwife's responsibilities include periodic examinations during the term of the pregnancy and instructing the patient in proper care, nutrition, and exercise to insure a delivery as normal and comfortable as possible. This nurse monitors the results of laboratory tests to assure that the patient is making normal progress. If evidence of complication does appear, in collaboration with the obstetrician, the nurse works out corrective procedures to alleviate the complication.

The nurse-midwife stays with the patient during labor and delivery providing emotional support and care of physical needs, including administration of needed medication. Under supervision of the obstetrician, the nurse-midwife delivers babies if the delivery is uncomplicated. In the case of complications, the nurse-midwife administers emergency measures and sees that the obstetrician is notified immediately.

Following the delivery of the baby, the nurse-midwife performs routine examinations of the patient, instructs the new mother in infant care, and may conduct classes for mothers and other family members in the care of the newborn. Postpartum care may include home visits to monitor progress of the mother and the child. Information and advice on contraception and family planning are part of the aftercare.

Nurse-midwives typically work in hospitals, birthing centers, public health departments, private practices, health maintenance organizations, and clinics.

For further career information, write to the American College of Nurse-Midwives, 1522 "K" Street NW, Washington, DC 20005.

The Nurse Nuclear Medical Technologist

The nurse who becomes a *nuclear medical technologist* (NMT) has received special training in the use of radioactive materials for diagnosis and treatment.

The nuclear medical technologist, working under the direction of a radiologist, performs analyses of biological specimens such as blood and urine by combining them with radioactive drugs (also called radiopharmaceuticals) to detect such substances as hormones, drugs, or other chemicals.

The NMT also administers radioactive materials that localize in a particular organ, and is then photographed or "imaged" by scanners or cameras so that the physician can study the structure and function of the organ to diagnose disease or structural abnormalities. This procedure subjects the patient to minimal radiation and is not painful.

This nurse administers radioactive materials in the treatment of disease. Other responsibilities include assuring radiation safety; preparation, administration, and disposal of radioactive materials; use of nuclear instruments; and the preparation of specimens for laboratory study. The data from these studies are prepared for the physician's use in diagnosis.

The Nurse Practitioner

The *nurse practitioner* is usually defined as a registered nurse (RN) with education and experience enabling nursing performance in an expanded role. This nurse is competent to work without supervision in many of the nursing services. For many years in rural areas, ghettos, and other places where a physician is not readily available, nurses have worked with independence, being the main source of medical care in some isolated regions. The nurse practitioner works in many settings, including clinics, health centers, public health agencies, physicians' offices, emergency departments, nursing homes, prisons, industry, and isolated rural areas.

The nurse practitioner assesses the health status of patients by taking health histories, performing physical examinations, and ordering and interpreting diagnostic tests. This nurse consults with the physician and plans treatment, establishes a healthcare plan including preventive and maintenance measures, and, with approval of the physician, implements such plans. The nurse recommends medication and other types of treatment such as physical therapy or psychotherapy. This nurse may make referrals to specialists for treatment of conditions beyond the scope of the nurse practitioner and maintains records of patient's condition, treatment, and prognosis.

Nurse practitioners have a teaching and counseling role in helping patients in maintaining health and preventing illness, assisting parents to develop better physical and emotional health for their children, and counseling the elderly in maintaining good health during the aging process. These nurses may counsel the terminally ill and their families to help them through the death of the patient. They may manage the care of women with normal pregnancies.

Nurse practitioners work with and under the guidance of a licensed physician. However, there are some states in which the state law permits them to engage in independent practice. Persons interested in this career should contact their state licensure board to determine what a nurse practitioner can do in their state.

The Nurse Supervisor

The *nurse supervisor* works in a hospital or health agency supervising the delivery of nursing services for patient care units and assuring that the staff provides quality care to the patients. The supervisor coordinates the nursing activities on a unit as well as coordinating activities with other units in the hospital.

The nurse supervisor evaluates the performance of the unit nursing staff, participates in planning in-service training and education programs to insure staff development, and offers guidance for nurses seeking ways of advancing in their profession. The supervisor is also involved in preparation of the budget for the unit or units supervised and may participate in studies or surveys to contribute to nursing research designed to promote better nursing programs.

The nurse supervisor may be in charge of a unit specializing in a particular area of nursing, such as obstetrics, coronary care, or surgery. The nurse who supervises such a specialty unit will need to have experience as well as special academic preparation in the specialty.

The Obstetric Nurse

The *obstetric nurse* is a registered nurse (RN) who works in hospitals, physicians' offices, public health departments, family planning clinics, homes, and community agencies furnishing nursing services to women during pregnancy, delivery, and the postpartum period.

Obstetric nurses may begin to work with patients in early pregnancy, counseling them on diet, exercise, and the physical changes that will take place as the pregnancy progresses. They help prepare mothers for the processes of labor and delivery and may conduct classes in natural childbirth that include the fathers and any other members of the family who may want to be a part of the birth experience. In this phase of obstetric care, nurses may work with high-risk patients and have responsibility for the close monitoring of these patients to ascertain any conditions that may require the care of the physician.

The obstetric nurse may work in the delivery room to assist the mother in having a delivery that is as safe and comfortable as possible. Since childbirth is certainly an emotional and may be a difficult time, the role of the nurse in offering support and comfort to the patient is a vital one.

Following the birth of the baby, these nurses assist the mother during the healing process. They assess the mother's physical and emotional condition and lend whatever assistance the mother needs in adapting to her new baby and its needs. Counseling and education for the mother in this situation may also include the father and siblings.

For further information, write to the Nurses Association of the American College of Obstetricians & Gynecologists, 409 Twelfth Street SW, Washington, DC 20024-2188.

The Occupational Health Nurse

Occupational health nurses, formerly called *industrial nurses*, provide nursing services to workers in department stores, factories, large office complexes, or other places of employment

302

that have large numbers of employees.

The most important objectives of the occupational health nurse are the prevention of illness and the maintenance of the highest possible level of good health for the work force. Since employee ill health and its accompanying absentee rate are very costly to the employer, the role of the occupational health nursing staff in the counseling and education of employees in matters of good health cannot be overestimated.

The occupational health nurse works closely with the personnel department to discover and deal with such problems as alcoholism, chronic health problems, and emotional and mental instability in an effort to prevent them from progressing to insolubility.

It is important for the occupational health nurse to maintain cooperative relationships with local physicians, community health centers, and other health agencies These may be needed for referral of clients for care beyond the scope of the nurse.

Occupational health nurses render competent nursing care to persons who may become ill or injured at the place of employment. After administering first aid in the case of an accident, they see that patients are transported to a physician or hospital for needed additional care. After treatment by a physician these nurses may, under direction of the physician, apply subsequent dressings to wounds.

The nurse may visit homes of employees to determine cause of prolonged absence and need for referral services, and to give guidance to employees and their families in health care. It is necessary to keep complete records of treatment given employees and to prepare accident reports and other reports for worker's compensation, insurance coverage, and so forth.

The occupational health nurse organizes or participates in programs of accident prevention, health examination, or group immunization. The nurse who enters this field of work must be prepared to view the prevention of accidents and illness and the maintenance of good health as important as treatment of the patient after the onset of ill health. The occupational health nurse may be called upon to participate in seminars for supervisors and managers aimed at education on the early detection of physical or mental conditions and behavior patterns that may point to impending greater health problems and their resulting absenteeism. The nurse in this profession must exercise exceptionally good human relations skills.

For further details, write to the American Association of Occupational Health Nurses, 50 Lenox Pointe, Atlanta, Georgia 30324.

The Office Nurse

The *office nurse* who is employed in a busy physician's office fills many roles: functioning at times like a physician's assistant, at others like a laboratory technician, and at times, like a secretary, bookkeeper, or receptionist.

The office nurse prepares patients for examination, assists the physician during examination, and instructs the patient regarding medication or home care following office treatment. The office nurse may, under instructions from the physician, administer injections or other medication, dress wounds, and remove stitches.

Office nurses assist the doctor with minor surgical procedures performed in the office and maintain office records of patient diagnosis, treatment, and prognosis. They check and requisition supplies, clean and sterilize equipment, and may develop x-rays and perform routine laboratory tests such as urinalysis and blood counts.

The duties of the office nurse vary with the employment situation. In a small office with limited staff the office nurse may perform receptionist and secretarial duties and send out the monthly bills; in an office with more help, these duties will be performed by clerical staff.

The office nurse works under the supervision of the physician and may, in turn, supervise nursing assistants or clerical help. This nurse may be allowed to work with varying degrees of independence, depending on the nurse's experience and the inclination of the employing physician. Some persons prefer this one-boss arrangement to the layers of supervision and management in a hospital setting.

Persons entering this field of nursing need to be emotionally stable, able to handle emergencies in the absence of the doctor, have the ability to work well with people, and have a genuine liking for people. This nurse will often deal with many members of the same family over a period of years and may be called upon to give counseling and reassurance to the patient and family.

Some nurses derive a high degree of job satisfaction from this work. They become a valued assistant to the physician, relied upon by the patients to take care of their minor problems when the doctor is not available.

The Oncology Nurse

Oncology nurses administer various cancer treatments, manage their patient's pain, and counsel the patient and family. They also perform many traditional nursing duties such as taking temperatures, blood pressure readings, and pulse rates. Some oncology nurses consult with hospitals about oncology programs.

Oncology nurses are employed in hospitals, hospices, physicians' offices, schools of nursing, comprehensive cancer centers, and outpatient care clinics.

The oncology nurse prepares the cancer patient, both physiologically and psychologically for surgery. Following surgery, the nurse assists the patient through the postoperative period by giving medication, comfort, and reassurance. The nurse cares for the tracheostomy, laryngectomy, mastectomy, and colostomy and teaches the patient home care of these conditions.

There is probably no nursing specialty that requires as much warmth and understanding on the part of the nurse. The disease is so threatening that family relationships may become very strained. The nurse is often the intermediary for communication between patient and family as well as between patient and doctor. This nurse must be able to communicate with the family so that they understand the situation and how important their support is to the patient at this time.

When the patient is ready for discharge, this nurse instructs the patient and family in home care. The nurse also counsels the family on its attitude toward the patient and the necessity of maintaining a positive outlook, along with tolerance for the behavior of the patient trying to adjust to a very traumatic situation. The family must be made to understand the importance of the patient's return to activity that is as nearly normal as possible.

For more information, write to the Oncology Nursing Society, 501 Holiday Drive, Pittsburgh, Pennsylvania 15220-2749.

The Orthopedic Nurse

The *orthopedic nurse* is a registered nurse who has received special training in the care and treatment of musculoskeletal difficulties, deformities, and chronic diseases of the joints and spine.

Orthopedic nurses work with patients who have arthritis, bursitis, fractures, dislocations, and congenital deformities. Before the introduction of the Salk vaccine in 1955, a large part of orthopedic nursing was devoted to work with patients crippled by poliomyelitis. Following the virtual disappearance of polio, the emphasis shifted to working with birth defects and with orthopedic conditions in the elderly.

This nurse teaches the patient to use crutches, walkers, braces, and other equipment in the orthopedic unit. For patients who have had orthopedic surgery, the nurse helps care for the patient while in the hospital and instructs the patient in home care upon discharge.

Orthopedic patients frequently have conditions that require a change in life-style. It is the orthopedic nurse's responsibility to prepare them for this change, working with the family so that they are ready for the patient's return and are prepared to share in the adjustments they may have to make to accommodate the patient's new life-style. The orthopedic nurse must be prepared to give psychological support to patients while they make these changes.

The Pediatric Nurse

Pediatric nurses are registered nurses specially trained to furnish nursing services to infants, children, and adolescents. They may work in hospitals, public health agencies, well-child clinics, family clinics, long-term care facilities, and physicians' offices.

Pediatric nurses perform traditional nursing functions such as taking temperatures, blood pressures, and respiratory rates and recording this data. They bathe patients, weigh them, feed them or persuade them to eat, and give medication as prescribed by the physician. Pediatric nurses must thoroughly understand the growth and development patterns of the child in order to assess the significance of behavior in relation to the child's illness.

The pediatric nurse must be able to communicate with the child and be able to understand his or her nonverbal communication since the patient may be too young to talk or just too intimidated by the situation to complain. This increases the importance of close observation of appearance and behavior. A large part of pediatric nursing is allaying the anxiety of the children by explaining the procedures being used and reassuring and supporting them. The pediatric nurse's training in child psychology enables him or her to assess the behavior of the patient under treatment.

The pediatric nurse must also be able to reassure and support the parents as well as explain to them the procedures being used to treat their child. This avoids having fearful parents transfer anxiety to their children.

Pediatric nurses may work in the nursery in the care of the new-born, with older children, or with adolescents. Nurses working this area must have a thorough understanding of the physical and emotional development of the adolescent.

The Private Duty Nurse

The *private duty nurse* makes a private contract to furnish nursing services at home or in a hospital. Usually this will be for nursing one patient only.

The private duty nurse works under the supervision of a physician to administer prescribed medication and other treatment to the patient. The nurse monitors the patient, noting changes in condition, evaluates and records these changes, initiates emergency measures if needed, and notifies the physician immediately of the patient's condition.

The private duty nurse instructs the patient and family in the procedures needed to restore and maintain the patient in a state of good health. If the nurse is working in a private home, they may supervise the diet of the patient. This nurse cooperates with any community agencies furnishing services to the family.

The Psychiatric Nurse

The *psychiatric nurse* is a registered nurse who delivers nursing service to patients having mental health problems. The psychiatric nurse may work in mental hospitals, the psychiatric wards of general hospitals, health clinics, community mental health centers, nursing homes, and private homes.

The psychiatric nurse performs many of the same nursing functions as the general duty nurse, such as administering medication prescribed by the physician, and taking and recording temperatures, pulse rates, blood pressures, and other vital signs affecting the physical health of the patient. In addition, the psychiatric nurse works with individual patients and with groups to assist them in understanding their problems, developing better self concepts, and learning the coping skills necessary to move back toward mental health.

The psychiatric nurse observes and assesses the behavior of the patient and, on the basis of this observation and assessment, forms a nursing diagnosis. Then, working with the physician and other members of the nursing team, the nurse devises a nursing plan for each individual patient.

The psychiatric nurse must be both teacher and counselor in addition to being a nurse in the traditional sense. Working with the patients in a warm accepting manner helps them make a more socially acceptable adjustment to their environment and the people with whom they come in contact. This nurse is trained in listening and communication skills, to assist the client in socializing with others and developing better interpersonal relations skills.

The Quality Assurance Coordinator

The *quality assurance coordinator* is a registered nurse (RN) who determines and implements the quality assurance standards of the healthcare facility. It is his or her responsibility to ensure that patients receive quality care. He or she reviews and examines the health care facility's current policies, procedures, and quality assurance standards, writing new quality assurance policies and procedures if necessary. To ensure that quality assurance standards are being applied, he or she reviews and evaluates patients' medical records and oversees staff reviewing of patients' medical records. He or she may question patients and staff to measure the effectiveness of the facility's quality assurance program. The quality assurance coordinator may also collect statistical information; write reports; and select specific subjects to be reviewed, such as drugs, high risk cases, and problem procedures.

The Rehabilitation Nurse

The *rehabilitation nurse* is a registered nurse who provides services to persons needing restoration of physical or mental functioning to a state as nearly normal as possible. These patients have suffered trauma as a result of disease, birth defects, or accidental injury.

Rehabilitation nurses work in hospitals, rehabilitation centers, nursing homes, community health agencies, schools, clinics, and hospices. They perform many tasks performed by regular staff nurses, such as administering medication prescribed by the physician; taking temperatures, blood pressures, pulse rates, and other vital signs; and keeping records of patient care. In addition, they are especially trained in rehabilitation nursing techniques, including assisting the patient in use of prostheses, physical therapy, and special exercises to restore function in impaired body parts.

Some of the conditions the rehabilitation nurse will work with include arthritis, drug addiction, birth defects, cerebral palsy, cancer, epilepsy, spinal cord injuries, alcoholism, blindness, deafness, and disabilities resulting from deteriorating disease processes and accidental injuries.

The rehabilitation nurse is trained in the use of a wide variety of machines and equipment designed to help the patient's recovery. The nurse instructs the patient in the use of such aids as braces, walkers, respirators, and artificial limbs and other prostheses.

Being a rehabilitation nurse calls for good counseling skills. If the patient has psychological problems related to his or her disability, they must be worked through so they will not stand in the way of rehabilitation and resumption of a nearly normal life. Teaching skills are necessary to teach the patient the use of new equipment, new methods of doing things, and sometimes a whole new life-style compatible with the patient's capabilities.

This nurse must be infinitely patient, able to derive encouragement from the patient's minimal improvement and able to persuade the patient to share this encouragement. Patients who have been disabled from birth or early childhood may have built up such highly defensive behavior that it interferes with socialization or employment. The nurse assists the patient in developing a better self-concept by setting achievable goals and assisting the patient in reaching these goals.

The Respiratory Therapy Nurse

The *respiratory therapy nurse* is a registered nurse who has been trained to administer diagnostic and treatment procedures to persons with cardiopulmonary problems that affect their ability to breathe normally. Most respiratory therapy nurses are employed in hospitals, but some will be found in medical clinics, nursing homes, industry, military service, and physicians' offices.

The respiratory therapy nurse is a member of the critical care staff, working with patients who require life-support measures to maintain clear airways. They provide artificial ventilation for patients who cannot breathe normally. This requires highly specialized knowledge in the use of very sophisticated ventilation equipment as well as a thorough understanding of the underlying physiology involved in cardiopulmonary dysfunctions.

In addition to management of critical cases in which life is threatened, respiratory nurses work in the routine care of patients with respiratory disorders. They administer oxygen, supervise exercises, and perform cardiopulmonary resuscitation.

Respiratory nurses treat such conditions as cardiac failure, emphysema, stroke, asthma, drowning, and shock. They conduct such diagnostic procedures as screening of lungs, measurement of lung capacity, and securing of secretion samples for cancer diagnosis.

The School Nurse

The *school nurse* is a registered nurse (RN) who is employed in an elementary school, junior high school, high school, or college. The school nurse works more with healthy than with sick patients, a large part of this job being preventive medicine such as assisting in immunization and safety programs, counseling, and educating the student body regarding the maintenance of good health.

School nurses perform physical examinations, give vision and hearing tests, render first aid following accidents on the school property, and refer students to a physician if treatment beyond first aid is indicated.

Students who are having problems in classes, such as inattention, disruptive behavior, drug abuse, or apparent emotional instability may be referred to the school or college nurse so that the underlying physical or emotional condition that may be responsible for the student's inappropriate behavior may be discovered. Duties of the college nurse will also include sex education and contraceptive information.

The school nurse works with school administrative officials to establish standards and policies for a school health program, then monitors and evaluates that program. Part of the work of these nurses is health education and they may instruct classes in home healthcare, child care, and the general maintenance of good health.

School nurses are usually involved in the community and work with its agencies to plan activities for children outside the school. They may also be involved in devising special programs designed to aid handicapped children.

These nurses need to have counseling skills, a liking for youth of the age with which they work, and good interpersonal relations skills. Persons considering entering this field would do well to examine their attitudes toward the elementary school child, the adolescent, and the college student. While nursing skills for all groups may be the same, relating to the attitudes and emotions of the various age groups requires different approaches incorporating a good understanding of developmental psychology.

The Staff Nurse

Staff nurses are employed in the hospital, infirmary, nursing home, community health agency, or other similar institution giving general nursing care to patients. They work under the supervision of nursing supervisors and physicians.

The staff nurse observes the condition of the patient, takes temperature, pulse rate, blood pressure, and any other vital signs needed to evaluate the progress of the patient. The nurse records data from these observations on patients' charts and notifies the supervisor or physician of any change indicating the need for special attention. These nurses prepare the patient for examination, assist the physician during examination and treatment, and administer medications and treatments under the direction of the physician.

Duties will vary according to the size and type of institution. In a large, fully staffed hospital with many nursing aides (assistants), the nurse's duties may be almost exclusively patient treatment. In a smaller institution with less support staff, duties may include sterilization of instruments, bed making, feeding and bathing patients, and preparation of rooms for occupancy.

The staff nurse may be assigned to work in a special section of the hospital, such as surgery, pediatrics, obstetrics, psychiatry, or the admitting office. The nurse who works in several of these sections gets a broad scope of nursing specialties and is able to make a more informed decision as to which of the clinical areas to choose for further study and specialization.

Persons who enter the career field of staff nursing should have a genuine liking for people, and should be emotionally stable, enabling them to cope with ill patients and their distressed families. They should be able to work under pressure, be responsible and resourceful, be able to direct the activities of the nursing aides (assistants), as well as be able to take precise orders from superiors and execute them exactly. The staff nurse needs a lot of physical stamina as the occupation requires much walking and standing as well as lifting and moving patients. During periods of disaster or epidemics, the nurse may be required to work prolonged shifts until the emergency passes.

The Surgical Nurse

The *surgical nurse* is a registered nurse (RN) who has special training and experience working with patients hospitalized for surgery. The work of the surgical nurse falls into three phases-preoperative nursing, operating room duties, and postoperative care.

The goal of the preoperative phase is to prepare the patient physically and psychologically for surgery. The nurse interviews the patient in depth to uncover any indications of problems that might surface during surgery or in the postoperative period. All available previous medical records are reviewed by the nurse to alert the physician to any past medical history that might impinge on the planned procedures. The importance of this interview cannot be overemphasized. Such things as allergies to medication, unreasonable fears of anesthesia, and emotional pressures will surface in the good interview, offering the nurse the opportunity to explain to patients each procedure they can expect to experience. The manner in which this interview is handled by the nurse will determine to a great extent the degree of anxiety patients will take with them to the operating room. Communicating with the families of patients is important to allay their anxiety, since their fears may be transferred to the patient. This nurse needs counseling skills so that the fears and anxieties of the patient can be acknowledged as normal for the situation, and the patient can be allowed to talk through these fears to the extent possible. The nurse should be sensitive to the spiritual needs of the patient and should react to the patient's suggestions, however veiled, that the services of a clergyman would be welcome.

The second phase of surgical nursing is the operating room phase. The scrub nurse, who must be experienced and know what equipment the surgeon will need for each specific procedure, sees that such equipment is in place before the surgery. During the surgery this nurse hands the instruments, sutures, sponges, and other needed supplies to the physician. The efficient scrub nurse observes the surgeon closely to know what is needed before it is requested. The maneuvers must be accomplished with careful speed so that no time is wasted but no accidents occur due to haste or carelessness. It is also the responsibility of the scrub nurse to see that sterile conditions are maintained in the operating room.

In addition to the scrub nurse, there is the circulating nurse who supervises the preparation of the operating room, insuring that the room and all its equipment are scrupulously clean and properly prepared for the surgery. Following the operation, the circulating nurse supervises clean-up and preparation for the next scheduled patient. This nurse is usually a senior nurse with several years of experience.

The third phase of surgical nursing is the postoperative phase. It starts with the recovery room (or the intensive care unit if the patient has complications) and includes care of the surgical wound, measurements to guard against infection, support and reassurance for the patient, and the teaching of home care after hospital discharge.

Foreign Nurses

Due to the shortage of nurses in this country, persons who are licensed nurses in foreign countries are given preference status by the immigration system to come to the United States to practice nursing. Admitted into the states on this basis, nurses get work permits and may work as registered nurses (RNs) as soon as they pass the state board nursing examination.

The Commission on Graduates of Foreign Nursing Schools (CGFNS) has set up a procedure by which foreign nursing school graduates can take a screening examination to determine their chances of passing a state examination in the United States. Upon passing the CGFNS preliminary examination, the nurse is given a certificate to be presented to the U.S. Immigration and Naturalization Service for a preference visa and to the U.S. Labor Department for a work permit.

To qualify to take the screening examination, nurses must be educated and registered as a first-level, general nurse. (A first-level nurse is known as a Registered or Professional nurse in most countries.) CGFNS's educational requirements are: successful completion of a full, secondary school education that is separate from the nursing education; graduation from a two year government-approved general nursing program; and theory and clinical education in medical ,surgical, obstetric, pediatric, and psychiatric nursing. The examination takes one entire day and covers nursing proficiency and English comprehension.

Application to take the examination may be made by contacting a U.S. embassy or consulate, national nurses' associations, or writing to CGFNS for application forms. A fee is required for taking the examination the first time. Each applicant is notified of passing or failing eight to ten weeks after taking the exam.

Detailed information on the CGFNS examination, examination sites and dates, and entry into the United States for the purpose of practicing nursing may be obtained by writing to the Commission on Graduates of Foreign Nursing Schools (CGFNS), 3600 Market Street, Suite 400, Philadelphia, Pennsylvania 19104-2651, U.S.A.

Nursing Aide/Orderly

The *nursing aide/orderly* works as an auxiliary employee in an entry-level position in a department of nursing, helping the professional nursing staff in the care of sick, disabled, or infirmed patients. Nursing aides/orderlies may also be referred to as *nursing assistants, hospital attendants,* or in the case of mental health facilities, nursing homes or home-healthcare agencies, as *psychiatric aides, geriatric aides* or *home-health aides,* respectively. Refer to the chapters titled Mental Health and Homemaker Home-Health Aide Services for more information on the positions of psychiatric aide and home-health aide.

Depending on the type of health facility and the type of patient being cared for, the duties of the nursing aide/orderly vary from cleaning patients' rooms and other household tasks to assisting in patient care.

Under direct supervision of the nursing staff, the nursing aide performs routine duties such as answering patient bell calls, delivering messages, serving and collecting food trays, feeding patients who are unable to feed themselves, assisting patients with their personal hygiene, giving massages and alcohol rubs, and reporting all unusual conditions and reactions of patients to the nurses in charge. In assisting in basic patient care, the nursing aide may administer catheterization treatments; take and record temperature, blood pressure, pulse, and respiration rates; and accompany patients during exercise periods.

The orderly performs the same functions as the nursing aide, but with emphasis on the personal care of male patients. The orderly also does the lifting and heavy work such as transporting patients in wheelchairs and stretchers, lifting and turning patients in bed, and carrying mattresses to the sterilization room. With special training the orderly may also transport and set up catheterization, sterilization, respiratory, traction, and mobile X-ray equipment.

Most nursing aides/orderlies work in hospitals, while others are employed in nursing homes and other long-term care facilities.

After being hired by a hospital or nursing home, the nursing aide/orderly is trained on-the-job. Some employers prefer their aides/orderlies to be recent high school graduates. Nursing homes and psychiatric hospitals prefer to hire more mature individuals as their aides/orderlies.

Many vocational schools, community colleges, and other post-secondary institutions throughout the United States have training programs for the nursing aide/orderly. Interested students should check with schools in their area for further information.

The nursing aide/orderly has limited opportunities for promotion and better salaries without additional education and training. The nursing aide/orderly may, for example, take specialized courses or on-the-job training and become a cardiographic technician or radiographer (X-ray technician).

For additional information on the job opportunities, persons interested in a career as a nursing aide/orderly should contact the Personnel Director of their local healthcare facility or talk with faculty or career counselors at post-secondary educational institutions in their area offering nursing aide/orderly training programs.

SOURCES:

Alperin Stanley, *Careers in Nursing*, Ballinger Publishing Company,
  Cambridge, Massachusetts
American Association of Legal Nurse Consultants
American Association of Nurse Anesthetists
American Association of Occupational Health Nurses
American College of Nurse-Midwives
American College of Obstetrics and Gynecologists
American Nurses' Association
Commission on Graduates of Foreign Nursing Schools
Dictionary of Occupational Titles
Emergency Nurses Association
National Federation of Licensed Practical Nurses
National League for Nursing
Nurses Association of the American College of Obstetrics and
  Gynecologists
Occupational Outlook Handbook
Oncology Nursing Society

OCCUPATIONAL SAFETY AND HEALTH

Occupational safety and health is concerned with the maintenance of optimal health standards in all of today's working environments. To protect workers from undue hazards and dangerous working conditions in industry, manufacturing, mining, construction, transportation, and scientific research, safety and health regulations are established to prevent or reduce work-related accidents, injuries, and illnesses. In this field of allied health there are several closely related careers, including those of the *safety professional,* the *industrial hygienist,* the *occupational safety* and *health technician,* and the *industrial hygiene technician;* all of these are discussed below.

Safety Professional

Known as a *safety engineer,* a *safety specialist,* or a *safety manager,* the safety professional plans and administers accident-prevention and injury-control programs in industrial and other settings. He or she investigates health and safety conditions and the potential for accidents and for the loss of time, materials, or equipment in working environments. Such hazards as faulty equipment, poor facility design, dangerous materials, unsafe work practices, and the nonobservance of safety and health regulations are all the concern of the safety professional. The safety professional develops and implements programs that will eliminate or reduce the chances of an accident by informing management of problems, by enforcing safety standards, by recommending the use of safer equipment or more stringent control procedures, and/or by conducting intensive educational programs to increase and stimulate awareness and interest in occupational safety and health among both employers and employees.

The safety professional also coordinates safety activities with others who participate in safety and health, including managers, industrial hygienists, physicians, nurses, and fire and security personnel. Finally, as a *safety consultant* he or she offers advice on the design, construction, or installation of working facilities or equipment and on the safety of manufactured products.

Safety professionals work in a variety of locations including industrial and manufacturing

313

plants, construction and mining sites, insurance companies, research and educational institutions, and in all levels of government, establishing and maintaining safety and health regulations.

Recommended high school courses for students interested in a career as a safety professional include mathematics, biology, chemistry, physics, and English.

The minimum educational requirement for a safety professional is a bachelor's degree. Graduate programs are available for those who wish to obtain high level jobs in the various fields of occupational safety and health.

According to a 1990 survey by the American Society of Safety Engineers the average annual compensation of safety professionals, including cash incentives and commissions, ranged from $42,200 to $43,447.

For further information on a career as a safety professional, write to the American Society of Safety Engineers, 1800 East Oakton Street, Des Plaines, Illinois 60018-2187, or the National Institute for Occupational Safety and Health, Robert A. Taft Laboratories, 4676 Columbia Parkway, Cincinnati, Ohio 45226-1998.

Following is a list of colleges and universities offering safety degree programs, compiled from data from the American Society of Safety Engineers.

SOURCES:

American Society of Safety Engineers
National Institute for Occupational Safety and Health

Safety Degree Programs

ALABAMA

Industrial Engineering Program
Auburn University
School of Engineering
Auburn, Alabama 36849-5346

Occupational Health & Safety Program
University of Alabama-Birmingham
School of Public Health
Birmingham, Alabama 35294

CALIFORNIA

Environmental Health Studies Program
University of California-Berkeley
School of Public Health
Berkeley, California 94720

Occupational Safety & Health Program
California State University-Fresno
Dept. of Health Science
School of Health & Social Work
2345 East San Ramon
Fresno, California 93740-0030

Occupational Safety & Health Program
California State University-LA
Health & Science Dept.
5151 State University
Los Angeles, California 90032

Occupational Safety & Health Program
University of Southern California
University Park
Los Angeles, California 90089-0021

Environmental Health Program
California State University-Northridge
Health Science Dept.
18111 Nordhoff Street
Northridge, California 91330

Occupational Safety & Health Program
Merritt College
Technical Division
12500 Campus Drive
Oakland, California 94619

Occupational Safety & Health Program
National University
School of Engineering & Computer
  Science
4141 Camino Del Rio South
San Diego, California 92108

COLORADO

Environmental Health Program
Colorado State University
College of Veterinary Medicine &
  Biomed Sciences
Ft. Collins, Colorado 80523

Occupational Safety Program
Trinidad State Junior College
600 Prospect
Trinidad, Colorado 81082

CONNECTICUT

Occupational Safety & Health Program
Central Connecticut State University
School of Technology
Central Connecticut State University
1615 Stanley Street
New Britain, Connecticut 06050

Occupational Safety & Health Program
University of New Haven
School of Professional Studies
300 Orange Avenue
West Haven, Connecticut 06516

FLORIDA

Fire Science Technology Program
Miami-Dade Community College
Academy of Science
11011 SW 104th Street
Miami, Florida 33176

Fire Safety Program
Hillsborough Community College
Fire Safety Dept.
2001 North 14th Street
Tampa, Florida 33605

GEORGIA

Environmental Health Program
University of Georgia
College of Agriculture
Room 206 Dairy Science Building
Athens, Georgia 30602

Environmental Engineering Program
Georgia Institute of Technology
School of Civil Engineering
790 Atlantic Drive
Atlanta, Georgia 30332

HAWAII

Environmental Health Program
University of Hawaii
School of Public Health
1960 East-West Road
Honolulu, Hawaii 96822

ILLINOIS

Industrial Technology Program
Southern Illinois University
College of Engineering & Technology
Carbondale, Illinois 62901

315

Occupational Safety & Health Program
University of Illinois-Chicago
Environ & Occupational Health Dept.
School of Public Health West
2121 West Taylor
Chicago, Illinois 60612

Industrial Technology Program
Northern Illinois University
Dept. of Technology
DeKalb, Illinois 60115-1349

Health Sciences Program
Western Illinois University
Macomb, Illinois 61455

Environmental Health & Safety Program
Illinois State University
Health Sciences Dept.
College of Applied Science &
  Technology
Normal, Illinois 61761

Environmental Engineering & Science
  Program
University of Illinois-Champaign
Civil Engineering Department
205 North Matthews
Urbana, Illinois 61801

INDIANA

Occupational Safety & Health Program
Indiana University-Bloomington
College of Health, PE & Recreation
Bloomington, Indiana 47405

Industrial Health & Safety Mgmt
  Program
Indiana State University
Applied Health Science Dept.
School of Health, PE & Recreation
Terre Haute, Indiana 47809

Occupational Safety & Health Program
Purdue University
School of Health
West Lafayette, Indiana 47907

IOWA

Occupational Safety Program
Iowa State University
School of Education
1013 Hunziker
Ames, Iowa 50010

Safety Education Program
University of Northern Iowa
Curriculum & Instruction Dept.
School of Education
Cedar Falls, Iowa 50614

KENTUCKY

Occupational Health & Safety Program
Western Kentucky University
Health & Safety Dept.
Ogden College of Science, Technology
  & Health
Bowling Green, Kentucky 42101

Environmental Studies Program
Morehead State University
College of Arts & Science
Morehead, Kentucky 40351

Occupational Safety & Health Program
Murray State University
Murray, Kentucky 42071

Fire & Safety Engineering Technology
  Program
Eastern Kentucky University
Loss Prevention & Safety Dept.
College of Law Enforcement
Richmond, Kentucky 40475

LOUISIANA

Industrial Technology Program
Louisiana State University
Dept. of Agriculture-Engineering
Baton Rouge, Louisiana 70803

316

Petroleum Safety Program
Nicholls State University
Petroleum Services Department
University Station
P.O. Box 2094
Thibodaux, Louisiana 70301

MARYLAND

Environmental Engineering Program
John Hopkins University
School of Hygiene & Public Health
615 North Wolfe Street
Baltimore, Maryland 21205

Industrial Technology Program
University of Maryland
Industrial, Tech & Occup Education
  Dept.
College of Education
3216 JM Patterson
College Park, Maryland 20742

MASSACHUSETTS

Fire Protection Safety Program
North Shore Community College
Three Essex Street
Beverly, Massachusetts 01915

Human Factors Program
Tufts University
Engineering Design Department
College of Engineering
Medford, Massachusetts 02155

Fire Protection Engineering Program
Worcester Polytechnic Institute
School of Fire Protect Engineering
100 Institute Road
Worcester, Massachusetts 01609

MICHIGAN

Occupational Safety & Health Program
Grand Valley State University
School of Health Sciences
College Landing
Allendales, Michigan 49401-9403

Occupational Safety Engineering
  Program
University of Michigan-Ann Arbor
School of Engineering
1205 Beal Street, 10E Bldg.
Ann Arbor, Michigan 48109

Environment & Industrial Health
  Program
University of Michigan-Ann Arbor
School of Public Health
Ann Arbor, Michigan 48109

Occupational Safety & Health Program
Ferris State College
School of Allied Health
Big Rapids, Michigan 49307

Fire Science Program
Henry Ford Community College
Management Development Division
22586 Ann Arbor Trail
Dearborn Heights, Michigan 48127

Occupational & Environmental Health
  Program
Wayne State University
College of Pharmacy & Allied Health
Detroit, Michigan 48202

Occupational Safety & Health Program
Madonna College
Division of Science & Technology
36600 Schoolcraft Road
Livonia, Michigan 48150

Industrial Management & Technology
Program
Central Michigan University
Industrial Engineering & Technology
Dept.
Mount Pleasant, Michigan 48859

Industrial Health Program
Oakland University
School of Health Sciences
Rochester, Michigan 48309-4401

MINNESOTA

Industrial & Technical Studies Program
University of Minnesota-Duluth
Duluth, Minnesota 55812

MISSISSIPPI

Occupational Safety Program
University of Southern Mississippi
Center for Community Health
College of Health & Human Services
P.O. Box 5122
Hattiesburg, Mississippi 39406-5122

MISSOURI

Industrial Science Program
Northeast Missouri State University
Kirksville, Missouri 63501

Fire Protection Safety Program
St. Louis Community College-Forest
Park
Municipal Services
3600 Oakland
St. Louis, Missouri 63110

Safety Science & Technology Program
Central Missouri State
Warrensburg, Missouri 64093

MONTANA

Occupational Safety & Health Program
Montana College of Mineral Science &
Technology
Environmental Engineering & Natural
Science Dept.
Butte, Montana 59701

NEBRASKA

Occupational Safety & Health Program
Kearney Safety College
Nebraska Safety Center
West Center
Kearney, Nebraska 68849

NEVADA

Fire Protection Safety Program
Clark County Community College
Social Sciences & Service Occupation
Div.
3200 East Cheyenne Avenue
North Las Vegas, Nevada 89030

NEW HAMPSHIRE

Occupational Safety & Health Program
Keene State College
Safety Center
229 Main Street
Keene, New Hampshire 03431

NEW JERSEY

Occupational Safety Program
Cameden County College
Information Services
P.O. Box 200
Blackwood, New Jersey 08012

Radiation Science Program
Rutgers, The State University of New
Jersey
Bldg. 4087, Kilmer Campus
New Brunswick, New Jersey 08093

318

NEW YORK

Occupational Safety & Health Program
Broome Community College
Special Career Programs Dept.
P.O. Box 1017
Binghamton, New York 13902

Public Safety Program
Mercy College
Criminal Justice & Public Safety Dept.
555 Broadway
Dobbs Ferry, New York 10522

Environmental Health & Safety Program
Columbia University
600 West 168 Street
New York, New York 10032

Environmental Studies Program
University of Rochester
Toxicology Division
Radiation & Biophysics Dept.
School of Medicine
Rochester, New York 14642

NORTH CAROLINA

Environmental Engineering Program
University of North Carolina-Chapel Hill
School of Public Health
P.O. Box 2688
Chapel Hill, North Carolina 27599-7400

Industrial Safety Program
Central Piedmont Community College
P.O. Box 350009
Charlotte, North Carolina 28235

Occupational Safety Program
Western Carolina University
Industrial Technology Dept.
Cullowhee, North Carolina 28723

Occupational Safety & Health Program
North Carolina A&T State University
1601 East Market Street
Greensborough, North Carolina 27411

Environmental Health Program
East Carolina University
East Fifth Street
Greenville, North Carolina 27834

NORTH DAKOTA

Industrial Hygiene Program
North Dakota State College of Science
Wahpeton, North Dakota 58076

OHIO

Fire Science Technology Program
University of Cincinnati
College of Applied Science
2220 Victory Parkway ML 103
Cincinnati, Ohio 45206

Environmental Health Sciences Program
Wright State University
Biological Sciences Dept.
Colonel Glenn Highway
Dayton, Ohio 45435

OKLAHOMA

Environmental Science Program
East Central University
Physical & Environmental Sciences
 Dept.
Ada, Oklahoma 74820

Industrial Technology Program
Central State University
College of Education
100 North University Drive
Edmond, Oklahoma 73034-0185

Environmental Science Engineering
University of Oklahoma
Civil Engineering & Environmental
 Sciences Dept.
202 West Boyd Street
Norman, Oklahoma 73109

Occupational & Environmental Health
Program
University of Oklahoma-Oklahoma City
P.O. Box 25901
Oklahoma City, Oklahoma 73190

Fire & Protection Safety Program
Oklahoma State University
Academic Services
Engineering Technology Dept.
Stillwater, Oklahoma 74078

OREGON

Fire Science Program
Southwestern Oregon Community
College
Coos Bay, Oregon 97420

Safety Studies Program
Oregon State University
Health Department
College of Health & Human
Performance
Corvallis, Oregon 97331-6404

PENNSYLVANIA

Safety Science Program
Indiana University of Pennsylvania
College of Human Ecology & Health
Science
Indiana, Pennsylvania 15705

Occupational Safety Program
Millersville University of Pennsylvania
Industry & Technology Department
Millersville, Pennsylvania 17551

Occupational Health & Safety Mgmt.
Program
Slippery Rock University of
Pennsylvania
Allied Health Dept.
College of Education & Human Services
Professionals
Slippery Rock, Pennsylvania 16057

SOUTH CAROLINA

Occupational Safety & Health Program
Clemson University
Management Dept.
College of Commerce & Industry
Clemson, South Carolina 29634-1305

TENNESSEE

Environmental Health Program
East Tennessee State University
School of Public & Allied Health
Johnson City, Tennessee 37614

Safety Education Program
University of Tennessee-Knoxville
Health, Leisure & Safety Division
School of Health, PE & Recreation
1914 Andy Holt Drive
Knoxville, Tennessee 37996-2700

TEXAS

Occupational Safety & Health Program
Lamar University
Fire & Safety Institute
P.O. Box 10043
Beaumont, Texas 77710

Safety Engineering Program
Texas A&M University
Nuclear Engineering
College Station, Texas 77843-3133

Occupational Safety & Health Program
San Jacinto College Central
Industrial Technology Division
8060 Spencer Highway
Pasadena, Texas 77505

Occupational Safety & Health Program
Texas State Technical Institute
Waco Campus
Waco, Texas 76705

VIRGINIA

Safety & Risk Administration Program
Virginia Commonwealth University
Justice/Risk Administration Dept.
School of Community & Public Affairs
P.O. Box 2017
Richmond, Virginia 23284

WASHINGTON

Environmental Health Program
Central Washington University
Central Safety Center
Ellensburg, Washington 98926

Environmental Health Program
University of Washington
Environmental Health Dept.
School of Public Health & Community
  Medicine
Seattle, Washington 98195

WEST VIRGINIA

Occupational Safety Engineering
  Program
Fairmont State College
Technology Division
Locust Avenue
Fairmont, West Virginia 26554

Occupational Safety & Health Program
Marshall University
Safety Technology Department
College of Education
Huntington, West Virginia 25701

Occupational Safety & Health Program
West Virginia University
Safety Studies Dept.
Morgantown, West Virginia 26505

WISCONSIN

Health & Related Programs
University of Wisconsin-Parkside
Allied Health Dept.
P.O. Box 1000
Kenosha, Wisconsin 53141

Occupational Safety & Health Program
University of Wisconsin-Stout
Safety & Loss Control Center
Industrial Management Dept.
205 Communications Center
Menomonie, Wisconsin 54751

Industrial Technology Management
  Program
University of Wisconsin-Platteville
Industrial Studies Department
Platteville, Wisconsin 53818

Driver Safety Education Program
University of Wisconsin-Steven's Point
Traffic Safety Education
Health, PE & Recreation Dept.
Steven's Point, Wisconsin 54481

Industrial Safety Program
University of Wisconsin-Whitewater
800 West Main Street
Whitewater, Wisconsin 53190

Industrial Hygienist

As a member of the occupational safety team, the *industrial hygienist* recognizes, evaluates, and controls environmental factors that affect the safety and health of workers. The industrial hygienist performs many duties similar to the safety professional, such as conducting safety and health inspections, recommending changes to equipment or to processes, implementing control procedures, and advising on the design and construction of new facilities. Where their respective duties differ however is in the industrial hygienist's particular concern with the controlling of chemical, physical, and biological agents that cause illness, injuries, discomfort, and fatigue to workers. The industrial hygienist strives to minimize radiation, fungi, air and noise pollution, vibration, poor lighting and other unsanitary, unhealthy, and hazardous working conditions.

Industrial hygienists are employed in universities, government, business, and factories. Some are self-employed as consultants.

Some colleges offer a two year degree in industrial hygiene, health, or engineering, but a bachelor's degree in one of the sciences such as engineering, chemistry, or physical science is generally the minimum educational requirement for the industrial hygienist. Continued professional development is available through a number of graduate degree programs.

Recommended high school courses include chemistry, biology, math, and the physical sciences.

Salaries for the industrial hygienist vary depending upon education, experience, and location. Entry level positions average $24,000 to $31,000 annually, while executive salaries may reach $90,000 annually.

For further information on a career as an industrial hygienist, write to the American Industrial Hygiene Foundation, 2700 Prosperity Avenue, Suite 250, Fairfax, Virginia 22031.

Following the Occupational Safety and Health Technician/Industrial Hygiene Technician chapter, is a list compiled by the American Industrial Hygiene Foundation of educational programs in Industrial Hygiene.

SOURCE:

American Industrial Hygiene Foundation

Occupational Safety and Health Technician
Industrial Hygiene Technician

The *occupational safety and health technician* and the *industrial hygiene technician* support and work in construction, manufacturing, government, organized labor, insurance, and other sectors of the economy. Both technicians are concerned with maintenance of safety and health standards and with accident prevention and perform such duties as inspecting working conditions; collecting samples of physical, chemical, and biological agents for testing; operating instruments that detect and measure levels of noise, radiation, air flow, light, and gas; keeping records of the amounts of hazardous agents to which workers could be exposed; and investigating work-related accidents. Both technicians also teach workers the principles and techniques of disease and accident prevention.

An associate degree from an accredited institution in health and safety or other technical and scientific discipline is generally the minimum educational requirement for both the occupational safety and health technician and the industrial hygiene technician.

Recommended high school courses include algebra, trigonometry, biology, chemistry, and physics.

Following is a list of programs in occupational health and safety and in industrial hygiene, compiled by the American Industrial Hygiene Foundation. The two fields are closely related and most programs, whatever their title, offer courses in both. Persons interested in a specific program should contact it directly and inquire about its particular specialties and degree offered.

SOURCES:

American Board of Industrial Hygiene
American Industrial Hygiene Foundation

Occupational and Industrial Safety and Health Technician Programs

ALABAMA

Industrial Engineering Program
Auburn University
Auburn University, Alabama 36849

Environmental Health Sciences Program
University of Alabama at Birmingham
Department of Environmental Health
Sciences
720-20th Street South
UAB Station
Birmingham, Alabama 35294-0008

Industrial Hygiene Program
University of North Alabama
Dept. of Chemistry & Industrial Hygiene
UNA-Box 5049
Florence, Alabama 35632-0001

ARIZONA

Industrial Hygiene Program
University of Arizona
School of Health Related Professionals
1435 North Fremont Avenue
Tucson, Arizona 85719

ARKANSAS

Occupational & Environmental Health
Program
University of Arkansas for Medical
Sciences
UAMS Division of Toxicology
4301 West Markham Street
Mail Slot #638
Little Rock, Arkansas 72205-7199

CALIFORNIA

Environmental & Occupational Health
Program
California State University, Northridge
18111 Nordhoff Street
Northridge, California 91311

Industrial Hygiene Program
San Diego State University
Graduate School of Public Health
San Diego, California 92182-0405

Environmental Health Science Program
University of California at Berkeley
Berkeley, California 94720

COLORADO

Industrial Hygiene Program
Colorado State University
Occupational Health & Safety Section
Ft. Collins, Colorado 80526

Risk & Safety Management Program
Pikes Peak Community College
5675 South Academy Boulevard
Colorado Springs, Colorado 80909

Public Health Program
University of Colorado
Dept. of Preventive Medicine &
Biometrics
4200 East Ninth Avenue, Box C245
Denver, Colorado 80262

CONNECTICUT

Public Health Program
University of Connecticut
University of Connecticut Health Center
School of Medicine
Farmington, Connecticut 06030

Occupational Safety & Health Program
University of New Haven
300 Orange Avenue
West Haven, Connecticut 06516

FLORIDA

Public Health Program
Florida International University
North Miami Campus
North Miami, Florida 33181

Environmental Health & Safety Program
University of Miami
Dept. of Industrial Engineering
1251 Memorial Drive
Coral Gables, Florida 33145

Industrial Hygiene & Safety
Management Program
University of South Florida
College of Public Health
13201 Bruce B. Downs Boulevard
Tampa, Florida 33612

HAWAII

Fire Science Program
University of Hawaii
874 Dillingham
Honolulu, Hawaii 96817

IDAHO

Industrial Technology Program
University of Idaho
Idaho Falls Center
Box 50778
1776 Science Center Drive
Idaho Falls, Idaho 83405

ILLINOIS

Environmental Health Program
Illinois State University
Dept. of Health Sciences
Normal, Illinois 61761-6901

Community Health Program
Northern Illinois University
School of Allied Health Professions
DeKalb, Illinois 60115

Industrial Safety & Health Program
Rock Valley College
5279-28th Avenue
Rockford, Illinois 61109

Environmental & Occupational Health
Program
The University of Illinois at Chicago
School of Public Health
P.O. Box 6998
Chicago, Illinois 60680

INDIANA

Environmental Protection Program
Ball State University
Dept. of Natural Resources
Muncie, Indiana 47306

Hazard Control Program
Indiana University
400 East Seventh Street
Bloomington, Indiana 47405

Industrial Hygiene Program
Purdue University
School of Health Sciences
West Lafayette, Indiana 47907

IOWA

Occupational & Environmental Health
Program
The University of Iowa
Institute of Agricultural Medicine &
Occupational Health
Oakdale Campus
Iowa City, Iowa 52242

KENTUCKY

Environmental Health Science Program
Eastern Kentucky University
College of Allied Health & Nursing
Richmond, Kentucky 40475

LOUISIANA

Environmental Sciences Program
McNeese State University
P.O. Box 92000
Lake Charles, Louisiana 70690-2000

MAINE

Occupational Health & Safety Program
Central Maine Technical College
1250 Turner Street
Auburn, Maine 04210

MARYLAND

Industrial Hygiene Program
Johns Hopkins University
School of Hygiene and Public Health
615 North Wolfe Street
Baltimore, Maryland 21205

Public Health Program
Uniformed Services University of the
Health Sciences
F. Edward Hebert School of Medicine
4301 Jones Bridge Road
Bethesda, Maryland 20814-4799

MASSACHUSETTS

Industrial Hygiene Program
Harvard School of Public Health
665 Huntington Avenue
Boston, Massachusetts 02115

MICHIGAN

Occupational Health & Safety Program
Grand Valley State University
Allendale, Michigan 49401

Occupational Safety Program
Madonna University
36600 Schoolcraft Road
Livonia, Michigan 48150-1173

Industrial Health Program
University of Michigan
Dept. of Environmental & Industrial
Health
School of Public Health
Ann Arbor, Michigan 48109-2029

Occupational & Environmental Health
Program
Wayne State University
1400 Chrysler Drive
Detroit, Michigan 48202

MINNESOTA

Industrial Hygiene Program
University of Minnesota
Box 197 Mayo
420 Delaware Street SE
Minneapolis, Minnesota 55455

MISSISSIPPI

Environmental Health Program
Mississippi Valley State University
Dept. of Natural Science &
Environmental Health
Highway 82 West
Box 1240 MVSU
Itta Bena, Mississippi 38941

MISSOURI

Safety Science & Technology Program
Central Missouri State University
Warrensburg, Missouri 64093

MONTANA

Industrial Hygiene Program
Montana College of Mineral Science &
Technology
Montana Tech Campus
Butte, Montana 59701

NEW JERSEY

Occupational Safety & Health
Engineering Program
New Jersey Institute Of Technology
Dept. of Mechanical & Industrial
Engineering
323 King Boulevard
Newark, New Jersey 07102

NEW YORK

Environmental Health Program
City University of New York, York
College
94-20 Guy R. Brewer Boulevard
Jamaica, New York 11451

Industrial Hygiene Program
Clarkson University
Potsdam, New York 13699-5805

Environmental Health Science Program
New York University
Institute of Environmental Medicine
Long Meadow Road
Tuxedo, New York 10987

NORTH CAROLINA

Environmental Health Program
Dept. of Environmental Health
East Carolina University
Greenville, North Carolina 27858

Construction Management/Safety
Program
North Carolina A&T State University
1601 East Market Street
Greensboro, North Carolina 27411

Occupational Safety Program
North Carolina State University
Dept. of Industrial Engineering
Box 7906
Raleigh, North Carolina 27695

Industrial Hygiene & Safety Program
St. Augustine's College
Box 14
Raleigh, North Carolina 27610-2298

Industrial Hygiene Program
University of North Carolina
Chapel Hill, North Carolina 27514

OHIO

Environmental Health Program
Bowling Green State University
102 Health Center
Bowling Green, Ohio 43403

Occupational Health
Medical College of Ohio at Toledo
3000 Arlington Avenue
Toledo, Ohio 43614

Industrial Hygiene Program
Ohio University
School of Health & Sport Sciences
189 Convocation Center
Athens, Ohio 45701-2979

OKLAHOMA

Environmental Science Program
East Central University
Box N-4
Ada, Oklahoma 74820

OREGON

Environmental Health Program
Oregon State University
Corvallis, Oregon 97331-6406

PENNSYLVANIA

Safety Sciences Program
Indiana University of Pennsylvania
Indiana, Pennsylvania 15705

Occupational Safety & Hygiene Program
Millersville University of Pennsylvania
Lancaster County
Millersville, Pennsylvania 17551

Environmental Health Program
Temple University
College of Engineering
Philadelphia, Pennsylvania 19122

SOUTH CAROLINA

Industrial Hygiene Program
University of South Carolina
Dept. of Environmental Health Sciences
Columbia, South Carolina 29208

TENNESSEE

Environmental Health Program
East Tennessee State University
Dept. of Environmental Health
P.O. Box 24,449
Johnson City, Tennessee 37614

Public Health Program
University of Tennessee, Knoxville
Dept. of Health, Leisure, & Safety
1914 Andy Holt Avenue
Knoxville, Tennessee 37996-2700

TEXAS

Industrial Hygiene Program
Texas A&M University
Nuclear Engineering Department
College Station, Texas 77843-3133

Industrial Engineering Program
Texas Tech University
Lubbock, Texas 79409

Industrial Hygiene & Safety Program
University of Houston, Clearlake
2700 Bay Area Boulevard
Box 59
Houston, Texas 77058

Environmental Engineering Program
The University of Texas at Austin
Civil Engineering Department
Austin, Texas 78712

UTAH

Industrial Hygiene Program
University of Utah
Rocky Mountain Center for
Occupational & Environmental Health
Salt Lake City, Utah 84112

Industrial Hygiene Program
Utah State University
Dept. of Biology/Public Health
Logan, Utah 84322-5305

VIRGINIA

Environmental/Occupational Health
Program
Old Dominion University
School of Medical Laboratory
Sciences and Environmental Health
Norfolk, Virginia 23529

Industrial Hygiene Program
Virginia Commonwealth University
Medical College of Virginia
School of Basic Health Sciences
Richmond, Virginia 23298-0694

Industrial Engineering Program
Virginia Tech
Dept. of I.S.E.
Blacksburg, Virginia 24060

WASHINGTON

Industrial Hygiene Program
University of Washington
Dept. of Environmental Health
Seattle, Washington 98195

WEST VIRGINIA

Occupational Health & Safety Program
West Virginia University
P.O. Box 6101
Morgantown, West Virginia 26506

WISCONSIN

Safety Technical Program
University of Wisconsin-Stout
Loss Control Center
Menomonie, Wisconsin 54751

CANADA

Occupational Health Program
University of Alberta
Edmonton, Alberta
Canada T6G 2G3

Occupational Hygiene Program
University of British Columbia
C/O Faculty of Graduate Studies
2075 Wesbrook Mall
Vancouver, British Columbia
Canada V6T 1Z3

Occupational Health & Safety Program
University of Toronto
Dept. of Chemical Engineering
200 College Street
Toronto, Ontario
Canada M5S 1A4

✚ OCCUPATIONAL THERAPY

Occupational therapy is a health profession concerned with the physical and psychological rehabilitation of individuals who suffer from injury or illness, or from emotional, mental, or developmental problems. In occupational therapy, rehabilitation employs the use of educational, vocational, and recreational activities or "occupations". There are three career classifications in occupational therapy: *Occupational therapist, occupational therapy assistant,* and *occupational therapy aide.*

Occupational Therapist

The *occupational therapist* attempts to restore a medical patient's health, independence, and self-reliance by first evaluating the patient's needs, and then teaching the patient to understand and compensate for their disability through planned activities and therapy. By teaching specially designed occupations such as manual and creative activities, the occupational therapist can, for example, help a patient restore the mobility and coordination of an injured limb. For the mentally ill or emotionally disturbed, such as substance abusers and those disabled by stress, depression, or eating disorders, the occupational therapist may emphasize time management skills, use of public transportation, homemaking, and shopping. For people with permanent functional disabilities, such as cerebral palsy, muscular dystrophy, or spinal cord injuries, occupational therapists may teach patients to operate computer-aided devices that aid patients in walking, communicating, and operating telephones and television sets. Therapists also provide equipment such as wheelchairs and aids for dressing and eating. The occupational therapist assists with the physical, psychological, and social development of physically and mentally handicapped children and children with learning disabilities. A common therapy involves helping the disabled child develop sensory, motor, and perceptual skills, all essential for further growth and development. Occupational therapists use activities of all kinds as treatment, ranging from cooking to using a computer. No matter what the impairment or disability, whether mental or physical, occupational therapy attempts to rehabilitate and to provide restorative services so that the patient may achieve full or partial

329

functional independence and learn to lead, or return to leading, a satisfying productive life.

The occupational therapist has the opportunity to work with a variety of members of a professional health team, including physicians, physical therapists, psychologists, nurses, speech pathologists, teachers, and others. Although most work in hospitals, the occupational therapist can also work in public and private schools, rehabilitation facilities, clinics, long-term care facilities, colleges and universities, and the patients' own homes.

An individual can become an occupational therapist by completing either a bachelor's degree program, a post-baccalaureate certificate program, or an entry-level master's degree program. All programs include a supervised clinical internship.

Upon completion of an accredited educational program graduates are eligible to take a national certification examination to become a registered occupational therapist (OTR) and to practice occupational therapy.

Many states also require occupational therapists to be licensed. Licensure applicants must generally complete an accredited occupational therapy program and successfully pass the American Occupational Therapy Certification Board's national certification examination. Contact the state's occupational therapy licensing division for more specifics on licensure.

High school students who are interested in a career in occupational therapy should take courses in biology, chemistry, physics, health, social sciences, and art. They also should try to maintain above-average grades, especially in the science fields.

According to the 1991 Committee on Allied Health Education and Accreditation's annual supplemental survey, entry level salaries for occupational therapists averaged $32,400 a year.

Employment opportunities for occupational therapists are expected to increase due to increasing demands for long-term care services and rehabilitation.

For further information on occupational therapy careers as well as financial aid and scholarship information for occupational therapy students, write to the American Occupational Therapy Association, 1383 Piccard Drive, P.O. Box 1725, Rockville, Maryland 20849-1725.

Following is a list of educational programs in occupational therapy accredited by the Committee on Allied Health Education and Accreditation of the American Medical Association in collaboration with the American Occupational Therapy Association.

Key:

(1)   Baccalaureate Degree Program.
(2)   Post-Baccalaureate Certificate Program
(3)   Professional Master's Degree Program
(4)   Combined Baccalaureate/Master's Degree Program
(5)   Certificate awarded to students in partial fulfillment of Master's degree

SOURCE:

Occupational Outlook Handbook

Occupational Therapist Programs

ALABAMA

Occupational Therapy Program (1)
University of Alabama at Birmingham
School of Health Related Professions
Birmingham, Alabama 35294-1270

Occupational Therapy Program (1)
Tuskegee University
Division of Allied Health
School of Nursing and Allied Health
Tuskegee, Alabama 36088-1696

ARKANSAS

Occupational Therapy Program (1)
University of Central Arkansas
Box 5001
Conway, Arkansas 72035-0001

CALIFORNIA

Occupational Therapy Program (1,2)
Loma Linda University
School of Allied Health Professions
Loma Linda, California 92350-0001

Occupational Therapy Program (1,3)
San Jose State University
College of Applied Sciences and Arts
One Washington Square
San Jose, California 95192-0059

Occupational Therapy Program (1,3,5)
University of Southern California
2250 Alcazar
Los Angeles, California 90033

COLORADO

Occupational Therapy Program (1,3)
Colorado State University
Ft. Collins, Colorado 80523

CONNECTICUT

Occupational Therapy Program (1,2)
Quinnipiac College
School of Allied Health and Natural
  Sciences
Hamden, Connecticut 06518

DISTRICT OF COLUMBIA

Occupational Therapy Program (1)
Howard University
College of Allied Health Sciences
Sixth and Bryant Streets, NW
Washington, DC 20059

FLORIDA

Occupational Therapy Program (1)
Florida Agricultural and Mechanical
  University
Tallahassee, Florida 32307

Occupational Therapy Program (1,5)
Florida International University
University Park Campus
Miami, Florida 33199

Occupational Therapy Program (1,5)
University of Florida
Box 100164, JHMHC
Gainesville, Florida 32610-0164

GEORGIA

Occupational Therapy Program (1)
The Medical College of Georgia
School of Allied Health Sciences
Augusta, Georgia 30912-0700

ILLINOIS

Occupational Therapy Program (1)
Chicago State University
College of Allied Health
95th Street at King Drive
Chicago, Illinois 60628-1598

Occupational Therapy Program (1)
University of Illinois at Chicago
College of Associated Health Professions
1919 West Taylor Street
Chicago, Illinois 60612-3833

Occupational Therapy Program (3)
Rush University
Rush-Presbyterian-St. Luke's Medical
  Center
1653 West Congress Parkway
Chicago, Illinois 60612-3833

INDIANA

Occupational Therapy Program (1)
Indiana University School of Medicine
School of Allied Health Sciences
1140 West Michigan Street
Indianapolis, Indiana 46202-5119

Occupational Therapy Program (3)
University of Indianapolis
1400 East Hanna Avenue
Indianapolis, Indiana 46227-3697

IOWA

Occupational Therapy Program (1)
St. Ambrose University
518 West Locust
Davenport, Iowa 52803

KANSAS

Occupational Therapy Program (1)
University of Kansas Medical Center
School of Allied Health
3901 Rainbow Boulevard
Kansas City, Kansas 66160-7602

KENTUCKY

Occupational Therapy Program (1,5)
Eastern Kentucky University
Richmond, Kentucky 40475-3135

LOUISIANA

Occupational Therapy Program (1)
Louisiana State University Medical
  Center
School of Allied Health Professions
1900 Gravier Street
New Orleans, Louisiana 70112-2223

Occupational Therapy Program (1)
Northeast Louisiana University
School of Allied Health Sciences
Monroe, Louisiana 71209-0430

MAINE

Occupational Therapy Program (1)
University of New England
College of Arts and Sciences
Biddeford, Maine 04005-9599

MARYLAND

Occupational Therapy Program (1,3)
Towson State University
Towson, Maryland 21204-7097

MASSACHUSETTS

Occupational Therapy Program (1,3)
Boston University
Sargent College of Allied Health
  Professions
635 Commonwealth Avenue
Boston, Massachusetts 02215

Occupational Therapy Program (3,4)
Springfield College
263 Alden Street
Springfield, Massachusetts 01109-3797

Occupational Therapy Program (3)
Tufts University
Boston School of Occupational Therapy
26 Winthrop Street
Medford, Massachusetts 02155

Occupational Therapy Program (1)
Worcester State College
486 Chandler Street
Worcester, Massachusetts 01602-2597

MICHIGAN

Occupational Therapy Program (1)
Eastern Michigan University
Department of Associated Health
  Professions
Ypsilanti, Michigan 48197-2239

Occupational Therapy Program (1,2)
Wayne State University
College of Pharmacy and Allied Health
  Professions
Detroit, Michigan 48202-3489

Occupational Therapy Program (1,3,4)
Western Michigan University
Kalamazoo, Michigan 49008-5051

MINNESOTA

Occupational Therapy Program (1)
University of Minnesota
Health Sciences Center
Box 388, UMHC
Minneapolis, Minnesota 55455-0392

Occupational Therapy Program (1,2)
The College of St. Catherine
2004 Randolph Avenue
St. Paul, Minnesota 55105-1794

MISSISSIPPI

Occupational Therapy Program (1)
University of Mississippi
Medical Center
2500 North State Street
Jackson, Mississippi 39216-4505

MISSOURI

Occupational Therapy Program (1)
University of Missouri-Columbia
School of Health Related Professions
Columbia, Missouri 65211

Occupational Therapy Program (1,3)
Washington University School of
  Medicine
4567 Scott Avenue
St. Louis, Missouri 63110-1093

NEBRASKA

Occupational Therapy Program (1)
Creighton University
School of Pharmacy and Allied Health
California at 24th Street
Omaha, Nebraska 68178-0259

NEW HAMPSHIRE

Occupational Therapy Program (1)
University of New Hampshire
School of Health and Human Services
Durham, New Hampshire 03824-3563

NEW JERSEY

Occupational Therapy Program (1,2)
Kean College of New Jersey
Morris Avenue
Union, New Jersey 07083-9982

NEW YORK

Occupational Therapy Program (3)
Columbia University
College of Physicians and Surgeons
630 West 168th Street
New York, New York 10032

Occupational Therapy Program (1)
Dominican College
10 Western Highway
Orangeburg, New York 10962

Occupational Therapy Program (4)
D'Youville College
One D'Youville Square
320 Porter Avenue
Buffalo, New York 14201-1084

Occupational Therapy Program (1)
Keuka College
Keuka Park, New York 14478-0098

Occupational Therapy Program (1,3)
New York University
School of Education, Health, Nursing,
  and Arts Professions
35 West Fourth Street, 11th Floor
New York, New York 10003-0152

Occupational Therapy Program (1)
State University of New York
Health Science Center at Brooklyn
450 Clarkson Avenue, Box 81
Brooklyn, New York 11203-2098

Occupational Therapy Program (4)
Touro College
Building #10
135 Carman Road
Dix Hills, New York 11746

Occupational Therapy Program (1)
University at Buffalo
State University of New York
3435 Main Street
Buffalo, New York 14214-3079

Occupational Therapy Program (1)
Utica College of Syracuse University
Division of Health Sciences
Burrstone Road
Utica, New York 13502-4892

Occupational Therapy Program (1)
York College of the City University of
  New York
94-20 Guy R. Brewer Boulevard
Jamaica, New York 11451-9902

NORTH CAROLINA

Occupational Therapy Program (1)
East Carolina University
School of Allied Health Sciences
Greenville, North Carolina 27858

Occupational Therapy Program (3)
University of North Carolina at Chapel
  Hill
Medical School
Chapel Hill, North Carolina 27599-7120

NORTH DAKOTA

Occupational Therapy Program (1)
University of North Dakota
Box 8036, University Station
Grand Forks, North Dakota 58202

OHIO

Occupational Therapy Program (1,2)
Cleveland State University
Euclid Avenue at East 24th Street
Cleveland, Ohio 44115-2440

Occupational Therapy Program (1,2)
Ohio State University
School of Allied Medical Professions
1583 Perry Street
Columbus, Ohio 43210-1234

OKLAHOMA

Occupational Therapy Program (1)
University of Oklahoma
Health Sciences Center
College of Allied Health
P.O. Box 26901
Oklahoma City, Oklahoma 73190

OREGON

Occupational Therapy Program (1)
Pacific University
2043 College Way
Forest Grove, Oregon 97116-1797

PENNSYLVANIA

Occupational Therapy Program (1)
Elizabethtown College
One Alpha Drive
Elizabethtown, Pennsylvania 17022-2298

Occupational Therapy Program (1)
College Misericordia
Division of Allied Health Professions
Dallas, Pennsylvania 18612

Occupational Therapy Program (1)
University of Pittsburgh
School of Health and Rehabilitation
  Sciences
Pittsburgh, Pennsylvania 15261-1813

Occupational Therapy Program (1,5)
Temple University
College of Allied Health Professions
Health Sciences Campus
3307 North Broad Street
Philadelphia, Pennsylvania 19140

Occupational Therapy Program (1,5)
Thomas Jefferson University
College of Allied Health Sciences
130 South Ninth Street
Philadelphia, Pennsylvania 19107-5233

PUERTO RICO

Occupational Therapy Program (1)
University of Puerto Rico
Medical Sciences Campus
College of Health Related Professions
Physical and Occupational Therapy
  Department
P.O. Box 365067
San Juan, Puerto Rico 00936-5067

SOUTH CAROLINA

Occupational Therapy Program (1)
Medical University of South Carolina
College of Health Related Professions
171 Ashley Avenue
Charleston, South Carolina 29425-2701

TENNESSEE

Occupational Therapy Program (1)
University of Tennessee-Memphis
The Health Science Center
College of Allied Health Sciences
Dept. of Rehabilitation Services
822 Beale Street
Memphis, Tennessee 38163

TEXAS

Occupational Therapy Program (1)
Texas Tech University
Health Sciences Center
School of Allied Health
3601 Fourth Street
Lubbock, Texas 79430-0001

Occupational Therapy Program (1,2,3)
Texas Woman's University
School of Occupational Therapy
Box 23718, TWU Station
Denton, Texas 76204-1718

Occupational Therapy Program (1)
University of Texas Health Science
   Center at San Antonio
7703 Floyd Curl Drive
San Antonio, Texas 78284-7770

Occupational Therapy Program (1)
University of Texas School of Allied
   Health Sciences at Galveston
University of Texas Medical Branch at
   Galveston
Galveston, Texas 77555-1028

VIRGINIA

Occupational Therapy Program (1,3)
Virginia Commonwealth University
Box 8, MCV Station
Richmond, Virginia 23298-0008

WASHINGTON

Occupational Therapy Program (1,2,3)
University of Puget Sound
1500 North Warner
Tacoma, Washington 98416

Occupational Therapy Program (1)
University of Washington
University Hospital
Seattle, Washington 98195

WISCONSIN

Occupational Therapy Program (1)
Mount Mary College
2900 North Menomonee River Parkway
Milwaukee, Wisconsin 53222-4597

Occupational Therapy Program (1)
University of Wisconsin-Madison
1300 University Avenue
Madison, Wisconsin 53706-1532

Occupational Therapy Program (1)
University of Wisconsin-Milwaukee
School of Allied Health Professions
P.O. Box 413
Milwaukee, Wisconsin 53201-0413

Occupational Therapy Assistant

The *occupational therapy assistant* works under the supervision of the professional occupational therapist and helps in the planning and implementing of rehabilitation programs. The occupational therapy assistant teaches self-care and creative and work-related skills and directs participation in selected tasks to restore, reinforce, and enhance performance and to promote and maintain health.

Most occupational therapy assistants work in hospitals while others may work in nursing homes, clinics, rehabilitation facilities, schools, community agencies, and private homes.

To become an occupational therapy assistant, one may complete either a two-year associate degree program or a twelve to fourteen month certificate program. All programs include a supervised clinical internship.

Graduates of an accredited educational program are eligible to take the American Occupational Therapy Association's examination to become a certified occupational therapy assistant (COTA).

According to a 1992 study by the American Occupational Therapy Association, the average annual salary for entry level occupational therapy assistants was $21,000.

For more information about becoming an occupational therapy assistant, write to the Occupational Therapy Association, 1383 Piccard Drive, P.O. Box 1725, Rockville, Maryland 20849-1725.

Following is a list provided by the American Occupational Therapy Association, of approved educational facilities that offer occupational therapy assistant programs.

KEY:

(1)   Associate Degree Program
(2)   Certificate Program

SOURCES:

American Occupational Therapy Association
Occupational Outlook Handbook

Occupational Therapy Assistant Programs

ALABAMA

Occupational Therapy Assistant Program (1,2)
University of Alabama at Birmingham
School of Health Related Professions
Birmingham, Alabama 35294-1270

CALIFORNIA

Occupational Therapy Program (1)
Loma Linda University
School of Allied Health Professions
Loma Linda, California 92350-0001

Occupational Therapy Program (1,2)
Mount St. Mary's College
Doheny Campus
10 Chester Place
Los Angeles, California 90007-2598

Occupational Therapy Program (1)
Sacramento City College
3835 Freeport Boulevard
Sacramento, California 95822

COLORADO

Occupational Therapy Program (1)
Denver Institute of Technology
7350 North Broadway
Denver, Colorado 80221-3653

Occupational Therapy Program (1)
Pueblo Community College
900 West Orman Avenue
Pueblo, Colorado 81004-1499

CONNECTICUT

Occupational Therapy Program (1)
Manchester Community College
P.O. Box 1046
60 Bidwell Street
Manchester, Connecticut 06040-1046

DELAWARE

Occupational Therapy Program (1)
Delaware Technical and Community
  College
Southern Campus
P.O. Box 610
Georgetown, Delaware 19947

FLORIDA

Occupational Therapy Program (1)
Hillsborough Community College
P.O. Box 30030
Tampa, Florida 33630-3030

Occupational Therapy Program (1)
Palm Beach Community College
4200 South Congress Avenue
Lake Worth, Florida 33461-4796

GEORGIA

Occupational Therapy Program (1)
Medical College of Georgia
School of Allied Health Sciences
Augusta, Georgia 30912-0700

HAWAII

Occupational Therapy Program (1)
University of Hawaii/Kapiolani
  Community College
Allied Health Department
4303 Diamond Head Road
Honolulu, Hawaii 96816

KANSAS

Occupational Therapy Program (1)
Barton County Community College
Great Bend, Kansas 67530

ILLINOIS

Occupational Therapy Program (1)
College of DuPage
Occupational and Vocational Education
22nd Street and Lambert Road
Glen Ellyn, Illinois 60137-6599

Occupational Therapy Program (1)
Illinois Central College
One College Drive
East Peoria, Illinois 61635-0001

Occupational Therapy Program (1)
Parkland College
2400 West Bradley Avenue
Champaign, Illinois 61821-1899

Occupational Therapy Program (1)
South Suburban College of Cook County
15800 South State Street
South Holland, Illinois 60473-1262

Occupational Therapy Program (1)
Wright College
3400 North Austin
Chicago, Illinois 60634-4276

IOWA

Occupational Therapy Program (1)
Kirkwood Community College
P.O. Box 2068
6301 Kirkwood Boulevard SW
Cedar Rapids, Iowa 52406-9973

LOUISIANA

Occupational Therapy Program (1)
Northeast Louisiana University
School of Allied Health Sciences
College of Pharmacy and Health
  Sciences
Monroe, Louisiana 71209-0430

MAINE

Occupational Therapy Program (1)
Kennebec Valley Technical College
Western Avenue
P.O. Box 29
Fairfield, Main 04937-0029

MARYLAND

Occupational Therapy Program (1)
Catonsville Community College
800 South Rolling Road
Baltimore, Maryland 21228-9987

MASSACHUSETTS

Occupational Therapy Program (1)
Becker College
61 Sever Street, Box 15071
Worcester, Massachusetts 01615-0071

Occupational Therapy Program (2)
Middlesex Community College
Springs Road
Bedford, Massachusetts 01730

Occupational Therapy Program (1)
Mount Ida College
Junior College Division
777 Dedham Street
Newton Centre, Massachusetts 02159-3310

Occupational Therapy Program (1)
North Shore Community College
One Ferncroft Road
Danvers, Massachusetts 01923

Occupational Therapy Program (1)
Quinsigamond Community College
670 West Boylston Street
Worcester, Massachusetts 01606

MICHIGAN

Occupational Therapy Program (1)
Grand Rapids Community College
143 Bostwick NE
Grand Rapids, Michigan 49503-3295

Occupational Therapy Program (1)
Lake Michigan College
South Campus
111 Spruce Street
Niles, Michigan 49120

Occupational Therapy Program (1)
Schoolcraft College
1751 Radcliff Street
Garden City, Michigan 48135-1197

Occupational Therapy Program (1)
Wayne County Community College
1001 West Fort Street
Detroit, Michigan 48226-9975

MINNESOTA

Occupational Therapy Program (1)
Anoka Technical College
1355 West Highway 10
Anoka, Minnesota 55303

Occupational Therapy Program (1)
Austin Community College
1600 Eighth Avenue NW
Austin, Minnesota 55912-1407

Occupational Therapy Program (1)
Duluth Technical College
2101 Trinity Road
Duluth, Minnesota 55811-3399

Occupational Therapy Program (1)
St. Mary's Campus of the College of St.
  Catherine
2500 South Sixth Street
Minneapolis, Minnesota 55454-1494

MISSOURI

Occupational Therapy Program (1)
Penn Valley Community College
3201 Southwest Trafficway
Kansas City, Missouri 64111

Occupational Therapy Program (1)
St. Louis Community College at
  Meramec
11333 Big Bend Boulevard
St. Louis, Missouri 63122

MONTANA

Occupational Therapy Program (1)
Great Falls Vocational-Technical Center
2100-16th Avenue South
Great Falls, Montana 59405-4998

NEW HAMPSHIRE

Occupational Therapy Program (1)
New Hampshire Technical College-
Claremont
One College Drive
RR 3, Box 550
Claremont, New Hampshire 03743-9707

NEW JERSEY

Occupational Therapy Program (1)
Atlantic Community College
Allied Health Division
Mays Landing, New Jersey 08330-9888

Occupational Therapy Program (1)
Union County College
1700 Raritan Road
Scotch Plains, New Jersey 07060

NEW MEXICO

Occupational Therapy Program (1)
Western New Mexico University
P.O. Box 680
Silver City, New Mexico 88062

NEW YORK

Occupational Therapy Program (1)
Erie Community College
6205 Main Street
Williamsville, New York 14221-7095

Occupational Therapy Program (1)
Herkimer County Community College
Herkimer, New York 13350-1598

Occupational Therapy Program (1)
LaGuardia Community College
31-10 Thomson Avenue
Long Island City, New York 11101-
3083

Occupational Therapy Program (1)
Maria College
700 New Scotland Avenue
Albany, New York 12208-1798

Occupational Therapy Program (1)
Orange County Community College
115 South Street
Middletown, New York 10940-6404

Occupational Therapy Program (1)
Rockland Community College
145 College Road
Suffern, New York 10901-3699

NORTH CAROLINA

Occupational Therapy Program (1)
Caldwell Community College and
  Technical Institute
1000 Hickory Boulevard
Hudson, North Carolina 28638

Occupational Therapy Program (1)
Pitt Community College
P.O. Drawer 7007
Highway 11, South
Greenville, North Carolina 27835-7007

Occupational Therapy Program (1)
Stanly Community College
Route 4, Box 55
Albemarle, North Carolina 28001-9402

NORTH DAKOTA

Occupational Therapy Program (1)
North Dakota State College of Science
Wahpeton, North Dakota 58076-3695

OHIO

Occupational Therapy Program (1)
Cincinnati Technical College
3520 Central Parkway
Cincinnati, Ohio 45223

Occupational Therapy Program (1)
Cuyahoga Community College
2900 Community College Avenue
Cleveland, Ohio 44115-3196

Occupational Therapy Program (1)
Kent State University
East Liverpool Campus
400 East Fourth Street
East Liverpool, Ohio 43920-3497

Occupational Therapy Program (1)
Lourdes College
6832 Convent Boulevard
Sylvania, Ohio 43560-2898

Occupational Therapy Program (1)
Muskingum Area Technical College
1555 Newark Road
Zanesville, Ohio 43701-2694

Occupational Therapy Program (1)
Shawnee State University
940 Second Street
Portsmouth, Ohio 45662

Occupational Therapy Program (1)
Sinclair Community College
444 West Third Street
Dayton, Ohio 45402-1460

Occupational Therapy Program (1)
Stark Technical College
6200 Frank Avenue NW
Canton, Ohio 44720-7299

OKLAHOMA

Occupational Therapy Program (1)
Oklahoma City Community College
Health, Social Sciences, and Human
   Services Division
7777 South May Avenue
Oklahoma City, Oklahoma 73159

Occupational Therapy Program (1)
Tulsa Junior College
Allied Health Services Division
909 South Boston Avenue
Tulsa, Oklahoma 74119-2095

OREGON

Occupational Therapy Program (1)
Mount Hood Community College
26000 SE Stark Street
Gresham, Oregon 97030-3300

PENNSYLVANIA

Occupational Therapy Program (1)
Community College of Allegheny
   County/Boyce Campus
595 Beatty Road
Monroeville, Pennsylvania 15146-1395

Occupational Therapy Program (1)
Harcum Junior College
Bryn Mawr, Pennsylvania 19010

Occupational Therapy Program (1)
Lehigh County Community College
2370 Main Street
Schnecksville, Pennsylvania 18078-2598

Occupational Therapy Program (1)
Mount Aloysius College
Cresson, Pennsylvania 16630

Occupational Therapy Program (1)
Pennsylvania College of Technology
One College Avenue
Williamsport, Pennsylvania 17701-5799

Occupational Therapy Program (1)
Pennsylvania State University
Berk Campus
Tulpehocken Road
P.O. Box 7009
Reading, Pennsylvania 19610-6009

PUERTO RICO

Occupational Therapy Program (1)
Humacao University College
University of Puerto Rico
CUH Postal Station
Humacao, Puerto Rico 00791

SOUTH CAROLINA

Occupational Therapy Program (1)
Trident Technical College
P.O. Box 10367
Charleston, South Carolina 29411

TENNESSEE

Occupational Therapy Program (1)
Roane State Community College
RR 8, Box 69, Patton Lane
Harriman, Tennessee 37748-5011

Occupational Therapy Program (1)
Nashville State Technical Institute
120 White Bridge Road
P.O. Box 90285
Nashville, Tennessee 37209-4515

TEXAS

Occupational Therapy Program (2)
Academy of Health Sciences, U.S. Army
Army Medical Specialist Corps Division
Ft. Sam Houston, Texas 78234-6100

Occupational Therapy Program (1)
Austin Community College
7748 Highway 290 West
Austin, Texas 78736-3290

Occupational Therapy Program (1)
Cooke County College
P.O. Box 22786
TWU Station
Denton, Texas 76201

Occupational Therapy Program (2)
Houston Community College
Health Careers Division
3100 Shenandoah
Houston, Texas 77021-1098

Occupational Therapy Program (1)
St. Philip's College
1801 Martin Luther King Street
San Antonio, Texas 78203-2098

UTAH

Occupational Therapy Program (1)
Salt Lake Community College
4600 South Redwood Road
P.O. Box 30808
Salt Lake City, Utah 84130-0808

VIRGINIA

Occupational Therapy Program (1)
College of Health Sciences
Community Hospital of Roanoke Valley
P.O. Box 13186
Roanoke, Virginia 24031-3186

Occupational Therapy Program (1)
J. Sargeant Reynolds Community
    College
P.O. Box 85622
Richmond, Virginia 23285-5622

WASHINGTON

Occupational Therapy Program (1)
Green River Community College
12401 SE 320th Street
Auburn, Washington 98002-4815

Occupational Therapy Program (1)
Yakima Valley Community College
Sixteenth Avenue and Nob Hill
  Boulevard
P.O. Box 1647
Yakima, Washington 98907

WISCONSIN

Occupational Therapy Program (1)
Fox Valley Technical College
1825 North Bluemound Drive
P.O. Box 2277
Appleton, Wisconsin 54913-2277

Occupational Therapy Program (1)
Madison Area Technical College
211 North Carroll Street
Madison, Wisconsin 53703-2285

Occupational Therapy Program (1)
Milwaukee Area Technical College
700 West State Street
Milwaukee, Wisconsin 53233

Occupational Therapy Aide

The *occupational therapy aide* performs mostly routine work, ordering supplies, maintaining the work area, preparing work materials, transporting patients, and maintaining the tools and equipment used in the therapy. The occupational therapy aide generally has no direct patient care responsibilities.

Occupational therapy aides are employed mainly in hospitals, but they may also work in other healthcare facilities where occupational therapy is conducted.

Training to become an occupational therapy aide is usually done on-the-job in hospitals and other healthcare facilities. The length and content of training programs depends upon the duties for which the aide will be responsible. Persons interested in becoming occupational therapy aides should contact the Chief Occupational Therapist or the Personnel Director of their local hospital.

SOURCE:

Occupational Outlook Handbook

ORIENTATION AND MOBILITY INSTRUCTION

Orientation and mobility instruction teaches blind and visually impaired individuals to move about safely and independently. Orientation and mobility skills are taught by an *orientation and mobility specialist*. In the closely related professions of special education, rehabilitation teaching, and rehabilitation counseling, the blind and visually impaired are taught to achieve independence in communication, personal, and management skills. The *special educator, rehabilitation teacher, and rehabilitation counselor* may teach their students or clients to read Braille or to use computers and other electrical devices that aid the blind and visually impaired. They may also teach personal and home management skills and provide counseling and career guidance. The goals of the *orientation and mobility specialist, special educator, rehabilitation teacher,* and *rehabilitation counselor* are to help the blind and visually impaired lead more productive, independent, and satisfying lives.

Orientation and Mobility Specialist

The *orientation and mobility specialist* may also be known as an *orientor, instructor of the blind, orientation therapist for the blind, therapist for the blind, orientation and mobility instructor,* and *orientation and mobility therapist for the blind.* He or she instructs the blind and the visually impaired individual to move about safely and independently and to achieve personal adjustment in daily living. The orientation and mobility specialist first interviews the client, administers assessment tests, and analyzes the client's lifestyle to determine which orientation and mobility skills are needed. The orientation and mobility specialist then develops and implements an instructional program. The blind or visually impaired individual is taught how to travel alone using such travel aids as laser canes, special sensors, and guide dogs. The student is taught to be aware of his or her physical environment through sense of smell, hearing, and touch. In a suburban neighborhood, the blind or visually impaired individual may be taught how to interpret the sounds of traffic in order to cross the street or how to use public transportation. The orientation and mobility specialist teaches the client to protect his or her body by using arms and hands to detect obstacles. The orientation and

345

mobility specialist also teaches the client to read and write Braille and how to use reading machines and other electrical devices. He or she teaches the client such personal and home management skills as cooking, cleaning, sewing, eating, grooming, dressing, use of bathroom facilities, use of the telephone, and coin and money identification. To improve the client's coordination, motor skills, and sense of touch, the orientation and mobility instructor may teach recreational skills, arts and crafts, and how to play musical instruments such as the piano. He or she may also instruct group activities such as dancing, swimming, and modified sports activities to encourage social participation and increase general health. The orientation and mobility instructor prepares a progress report to allow rehabilitation professionals to evaluate the client's ability to perform the activities that are essential to daily living.

Orientation and mobility specialists may work with children, teenagers, adults, and their family members. They are employed in rehabilitation agencies, private schools, public schools, clients' homes, and in private consulting. Orientation and mobility specialists may also work with teachers, therapists, rehabilitation specialists, and other professionals.

Valuable job experience can and should be obtained by volunteering to work with the blind or visually impaired in schools, rehabilitation centers, senior centers, and summer camps for blind children.

The educational requirements for the orientation and mobility specialist may be fulfilled at the undergraduate or graduate level. Graduate programs do not require a particular major. Some universities offer special financial assistance funds to qualifying students. Contact individual schools for more information on financial aid.

Salaries for the orientation and mobility specialist vary according to experience, place of employment, and geographic location, but are generally comparable to teacher salaries.

For more information on becoming an orientation and mobility specialist, contact the American Foundation for the Blind, 15 West 16th Street, New York, New York 10011, or the Association for Education and Rehabilitation of the Blind and Visually Impaired, 206 North Washington Street, Suite 320, Alexandria, Virginia 22314.

Following the special educator, rehabilitation teacher, and rehabilitation counselor chapter is a list compiled by the American Foundation for the Blind (AFB) and the Association for Education and Rehabilitation of the Blind and Visually Impaired (AER). The list contains educational institutions offering undergraduate and graduate programs in orientation and mobility.

SOURCES:

American Foundation for the Blind
Association for Education and Rehabilitation of the Blind and Visually Impaired
Dictionary of Occupational Titles

Special Educator
Rehabilitation Teacher
Rehabilitation Counselor

The *special educator* instructs blind and visually impaired children in elementary and secondary school subjects and in the skills used in everyday living. He or she teaches visually impaired students how to use their remaining vision in the most effective ways possible and how to read and write, by using magnification equipment and large print material. The special educator teaches blind students how to read and write Braille, sometimes using a computer to provide speech or Braille output. He or she may meet with parents to discuss how he or she intends to carry out educational programs suited to the needs of the blind or visually impaired child and how parents can encourage their child's independence. The special educator also discusses individual programs for the blind or visually impaired child with social workers, administrators, and testing specialists. The special educator may help other teachers adapt materials and techniques to the needs of the blind or visually impaired students in classes with non-disabled students. He or she may also arrange field trips, transcribe lessons and other material into Braille or large print, and counsel students. The special educator may also teach such daily living skills as cooking, cleaning, safety, and hygiene.

The special educator works on a one-on-one basis or with a small group of students and may be employed in hospitals, public schools, or residential schools. Some special educators teach in resource rooms or special classrooms; others may travel from school to school. Some special educators may even work in the home of the student.

The *rehabilitation teacher* works with blind and visually impaired adults, usually with one student at a time or in very small groups. The rehabilitation teacher helps the blind and visually impaired individual to adjust emotionally to his or her loss of vision. Based on what the client wishes to accomplish, and working with family members and other professionals, the rehabilitation teacher develops a plan that will enable a blind or visually impaired individual to lead a more productive, independent, and satisfying life. The rehabilitation teacher teaches the skills necessary in maintaining personal and home life. He or she may teach the client how to cook, organize a kitchen, measure ingredients in a recipe, and how to put Braille markings on a stove. He or she may also teach the client how to read and write Braille, how to use a typewriter, and other skills such as shopping, managing money and using community resources.

The rehabilitation teacher may work in rehabilitation agencies, residential facilities, state agencies, private non-profit organizations, and clients' homes.

The *rehabilitation counselor* provides counseling and career guidance to blind and visually impaired individuals. The rehabilitation counselor locates and sets up vocational training and jobs with employers within the community. He or she may assist the client in finding individual services such as medical treatment, psychological treatment, and eye evaluations. The rehabilitation counselor may also locate various appliances and aids, such as laser canes, Braille typewriters or large print materials, that are necessary to the client in overcoming his or her visual impairment.

The rehabilitation counselor works in state agencies, rehabilitation facilities, and private non-profit organizations.

Volunteer opportunities are available in many communities for students interested in pursuing a career in special education, rehabilitation, and counseling for the blind and visually impaired. Such opportunities include: reading for the blind and visually impaired in senior centers, becoming a student helper for a teacher of blind children, assisting with recreation programs at local rehabilitation centers, and volunteering at summer camps for blind children.

Educational requirements for the special educator, rehabilitation teacher, and rehabilitation counselor vary according to profession, but generally include a bachelor's degree in special education, rehabilitation education, and rehabilitation counseling. Master's degree programs are also available. Special financial aid funds are available through some universities for qualifying students. Contact individual universities for more information on financial aid and degrees offered.

Salaries for theses professions vary according to employer and geographic location, but are generally comparable to salaries of teachers.

For more information on the careers of special educator, rehabilitation teacher, and rehabilitation counselor, contact the American Foundation for the Blind, 15 West 16th Street, New York, New York 10011 or the Association for Education and Rehabilitation of the Blind and Visually Impaired, 206 North Washington Street, Suite 320, Alexandria, Virginia 22314.

The following is a list supplied by the American Foundation for the Blind (AFB) and the Association for Education and Rehabilitation of the Blind and Visually Impaired (AER). The list contains educational institutions offering undergraduate and graduate training programs in orientation and mobility. Special education, rehabilitation teaching, and rehabilitation counseling programs are included in this list also. For specific information on programs, contact the individual schools.

KEY:

(G) Graduate Program
(U) Undergraduate Program

SOURCES:

American Foundation for the Blind
Association for Education and Rehabilitation of the Blind and Visually Impaired
Dictionary of Occupational Titles

Orientation and Mobility Training Programs

ALABAMA

University of Alabama (G)
Department of Special Education
Birmingham, Alabama 35294

ARIZONA

University of Arizona (G)
Department of Special Education
Tucson, Arizona 85721

ARKANSAS

University of Arkansas at Little
 Rock   (G)
Department of Rehabilitation and
Special Education
2801 South University
Little Rock, Arkansas 72204

CALIFORNIA

California State University,
 Los Angeles   (G)
Department of Special Education
5151 State University Drive
Los Angeles, California 90032

Sacramento State University (G)
Department of Special Services
6000 J Street
Sacramento, California 95819

San Francisco State University (G)
Department of Special Education
1600 Holloway Avenue
San Francisco, California 94132

COLORADO

University of Northern Colorado (G)
Division of Special Education
College of Education
Greeley, Colorado 80639

FLORIDA

Florida State University (G) (U)
Mobility Education
Department of Special Education
Tallahassee, Florida 32306

GEORGIA

University of Georgia (G)
Rehabilitation Teaching Program
Athens, Georgia 30602

ILLINOIS

Illinois State University (G) (U)
Dept. of Specialized Educational
Development
Normal, Illinois 61761

Northern Illinois University (G) (U)
Department of E.P.C.S.E.
DeKalb, Illinois 60115-2867

Southern Illinois University (G) (U)
Rehabilitation Institute
Carbondale, Illinois 62901

INDIANA

Butler University
Visually Handicapped Studies
7725 North College
Indianapolis, Indiana 46240

KENTUCKY

University of Louisville (G) (U)
Department of Special Education
Louisville, Kentucky 40292

MARYLAND

Johns Hopkins University (G)
Dept. of Visually Handicapped Studies
Baltimore, Maryland 21218

MASSACHUSETTS

Boston College (G)
Division of Special Education and
Rehabilitation
Chester Hill, Massachusetts 02167

Northeastern University (G) (U)
Dept. of Counseling Psychology,
Rehabilitation & Special Education
Boston, Massachusetts 02115

University of Massachusetts (G)
Graduate School of Education
Harbor Campus
Boston, MA 02125

MICHIGAN

Eastern Michigan University (G) (U)
Department of Special Education
Ypsilanti, Michigan 48197

Michigan State University (G) (U)
Department of C.E.P.S.E.
East Lansing, Michigan 48824

Wayne State University (G) (U)
Teacher Education Division
Detroit, Michigan 48202

Western Michigan University (G) (U)
Department of Special Education and
Rehabilitation
College of Health & Human Services
Kalamazoo, Michigan 49008

MINNESOTA

Mankato State University (G)
Rehabilitation Counseling Department
Box 52
Mankato, Minnesota 56001

University of Minnesota (G)
College of Education
Minneapolis, Minnesota 53455

MISSISSIPPI

Jackson State University (G) (U)
1325 Lynch Street
P.O. Box 17501
Jackson, Mississippi 39217

Mississippi State University (G)
Rehabilitation Counseling Program
P.O. Drawer GE
Mississippi State, Mississippi 39762

NEBRASKA

University of Nebraska, Lincoln (G)
Department of Special Education
Lincoln, Nebraska 68583

NEW YORK

D'Youville College (U)
Division of Education
320 Porter Avenue
Buffalo, New York 14201

Dominican College (U)
Orientation and Mobility Training
Program
10 Western Highway
Orangeburg, New York 10962

Hunter College (G)
Department of Special Education
695 Park Avenue
Box 1487
New York, New York 10021

New York University (G) (U)
School of Education, Health & Nursing
Arts Professionals
Rehabilitation Counseling Department
50 West Fourth Street
New York, New York 10003

Teachers College Columbia
University   (G)
525 West 120th Street
Box 223
New York, New York 10027

NORTH DAKOTA

University of North Dakota (G) (U)
Department of Special Education
Grand Forks, North Dakota 58201

OHIO

Ohio State University (G)
Department of Human Services Ed.
154 West 12th Avenue
Columbus, Ohio 43210

University of Toledo (G) (U)
Department of Special Education
College of Education & Allied
Professionals
2801 West Bancroft Street
Toledo, Ohio 43606

OREGON

Portland State University (G)
Department of Special Education
Box 751
Portland, Oregon 97207

PENNSYLVANIA

Kutztown State University (U)
Department of Special Education
Kutztown, Pennsylvania 19530

Pennsylvania College of
Optometry   (G)
Institute for the Visually Impaired
1200 West Godfrey Avenue
Philadelphia, Pennsylvania 19141

University of Pittsburgh (G)
Program in Special Education
230 South Bouquet Street
Pittsburgh, Pennsylvania 15260

PUERTO RICO

University of Puerto Rico
P.O. Box 22484
San Juan, Puerto Rico 99031

SOUTH CAROLINA

South Carolina State College (G)
Department of Human Services
300 College Street NE
Orangeburg, South Carolina 29117

University of South Carolina (G)
College of Education, Box 57
Columbia, South Carolina 29208

SOUTH DAKOTA

Northern State University
Department of Special Education
Aberdeen, South Dakota 57401

TENNESSEE

Middle Tennessee State
University   (G) (U)
Elementary & Special Education
Department
P.O. Box 69
Murfreesboro, Tennessee 37132

Vanderbilt University (G)
George Peabody College for Teachers
Department of Special Education
Box 328, Peabody College
Nashville, Tennessee 37203

TEXAS

Stephen F. Austin State
University   (U)
Dept of Counseling & Special Education
Programs
P.O. Box 13019
Nacogdoches, Texas 75962

Texas Tech University (G)
College of Education
P.O. Box 41071
Lubbock, Texas 79409-1071

University of Texas at Austin (G)
Department of Special Education
Austin, Texas 78712

CANADA

University of British Columbia
Department of Special Education
Vancouver, British Columbia
V6T 1Z5 Canada

University of Calgary
Department of Educational Psychology
Calgary, Alberta
Canada

University of Western Ontario
W. Ross MacDonald School for the
Visually Handicapped
Brant Avenue
Brantford, Ontario
N3T 3J9 Canada

ORTHOTIC AND PROSTHETIC TECHNOLOGY

Orthotics and prosthetics are allied health professions concerned with the making and fitting of orthopedic braces and other supportive appliances (orthoses) and of artificial limbs (prostheses). The orthotist and prosthetist are members of a healthcare rehabilitation team, which may incorporate skills of a physician, surgeon, physical and occupational therapist, and social worker. An individual can be trained as either an orthotist, prosthetist, or both. Summarized below are two career classifications in each profession: *orthotist* and *prosthetist* and *orthotic technician* and *prosthetic technician*.

Orthotist And Prosthetist

The *orthotist/prosthetist* designs, fabricates, fits, and repairs orthoses and prostheses. These appliances are designed to support or replace a patient's limbs or other bodily features that have been disabled or lost through injury, abnormality, or disease.

Following the physician's prescription the orthotist/prosthetist selects an appliance, taking into consideration function, efficiency, and comfort as well as cosmetic appearance. In deciding upon the correct prescription for a specific patient, the physician will often consult with the orthotist/prosthetist on the design and material of the orthoses/prostheses. After the appliance has been made and approved by the physician, the orthotist/prosthetist is responsible for evaluating its performance and also for initially assisting the physical therapist and/or occupational therapist in training the patient to use and care for the new orthoses/prostheses.

The orthotist/prosthetist must possess a high degree of manual dexterity and mechanical skill to operate the specialized tools that are used in the manufacture of braces and artificial limbs.

Orthotists and prosthetists are employed in hospitals, laboratories, and rehabilitation centers. Responsibilities of the orthotist/prosthetist may vary depending upon the size of the healthcare facility. In a small office or department, the orthotist/prosthetist may design, fabricate, and fit the appliance. In a larger facility, the orthotist/prosthetist may only be responsible for designing, measuring, and fitting the appliance. He or she may hire technicians to fabricate the orthoses or prostheses.

A practitioner of orthotics/prosthetics can become certified by the American Board for Certification in Orthotics and Prosthetics as either a certified orthotist (CO), a certified prosthetist (CP), or a certified prosthetist-orthotist (CPO).

There are several options available concerning the amount of training and work experience required to take the American Board for Certification in Orthotics and Prosthetics certification exam. At present, applicants for certification must have either (1) a bachelor's degree in orthotics/prosthetics from an accredited program, plus one year's work experience, or (2) a bachelor's degree in any field plus a certificate obtained by successfully completing an accredited long term certificate program and one year's work experience in the selected discipline (orthotics or prosthetics), or (3) possess a combination of education, clinical experience, and professional training equivalent to the qualifications listed above.

Following the Orthotic and Prosthetic Technician chapter, is a list of orthotic and prosthetic educational programs accredited by the American Board for Certification in Orthotics and Prosthetics. For more information on training programs contact either the individual schools or the American Board for Certification in Orthotics and Prosthetics at 1650 King Street, Suite 500, Alexandria, Virginia 22314-2747.

Orthotic and Prosthetic Technician

Supervised by the orthotist/prosthetist, the *orthotic/prosthetic technician* aids in the fabricating, maintenance, and repair of orthoses and prostheses. The orthotic/prosthetic technician is employed in the same locations as the orthotist/prosthetist, and must similarly possess the mechanical skills needed to use specialized device-making tools.

Registration as an *orthotic technician*, a *prosthetic technician*, or an *orthotic/prosthetic technician* requires that the candidate possess at least a high school degree or equivalent; have completed an accredited training program, or applicable experience; and have successfully passed the technician examination.

Salaries for orthotic/prosthetic technicians are just below the salary levels of orthotic/prosthetic practitioners.

For further information on the technician examination, training facilities, and career opportunities contact the American Board for Certification in Orthotics and Prosthetics, 1650 King Street, Suite 500, Alexandria, Virginia 22314-2747.

KEY:
(1)   Bachelor degree program
(2)   Certificate program
(3)   Orthotic program only
(4)   Technician program

SOURCE:
American Board for Certification in Orthotics and Prosthetics

---

Orthotic And Prosthetic Programs

CALIFORNIA

Orthotic/Prosthetic Program (1)
California State University
1000 East Victoria Street
Dominguez Hills, California 90747

Orthotic/Prosthetic Program (2,3)
Rancho Los Amigos Hospital
Orthotics Department
7450 Leeds Street
Downey, California 90242

FLORIDA

Orthotic/Prosthetic Program (1,2)
Florida International University
College of Health
Miami, Florida 33199

ILLINOIS

Orthotic/Prosthetic Program (2)
Northwestern University Medical School
Orthotic/Prosthetic Center
345 East Superior Street
Chicago, Illinois 60611

MINNESOTA

Orthotic/Prosthetic Program
Northeast Metro Technical College
3300 Century Avenue North
White Bear Lake, Minnesota 55110

TENNESSEE

Orthotic/Prosthetic Program (2)
Shelby State Community College
P.O. Box 40568
Memphis, Tennessee 38174

TEXAS

Orthotic/Prosthetic Program
University of Texas
School of Allied Health Services
Orthotics & Prosthetics Department
6011 Harry Hines Boulevard
Dallas, Texas 75235-9091

WASHINGTON

Orthotic/Prosthetic Program (4)
Spokane Falls Community College
W. 3410 Ft. George Wright Drive
Spokane, Washington 99204-5288

Orthotic/Prosthetic Program (1)
University of Washington
School of Medicine
Division of Orthotics & Prosthetics
Seattle, Washington 98195

✚ PATIENT REPRESENTATION

Patient representation balances the problems, concerns, and unmet needs of the patient with the solutions provided by the hospital. The *patient representative* serves as a liaison between the patient and the facility, and between the facility and the community it serves.

Patient Representative

The *patient representative* works with patients on a one-on-one basis, acting as a mediator between patients and hospital administration. He or she evaluates patient satisfaction with the hospital experience and investigates patient complaints involving the staff or facility. He or she may also evaluate reports from patients and staff which conflict. The patient representative directs inquiries and complaints to the appropriate resources and services within the hospital. He or she also explains the hospital policies, procedures, and services to patients, providing translators to non-English speaking patients if necessary.

Through new employee orientation and ongoing training programs, the patient representative educates the staff on patients' perceptions of the hospital experience. The patient representative also collects and compiles data on patient care problems. He or she may then make recommendations to supervisors, directors, administrators, and appropriate departments to institute changes in the facility's policies and procedures. The patient representative also encourages the staff to adhere to the hospital's philosophy on patients' rights and responsibilities.

Depending upon the particular healthcare institution in which he or she is employed, the patient representative may act as a patient advocate or as a representative of the healthcare facility. Acting as a patient advocate, the patient representative considers the patient's interest before the institution's interest. He or she may attempt to protect the patient from further errors or mishaps, and recommend alternative policies and procedures in order to improve service to the patient. The patient representative may also inform the patient of his or her recourse to legal action. The patient representative that acts as a representative of the healthcare institution, considers the institution's interest before the patient's interest. In order to prevent possible legal action by the patient and reduce individual and community hostility, the patient representative may investigate problem sources, explain policies and procedures, and attempt to placate the patient.

The patient representative is employed in hospitals as well as in ambulatory health facilities, nursing homes, health maintenance organizations, health centers, government health agencies, volunteer health agencies, programs for the disabled, and programs for the elderly.

Educational requirements for the patient representative vary amongst healthcare facilities. Some employers may only require a high school education, while others may require a Bachelor's or Master's degree. Some may also require previous hospital experience or a knowledge of the inner workings of a hospital. A background in human behavior, psychology, or sociology may be helpful. For more information on educational and experience requirements, contact individual hospitals.

Recommended high school courses for the student interested in pursuing a career in patient representation include psychology, sociology, and human behavior.

A Graduate degree program in the field of health advocacy is offered by The Sarah Lawrence College in Bronxville, New York. The program is designed for students interested in careers in health advocacy and the related field of patient representation. Students can earn either a Master of Arts or a Master of Professional Studies degree. Educational prerequisites include a bachelor's degree; coursework in economics, biology, psychology, sociology, or anthropology; the ability to speak a foreign language-preferably Spanish; and experience in a health care setting. Financial aid for those who qualify includes higher education loans, limited institutional aid, and special scholarships. For more information on financial aid, prerequisite requirements, and curriculum plan, contact the Sarah Lawrence College, Health Advocacy Program, Bronxville, New York 10708.

For more information on a career as a patient representative, contact the National Society for Patient Representation and Consumer Affairs, American Hospital Association, 840 North Lake Shore Drive, Chicago, Illinois 60611.

SOURCE:

National Society for Patient Representation and Consumer Affairs

Physical therapy is the allied health profession concerned with the rehabilitation of individuals who have been physically disabled by disease or accident, or who are born with a physical handicap. By attempting to restore function and prevent further disability, physical therapy assists patients in reaching their maximum performance in learning to live a normal life within the limits of their capabilities. There are two levels of physical therapy practitioners: the professionally qualified *physical therapist* and the *physical therapist assistant*. Both require graduation from an accredited training program, with on-the-job training offered by some hospitals for the non-professional position of *physical therapy aide* (listed at the end of this chapter).

Physical Therapist

Upon referral by a physician, the *physical therapist* evaluates the extent of the patient's disability in such areas as neuromuscular, musculoskeletal, sensorimotor, cardiovascular, and respiratory functions. The physical therapist then plans, implements, and evaluates an appropriate treatment program that may include one or more of the following: exercises for increasing muscle strength, endurance, and coordination; electrical stimulation to activate paralyzed muscles; instruction in the use of assistive devices; and the application of massage, heat, cold, sound, water, ultrasound, or electricity; all of which are designed to relieve pain or to change the patient's physiological condition. The physical therapist must also be supportive and sensitive to a patient's emotional as well as physical well-being.

The physical therapist may treat patients with a wide variety of disabilities or may specialize in geriatrics, pediatrics, orthopedics, athletic training, (refer to chapter titled Athletic Training), neurology, or cardiopulmonary disease. The physical therapist most often works in general, specialized, or long-term care hospitals, but may also find employment in nursing homes, rehabilitation or research centers, schools for handicapped children, pediatric centers, sports facilities, clinics, home-health agencies, school systems, and private practice.

For the next few years most physical therapy graduates will continue to come from bachelor's degree programs. However, it is likely that most bachelor's degree programs will eventually be extended to master's degree programs because it is believed that a master's degree is better for preparing students for independent practice.

Recommended high school subjects include mathematics, health, biology, anatomy, chemistry, physics, and social sciences. Admission into physical therapy programs is competitive, and applicants should have good grades in the above courses.

Licensure or registration as a physical therapist is attained after candidates graduate from an accredited education program and pass a state administered national exam. Other requirements for physical therapy practice vary from state to state. Contact the state licensing board (located in the state capitol) for more information on licensing requirements.

In 1991 annual salaries of physical therapists employed full-time in private hospitals averaged $17 an hour. Salaries may vary because of geographic location, level of experience, and type of facility.

Outlook for physical therapy employment is good. Employment is expected to grow much faster than the average for all occupations through the year 2005. For more information on physical therapy careers or certification requirements, write to the American Physical Therapy Association, 1111 North Fairfax Street, Alexandria, Virginia 22314.

Following is a list of college and university physical therapy programs accredited by the Commission on Accreditation in Physical Therapy Education.

KEY:

(1A) Bachelor's degree program
(1B) Accepts candidates for second bachelor's degree
(2A) Certificate program
(2B) Certificate awarded to graduates holding bachelor's degree in another field
(3) Bachelor's degree available from affiliating college or university
(4) Accepts women students only
(5) Entry-level master's degree program

SOURCES:

American Physical Therapy Association
Occupational Outlook Handbook

Physical Therapist Programs

ALABAMA

Physical Therapy Program (5)
University of Alabama at Birmingham
School of Health Related Professions
UAB Station, Alabama 35294-1270

Physical Therapy Program (1A, 1B)
University of South Alabama
College of Allied Health Professions
Mobile, Alabama 36688

ARIZONA

Physical Therapy Program (5)
Northern Arizona University
C.U. Box 15105
Flagstaff, Arizona 86011

ARKANSAS

Physical Therapy Program (5)
University of Central Arkansas
Conway, Arkansas 72032

CALIFORNIA

Physical Therapy Program (1A)
California State University, Fresno
2345 East San Ramon
Fresno, California 93740

Physical Therapy Program (1A)
California State University at Long
  Beach
School of Allied Arts & Sciences
1250 Bellflower Boulevard
Long Beach, California 90840

Physical Therapy Program (1A, 1B)
Department of Health Science
California State University, Northridge
Northridge, California 91330

Physical Therapy Program (5)
Children's Hospital of Los
  Angeles/Chapman College
4650 Sunset Boulevard
Los Angeles, California 90027

Physical Therapy Program (5)
Loma Linda University
School of Allied Health Professions
Loma Linda, California 92350

Physical Therapy
  Program (1A, 1B, 4, 5)
Mount St. Mary's College
12001 Chalon Road
Los Angeles, California 90049

Physical Therapy Program (5)
Samuel Merritt College
370 Hawthorne Avenue
Oakland, California 94609

Physical Therapy Program (5)
University of California San Francisco
School of Medicine
Box 0736
San Francisco, California 94143

Physical Therapy Program (5)
San Francisco State University
1600 Holloway Avenue
San Francisco, California 94132

Physical Therapy Program (5)
University of the Pacific
Stockton, California 95211

Physical Therapy Program (5)
University of Southern California
Department of Physical Therapy
2025 Zonal Avenue
Los Angeles, California 90033

COLORADO

Physical Therapy Program (5)
University of Colorado
Health Science Center
4200 East Ninth Avenue, Box E244
Denver, Colorado 80262

CONNECTICUT

Physical Therapy Program (1A)
Quinnipiac College
School of Allied Health and Natural
  Sciences
Hamden, Connecticut 06518

Physical Therapy Program (1A)
University of Connecticut
School of Allied Health Professions
Storrs, Connecticut 06269-2101

361

DELAWARE

Physical Therapy Program (5)
University of Delaware
School of Life and Health Sciences
Newark, Delaware 19716

DISTRICT OF COLUMBIA

Physical Therapy Program (1A)
Howard University
College of Allied Health Sciences
Sixth and Bryant Streets, NW
Washington, DC 20059

FLORIDA

Physical Therapy Program (1A)
Florida A&M University
Tallahassee, Florida 32307

Physical Therapy Program (1A, 1B)
Florida International University
College of Health Sciences
Miami, Florida 33199

Physical Therapy Program (1A, 1B)
University of Florida
College of Health Related Professions
Box 100154
Gainesville, Florida 32610-0154

Physical Therapy Program (5)
University of Miami
Department of Orthopaedics & Rehab.
School of Medicine
5915 Ponce de Leon Boulevard
5th Floor
Coral Gables, Florida 33146

GEORGIA

Physical Therapy Program (5)
Emory University
1441 Clifton Road SE
Atlanta, Georgia 30322

Physical Therapy Program (1A, 1B)
Georgia State University
University Plaza
Atlanta, Georgia 30303

Physical Therapy Program (1A, 1B)
Medical College of Georgia
Augusta, Georgia 30912-0800

IDAHO

Physical Therapy Program (5)
Idaho State University
Box 8002
Pocatello, Idaho 83209

ILLINOIS

Physical Therapy Program (1A, 1B)
Northern Illinois University
School of Allied Health Professions
DeKalb, Illinois 60115

Physical Therapy Program (5)
Northwestern University
345 East Superior Street
Chicago, Illinois 60611

Physical Therapy Program (1A, 1B)
University of Health Sciences
Chicago Medical School
School of Related Health Sciences
3333 Green Bay Road
North Chicago, Illinois 60064

Physical Therapy Program (1A, 1B)
University of Illinois at Chicago
1919 West Taylor Street
Chicago, Illinois 60612

INDIANA

Physical Therapy Program (1A, 1B)
Indiana University
1140 West Michigan Street
Indianapolis, Indiana 46223

Physical Therapy Program (1A, 1B, 5)
University of Evansville
1800 Lincoln Avenue
Evansville, Indiana 47722

Physical Therapy Program (5)
University of Indianapolis
1400 East Hanna Avenue
Indianapolis, Indiana 46227-3697

IOWA

Physical Therapy Program (5)
University of Iowa
College of Medicine
Iowa City, Iowa 52242

Physical Therapy Program (5)
University of Osteopathic Medicine &
  Health Sciences
College of Biological Sciences
3200 Grand Avenue
Des Moines, Iowa 50312

KANSAS

Physical Therapy Program (5)
University of Kansas Medical Center
Kansas City, Kansas 66103

Physical Therapy Program (5)
Wichita State University
College of Health Professions
Wichita, Kansas 67260-0043

KENTUCKY

Physical Therapy Program (1A, 1B)
University of Kentucky Medical Center
Lexington, Kentucky 40536-0079

Physical Therapy Program (1A, 1B)
University of Louisville
Division of Allied Health Science
525 East Madison Street
Louisville, Kentucky 40292

LOUISIANA

Physical Therapy Program (1A)
Louisiana State University Medical
  Center
School of Allied Health Professions
P.O. Box 33932
Shreveport, Louisiana 71130-3932

MAINE

Physical Therapy Program (1A)
University of New England
11 Hills Beach Road
Biddeford, Maine 04005

MARYLAND

Physical Therapy Program (1A)
University of Maryland
School of Medicine
100 Penn Street
Baltimore, Maryland 21201

Physical Therapy Program (1A)
University of Maryland Eastern Shore
Princess Anne, Maryland 21853

MASSACHUSETTS

Physical Therapy Program (5)
Boston University
Sargent College of Allied Health
  Professions
635 Commonwealth Avenue
Boston, Massachusetts 02215

Physical Therapy Program (1A)
Northeastern University
360 Huntington Avenue
Boston, Massachusetts 02115

Physical Therapy Program (5)
Simmons College
Graduate School for Health Studies
300 The Fenway
Boston, Massachusetts 02115

Physical Therapy Program (5)
Springfield College
263 Alden Street
Springfield, Massachusetts 01109

Physical Therapy Program (5)
University of Massachusetts-Lowell
South Campus
Lowell, Massachusetts 01854

MICHIGAN

Physical Therapy Program (5)
Andrews University
Berrien Springs, Michigan 49104

Physical Therapy Program (5)
Grand Valley State University
Allendale, Michigan 49401

Physical Therapy Program (5)
Oakland University
School of Health Sciences
Rochester, Michigan 48309-4401

Physical Therapy Program (5)
University of Michigan-Flint
School of Health Professions and Studies
Flint, Michigan 48502-2186

Physical Therapy Program (1A, 1B)
Wayne State University
College of Pharmacy and Allied Health
  Professions
Detroit, Michigan 48202

MINNESOTA

Physical Therapy Program (5)
College of St. Scholastica
1200 Kenwood Avenue
Duluth, Minnesota 55811

Physical Therapy Program (5)
Mayo School of Health Related Sciences
Rochester, Minnesota 55905

Physical Therapy Program (1A, 1B)
University of Minnesota
Box 388
Minneapolis, Minnesota 55455

MISSISSIPPI

Physical Therapy Program (1A, 1B)
University of Mississippi Medical Center
School of Health Related Professions
2500 North State Street
Jackson, Mississippi 39216

MISSOURI

Physical Therapy Program (1A, 1B)
Maryville University
13550 Conway Road
St. Louis, Missouri 63141

Physical Therapy Program (1A)
Rockhurst College
1100 Rockhurst Road
Kansas City, Missouri 64110

Physical Therapy Program (1A, 1B)
St. Louis University Medical Center
1504 South Grand Boulevard
St. Louis, Missouri 63104

Physical Therapy Program (1A, 1B)
University of Missouri-Columbia
School of Health Related Professions
Columbia, Missouri 65211

Physical Therapy Program (5)
Washington University
School of Medicine
4525 Scott Avenue
St. Louis, Missouri 63110

MONTANA

Physical Therapy Program (1A)
University of Montana
Missoula, Montana 59812

NEBRASKA

Physical Therapy Program (5)
University of Nebraska Medical Center
College of Medicine
600 South 42nd
Omaha, Nebraska 68198-4420

NEW JERSEY

Physical Therapy Program (1A, 1B)
Kean College of New Jersey
University of Medicine & Dentistry of
  New Jersey
School of Allied Health Related
  Professions
65 Bergen Street
Newark, New Jersey 07103-3007

Physical Therapy Program (5)
Rutgers University, UM&D
401 Haddon Avenue
Camden, New Jersey 08103-1506

Physical Therapy Program (1A, 1B)
Stockton State College
Pomana, New Jersey 08240

NEW MEXICO

Physical Therapy Program (1A, 1B)
University of New Mexico
School of Medicine
Albuquerque, New Mexico 87131

NEW YORK

Physical Therapy Program (5)
Columbia University
630 West 168th Street
New York, New York 10032

Physical Therapy Program (1A)
Daemen College
4380 Main Street
Amherst, New York 14226

Physical Therapy Program (5)
D'Youville College
One D'Youville Square
320 Porter Avenue
Buffalo, New York 14201-1084

Physical Therapy Program (1A, 2B)
Hunter College
School of Health Sciences
425 East 25th Street
New York, New York 10010

Physical Therapy Program (5)
Ithaca College
Ithaca, New York 14850-7183

Physical Therapy Program (5)
Long Island University
University Plaza
Brooklyn, New York 11201

Physical Therapy Program (1A, 1B)
421 First Avenue
New York, New York 10010

Physical Therapy Program (1A, 4)
Russell Sage College
Troy, New York 12180

Physical Therapy Program (1A, 1B)
State University of New York
Department of Physical Therapy and
  Exercise Science
Main Street Campus
Buffalo, New York 14214

Physical Therapy Program (1A, 1B)
State University of New York
Health Science Center at Brooklyn
Box 16
450 Clarkson Avenue
Brooklyn, New York 11203

Physical Therapy Program (1A, 1B)
State University of New York at Stony
  Brook
School of Allied Health Professions
Health Science Center
Stony Brook, New York 11794

Physical Therapy Program (1A, 1B)
State University of New York
Health Science Center at Syracuse
College of Health Related Professions
750 East Adams Street
Syracuse, New York 13210

Physical Therapy Program (5)
Touro College
School of Allied Health Sciences
135 Carman Road
Dix Hills, New York 11746

NORTH CAROLINA

Physical Therapy Program (5)
Duke University
P.O. Box 3965
Durham, North Carolina 27710

Physical Therapy Program (1A, 1B)
East Carolina University
School of Allied Health Sciences
Greenville, North Carolina 27858-4353

Physical Therapy Program (1A, 1B)
University of North Carolina at Chapel
  Hill
Medical School
Chapel Hill, North Carolina 27599-7135

NORTH DAKOTA

Physical Therapy Program (1A, 1B, 5)
School of Medicine
Grand Forks, North Dakota 58203

OHIO

Physical Therapy Program (1A, 1B, 2B)
Cleveland State University
Department of Health Sciences
1983 East 24th Street
Cleveland, Ohio 44115

Physical Therapy Program (1A, 1B, 3)
Medical College of Ohio
P.O. Box 10008
Toledo, Ohio 43699-0008

Physical Therapy Program (1A, 1B)
Ohio University
Athens, Ohio 45701

Physical Therapy Program (1A, 1B, 2B)
Ohio State University
306 Allied Medical Professions
1583 Perry Street
Columbus, Ohio 43210

OKLAHOMA

Physical Therapy Program (1A)
Langston University
Langston, Oklahoma 73050

Physical Therapy Program (1A)
University of Oklahoma
College of Allied Health
Health Science Center
P.O. Box 26901
Oklahoma City, Oklahoma 73190

OREGON

Physical Therapy Program (5)
Pacific University
2043 College Way
Forest Grove, Oregon 97116

PENNSYLVANIA

Physical Therapy Program (5)
Beaver College
Glenside, Pennsylvania 19038

Physical Therapy Program (5)
Hahnemann University
201 North 15th Street
Philadelphia, Pennsylvania 19102

Physical Therapy Program (5)
Philadelphia College of Pharmacy and
  Science
43rd Street and Woodland Avenue
Philadelphia, Pennsylvania 19104

Physical Therapy Program (5)
Slippery Rock University
School of Physical Therapy
Suite 100, North Road
Slippery Rock, Pennsylvania 16057

Physical Therapy Program (5)
Temple University
College of Allied Health Professions
3307 North Broad Street
Philadelphia, Pennsylvania 19140

Physical Therapy Program (5)
Thomas Jefferson University
College of Allied Health Sciences
103 South Ninth Street
Philadelphia, Pennsylvania 19107

Physical Therapy Program (5)
University of Pittsburgh
Pittsburgh, Pennsylvania 15261

Physical Therapy Program (5)
University of Scranton
800 Linden Street
Scranton, Pennsylvania 18510-4586

PUERTO RICO

Physical Therapy Program (1A)
University of Puerto Rico
College of Health Related Professions
Medical Sciences Campus
GPO Box 365067
San Juan, Puerto Rico 00936

RHODE ISLAND

Physical Therapy Program (5)
University of Rhode Island
Kingston, Rhode Island 02881-0180

SOUTH CAROLINA

Physical Therapy Program (1A, 1B)
Medical University of South Carolina
171 Ashley Avenue
Charleston, South Carolina 29425

TENNESSEE

Physical Therapy Program (1)
Tennessee State University
3500 John A. Merritt Boulevard
Nashville, Tennessee 37209-1561

Physical Therapy Program (1A, 1B)
University of Tennessee
822 Beale Street, 3rd Floor
Memphis, Tennessee 38163

Physical Therapy Program (1A, 1B)
University of Tennessee/Chattanooga
615 McCallie Avenue
Chattanooga, Tennessee 37403-2598

TEXAS

Physical Therapy Program (1A, 1B)
Southwest Texas State University
Health Science Center
601 University Drive
San Marcos, Texas 78666

Physical Therapy Program (1A, 1B)
Texas Tech University Health Sciences
  Center
School of Allied Health
Lubbock, Texas 79430

Physical Therapy Program (5)
Texas Woman's University
Box 22487, TWU Station
Denton, Texas 76204

Physical Therapy Program (1A, 1B)
University of Texas Southwestern
  Medical Center at Dallas
School of Allied Health Sciences
5323 Harry Hines Boulevard
Dallas, Texas 75235

Physical Therapy Program (1A, 1B)
University of Texas Health Science
  Center at San Antonio
7703 Floyd Curl Drive
San Antonio, Texas 78284

Physical Therapy Program (5)
University of Texas Medical Branch at
  Galveston
School of Allied Health Sciences
Galveston, Texas 77550

Physical Therapy Program (5)
U.S. Army-Baylor University
AMSC Division
Academy of Health Sciences
Ft. Sam Houston, Texas 78234

UTAH

Physical Therapy Program (1A, 1B)
University of Utah
College of Health
Salt Lake City, Utah 84112

VERMONT

Physical Therapy Program (1A, 1B)
University of Vermont
School of Allied Health Sciences
Burlington, Vermont 05405

VIRGINIA

Physical Therapy Program (1A, 5)
Old Dominion University
School of Community Health
  Professions and Physical Therapy
Norfolk, Virginia 23529-0288

Physical Therapy Program (1A, 5)
Virginia Commonwealth University
Box 224, MCV Station
Richmond, Virginia 23298

WASHINGTON

Physical Therapy Program (1A, 1B)
Eastern Washington University
Mail Stop 4
Cheney, Washington 99004

Physical Therapy Program (5)
University of Puget Sound
1500 North Warner
Tacoma, Washington 98416

Physical Therapy Program (1A, 1B)
University of Washington
Department of Rehabilitation Medicine
Seattle, Washington 98195

WEST VIRGINIA

Physical Therapy Program (1A)
West Virginia University Medical Center
School of Medicine
P.O. Box 9226
Morgantown, West Virginia 26506-9226

WISCONSIN

Physical Therapy Program (1A)
Marquette University
Milwaukee, Wisconsin 53233

Physical Therapy Program (1A, 1B)
University of Wisconsin at LaCrosse
LaCrosse, Wisconsin 54601

Physical Therapy Program (1A, 1B)
University of Wisconsin-Madison
1300 University Avenue
Madison, Wisconsin 53706

CANADA

Physical Therapy Program (1A)
McGill University
3654 Drummond Street
Montreal, Quebec
Canada H3G 1Y5

Physical Therapist Assistant

The *physical therapist assistant* works under the supervision of a professional physical therapist in the rehabilitation of disabled persons. The assistant helps with complicated therapeutic procedures but may perform routine procedures independently. She or he helps test and evaluate patients' disabilities, applies stimulants, assists patients in performing exercises, trains patients to adapt to splints, braces, and artificial limbs, and observes and reports to the supervising physical therapist, the patient's response.

Most physical therapist assistants work in general and specialized hospitals, while others work in the same range of healthcare facilities as the professional physical therapist, including clinics, health maintenance organizations, nursing homes, rehabilitation centers, schools for handicapped children, and private practices.

The educational requirement to become a physical therapist assistant is the completion of a two year associate degree program at an accredited community or junior college, university, vocational-technical school, or Armed Forces sponsored college program. Some states require physical therapist assistants to be licensed; that is, they must have graduated from an accredited associate degree program and passed a certification examination. Contact the state's licensing board (located in the state capitol) for more information on licensing requirements.

Recommended high school subjects include health, mathematics, English, and the biological, physical and social sciences.

Following is a list of educational programs that have received accreditation from the Commission on Accreditation in Physical Therapy Education.

For more information on a career as a physical therapist assistant, write to the American Physical Therapy Association, 1111 North Fairfax Street, Alexandria, Virginia 22314.

SOURCES:

American Physical Therapy Association
Occupational Outlook Handbook

Physical Therapist Assistant Programs

ALABAMA

Physical Therapist Assistant Program
Bishop State Community College
351 North Broad Street
Mobile, Alabama 36603-5898

Physical Therapist Assistant Program
University of Alabama at Birmingham
University Station, Alabama 35294

Physical Therapist Assistant Program
Wallace State Community College
801 Main Street NW
Hanceville, Alabama 35077

ARKANSAS

Physical Therapist Assistant Program
University of Central Arkansas
Conway, Arkansas 72032

CALIFORNIA

Physical Therapist Assistant Program
Cerritos College
Health Occupations Division
11110 Alondra Boulevard
Norwalk, California 90650

Physical Therapist Assistant Program
DeAnza Community College
21250 Stevens Creek Boulevard
Cupertino, California 95014

Physical Therapist Assistant Program
Loma Linda University
Loma Linda, California 92350

Physical Therapist Assistant Program
Mount St. Mary's College
10 Chester Place
Los Angeles, California 90007

Physical Therapist Assistant Program
San Diego Mesa College
7250 Mesa College Drive
San Diego, California 92111-4998

COLORADO

Physical Therapist Assistant Program
Arapahoe Community College
5900 South Santa Fe Drive
Littleton, Colorado 80160-9002

Physical Therapist Assistant Program
Morgan Community College
17800 Road 20
Ft. Morgan, Colorado 80701

Physical Therapist Assistant Program
Pueblo Community College
900 West Orman Avenue
Pueblo, Colorado 81004

CONNECTICUT

Physical Therapist Assistant Program
Housatonic Community College
510 Barnum Avenue
Bridgeport, Connecticut 06608

DELAWARE

Physical Therapist Assistant Program
Delaware Technical & Community
  College
333 Shipley Street
Wilmington, Delaware 19801

FLORIDA

Physical Therapist Assistant Program
Broward Community College
Allied Health Center Campus
3501 SW Davie Road
Ft. Lauderdale, Florida 33314

Physical Therapist Assistant Program
Miami-Dade Community College
Medical Center Campus
950 NW 20th Street
Miami, Florida 33127

Physical Therapist Assistant Program
Pensacola Junior College
Warrington Campus
5555 West Highway 98
Warrington, Florida 32507

Physical Therapist Assistant Program
St. Petersburg Junior College
P.O. Box 13489
St. Petersburg, Florida 33733

GEORGIA

Physical Therapist Assistant Program
Gwinnett Technical Institute
1250 Adkinson Road, Box 1505
Lawrenceville, Georgia 30246

Physical Therapist Assistant Program
Medical College of Georgia
School of Allied Health Sciences
Medical College of Georgia
Augusta, Georgia 30912-3100

Physical Therapist Assistant Program
Thomas Technical Institute
P.O. Box 1578
Thomasville, Georgia 31799

HAWAII

Physical Therapist Assistant Program
Kapiolani Community College
4303 Diamond Head Road
Honolulu, Hawaii 96816

ILLINOIS

Physical Therapist Assistant Program
Belleville Area College
2500 Carlyle Road
Belleville, Illinois 62221

Physical Therapist Assistant Program
Illinois Central College
East Peoria, Illinois 61635

Physical Therapist Assistant Program
Morton College
3801 South Central Avenue
Cicero, Illinois 60650

Physical Therapist Assistant Program
Oakton Community College
1600 East Golf Road
Des Plaines, Illinois 60016

Physical Therapist Assistant Program
Southern Illinois University
Clinical Center
Carbondale, Illinois 62901

INDIANA

Physical Therapist Assistant Program
University of Evansville
1800 Lincoln Avenue
Evansville, Indiana 47722

Physical Therapist Assistant Program
Vincennes University
Health Occupations Department
Vincennes, Indiana 47591

IOWA

Physical Therapist Assistant Program
Indian Hills Community College
Health Occupations Department
Ottumwa Campus
525 Grandview
Ottumwa, Iowa 52501

KANSAS

Physical Therapist Assistant Program
Colby Community College
1255 South Range
Colby, Kansas 67701

Physical Therapist Assistant Program
Washburn University
School of Applied and Continuing
  Education
Topeka, Kansas 66621

KENTUCKY

Physical Therapist Assistant Program
Jefferson Community College
109 East Broadway Street
Louisville, Kentucky 40202-2000

Physical Therapist Assistant Program
Paducah Community College
West Kentucky State Technical School
P.O. Box 7408
Paducah, Kentucky 42002-7408

Physical Therapist Assistant Program
Somerset Community College
808 Monticello Road
Somerset, Kentucky 42501

MARYLAND

Physical Therapist Assistant Program
Baltimore City Community College
2901 Liberty Heights Avenue
Baltimore, Maryland 21215

MASSACHUSETTS

Physical Therapist Assistant Program
Becker College
61 Sever Street
Worcester, Massachusetts 01609

Physical Therapist Assistant Program
Berkshire Community College
1350 West Street
Pittsfield, Massachusetts 01201-5786

Physical Therapist Assistant Program
Lasell College
Newton, Massachusetts 02166

Physical Therapist Assistant Program
Newbury College
12 First Avenue
Brookline, Massachusetts 02146

Physical Therapist Assistant Program
North Shore Community College
One Ferncroft Road
Danvers, Massachusetts 01923-4093

Physical Therapist Assistant Program
Springfield Technical Community
  College
One Amory Square
Springfield, Massachusetts 01105

MICHIGAN

Physical Therapist Assistant Program
Delta College
University Center, Michigan 48710

Physical Therapist Assistant Program
Henry Ford Community College
22586 Ann Arbor Trail
Dearborn Heights, Michigan 48127-2598

Physical Therapist Assistant Program
Kellogg Community College
450 North Avenue
Battle Creek, Michigan 49017

Physical Therapist Assistant Program
Macomb Community College
44575 Garfield Road
Mount Clemens, Michigan 48044-3179

MINNESOTA

Physical Therapist Assistant Program
Anoka Technical College
1355 West Main Street
Anoka, Minnesota 55303

Physical Therapist Assistant Program
Duluth Technical College
2101 Trinity Road
Duluth, Minnesota 55811

Physical Therapist Assistant Program
St. Mary's Campus of the College of St.
  Catherine
2500 South Sixth Street
Minneapolis, Minnesota 55454

MISSOURI

Physical Therapist Assistant Program
Penn Valley Community College
3201 Southwest Trafficway
Kansas City, Missouri 64111

Physical Therapist Assistant Program
St. Louis Community College at
  Meramec
11333 Big Bend Boulevard
St. Louis, Missouri 63122

NEVADA

Physical Therapist Assistant Program
Community College of Southern Nevada
West Charleston Boulevard
Las Vegas, Nevada 89102

NEW HAMPSHIRE

Physical Therapist Assistant Program
New Hampshire Technical College
One College Drive
Claremont, New Hampshire 03743-9707

NEW JERSEY

Physical Therapist Assistant Program
Atlantic Community College
Mays Landing, New Jersey 08330

Physical Therapist Assistant Program
Essex County Community College
303 University Avenue
Newark, New Jersey 07102

Physical Therapist Assistant Program
Fairleigh-Dickinson University
285 Madison Avenue
Madison, New Jersey 07940

Physical Therapist Assistant Program
Union County College
232 East Second Street
Plainfield, New Jersey 07060

NEW YORK

Physical Therapist Assistant Program
Broome Community College
P.O. Box 1017
Binghamton, New York 13902

Physical Therapist Assistant Program
Genesee Community College
One College Road
Batavia, New York 14020-9704

Physical Therapist Assistant Program
Herkimer County Community College
Reservoir Road
Herkimer, New York 13350

Physical Therapist Assistant Program
Institute of Rehabilitation Medicine
New York University Medical Center
400 East 34th Street
New York, New York 10016

Physical Therapist Assistant Program
LaGuardia Community College
31-10 Thomson Avenue
Long Island City, New York 11101

Physical Therapist Assistant Program
Maria College
700 New Scotland Avenue
Albany, New York 12208-1798

Physical Therapist Assistant Program
Nassau Community College
Garden City, New York 11530

Physical Therapist Assistant Program
Niagara County Community College
3111 Saunders Settlement Road
Sanborn, New York 14132

Physical Therapist Assistant Program
Onondaga Community College
Syracuse, New York 13215

Physical Therapist Assistant Program
Orange County Community College
115 South Street
Middletown, New York 10940

Physical Therapist Assistant Program
Suffolk County Community College
Department of Health Careers
533 College Road
Selden, New York 11784

NORTH CAROLINA

Physical Therapist Assistant Program
Caldwell Technical Institute
1000 Hickory Boulevard
Hudson, North Carolina 28638-1399

Physical Therapist Assistant Program
Central Piedmont Community College
P.O. Box 35009
Charlotte, North Carolina 28235

Physical Therapist Assistant Program
Fayetteville Technical Community
  College
P.O. Box 35236
Fayetteville, North Carolina 28303

Physical Therapist Assistant Program
Martin Community College
Kehukee Park Road
Williamston, North Carolina 27892

Physical Therapist Assistant Program
Nash Community College
Old Carriage Road
P.O. Box 7488
Rocky Mount, North Carolina 27804-
0488

Physical Therapist Assistant Program
Southwestern Community College
275 Webster Road
Sylva, North Carolina 28779-9578

Physical Therapist Assistant Program
Stanly Community College
141 College Drive
Albemarle, North Carolina 28001

OHIO

Physical Therapist Assistant Program
Central Ohio Technical College
Dept. of Allied Health & Public Service
University Drive
Newark, Ohio 43055

Physical Therapist Assistant Program
Cuyahoga Community College
2900 Community College Drive
Cleveland, Ohio 44115

Physical Therapist Assistant Program
Kent State University
East Liverpool Regional Campus
400 East Fourth Street
P.O. Box 769
East Liverpool, Ohio 43920-3497

Physical Therapist Assistant Program
Professional Skills Institute
1232 Flaire Drive
Toledo, Ohio 43615

Physical Therapist Assistant Program
Shawnee State University
940 Second Street
Portsmouth, Ohio 45662

Physical Therapist Assistant Program
Sinclair Community College
444 West Third Street
Dayton, Ohio 45402

Physical Therapist Assistant Program
Stark Technical College
Allied Health Technologies
6200 Frank Avenue NW
Canton, Ohio 44720

Physical Therapist Assistant Program
Michael J. Owens Technical College
Caller #10,000, Oregon Road
Toledo, Ohio 43699

Physical Therapist Assistant Program
University of Cincinnati
Cincinnati, Ohio 45221-0168

OKLAHOMA

Physical Therapist Assistant Program
Oklahoma City Community College
7777 South May Avenue
Oklahoma City, Oklahoma 73159

Physical Therapist Assistant Program
Tulsa Junior College
909 South Boston Avenue
Tulsa, Oklahoma 74119

OREGON

Physical Therapist Assistant Program
Mount Hood Community College
26000 SE Stark Street
Gresham. Oregon 97030

PENNSYLVANIA

Physical Therapist Assistant Program
Alvernia College
Reading, Pennsylvania 19607

Physical Therapist Assistant Program
Central Pennsylvania Business School
School College Hill
Summerdale, Pennsylvania 17093-0309

Physical Therapist Assistant Program
Community College of Allegheny
  County
595 Beatty Road
Monroeville, Pennsylvania 15146

Physical Therapist Assistant Program
Hahnemann University
Broad and Vine Streets
Philadelphia, Pennsylvania 19102-1192

Physical Therapist Assistant Program
Harcum Junior College
Bryn Mawr, Pennsylvania 19010

Physical Therapist Assistant Program
Lehigh County Community College
4525 Education Park Drive
Schnecksville, Pennsylvania 18078-2598

Physical Therapist Assistant Program
Pennsylvania State University-Hazleton
Box 704-A
Hazleton, Pennsylvania 18201

Physical Therapist Assistant Program
Pennsylvania State University
Mont Alto Campus
Mont Alto, Pennsylvania 17237

PUERTO RICO

Physical Therapist Assistant Program
Humacao University College
CUH Postal Station
Humacao, Puerto Rico 00791

Physical Therapist Assistant Program
Ponce Technological University College
P.O. Box 7186
Ponce, Puerto Rico 00732

SOUTH CAROLINA

Physical Therapist Assistant Program
Greenville Technical College
P.O. Box 5616, Station B
Greenville, South Carolina 29606-5616

Physical Therapist Assistant Program
Trident Technical College
P.O. Box 10367
Charleston, South Carolina 29411

TENNESSEE

Physical Therapist Assistant Program
Chattanooga State Technical Community
  College
Nursing and Allied Health Division
4501 Amnicola Highway
Chattanooga, Tennessee 37406-1097

Physical Therapist Assistant Program
Jackson State Community College
2046 North Parkway
Jackson, Tennessee 38301-3797

Physical Therapist Assistant Program
Roane State Community College
Patton Lane
Harriman, Tennessee 37748

Physical Therapist Assistant Program
Shelby State Community College
P.O. Box 40568
Memphis, Tennessee 38174-0568

Physical Therapist Assistant Program
Volunteer State Community College
Nashville Pike
Gallatin, Tennessee 37066

Physical Therapist Assistant Program
Walters State Community College
500 South Davy Crockett Parkway
Morristown, Tennessee 37813-6899

TEXAS

Physical Therapist Assistant Program
Amarillo College
P.O. Box 447
Amarillo, Texas 79178

Physical Therapist Assistant Program
Austin Community College
Pinnacle Campus
7748 Highway 290 West
Austin, Texas 78736-3290

Physical Therapist Assistant Program
Community College of the Air Force
Sheppard Air Force Base, Texas 76311-
5465

Physical Therapist Assistant Program
El Paso Community College
P.O. Box 20500
El Paso, Texas 79998

Physical Therapist Assistant Program
Houston Community College System
3100 Shenandoah
Houston, Texas 77021-1098

Physical Therapist Assistant Program
Kilgore College
1100 Broadway
Kilgore, Texas 75662

Physical Therapist Assistant Program
Laredo Junior College
West End Washington Street
Laredo, Texas 78040

Physical Therapist Assistant Program
McLennan Community College
1400 College Drive
Waco, Texas 76708

Physical Therapist Assistant Program
Odessa College
201 West University
Odessa, Texas 79764

Physical Therapist Assistant Program
St. Philip's College
1801 Martin Luther King Boulevard
San Antonio, Texas 76054

Physical Therapist Assistant Program
Tarrant County Junior College
828 Harwood Road
Northeast Campus
Hurst, Texas 76054

Physical Therapist Assistant Program
Wharton County Junior College
911 Boling Highway
Wharton, Texas 77488

Physical Therapist Assistant Program
University of Texas-Pan American
Division of Health Related Professions
1201 West University Drive
Edinburg, Texas 78539

VIRGINIA

Physical Therapist Assistant Program
College of Health Sciences/Community
  Hospital of Roanoke Valley
College of Health Sciences
P.O. Box 13186
Roanoke, Virginia 24031

Physical Therapist Assistant Program
John Tyler Community College
13101 Jefferson Davis Highway
Chester, Virginia 23831

Physical Therapist Assistant Program
Northern Virginia Community College
8333 Little River Turnpike
Annandale, Virginia 22003

Physical Therapist Assistant Program
Tidewater Community College
1700 College Crescent
Virginia Beach, Virginia 23456

Physical Therapist Assistant Program
Wytheville Community College
Wytheville, Virginia 24382

WASHINGTON

Physical Therapist Assistant Program
Green River Community College
Health Occupations Division
12401 Southeast 320th Street
Auburn, Washington 98002

WISCONSIN

Physical Therapist Assistant Program
Blackhawk Technical College
6004 Prairie Road
P.O. Box 5009
Janesville, Wisconsin 53547

Physical Therapist Assistant Program
Milwaukee Area Technical College
Health Occupations Division
1015 North Sixth Street
Milwaukee, Wisconsin 53233

Physical Therapist Assistant Program
Northeast Wisconsin Technical College
2740 West Mason Street
Green Bay, Wisconsin 54307

Physical Therapy Aide

The *physical therapy aide* is a non-licensed employee who works under the supervision of a professional physical therapist. The aide carries out designated routine tasks such as helping patients prepare for treatment, transporting patients to and from treatment areas, maintaining, cleaning, and assembling devices and equipment used in treatment, and performing clerical duties.

Usually a high school graduate or equivalent, the physical therapy aide must have completed on-the-job training in a hospital or clinic facility. Length and content of training programs depend upon the duties the aide will be expected to perform. Employers usually prefer that potential aides have some previous hospital experience.

Individuals interested in becoming physical therapy aides should contact the Chief Physical Therapist or the Personnel Director of their local hospital or healthcare facility.

SOURCE:

Occupational Outlook Handbook

Physician extender services provide clinical support to physicians in a wide variety of healthcare settings. Physician extender personnel are trained to function as physician assistants, as surgeon's assistants, or with additional training and education as assistants for various medical specialties including orthopedics, urology, pediatrics and emergency medicine. Two of these careers, *physician assistant* and *surgeon's assistant* are discussed in this chapter. For further information on careers and training of specialized physician assistants, interested persons should contact the American Academy of Physician Assistants, 950 North Washington Street, Alexandria, Virginia 22314-1552. The career of *Surgical Technologist* is listed at the end of this chapter.

Physician Assistant

The physician assistant, sometimes referred to as a *physician associate*, is a skilled health practitioner under the physician's supervision who is qualified by academic and clinical training to provide routine patient services traditionally performed by a licensed physician. By utilizing the skills of the physician assistant, the physician has more time to deal with patients with more complex problems.

The wide range of routine medical procedures that the assistant performs depends upon the particular medical practice of the physician and state regulations but usually includes taking medical histories, performing physical examinations, assisting in laboratory procedures, administering injections and immunizations, suturing and caring for wounds, referring patients to other healthcare facilities, counseling patients, and performing emergency medical care. In some states, physician assistants are permitted to prescribe certain medications.

Physician assistants work mainly with family physicians and internists. The rest work in hospitals, health maintenance organizations, community health centers, industrial health clinics, prisons, and with the armed forces.

Medical schools, universities, community colleges, hospitals, and vocational-technical schools offer training programs for the physician assistant. These programs award certificates, associate degrees, and/or bachelor's degrees and have a variety of entrance requirements. The typical program lasts 24 month, although some programs range form 12-24 months, depending upon the type of award offered.

The minimum educational requirement for physician assistant training programs is generally two years of college with course emphasis in the physical and biological sciences and some health care experience.

Certification as a "Physician Assistant-Certified" or "PA-C" is awarded by the National Committee on Certification of Physician's Assistants after graduating from an accredited physician assistant training program and successfully passing a national certifying examination. Many states require registration (certification) or licensure for employment and interested persons should inquire with their state's licensing division or board of medical examiners. For additional certification information, write to the National Commission on Certification of Physician Assistants, 2845 Henderson Mill Road, NE, Atlanta, Georgia 30341.

Salaries for physician assistants vary because of geographic location, years of experience, education and type of facility. Recent studies indicate that average starting annual salaries equaled approximately $33,000. Physician assistants with several years hospital experience may earn from $40,000 to $60,000.

Following is a list provided by the American Academy of Physician Assistants of physician assistant programs accredited by the American Medical Association's Committee on Allied Health Education and Accreditation.

For further information on physician assistant careers, contact the American Academy of Physician Assistants, 950 North Washington Street, Alexandria, Virginia 22314-1552. The Association of Physician Assistant Programs is located at the same address.

SOURCES:

American Academy of Physician Assistants
Occupational Outlook Handbook

Physician Assistant Programs

CALIFORNIA

Physician Assistant Program
Charles R. Drew University of Medicine
 and Science
School of Allied Health
1621 East 120th Street
Los Angeles, California 90059

Primary Care Physician Assistant
 Program
University of Southern California School
 of Medicine
1975 Zonal Avenue
Los Angeles, California 90033

Physician Assistant Program
College of Osteopathic Medicine of the
 Pacific
College Plaza
Pomona, California 91766-1889

Physician Assistant Program
University of California
Davis Medical Center
Department of Family Practice
2270 Stockton Boulevard
Sacramento, California 95817

Physician Assistant Program
Naval School of Health Sciences
San Diego, California 92134-6000

Physician Assistant Program
Stanford University School of Medicine
703 Welch Road
Palo Alto, California 94304-1760

COLORADO

Child Health Associate Program
University of Colorado School of
  Medicine
Box C-219
4200 East Ninth Avenue
Denver, Colorado 80262

CONNECTICUT

Physician Assistant Program
Yale University School of Medicine
382 Congress Avenue
P.O. Box 3333
New Haven, Connecticut 06510

DISTRICT OF COLUMBIA

Physician Assistant Program
George Washington University
2300 Eye Street, NW
Washington, DC 20037

Physician Assistant Program
Howard University
2041 Georgia Avenue NW
Washington, DC 20060

FLORIDA

Physician Assistant Program
University of Florida
Box 100176
Gainesville, Florida 32610-0176

GEORGIA

Physician Assistant Program
Emory University School of Medicine
P.O. Drawer XX
Atlanta, Georgia 30322

Physician Assistant Program
Medical College of Georgia
Augusta, Georgia 30912

ILLINOIS

Physician Assistant Program
Cook County Hospital/Malcom X
  College
Health Services Institute
1900 West Polk Street
Chicago, Illinois 60612

IOWA

Physician Assistant Program
University of Iowa
Iowa City, Iowa 52242

Physician Assistant Program
University of Osteopathic Medicine &
  Health Sciences
3200 Grand Avenue
Des Moines, Iowa 50312

KANSAS

Physician Assistant Program
Wichita State University
College of Health Professions
Wichita, Kansas 67208

KENTUCKY

Physician Assistant Program
University of Kentucky
A.B. Chandler Medical Center
Lexington, Kentucky 40536-0080

MARYLAND

Physician Assistant Program
Essex Community College
7201 Rossville Boulevard
Baltimore, Maryland 21237

MASSACHUSETTS

Physician Assistant Program
Northeastern University
Boston, Massachusetts 02115

MICHIGAN

Physician Assistant Program
University of Detroit
8200 West Outer Drive
Detroit, Michigan 48219

Physician Assistant Program
Western Michigan University
Kalamazoo, Michigan 49008-5138

MISSOURI

Physician Assistant Program
St. Louis University
School of Allied Health Professions
1504 South Grand Boulevard
St. Louis, Missouri 63401

NEBRASKA

Physician Assistant Program
University of Nebraska Medical Center
600 South 42nd Street
Omaha, Nebraska 68198-4300

NEW JERSEY

Physician Assistant Program
Rutgers University
University of Medicine and Dentistry of
  New Jersey
Robert Wood Johnson Medical School
675 Hoes Lane
Piscataway, New Jersey 08854-5635

NEW YORK

Physician Assistant Program
Albany-Hudson Valley
Albany Medical College
47 New Scotland Avenue
Albany, New York 12208

Physician Assistant Program
Brooklyn Hospital Center
Long Island University
121 DeKalb Avenue
Brooklyn, New York 11201

Physician Assistant Program
Touro College School of Health
  Sciences
135 Carman Road
Dix Hills, New York 11746

Physician Assistant Program
CUNY/Harlem Hospital Center
506 Lenox Avenue
New York, New York 10037

Physician Assistant Program
Bayley Seton Hospital
75 Vanderbilt Avenue
Staten Island, New York 10304

Physician Assistant Program
HSC, University at Stony Brook
School of Allied Health Professions
Stony Brook, New York 11794-8202

Physician Assistant Program
State University of New York
Health Science Center at Brooklyn
450 Clarkson Avenue
Brooklyn, New York 11234

NORTH CAROLINA

Physician Assistant Program
Duke University Medical Center
2200 West Main Street
First Union Plaza
Durham, North Carolina 27705

Physician Assistant Program
Bowman Gray School of Medicine of
  Wake Forest University
1990 Beach Street
Winston-Salem, North Carolina 27103

NORTH DAKOTA

Physician Assistant Program
University of North Dakota School of
  Medicine
Department of Community Medicine and
  Rural Health
501 North Columbia Road
Grand Forks, North Dakota 58203

OHIO

Physician Assistant Program
Kettering College of Medical Arts
3737 Southern Boulevard
Kettering, Ohio 45429

Physician Assistant Program
Cuyahoga Community College
11000 Pleasant Valley Road
Parma, Ohio 44130

OKLAHOMA

Physician Assistant Program
University of Oklahoma
Health Sciences Center
P.O. Box 26901
Oklahoma City, Oklahoma 73190

PENNSYLVANIA

Physician Assistant Program
Gannon University
Erie, Pennsylvania 16541

Physician Assistant Program
St. Francis College
Loretto, Pennsylvania 15940

Physician Assistant Program
Hahnemann University
School of Health Sciences and
  Humanities
Broad & Vine Streets
Philadelphia, Pennsylvania 19102

Physician Assistant Program
King's College
133 North River Street
Wilkes-Barre, Pennsylvania 18711

TENNESSEE

Physician Assistant Program
Trevecca Nazarene College
333 Murfreesboro Road
Nashville, Tennessee 37210-2877

TEXAS

Physician Assistant Program
Southwestern Medical Center
University of Texas
5323 Harry Hines Boulevard
Dallas, Texas 75235

Physician Assistant Program
Academy of Health Sciences
Fort Sam Houston, Texas 78234

Physician Assistant Program
University of Texas Medical Branch
School of Allied Health Services
Galveston, Texas 77550

Physician Assistant Program
Baylor College of Medicine
Dept. of Community Medicine
One Baylor Plaza
Houston, Texas 77030

Physician Assistant Program
3790 MSTW/MSM
Sheppard AFB, Texas 76311

UTAH

Physician Assistant Program
University of Utah School of Medicine
50 North Medical Drive
Salt Lake City, Utah 84132

WASHINGTON

Physician Assistant Program
University of Washington
3731 University Way, NE
Seattle, Washington 98105

WEST VIRGINIA

Physician Assistant Program
Alderson-Broaddus College
P.O. Box 578
Philippi, West Virginia 26414

WISCONSIN

Physician Assistant Program
University of Wisconsin/Madison
1300 University Avenue
Madison, Wisconsin 53706

Surgeon's Assistant

The *surgeon's assistant* is a specialized physician assistant who is qualified by academic and clinical training to provide patient services under the supervision and responsibility of a surgeon. Working in any medical setting for which the surgeon is responsible, the surgeon's assistant gathers diagnostic data for the surgeon and assists the surgeon in appropriate treatment. As such the assistant obtains medical histories, carries out physical examinations, and helps evaluate the effectiveness of the surgery during the postoperative examinations, and helps evaluate the effectiveness of the surgery during the postoperative period. The surgeon assistant may also accompany the surgeon during visits to the patients' rooms, record notes on their progress, and compile data for case summaries.

Through preparation in surgeon's assistant training programs, the student gains experience in both general and specialty surgical services as well as in emergency room procedures. At present there are three surgeon's assistant training programs accredited by the Committee on Allied Health Education and Accreditation of the American Medical Association. These programs are generally two years in length. For specific guidelines governing undergraduate surgeon assistant programs, contact the American College of Surgeons, 55 East Erie Street, Chicago, Illinois 60611; or the American Medical Association, 535 North Dearborn Street, Chicago, Illinois 60610.

Most states require that surgeon's assistants be certified as a Physician Assistant. Certification requirements include graduation from an approved surgeon's assistant program

384

and successful completion of the national certification examination. Contact the state's licensing division or board of medical examiners for more specifics. The examination is administered by the National Commission on Certification of Physician Assistants at 2845 Henderson Mill Road, NE, Atlanta, Georgia 30341.

For more information on a career as a surgeon's assistant, contact the Association of Physician Assistants, 950 North Washington Street, Alexandria, Virginia 22314.

SOURCE:

American Association of Surgeon Assistants

Surgeon's Assistant Programs

ALABAMA

Surgeon's Assistant Program
University of Alabama School of
  Medicine
School of Community and Allied Health
619 South 19th Street
Birmingham, Alabama 35294

NEW YORK

Surgeon's Assistant Program
Cornell University Medical College
1300 York Avenue
New York, New York 10021

OHIO

Surgeon's Assistant Program
Cuyahoga Community College
11000 Pleasant Valley Road
Parma, Ohio 44130

Surgical Technologist

The surgical technologist, a member of the surgical healthcare team, provides technical support to surgeons, registered nurses, and anesthesiologists, in an operating room setting. The *surgical technologist,* also referred to as a *surgical technician* or *operating room technician,* is supervised by a registered nurse and performs tasks that are essential to the continuity of the surgical procedure.

In the operating room the technologist arranges supplies and instruments, keeping an accurate count of the latter at all times; helps the surgical team members scrub and dress for surgery; passes instruments and other sterile supplies to the surgeon during the operation;

helps apply dressings; and helps prepare and preserve specimens taken for testing. The technologist if qualified, may also operate sterilizers, lights, suction machines, and diagnostic equipment and may become specialized in certain areas of operating room surgery. After the operation the technologist may transfer the patient and help restock the operating room and maintain its aseptic conditions. Under close supervision the technologist may also assist in patient care in the operating room and in the delivery room.

Surgical technologists work in hospitals and other institutions that have operating rooms, delivery rooms, and emergency room facilities.

Training programs are offered by community and junior colleges, vocational-technical schools, the Armed Forces, as well as some hospital based programs. The programs include both classroom instruction and clinical training and generally last one to two years, awarding a certificate or associate degree.

Certification by examination is voluntary and available from the Liaison Council on Certification, the certifying body of the Association of Surgical Technologists. The credentials of CST (Certified Surgical Technologist) is granted after graduating from an approved academic program and successfully passing a written examination. For further information on certification, contact the Liaison Council on Certification, Association of Surgical Technologists, 7108-C South Alton Way, Englewood, Colorado 80112.

For high school students interested in this career, recommended courses include health, math, biology, and chemistry. Since operating room procedures require precise work and may last several hours, the surgical technologist should have physical stamina, be able to work quickly and accurately under pressure, and be detail oriented.

Salaries for the surgical technologist vary depending on location, education, experience, and responsibilities of the position. According to a 1991 survey by the Committee on Allied Health Education and Accreditation, entry level salaries averaged $17,400 a year.

Following is a list, provided by the Accreditation Review Committee on Education in Surgical Technology, of academic programs accredited by the Committee on Allied Health Education and Accreditation of the American Medical Association.

For further information on training and career opportunities contact the Association of Surgical Technologists, 7108-C South Alton Way, Englewood, Colorado 80112.

SOURCES:

Association of Surgical Technologists
Occupational Outlook Handbook

Surgical Technologist Programs

ARKANSAS

Surgical Technologist Program
Westark Community College
P.O. Box 3649
Ft. Smith, Arkansas 72193

Surgical Technologist Program
University of Arkansas
School of Health Related Professions
Veterans Medical Center
2200 Fort Roots Drive
North Little Rock, Arkansas 72114-1706

CALIFORNIA

Surgical Technologist Program
California Paramedical & Technical
  College
3745 Long Beach Boulevard
Long Beach, California 90807

Surgical Technologist Program
Naval School Health Sciences
San Diego Detachment
Oakland, California 94627-5000

Surgical Technologist Program
Simi Valley Adult School
3150 School Street
Simi Valley, California 93065

Surgical Technologist Program
Naval School of Health Sciences
San Diego, California 92134-6000

COLORADO

Surgical Technologist Program
Community College-Denver
1111 West Colfax
Denver, Colorado 80204

CONNECTICUT

Surgical Technologist Program
Danbury Hospital
24 Hospital Avenue
Danbury, Connecticut 06810

Surgical Technologist Program
Manchester Community College
60 Bidwell Street
Mail Station 19
Manchester, Connecticut 06040

Surgical Technologist Program
St. Mary's Hospital
56 Franklin Street
Waterbury, Connecticut 06706

FLORIDA

Surgical Technologist Program
Daytona Beach Community College
1200 Volusia Avenue
P.O. Box 2811
Daytona Beach, Florida 32120

Surgical Technologist Program
Lindsey Hopkins Technical Education
  Center
Dade County Public Schools
750 Northwest 20th Street
Miami, Florida 33127

Surgical Technologist Program
David G. Erwin Technical Center
2010 East Hillsborough Avenue
Tampa, Florida 33610-8299

GEORGIA

Surgical Technologist Program
DeKalb Technical Institute
495 North Indian Creek Drive
Clarkston, Georgia 30021

Surgical Technologist Program
Savannah Technical Institute
5717 White Bluff Road
Savannah, Georgia 31499

Surgical Technologist Program
Thomas Technical Institute
P.O. Box 1578
Thomasville, Georgia 31799

IDAHO

Surgical Technologist Program
Boise State University
1910 University Drive
Boise, Idaho 83725

ILLINOIS

Surgical Technologist Program
Central DuPage Hospital
25 North Winfield Road
Winfield, Illinois 60190

Surgical Technologist Program
Swedish-American Hospital
1400 Charles Street
Rockford, Illinois 61101

Surgical Technologist Program
Parkland College
2400 West Bradley Avenue
Champaign, Illinois 61821

Surgical Technologist Program
Illinois Central College
P.O. Box 2400
East Peoria, Illinois 61635

Surgical Technologist Program
United Medical Center
510 Tenth Avenue
Moline, Illinois 61265

Surgical Technologist Program
Triton College
2000 North Fifth Avenue
River Grove, Illinois 60171

INDIANA

Surgical Technologist Program
Indiana Vo-Tech College SW
3501 First Avenue
Evansville, Indiana 47710

Surgical Technologist Program
Lutheran College of Health Professions
535 Home Avenue
Ft. Wayne, Indiana 46807

Surgical Technologist Program
Indiana Vo-Tech College
One West 26th Street
P.O. Box 1763
Indianapolis, Indiana 46206

Surgical Technologist Program
Indiana Vo-Tech College
3208 Ross Road
P.O. Box 6299
Lafayette, Indiana 47903

Surgical Technologist Program
Indiana Vo-Tech College NW
2401 Valley Drive
Valparaiso, Indiana 46383

IOWA

Surgical Technologist Program
Marshalltown Community College
3700 South Center Street
Marshalltown, Iowa 50158

Surgical Technologist Program
Western Iowa Technical Community
  College
4647 Stone Avenue
Sioux City, Iowa 51105

KANSAS

Surgical Technologist Program
Wichita Area Vo-Tech School
324 North Emporia
Wichita, Kansas 67202

KENTUCKY

Surgical Technologist Program
Bowling Green State Vo-Tech School
1845 Loop Drive
Bowling Green, Kentucky 42101-3601

Surgical Technologist Program
Kentucky Tech-Central Campus
104 Vo-Tech Road
Lexington, Kentucky 40511

Surgical Technologist Program
Health Occupations School
701 North Laffoon Street
Madisonville, Kentucky 42431

Surgical Technologist Program
West Kentucky Vo-Tech School
P.O. Box 7408
Paducah, Kentucky 42001

Surgical Technologist Program
Cumberland Valley Health Occupations
  Center
P.O. Box 187
Pineville, Kentucky 40977

LOUISIANA

Surgical Technologist Program
Alton Ochsner Medical Foundation
1516 Jefferson Highway
New Orleans, Louisiana 70121

Surgical Technologist Program
Our Lady of the Lake Regional Medical
  Center
5000 Hennessy Boulevard
Baton Rouge, Louisiana 70808

MAINE

Surgical Technologist Program
Maine Medical Center
22 Bramhall Street
Portland, Maine 04102

MARYLAND

Surgical Technologist Program
Naval School of Health Sciences
Bethesda, Maryland 20889-5033

MASSACHUSETTS

Surgical Technologist Program
Quincy College
50 Saville Avenue
Quincy, Massachusetts 02169

Surgical Technologist Program
Springfield Technical Community
  College
One Armory Square
Springfield, Massachusetts 01105

MICHIGAN

Surgical Technologist Program
Delta College
University Center, Michigan 48710

Surgical Technologist Program
Highland Park Community College
Glendale at Third
Highland Park, Michigan 48203

MINNESOTA

Surgical Technologist Program
Anoka Technical College
1355 West Highway 10
Anoka, Minnesota 55303

Surgical Technologist Program
East Grand Forks Technical College
Highway 220 North
East Grand Forks, Minnesota 56721

Surgical Technologist Program
Minnesota Riverland Technical College
Rochester, Minnesota 55904

Surgical Technologist Program
St. Cloud Technical College
1540 Northway Drive
St. Cloud, Minnesota 56301

MISSISSIPPI

Surgical Technologist Program
Hinds Community College
Vo-Tech Jackson Branch
1750 Chadwick Drive
Jackson, Mississippi 39204

MISSOURI

Surgical Technologist Program
St. Louis Community College at Forest
  Park
5600 Oakland Avenue
St. Louis, Missouri 63110

MONTANA

Surgical Technologist Program
Missoula Vo-Tech Center
909 South Avenue West
Missoula, Montana 59801

NEBRASKA

Surgical Technologist Program
Southeast Community College
8800 "O" Street
Lincoln, Nebraska 68520

Surgical Technologist Program
Metropolitan Community College
P.O. Box 3777
Omaha, Nebraska 68103

NEW JERSEY

Surgical Technologist Program
Bergen Community College
400 Paramus Road
Paramus, New Jersey 07652

Surgical Technologist Program
University of Medicine and Dentistry of
New Jersey
65 Bergen Street
Newark, New Jersey 07107-3006

NEW YORK

Surgical Technologist Program
Nassau Community College
Stewart Avenue
Garden City, New York 11530

Surgical Technologist Program
Niagara County Community College
P.O. Box 5236
3111 Saunders Settlement Road
Sanborn, New York 14132

Surgical Technologist Program
Onondaga Community College
Onondaga Road
Syracuse, New York 13215

Surgical Technologist Program
Trocaire College
110 Red Jacket Parkway
Buffalo, New York 14220

NORTH CAROLINA

Surgical Technologist Program
Fayetteville Technical Community
College
P.O. Box 35236
Fayetteville, North Carolina 28303

Surgical Technologist Program
Coastal Carolina Community College
444 Western Boulevard
Jacksonville, North Carolina 28546-6877

Surgical Technologist Program
Lenoir Community College
P.O. Box 188
Kinston, North Carolina 28501

Surgical Technologist Program
Sandhills Community College
2200 Airport Road
Pinehurst, North Carolina 28374

Surgical Technologist Program
Presbyterian Hospital
P.O. Box 33549
Charlotte, North Carolina 28233

OHIO

Surgical Technologist Program
Cincinnati Technical College
3520 Central Parkway
Cincinnati, Ohio 45223

Surgical Technologist Program
Sinclair Community College
444 West Third Street
Dayton, Ohio 45402

Surgical Technologist Program
University of Akron
East Buchtel Avenue
Akron, Ohio 44325

Surgical Technologist Program
Michael J. Owens Technical College
Oregon Road
Toledo, Ohio 43699

Surgical Technologist Program
Youngstown Public School
200 East Wood Street
Youngstown, Ohio 44503

OKLAHOMA

Surgical Technologist Program
Great Plains Area Vo-Tech
4500 West Lee Boulevard
Lawton, Oklahoma 73505

Surgical Technologist Program
Tulsa County Area Vo-Tech School
3420 South Memorial Drive
Tulsa, Oklahoma 74145

OREGON

Surgical Technologist Program
Mt. Hood Community College
26000 SE Stark Street
Gresham, Oregon 97030

PENNSYLVANIA

Surgical Technologist Program
Sacred Heart Hospital
421 Chew Street
Allentown, Pennsylvania 18102

Surgical Technologist Program
Conemaugh Valley Memorial Hospital
1086 Franklin Street
Johnstown, Pennsylvania 15905

Surgical Technologist Program
Delaware County Community College
Media, Pennsylvania 19063

Surgical Technologist Program
Community College of Allegheny
Boyce Campus
595 Beatty Road
Monroeville, Pennsylvania 15146

Surgical Technologist Program
Mt. Aloysius Junior College
William Penn Highway
Cresson, Pennsylvania 16630

SOUTH CAROLINA

Surgical Technologist Program
Tri-County Technical College
Anderson Memorial Hospital
800 North Fant Street
Anderson, South Carolina 29621

Surgical Technologist Program
Midlands Technical College
P.O. Box 2408
Columbia, South Carolina 29202

Surgical Technologist Program
Florence-Darlington Technical College
P.O. Box 100548
Florence, South Carolina 29501-0548

Surgical Technologist Program
Greenville Technical College
P.O. Box 5616
Greenville, South Carolina 29606-5616

Surgical Technologist Program
Spartanburg Technical College
Drawer 4386
Spartanburg, South Carolina 29305

TENNESSEE

Surgical Technologist Program
East Tennessee State University
1000 West E. Street
Elizabethton, Tennessee, 37643

Surgical Technologist Program
Memphis Area Vo-Tech School
620 Mosby Avenue
Memphis, Tennessee 38105

TEXAS

Surgical Technologist Program
Amarillo College
P.O. Box 447
Amarillo, Texas 79178

Surgical Technologist Program
Austin Community College
Pinnacle Campus
7748 Highway 290 West
Austin, Texas 78736

Surgical Technologist Program
Del Mar College
Baldwin and Ayers
Corpus Christi, Texas 78404

Surgical Technologist Program
El Centro College
Main and Lamar Streets
Dallas, Texas 75202

Surgical Technologist Program
El Paso Community College
P.O. Box 20500
El Paso, Texas 79998

Surgical Technologist Program
Houston Community College
3100 Shenandoah
Houston, Texas 77021

Surgical Technologist Program
Tarrant County Junior College
828 Harwood Road
Hurst, Texas 76054

Surgical Technologist Program
Odessa College
201 West University
Odessa, Texas 79764

Surgical Technologist Program
San Jacinto College
8060 Spencer Highway
Pasadena, Texas 77501-2007

Surgical Technologist Program
St. Philip's College
1001 Martin Luther King Drive
San Antonio, Texas 78203

Surgical Technologist Program
South Plains College
1302 Main Street
Lubbock, Texas 79401-3298

Surgical Technologist Program
Temple Junior College
2600 South First
Temple, Texas 76504

Surgical Technologist Program
The Victoria College
2200 East Red River
Victoria, Texas 77901

Surgical Technologist Program
Trinity Valley Community College
800 Highway 243 West
Kaufman, Texas 75142

Surgical Technologist Program
Sheppard Air Force Base
3790th Medical Services Training Wing
Wichita Falls, Texas 76311

UTAH

Surgical Technologist Program
Salt Lake Community College
P.O. Box 30808
Salt Lake City, Utah 84130

VIRGINIA

Surgical Technologist Program
Riverside Hospital
Newport News Public Schools
500 J. Clyde Morris Boulevard
Newport News, Virginia 23601

Surgical Technologist Program
Naval School of Health Sciences
Portsmouth, Virginia 23708-5000

Surgical Technologist Program
Winchester Medical Center
1840 Amherst Street
P.O. Box 3340
Winchester, Virginia 22601

Surgical Technologist Program
Sentara-Norfolk General Hospital
600 Gresham Drive
Norfolk, Virginia 23507

WASHINGTON

Surgical Technologist Program
Seattle Central Community College
1701 Broadway
Seattle, Washington 98122

Surgical Technologist Program
Spokane Community College
North 1810 Greene Street
Spokane, Washington 99207

Surgical Technologist Program
Renton Technical College
3000 NE Fourth Street
Renton, Washington 98056

Surgical Technologist Program
West Virginia Northern Community
  College
15th & Jacob Streets
Wheeling, West Virginia 26003

WISCONSIN

Surgical Technologist Program
Gateway Technical College
3520 30th Avenue
Kenosha, Wisconsin 53144-1690

Surgical Technologist Program
Western Wisconsin Technical College
304 North Sixth Street
LaCrosse, Wisconsin 54602

Surgical Technologist Program
Milwaukee Area Technical College
700 West State Street
Milwaukee, Wisconsin 53233

Surgical Technologist Program
Waukesha Technical College
800 Main Street
Pewaukee, Wisconsin 53072

Surgical Technologist Program
Mid-State Technical College
2600 West Fifth Street
Marshfield, Wisconsin 54449

Surgical Technologist Program
Northeast Wisconsin Technical College
2740 West Mason Street
P.O. Box 19042
Green Bay, Wisconsin 54307-9042

Surgical Technologist Program
Northcentral Technical College
1000 Campus Drive
Wausau, Wisconsin 54401

PUBLIC HEALTH

Made up of federal, state and local health and environmental agencies, the field of public health is concerned with the maintenance and promotion of high quality health standards in the community. Public health encompasses many varied facets of healthcare and research including biomedical and laboratory sciences, biostatistics, dental public health, environmental health, epidemiology (the study of epidemic disease cause and control), health services administration, health policy and planning, mental health, nutrition, occupational safety and health, population studies, AIDS research, and public health education. Because of its diverse nature the public health work force includes physicians, nurses, planners, administrators, educators, social workers, therapists, technicians, and many more kinds of specialists and paraprofessionals, all of whom work towards conserving and improving the health of the public. Most available careers in public health are discussed in this handbook under their respective occupational title.

Public health professionals are employed in the public sector in health departments, and with voluntary and government health agencies.

Schools of public health are primarily graduate institutions. Applicants to these schools generally have a health background and several years experience.

Following is a list of schools of Public Health accredited by the Council on Education for Public Health. Persons interested in a master's degree program in public health at a specific school should contact the school directly to determine the specific area of public health it specializes in teaching.

For further information on a career in Public Health, write to the American Public Health Association, 1015 15th Street NW, Washington, DC 20005.

SOURCES:

Council on Education for Public Health

Public Health Programs

ALABAMA

Public Health Program
University of Alabama at Birmingham
720 South 20th Street
Birmingham, Alabama 35294-0008

CALIFORNIA

Public Health Program
Loma Linda University
Loma Linda, California 92350

Public Health Program
San Diego State University
San Diego, California 92182-0405

Public Health Program
University of California at Berkeley
Berkeley, California 94720

Public Health Program
University of California at Los Angeles
Center for the Health Sciences
Los Angeles, California 90024-1772

CONNECTICUT

Public Health Program
Yale University
Department of Epidemiology and Public
  Health
School of Medicine
P.O. Box 3333
60 College Street
New Haven, Connecticut 06510

FLORIDA

Public Health Program
University of South Florida
13201 Bruce B. Downs Boulevard
Tampa, Florida 33612-3805

GEORGIA

Public Health Program
Emory University
1599 Clifton Road
Atlanta, Georgia 30329

HAWAII

Public Health Program
University of Hawaii
1960 East-West Road
Honolulu, Hawaii 96822

ILLINOIS

Public Health Program
University of Illinois at Chicago
Box 6998
Chicago, Illinois 60680

LOUISIANA

Public Health Program
Tulane University
1430 Tulane Avenue
New Orleans, Louisiana 70112

MARYLAND

Public Health Program
Johns Hopkins University
615 North Wolfe Street
Baltimore, Maryland 21205-2179

MASSACHUSETTS

Public Health Program
Boston University
School of Medicine
80 East Concord Street
Boston, Massachusetts 02118-02394

Public Health Program
Harvard University
677 Huntington Avenue
Boston, Massachusetts 02115

Public Health Program
University of Massachusetts
School of Health Sciences
Amherst, Massachusetts 01003-0037

MICHIGAN

Public Health Program
University of Michigan
109 South Observatory Street
Ann Arbor, Michigan 48109-2029

MINNESOTA

Public Health Program
University of Minnesota
Box 197
420 Delaware Street, SE
Minneapolis, Minnesota 55455-0381

MISSOURI

Public Health Program
St. Louis University
3663 Lindell Avenue
St. Louis, Missouri 63108

NEW YORK

Public Health Program
Columbia University
600 West 168th Street
New York, New York 10032

NORTH CAROLINA

Public Health Program
University of North Carolina
Chapel Hill, North Carolina 27599-7400

OKLAHOMA

Public Health Program
University of Oklahoma
801 NE 13th Street
Oklahoma City, Oklahoma 73104-5072

PENNSYLVANIA

Public Health Program
University of Pittsburgh
130 De Soto Street
Pittsburgh, Pennsylvania 15261

PUERTO RICO

Public Health Program
University of Puerto Rico
Medical Sciences Campus
Box 5067
San Juan, Puerto Rico 00936

SOUTH CAROLINA

Public Health Program
University of South Carolina
Columbia, South Carolina 29208

TEXAS

Public Health Program
University of Texas
Health Science Center at Houston
P.O. Box 20186
Houston, Texas 77225

WASHINGTON

Public Health Program
University of Washington
Seattle, Washington 98195

RADIOLOGIC TECHNOLOGY

Radiologic technology is the allied health profession concerned with the use of ionizing radiation, radioactive isotopes, or sound waves for diagnostic and therapeutic purposes. There are four allied health careers in the field of radiologic technology: *radiographers* take radiographs (X-rays) of the internal structures of the body for diagnostic imaging purposes; *radiation therapy technologists* use prescribed doses of ionizing radiation to treat diseases, mainly cancer; *nuclear medicine technologists* work with radioactive materials for both diagnostic imaging and treatment; and *ultrasound technologists* operate non-ionizing equipment that utilizes sound waves to produce images. These occupations are generally supervised by the radiologist.

Diagnostic Radiologic Technologist or Radiographer

Also known as an *X-ray technologist,* the radiographer assists the radiologist in the use of X-ray equipment in the diagnostic imaging of such medical problems as broken bones, ulcers, tumors, and other illnesses. These images may be recorded on film or video tape. The radiologist interprets the radiographs (X-rays) and may make a diagnosis based on the results. In using the radiographic equipment, the technologist positions the patient on the X-ray machine, determines proper voltage current and exposure time, takes the X-ray, and processes the X-ray film. The technologist pays careful attention to safety while handling the X-ray equipment. Lead shields and other protective devices are furnished to patients to protect them from excess exposure to radiation during the procedure.

Sometimes mobile X-ray equipment may have to be used in such places as emergency rooms, surgery, or at the patient's bedside. The technologist is also responsible for maintaining the equipment in good working order, except for major repairs, and for keeping radiograph records, ordering supplies, and possibly mixing processing solutions. Other duties may include providing patient education and managing a radiographic quality assurance program.

Most radiographers work in hospitals, but there are also positions available in clinics, private physician's offices, the government, industry, public health facilities, laboratories, and in radiographic equipment sales.

Educational programs in radiography are available in hospitals, colleges and universities, vocational-technical schools, community and junior colleges, and in the military. Most training programs last twenty-four months, but some schools also offer bachelor's degree programs. The applicant to a training program must be a high school graduate or the equivalent.

Graduating from an educational program approved by the American Medical Association's Committee on Allied Health Education and Accreditation and successfully passing a qualifying examination are the requirements for certification as a radiographer.

Certification by the American Registry of Radiologic Technologists is a prerequisite for obtaining highly skilled and specialized positions. Check with the state licensing division or contact the American Registry of Radiologic Technologists, 2600 Wayzata Boulevard, Minneapolis, Minnesota 55405, for further details on licensure.

Recommended high school courses include algebra, geometry, physics, chemistry, biology and computer science.

In addition to X-ray equipment, many radiographers are being trained to use sophisticated computer imaging machines such as the CT Scanner (computed tomographer) and the MRI (magnetic resonance imager). These machines provide detailed information about the body's anatomy using computer technology.

According to the 1991 Committee on Allied Health Education and Accreditation's annual supplemental survey, entry level salaries for radiographers average $21,800 a year, while those with several years experience and specialized training may earn more.

Following is a list of programs in radiography approved by the Committee on allied Health Education and Accreditation of the American Medical Association. Contact each school directly for entrance requirements, length of program, and type of certificate or degree awarded.

SOURCES:

American Society of Radiologic Technologists
Occupational Outlook Handbook

Radiographer Programs

ALABAMA

Radiographer Program
Carraway Methodist Medical Center
1600 26th Street North
Birmingham, Alabama 35234

Radiographer Program
Jefferson State Community College
2601 Carson Road
Birmingham, Alabama 35215

Radiographer Program
University of Alabama at Birmingham
School of Health Related Professions
UAB Station
Birmingham, Alabama 35294

Radiographer Program
Gadsden State Community College
P.O. Box 227
Gadsen, Alabama 35999-0227

Radiographer Program
Wallace State Community College
P.O. Box 250
Hanceville, Alabama 35077

Radiographer Program
Huntsville Hospital
101 Sivley Road
Huntsville, Alabama 35801

Radiographer Program
University of South Alabama
1504 Springhill Avenue
Mobile, Alabama 36604

Radiographer Program
Baptist Medical Center
School of Radiologic Tech.
Montgomery, Alabama 36198

Radiographer Program
Humana Hospital-Montgomery
301 South Ripley Street
Drawer 311
Montgomery, Alabama 36104

Radiographer Program
East Alabama Medical Center
2000 Pepperell Parkway
Opelika, Alabama 36802-3201

Radiographer Program
DCH Regional Medical Center
809 University Boulevard E
Tuscaloosa, Alabama 35403

ARIZONA

Radiographer Program
Gateway Community College
108 North 40th Street
Phoenix, Arizona 85034

Radiographer Program
Pima Medical Institute-Tempe
2300 East Broadway Road
Tempe, Arizona 85282

Radiographer Program
Pima Community College
2202 West Anklam Road
Tucson, Arizona 85709

Radiographer Program
Pima Medical Institute-Tucson
3350 East Grant Road
Tucson, Arizona 85716

ARKANSAS

Radiographer Program
S Arkansas University Eldorado Branch
300 South West Avenue
El Dorado, Arkansas 71730

Radiographer Program
Sparks Regional Medical Center
School of Radiology
1311 South "I" Street
P.O. Box 17006
Ft. Smith, Arkansas 72901-7006

Radiographer Program
St. Edward Mercy Medical Center
7301 Rogers Avenue
P.O. Box 17000
Ft. Smith, Arkansas 72917-7000

Radiographer Program
Garland County Community College
400 Mid-America Boulevard
Hot Springs, Arkansas 71913-9120

Radiographer Program
Baptist Medical System
11900 Colonel Glenn Road, Suite 1000
Little Rock, Arkansas 72210-2820

Radiographer Program
St. Vincent Infirmary Medical Center
Two St. Vincent Circle
Little Rock, Arkansas 72205-5499

Radiographer Program
University of Arkansas for Med Sciences
4301 West Markham
Little Rock, Arkansas 72205

Radiographer Program
Jefferson Regional Medical Center
1515 West 42nd Avenue
Pine Bluff, Arkansas 71603

Radiographer Program
Arkansas State University
College of Nursing & Health Professions
P.O. Box 69
State University, Arkansas 72467

CALIFORNIA

Radiographer Program
Cabrillo College
6500 Soquel Drive
Aptos, California 95003

Radiographer Program
Bakersfield College
1801 Panorama Drive
Bakersfield, California 93305

Radiographer Program
Mills-Peninsula Hospitals
1783 El Camino Real
Burlingame, California 94010

Radiographer Program
Enloe Hospital
West Fifth Avenue & The Esplanade
Chico, California 94926

Radiographer Program
Orange Coast College
2701 Fairview Road
Costa Mesa, California 92626

Radiographer Program
Cypress College
9200 Valley View Street
Cypress, California 90630

Radiographer Program
San Joaquin General Hospital
500 West Hospital Road
French Camp, California 95231

Radiographer Program
Fresno City College
1101 East University
Fresno, California 93741

Radiographer Program
Daniel Freeman Memorial Hospital
333 North Prairie Avenue
Inglewood, California 90301

Radiographer Program
Loma Linda University
Loma Linda, California 92350

Radiographer Program
Long Beach City College
4901 East Carson Street
Long Beach, California 90808

Radiographer Program
Foothill Community College
12345 El Monte Road
Los Altos Hills, California 94022

Radiographer Program
Charles R. Drew U of Medicine &
  Science
College of Allied Health Medical
  Imaging Tech
1621 East 120th Street
Los Angeles, California 90059

Radiographer Program
Children's Hospital of Los Angeles
4650 Sunset Boulevard
Los Angeles, California 90027

Radiographer Program
Los Angeles City College
855 North Vermont Avenue
Los Angeles, California 90029

Radiographer Program
Los Angeles County-USC Medical
  Center
1200 North State Street
Los Angeles, California 90033

Radiographer Program
UCLA Center for Health Sciences
10833 Le Conte Avenue
Los Angeles, California 90024-1721

Radiographer Program
VA Medical Center West Los Angeles
Wadsworth Division
Wilshire & Sawtelle Boulevards
Los Angeles, California 90073

Radiographer Program
Yuba College
2088 North Beal Road
Marysville, California 95901

Radiographer Program
Merced College
3600 "M" Street
Merced, California 95348-2898

Radiographer Program
California State University-Northridge
18111 Nordhoff Street
Northridge, California 91330

Radiographer Program
Merritt College
12500 Campus Drive
Oakland, California 94619

Radiographer Program
St. John's Regional Medical Center
333 North "F" Street
Oxnard, California 93030

Radiographer Program
Huntington Memorial Hospital
100 Congress Street
Pasadena, California 91105

Radiographer Program
Pasadena City College
1570 East Colorado Boulevard
Pasadena, California 91106

Radiographer Program
Chaffey Community College
5885 Haven Avenue
Rancho Cucamonga, California 91701

Radiographer Program
Canada College
4200 Farm Hill Boulevard
Redwood City, California 94061

Radiographer Program
Kaiser Permanente Medical Center
1330 Cutting Boulevard
Richmond, California 94804

Radiographer Program
Sutter Community Hospitals
2800 L Street, Room 242
Sacramento, California 95816

Radiographer Program
San Bernardino County Medical Center
780 East Gilbert Street
San Bernardino, California 92404

Radiographer Program
Naval Health Science Education &
  Training Command
Naval School of Health Sciences
San Diego, California 92134-6000

Radiographer Program
San Diego Mesa College
7250 Mesa College Drive
San Diego, California 92111

Radiographer Program
City College of San Francisco
50 Phelan Avenue
San Francisco, California 94112

Santa Barbara City College
721 Cliff Drive
Santa Barbara, California 93109-9990

Radiographer Program
Santa Rosa Junior College
1501 Mendocino Avenue
Santa Rosa, California 95401

Radiographer Program
Sepulveda VA Medical Center
16111 Plummer Street
Sepulveda, California 91343

Radiographer Program
El Camino College
16007 Crenshaw Boulevard
Torrance, California 90506

Radiographer Program
LA County Harbor UCLA Medical
  Center
1000 West Carson Street
P.O. Box 22
Torrance, California 90509

Radiographer Program
Mt. San Antonio College
1100 North Grand Avenue
Walnut, California 91789

COLORADO

Radiographer Program
Memorial Hospital
1400 East Boulder Street
P.O. Box 1326
Colorado Springs, Colorado 80909

Radiographer Program
Community College of Denver-Auraria
  Campus
1111 West Colfax Avenue
Denver, Colorado 80204

Radiographer Program
Pima Medical Institute-Denver
7290 Samuel Drive, Suite 200
Denver, Colorado 80221

Radiographer Program
Presbyterian/St. Luke Center for Health
  Science Education
1719 East 19th Avenue
Denver, Colorado 80218

Radiographer Program
St. Anthony Hospital Systems
4231 West 16th Avenue
Denver, Colorado 80204

Radiographer Program
Mesa State College
P.O. Box 2647
Grand Junction, Colorado 81502

Radiographer Program
Aims Community College
P.O. Box 69
Greeley, Colorado 80631

Radiographer Program
Pueblo Community College
900 West Orman Avenue
Pueblo, Colorado 81004

Radiographer Program
Lutheran Medical Center
8300 West 36th Avenue
Wheat Ridge, Colorado 80033

CONNECTICUT

Radiographer Program
St. Vincent's Medical Center
2800 Main Street
Bridgeport, Connecticut 06606

Radiographer Program
Danbury Hospital
24 Hospital Avenue
Danbury, Connecticut 06810

Radiographer Program
Quinnipiac College
Mt. Carmel Avenue
Hamden, Connecticut 06518

Radiographer Program
Hartford Hospital
Education & Resource Center
560 Hudson Street
Hartford, Connecticut 06106-0729

Radiographer Program
Mt. Sinai Hospital
500 Blue Hills Avenue
Hartford, Connecticut 06112

Radiographer Program
Manchester Memorial Hospital
71 Haynes Street
Manchester, Connecticut 06040-4188

Radiographer Program
Veterans Memorial Medical Center
One King Place
P.O. Box 1009
Meriden, Connecticut 06450-1009

Radiographer Program
Middlesex Community College
100 Training Hill Road
Middletown, Connecticut 06457

Radiographer Program
New Britain General Hospital
100 Grand Street
New Britain, Connecticut 06050

Radiographer Program
South Central Community College
60 Sargent Drive
New Haven, Connecticut 06511

Radiographer Program
Lawrence & Memorial Hospitals
365 Montauk Avenue
New London, Connecticut 06320

Radiographer Program
Stamford Hospital
Shelburne Road
P.O. Box 9317
Stamford, Connecticut 06904

Radiographer Program
University of Hartford/Mt. Sinai
 Hospital
200 Bloomfield Avenue
West Hartford, Connecticut 06117

Radiographer Program
Mattatuck Community College
750 Chase Parkway
Waterbury, Connecticut 06708

Radiographer Program
Windham Community Memorial
 Hospital
112 Mansfield Avenue
Willimantic, Connecticut 06226

DELAWARE

Radiographer Program
Delaware Technical Community College
Southern Campus
P.O. Box 610
Georgetown, Delaware 19947

Radiographer Program
Delaware Technical Community College
Wilmington
333 Shipley Street
Wilmington, Delaware 19801

Radiographer Program
St. Francis Hospital
Seventh & Clayton Streets
Wilmington, Delaware 19805

DISTRICT OF COLUMBIA

Radiographer Program
Howard University
2400 Sixth Street NW
Washington, DC 20007

Radiographer Program
University of the District of Columbia
4200 Connecticut Avenue NW
Washington, DC 20008

Radiographer Program
Washington Hospital Center
110 Irving Street NW
Washington, DC 20010

FLORIDA

Radiographer Program
West Boca Medical Center
21644 State Road 7
Boca Raton, Florida 33428

Radiographer Program
Bethesda Memorial Hospital
2815 South Seacrest Boulevard
Boynton Beach, Florida 33435

Radiographer Program
Manatee Community College
5840 26th Street West
P.O. Box 1849
Bradenton, Florida 34206

Radiographer Program
Brevard Community College
1519 Clearlake Road
Cocoa, Florida 32922

Radiographer Program
Broward Community College
3501 SW Davie Road
Davie, Florida 33314

Radiographer Program
Halifax Medical Center
303 North Clyde Morris Boulevard
P.O. Box 2830
Daytona Beach, Florida 32115

Radiographer Program
Lee Memorial Hospital
2776 Cleveland Avenue
Ft. Myers, Florida 33902

Radiographer Program
Indian River Community College
3209 Virginia Avenue
Ft. Pierce, Florida 34981-5999

Radiographer Program
Santa Fe Community College
3000 NW 83rd Street
Gainesville, Florida 32602

Radiographer Program
Baptist Medical Center
800 Prudential Drive
Jacksonville, Florida 32207

Radiographer Program
St. Vincent's Medical Center
1800 Barrs Street
P.O. Box 2982
Jacksonville, Florida 32203

Radiographer Program
University Medical Center
655 West Eighth Street
Jacksonville, Florida 32209

Radiographer Program
Lakeland Regional Medical Center
1324 Lakeland Hills Road
P.O. Box 95448
Lakeland, Florida 33804

Radiographer Program
Miami-Dade Community College
950 NW 20th Street
Miami, Florida 33127

Radiographer Program
U of Miami-Jackson Memorial Med
  Center
1611 NW 12th Avenue
Miami, Florida 33136

Radiographer Program
Mt. Sinai Medical Center of Greater
  Miami
4300 Alton Road
Miami Beach, Florida 33140

Radiographer Program
Marion County School of Radiologic
  Technology
438 SW Third Street
Ocala, Florida 32674

Radiographer Program
Florida Hospital Medical Center
601 East Rollins
Orlando, Florida 32803

Radiographer Program
University of Central Florida
P.O. Box 25000
Orlando, Florida 32816

Radiographer Program
Valencia Community College
1800 South Kirkman Road
Orlando, Florida 32811

Radiographer Program
Gulf Coast Community College
5230 West US Highway 98
Panama City, Florida 32401-1041

Radiographer Program
Pensacola Junior College
Warrington Campus
5555 West Highway 98
Pensacola, Florida 32507-1097

Radiographer Program
St. Petersburg Junior College
P.O. Box 13489
St. Petersburg, Florida 33733

Radiographer Program
Hillsborough Community College
P.O. Box 30030
Tampa, Florida 33630

Radiographer Program
St. Mary's Hospital
901 45th Street
West Palm Beach, Florida 33407

Radiographer Program
Polk Community College
999 Avenue "H" NE
Winter Haven, Florida 33881

GEORGIA

Radiographer Program
Albany Technical Institute
1021 Lowe Road
Albany, Georgia 31708

Radiographer Program
Athens Area Technical Institute
US Highway 29 North
Athens, Georgia 30610-0399

Radiographer Program
Emory University
School of Medicine
1364 Clifton Road NE
Atlanta, Georgia 30322

Radiographer Program
Georgia Baptist Medical Center
300 Boulevard NE
Box 51
Atlanta, Georgia 30312-1206

Radiographer Program
Grady Memorial Hospital
80 Butler Street SE
Atlanta, Georgia 30335

Radiographer Program
Medical College of Georgia
Dept of Rad Techs
School of Health Sciences
Augusta, Georgia 30912-0600

Radiographer Program
University Hospital
1350 Walton Way
Augusta, Georgia 30910

Radiographer Program
Brunswick College
Atlanta at Fourth Street
Brunswick, Georgia 31520

Radiographer Program
The Medical Center
P.O. Box 951
Columbus, Georgia 31994-2299

Radiographer Program
De Kalb Medical Center
2701 North Decatur Road
Decatur, Georgia 30030

Radiographer Program
Griffin Technical Institute
501 Varsity Road
Griffin, Georgia 30223

Radiographer Program
West Georgia Technical Institute
Fort Drive
LaGrange, Georgia 30240

Radiographer Program
Gwinnett Tech
1250 Atkinson Road
P.O. Box 1505
Lawrenceville, Georgia 30246

Radiographer Program
Medical Center of Central Georgia
777 Hemlock Street
Macon, Georgia 31206

Radiographer Program
Kennestone Regional Health Care
  System
677 Church Street
Marietta, Georgia 30060

Radiographer Program
Floyd Medical Center
Turner McCall Boulevard
Rome, Georgia 30161

Radiographer Program
Armstrong State College
11935 Abercorn Street
Savannah, Georgia 31406

Radiographer Program
Thomas Technical Institute
Box 1578
Thomasville, Georgia 31799

Radiographer Program
Valdosta Technical Institute
Route 12, Box 1273
Valdosta, Georgia 31602

Radiographer Program
Okefenokee Technical Institute
1701 Carswell Avenue
Waycross, Georgia 31501

HAWAII

Radiographer Program
Kapiolani Community College
4303 Diamond Head Road
Honolulu, Hawaii 96816

IDAHO

Radiographer Program
Boise State University
1910 University Drive
Boise, Idaho 83725

Radiographer Program
Idaho State University
Pocatello, Idaho 83209

ILLINOIS

Radiographer Program
Northwest Community Hospital
800 West Central Road
Arlington Heights, Illinois 60005

Radiographer Program
Belleville Area College
2500 Carlyle Road
Belleville, Illinois 62221

Radiographer Program
Southern Illinois University at
    Carbondale
College of Technical Careers
Douglas Drive
Carbondale, Illinois 62901

Radiographer Program
Kaskaskia College
Shattuc Road
Centralia, Illinois 62801

Radiographer Program
Parkland College
2400 West Bradley Avenue
Champaign, Illinois 61820

Radiographer Program
Cook County Hospital
1825 West Harrison Street
Chicago, Illinois 60612

Radiographer Program
Malcolm X College
1900 West Van Buren Street
Chicago, Illinois 60612

Radiographer Program
Ravenswood Hospital Medical Center
4550 North Winchester Avenue
Chicago, Illinois 60640

Radiographer Program
South Chicago Community Hospital
Evangelical Health Care System
2320 East 93rd Street
Chicago, Illinois 60617

Radiographer Program
Wilbur Wright College
3400 North Austin Avenue
Chicago, Illinois 60634

Radiographer Program
United Samaritans Medical Center
812 North Logan Avenue
Danville, Illinois 61832

Radiographer Program
Decatur Memorial Hospital
2300 North Edward Street
Decatur, Illinois 62526

Radiographer Program
Sauk Valley Community College
173 IL Route #2
Dixon, Illinois 61021

Radiographer Program
Illinois Central College
East Peoria, Illinois 61635

Radiographer Program
St. Joseph Hospital
77 North Airlite Street
Elgin, Illinois 60120

Radiographer Program
St. Francis Hospital
355 Ridge Avenue
Evanston, Illinois 60202

Radiographer Program
Carl Sandburg College
2232 South Lake Storey Road
Galesburg, Illinois 61402

Radiographer Program
College of Du Page
22nd Street & Lambert Road
Glen Ellyn, Illinois 60137-6599

Radiographer Program
College of Lake County
19351 West Washington Street
Grayslake, Illinois 60030-1198

Radiographer Program
Hinsdale Hospital
120 North Oak Street
Hinsdale, Illinois 60521

Radiographer Program
Kankakee Community College
River Road
P.O. Box 888
Kankakee, Illinois 60901-0888

Radiographer Program
McDonough District Hospital
525 East Grant Street
Macomb, Illinois 61455

Radiographer Program
Kishwaukee College
Route 38 & Malta Road
Malta, Illinois 60150

Radiographer Program
United Medical Center
501 Tenth Avenue
Moline, Illinois 61265

Radiographer Program
Bloomington-Normal School of
  Radiography
900 Franklin Avenue
Normal, Illinois 61761

Radiographer Program
Olney Central College
RR #3
Olney, Illinois 62450

Radiographer Program
Moraine Valley Community College
10900 South 88th Avenue
Palos Hills, Illinois 60465

Radiographer Program
St. Francis Medical Center
530 NE Glen Oak Avenue
Peoria, Illinois 61637

Radiographer Program
Blessing Hospital
Broadway at 11th Street
Quincy, Illinois 62305

Radiographer Program
St. Mary Hospital
1415 Vermont Street
Quincy, Illinois 62301

Radiographer Program
Triton College
2000 North Fifth Avenue
River Grove, Illinois 60171

Radiographer Program
Franciscan Medical Center
2701 17th Street
Rock Island, Illinois 61201

Radiographer Program
Rockford Memorial Hospital
2400 North Rockton Avenue
Rockford, Illinois 61103

Radiographer Program
Swedish American Hospital
1400 Charles Street
Rockford, Illinois 61101

Radiographer Program
South Suburban College of Cook County
15800 South State Street
South Holland, Illinois 60473

Radiographer Program
Lincoln Land Community College
Shepherd Road
Springfield, Illinois 62708

Radiographer Program
Memorial Medical Center
800 North Rutledge
Springfield, Illinois 62781

INDIANA

Radiographer Program
University of Southern Indiana
8600 University Boulevard
Evansville, Indiana 47712

Radiographer Program
Welborn Baptist Hospital
401 SE Sixth Street
Evansville, Indiana 47713

Radiographer Program
Ft. Wayne School of Radiography
2200 Randallia Drive
Ft. Wayne, Indiana 46805

Radiographer Program
Lutheran College of Health Professions
535 Home Avenue
Ft. Wayne, Indiana 46807

Radiographer Program
Indiana University Northwest
3400 Broadway
Gary, Indiana 46408

Radiographer Program
Hancock Memorial Hospital
801 North State Street
Greenfield, Indiana 46140

Radiographer Program
Ball State University
Methodist Hospital of Indiana
1701 North Senate Boulevard
Indianapolis, Indiana 46202

Radiographer Program
Community Hospital Indianapolis
1500 North Ritter Avenue
Indianapolis, Indiana 46219

Radiographer Program
Indiana University School of Medicine
541 Clinical Drive
Indianapolis, Indiana 46202-5111

Radiographer Program
Indiana Vo-Tech College-Indianapolis
One West 26th Street
P.O. Box 1763
Indianapolis, Indiana 46206-1763

Radiographer Program
Marian College
3200 Cold Spring Road
Indianapolis, Indiana 46222

Radiographer Program
St. Joseph Hospital & Health Center
1907 West Sycamore Street
Kokomo, Indiana 46901

Radiographer Program
King's Daughter Hospital
One King's Daughter's Drive
P.O. Box 447
Madison, Indiana 47250

Radiographer Program
Ball Memorial Hospital
2401 University Avenue
Muncie, Indiana 47303

Radiographer Program
Reid Memorial Hospital
1401 Chester Boulevard
Richmond, Indiana 47374

Radiographer Program
Memorial Hospital of South Bend
1700 Mishawaka Avenue
P.O. Box 7111
South Bend, Indiana 46634-7111

Radiographer Program
Indiana Vo-Tech College-Terre Haute
7377 South Dixie Bee Road
Terre Haute, Indiana 47802

Radiographer Program
Porter Memorial Hospital
814 La Porte Avenue
Valparaiso, Indiana 46383

Radiographer Program
Good Samaritan Hospital
520 South Seventh Street
Vincennes, Indiana 47591

Radiographer Program
N. Indiana School of Radiologic
  Technology
Purdue U-N Central Campus
Westville, Indiana 46391

IOWA

Radiographer Program
Scott Community College
500 Belmont Road
Bettendorf, Iowa 52722-5649

Radiographer Program
St. Luke's Hospital
1025 "A" Avenue NE
Cedar Rapids, Iowa 52402

Radiographer Program
Jennie Edmundson Memorial Hospital
933 East Pierce Street
Council Bluffs, Iowa 51501

Radiographer Program
Iowa Methodist Medical Center
1200 Pleasant Street
Des Moines, Iowa 50309

Radiographer Program
Mercy Hospital Medical Center
928 Sixth Avenue
Des Moines, Iowa 50309

Radiographer Program
University of Iowa Hospitals and Clinic
Iowa City, Iowa 52242

Radiographer Program
St. Joseph Mercy Hospital
84 Beaumont Drive
Mason City, Iowa 50401

Radiographer Program
Indian Hills Community College
Ottumwa Campus
525 Grandview
Ottumwa, Iowa 52501

Radiographer Program
Northeast Iowa Community College
10250 Sundown Road
Peosta, Iowa 52068

Radiographer Program
Marian Health Center
801 Fifth Street
Sioux City, Iowa 51101

Radiographer Program
Allen Memorial Hospital
1825 Logan Avenue
Waterloo, Iowa 50703

Radiographer Program
Covenant Medical Center-Kimball
2101 Kimball Avenue
Waterloo, Iowa 50702

KANSAS

Radiographer Program
Ft. Hays State University
600 West Park Street
Hays, Kansas 67601

Radiographer Program
Hutchinson Community College
1300 North Plum
Hutchinson, Kansas 67501

Radiographer Program
Bethany Medical Center
51 North 12th Street
Kansas City, Kansas 66102

Radiographer Program
Labette Community College
200 South 14th Street
Parsons, Kansas 67357

Radiographer Program
Washburn University
1700 College Avenue
Topeka, Kansas 66621

Radiographer Program
HCA Wesley Medical Center
550 North Hillside Avenue
Wichita, Kansas 67214

Radiographer Program
St. Francis Regional Medical Center
929 North St. Francis Avenue
Wichita, Kansas 67214

Radiographer Program
St. Joseph Medical Center
3600 East Harry
Wichita, Kansas 67218

KENTUCKY

Radiographer Program
King's Daughter's Medical Center
2201 Lexington Avenue
Ashland, Kentucky 41101

Radiographer Program
Bowling Green State Vo-Tech School
1845 Loop Drive
Bowling Green, Kentucky 42101

Radiographer Program
Northern Kentucky University
Nunn Drive
Highland Heights, Kentucky 41076

Radiographer Program
Lexington Community College
Cooper Drive
Lexington, Kentucky 40506

Radiographer Program
St. Joseph Hospital
One St. Joseph Drive
Lexington, Kentucky 40504

Radiographer Program
University of Louisville
Division of Allied Health
Louisville, Kentucky 40292

Radiographer Program
Health Occupations School
701 North Laffoon Street
Madisonville, Kentucky 42431

Radiographer Program
Morehead State University
Morehead, Kentucky 40351

Radiographer Program
West Kentucky State Vocational
  Technical
P.O. Box 7408
Blandville Road
Paducah, Kentucky 42002-7408

Radiographer Program
Cumberland Valley Health Occupations
  Center
US 25 E South
P.O. Box 187
Pineville, Kentucky 40977

LOUISIANA

Radiographer Program
Rapides Regional Medical Center
211 Fourth Street
Alexandria, Louisiana 71306

413

Radiographer Program
Baton Rouge General Medical Center
3600 Florida Street
Baton Rouge, Louisiana 70806

Radiographer Program
Seventh Ward General Hospital
Highway 51 South
Hammond, Louisiana 70401

Lafayette General Medical Center
1214 Coolidge Avenue
Lafayette, Louisiana 70505

Radiographer Program
University Medical Center
2390 West Congress
P.O. Box 4016-C
Lafayette, Louisiana 70502

Radiographer Program
McNeese State University
P.O. Box 92000
Lake Charles, Louisiana 70609

Radiographer Program
Northeast Louisiana University
700 University Avenue
Monroe, Louisiana 71209

Radiographer Program
Alton Ochsner Medical Foundation
1516 Jefferson Highway
New Orleans, Louisiana 70121

Radiographer Program
Delgado Community College
615 City Park Avenue
New Orleans, Louisiana 70119

Radiographer Program
Louisiana U Medical Center-Shreveport
1541 Kings Highway
Shreveport, Louisiana 71130

Radiographer Program
Northwestern State University
Dept. of Biology & Microbiology
915 Margaret Place
Shreveport, Louisiana 71120

Radiographer Program
Southern University
3050 Martin Luther King Jr. Drive
Shreveport, Louisiana 71107

MAINE

Radiographer Program
Eastern Maine Technical College
354 Hogan Road
Bangor, Maine 04401

Radiographer Program
Central Maine Medical Center
300 Main Street
Lewiston, Maine 04240

Radiographer Program
St. Mary's Hospital
Campus Avenue
Lewiston, Maine 04240

Radiographer Program
Mercy Hospital
144 State Street
Portland, Maine 04101

Radiographer Program
Southern Main Technical College
Fort Road
South Portland, Maine 04106

Radiographer Program
Mid Maine Medical Center Thayer Unit
North Street
Waterville, Maine 04901

MARYLAND

Radiographer Program
Essex Community
7201 Rossville Boulevard
Baltimore, Maryland 21237

Radiographer Program
Greater Baltimore Medical Center
6701 North Charles Street
Baltimore, Maryland 21204

Radiographer Program
Harbor Hospital Center
3001 South Hanover Street
Baltimore, Maryland 21230

Radiographer Program
Johns Hopkins Hospital
600 North Wolfe Street
Baltimore, Maryland 21205

Radiographer Program
Maryland General Hospital
827 Linden Avenue
Baltimore, Maryland 21202

Radiographer Program
Mercy Medical Center
301 St. Paul Street
Baltimore, Maryland 21202-2165

Radiographer Program
Allegany Community College
Willowbrook Road
Cumberland, Maryland 21502-2596

Radiographer Program
Hagerstown Junior College
11400 Robinwood Drive
Hagerstown, Maryland 21742-6590

Radiographer Program
Prince George's Community College
301 Largo Road
Largo, Maryland 20772-2199

Radiographer Program
Wor Wic Tech Community College
1409 Wesley Drive
Salisbury, Maryland 21801-7131

Radiographer Program
Holy Cross Hospital of Silver Spring
1500 Forest Glen Road
Silver Spring, Maryland 20910

Radiographer Program
Montgomery College
Takoma Park Campus
Takoma Avenue at Fenton Street
Takoma Park, Maryland 20912

Radiographer Program
Washington Adventist Hospital
7600 Carroll Avenue
Takoma Park, Maryland 20912

Radiographer Program
Chesapeake College
P.O. Box 8
Wye Mills, Maryland 21679

MASSACHUSETTS

Radiographer Program
Middlesex Community College
Springs Road
Bedford, Massachusetts 01730

Radiographer Program
Bunker Hill Community College
New Rutherford Avenue
Boston, Massachusetts 02129

Radiographer Program
Northeastern University
360 Huntington Avenue
Boston, Massachusetts 02215

Radiographer Program
Massasoit Community College
One Massasoit Boulevard
Brockton, Massachusetts 02402

Radiographer Program
Mt. Auburn Hospital
330 Mt. Auburn Street
Cambridge, Massachusetts 02138

Radiographer Program
North Shore Community College
One Ferncroft Road
Danvers, Massachusetts 01923

Radiographer Program
Northern Essex Community College
100 Elliot Way
Haverhill, Massachusetts 01830

Radiographer Program
Holyoke Community College
303 Homestead Avenue
Holyoke, Massachusetts 01040

Radiographer Program
Springfield Tech Community College
One Armory Square
Springfield, Massachusetts 01105

Radiographer Program
Massachusetts Bay Community College
50 Oakland Street
Wellesley Hills, Massachusetts 02181

Radiographer Program
Quinsigamond Community College
670 West Boylston Street
Worcester, Massachusetts 01606

MICHIGAN

Radiographer Program
Washtenaw Community College
4800 East Huron River Drive
Ann Arbor, Michigan 48106

Radiographer Program
Kellogg Community College
450 North Avenue
Battle Creek, Michigan 49017

Radiographer Program
Lake Michigan College
2755 East Napier Avenue
Benton Harbor, Michigan 49022

Radiographer Program
Ferris State University
901 South State
Big Rapids, Michigan 49307

Radiographer Program
Oakwood Hospital
18101 Oakwood Boulevard
Dearborn, Michigan 48124-2500

Radiographer Program
Grace Hospital
6071 West Outer Drive
Detroit, Michigan 48235

Radiographer Program
Henry Ford Hospital
2799 West Grand Boulevard
Detroit, Michigan 48202

Radiographer Program
Marygrove College
8425 West McNichols Road
Detroit, Michigan 48221-2599

Radiographer Program
St. John Hospital and Medical Center
22101 Moross Road
Detroit, Michigan 48236

Radiographer Program
Hurley Medical Center
Number One Hurley Plaza
Flint, Michigan 48502

Radiographer Program
St. Joseph Hospital
302 Kensington Avenue
Flint, Michigan 48502

Radiographer Program
Grand Rapids Community College
143 Bostwick Avenue NE
Grand Rapids, Michigan 48502

Radiographer Program
Mid Michigan Community College
1375 South Clare Avenue
Harrison, Michigan 48625

Radiographer Program
Jackson Community College
2111 Emmons Road
Jackson, Michigan 49201

Radiographer Program
Bronson Methodist Hospital
252 East Lovell Street
Kalamazoo, Michigan 49007

Radiographer Program
Lansing Community College
Department of Health Careers
P.O. Box 40010
Lansing, Michigan 48901

Radiographer Program
Marquette General Hospital
420 West Magnetic Street
Marquette, Michigan 49855

Radiographer Program
Port Huron Hospital
1001 Kearney Street
P.O. Box 5011
Port Huron, Michigan 48061-5011

Radiographer Program
William Beaumont Hospital
3601 West 13 Mile Road
Royal Oak, Michigan 48073

Radiographer Program
Oakland Community College
Southfield Campus
22322 Rutland Avenue
Southfield, Michigan 48075

Radiographer Program
Providence Hospital
16001 West Nine Mile Road
Southfield, Michigan 48037

Radiographer Program
Delta College
University Center, Michigan 48710

Radiographer Program
Oakwood-United Hospitals
33155 Annapolis Avenue
Wayne, Michigan 48184

MINNESOTA

Radiographer Program
Hibbing Community College
Duluth Community College Center
1309 Rice Lake Road
Duluth, Minnesota 55811

Radiographer Program
East Grand Forks Technical College
Highway 220 North
P.O. Box 111
East Grand Forks, Minnesota 56721

Radiographer Program
Abbott Northwestern Hospital
800 East 28th Street
Minneapolis, Minnesota 55407

Radiographer Program
Minneapolis Veterans Affairs Medical
  Center
One Veteran's Drive
Minneapolis, Minnesota 55417

Radiographer Program
U of Minnesota Health Science Center
Harvard at East River Road
Minneapolis, Minnesota 55455

Radiographer Program
North Memorial Medical Center
3300 Oakdale North
Robbinsdale, Minnesota 55422

Radiographer Program
Mayo Foundation
School of Health Related Sciences
200 First Street SW
Rochester, Minnesota 55905

Radiographer Program
St. Cloud Hospital
1406 Sixth Avenue North
St. Cloud, Minnesota 56303

Radiographer Program
Methodist Hospital
6500 Excelsior Boulevard
St. Louis Pk., Minnesota 55426

Radiographer Program
Lakewood Community College
3401 Century Avenue
White Bear Lake, Minnesota 55110

Radiographer Program
Rice Memorial Hospital
301 Becker Avenue SW
Willmar, Minnesota 56201

MISSISSIPPI

Radiographer Program
Itawamba Community College
Fulton, Mississippi 38843

Radiographer Program
Mississippi Gulf Coast Community
  College
P.O. Box 100
Gautier, Mississippi 39553

Radiographer Program
Hattiesburg Radiology Group
5000 West Fourth Street
Hattiesburg, Mississippi 39402

Radiographer Program
Mississippi Baptist Medical Center
1225 North State Street
Jackson, Mississippi 39201

Radiographer Program
University of Mississippi Medical Center
2500 North State Street
Jackson, Mississippi 39216

Radiographer Program
South Central Regional Medical Center
P.O. Box 607
Laurel, Mississippi 39440

Radiographer Program
Meridian Community College
910 Highway 19 North
Meridian, Mississippi 39307

Radiographer Program
Mississippi Delta Community College
P.O. Box 668
Moorhead, Mississippi 38761

Radiographer Program
Copiah-Lincoln Community College
P.O. Box 457
Wesson, Mississippi 39191

MISSOURI

Radiographer Program
University of Missouri-Columbia
Columbia, Missouri 65211

Radiographer Program
Mineral Area Regional Medical Center
1212 Weber Road
Farmington, Missouri 63640

Radiographer Program
Missouri Southern State College
Newman & Duquesne Roads
Joplin, Missouri 64801-1595

Radiographer Program
Avila College
11901 Wornall Road
Kansas City, Missouri 64145

Radiographer Program
Penn Valley Community College
3201 SW Trafficway
Kansas City, Missouri 64111

Radiographer Program
Research Medical Center
2316 East Meyer Boulevard
Kansas City, Missouri 64132

Radiographer Program
St. Luke's Hospital of Kansas City
4400 Wornall Road
Kansas City, Missouri 64111

Radiographer Program
North Kansas City Hospital
2800 Clay Edwards Drive
North Kansas City, Missouri 64116

Radiographer Program
Rolla Area Vocational-Technical School
1304 East Tenth Street
Rolla, Missouri 65401-3699

Radiographer Program
Cox Medical Centers
1423 North Jefferson
Springfield, Missouri 65802

Radiographer Program
St. John's Regional Health Center
1235 East Cherokee
Springfield, Missouri 65802

Radiographer Program
Mallinckrodt Institute of Radiology
510 South Kingshighway Boulevard
St. Louis, Missouri 63110

Radiographer Program
St. John's Mercy Medical Center
615 South New Ballas Road
St. Louis, Missouri 63141-8221

Radiographer Program
St. Louis Community College at Forest
  Park
5600 Oakland Avenue
St. Louis, Missouri 63110

MONTANA

Radiographer Program
St. Vincent Hospital & Health Center
1233 North 30th Street
Billings, Montana 59107

Radiographer Program
Columbus Hospital
500 15th Avenue South
Great Falls, Montana 59403

Radiographer Program
Montana Deaconess Medical Center
1101 26th Street South
Great Falls, Montana 59405

Radiographer Program
St. Patrick Hospital
500 West Broadway
Missoula, Montana 59806

NEBRASKA

Radiographer Program
Mary Lanning Memorial Hospital
715 North St. Joseph
Hastings, Nebraska 68901

Radiographer Program
Southeast Community College
8800 "O" Street
Lincoln, Nebraska 68520

Radiographer Program
Bergan Mercy Medical Center
7500 Mercy Road
Omaha, Nebraska 68124

Radiographer Program
Immanuel Medical Center
6901 North 72nd Street
Omaha, Nebraska 68122

Radiographer Program
St. Joseph Hospital
601 North 30th Street
Omaha, Nebraska 68131

Radiographer Program
University of Nebraska Medical Center
600 South 42nd Street
Omaha, Nebraska 68198-1045

Radiographer Program
Regional West Medical Center
4021 Avenue "B"
Scottsbluff, Nebraska 69361

NEVADA

Radiographer Program
University of Nevada
4505 Maryland Parkway
Las Vegas, Nevada 89154

Radiographer Program
Truckee Meadows Community College
7000 Dandini Boulevard
Reno, Nevada 89512

NEW HAMPSHIRE

Radiographer Program
New Hampshire Technical Institute
Institute Drive
P.O. Box 2039
Concord, New Hampshire 03302-2039

NEW JERSEY

Radiographer Program
Atlantic City Medical Center
1925 Pacific Avenue
Atlantic City, New Jersey 08401

Radiographer Program
Hudson Area School of Radiologic
  Technology
29 East 29th Street
Bayonne, New Jersey 07002

Radiographer Program
South Jersey Hospital System
Bridgeton Hospital Division
Irving Avenue
Bridgeton, New Jersey 08302

Radiographer Program
Cooper Hospital/University Medical
  Center
One Cooper Plaza
Camden, New Jersey 08103

Radiographer Program
West Jersey Hospital System
Mt. Ephraim & Atlantic Avenues
Camden, New Jersey 08104

Radiographer Program
Burdette Tomlin Memorial Hospital
Route 9 & Stone Harbor Boulevard
Cape May Court House, New Jersey
  08210

Radiographer Program
Middlesex County College
155 Mill Road
P.O. Box 3050
Edison, New Jersey 08818-3050

Radiographer Program
Elizabeth General Medical Center
925 East Jersey Street
Elizabeth, New Jersey 07201

Radiographer Program
Englewood Hospital Association
350 Engle Street
Englewood, New Jersey 07631

Radiographer Program
Mountainside Hospital
Bay & Highland Avenues
Glen Ridge/Montclair, New Jersey
  07042

Hackensack Medical Center
30 Prospect Avenue
Hackensack, New Jersey 07601

Radiographer Program
Monmouth Medical Center
One Centennial Way
Long Branch, New Jersey 07740

Radiographer Program
Fairleigh Dickinson University
285 Madison Avenue
Madison, New Jersey 07960

Radiographer Program
Morristown Memorial Hospital
100 Madison Avenue
Morristown, New Jersey 07962-1956

Radiographer Program
Memorial Hospital of Burlington County
175 Madison Avenue
Mount Holly, New Jersey 08060

Radiographer Program
Essex County College
303 University Avenue
Newark, New Jersey 07102

Radiographer Program
St. Michael's Medical Center
268 Dr. Martin Luther King Boulevard
Newark, New Jersey 07102

Radiographer Program
U of Medicine & Dentistry of New
  Jersey
School of Health Related Professions
100 Bergen Street
Newark, New Jersey 07103

Radiographer Program
Bergen County Community College
400 Paramus Road
Paramus, New Jersey 07652

Radiographer Program
Passaic County Community College
College Boulevard
Paterson, New Jersey 07509

Radiographer Program
Muhlenberg Regional Medical Center
Park Avenue & Randolph Road
Plainfield, New Jersey 07061

Radiographer Program
Riverview Medical Center
One Riverview Plaza
Red Bank, New Jersey 07701

Radiographer Program
Valley Hospital
223 North Van Dien Avenue
Ridgewood, New Jersey 07450

Radiographer Program
Overlook Hospital
99 Beauvoir Avenue
P.O. Box 220
Summit, New Jersey 07902-0220

Radiographer Program
Helene Fuld Medical Center
750 Brunswick Avenue
Trenton, New Jersey 08638

Radiographer Program
Mercer County Community College
1200 Old Trenton Road
P.O. Box B
Trenton, New Jersey 08690

Radiographer Program
St. Francis Medical Center
601 Hamilton Avenue
Trenton, New Jersey 08629-1986

Radiographer Program
Cumberland County College
College Drive
P.O. Box 517
Vineland, New Jersey 08360-0317

Radiographer Program
Pascack Valley Hospital
Old Hook Road
Westwood, New Jersey 07675

NEW MEXICO

Radiographer Program
Pima Medical Institute-Albuquerque
2201 San Pedro NE
Albuquerque, New Mexico 87110

Radiographer Program
U of New Mexico School of Medicine
Albuquerque, New Mexico 87131

Radiographer Program
Clovis Community College
417 Schepps Boulevard
Clovis, New Mexico 88101

Radiographer Program
Northern New Mexico Community
  College
1002 North Onate Street
Espanola, New Mexico 87532

Radiographer Program
Dona Ana Branch Community College
Box 30001
Las Cruces, New Mexico 88003

Radiographer Program
Eastern New Mexico Medical Center
405 West Country Club Road
Roswell, New Mexico 88201-9981

NEW YORK

Radiographer Program
Albany Memorial Hospital
600 Northern Boulevard
Albany, New York 12204

Radiographer Program
Broome Community College
Business Building
P.O. Box 1017
Binghamton, New York 13902

Radiographer Program
CUNY Bronx Community College
University Avenue & West 181 Street
Bronx, New York 10453

Radiographer Program
Hostos Community College of CUNY
475 Grand Concourse
Bronx, New York 10451

Radiographer Program
CUNY New York City Technical
  College
300 Jay Street
Brooklyn, New York 11201

Radiographer Program
Long Island College Hospital
340 Henry Street
Brooklyn, New York 11201

Radiographer Program
Methodist Hospital of Brooklyn
506 Sixth Street
Brooklyn, New York 11215

Radiographer Program
Long Island University
C.W. Post Campus
Northern Boulevard
Brookville, New York 11548

Radiographer Program
Millard Fillmore Hospital
Three Gates Circle
Buffalo, New York 14209

Radiographer Program
Trocaire College
110 Red Jacket Parkway
Buffalo, New York 14220-2094

Radiographer Program
Arnot Ogden Medical Center
Roe Avenue
Elmira, New York 14905-1676

Radiographer Program
Peninsula Hospital Center
51-15 Beach Channel Drive
Far Rockaway, New York 11691

Radiographer Program
Nassau Community College
Stewart Avenue
Garden City, New York 11530

Radiographer Program
Glens Falls Hospital
100 Park Street
Glens Falls, New York 12801

St. James Mercy Hospital
411 Canisteo Street
Hornell, New York 14843

Radiographer Program
Tompkins Community Hospital
101 Dates Drive
Ithaca, New York 14850

Radiographer Program
Women's Christian Association Hospital
207 Foote Avenue
Jamestown, New York 14701

Radiographer Program
Orange County Community College
115 South Street
Middletown, New York 10940

Radiographer Program
Winthrop University Hospital
259 First Street
Mineola, New York 11501

Radiographer Program
Bellevue Hospital Center
First Avenue & 27th Street
New York, New York 10016

Radiographer Program
Harlem Hospital Center
506 Lenox Avenue
New York, New York 10037

Radiographer Program
Northport VA Medical Center
Middleville Road
Northport, New York 11768

Radiographer Program
South Nassau Communities Hospital
2445 Oceanside Road
Oceanside, New York 11572

Radiographer Program
Champlain Valley Phys Hospital Med
   Ctr
100 Beekman Street
Plattsburgh, New York 12901

Radiographer Program
United Hospital Medical Center
406 Boston Post Road
Port Chester, New York 10573

Radiographer Program
Central Suffolk Hospital
1300 Roanoke Avenue
Riverhead, New York 11901

Radiographer Program
Genesee Hospital
224 Alexander Street
Rochester, New York 14607

Radiographer Program
Monroe Community College
1000 East Henrietta Road
Rochester, New York 14623

Radiographer Program
Mercy Hospital
1000 North Village Avenue
Rockville Centre, New York 11570

Radiographer Program
North County Community College
20 Winona Avenue
Saranac Lake, New York 12983

Radiographer Program
Staten Island University Hospital-North
475 Seaview Avenue
Staten Island, New York 10305

Radiographer Program
SUNY Health Science Center at
  Syracuse
750 East Adams Street
Syracuse, New York 13210

Radiographer Program
Hudson Valley Community College
Vandenburgh Avenue
Troy, New York 12180

Radiographer Program
St. Elizabeth Hospital
2209 Genesee Street
Utica, New York 13501

Radiographer Program
St. Luke's Memorial Hospital Center
Champlin Avenue
P.O. Box 479
Utica, New York 13503

Radiographer Program
Westchester Community College
75 Grasslands Road
Valhalla, New York 10595

Radiographer Program
Catholic Medical Center
89-15 Woodhaven Boulevard
Woodhaven, New York 11421

NORTH CAROLINA

Radiographer Program
Asheville Buncombe Technical
  Community College
340 Victoria Road
Asheville, North Carolina 28801

Radiographer Program
University of North Carolina
Medical Allied Health Professions
Chapel Hill, North Carolina 27599-7120

Radiographer Program
Carolinas Medical Center
Box 32861
Charlotte, North Carolina 28232

Radiographer Program
Presbyterian Hospital
200 Hawthorne Lane
P.O. Box 33549
Charlotte, North Carolina 28233-3549

Radiographer Program
Durham County General Hospital
3643 North Roxboro Street
Durham, North Carolina 27704

Radiographer Program
Fayetteville Technical Community
  College
P.O. Box 35236
Fayetteville, North Carolina 28303

Radiographer Program
Gaston Memorial Hospital
2525 Court Drive
P.O. Box 1747
Gastonia, North Carolina 28053-1747

Radiographer Program
Moses H. Cone Memorial Hospital
1200 North Elm Street
Greensboro, North Carolina 27401

Radiographer Program
Pitt Community College
P.O. Drawer 7007
Highway 11 South
Greenville, North Carolina 27834

Radiographer Program
Vance Granville Community College
P.O. Box 917
Henderson, North Carolina 27536

Radiographer Program
Caldwell Comm College & Tech
  Institute
1000 Hickory Boulevard
Husdon, North Carolina 28638

Radiographer Program
Lenoir Memorial Hospital
100 Airport Road
Kinston, North Carolina 28501

Radiographer Program
Carteret Community College
3505 Arendell Street
Morehead City, North Carolina 28557

Radiographer Program
Wilkes Regional Medical Center
Box 609
North Wildesboro, North Carolina 28659

Radiographer Program
Sandhills Community College
2200 Airport Road
Pinehurst, North Carolina 28374

Radiographer Program
Wake Technical Community College
9101 Fayetteville Road
Raleigh, North Carolina 27603

Radiographer Program
Rowan Cabarrus Community College
P.O. Box 1595
Salisbury, North Carolina 28145-1595

Radiographer Program
Cleveland Community College
137 South Post Road
Shelby, North Carolina 28150

Radiographer Program
Johnston Community College
Box 2350
Smithfield, North Carolina 27577

Radiographer Program
Southwestern Community College
275 Webster Road
Sylva, North Carolina 28779

Radiographer Program
Edgecombe Community College
P.O. Box 550
Tarboro, North Carolina 27886

Radiographer Program
Forsyth Technical Community College
2100 Silas Creek Parkway
Winston-Salem, North Carolina 27103

NORTH DAKOTA

Radiographer Program
Q&R Clinic
300 North Seventh Street
Bismarck, North Dakota 58501

Radiographer Program
St. Alexius Medical Center
900 East Broadway
Bismarck, North Dakota 58502-5510

Radiographer Program
Fargo Clinic/St. Lukes Hospital
  Meritcare
720 Fourth Street North
Fargo, North Dakota 58122

Radiographer Program
Minot School for Allied Health
20 Burdick Expressway West, Suite 603
Minto, North Dakota 58701

OHIO

Radiographer Program
Akron General Medical Center
400 Wabash Avenue
Akron, Ohio 44307

Radiographer Program
Children's Hospital Medical Ctr of
  Akron
281 Locust Street
Akron, Ohio 44308

Radiographer Program
Summa Health System
525 East Market Street
P.O. Box 2090
Akron, Ohio 44309-2090

Radiographer Program
Aultman Hospital
2600 Sixth Street SW
Canton, Ohio 44710

Radiographer Program
Timken Mercy Medical Center
1320 Timken Mercy Drive NW
Canton, Ohio 44708

Radiographer Program
U of Cincinnati
Raymond Walters College
234 Goodman Street
Cincinnati, Ohio 45267-0579

Radiographer Program
Xavier University
3800 Victory Parkway
Cincinnati, Ohio 45207

Radiographer Program
Cuyahoga Community College
11000 Pleasant Valley Road
Cleveland, Ohio 44130

Radiographer Program
Metro Health Medical Center
3395 Scranton Road
Cleveland, Ohio 44109

Radiographer Program
University Hospitals of Cleveland
2074 Abington Road
Cleveland, Ohio 44106

Radiographer Program
Ohio State University
1583 Perry Street
Columbus, Ohio 43210

Radiographer Program
Riverside Methodist Hospital
3535 Olentangy River Road
Columbus, Ohio 43214

Radiographer Program
Sinclair Community College
444 West Third Street
Dayton, Ohio 45402

Radiographer Program
Lorain County Community College
1005 North Abbe Road
Elyria, Ohio 44035

Radiographer Program
Meridia Euclid Hospital
18901 Lake Shore Boulevard
Euclid, Ohio 44119

Radiographer Program
Mercy Hospital
P.O. Box 418
Hamilton, Ohio 45012

426

Radiographer Program
Kettering College of Medical Arts
3737 Southern Boulevard
Kettering, Ohio 45429

Radiographer Program
Lima Technical College
4240 Campus Drive
Lima, Ohio 45804

Radiographer Program
North Central Technical College
2441 Kenwood Circle
P.O. Box 698
Mansfield, Ohio 44901

Radiographer Program
Marietta Memorial Hospital
401 Matthew Street
Marietta, Ohio 45750

Radiographer Program
Marion General Hospital
McKinley Park Drive
Marion, Ohio 43302

Radiographer Program
Meridia Hillcrest Hospital
6780 Mayfield Road
Mayfield Heights, Ohio 44124

Radiographer Program
Southwest General Hospital
18697 East Bagley Road
Middleburg Hts, Ohio 44130

Radiographer Program
Middletown Regional Hospital
105 McKnight Drive
Middletown, Ohio 45042

Radiographer Program
Central Ohio Technical College
University Drive
Newark, Ohio 43055

Radiographer Program
Shawnee State University
940 Second Street
Portsmouth, Ohio 45662

Radiographer Program
Richmond Heights General Hospital
27100 Chardon Road
Richmond Heights, Ohio 44143

Radiographer Program
Kent State University
2491 State Rt. 45 South
Salem, Ohio 44460

Radiographer Program
Providence Hospital
1912 Hayes Avenue
Sandusky, Ohio 44870

Radiographer Program
Comm Hosp of Springfield & Clark
  County
2615 East High Street
Springfield, Ohio 45501

Radiographer Program
Jefferson Technical College
4000 Sunset Boulevard
Steubenville, Ohio 43952

Radiographer Program
Michael J. Owens Technical College
Oregon Road
Toledo, Ohio 43699

Radiographer Program
St. Vincent Medical Center
2213 Cherry Street
Toledo, Ohio 43608

Radiographer Program
Trumbull Memorial Hospital
1350 East Market Street
Warren, Ohio 44482

Radiographer Program
St. Elizabeth Hospital Medical Center
1044 Belmont Avenue
Youngstown, Ohio 44501

Radiographer Program
Western Reserve Care System
500 Gypsy Lane
Youngstown, Ohio 44501

Radiographer Program
Muskingum Area Technical College
1555 Newark Road
Zanesville, Ohio 43701

OKLAHOMA

Radiographer Program
O.T. Autry Area Vo-Tech Center
1201 West Willow
Enid, Oklahoma 73703

Radiographer Program
Great Plains Area Vo-Tech School
4500 West Lee Boulevard
Lawton, Oklahoma 73505

Rose State College
6420 SE 15th Street
Midwest City, Oklahoma 73110-2797

Radiographer Program
Bacone College
Muskogee, Oklahoma 74403-1597

Radiographer Program
HCA Presbyterian Hospital
700 NE 13th Street
Oklahoma City, Oklahoma 73104

Radiographer Program
University of Oklahoma at Oklahoma
  City
Box 26901
Oklahoma City, Oklahoma 73190

Radiographer Program
Southwestern Oklahoma State University
409 East Mississippi
Sayre, Oklahoma 73662

Radiographer Program
Indian Meridian Vo-Tech Center
1312 South Sangre Street
Stillwater, Oklahoma 74074

Radiographer Program
Tulsa County Area Vo-Tech
3420 South Memorial Drive
Tulsa, Oklahoma 74145

Radiographer Program
Tulsa Junior College
909 South Boston Avenue
Tulsa, Oklahoma 74119

OREGON

Radiographer Program
Oregon Institute of Technology
3201 Campus Drive
Klamath Falls, Oregon 97601-8801

Radiographer Program
Portland Community College
12000 SW 49th Avenue
Portland, Oregon 97219

PENNSYLVANIA

Radiographer Program
Abington Memorial Hospital
1200 Old York Road
Abington, Pennsylvania 19001

Radiographer Program
Aliquippa Hospital
2500 Hospital Drive
Aliquippa, Pennsylvania 15001

The Allentown Hospital
Lehigh Valley Hospital Center
17th & Chew Streets
Allentown, Pennsylvania 18102

428

Radiographer Program
Mercy Hospital
2500 Seventh Avenue
Altoona, Pennsylvania 16603

Radiographer Program
The Medical Center Beaver PA
1000 Dutch Ridge Road
Beaver, Pennsylvania 15009

Radiographer Program
Northampton Community College
3835 Green Pond Road
Bethlehem, Pennsylvania 18017

Radiographer Program
Bradford Hospital
116-156 Interstate Parkway
Bradford, Pennsylvania 16701

Radiographer Program
The Bryn Mawr Hospital
130 South Bryn Mawr Avenue
Bryn Mawr, Pennsylvania 19010

Radiographer Program
Holy Spirit Hospital
North 21st Street
Camp Hill, Pennsylvania 17011

Radiographer Program
Carlisle Hospital
246 Parker Street
P.O. Box 310
Carlisle, Pennsylvania 17013-0310

Radiographer Program
Chambersburg Hospital
112 North Seventh Street
Chambersburg, Pennsylvania 17201-
0187

Radiographer Program
Sacred Heart Medical Center
Ninth & Wilson Streets
Chester, Pennsylvania 19013

Radiographer Program
Clearfield Hospital
P.O. Box 992
Clearfield, Pennsylvania 16830

Radiographer Program
Brandywine Hospital and Trauma Center
Route 30 Bypass
Coatesville, Pennsylvania 19320-1536

Radiographer Program
College Misericordia
Lake Street
Dallas, Pennsylvania 18612

Radiographer Program
Geisinger Medical Center
North Academy Avenue
Danville, Pennsylvania 17822-2007

Radiographer Program
Doylestown Hospital
595 West State Street
Doylestown, Pennsylvania 18901

Radiographer Program
Rolling Hill Hospital
60 East Township Line Road
Elkins Park, Pennsylvania 19117

Radiographer Program
Gannon University
University Square
Erie, Pennsylvania 16541

Radiographer Program
Franklin Regional Medical Center
One Spruce Street
Franklin, Pennsylvania 16323

Radiographer Program
Harrisburg Hospital
South Front Street
Harrisburg, Pennsylvania 17101

Radiographer Program
Polyclinic Medical Center
2601 North Third Street
Harrisburg, Pennsylvania 17105

Radiographer Program
Hazleton-St. Joseph Medical Center
687 North Church Street
Hazelton, Pennsylvania 18201

Radiographer Program
M.S. Hershey Medical Center
Penn State U
Hershey, Pennsylvania 17033

Radiographer Program
Monsour Medical Center
70 Lincoln Way East
Jeannette, Pennsylvania 15644

Radiographer Program
Conemaugh Valley Memorial Hospital
1086 Franklin Street
Johnstown, Pennsylvania 15905

Radiographer Program
Lee Hospital
320 Main Street
Johnstown, Pennsylvania 15901

Radiographer Program
Armstrong County Memorial Hospital
RD #8/Box 50
Kittanning, Pennsylvania 16201

Radiographer Program
Lancaster General Hospital
555 North Duke Street
Lancaster, Pennsylvania 17603

Radiographer Program
St. Joseph Hospital & Health Care
  Center
250 College Avenue
Lancaster, Pennsylvania 17604

Radiographer Program
Mansfield University
Mansfield, Pennsylvania 16933

Radiographer Program
Ohio Valley General Hospital
R. Morris College
Heckel Road
McKees Rocks, Pennsylvania 15136

Radiographer Program
Community College of Allegheny Cnty
Boyce Campus
595 Beatty Road
Monroeville, Pennsylvania 15146

Radiographer Program
Allegheny Valley Hospital
1301 Carlisle Street
Natrona Heights, Pennsylvania 15065

Radiographer Program
St. Francis Hospital of New Castle
1000 South Mercer Street
New Castle, Pennsylvania 16101

Radiographer Program
Penn State U-New Kensington Campus
3550 Seventh St Road
New Kensington, Pennsylvania 15068

Radiographer Program
Albert Einstein Med Ctr Northern Div
York & Tabor Roads
Philadelphia, Pennsylvania 19141

Radiographer Program
Community College of Philadelphia
1700 Spring Garden Street
Philadelphia, Pennsylvania 19130

Radiographer Program
Germantown Hospital & Medical Center
One Penn Boulevard
Philadelphia, Pennsylvania 19144

Radiographer Program
Hahnemann University
Broad & Vine Streets
Philadelphia, Pennsylvania 19102

Holy Family College
Grant & Frankford Avenues
Philadelphia, Pennsylvania 19114

Radiographer Program
Lankenau Hospital
Lancaster Avenue W of City Line
Philadelphia, Pennsylvania 19151

Radiographer Program
Temple University Hospital
3401 North Broad Street
Philadelphia, Pennsylvania 19140

Radiographer Program
Thomas Jefferson University
130 South Ninth Street
Philadelphia, Pennsylvania 19107

Radiographer Program
Allegheny General Hospital
320 East North Avenue
Pittsburgh, Pennsylvania 15212

Radiographer Program
Presbyterian Univ Hospital of Pittsburgh
Desota at O'Hara Streets
Pittsburgh, Pennsylvania 15213

Radiographer Program
Community General Hospital
145 North Sixth Street
Reading, Pennsylvania 19601

Radiographer Program
Reading Hospital and Medical Center
P.O. Box 16052
Reading, Pennsylvania 19612-6052

Radiographer Program
St. Joseph Hospital
12th & Walnut Street
P.O. Box 316
Reading, Pennsylvania 19603

Radiographer Program
Penn State University-Schuylkill
200 University Drive
Schuylkill Haven, Pennsylvania 17972-
2208

Radiographer Program
Community Medical Center
1822 Mulberry Street
Scranton, Pennsylvania 18510

Radiographer Program
Sewickley Valley Hospital
Blackburn Road
Sewickley, Pennsylvania 15143

Radiographer Program
Sharon Regional Health System
740 East State Street
Sharon, Pennsylvania 16146

Radiographer Program
Somerset Hospital Center for Health
225 South Center Avenue
Somerset, Pennsylvania 15501

Radiographer Program
Crozer-Chester Medical Center
One Medical Center Boulevard
Upland, Pennsylvania 19013

Radiographer Program
Washington Hospital
155 Wilson Avenue
Washington, Pennsylvania 15301

Radiographer Program
Wilkes Barre General Hospital
North River & Auburn Streets
Wilkes-Barre, Pennsylvania 18764

Radiographer Program
Pennsylvania College of Technology
One College Avenue
Williamsport, Pennsylvania 17701-5799

Radiographer Program
York Hospital
1001 South George Street
York, Pennsylvania 17405

PUERTO RICO

Radiographer Program
Universidad Central del Caribe
Bayamon, Puerto Rico 00621-6032

Radiographer Program
University of Puerto Rico
GPO Box 5067
San Juan, Puerto Rico 00936

RHODE ISLAND

Radiographer Program
Community College of Rhode Island
1762 Louisquisset Pike
Lincoln, Rhode Island 02865

Radiographer Program
Rhode Island Hospital
593 Eddy Street
Providence, Rhode Island 02902

SOUTH CAROLINA

Radiographer Program
Anderson Memorial Hospital
800 North Fant Street
Anderson, South Carolina 29621

Radiographer Program
Pettit School Radiologic Tech
Roper Hospital
316 Calhoun Street
Charleston, South Carolina 29401

Radiographer Program
Trident Technical College
P.O. Box 10367
Charleston, South Carolina 29411

Radiographer Program
Baptist Medical Center at Columbia
Taylor at Marion
Columbia, South Carolina 29220

Radiographer Program
Midlands Technical College
P.O. Box 2408
Columbia, South Carolina 29202

Radiographer Program
Florence Darlington Technical College
P.O. Box 100548
Florence, South Carolina 29501

Radiographer Program
Greenville Technical College
P.O. Box 5616
Greenville, South Carolina 29606

Radiographer Program
Piedmont Technical College
P.O. Drawer 1467
Emerald Road
Greenwood, South Carolina 29646

Radiographer Program
Orangeburg Calhoun Technical College
3250 St. Matthews Road
Orangeburg, South Carolina 29115

Radiographer Program
York Technical College
452 South Anderson Road
Rock Hill, South Carolina 29730

Radiographer Program
Spartanburg Technical College
P.O. Drawer 4386
Spartanburg, South Carolina 29305-4386

SOUTH DAKOTA

St. Luke's-Midland Regional Medical
  Ctr
305 South State Street
Aberdeen, South Dakota 57401

Radiographer Program
St. Joseph Hospital
Fifth & Foster
Mitchell, South Dakota 57301

Radiographer Program
Rapid City Regional Hospital
353 Fairmont Boulevard
Rapid City, South Dakota 57709

Radiographer Program
Mckennan Hospital
800 East 21st Street
Sioux Falls, South Dakota 57101

Radiographer Program
Sioux Valley Hospital
1100 South Euclid Avenue
Sioux Falls, South Dakota 57117

Radiographer Program
Sacred Heart Hospital
501 Summit Street
Yankton, South Dakota 57078

TENNESSEE

Radiographer Program
Chattanooga State Technical Comm
  College
4501 Amnicola Highway
Chattanooga, Tennessee 37406

Radiographer Program
Columbia State Community College
P.O. Box 1315
Columbia, Tennessee 38401

Radiographer Program
Cumberland Medical Center
811 South Main Street
Crossville, Tennessee 38555

Radiographer Program
East Tennessee State University
1000 West E Street
Elizabethton, Tennessee 37643

Radiographer Program
Volunteer State Community College
Nashville Pike
Gallatin, Tennessee 37066

Radiographer Program
Roane State Community College
Patton Lane
Harriman, Tennessee 37748

Radiographer Program
Jackson State Community College
2046 North Parkway Street
Jackson, Tennessee 38301-3797

Radiographer Program
U of Tennessee Medical Ctr at
  Knoxville
1924 Alcoa Highway
Knoxville, Tennessee 37920

Radiographer Program
Baptist Memorial Hospital
899 Madison Avenue
Memphis, Tennessee 38146

Radiographer Program
Methodist Hospital of Memphis
1265 Union Avenue
Memphis, Tennessee 38104

Radiographer Program
Shelby State Community College
P.O. Box 40568
Memphis, Tennessee 38174-0568

Radiographer Program
St. Joseph Hospital
220 Overton Avenue
P.O. Box 178
Memphis, Tennessee 38105

Radiographer Program
Metropolitan Nashville General Hospital
72 Hermitage Avenue
Nashville, Tennessee 37210

TEXAS

Radiographer Program
Hendrick Medical Center
1242 North 19th
Abilene, Texas 79601

Radiographer Program
Amarillo College
2200 South Washington
P.O. Box 447
Amarillo, Texas 79178-0001

Radiographer Program
Austin Community College
P.O. Box 140647
Austin, Texas 78714

Radiographer Program
Baptist Hospital of Southeast Texas
P.O. Drawer 1591
Beaumont, Texas 77704

Radiographer Program
Lamar University
Box 10096
Beaumont, Texas 77710

Radiographer Program
Scenic Mountain Medical Center
1601 West 11th Place
Big Spring, Texas 79720

Radiographer Program
Texas Southmost College
80 Ft. Brown
Brownsville, Texas 78520

Radiographer Program
Blinn College
2901 East 29th Street
Bryan, Texas 77802

Radiographer Program
Del Mar College
Baldwin & Ayers
Corpus Christi, Texas 78404

Radiographer Program
Baylor University Medical Center
3500 Gaston Avenue
Dallas, Texas 75246

Radiographer Program
El Centro College
Main & Lamar Streets
Dallas, Texas 75202-3604

Radiographer Program
Parkland Memorial Hospital
5201 Harry Hines Boulevard
Dallas, Texas 75235

Radiographer Program
El Paso Community College
P.O. Box 20500
El Paso, Texas 79998

Radiographer Program
Academy of Health Sciences, U.S. Army
Medicine & Surgery Division
Ft. Sam Houston, Texas 78234-6100

Radiographer Program
Galveston College-University of Texas
4015 Avenue "Q"
Galveston, Texas 77550

Radiographer Program
Houston Community College System
3100 Shenandoah
Houston, Texas 77021

Radiographer Program
Memorial Hospital System
7777 SW Freeway
Houston, Texas 77074

Radiographer Program
U of Texas Hlth Sciences Ctr at Houston
Box 20708
Houston, Texas 77225

Radiographer Program
Tarrant County Junior College
North East Campus
828 Harwood Road
Hurst, Texas 76054

Radiographer Program
Kilgore College
1100 Broadway
Kilgore, Texas 75662

Radiographer Program
Laredo Junior College
West End Washington Street
Laredo, Texas 78040

Radiographer Program
Methodist Hospital
3615 19th Street
P.O. Box 1201
Lubbock, Texas 79408

Radiographer Program
South Plains College
1302 Main Street
Lubbock, Texas 79401

Radiographer Program
Angelina College
P.O. Box 1768
Lufkin, Texas 75901

Radiographer Program
Midland College
3600 North Garfield
Midland, Texas 79705

Radiographer Program
Odessa College
201 West University
Odessa, Texas 79764

Radiographer Program
San Jacinto College Central Campus
8060 Spencer Highway
Pasadena, Texas 77505-2007

Radiographer Program
Baptist Memorial Hospital System
111 Dallas Street
San Antonio, Texas 78205

Radiographer Program
St. Philip's College
2111 Nevada Street
San Antonio, Texas 78203

Radiographer Program
Wadley Regional Medical Center
1000 Pine Street
Texarkana, Texas 75501

Radiographer Program
Tyler Junior College
P.O. Box 9020
Tyler, Texas 75701

Radiographer Program
Citizens Medical Center
2701 Hospital Drive
Victoria, Texas 77901-5749

Radiographer Program
McLennan Community College
1400 College Drive
Waco, Texas 76708

Radiographer Program
Wharton County Junior College
911 Boling Highway
Wharton, Texas 77488

Radiographer Program
School of Health Care Sciences
Sheppard Air Force Base
Wichita Falls, Texas 76311

Radiographer Program
Midwestern State University
3400 Taft Boulevard
Wichita Falls, Texas 76308-2099

UTAH

Radiographer Program
Weber State University
School of Allied Health Sciences
Ogden, Utah 84408-1602

Radiographer Program
Utah Valley Regional Medical Center
1034 N 500 West
Provo, Utah 84603

VERMONT

Radiographer Program
Champlain College
163 South Willard Street
Burlington, Vermont 05402

Radiographer Program
Rutland Regional Medical Center
160 Allen Street
Rutland, Vermont 05701

VIRGINIA

Radiographer Program
Northern Virginia Community College
8333 Little River Turnpike
Annandale, Virginia 22003

Radiographer Program
University of Virginia
Health Science Center
Jefferson Pk Avenue
Charlottesville, Virginia 22908

Radiographer Program
Memorial Hospital
142 South Main Street
Danville, Virginia 24541

Radiographer Program
Rockingham Memorial Hospital
235 Cantrell Avenue
Harrisonburg, Virginia 22801

Radiographer Program
Alleghany Regional Hospital
P.O. Box 7
Low Moor, Virginia 24457

Radiographer Program
Central Virginia Community College
3506 Wards Road
Lynchburg, Virginia 24502

Radiographer Program
Mary Immaculate Hospital
800 Denbigh Boulevard
Newport News, Virginia 23602

Radiographer Program
Newport News Pub Sch
Riverside Reg Med Ctr
500 J. Clyde Morris Boulevard
Newport News, Virginia 23601

Radiographer Program
DePaul Medical Center
150 Kingsley Lane
Norfolk, Virginia 23505

Radiographer Program
Sentara Norfolk General Hospital
600 Gresham Drive
Norfolk, Virginia 23507

Radiographer Program
Southside Regional Medical Center
801 South Adams Street
Petersburg, Virginia 23803

Radiographer Program
Navla Hlth Sci Educ & Training
  Command
Naval Sch of Hlth Sciences
Portsmouth, Virginia 23708-5000

Radiographer Program
Southwest Virginia Community College
P.O. Box SVCC
Richlands, Virginia 24641

Radiographer Program
Medical College of Virginia
Virginia Commonwealth University
Dept. of Radiation Sciences
Richmond, Virginia 23298-0495

Radiographer Program
St. Mary's Hospital
5801 Bremo Road
Richmond, Virginia 23226

Radiographer Program
Carilion Health Systems
Roanoke Memorial Hospitals
P.O. Box 13367
Roanoke, Virginia 24033

Radiographer Program
Virginia Western Community College
3095 Colonial Avenue SW
P.O. Box 14007
Roanoke, Virginia 24038

Radiographer Program
Tidewater Community College
1700 College Crescent
Virginia Beach, Virginia 23456

Radiographer Program
Winchester Medical Center
1840 Amherst Street
P.O. Box 3340
Winchester, Virginia 22601-2540

WASHINGTON

Radiographer Program
Bellevue Community College
3000 Landerholm Circle SE
Bellevue, Washington 98007

Radiographer Program
Holy Family Hospital
N 5633 Lidgerwood Avenue
Spokane, Washington 99207

Radiographer Program
Tacoma Community College
5900 South 12th Street
Tacoma, Washington 98465

Radiographer Program
Wenatchee Valley College
1300 Fifth Street
Wenatchee, Washington 98801

Radiographer Program
Yakima Valley Community College
P.O. Box 1647
Yakima, Washington 98907

WEST VIRGINIA

Radiographer Program
Bluefield State College
Rock Street
Bluefield, West Virginia 24701

Radiographer Program
University of Charleston
2300 MacCorkle Avenue SE
Charleston, West Virginia 25304

Radiographer Program
United Hospital Center
#3 Hospital Plaza Route 19 South
Clarkesburg, West Virginia 26301

Radiographer Program
St. Mary's Hospital
2900 First Avenue
Huntington, West Virginia 25701

Radiographer Program
West Virginia University Hospital
Medical Center Drive
Box 6401
Morgantown, West Virginia 26506

Radiographer Program
Camden Clark Memorial Hospital
800 Garfield Avenue
Parkersburg, West Virginia 26101

Radiographer Program
Ohio Valley Medical Center
2000 Eoff Street
Wheeling, West Virginia 26003

Radiographer Program
Wheeling Hospital
Medical Park
Wheeling, West Virginia 26003

WISCONSIN

Radiographer Program
Beloit Memorial Hospital
1969 West Hart Road
Beloit, Wisconsin 53511

Radiographer Program
Chippewa Valley Technical College
620 West Clairmont Avenue
Eau Claire, Wisconsin 54701-1098

Radiographer Program
Luther Hospital
1221 Whipple Street
Eau Claire, Wisconsin 54702-4105

Radiographer Program
Bellin Memorial Hospital
744 South Webster
P.O. Box 1700
Green Bay, Wisconsin 54305

Radiographer Program
St. Catherine's Hospital
3556 Seventh Avenue
Kenosha, Wisconsin 53140

Radiographer Program
Western Wisconsin Technical College
304 North Sixth Street
P.O. Box 908
La Crosse, Wisconsin 54602

Radiographer Program
Madison Area Technical College
3550 Anderson Street
Madison, Wisconsin 53791

Radiographer Program
University of Wisconsin Hosp & Clinics
600 Highland Avenue
Madison, Wisconsin 53792

Radiographer Program
St. Joseph's Hospital
611 St. Joseph Avenue
Marshfield, Wisconsin 54449

Radiographer Program
Clement J. Zablocki VA Medical Center
5000 West National Avenue
Milwaukee, Wisconsin 53295

Radiographer Program
Columbia Hospital
2025 East Newport Avenue
Milwaukee, Wisconsin 53211

Radiographer Program
Milwaukee Area Technical College
700 West State Street
Milwaukee, Wisconsin 53233

Radiographer Program
Milwaukee County Medical Complex
8700 West Wisconsin Avenue
Milwaukee, Wisconsin 53226

Radiographer Program
St. Luke's Medical Center
2900 West Oklahoma Avenue
Milwaukee, Wisconsin 53215

Radiographer Program
St. Mary's Hospital
2323 North Lake Drive
P.O. Box 503
Milwaukee, Wisconsin 53211

Radiographer Program
St. Michael Hospital
2400 West Villard Avenue
Milwaukee, Wisconsin 53209

Radiographer Program
Theda Clark Regional Medical Center
130 Second Street
Neenah, Wisconsin 54956

Radiographer Program
Mercy Medical Center
P.O. Box 1100
Oshkosh, Wisconsin 54902

Radiographer Program
St. Luke's Memorial Hospital
1320 South Wisconsin Avenue
Racine, Wisconsin 53403

Radiographer Program
St. Mary's Medical Center
3801 Spring Street
Racine, Wisconsin 53405

Radiographer Program
Northcentral Technical College
1000 Campus Drive
Wausau, Wisconsin 54401

WYOMING

Radiographer Program
Casper College
125 College Drive
Casper, Wyoming 82601

Radiographer Program
Laramie County Community College
1400 East College Drive
Cheyenne, Wyoming 82001

Radiographer Program
West Park Hospital
707 Sheridan Avenue
Cody, Wyoming 82414

Radiographer Program
Western Wyoming Community College
2500 College Drive
P.O. Box 428
Rock Springs, Wyoming 82902-0428

Radiation Therapy Technologist

As part of the cancer treatment team, which may include physicians, nurses, radiologists, oncologists (physicians who specialize in treating cancer), and clinical physicists, the *radiation therapy technologist* uses radiation producing equipment to treat, mainly, cancer patients. Radiation therapy may be used separately or in combination with surgery or drug therapy (chemotherapy). After positioning the patient and the equipment, the technologist is directed by the radiologist to administer prescribed concentrations of X-rays or other forms of ionizing radiation to the diseased areas of the patient's body. Different levels of radiation are used depending upon the treatment required. The technologist sets the controls for a specific intensity and exposure time, and monitors these controls throughout the duration of the treatment. Throughout the procedure the technologist is responsible for the safety of the patient and the other medical personnel. The technologist keeps records of all treatments, and maintains equipment. Radiation therapy technologists work mainly in cancer treatment centers or large hospitals.

There are currently two types of approved educational programs in radiation therapy technology. Admission into the twelve month program generally requires that the applicant be either a graduate of an approved radiologic technology program or a registered nurse. Other health professionals wishing to apply to these programs should contact the program director for specific requirements. Admission into the twenty-four month program requires that the applicant be a high school graduate or equivalent, with an acceptable background in basic sciences and mathematics. Graduates of approved educational programs in radiation therapy technology may become certified by the American Registry of Radiologic Technologists. Certification is granted to radiation therapy technologists after graduating from a radiation therapy program accredited by the American Medical Association's Committee on Allied Health Education and Accreditation, and successfully passing a qualifying examination. Some states require radiation therapy technologists to be licensed. For additional information on certification, contact the American Registry of Radiologic Technologists, 1255 Northland Drive, Mendota, Minnesota 55120.

Recommended high school subjects include algebra, geometry, physics, chemistry, biology and computer science.

According to a 1991 survey by the Committee on Allied Health Education and Accreditation, starting salaries for radiation therapy technologists averaged $29,300.

Following is a list of college, university, and hospital based programs approved by the American Medical Association's Committee on Health Education and Accreditation. Contact the program directly for entrance requirements, length of program, and type of certificate/degree awarded.

For more information on a career as a radiation therapy technologist, write to the American Society of Radiologic Technologists, 15000 Central Avenue SE, Albuquerque, New Mexico 87123-3909.

SOURCES:

American Society of Radiologic Technologists
Occupational Outlook Handbook

Radiation Therapy Technologist Programs

ALABAMA

Radiation Therapy Technologist Program
University of Alabama at Birmingham
School of Health Related Professions
UAB Station
Birmingham, Alabama 35294

Radiation Therapy Technologist Program
Mobile Infirmary Medical Center
P.O. Box 2144
Mobile, Alabama 36652

ARKANSAS

Radiation Therapy Technologist
  Program
CARTI School of Radiation Therapy
  Tech
Markham & U Box 5210
Little Rock, Arkansas 72215

CALIFORNIA

Radiation Therapy Technologist Program
City of Hope National Medical Center
1500 East Duarte Road
Duarte, California 91010

Radiation Therapy Technologist Program
Loma Linda University
Loma Linda, California 92350

Radiation Therapy Technologist Program
Foothill Community College
12345 El Monte Road
Los Altos Hills, California 94022

Radiation Therapy Technologist Program
Los Angeles County-USC Medical
  Center
1200 North State Street
Los Angeles, California 90033

Radiation Therapy Technologist Program
Radio Assoc of Sacramento Medical
  Group
1800 "I" Street
Sacramento, California 95814

Radiation Therapy Technologist Program
City College of San Francisco
50 Phelan Avenue
San Francisco, California 94112

Radiation Therapy Technologist Program
Cancer Foundation of Santa Barbara
300 East Pueblo Street
P.O. Box 837
Santa Barbara, California 93105

COLORADO

Radiation Therapy Technologist Program
Community Coll of Denver-Auraria
  Campus
P.O. Box 173363
Denver, Colorado 80217-3363

CONNECTICUT

Radiation Therapy Technologist Program
Danbury Hospital
24 Hospital Avenue
Danbury, Connecticut 06810

Radiation Therapy Technologist Program
Hartford Hospital
80 Seymour Street
Hartford, Connecticut 06115

Radiation Therapy Technologist Program
South Central Community College
60 Sargent Drive
New Haven, Connecticut 06511

DISTRICT OF COLUMBIA

Radiation Therapy Technologist Program
George Washington University Med Ctr
901 23rd Street NW
Washington, DC 20037

Radiation Therapy Technologist Program
Howard University
Sixth & Bryant Streets, NW
Washington, DC 20059

FLORIDA

Radiation Therapy Technologist Program
Halifax Medical Center
303 North Clyde Morris Boulevard
P.O. Box 2830
Daytona Beach, Florida 32115-2830

Radiation Therapy Technologist Program
Radiation Therapy Regional Centers
School of Radiation Therapy
 Technology
7341 Gladiolus Drive
Ft. Meyers, Florida 33908

Radiation Therapy Technologist Program
Santa Fe Community College
P.O. Box 1530
Gainesville, Florida 32602

Radiation Therapy Technologist Program
St. Vincent's Medical Center
1800 Barrs Street
P.O. Box 2982
Jacksonville, Florida 32203

Radiation Therapy Technologist Program
Miami-Dade Community College
950 NW 20th Street
Miami, Florida 33127

Radiation Therapy Technologist Program
Hillsborough Community College
P.O. Box 30030
Tampa, Florida 33630

GEORGIA

Radiation Therapy Technologist Program
Grady Memorial Hospital
80 Butler Street SE
Atlanta, Georgia 30335-3801

Radiation Therapy Technologist Program
Medical College of Georgia
Augusta, Georgia 30912-3965

IDAHO

Radiation Therapy Technologist Program
St. Luke's Regional Medical Center
Mountain State Tumor Institute
151 East Bannock Street
Boise, Idaho 83712

ILLINOIS

Radiation Therapy Technologist Program
Chicago State University
95th Street & King Drive
Chicago, Illinois 60628

Radiation Therapy Technologist Program
Humana Hospital-Michael Reese
Lake Shore Drive at 31st Street
Chicago, Illinois 60616

Radiation Therapy Technologist Program
St. Joseph Hospital
77 North Airlite Street
Elgin, Illinois 60123

Radiation Therapy Technologist Program
National-Louis University
2840 North Sheridan Road
Evanston, Illinois 60201

Radiation Therapy Technologist Program
Edward Hines Jr. VA Hospital
Fifth Avenue & Roosevelt Road
Hines, Illinois 60141

Radiation Therapy Technologist Program
Swedish American Hospital
1400 Charles Street
Rockford, Illinois 61104

INDIANA

Radiation Therapy Technologist Program
Indiana University School of Medicine
535 Barnhill Drive, Rte 071
Indianapolis, Indiana 46223

Radiation Therapy Technologist Program
Methodist Hospital of Indiana
1701 North Senate Boulevard
Box 1367
Indianapolis, Indiana 46206

Radiation Therapy Technologist Program
Memorial Hospital of South Bend
615 North Michigan Avenue
South Bend, Indiana 46601

IOWA

Radiation Therapy Technologist Program
University of Iowa Hospitals and Clinic
Iowa City, Iowa 52242

KANSAS

Radiation Therapy Technologist Program
University of Kansas Medical Center
39th Street & Rainbow Boulevard
Kansas City, Kansas 66103

Radiation Therapy Technologist Program
Washburn University
1700 College Avenue
Topeka, Kansas 66621

KENTUCKY

Radiation Therapy Technologist Program
University of Kentucky
800 Rose Street
Lexington, Kentucky 40536-0084

Radiation Therapy Technologist Program
James Graham Brown Cancer Center
529 South Jackson Street
Louisville, Kentucky 40202

Radiation Therapy Technologist Program
St. Anthony Medical Center
1313 St. Anthony Place
Louisville, Kentucky 40204

LOUISIANA

Radiation Therapy Technologist Program
Alton Ochsner Medical Foundation
1516 Jefferson Highway
New Orleans, Louisiana 70121

MAINE

Radiation Therapy Technologist Program
Southern Maine Technical College
Two Fort Road
South Portland, Maine 04106

MARYLAND

Radiation Therapy Technologist Program
Essex Community College
7201 Rossville Boulevard
Baltimore, Maryland 21237

MASSACHUSETTS

Radiation Therapy Technologist Program
Catherine Laboure College
2120 Dorchester Avenue
Boston, Massachusetts 02124

Radiation Therapy Technologist Program
Mass Coll of Pharmacy & Allied Health
179 Longwood Avenue
Boston, Massachusetts 02115

Radiation Therapy Technologist Program
Springfield Tech Community College
One Armory Square
Springfield, Massachusetts 01105

Radiation Therapy Technologist Program
U Mass Med Center/Worcester State
  Coll
55 Lake Avenue North
Worcester, Massachusetts 01605

MICHIGAN

Radiation Therapy Technologist Program
University of Michigan Medical Center
Ann Arbor, Michigan 48109

Radiation Therapy Technologist Program
Henry Ford Hospital
2799 West Grand Boulevard
Detroit, Michigan 48202

Radiation Therapy Technologist Program
Wayne State University
Detroit, Michigan 48202

Radiation Therapy Technologist Program
Lansing Community College
Department of Health Careers
P.O. Box 40010
Lansing, Michigan 48901

MINNESOTA

U of Minnesota Health Science Center
Harvard Street at E River Road
Minneapolis, Minnesota 55455

Radiation Therapy Technologist Program
Mayo Foundation
School of Health Related Sciences
200 First Street SW
Rochester, Minnesota 55905

MISSISSIPPI

Radiation Therapy Technologist Program
University of Mississippi Medical Center
2500 North State Street
Jackson, Mississippi 39216

MISSOURI

Radiation Therapy Technologist Program
St. Luke's Hospital of Kansas City
4400 Wornall Road
Kansas City, Missouri 64111

Radiation Therapy Technologist Program
Mallinckrodt Institute of Radiology
510 South Kingshighway Boulevard
St. Louis, Missouri 63110

NEBRASKA

Radiation Therapy Technologist Program
University of Nebraska Medical Center
600 South 42nd Street
Omaha, Nebraska 68198-1045

NEW JERSEY

Radiation Therapy Technologist Program
Cooper Hospital/University Medical
  Center
School of Radiation Therapy Tech
One Cooper Plaza
Camden, New Jersey 08103

Radiation Therapy Technologist Program
St. Barnabas Medical Center
Old Short Hills Road
Livingston, New Jersey 07039

Radiation Therapy Technologist Program
St. Peter's Medical Center
254 Easton Avenue
New Brunswick, New Jersey 08901

NEW MEXICO

Radiation Therapy Technologist Program
U of New Mexico School of Medicine
Albuquerque, New Mexico 87131

NEW YORK

Radiation Therapy Technologist Program
Montefiore Medical Center
111 East 210th Street
Bronx, New York 10467

Radiation Therapy Technologist Program
Methodist Hospital of Brooklyn
506 Sixth Street
Brooklyn, New York 11215

Radiation Therapy Technologist Program
Erie Community College
121 Ellicott Street
City Campus
Buffalo, New York 14203

Radiation Therapy Technologist Program
Nassau Community College
Stewart Avenue
Garden City, New York 11530

Radiation Therapy Technologist Program
Memorial Sloan-Kettering Cancer Center
1275 York Avenue
New York, New York 10021

Radiation Therapy Technologist Program
University of Rochester
601 Elmwood Avenue
P.O. Box 647
Rochester, New York 14642

Radiation Therapy Technologist Program
SUNY Health Science Center at
  Syracuse
750 East Adams Street
Syracuse, New York 13210

NORTH CAROLINA

Radiation Therapy Technologist Program
University of North Carolina Hospitals
101 Manning Drive
Chapel Hill, North Carolina 27514

Radiation Therapy Technologist Program
Pitt Community College
P.O. Drawer 7007
Greenville, North Carolina 27835-7007

Radiation Therapy Technologist Program
Forsyth Technical Community College
2100 Silas Creek Parkway
Winston-Salem, North Carolina 27103

OHIO

Radiation Therapy Technologist Program
Aultman Hospital
2600 Sixth Street SW
Canton, Ohio 44710

Radiation Therapy Technologist Program
U of Cincinnati/Raymond Walters
  College
234 Goodman Street
Cincinnati, Ohio 45267

Radiation Therapy Technologist Program
Cleveland Clinic Foundation
One Clinic Center
9500 Euclid Avenue
Cleveland, Ohio 44195-5130

Radiation Therapy Technologist Program
University Hospitals of Cleveland
2074 Abington Road
Cleveland, Ohio 44106

Radiation Therapy Technologist Program
Ohio State University Hospitals
A.G. James Cancer Hosp & Res Inst
300 West Tenth Avenue
Columbus, Ohio 43210-1228

Radiation Therapy Technologist Program
Michael J. Owens Technical College
Oregon Road
Toledo, Ohio 43699-1947

OKLAHOMA

Radiation Therapy Technologist Program
University of Oklahoma at Oklahoma
  City
Box 26901
Oklahoma City, Oklahoma 73190

OREGON

Radiation Therapy Technologist Program
Oregon Health Sciences University
3181 SW Sam Jackson Pk Road
Portland, Oregon 97201

PENNSYLVANIA

Radiation Therapy Technologist Program
Mercy Hospital
2500 Seventh Avenue
Altoona, Pennsylvania 16603-2099

Radiation Therapy Technologist Program
Geisinger Medical Center
North Academy Avenue
Danville, Pennsylvania 17822-2007

Radiation Therapy Technologist Program
Gwynedd-Mercy College
Sumneytown Pike
Gwynedd Valley, Pennsylvania 19437

Radiation Therapy Technologist Program
Comm Coll of Allegheny Cty-Alleg
  Campus
808 Ridge Avenue
Pittsburgh, Pennsylvania 15212

Radiation Therapy Technologist Program
Western Pennsylvania Hospital
4800 Friendship Avenue
Pittsburgh, Pennsylvania 15224

RHODE ISLAND

Radiation Therapy Technologist Program
Rhode Island Hospital
593 Eddy Street
Providence, Rhode Island 02902

SOUTH CAROLINA

Radiation Therapy Technologist Program
Medical University of South Carolina
Coll Hlth Related Professions
171 Ashley Avenue
Charleston, South Carolina 29425

TENNESSEE

Radiation Therapy Technologist Program
Baptist Memorial Hospital
899 Madison Avenue
Memphis, Tennessee 38146

Radiation Therapy Technologist Program
Methodist Hospital of Memphis
1265 Union Avenue
Memphis, Tennessee 38104

Radiation Therapy Technologist Program
Vanderbilt University Medical Center
Radiation Oncology
The Vanderbilt Clinic
Nashville, Tennessee 37232-5671

TEXAS

Radiation Therapy Technologist Program
Amarillo College
2200 South Washington
P.O. Box 447
Amarillo, Texas 79178-0001

Radiation Therapy Technologist Program
Allan Shivers Radiation Therapy Center
2600 East Martin Luther King Blvd.
Austin, Texas 78702

Radiation Therapy Technologist Program
Baylor University Medical Center
3500 Gaston Avenue
Dallas, Texas 75246

Radiation Therapy Technologist Program
El Paso Community College
P.O. Box 20500
El Paso, Texas 79998

Radiation Therapy Technologist Program
Moncrief Radiation Center
1450 Eighth Avenue
Ft. Worth, Texas 76104

Radiation Therapy Technologist Program
Galveston College-University of Texas
4015 Avenue "Q"
Galveston, Texas 77550

Radiation Therapy Technologist Program
U Texas M.D. Anderson Cancer Center
1515 Holcombe Boulevard
Houston, Texas 77030

Radiation Therapy Technologist Program
Methodist Hospital
3615 19th Street
Lubbock, Texas 79410

Radiation Therapy Technologist Program
Cancer Therapy & Research Center
4450 Medical Drive
San Antonio, Texas 78229

UTAH

Radiation Therapy Technologist Program
Weber State University
Ogden, Utah 84408-1602

Radiation Therapy Technologist Program
LDS Hospital
Eighth Avenue & C Street
Salt Lake City, Utah 84143

Radiation Therapy Technologist Program
Univ of Utah Health Sciences Center
50 North Medical Drive
Salt Lake City, Utah 84132

VERMONT

Radiation Therapy Technologist Program
University of Vermont
Burlington, Vermont 05405

VIRGINIA

Radiation Therapy Technologist Program
University of Virginia Health Science
    Center
Jefferson Park Avenue
Charlottesville, Virginia 22908

Radiation Therapy Technologist Program
Sentara Norfolk General Hospital
600 Gresham Drive
Norfolk, Virginia 23507

Radiation Therapy Technologist Program
Med Coll of VA
Virginia Commonwealth University
Dept. of Radiation Sciences
Richmond, Virginia 23298-0495

Radiation Therapy Technologist Program
Carillion Health Systems
Roanoke Memorial Hospitals
Belleview at Jefferson Street
Roanoke, Virginia 24033

WASHINGTON

Radiation Therapy Technologist Program
Bellevue Community College
V. Mason Clinic
3000 Landerholm Circle SE
Bellevue, Washington 98007-6484

WEST VIRGINIA

Radiation Therapy Technologist Program
West Virginia University Hospital
1244 U Hospital
Morgantown, West Virginia 26506-8150

WISCONSIN

Radiation Therapy Technologist Program
University of Wisconsin Hosp & Clinics
600 Highland Avenue
Madison, Wisconsin 53792

Radiation Therapy Technologist Program
Medical College of Wisconsin
8701 Watertown Plank Road
Milwaukee, Wisconsin 53226

Radiation Therapy Technologist Program
St. Joseph's Hospital
5000 West Chambers Street
Milwaukee, Wisconsin 53210

Nuclear Medicine Technology

Nuclear medicine technology is the allied health specialty concerned with the use of radioactive materials for diagnostic purposes.

Radiopharmaceuticals are used to treat and diagnose diseases of the brain, heart, kidneys, liver, lungs, spleen, pancreas, thyroid, bone and gastrointestinal system. Visualization of these structures is achieved with the patient ingesting, inhaling, or being injected with a small amount of radioactive material and measured with a radiation detection instrument.

Other diagnostic procedures involve radioactive analysis of biologic specimens, such as blood or urine collected from a patient. The specimen is mixed with radioactive materials to measure presence and amounts of hormones, drugs, blood constituents and other components.

The allied health career that employs nuclear medicine technology is the *nuclear medicine technologist.*

Nuclear Medicine Technologist

Under supervision of a radiologist, the *nuclear medicine technologist* assists with the administration and detection of radioactive materials in diagnosis and therapy. The technologist verifies patients' records, prepares and administers the radiopharmaceutical in prescribed dosages, positions the patient for imaging procedures, and operates the nuclear

448

instruments. The technologist prepares the results and presents them to the radiologist. In therapy, the nuclear medicine technologist administers radioactive materials to treat specific diseases, and is responsible for the protection of the patient and medical personnel from excessive radiation.

The technologist is careful about radiation safety and quality control. He or she keeps inventory of the radiopharmaceuticals and is responsible for their safe storage and use and for the disposal of radioactive waste. Although mainly employed in large hospitals, nuclear medicine technologists also work in small community hospitals, laboratories, research centers, physicians' offices and clinics.

The educational program for nuclear medicine technology includes classroom, laboratory, and supervised experience in a clinical setting. Programs available include a one-year certificate, two-year associate degree, and a four-year bachelor's degree. Admission into a nuclear medicine school requires a high school degree or equivalent plus post secondary competencies in science, mathematics, and communications.

Certification is offered by two organizations: the American Registry of Radiologic Technologists, and the Nuclear Medicine Technology Certification Board. Certification with one of these is a job prerequisite in almost all nuclear medicine departments. Certification is granted to nuclear medicine technologists after graduating from a nuclear medicine technology program accredited by the Committee on Allied Health Education and Accreditation of the American Medical Association, and successfully passing a qualifying examination. The Nuclear Medicine Technology Certification Board also requires clinical experience as a certification requirement. Certification information is available from the American Registry of Radiologic Technologists, 1255 Northland Drive, Mendota Heights, Minnesota 55120, or the Nuclear Medicine Technology Certification Board, 2970 Clairmont Road, Suite 610, Atlanta, Georgia 30329-1634.

Recommended high school courses include English, mathematics, chemistry, biology, physiology, and physics.

According to a 1991 survey by the Committee on Allied Health Education and Accreditation, starting salaries for nuclear medicine technologists averaged $27,300 a year.

Following is a list of accredited nuclear medicine technology educational programs, supplied by the Joint Review Committee on Educational Programs in Nuclear Medicine Technology.

For more information on a career in nuclear medicine technology, contact the American Society of Radiologic Technologists, 15000 Central Avenue SE, Albuquerque, New Mexico 87123, or the Society of Nuclear Medicine, 136 Madison Avenue, New York, New York 10016.

SOURCES:

American Society of Radiologic Technologists
Joint Review Committee on Ed Programs in Nuclear Med Technology
Nuclear Medicine Technology Certification Board
Occupational Outlook Handbook

Nuclear Medicine Technologist Programs

ALABAMA

Nuclear Medicine Technologist Program
University of Alabama-Birmingham
School of Health Related Professions
1714 Ninth Avenue South
Birmingham, Alabama 35294-1270

ARIZONA

Nuclear Medicine Technologist Program
Gateway Community College
108 North 40th Street
Phoenix, Arizona 85034

ARKANSAS

Nuclear Medicine Technologist Program
Baptist Medical Center
11900 Colonel Glenn Road, Suite 1000
Little Rock, Arkansas 72210-2820

Nuclear Medicine Technologist Program
University of Arkansas
St. Vincent Infirmary Medical Center
College of Health Related Professions
4301 West Markham
Little Rock, Arkansas 72205

CALIFORNIA

Nuclear Medicine Technologist Program
California State University-Dominguez
 Hills
Dept. of Clinical Sciences
1000 East Victoria Street
Carson, California 90747-3748

Nuclear Medicine Technologist Program
Loma Linda University
Dept. of Radiation Technology
Loma Linda, California 92350

Nuclear Medicine Technologist Program
Charles R. Drew University of Medicine
 & Science
1621 East 120th Street
Los Angeles, California 90059

Nuclear Medicine Technologist Program
LA County Univ of So CA Medical
 Center
School of Nuclear Medicine Technology
1200 North State Street
Los Angeles, California 90033-1084

Nuclear Medicine Technologist Program
VAMC West Los Angeles Wadsworth
 Division
Dept. of Veterans Affairs
Medical Center West Los Angeles
Wilshire & Sawtelle Boulevards
Los Angeles, California 90073

Nuclear Medicine Technologist Program
Sutter Community Hospitals
School of Nuclear Medicine Technology
2801 "L" Street
Sacramento, California 95816

Nuclear Medicine Technologist Program
University of CA San Diego Med Center
225 Dickinson Street
San Diego, California 92103-8758

Nuclear Medicine Technologist Program
Medical Ctr at Univ of CA San
 Francisco
505 Parnassus Avenue
P.O. Box 0252
San Francisco, California 94143-0252

Nuclear Medicine Technologist Program
Cancer Foundation of Santa Barbara
300 West Pueblo
P.O. Box 837
Santa Barbara, California 93105

COLORADO

Nuclear Medicine Technologist Program
Community College of Denver
Auraria Campus
1111 West Colfax Avenue
Denver, Colorado 80204

CONNECTICUT

Nuclear Medicine Technologist Program
St. Vincents Medical Center
School of Nuclear Medicine Technology
2800 Main Street
Bridgeport, Connecticut 06606

Nuclear Medicine Technologist Program
Middlesex Community College
100 Training Hill Road
Middletown, Connecticut 06457

Nuclear Medicine Technologist Program
Gateway Community Technical College
60 Sargent Drive
New Haven, Connecticut 06511

DELAWARE

Nuclear Medicine Technologist Program
Delaware Technical & Community
  College
333 Shipley Street
Wilmington, Delaware 19801

DISTRICT OF COLUMBIA

Nuclear Medicine Technologist Program
George Washington University
School of Medicine & Health Sciences
2300 Eye Street NW
Washington, DC 20037-2337

FLORIDA

Nuclear Medicine Technologist Program
Santa Fe Community College
3000 NW 83rd Street
Gainesville, Florida 32606-6200

Nuclear Medicine Technologist Program
University of Miami Jackson Mem Med
  Ctr
School of Technological Radiology
1611 NW 12th Avenue
Miami, Florida 33136

Nuclear Medicine Technologist Program
Mount Sinai Medical Center
4300 Alton Road
Miami Beach, Florida 33140

Nuclear Medicine Technologist Program
Valencia Community College
Dept. of Nuclear Medicine
1800 South Kirkman Road
Orlando, Florida 32811

Nuclear Medicine Technologist Program
Hillsborough Community College
P.O. Box 30030
Tampa, Florida 33630

GEORGIA

Nuclear Medicine Technologist Program
Medical College of Georgia
School of Allied Health Sciences
1120 15th Street
Augusta, Georgia 30912-0070

ILLINOIS

Nuclear Medicine Technologist Program
College of Dupage
22nd Street & Lambert Road
Glen Ellyn, Illinois 60137-6599

Nuclear Medicine Technologist Program
Edward Hines Jr. VA Hospital
Fifth Avenue & Roosevelt Road
Hines, Illinois 60141-5000

Nuclear Medicine Technologist Program
St. Francis Medical Center
530 NE Glen Oak Avenue
Peoria, Illinois 61637

Nuclear Medicine Technologist Program
Triton College
2000 North Fifth Avenue
River Grove, Illinois 60171

INDIANA

Nuclear Medicine Technologist Program
Indiana University
Radiological Sciences
541 Clinical Drive
Indianapolis, Indiana 46202-5111

Nuclear Medicine Technologist Program
Ball State University
Physiology & Health Science
  Department
Muncie, Indiana 47306

IOWA

Nuclear Medicine Technologist Program
University of Iowa
Dept. of Radiology
200 Hawkins Drive
Iowa City, Iowa 52242-1009

KENTUCKY

Nuclear Medicine Technologist Program
Lexington Community College
Cooper Drive
Lexington, Kentucky 40506-0235

Nuclear Medicine Technologist Program
University of Louisville
Division of Allied Health
Louisville, Kentucky 40292

LOUISIANA

Nuclear Medicine Technologist Program
Delgado Community College
Allied Health Department
615 City Park Avenue
New Orleans, Louisiana 70119-4399

Nuclear Medicine Technologist Program
Alton Ochsner Medical Center
School of Allied Health Sciences
1516 Jefferson Highway
New Orleans, Louisiana 70121

Nuclear Medicine Technologist Program
Overton Brooks VA Medical Center
510 East Stoner Avenue
Shreveport, Louisiana 71101-4295

MARYLAND

Nuclear Medicine Technologist Program
Johns Hopkins Hospital
Essex Community College
600 North Wolfe Street
Baltimore, Maryland 21205

Nuclear Medicine Technologist Program
Naval School of Health Sciences
Technical Training Department
Bethesda, Maryland 20814-5033

Nuclear Medicine Technologist Program
Prince Georges Community College
Division of Health Technology
301 Largo Road
Largo, Maryland 20772

MASSACHUSETTS

Nuclear Medicine Technologist Program
Massachusetts College Pharm & Allied
  Hlth
179 Longwood Avenue
Boston, Massachusetts 02115

Nuclear Medicine Technologist Program
Bunker Hill Community College
Rutherford Avenue
Charlestown, Massachusetts 02129

Nuclear Medicine Technologist Program
Salem State College
Biology Department
352 Lafayette Street
Salem, Massachusetts 01970

452

Nuclear Medicine Technologist Program
Springfield Technical Community
  College
One Armory Square
P.O. Box 9000
Springfield, Massachusetts 01101-9000

Nuclear Medicine Technologist Program
University of MA Medical Center
Worcester State College
55 Lake Avenue North
Worcester, Massachusetts 01655

MICHIGAN

Nuclear Medicine Technologist Program
Ferris State College
Hospital Related Programs
College of Allied Health Sciences
200 Ferris Drive
Big Rapids, Michigan 49307-2740

Nuclear Medicine Technologist Program
St. John Hospital & Medical Center
22101 Moross Road
Detroit, Michigan 48236-2172

Nuclear Medicine Technologist Program
William Beaumont Hospital
3601 West 13 Mile Road
Royal Oak, Michigan 48073-6769

MINNESOTA

Nuclear Medicine Technologist Program
Mayo Clinic Foundation
200 First Street SW
Rochester, Minnesota 55905

Nuclear Medicine Technologist Program
St. Mary's College of Minnesota
700 Terrace Heights
Winona, Minnesota 55987-1399

MISSISSIPPI

Nuclear Medicine Technologist Program
University of Mississippi Medical Center
2500 North State Street
Jackson, Mississippi 39216-4505

MISSOURI

Nuclear Medicine Technologist Program
University of Missouri-Columbia
School of Health Related Professions
Columbia, Missouri 65211-0001

Nuclear Medicine Technologist Program
Research Medical Center
2316 East Meyer Boulevard
Kansas City, Missouri 64132

Nuclear Medicine Technologist Program
St. Lukes Hospital of Kansas City
44th & Wornall Road
Kansas City, Missouri 64111

Nuclear Medicine Technologist Program
St. Louis University
School of Allied Health Professions
1504 South Grand Boulevard
St. Louis, Missouri 63104-1395

NEBRASKA

Nuclear Medicine Technologist Program
University of Nebraska Medical Center
600 South 42nd Street
Omaha, Nebraska 68198

NEVADA

Nuclear Medicine Technologist Program
University of Nevada-Las Vegas
College of Health Sciences
4505 South Maryland Parkway
Las Vegas, Nevada 89154

NEW JERSEY

Nuclear Medicine Technologist Program
University of Medicine & Dentistry of
 NJ
School of Health Related Professions
65 Bergen Street
Newark, New Jersey 07107-3006

Nuclear Medicine Technologist Program
Riverview Medical Center
One Riverview Plaza
Red Bank, New Jersey 07701

Nuclear Medicine Technologist Program
Gloucester County College
RR #4 Box 203
Tanyard Road
Sewell, New Jersey 08080

Nuclear Medicine Technologist Program
Overlook Hospital
99 Beauvoir Avenue at Sylan Road
Summit, New Jersey 07901-0220

NEW MEXICO

Nuclear Medicine Technologist Program
University New Mexico School of
 Medicine
Dept. of Radiology
Albuquerque, New Mexico 87131-5656

NEW YORK

Nuclear Medicine Technologist Program
Bronx Community College of the City
 Univ of NY
University Avenue & West 181 Street
Bronx, New York 10453

Nuclear Medicine Technologist Program
SUNY Health Science Center at
 Brooklyn
Box 1226
450 Clarkson Avenue
Brooklyn, New York 11203

Nuclear Medicine Technologist Program
SUNY at Buffalo
3435 Main Street
Buffalo, New York 14214-3000

Nuclear Medicine Technologist Program
Institute of Allied Medical Professions
106 Central Park South
New York, New York 10019

Nuclear Medicine Technologist Program
New York University Medical Center
560 First Avenue
New York, New York 10016

Nuclear Medicine Technologist Program
St. Vincents Hospital & Medical Center
153 West 11th Street
New York, New York 10011

Nuclear Medicine Technologist Program
Veterans Administration Medical Center
79 Middleville Road
Northport, New York 11768

Nuclear Medicine Technologist Program
Manhattan College
Dept. of Radiological & Health Sciences
Manhattan College Parkway
Riverdale, New York 10471-4098

Nuclear Medicine Technologist Program
Rochester Institute of Technology
One Lomb Memorial Drive
P.O. Box 9887
Rochester, New York 14623-0887

Nuclear Medicine Technologist Program
SUNY Health Science Center at
 Syracuse
750 East Adams Street
Syracuse, New York 13210

NORTH CAROLINA

Nuclear Medicine Technologist Program
University North Carolina Hospitals
Imaging Division/Radiology Department
101 Manning Drive
Chapel Hill, North Carolina 27514

Nuclear Medicine Technologist Program
Forsyth Technical Community College
2100 Silas Creek Parkway
Winston-Salem, North Carolina 27103

OHIO

Nuclear Medicine Technologist Program
Aultman Hospital
2600 Sixth SW
Canton, Ohio 44710-1799

Nuclear Medicine Technologist Program
University of Cincinnati Medical Center
234 Goodman Street
Cincinnati, Ohio 45267

Nuclear Medicine Technologist Program
Ohio State University Hospitals
410 West Tenth Avenue
Columbus, Ohio 43210-1228

Nuclear Medicine Technologist Program
Nuclear Medicine Institute
University of Findlay
1000 North Main Street
Findlay, Ohio 45840-3695

Nuclear Medicine Technologist Program
St. Elizabeth Hospital Medical Center
1044 Belmont Avenue
Youngstown, Ohio 44501-1790

OKLAHOMA

Nuclear Medicine Technologist Program
University of Oklahoma
College of Allied Health
P.O. Box 26901
Oklahoma City, Oklahoma 73190

OREGON

Nuclear Medicine Technologist Program
Veterans Administration Medical Center
P.O. Box 1034
Portland, Oregon 97207

PENNSYLVANIA

Nuclear Medicine Technologist Program
Cedar Crest College
100 College Drive
Allentown, Pennsylvania 18104-6196

Nuclear Medicine Technologist Program
South Central PA Consortium for
   Nuclear Medicine Technology Training
Harrisburg Hospital
111 South Front Street
Harrisburg, Pennsylvania 17101-2099

Nuclear Medicine Technologist Program
Hospital of the University of PA
3400 Spruce Street
Philadelphia, Pennsylvania 19104

Nuclear Medicine Technologist Program
Temple University Hospital
Dept. of Diagnostic Imaging
3401 North Broad Street
Philadelphia, Pennsylvania 19140-5192

Nuclear Medicine Technologist Program
Community College of Allegheny
   County
808 Ridge Avenue
Pittsburgh, Pennsylvania 15212

Nuclear Medicine Technologist Program
Western Pennsylvania Hospital
4800 Friendship Avenue
Pittsburgh, Pennsylvania 15224

Nuclear Medicine Technologist Program
Wilkes Barre General Hospital
North River & Auburn Streets
Wilkes Barre, Pennsylvania 18764

PUERTO RICO

Nuclear Medicine Technologist Program
University of Puerto Rico
College of Health Related Professions
Medical Sciences Campus
P.O. Box 365067
San Juan, Puerto 00936-5067

RHODE ISLAND

Nuclear Medicine Technologist Program
Rhode Island Hospital
593 Eddy Street
Providence, Rhode Island 02902

SOUTH CAROLINA

Nuclear Medicine Technologist Program
Midlands Technical College
P.O. Box 2408
Columbia, South Carolina 29202

SOUTH DAKOTA

Nuclear Medicine Technologist Program
Southeast Vocational Technical Institute
2301 Career Place
Sioux Falls, South Dakota 57101

TENNESSEE

Nuclear Medicine Technologist Program
University of Tennessee Medical Center
1924 Alcoa Highway
Knoxville, Tennessee 37920-6999

Nuclear Medicine Technologist Program
Baptist Memorial Hospital
899 Madison Avenue
Memphis, Tennessee 38146

Nuclear Medicine Technologist Program
Methodist Hospitals of Memphis
1265 Union Avenue
Memphis, Tennessee 38104

Nuclear Medicine Technologist Program
Vanderbilt University Medical Center
21st Avenue South
Nashville, Tennessee 37323

TEXAS

Nuclear Medicine Technologist Program
Galveston College
4015 Avenue Q
Galveston, Texas 77550-2782

Nuclear Medicine Technologist Program
Baylor College of Medicine
Center for Allied Health Professions
One Baylor Plaza
Houston, Texas 77030

Nuclear Medicine Technologist Program
Houston Community College System
3100 Shenandoah
Houston, Texas 77021-1042

Nuclear Medicine Technologist Program
Incarnate Word the College
4301 Broadway
San Antonio, Texas 78209-6397

UTAH

Nuclear Medicine Technologist Program
Weber State College
Ogden, Utah 84408-1602

Nuclear Medicine Technologist Program
University of Utah
50 North Medical Drive
Salt Lake City, Utah 84132

VERMONT

Nuclear Medicine Technologist Program
University of Vermont
Burlington, Vermont 05405

VIRGINIA

Nuclear Medicine Technologist Program
University of Virginia Medical Center
Box 486
Charlottesville, Virginia 22908

Nuclear Medicine Technologist Program
Old Dominion University
College of Health Sciences
Norfolk, Virginia 23529-0286

Nuclear Medicine Technologist Program
Medical College of Virginia
Virginia Commonwealth University
MCV Station Box 495
Richmond, Virginia 23298-0495

Nuclear Medicine Technologist Program
Roanoke Memorial Hospitals
Jefferson at Belleview
P.O. Box 13367
Roanoke, Virginia 24033-3367

WASHINGTON

Nuclear Medicine Technologist Program
Bellevue Community College
P.O. Box 92700
Bellevue, Washington 98009-2037

WEST VIRGINIA

Nuclear Medicine Technologist Program
West Virginia State College
Institute, West Virginia 25122-1000

Nuclear Medicine Technologist Program
West Virginia University Hospitals
Dept. of Radiology
P.O. Box 6401
Morgantown, West Virginia 26506

Nuclear Medicine Technologist Program
Wheeling Jesuit College
316 Washington Avenue
Wheeling, West Virginia 26003

WISCONSIN

Nuclear Medicine Technologist Program
St. Joseph's Hospital
611 St. Joseph Avenue
Marshfield, Wisconsin 54449

Nuclear Medicine Technologist Program
Milwaukee County Medical Complex
8700 West Wisconsin Avenue
Milwaukee, Wisconsin 53226

Nuclear Medicine Technologist Program
St. Lukes Medical Center
2900 West Oklahoma Avenue
Milwaukee, Wisconsin 53201-2901

Nuclear Medicine Technologists
  Program
St. Mary's Hospital
P.O. Box 503
Milwaukee, Wisconsin 53201-0503

Diagnostic Ultrasound

Diagnostic ultrasound is the technique that uses high frequency sound waves (ultrasound) for diagnostic purposes. By transmitting ultrasound through various parts of the body, images are created on video screens that show the shape and composition of organs, tissues, and other bodily masses such as fluid accumulations. These images are then used by a licensed physician (one who has been trained to interpret ultrasound images) to diagnose disease, injury, or other physical conditions. Unlike X-rays (which use radiation to create images on film) ultrasound is noninvasive (it does not invade healthy tissue). The technical practitioner of diagnostic ultrasound is the *diagnostic medical sonographer.*

Diagnostic Medical Sonographer

Also called an *ultrasound technologist,* the diagnostic medical sonographer works under the direction of a physician to provide quality imaging techniques in ultrasound diagnoses. The sonographer may perform a variety of studies, including the examination of the contour and inner structures of the brain (neurosonography); examination of the heart and its structures (echocardiography); examination of the soft tissue structures of the abdomen such as the liver, spleen, kidneys and pancreas; examination of the female anatomy and of pregnant females (gynecology and obstetrics); and the examination of the eyes (ophthalmology). The diagnostic medical sonographer is well knowledgeable of the human anatomy.

The medical sonographer is responsible for the personal comfort of the patient in his or her care. The sonographer prepares the patient for the examination, explains the procedure, scans the patient with the ultrasound equipment, and provides the physician with the final results. He or she may also perform clerical duties such as keeping records of the patients and of the imaging films. The medical sonographer should be capable of working with little supervision within the rules set by the physician or department head.

Diagnostic medical sonographers work in all health facilities that utilize ultrasound devices-mainly large hospitals and medical centers. A few are employed in smaller rural hospitals, private physician practices, public health services, industry, and sales.

Training programs in diagnostic ultrasound are offered by universities, radiological institutes, and hospitals. The prerequisites for the one year program include high school graduation or the equivalent and qualifications in a related allied health profession. Programs may also be two or four years in duration depending on the degree or certificate awarded.

Satisfactory completion of specific educational and clinical experience requirements qualifies the candidate to take the registry examination and if successfully passed, apply for registration as a Registered Diagnostic Medical Sonographer (RDMS) with the American Registry of Diagnostic Medical Sonographers. The registry credential of Registered Vascular Technologist (RVT) is also available after successfully passing the Vascular Physical Principles and Instrumentation exam and the Vascular Technology exam.

The following is a summary of the educational and clinical prerequisites needed to take the registry examinations:

(1) Graduation from a training program in diagnostic medical sonography or vascular technology, accredited by the American Medical Association's Committee on Allied Health

458

Education and Accreditation (CAHEA), or (2) Completion of a two year patient related allied health occupation such as diagnostic medical sonographer, registered nurse, radiologic technologist, respiratory therapist, physical therapist or occupational therapist and 12 months clinical ultrasound/vascular experience, or (3) Completion of a bachelor's degree in sonography/vascular technology or in a radiology degree program with a minor in sonography and at least 12 months clinical ultrasound/vascular experience, or (4) Completion of a two-year college degree, plus 24 months clinical ultrasound/vascular experience.

For more information on registration requirements contact the American Registry for Diagnostic Medical Sonographers, 2368 Victory Parkway, Suite 510, Cincinnati, Ohio 45206.

Recommended high school subjects for a career in ultrasound technology are physics, chemistry, biology and mathematics.

According to a 1991 survey by the Committee on Allied Health Education and Accreditation, entry level salaries for diagnostic medical sonographers averaged $26,800 a year. Many factors, might, effect salary levels including education, experience, and geographic location.

Following is a list, provided by the Society of Diagnostic Medical Sonographers, of educational programs in diagnostic medical sonography accredited by the American Medical Association's Committee on Allied Health Education and Accreditation.

For further information on a career as a diagnostic medical sonographer, contact the Society of Diagnostic Medical Sonographers, 12770 Coit Road, Suite 508, Dallas, Texas 75251.

SOURCES:

American Society of Radiologic Technologists
Occupational Outlook Handbook
Society of Diagnostic Medical Sonographers

Diagnostic Ultrasound Programs

ARIZONA

Diagnostic Ultrasound Program
Gateway Community College
108 North 40th Street
Phoenix, Arizona 85034

CALIFORNIA

Diagnostic Ultrasound Program
Grossmont College
8800 Grossmont College Drive
El Cajon, California 92020

Diagnostic Ultrasound Program
Loma Linda University
11234 Anderson Street
Loma Linda, California 92354

Diagnostic Ultrasound Program
Orange Coast College
2701 Fairview Road
Costa Mesa, California 92628-5005

Diagnostic Ultrasound Program
University of California, San Diego
Department of Radiology
225 Dickinson Street
San Diego, California 92103

COLORADO

Diagnostic Ultrasound Program
Penrose Hospital
School of Diagnostic Medical
  Sonography
P.O. Box 7021
Colorado Springs, Colorado 80933

DELAWARE

Diagnostic Ultrasound Program
Delaware Technical & Community
  College
Wilmington Campus-Allied
  Health/Science Dept.
333 Shipley Street
Wilmington, Delaware 19801

FLORIDA

Diagnostic Ultrasound Program
Broward Community College
3501 Southwest Davie Road
Davie, Florida 33314

Diagnostic Ultrasound Program
Hillsborough Community College
4001 Tampa Bay Boulevard
Tampa, Florida 33630

Diagnostic Ultrasound Program
Jackson Memorial Hospital
School of Technological Radiology
1611 NW 12th Avenue
Miami, Florida 33136-1094

Diagnostic Ultrasound Program
Orlando Regional Medical Center
Valencia Community College
1414 Kuhl Avenue
Orlando, Florida 32802

GEORGIA

Diagnostic Ultrasound Program
Grady Memorial Hospital
P.O. Box 26095
80 Butler Street SE
Atlanta, Georgia 30335

Diagnostic Ultrasound Program
Medical College of Georgia
School of Radiologic Technologies
Augusta, Georgia 30912

ILLINOIS

Diagnostic Ultrasound Program
Triton Community College
2000 Fifth Avenue
River Grove, Illinois 60171

Diagnostic Ultrasound Program
Wilbur Wright College
3400 North Austin
Chicago, Illinois 60634

IOWA

Diagnostic Ultrasound Program
University of Iowa Hospitals and Clinics
Department of Radiology
Iowa City, Iowa 52242-1077

KENTUCKY

Diagnostic Ultrasound Program
West Kentucky State Vocational
  Technology School
P.O. Box 7408
Paducah, Kentucky 42002-7408

LOUISIANA

Diagnostic Ultrasound Program
Alton Ochsner Medical Foundation
880 Commerce Road West
New Orleans, Louisiana 70123

MARYLAND

Diagnostic Ultrasound Program
Maryland Institute of Ultrasound
  Technology
5401 Wilkins Avenue
Baltimore, Maryland 21228

MASSACHUSETTS

Diagnostic Ultrasound Program
Middlesex Community College
Springs Road
Bedford, Massachusetts 01730

MICHIGAN

Diagnostic Ultrasound Program
Henry Ford Hospital
2799 West Grand Boulevard
Detroit, Michigan 48202

Diagnostic Ultrasound Program
Jackson Community College
2111 Emmons Road
Jackson, Michigan 49201

Diagnostic Ultrasound Program
Oakland Community College
Southeast Campus System
22322 Rutland Drive
Southfield, Michigan 48075

MINNESOTA

Diagnostic Ultrasound Program
Mayo Clinic/Mayo Foundation
School of Diagnostic Medical
  Sonography
200 First Street SW
Rochester, Minnesota 55905

MISSOURI

Diagnostic Ultrasound Program
St. Louis Community College at Forest
  Park
5600 Oakland Avenue
St. Louis, Missouri 63110

NEBRASKA

Diagnostic Ultrasound Program
University of Nebraska Medical Center
600 South 42nd Street
Omaha, Nebraska 68198-1045

NEW JERSEY

Diagnostic Ultrasound Program
Bergen Community College
400 Paramus Road
Paramus, New Jersey 07652

Diagnostic Ultrasound Program
University of Medicine & Dentistry of
  New Jersey
School of Health Related Professions
65 Bergen Street
Newark, New Jersey 07107

NEW MEXICO

Diagnostic Ultrasound Program
University of New Mexico School of
  Medicine
Albuquerque, New Mexico 87131

NEW YORK

Diagnostic Ultrasound Program
State University of New York
Health Science Center at Brooklyn
College of Health Related Professions
450 Clarkson Avenue
Brooklyn, New York 11203

Diagnostic Ultrasound Program
New York University Medical Center
342 East 26th Street
New York, New York 10010

Diagnostic Ultrasound Program
Rochester Institute of Technology
Department of Allied Health Sciences
Box 9887
Rochester, New York 14623-0887

NORTH CAROLINA

Diagnostic Ultrasound Program
Caldwell Community College &
  Technical Institute
1000 Hickory Boulevard
Hudson, North Carolina 28638-1399

Diagnostic Ultrasound Program
Pitt Community College
P.O. Drawer 7007
Greenville, North Carolina 27835

OHIO

Diagnostic Ultrasound Program
Aultman Hospital
2600 Sixth Street SW
Canto, Ohio 44710

Diagnostic Ultrasound Program
Central Ohio Technical College
1179 University Drive
Newark, Ohio 43055

Diagnostic Ultrasound Program
Kettering College of Medical Arts
3737 Southern Boulevard
Kettering, Ohio 45429

Diagnostic Ultrasound Program
Metrohealth Medical Center
2500 MetroHealth Drive
Cleveland, Ohio 44109

Diagnostic Ultrasound Program
Owens Technical College
P.O. Box 10,000 Oregon Road
Toledo, Ohio 43699

OKLAHOMA

Diagnostic Ultrasound Program
University of Oklahoma
College of Allied Health
P.O. Box 26901
Oklahoma City, Oklahoma 73190

PENNSYLVANIA

Diagnostic Ultrasound Program
Community College of Allegheny
  County
Boyce Campus
595 Beatty Road
Monroeville, Pennsylvania 15146

Diagnostic Ultrasound Program
Polyclinic Medical Center
2601 North Third Street
Harrisburg, Pennsylvania 17110

Diagnostic Ultrasound Program
Thomas Jefferson University
College of Allied Health Sciences
Department of Diagnostic Imaging
1020 Locust Street
Philadelphia, Pennsylvania 19107

TEXAS

Diagnostic Ultrasound Program
Austin Community College RVS
  Campus
Box 140647
Austin, Texas 78714

Diagnostic Ultrasound Program
Delmar College
101 Baldwin
Corpus Christi, Texas 78404

Diagnostic Ultrasound Program
El Centro College
Main & Lamar
Dallas, Texas 75202

UTAH

Diagnostic Ultrasound Program
Weber State University
Ogden, Utah 84408-1602

VIRGINIA

Diagnostic Ultrasound Program
Tidewater Community College
1700 College Crescent
Virginia Beach, Virginia 23456

WASHINGTON

Diagnostic Ultrasound Program
Bellevue Community College
School of Diagnostic Medical
  Sonography
Health Sciences Division
3000 Landerholm Circle
Bellevue, Washington 98009-2037

Diagnostic Ultrasound Program
Spokane Community College
North 1810 Greene Street
Spokane, Washington 99207

Diagnostic Ultrasound Program
Seattle University
Broadway & Madison
Seattle, Washington 98122

WEST VIRGINIA

Diagnostic Ultrasound Program
West Virginia University Hospitals
Department of Radiology
Morgantown, West Virginia 26506

WISCONSIN

Diagnostic Ultrasound Program
Chippewa Valley Technical College
620 West Clairemont Avenue
Eau Claire, Wisconsin 54701

Diagnostic Ultrasound Program
St. Francis Hospital School of
  Diagnostic Ultrasound
3237 South 16th Street
Milwaukee, Wisconsin 53215

Diagnostic Ultrasound Program
St. Luke's Medical Center
2900 Oklahoma Avenue
Milwaukee, Wisconsin 53215

Diagnostic Ultrasound Program
University of Wisconsin Hospital and
  Clinics
Department of Radiology
600 Highland Avenue
Madison, Wisconsin 53792

✚ RESPIRATORY THERAPY

Respiratory therapy is the healthcare specialty employed to treat seriously ill patients with lung problems. Under medical direction, respiratory therapy procedures involve the evaluation, diagnosis, treatment, control, and rehabilitation of breathing disorders such as asthma and emphysema, and also in the emergency care of cardiac failure, stroke, and shock.

Respiratory therapy is of immediate and crucial importance in the treatment of acute respiratory conditions arising from head injury, drowning, or drug poisoning. If breathing is not restored in three to five minutes, brain damage will likely occur. Death will occur if breathing is not restored in nine minutes. Respiratory therapy is also concerned with the medical problems associated with cigarette smoking and air pollution. There are three career classifications in this field: *respiratory therapist, respiratory therapy technician,* and *respiratory therapy aide.*

Respiratory Therapist

Under the direction of a physician, the *respiratory therapist* administers respiratory care treatments to patients. The respiratory therapist may also supervise technicians and aides, make recommendations for respiratory therapy, and evaluate patients' progress. In both emergency and temporary care the therapist is able to administer gas, aerosol, and humidity therapies, and intermittent positive-pressure breathing treatments, as well as cardiopulmonary resuscitation, long term continuous artificial ventilation, and other special therapeutic procedures.

Other responsibilities of a respiratory therapist often include providing instruction in breathing exercises, operating and maintaining special respiratory equipment such as mechanical ventilators and oxygen tents. With additional academic training and/or work experience, the respiratory therapist may perform administrative, teaching, and research duties, and advance from general care to the care of patients with difficult or unusual diagnostic problems.

Most respiratory therapists are employed in hospital respiratory therapy, anesthesiology, or pulmonary departments. Others work in physicians' offices, nursing homes, industries, or contracting firms that provide respiratory care services. Some therapists are employed by home healthcare agencies, providing at-home instruction to patients and their families.

Admittance into educational programs, accredited by the American Medical Association's Committee on Allied Health Education and Accreditation or holding a Letter of Review by the Joint Review Committee for Respiratory Therapy Education, requires a high school diploma or the equivalent. Formal training programs are offered by colleges and universities, community and junior colleges, vocational technical schools, trade schools, hospitals and the Armed Forces, and award either an associate or bachelor's degree for a two or four year program.

The National Board for Respiratory Care offers certification and registration to respiratory therapists who have satisfied the educational and experience requirements. Therapists must first be certified as a Certified Respiratory Therapy Technician (CRTT) before being eligible to take a separate exam to become a Registered Respiratory Therapist (RRT). Most entry level positions for respiratory therapists require the applicant to be a CRTT while supervisory and intensive care specialties positions require the RRT. For more details on certification requirements, write to the National Board for Respiratory Care, 8310 Nieman Road, Lenexa, Kansas 66214. High school students interested in a career in respiratory therapy are advised to take courses in health, biology, mathematics, physics, and chemistry.

According to a 1991 survey compiled by the Committee on Allied Health Education and Accreditation, entry level salaries for respiratory therapists averaged $24,000 a year.

Following is a list of formal training programs provided by the Joint Review Committee for Respiratory Therapy Education. Contact the schools directly for length of program and award granted.

SOURCES:

American Medical Association
Joint Review Committee for Respiratory Therapy Education
National Board for Respiratory Care
Occupational Outlook Handbook

Respiratory Therapist Programs

ALABAMA

Respiratory Therapist Program
University of Alabama at Birmingham
School of Health Related Professions
UAB Station
Birmingham, Alabama 35294

Respiratory Therapist Program
University of South Alabama
1504 Springhill Avenue
Mobile, Alabama 36604

Respiratory Therapist Program
Wallace College-Dothan
Dothan, Alabama 36303

Respiratory Therapist Program
Wallace State College
801 Main Street NW
Hanceville, Alabama 35077-9080

ARIZONA

Respiratory Therapist Program
Apollo College
8503 North 27th Avenue
Phoenix, Arizona 85051

Respiratory Therapist Program
Gateway Community College
108 North 40th Street
Phoenix, Arizona 85034

Respiratory Therapist Program
Pima Community College
2202 West Anklam Road
Tucson, Arizona 85709

Respiratory Therapist Program
Pima Medical Institute
3350 East Grant
Tucson, Arizona 85716

Respiratory Therapist Program
South West Academy of Technology
1660 South Alma School Road
Suite 227
Mesa, Arizona 85210

ARKANSAS

Respiratory Therapist Program
University of Arkansas for Medical
  Sciences
College of Health Related Professions
4301 West Markham
Little Rock, Arkansas 72205-7199

CALIFORNIA

Respiratory Therapist Program
American River College
4700 College Oak Drive
Sacramento, California 95841

Respiratory Therapist Program
Butte Community College
3536 Butte Campus Drive
Oroville, California 95965

Respiratory Therapist Program
California College for Health Sciences
222 West 24th Street
National City, California 92050

Respiratory Therapist Program
College of the Desert
43-500 Monterey Avenue
Palm Desert, California 92260

Respiratory Therapist Program
Crafton Hills College
11711 Sand Canyon Road
Yucalpa, California 92399

Respiratory Therapist Program
East Los Angeles College
1301 Brooklyn Avenue
Monterey Park, California 91754

Respiratory Therapist Program
El Camino College
16007 Crenshaw Boulevard
Torrance, California 90506

Respiratory Therapist Program
Foothill College
12345 El Monte Road
Los Altos Hills, California 94022

Respiratory Therapist Program
Fresno City College
1101 East University
Fresno, California 93741

Respiratory Therapist Program
Grossmont College
8800 Grossmont College Drive
El Cajon, California 92020

Respiratory Therapist Program
Loma Linda University
Loma Linda, California 92350

Respiratory Therapist Program
Los Angeles Valley College
5800 Fulton Avenue
Van Nuys, California 91401

Respiratory Therapist Program
Modesto Junior College
435 College Avenue
Modesto, California 95350

Respiratory Therapist Program
Mt. San Antonio College
1100 North Grand Avenue
Walnut, California 91789

Respiratory Therapist Program
Napa Valley College
Napa, California 94558

Respiratory Therapist Program
Ohlone College
43600 Mission Boulevard
Fremont, California 94539-0390

Respiratory Therapist Program
Orange Coast College
2701 Fairview Road
P.O. Box 5005
Costa Mesa, California 92626

Respiratory Therapist Program
Rio Hondo College
3600 Workman Mill Road
Whittier, California 90608

Respiratory Therapist Program
Skyline College
3300 College Drive
San Bruno, California 94066

Respiratory Therapist Program
UCLA/Santa Monica College
10833 LeConte Avenue
Los Angeles, California 90024

Respiratory Therapist Program
Victor Valley College
18422 Bear Valley Road
Victorville, California 92392-9699

COLORADO

Respiratory Therapist Program
Front Range Community College
North Campus
3645 West 112th Avenue
Westminster, Colorado 80030

Respiratory Therapist Program
Pueblo Community College
900 West Orman Avenue
Pueblo, Colorado 81004

CONNECTICUT

Respiratory Therapist Program
Manchester Community College
60 Bidwell Street
Manchester, Connecticut 06040

Respiratory Therapist Program
Norwalk Hospital
24 Maple Street
Norwalk, Connecticut 06856

Respiratory Therapist Program
Quinnipiac College
Mount Carmel Avenue
Hamden, Connecticut 06518

Respiratory Therapist Program
Sacred Heart University
St. Vincent's Consortium
5151 Park Avenue
Fairfield, Connecticut 06432-1000

Respiratory Therapist Program
University of Hartford
200 Bloomfield Avenue
West Hartford, Connecticut 06117

DELAWARE

Respiratory Therapist Program
Delaware Technical and Community
  College
Wilmington Campus
333 Shipley Street
Wilmington, Delaware 19801

DISTRICT OF COLUMBIA

Respiratory Therapist Program
University of the District of Columbia
4200 Connecticut Avenue Northwest
Washington, DC 20010

FLORIDA

Respiratory Therapist Program
ATI Health Education Centers
1395 NW 167 Street, Suite 200
Miami, Florida 33169

Respiratory Therapist Program
Brevard Community College
1519 Clearlake Road
Cocoa, Florida 32922

Respiratory Therapist Program
Broward Community College
3501 SW Davie Road
Ft. Lauderdale, Florida 33314

Respiratory Therapist Program
Daytona Beach Community College
1200 Volusia Avenue
Daytona Beach, Florida 32114

Respiratory Therapist Program
Edison Community College
8099 College Parkway SW
P.O. Box 06210
Ft. Myers, Florida 33906-6210

Respiratory Therapist Program
Flagler Career Institute
3225 University Boulevard South
Jacksonville, Florida 32216

Respiratory Therapist Program
Florida Agricultural and Mechanical
  University
School of Allied Health Sciences
Tallahassee, Florida 32307

Respiratory Therapist Program
Florida Community College at
  Jacksonville
North Campus
4501 Capper Road
Jacksonville, Florida 32218

Respiratory Therapist Program
Manatee Community College
5840 26th Street West
Bradenton, Florida 34207

Respiratory Therapist Program
Miami-Dade Community College
Medical Center Campus
950 Northwest 20th Street
Miami, Florida 33127

Respiratory Therapist Program
Palm Beach Community College
3160 PGA Boulevard
Palm Beach Gardens, Florida 33410

Respiratory Therapist Program
Pensacola Junior College
Allied Health/Dental Department
Warrington Campus
5555 West Highway 98
Pensacola, Florida 32507

Respiratory Therapist Program
Santa Fe Community College
Central Florida Community College
3800 NW 83rd Street
P.O. Box 1530
Gainesville, Florida 32602

Respiratory Therapist Program
Seminole Community College
100 Weldon Boulevard
Sanford, Florida 32772

Respiratory Therapist Program
St. Petersburg Junior College
P.O. Box 13489
St. Petersburg, Florida 33733

Respiratory Therapist Program
Tallahassee Community College
444 Appleyard Drive
Tallahassee, Florida 32301

Respiratory Therapist Program
University of Central Florida
Dept. of Cardiopulmonary Sciences
Box 25,000
Orlando, Florida 32816-0994

Respiratory Therapist Program
Valencia Community College
Health and Public Services
P.O. Box 3028
Orlando, Florida 32802

GEORGIA

Respiratory Therapist Program
Armstrong State College
11935 Abercorn Street
Savannah, Georgia 31419

Respiratory Therapist Program
Athens Area Technical Institute
U.S. Highway 29 North
Athens, Georgia 30610-0399

Respiratory Therapist Program
Columbus College
Algonquin Drive
Columbus, Georgia 31993-2399

Respiratory Therapist Program
Georgia State University
Dept. of Cardiopulmonary Care Sciences
School of Allied Health Professions
University Plaza
Atlanta, Georgia 30303

Respiratory Therapist Program
Medical College of Georgia
815 St. Sebastian Way
Augusta, Georgia 30912-0850

HAWAII

Respiratory Therapist Program
Kapiolani Community College
University of Hawaii
4303 Diamond Head Road
Honolulu, Hawaii 96816

IDAHO

Respiratory Therapist Program
Boise State University
1910 University Drive
Boise, Idaho 83725

ILLINOIS

Respiratory Therapist Program
Black Hawk College
6600 34th Avenue
Moline, Illinois 61265

Respiratory Therapist Program
Illinois Central College
One College Drive
East Peoria, Illinois 61635

Respiratory Therapist Program
Lincoln Land Community College
Shepherd Road
Springfield, Illinois 62794-9256

Respiratory Therapist Program
Malcolm X College
1900 West Van Buren Street
Chicago, Illinois 60612

Respiratory Therapist Program
Moraine Valley Community College
10900 South 88th Avenue
Palos Hills, Illinois 60465

Respiratory Therapist Program
National-Louis University
University of Chicago Hospitals
2840 Sheridan Road
Evanston, Illinois 60201

Respiratory Therapist Program
Parkland College
2400 West Bradley
Champaign, Illinois 61821-1899

Respiratory Therapist Program
Rock Valley College
3301 North Mulford
Rockford, Illinois 61111

Respiratory Therapist Program
Southern Illinois University at
  Carbondale
Division of Allied Health & Public
  Services
Allied Health Career Specialties
Carbondale, Illinois 62901-6615

Respiratory Therapist Program
Triton College
2000 North Fifth Avenue
River Grove, Illinois 60171

INDIANA

Respiratory Therapist Program
Ball State University
Dept. of Physiology and Health Science
Muncie, Indiana 47306

Respiratory Therapist Program
Indiana University Northwest
Division of Allied Health Sciences
3400 North Broadway
Gary, Indiana 46408

Respiratory Therapist Program
Indiana University School of Medicine
1140 West Michigan Street
Indianapolis, Indiana 46202-5119

Respiratory Therapist Program
Indiana Vocational Technical College
One West 26th Street
P.O. Box 1763
Indianapolis, Indiana 46206

Respiratory Therapist Program
Indiana Vocational Technical College
3800 North Anthony Boulevard
Ft. Wayne, Indiana 46805

Respiratory Therapist Program
Indiana Vocational Technical College
Northwest Region
Human Services and Health
  Technologies Division
2401 Valley Drive
Valparaiso, Indiana 46383

Respiratory Therapist Program
Marian College
3200 Cold Springs Road
Indianapolis, Indiana 46222

Respiratory Therapist Program
University of Southern Indiana
8600 University Boulevard
Evansville, Indiana 47712

Respiratory Therapist Program
Vincennes University
1002 North First Street
Vincennes, Indiana 47591

IOWA

Respiratory Therapist Program
Des Moines Area Community College
2006 South Ankeny Boulevard
Ankeny, Iowa 50021

Respiratory Therapist Program
Kirkwood Community College
6301 Kirkwood Boulevard Southwest
P.O. Box 2068
Cedar Rapids, Iowa 52406

KANSAS

Respiratory Therapist Program
Johnson County Community College
12345 College Boulevard and Quivira
Overland Park, Kansas 66210

Respiratory Therapist Program
Labette Community College
200 South 14th Street
Parsons, Kansas 67357

Respiratory Therapist Program
Seward County Community College
Box 1137
Liberal, Kansas 67905-1137

Respiratory Therapist Program
University of Kansas
College of Health Sciences and
Hospital School of Allied Health
39th and Rainbow Boulevard
Kansas City, Kansas 66103

Respiratory Therapist Program
Washburn University of Topeka
School of Applied and Continuing
  Education
1700 College
Topeka, Kansas 66621

Respiratory Therapist Program
Wichita State University
College of Health Professions
1845 Fairmount
Wichita, Kansas 67208

KENTUCKY

Respiratory Therapist Program
Jefferson Community College
University of Kentucky
109 East Broadway
Louisville, Kentucky 40202

Respiratory Therapist Program
Lexington Community College
University of Kentucky
Cooper Drive
Lexington, Kentucky 40506-0235

Respiratory Therapist Program
Madisonville Consortium for Respiratory
  Care Education
701 North Laffoon Street
Madisonville, Kentucky 42431

Respiratory Therapist Program
University of Louisville School of
  Medicine
Division of Allied Health
525 East Madison Street
Louisville, Kentucky 40292

LOUISIANA

Respiratory Therapist Program
Alton Ochsner Medical Foundation
School of Allied Health Sciences
1516 Jefferson Highway
New Orleans, Louisiana 70121

Respiratory Therapist Program
Delgado Community College
615 City Park Avenue
New Orleans, Louisiana 70119

Respiratory Therapist Program
Louisiana State University Medical
  Center
Dept. of Cardiopulmonary Science
1900 Gravier Street
New Orleans, Louisiana 70112-2262

Respiratory Therapist Program
Southern University
Shreveport-Bossier City Campus
3050 Martin Luther King Jr. Drive
Shreveport, Louisiana 71107

MAINE

Respiratory Therapist Program
Southern Maine Technical College
Fort Road
South Portland, Maine 04106

MARYLAND

Respiratory Therapist Program
Allegany Community College
Willow Brook Road
P.O. Box 1695
Cumberland, Maryland 21502

Respiratory Therapist Program
Columbia Union College
7600 Flower Avenue
Takoma Park, Maryland 20912

Respiratory Therapist Program
New Community College of Baltimore
2901 Liberty Heights Avenue
Baltimore, Maryland 21215-7893

Respiratory Therapist Program
Prince George's Community College
301 Largo Road
Largo, Maryland 20772

Respiratory Therapist Program
Salisbury State University
College and Camden Avenue
Salisbury, Maryland 21801

MASSACHUSETTS

Respiratory Therapist Program
Berkshire Community College
West Street
Pittsfield, Massachusetts 01201

Respiratory Therapist Program
Massasoit Community College
One Massasoit Boulevard
Brockton, Massachusetts 02402

Respiratory Therapist Program
Newbury College
129 Fisher Avenue
Brookline, Massachusetts 02146

Respiratory Therapist Program
North Shore Community College
One Ferncroft Road
Danvers, Massachusetts 01923

Respiratory Therapist Program
Northeastern University
College of Pharmacy and Allied Health
  Professions
360 Huntington Avenue
Boston, Massachusetts 02115

Respiratory Therapist Program
Northern Essex Community College
100 Elliott Street
Haverhill, Massachusetts 01830

Respiratory Therapist Program
Quinsigamond Community College
670 West Boylston Street
Worcester, Massachusetts 01606

Respiratory Therapist Program
Springfield Technical Community
  College
One Armory Square
P.O. Box 9000
Springfield, Massachusetts 01105

MICHIGAN

Respiratory Therapist Program
Charles Stewart Mott Community
  College
1401 East Court Street
Flint, Michigan 48503

Respiratory Therapist Program
Delta College
University Center, Michigan 48710

Respiratory Therapist Program
Ferris State University
College of Allied Health Sciences
Big Rapids, Michigan 49307

Respiratory Therapist Program
Henry Ford Community College
22586 Ann Arbor Trail
Dearborn Heights, Michigan 48127

Respiratory Therapist Program
Kalamazoo Valley Community College
6767 West "O" Avenue
Kalamazoo, Michigan 49009

Respiratory Therapist Program
Lansing Community College
419 North Capitol Avenue
P.O. Box 40010
Lansing, Michigan 48901

Respiratory Therapist Program
Macomb Community College
Detroit Macomb Hospital Corporation
44575 Garfield Road
Mt. Clemens, Michigan 48044-3197

Respiratory Therapist Program
Marygrove College
8425 West McNichols Road
Detroit, Michigan 48221

Respiratory Therapist Program
Monroe County Community College
1555 South Raisinville Road
Monroe, Michigan 48161

Respiratory Therapist Program
Muskegon Community College
221 South Quarterline Road
Muskegon, Michigan 49442

Respiratory Therapist Program
Oakland Community College
2480 Opdyke Road
Bloomfield Hills, Michigan 48013

Respiratory Therapist Program
Washtenaw Community College
P.O. Box D-1
4800 East Huron River Drive
Ann Arbor, Michigan 48106

MINNESOTA

Respiratory Therapist Program
Duluth Technical College
Hibbing Technical College
2101 Trinity Road
Duluth, Minnesota 55811

Respiratory Therapist Program
East Grand Forks Technical College
Highway 220 North
East Grand Forks, Minnesota 56721

Respiratory Therapist Program
Rochester Community College
Mayo Foundation
Highway 14 East
Rochester, Minnesota 55904

Respiratory Therapist Program
St. Mary's Campus of the College of St.
  Catherine
2500 South Sixth Street
Minneapolis, Minnesota 55454

Respiratory Therapist Program
St. Paul Technical College
235 Marshall Avenue
St. Paul, Minnesota 55102

MISSISSIPPI

Respiratory Therapist Program
Hinds Community College-Jackson
  Branch
Nursing Allied Health Center
1750 Chadwick Drive
Jackson, Mississippi 39204-3402

Respiratory Therapist Program
Itawamba Community College
Fulton, Mississippi 38843

Respiratory Therapist Program
Northwest Mississippi Community
   College
Highway 51 North
510 North Panola
Senatobia, Mississippi 38668

Respiratory Therapist Program
University of Mississippi Medical Center
School of Health Related Professions
2500 North State Street
Jackson, Mississippi 39216-4505

MISSOURI

Respiratory Therapist Program
Southwest Missouri School of
   Respiratory Care
Graff Area VT Center and Drury
   College
815 North Sherman
Springfield, Missouri 65802-3792

Respiratory Therapist Program
St. Louis Community College at Forest
   Park
5600 Oakland
St. Louis, Missouri 63110

Respiratory Therapist Program
University of Missouri-Columbia
School of Health Related Professions
Columbia, Missouri 65211

MONTANA

Respiratory Therapist Program
Great Falls Vocational Technical Center
2100 16th Avenue South
Great Falls, Montana 59405

NEBRASKA

Respiratory Therapist Program
Immanuel Medical Center
Midland Lutheran College
6901 North 72nd Street
Omaha, Nebraska 68122

Respiratory Therapist Program
Metropolitan Community College
P.O. Box 3777
Omaha, Nebraska 68103

Respiratory Therapist Program
Nebraska Methodist College of Nursing
   and Allied Health
8501 West Dodge Road
Omaha, Nebraska 68144

Respiratory Therapist Program
Southeast Community College
8800 "O" Street
Lincoln, Nebraska 68520

NEVADA

Respiratory Therapist Program
Clark County Community College
3200 East Cheyenne Avenue
North Las Vegas, Nevada 89030

NEW HAMPSHIRE

Respiratory Therapist Program
New Hampshire Technical College
One College Drive
Claremont, New Hampshire 03743

NEW JERSEY

Respiratory Therapist Program
Bergen Community College
400 Paramus Road
Paramus, New Jersey 07652

Respiratory Therapist Program
Brookdale Community College
765 Newman Springs Road
Lincroft, New Jersey 07738

Respiratory Therapist Program
Fairleigh Dickinson University
Florham-Madison Campus
285 Madison Avenue
Madison, New Jersey 07940

Respiratory Therapist Program
Union County College
Scotch Plains Campus
1700 Raritan Road
Scotch Plains, New Jersey 07060

Respiratory Therapist Program
University of Medicine and Dentistry of
  New Jersey
School of Health Related Professions
65 Bergen Street
Newark, New Jersey 07107-3001

Respiratory Therapist Program
University of Medicine and Dentistry of
  New Jersey
School of Health Related Professions
Box 200
Blackwood, New Jersey 08012

NEW MEXICO

Respiratory Therapist Program
Albuquerque Technical-Vocational
  Institute
515 Buena Vista Southeast
Albuquerque, New Mexico 87106

Respiratory Therapist Program
University of New Mexico
School of Medicine
Allied Health Science Center
Albuquerque, New Mexico 87131

NEW YORK

Respiratory Therapist Program
Borough of Manhattan
Community College of the City of New
  York
199 Chambers Street
New York, New York 10007

Respiratory Therapist Program
Erie Community College
Main and Youngs Road
Williamsville, New York 14221

Respiratory Therapist Program
Hudson Valley Community College
80 Vandenburgh Avenue
Troy, New York 12180

Respiratory Therapist Program
Long Island University
One University Plaza
Brooklyn, New York 11201

Respiratory Therapist Program
Molloy College
1000 Hempstead Avenue
Rockville Centre, New York 11570-1199

Respiratory Therapist Program
Nassau Community College
Stewart Avenue
Garden City, New York 11530

Respiratory Therapist Program
New York City Health and Hospitals
  Corp.
Empire State College
27th Street and First Avenue
New York, New York 10016

Respiratory Therapist Program
New York University Medical Center
342 East 26th Street
New York, New York 10016

Respiratory Therapist Program
Onondaga Community College
Onondaga Road
Syracuse, New York 13215

Respiratory Therapist Program
Rockland Community College
145 College Road
Suffern, New York 10901

Respiratory Therapist Program
State University of New York
Upstate Medical Center
750 East Adams Street
Syracuse, New York 13210

Respiratory Therapist Program
State University of New York at Stony
  Brook
Health Sciences Center
Stony Brook, New York 11794-8203

Respiratory Therapist Program
Westchester Community College
75 Grasslands Road
Valhalla, New York 10595-1698

NORTH CAROLINA

Respiratory Therapist Program
Carteret Community College
3505 Arendell Street
Morehead City, North Carolina 28557

Respiratory Therapist Program
Central Piedmont Community College
P.O. Box 35009
Charlotte, North Carolina 28235

Respiratory Therapist Program
Durham Technical Community College
P.O. Box 11307
1637 Lawson Street
Durham, North Carolina 27703

Respiratory Therapist Program
Edgecombe Community College
2009 West Wilson Street
Tarboro, North Carolina 27886

Respiratory Therapist Program
Fayetteville Technical Community
  College
P.O. Box 35236
Fayetteville, North Carolina 28303-0236

Respiratory Therapist Program
Forsyth Technical Community College
2100 Silas Creek Parkway
Winston-Salem, North Carolina 27103

Respiratory Therapist Program
Pitt Community College
P.O. Drawer 7007
Greenville, North Carolina 27835-7007

Respiratory Therapist Program
Robeson Community College
P.O. Box 1420
Lumberton, North Carolina 28359

Respiratory Therapist Program
Sandhills Community College
2200 Airport Road
Pinehurst, North Carolina 28374

Respiratory Therapist Program
Southwestern Community College
275 Webster Road
Sylva, North Carolina 28779

Respiratory Therapist Program
Stanly Community College
Route Four, Box 55
Albemarle, North Carolina 28001

NORTH DAKOTA

Respiratory Therapist Program
North Dakota School of Respiratory
  Care
University of Mary & St. Alexius
  Medical Center
900 East Broadway
P.O. Box 5510
Bismarck, North Dakota 58502-5510

Respiratory Therapist Program
North Dakota State University
St. Luke's Hospital MeritCare
720 Fourth Street North
Fargo, North Dakota 58122

OHIO

Respiratory Therapist Program
Bowling Green State University
Firelands College
901 Rye Beach Road
Huron, Ohio 44839-9791

Respiratory Therapist Program
Cincinnati Technical College
3520 Central Parkway
Cincinnati, Ohio 45223

Respiratory Therapist Program
Columbus State Community College
550 East Spring Street
Columbus, Ohio 43215-1609

Respiratory Therapist Program
Cuyahoga Community College
11000 Pleasant Valley Road
Parma, Ohio 44130

Respiratory Therapist Program
Jefferson Technical College
4000 Sunset Boulevard
Steubenville, Ohio 43952

Respiratory Therapist Program
Kettering College of Medical Arts
3737 Southern Boulevard
Kettering, Ohio 45429

Respiratory Therapist Program
Lakeland Community College
I-90 and SR 306
Mentor, Ohio 44060

Respiratory Therapist Program
Lima Technical College
4240 Campus Drive
Lima, Ohio 45804

Respiratory Therapist Program
North Central Technical College
2441 Kenwood Circle
P.O. Box 698
Mansfield, Ohio 44901-0698

Respiratory Therapist Program
Ohio State University
1583 Perry Street
Columbus, Ohio 43210-1234

Respiratory Therapist Program
Shawnee State University
940 Second Street
Portsmouth, Ohio 45662

Respiratory Therapist Program
Sinclair Community College
444 West Third Street
Dayton, Ohio 45402

Respiratory Therapist Program
Stark Technical College
600 Frank Road NW
Canton, Ohio 44720

Respiratory Therapist Program
University of Akron
325 East Buchtel Avenue
Akron, Ohio 44325

Respiratory Therapist Program
University of Toledo
Community and Technical College
2801 West Bancroft Street
Toledo, Ohio 43606-3390

Respiratory Therapist Program
Youngstown State University
410 Wick Avenue
Youngstown, Ohio 44555

OKLAHOMA

Respiratory Therapist Program
Rose State College
6420 Southeast 15th
Midwest, Oklahoma 73110

Respiratory Therapist Program
Tulsa Junior College
Sciences & Health Services Division
909 South Boston Avenue
Tulsa, Oklahoma 74119

OREGON

Respiratory Therapist Program
Lane Community College
4000 East 30th Avenue
Eugene, Oregon 97405

Respiratory Therapist Program
Rogue Community College
3345 Redwood Highway
Grants Pass, Oregon 97526

Respiratory Therapist Program
Mt. Hood Community College
26000 Southeast Stark Street
Gresham, Oregon 97030

PENNSYLVANIA

Respiratory Therapist Program
Community College of Allegheny
  County
Allegheny Campus
808 Ridge Avenue
Pittsburgh, Pennsylvania 15212

Respiratory Therapist Program
Community College of Philadelphia
1700 Spring Garden Street
Philadelphia, Pennsylvania 19130

Respiratory Therapist Program
Delaware County Community College
Crozer-Chester Medical Center
One Medical Center Boulevard
Upland Chester, Pennsylvania 19013

Respiratory Therapist Program
Gannon University
University Square
Erie, Pennsylvania 16541

Respiratory Therapist Program
Gwynedd Mercy College
Sumneytown Pike
Gwynedd Valley, Pennsylvania 19437

Respiratory Therapist Program
Harrisburg Area Community College
3300 Cameron Street Road
Harrisburg, Pennsylvania 17110-2999

Respiratory Therapist Program
Indiana University of Pennsylvania
Western Pennsylvania Hospital
4800 Friendship Avenue
Pittsburgh, Pennsylvania 15224

Respiratory Therapist Program
Lehigh County Community College
2370 Main Street
Schnecksville, Pennsylvania 18078

Respiratory Therapist Program
Mansfield University
Grant Science Center
Mansfield, Pennsylvania 16933

Respiratory Therapist Program
Millersville University
Millersville, Pennsylvania 17551

Respiratory Therapist Program
University of Pittsburgh at Johnstown
Johnstown, Pennsylvania 15904

Respiratory Therapist Program
West Chester University
Bryn Mawr Hospital
West Chester, Pennsylvania 19383

Respiratory Therapist Program
York College of Pennsylvania
Country Club Road
York, Pennsylvania 17403-3426

PUERTO RICO

Respiratory Therapist Program
Universidad Metropolitana
P.O. Box 21150
Rio Piedras, Puerto Rico 00928

RHODE ISLAND

Respiratory Therapist Program
Community College of Rhode Island
Flanagan Campus
1762 Louisquisset Pike
Lincoln, Rhode Island 02865

SOUTH CAROLINA

Respiratory Therapist Program
Florence-Darlington Technical College
P.O. Drawer F-8000
Florence, South Carolina 29501-0057

Respiratory Therapist Program
Greenville Technical College
P.O. Box 5616
Greenville, South Carolina 29606-5616

Respiratory Therapist Program
Midlands Technical College
P.O. Box 2408
Columbia, South Carolina 29202

Respiratory Therapist Program
Spartanburg Technical College
Drawer 4386
Spartanburg, South Carolina 29305-4386

Respiratory Therapist Program
Trident Technical College
P.O. Box 10367
Charleston, South Carolina 29411

SOUTH DAKOTA

Respiratory Therapist Program
Dakota State University
College of Natural Sciences
Madison, South Dakota 57042-1799

Respiratory Therapist Program
Mount Marty College
1105 West Eighth
Yankton, South Dakota 57078

TENNESSEE

Respiratory Therapist Program
Chattanooga State Technical Community
  College
4501 Amnicola Highway
Chattanooga, Tennessee 37406-1097

Respiratory Therapist Program
Christian Brothers University
650 East Parkway South
Memphis, Tennessee 38104

Respiratory Therapist Program
Columbia State Community College
P.O. Box 1315
Columbia, Tennessee 38402-1315

Respiratory Therapist Program
Jackson State Community College
2046 North Parkway Street
Jackson, Tennessee 38301-3797

Respiratory Therapist Program
Roane State Community College
35 Patton Lane
Harriman, Tennessee 37748-5000

Respiratory Therapist Program
Tennessee State University
3500 John A. Merritt Boulevard
P.O. Box 533
Nashville, Tennessee 37209-1561

TEXAS

Respiratory Therapist Program
Alvin Community College
3110 Mustang Road
Alvin, Texas 77511-4898

Respiratory Therapist Program
Amarillo College
P.O. Box 447
Amarillo, Texas 79178

Respiratory Therapist Program
Collin County Community College
  District
2200 West University Drive
McKinney, Texas 75070

Respiratory Therapist Program
Del Mar College
Baldwin and Ayers
Corpus Christi, Texas 78404

Respiratory Therapist Program
El Centro College
Main and Lamar Streets
Dallas, Texas 75202

Respiratory Therapist Program
El Paso Community College
P.O. Box 20500
El Paso, Texas 79998

Respiratory Therapist Program
Houston Community College System
Eastwood Center for Health Careers
3100 Shenandoah
Houston, Texas 77021

Respiratory Therapist Program
Lamar University
College of Health Behavioral Sciences
P.O. Box 10096
Beaumont, Texas 77710

Respiratory Therapist Program
Midland College
3600 North Garfield
Midland, Texas 79705

Respiratory Therapist Program
NHMCCD-Kingwood College
East Campus
20000 Kingwood Drive
Kingwood, Texas 77339

Respiratory Therapist Program
Odessa College
201 West University
Odessa, Texas 79764

Respiratory Therapist Program
San Jacinto College District
Central Campus
8060 Spencer Highway
Pasadena, Texas 77505-2007

Respiratory Therapist Program
South Plains College at Lubbock
1302 Main Street
Lubbock, Texas 79401

Respiratory Therapist Program
Southwest Texas State University
San Marcos, Texas 78666

Respiratory Therapist Program
Tarrant County Junior College
Northeast Campus
828 Harwood Road
Hurst, Texas 76054

Respiratory Therapist Program
Temple Junior College
2600 South First Street
Temple, Texas 76504-7435

Respiratory Therapist Program
Texas Southern University
3100 Cleburne
Houston, Texas 77004

Respiratory Therapist Program
Texas Southmost College
83 Fort Brown
Brownsville, Texas 78520

Respiratory Therapist Program
University of Texas Health Science
  Center at Houston
7000 Fannin
Houston, Texas 77030

Respiratory Therapist Program
Tyler Junior College
P.O. Box 9020
Tyler, Texas 75711

Respiratory Therapist Program
University of Texas Medical Branch
Galveston College
4015 Avenue "Q"
Galveston, Texas 77550

Respiratory Therapist Program
Victoria College
2200 East Red River
Victoria, Texas 77901

UTAH

Respiratory Therapist Program
Weber State University
School of Allied Health Sciences
Ogden, Utah 84408-3904

VIRGINIA

Respiratory Therapist Program
Community Hospital of Roanoke Valley
College of Health Sciences
P.O. Box 13186
Roanoke, Virginia 24301-3186

Respiratory Therapist Program
J. Sargeant Reynolds Community
  College
P.O. Box C-32040
Richmond, Virginia 23261-2040

Respiratory Therapist Program
Northern Virginia Community College
8333 Little River Turnpike
Annandale, Virginia 22003

Respiratory Therapist Program
Piedmont Virginia Community College
Route 6, Box 1A
Charlottesville, Virginia 22901

Respiratory Therapist Program
Shenandoah University
Winchester Medical Center
203 South Cameron Street
Winchester, Virginia 22601

Respiratory Therapist Program
Southwest Virginia Community College
Richlands, Virginia 24641-1510

Respiratory Therapist Program
Tidewater Community College
1700 College Crescent
Virginia Beach, Virginia 23456

WASHINGTON

Respiratory Therapist Program
Highline Community College
98000 South 240th Street
Des Moines, 98198-9800

Respiratory Therapist Program
Seattle Central Community College
1701 Broadway
Seattle, Washington 98122

Respiratory Therapist Program
Spokane Community College
North 1810 Greene Street
Spokane, Washington 99207

Respiratory Therapist Program
Tacoma Community College
5900 South 12th Street
Tacoma, Washington 98465

Respiratory Therapist Program
Walla Walla Community College
500 Tausick Way
Walla Walla, Washington 99362

WEST VIRGINIA

Respiratory Therapist Program
College of West Virginia
609 South Kanawha Street
Beckley, West Virginia 24801

Respiratory Therapist Program
University of Charleston
College of Health Sciences
2300 MacCorkle Avenue SE
Charleston, West Virginia 25304

Respiratory Therapist Program
West Virginia Northern Community
  College
College Square
Wheeling, West Virginia 26003

Respiratory Therapist Program
Wheeling Jesuit College
316 Washington Avenue
Wheeling, West Virginia 26003-6295

WISCONSIN

Respiratory Therapist Program
Madison Area Technical College
3550 Anderson Street
Madison, Wisconsin 53704

Respiratory Therapist Program
Mid-State Technical College
2600 West Fifth Street
Marshfield, Wisconsin 54449

Respiratory Therapist Program
Milwaukee Area Technical College
700 West State Street
Milwaukee, Wisconsin 53233

Respiratory Therapist Program
Northeast Wisconsin Technical College
2740 West Mason Street
P.O. Box 19042
Green Bay, Wisconsin 54307-9042

Respiratory Therapist Program
Western Wisconsin Technical College
304 North Sixth Street
La Crosse, Wisconsin 54601

WYOMING

Respiratory Therapist Program
Western Wyoming Community College
2500 College Drive
P.O. Box 428
Rock Springs, Wyoming 82901

Respiratory Therapy Technician

The *respiratory therapy technician* is often supervised by the respiratory therapist and is responsible for the majority of bedside patient care. The technician carries out most of the non-critical respiratory treatments, such as administering oxygen and other gases, delivering breathing treatments, and setting up and operating equipment. He or she also cleans, sterilizes, and maintains the respiratory therapy equipment, and keeps medical records of patient's therapies.

Training to become a respiratory therapy technician involves completion of high school and a 12 to 18 month certificate educational program. The educational programs are generally offered by hospitals and community and junior colleges. Certification by examination is available from the National Board for Respiratory Care after graduation from an approved respiratory therapy technician program. After successfully meeting all requirements, the respiratory therapy technician may use the title, "Certified Respiratory Therapy Technician (CRTT)".

According to a 1991 survey compiled by the Committee on Allied Health Education and Accreditation, entry level salaries for respiratory therapy technicians averaged $20,000 a year.

Following is a list of educational programs for respiratory therapy technicians provided by the Joint Review Committee for Respiratory Therapy Education.

SOURCES:

American Association for Respiratory Care
American Medical Association
Joint Review Committee for Respiratory Therapy Education
National Board for Respiratory Care

Respiratory Therapy Technician Programs

ARIZONA

Respiratory Therapy Technician Program
Apollo College
8503 North 27th Avenue
Phoenix, Arizona 85051

Respiratory Therapy Technician Program
Gateway Community College
108 North 40th Street
Phoenix, Arizona 85034

Respiratory Therapy Technician Program
Long Medical Institute
4126 North Black Canyon Highway
Phoenix, Arizona 85017

Respiratory Therapy Technician Program
Pima Medical Institute
3350 East Grant
Tucson, Arizona 85716

Respiratory Therapy Technician Program
South West Academy of Technology
1660 South Alma School Road
Suite 227
Mesa, Arizona 85210

ARKANSAS

Respiratory Therapy Technician Program
Arkansas Valley Vocational Technical
  School
P.O. Box 506
Ozark, Arkansas 72949

Respiratory Therapy Technician Program
Black River Vocational Technical
  School
P.O. Box 468
Highway 304 East
Pocohontas, Arkansas 72455

Respiratory Therapy Technician Program
Pulaski Technical College
3000 West Scenic Road
North Little Rock, Arkansas 72118

Respiratory Therapy Technician Program
Red River Vocational Technical School
P.O. Box 140
Highway 29 South
Hope, Arkansas 71801

Respiratory Therapy Technician Program
University of Arkansas for Medical
  Sciences
College of Health Related Professions
4301 West Markham
Little Rock, Arkansas 72205-7199

CALIFORNIA

Respiratory Therapy Technician Program
California College for Health Sciences
222 West 24th Street
National City, California 92050

Respiratory Therapy Technician Program
California Paramedical & Technical
  College-Riverside
4550 La Sierra Avenue
Riverside, California 92505

Respiratory Therapy Technician Program
California Paramedical College-Long
  Beach
3745 Long Beach Boulevard
Long Beach, California 90807

Respiratory Therapy Technician Program
Concorde Career Institute
4150 Lankershim Boulevard
North Hollywood, California 91602

Respiratory Therapy Technician Program
Crafton Hills College
11711 Sand Canyon Road
Yucalpa, California 92399

Respiratory Therapy Technician Program
Hacienda-La Puente Unified School
  District
Hacienda-La Puente Adult Education
15540 East Fairgrove Avenue
La Puente, California 91744

Respiratory Therapy Technician Program
Modesto Junior College
435 College Avenue
Modesto, California 95350

Respiratory Therapy Technician Program
San Joaquin Valley College
8400 West Mineral King
Visalla, California 93291

Respiratory Therapy Technician Program
Simi Valley Adult School
3150 School Street
Simi Valley, California 93065

COLORADO

Respiratory Therapy Technician Program
Medical Careers Training Center
4020 South College Avenue
Ft. Collins, Colorado 80525

Respiratory Therapy Technician Program
T.H. Pickens Technical Center
Aurora Public Schools
500 Buckley Road
Aurora, Colorado 80011

CONNECTICUT

Respiratory Therapy Technician Program
Mattatuck Community College
Waterbury/St. Mary's Hospital
750 Chase Parkway
Waterbury, Connecticut 06708

Respiratory Therapy Technician Program
Quinnipiac College
Mount Carmel Avenue
Hamden, Connecticut 06518

FLORIDA

Respiratory Therapy Technician Program
ATI Health Education Centers
1395 NW 167th Street, Suite 200
Miami, Florida 33169

Respiratory Therapy Technician Program
Broward Community College
3501 SW Davie Road
Ft. Lauderdale, Florida 33314

Respiratory Therapy Technician Program
D.G. Erwin Technical Center
2010 East Hillsborough Avenue
Tampa, Florida 33610

Respiratory Therapy Technician Program
Daytona Beach Community College
1200 Volusia Avenue
Daytona Beach, Florida 32114

Respiratory Therapy Technician Program
Flagler Career Institute
3225 University Boulevard South
Jacksonville, Florida 32216

Respiratory Therapy Technician Program
Gulf Coast Community College
5230 West U.S. Highway 98
Panama City, Florida 32401

Respiratory Therapy Technician Program
Miami-Dade Community College
Medical Center Campus
950 Northwest 20th Street
Miami, Florida 33127

Respiratory Therapy Technician Program
Palm Beach Community College
3160 PGA Boulevard
Palm Beach Gardens, Florida 33410

Respiratory Therapy Technician Program
Pensacola Junior College
Allied Health/Dental Department
Warrington Campus
5555 West Highway 98
Pensacola, Florida 32507

Respiratory Therapy Technician Program
Pinellas Technical Education Centers-St.
  Petersburg
901 34th Street South
St. Petersburg, Florida 33711-2298

Respiratory Therapy Technician Program
Seminole Community College
100 Weldon Boulevard
Sanford, Florida 32772

GEORGIA

Respiratory Therapy Technician Program
Athens Area Technical Institute
U.S. Highway 29 North
Athens, Georgia 30610-0399

Respiratory Therapy Technician Program
Augusta Technical Institute
3116 Deans Bridge Road
Augusta, Georgia 30906

Respiratory Therapy Technician Program
Coosa Valley Technical Institute
112 Hemlock Street
Rome, Georgia 30161

Respiratory Therapy Technician Program
Georgia State University
Dept. of Cardiopulmonary Care Sciences
School of Allied Health Professions
University Plaza
Atlanta, Georgia 30303

Respiratory Therapy Technician Program
Gwinnett Technical Institute
1250 Atkinson Road
P.O. Box 1505
Lawrenceville, Georgia 30246

Respiratory Therapy Technician Program
Thomas Technical Institute
Highway 19 at 319
Thomasville, Georgia 31799

HAWAII

Respiratory Therapy Technician Program
Kapiolani Community College
University of Hawaii
4303 Diamond Head Road
Honolulu, Hawaii 96816

IDAHO

Respiratory Therapy Technician Program
Boise State University
College of Technology
1910 University Drive
Boise, Idaho 83725

ILLINOIS

Respiratory Therapy Technician Program
Belleville Area College
St. Elizabeth Medical Center
2100 Madison Avenue
Granite City, Illinois 62040

Respiratory Therapy Technician Program
Black Hawk College
6600 34th Avenue
Moline, Illinois 61265

Respiratory Therapy Technician Program
College of DuPage
22nd Street and Lambert Road
Glen Ellyn, Illinois 60137

Respiratory Therapy Technician Program
Illinois Central College
One College Drive
East Peoria, Illinois 61635

Respiratory Therapy Technician Program
Illinois Medical Training Center
162 North State Street
Chicago, Illinois 60601

Respiratory Therapy Technician Program
Kankakee Community College
Box 888
River Road
Kankakee, Illinois 60901

Respiratory Therapy Technician Program
Malcolm X College
1900 West Van Buren Street
Chicago, Illinois 60612

Respiratory Therapy Technician Program
Rock Valley College
3301 North Mulford
Rockford, Illinois 61111

Respiratory Therapy Technician Program
South Chicago Community Hospital
2320 East 93rd Street
Chicago, Illinois 60617

Respiratory Therapy Technician Program
St. John's Hospital
Springfield College
800 East Carpenter
Springfield, Illinois 62704

INDIANA

Respiratory Therapy Technician Program
Indiana Vocational Technical College
P.O. Box 6299
3208 Ross Road
Lafayette, Indiana 47903-6299

Respiratory Therapy Technician Program
Indiana Vocational Technical College
One West 26th Street
P.O. Box 1763
Indianapolis, Indiana 46206

Respiratory Therapy Technician Program
Indiana Vocational Technical College
3800 North Anthony Boulevard
Ft. Wayne, Indiana 46805

Respiratory Therapy Technician Program
Indiana Vocational Technical College-
Northwest Region
Human Services and Health
  Technologies Division
2401 Valley Drive
Valparaiso, Indiana 46383

IOWA

Respiratory Therapy Technician Program
Hawkeye Institute of Technology
1501 East Orange Road
P.O. Box 8015
Waterloo, Iowa 50704

Respiratory Therapy Technician Program
Northeast Iowa Community College
10250 Sundown Road
Peosta, Iowa 52021

KANSAS

Respiratory Therapy Technician Program
Bethany Medical Center
51 North 12th Street
Kansas City, Kansas 66102

Respiratory Therapy Technician Program
Labette Community College
200 South 14th Street
Parsons, Kansas 67357

Respiratory Therapy Technician Program
Seward County Community College
Box 1137
Liberal, Kansas 67905-1137

Respiratory Therapy Technician Program
Washburn University of Topeka
School of Applied and Continuing
  Education
1700 College
Topeka, Kansas 66621

KENTUCKY

Respiratory Therapy Technician Program
Bowling Green State Vocational
  Technical School
1845 Loop Drive
P.O. Box 6000
Bowling Green, Kentucky 42101

Respiratory Therapy Technician Program
Cumberland Valley Health Occupations
  Center
US 25E South
P.O. Box 187
Pineville, Kentucky 40977

Respiratory Therapy Technician Program
Harry Sparks Area Vocational Education
  Center
P.O. Box 275
Mt. Vernon, Kentucky 40456

Respiratory Therapy Technician Program
Kentucky Tech-Central Campus
104 Vo-Tech Road
Lexington, Kentucky 40510

Respiratory Therapy Technician Program
Madisonville Consortium for Respiratory
  Care Education
701 North Laffoon Street
Madisonville, Kentucky 42431

Respiratory Therapy Technician Program
Rowan State Vocational Technical
  School
100 Vo-Tech Drive
Morehead, Kentucky 40351

Respiratory Therapy Technician Program
West Kentucky State Vocational
  Technical School
P.O. Box 7408
Blandville Road
Highway 62-W
Paducah, Kentucky 42002-7408

LOUISIANA

Respiratory Therapy Technician Program
Alton Ochsner Medical Foundation
School of Allied Health Sciences
1516 Jefferson Highway
New Orleans, Louisiana 70121

Respiratory Therapy Technician Program
Bossier Parish Community College
2719 Airline Drive North
Bossier City, Louisiana 71111

Respiratory Therapy Technician Program
Delgado Community College
615 City Park Avenue
New Orleans, Louisiana 70119

Respiratory Therapy Technician Program
Louisiana State University at Eunice
P.O. Box 1129
Eunice, Louisiana 70535

488

Respiratory Therapy Technician Program
Nicholls State University
P.O. Box 2143
Thibodaux, Louisiana 70310

Respiratory Therapy Technician Program
Southeastern Louisiana University
P.O. Box 784, SLU
Hammond, Louisiana 70402

Respiratory Therapy Technician Program
West Jefferson Technical Institute
475 Manhattan Boulevard
Harvey, Louisiana 70058

MAINE

Respiratory Therapy Technician Program
Kennebec Valley Technical College
P.O. Box 29
Western Avenue
Fairfield, Maine 04937-0029

MARYLAND

Respiratory Therapy Technician Program
Essex Community College
7201 Rossville Boulevard
Baltimore, Maryland 21237

Respiratory Therapy Technician Program
New Community College of Baltimore
2901 Liberty Heights Avenue
Baltimore, Maryland 21215-7893

MASSACHUSETTS

Respiratory Therapy Technician Program
Newbury College
129 Fisher Avenue
Brookline, Massachusetts 02146

Respiratory Therapy Technician Program
Northern Essex Community College
100 Elliott Street
Haverhill, Massachusetts 01830

MICHIGAN

Respiratory Therapy Technician Program
Lansing Community College
419 North Capitol Avenue
P.O. Box 40010
Lansing, Michigan 48901

Respiratory Therapy Technician Program
Monroe County Community College
1555 South Raisinville Road
Monroe, Michigan 48161

Respiratory Therapy Technician Program
Muskegon Community College
221 South Quarterline Road
Muskegon, Michigan 49442

Respiratory Therapy Technician Program
St. John Hospital
22101 Moross Road
Detroit, Michigan 48236

MINNESOTA

Respiratory Therapy Technician Program
Duluth Technical College
Hibbing Technical/Community College
2101 Trinity Road
Duluth, Minnesota 55811

Respiratory Therapy Technician Program
East Grand Forks Technical College
Highway 220 North
East Grand Forks, Minnesota 56721

Respiratory Therapy Technician Program
St. Paul Technical College
235 Marshall Avenue
St. Paul, Minnesota 55102

MISSISSIPPI

Respiratory Therapy Technician Program
Hinds Community College-Jackson
  Branch
Nursing Allied Health Center
1750 Chadwick Drive
Jackson, Mississippi 39204-3402

Respiratory Therapy Technician Program
Itawamba Community College
Fulton, Mississippi 38843

Respiratory Therapy Technician Program
Meridian Community College
5500 Highway 19 North
Meridian, Mississippi 39307

Respiratory Therapy Technician Program
Mississippi Gulf coast Community
  College
P.O. Box 67
Perkinson, Mississippi 39573

Respiratory Therapy Technician Program
Northeast Mississippi Community
  College
Cunningham Boulevard
Booneville, Mississippi 38829

Respiratory Therapy Technician Program
Pearl River Community College
5448 Highway 49 South
Hattiesburg, Mississippi 39401

Respiratory Therapy Technician Program
University of Mississippi Medical Center
School of Health Related Professions
2500 North State Street
Jackson, Mississippi 39216-4505

MISSOURI

Respiratory Therapy Technician Program
Cape Girardeau Area Vocational
  Technical School
301 North Clark Avenue
Cape Girardeau, Missouri 63701

Respiratory Therapy Technician Program
Hannibal Area Vocational Technical
  School
4500 McMasters Avenue
Hannibal, Missouri 63401

Respiratory Therapy Technician Program
Rolla Area Vocational-Technical School
1304 Tenth Street
Rolla, Missouri 65401

Respiratory Therapy Technician Program
Southwest Missouri School of
  Respiratory Care
Graff Area VT Center and Drury
  College
815 North Sherman
Springfield, Missouri 65802-3792

Respiratory Therapy Technician Program
State Fair Community College
3201 West 16th
Sedalia, Missouri 65301

MONTANA

Respiratory Therapy Technician Program
Great Falls Vocational Technical Center
2100 16th Avenue South
Great Falls, Montana 59405

Respiratory Therapy Technician Program
Missoula Vocational Technical Center
909 South Avenue West
Missoula, Montana 59801

NEBRASKA

Respiratory Therapy Technician Program
Metropolitan Community College
P.O. Box 3777
Omaha, Nebraska 68103

Respiratory Therapy Technician Program
Southeast Community College
8800 "O" Street
Lincoln, Nebraska 68520

NEVADA

Respiratory Therapy Technician Program
Clark County Community College
3200 East Cheyenne Avenue
North Las Vegas, Nevada 89030

NEW JERSEY

Respiratory Therapy Technician Program
Gloucester County College
Tanyard Road
Deptford Township
Sewell, New Jersey 08080

Respiratory Therapy Technician Program
Passaic County Community College
College Boulevard
Paterson, New Jersey 07509

Respiratory Therapy Technician Program
University of Medicine and Dentistry of
New Jersey
School of Health Related Professions
65 Bergen Street
Newark, New Jersey 07107-3001

NEW MEXICO

Respiratory Therapy Technician Program
Albuquerque Technical-Vocational
Institute
515 Buena Vista Southeast
Albuquerque, New Mexico 87106

NEW YORK

Respiratory Therapy Technician Program
Mohawk Valley Community College
1101 Sherman Drive
Utica, New York 13501

Respiratory Therapy Technician Program
Molloy College
1000 Hempstead Avenue
Rockville Centre, New York 11570-1199

Respiratory Therapy Technician Program
New York City Health and Hospitals
Corp.
Empire State College
27th Street and First Avenue
New York, New York 10016

Respiratory Therapy Technician Program
Onondaga Community College
Onondaga Road
Syracuse, New York 13215

NORTH CAROLINA

Respiratory Therapy Technician Program
Carteret Community College
3505 Arendell Street
Morehead City, North Carolina 28557

Respiratory Therapy Technician Program
Durham Technical Community College
P.O. Box 11307
1637 Lawson Street
Durham, North Carolina 27703

Respiratory Therapy Technician Program
Edgecombe Community College
2009 West Wilson Street
Tarboro, North Carolina 27886

Respiratory Therapy Technician Program
Robeson Community College
P.O. Box 1420
Lumberton, North Carolina 28359

Respiratory Therapy Technician Program
Southwestern Community College
275 Webster Road
Sylva, North Carolina 28779

Respiratory Therapy Technician Program
Stanly Community College
Route Four, Box 55
Albemarle, North Carolina 28001

OHIO

Respiratory Therapy Technician Program
Cincinnati Technical College
3520 Central Parkway
Cincinnati, Ohio 45223

Respiratory Therapy Technician Program
Columbus State Community College
550 East Spring Street
Columbus, Ohio 43215-1609

Respiratory Therapy Technician Program
Lima Technical College
4240 Campus Drive
Lima, Ohio 45804

Respiratory Therapy Technician Program
Stark Technical College
600 Frank Road NW
Canton, Ohio 44720

Respiratory Therapy Technician Program
University of Toledo
Community and Technical College
2801 West Bancroft Street
Toledo, Ohio 43606-3390

OKLAHOMA

Respiratory Therapy Technician Program
Francis Tuttle Vocational Technical
  Center
12777 North Rockwell Avenue
Oklahoma City, Oklahoma 73142-2710

Respiratory Therapy Technician Program
Rose State College
6420 Southeast 15th
Midwest City, Oklahoma 73110

Respiratory Therapy Technician Program
Tulsa Junior College
Sciences & Health Services Division
909 South Boston Avenue
Tulsa, Oklahoma 74119

OREGON

Respiratory Therapy Technician Program
Rogue Community College
3345 Redwood Highway
Grants Pass, Oregon 97526

PENNSYLVANIA

Respiratory Therapy Technician Program
Community College of Allegheny
  County
Allegheny Campus
808 Ridge Avenue
Pittsburgh, Pennsylvania 15212

Respiratory Therapy Technician Program
Greater Johnstown Area Vo-Tech School
445 Schoolhouse Road
Johnstown, Pennsylvania 15904-2998

Respiratory Therapy Technician Program
Gwynedd Mercy College
Sumneytown Pike
Gwynedd Valley, Pennsylvania 19437

Respiratory Therapy Technician Program
Harrisburg Area Community College
3300 Cameron Street Road
Harrisburg, Pennsylvania 17110-2999

Respiratory Therapy Technician Program
James Martin Adult Health Occupations
2600 Red Lion Road
Philadelphia, Pennsylvania 19114

Respiratory Therapy Technician Program
Lehigh County Community College
2370 Main Street
Schnecksville, Pennsylvania 18078

Respiratory Therapy Technician Program
Luzerne County Community College
Middle Road and Prospect Street
Nanticoke, Pennsylvania 18634

Respiratory Therapy Technician Program
St. Francis Medical Center
45th Street off Penn Avenue
Pittsburgh, Pennsylvania 15201

Respiratory Therapy Technician Program
Thiel College
75 College Avenue
Greenville, Pennsylvania 16125

Respiratory Therapy Technician Program
York College of Pennsylvania
Country Club Road
York, Pennsylvania 17403-3426

SOUTH CAROLINA

Respiratory Therapy Technician Program
Florence-Darlington Technical College
P.O. Drawer F-8000
Florence, South Carolina 29501-0057

Respiratory Therapy Technician Program
Greenville Technical College
P.O. Box 5616
Greenville, South Carolina 29606-5616

Respiratory Therapy Technician Program
Midlands Technical College
P.O. Box 2408
Columbia, South Carolina 29202

Respiratory Therapy Technician Program
Orangeburg-Calhoun Technical College
3250 St. Matthews Road
Orangeburg, South Carolina 29115

Respiratory Therapy Technician Program
Piedmont Technical College
P.O. Drawer 1467
Greenwood, South Carolina 29646

Respiratory Therapy Technician Program
Spartanburg Technical College
Drawer 4386
Spartanburg, South Carolina 29305-4386

SOUTH DAKOTA

Respiratory Therapy Technician Program
Mount Marty College
1105 West Eighth
Yankton, South Dakota 57078

TENNESSEE

Respiratory Therapy Technician Program
East Tennessee State University
Dept. of Health Related Professions
1000 West E Street
Elizabethton, Tennessee 37643

Respiratory Therapy Technician Program
Memphis Area Vocational Technical
  School
620 Mosby Avenue
Memphis, Tennessee 38105

Respiratory Therapy Technician Program
Roane State Community College
35 Patton Lane
Harriman, Tennessee 37748-5000

Respiratory Therapy Technician Program
Volunteer State Community College
Nashville Pike
Gallatin, Tennessee 37066

TEXAS

Respiratory Therapy Technician Program
Academy of Health Sciences
Brooke Army Medical Center
Ft. Sam Houston, Texas 78234-6200

Respiratory Therapy Technician Program
Alvin Community College
3110 Mustang Road
Alvin, Texas 77511-4898

Respiratory Therapy Technician Program
Angelina College
P.O. Box 1768
Lufkin, Texas 75902-1768

Respiratory Therapy Technician Program
Colin County Community College
  District
2200 West University Drive
McKinney, Texas 75070

Respiratory Therapy Technician Program
Del Mar College
Baldwin and Ayers
Corpus Christi, Texas 78404

Respiratory Therapy Technician Program
El Centro College
Main and Lamar Streets
Dallas, Texas 75202

Respiratory Therapy Technician Program
Houston Community College System
3100 Shenandoah
Houston, Texas 77021-1098

Respiratory Therapy Technician Program
Howard College
3197 Executive Drive
San Angelo, Texas 76904

Respiratory Therapy Technician Program
Lamar University
College of Health Behavioral Sciences
P.O. Box 10096
Beaumont, Texas 77710

Respiratory Therapy Technician Program
McLennan Community College
1400 College Drive
Waco, Texas 76708

Respiratory Therapy Technician Program
Midland College
3600 North Garfield
Midland, Texas 79705

Respiratory Therapy Technician Program
NHMCCD-Kingwood College
East Campus
20000 Kingwood Drive
Kingwood, Texas 77339

Respiratory Therapy Technician Program
Odessa College
201 West University
Odessa, Texas 79764

Respiratory Therapy Technician Program
San Jacinto College District
Central Campus
8060 Spencer Highway
Pasadena, Texas 77505-2007

Respiratory Therapy Technician Program
South Plains College at Lubbock
1302 Main Street
Lubbock, Texas 79401

Respiratory Therapy Technician Program
Southwest Texas State University
San Marcos, Texas 78666

Respiratory Therapy Technician Program
St. Philip's College
2111 Nevada Street
San Antonio, Texas 78203

Respiratory Therapy Technician Program
Texas Southmost College
83 Fort Brown
Brownsville, Texas 78520

Respiratory Therapy Technician Program
Tyler Junior College
P.O. Box 9020
Tyler, Texas 75711

Respiratory Therapy Technician Program
Victoria College
2200 East Red River
Victoria, Texas 77901

UTAH

Respiratory Therapy Technician Program
Weber State University
School of Allied Health Sciences
Ogden, Utah 84408-3904

VIRGINIA

Respiratory Therapy Technician Program
Central Virginia Community College
3506 Wards Road
Lynchburg, Virginia 24502-2498

Respiratory Therapy Technician Program
J. Sargeant Reynolds Community
  College
P.O. Box C-32040
Richmond, Virginia 23261-2040

Respiratory Therapy Technician Program
Mountain Empire Community College
Division of Business Tech & Health
  Sciences
Drawer 700
Big Stone Gap, Virginia 24219

Respiratory Therapy Technician Program
Northern Virginia Community College
8333 Little River Turnpike
Annandale, Virginia 22003

Respiratory Therapy Technician Program
Shenandoah University
Winchester Medical Center
203 South Cameron Street
Winchester, Virginia 22601

Respiratory Therapy Technician Program
Southwest Virginia Community College
Box SVCC
Richlands, Virginia 24641-1510

Respiratory Therapy Technician Program
Tidewater Community College
1700 College Crescent
Virginia Beach, Virginia 23456

WASHINGTON

Respiratory Therapy Technician Program
Tacoma Community College
5900 South 12th Street
Tacoma, Washington 98465

WEST VIRGINIA

Respiratory Therapy Technician Program
Carver Career and Technical Education
  Center
4799 Midland Drive
Charleston, West Virginia 25306

WISCONSIN

Respiratory Therapy Technician Program
Milwaukee Area Technical College
700 West State Street
Milwaukee, Wisconsin 53233

WYOMING

Respiratory Therapy Technician Program
Western Wyoming Community College
2500 College Drive
P.O. Box 428
Rock Springs, Wyoming 82901

Respiratory Therapy Aide

Supervised by respiratory therapists and respiratory therapy technicians and having little direct contact with patients, the respiratory therapy aide is mostly concerned with cleaning, disinfecting, sterilizing, and maintaining equipment. She or he may be responsible for the majority of the clerical duties and may also deliver oxygen tanks and other equipment and supplies to specific hospital locations.

A high school education is the usual prerequisite for admittance into on-the-job hospital training available in some areas. Persons interested in becoming respiratory therapy aides should contact the Chief Respiratory Therapist or the Personnel Director of their local hospital.

According to a recent salary survey compiled by the American Association for Respiratory Care, the average rate of pay for respiratory therapy aides was $6.50 per hour.

SOURCE:

American Association for Respiratory Care
Dictionary of Occupational Titles

SCIENTIFIC MASSAGE THERAPY

Scientific massage is a systematic manual manipulation of bodily tissues for the purpose of affecting the muscular and nervous systems and the general circulation of the body. It is a method of natural treatment that can be recommended by a physician as a means for restoring the function of muscles and joints, as well as relieving mental and physical fatigue. The qualified practitioner of scientific massage is known as a *massage therapist.*

Massage Therapist

Applying the principles and techniques of scientific massage, the *massage therapist* may be capable of relieving many health disorders and disturbances. The techniques the massage therapist uses may assist in the rehabilitation of sprains, strains, fractures, and dislocations, as well as help eliminate pain from neuritic, arthritic, and rheumatic conditions. The therapist may also be able to apply massage to relieve various forms of paralysis, insomnia, migraine headaches, and other conditions caused by poor functioning of the nervous system. By stimulating the circulatory system, the massage therapist may reduce convalescent periods and improve many conditions after surgery. Shortened recovery time for injured athletes may also be achieved with massage therapy. In addition, massage therapy can also provide relief of muscle tightness caused by stress.

The therapist works with various agents to complement massage, including hot packs, ice applications, saunas, steam baths and whirlpools.

Some massage therapists work in hospitals, clinics, physicians' offices, private practices, sanitariums, and nursing homes while others work in health clubs, spas, and Y.M.C.A.'s.

A massage therapist must acquire a balance of clinical skills and technical knowledge as well as sensitivity and awareness.

The American Massage Therapy Association's affiliated schools offer massage therapy programs which consist of at least 500 hours of classroom instruction including 300 hours of massage theory and technique, 100 hours of anatomy and physiology, and 100 hours of required courses to meet the school's specific program objectives. First aid and CPR education are also required. Contact individual schools for more information. For information on licensing, contact the state's licensing agency which is usually located in the state capital.

Salaries for massage therapists vary due to differences in geographic location, experience, and places of employment. Many massage therapists do however, charge fees based on hourly or half-hourly time periods.

The following is a list of schools with programs accredited or approved by the American Massage Therapy Association.

For more information about a career as a massage therapist, contact the American Massage Therapy Association, 820 Davis Street, Suite 100, Evanston, Illinois 60201-4444.

SOURCE:

American Massage Therapy Association

Massage Therapist Programs

ARIZONA

Massage Therapist Program
Desert Institute of the Healing Arts
639 North Sixth Avenue
Tucson, Arizona 85705

Massage Therapist Program
Phoenix Therapeutic Massage College
3150 North 24th Street, Suite 101
Phoenix, Arizona 85016

CALIFORNIA

Massage Therapist Program
American Institute of Massage Therapy
2156 Newport Boulevard
Costa Mesa, California 92627

Massage Therapist Program
Heartwood Institute
220 Harmony Lane
Garberville, California 95440

Massage Therapist Program
Integrative Therapy School
3000 "T" Street, Suite 104
Sacramento, California 95816

Massage Therapist Program
International Professional School of
 Bodywork
1366 Hornblend Street
San Diego, California 92109

Massage Therapist Program
Mueller College of Holistic Studies
4607 Park Boulevard
San Diego, California 92116

Massage Therapist Program
National Holistic Institute
5900 Hollis Street, Suite J
Emeryville, California 94608

COLORADO

Massage Therapist Program
Boulder School of Massage Therapy
3285 30th Street
Boulder, Colorado 80301-1451

Massage Therapist Program
Stress Massage Institute
P.O. Box 1304
934 Manitou Avenue
Manitou Springs, Colorado 80829

CONNECTICUT

Massage Therapist Program
Connecticut Center for Massage Therapy
75 Kitts Lane
Newington, Connecticut 06111

DISTRICT OF COLUMBIA

Potomac Massage Training Institute
7826 Eastern Avenue NW, Suite LL-1
Washington, DC 20012

FLORIDA

Massage Therapist Program
Educating Hands School of Massage
261 SW Eighth Street
Miami, Florida 33130-3513

Massage Therapist Program
Florida Institute of Massage Therapy and
 Esthetics
5453 North University Drive
Lauderhill, Florida 33351

Massage Therapist Program
Florida School of Massage
6421 SW 13th Street
Gainsville, Florida 32608

Massage Therapist Program
Humanities Center Institute of Allied
 Health
School of Massage
4045 Park Boulevard
Pinellas Park, Florida 34665

Massage Therapist Program
Reese Institute
425 Geneva Drive
Oviedo, Florida 32765

Massage Therapist Program
Sarasota School of Massage Therapy
1970 Main Street
Sarasota, Florida 34236

Massage Therapist Program
Seminar Network International
SNI School of Massage & Beauty
 Therapy
518 North Federal Highway
Lake Worth, Florida 33460

Massage Therapist Program
Suncoast School of Massage Therapy
4910 West Cypress Street
Tampa, Florida 33607

GEORGIA

Massage Therapist Program
Atlanta School of Massage
2300 Peachford Road, Suite 3200
Atlanta, Georgia 30338

HAWAII

Massage Therapist Program
Honolulu School of Massage
1123 11th Avenue, Suite 301
Honolulu, Hawaii 96816

ILLINOIS

Massage Therapist Program
Chicago School of Massage Therapy
2918 North Lincoln Avenue
Chicago, Illinois 60657

INDIANA

Massage Therapist Program
Alexandria School of Scientific
 Therapeutics
809 South Harrison
P.O. Box 287
Alexandria, Indiana 46001

Massage Therapist Program
Lewis School & Clinic of Massage
  Therapy
3400 Michigan Street
Hobart, Indiana 46342

IOWA

Massage Therapist Program
Carlson College of Massage Therapy
1756 First Avenue NE
Cedar Rapids, Iowa 52402

MAINE

Massage Therapist Program
Downeast School of Massage
197 Moose Meadow Lane
P.O. Box 24
Waldoboro, Maine 04572

MARYLAND

Massage Therapist Program
Baltimore School of Massage
6401 Dogwood Road
Baltimore, Maryland 21207

MASSACHUSETTS

Bancroft School of Massage Therapy
50 Franklin Street, Suite 370
Worcester, Massachusetts 01608

Massage Therapist Program
Massage Institute of New England
439 Cambridge Street
Cambridge, Massachusetts 02141

Massage Therapist Program
Muscular Therapy Institute
122 Rindge Avenue
Cambridge, Massachusetts 02140

Massage Therapist Program
Stillpoint Center School of Massage
P.O. Box 15
60 Main Street
Hatfield, Massachusetts 01038

MICHIGAN

Massage Therapist Program
Health Enrichment Center
408 Davis Lake Road
Lapeer, Michigan 48446

MINNESOTA

Massage Therapist Program
Northern Lights School of Massage
  Therapy
1313 SE Fifth Street, Suite 202
Minneapolis, Minnesota 55414

NEW HAMPSHIRE

Massage Therapist Program
New Hampshire Institute for Therapeutic
  Arts
School of Massage Therapy
153 Lowell Road
Hudson, New Hampshire 03051

NEW MEXICO

Massage Therapist Program
Dr. Jay Scherer's Academy of Natural
  Healing
1443 South St. Francis Drive
Santa Fe, New Mexico 87501

Massage Therapist Program
New Mexico Academy of Massage and
  Advanced Healing Arts
P.O. Box 932
Santa Fe, New Mexico 87504

Massage Therapist Program
New Mexico School of Natural
 Therapeutics
117 Richmond NE, Suite A
Albuquerque, New Mexico 87106

NEW YORK

Massage Therapist Program
New Center for Wholistic Health
 Education and Research
50 Maple Place
Manhasset, New York 11030

Massage Therapist Program
Swedish Institute
226 West 26th Street
New York, New York 10001

NORTH CAROLINA

Massage Therapist Program
Body Therapy Institute
P.O. Box 202
Saxapahaw, North Carolina 27340

Massage Therapist Program
Carolina School of Massage
103 West Weaver Street
Carrboro, North Carolina 27510

OHIO

Massage Therapist Program
Central Ohio School of Massage
1110 Morse Road
Columbus, Ohio 43229

Massage Therapist Program
Self-Health School of Medical Massage
P.O. Box 474
130 Cook Road
Lebanon, Ohio 45036

OREGON

Massage Therapist Program
East-West College of the Healing Arts
812 SW Tenth Avenue
Portland, Oregon 97205

PENNSYLVANIA

Massage Therapist Program
Pennsylvania School of Muscle Therapy
651 South Gulph Road
King of Prussia, Pennsylvania 19406

TEXAS

Massage Therapist Program
Asten Center of Natural Therapeutics
797 North Grove Road, Suite 101
Richardson, Texas 75081

Massage Therapist Program
Institute of Natural Healing Sciences
4100 Felps Road, Suite E
Colleyville, Texas 76034

UTAH

Massage Therapist Program
Utah College of Massage Therapy
124 S. 400 E., Suite 330
Salt Lake City, Utah 84111

WASHINGTON

Massage Therapist Program
Brenneke School of Massage
160 Roy Street
Seattle, Washington 98109

Massage Therapist Program
Brian Utting School of Massage
900 Thomas Street
Seattle, Washington 98109

Massage Therapist Program
Seattle Massage School
7120 Woodlawn Avenue, NE
Seattle, Washington 98115

Massage Therapist Program
Tri-City School of Massage
26 East Third Avenue
Kennewick, Washington 99336

WISCONSIN

Massage Therapist Program
Lakeside School of Natural Therapeutics
804 East Center Street
Milwaukee, Wisconsin 53212

CANADA

Massage Therapist Program
Canadian College of Massage &
  Hydrotherapy
85 Church Street
Sutton West, Ontario
Canada L0E 1R0

Massage Therapist Program
Sutherland-Chan School & Teaching
  Clinic
330 Dupont Street, Suite 400
Toronto, Ontario
Canada M5R 1V9

The use of alcohol and other drugs causes a variety of serious health problems within the United States today. Alcohol and drug use is also responsible for alcohol and drug-related motor vehicle accidents, suicides, birth defects, crime, and decreased worker productivity. In an effort to provide the knowledge and skills necessary to avoid alcohol and other drug problems, substance abuse prevention approaches are being aimed at individuals, peer groups, schools, the workplace, the family, and the community. Some professions that involve the prevention of substance abuse include community health educators, school health educators, social workers, and psychologists. Physicians, nurses, and other health care professionals may also be involved in substance abuse prevention. They can identify alcohol and drug problems among their patients, counsel patients concerning the risks of use, and serve as informational resources. The health care field however, offers few strictly substance abuse prevention careers. Substance abuse prevention is a new field and few standards and credentialing processes have been enacted. Two professions that are specific to the prevention and treatment of substance abuse are the *substance abuse counselor* and the *chemical dependency attendant*.

Substance Abuse Counselor

The *substance abuse counselor* helps people, who are physiologically or psychologically dependent upon alcohol or drugs, deal with the disease of chemical dependency. The substance abuse counselor also helps family members, former addicts, and those who are afraid they might become addicts.

The substance abuse counselor begins by interviewing the client and reviewing records in order to identify an abuse problem. Through counseling and the use of his or her knowledge of drug and alcohol abuse, the substance abuse counselor formulates a program for treatment and rehabilitation of the client. He or she may counsel the client individually, or in a group session, in the methods of overcoming alcohol and drug dependency. The substance abuse counselor also counsels family members in the methods of dealing with and supporting the individual. In order to evaluate the success of the therapy, the substance abuse counselor monitors the condition of the client and adapts treatment as needed. He or she may also refer the client to other support services such as employment services, social services, and medical treatment. The substance abuse counselor does not prescribe medicine or provide any medical therapy. The substance abuse counselor also prepares reports and case histories and may prepare documents for presentation in court. If necessary, he or she accompanies the client to court.

The substance abuse counselor may also be involved in providing business managers and supervisors with methods of handling employee drug and alcohol abuse problems. He or she may also conduct programs to promote prevention of alcohol and drug abuse within the workplace.

The substance abuse counselor must have a thorough knowledge and understanding of prevention, treatment, rehabilitation, and the addiction process, as well as the physiological and psychological effects of alcohol, depressants, cocaine, stimulants, opiates, and hallucinogens. He or she must also be knowledgeable of legal, judicial, and enforcement procedures.

Substance abuse counselors are employed in rehabilitation centers, halfway houses, hospitals, clinics, schools, universities, government agencies, business, and private practice.

The educational requirements for the substance abuse counselor vary greatly amongst employers. A high school education is the usual minimum requirement of employers who provide on-the-job training that ranges from six weeks to two years. An Associate or Bachelor's degree may be the minimum requirement of other employers. Many employers however, require a master's degree in substance abuse counseling. Accredited graduate programs in substance abuse counseling are comprised of supervised internship and practicum experiences, in addition to regular course study. Some employers may provide work-study programs that allow counselors to pursue their graduate degrees.

To become a National Certified Addiction Counselor (NCAC), candidates must hold current state certification or licensure as an alcoholism and/or drug abuse counselor, have acquired three years of full-time or 6,000 hours of supervised experience as an alcoholism and/or drug abuse counselor, and complete the written exam with a passing score. The written exam tests candidates' knowledge on the pharmacology of psychoactive substances, counseling practices, the theoretical base of counseling, and professional issues related to alcoholism and drug abuse treatment. The written exam is administered twice yearly.

Recommended high school courses for the student interested in pursuing a career as a substance abuse counselor include psychology, sociology, anatomy and physiology, and health.

Salaries of substance abuse counselors vary according to experience, education, and place of employment. According to a survey by the National Association of Alcoholism and Drug Abuse Counselors, senior counselors averaged approximately $32,000 annually, while intermediate counselors averaged $27,000 annually. The study found that while most counselors receive a salary from an employer, some may earn additional income from secondary employment and many are self-employed in private practice.

For more information on a career as a substance abuse counselor, contact the National Association of Alcoholism and Drug Abuse Counselors, 3717 Columbia Pike, Suite 300, Arlington, Virginia 22204-4254

SOURCES:

American Counseling Association
Dictionary of Occupation Titles
National Association of Alcoholism and Drug Abuse Counselors
Occupational Outlook Handbook

Chemical Dependency Attendant

The *chemical dependency attendant* works in substance abuse treatment programs, under the supervision of the medical or nursing staff. He or she works as a type of nursing aide or orderly performing nursing tasks and caring for the patients' eating, sleeping, and personal hygiene habits. He or she may also clean rooms and change linens. The chemical dependency attendant takes temperatures, blood pressure, pulse and respiration counts; draws blood samples; collects laboratory specimens; administers prescribed medications; and records information on patients' charts. He or she may also interview patients and record data upon admission. The chemical dependency attendant may also be required to restrain patients in order to prevent injuries to themselves, staff, and other patients. The chemical dependency attendant provides rehabilitation assistance in the patient's development of social relationships by encouraging participation in social and recreational activities. He or she also spends time talking with patients and accompanying them to activities and games. He or she may also accompany patients off grounds to shop or to attend church or medical and dental appointments. Training programs for the chemical dependency attendant are usually held on-the-job. For more information on qualifications, training, and salary, call the personnel departments of local hospitals and substance abuse treatment centers.

For information on other employment opportunities in the field of substance abuse prevention and treatment, interested individuals should contact substance abuse prevention organizations in their area. Information on these local organizations can be obtained from the following list of state substance abuse prevention coordinators.

SOURCE:

Dictionary of Occupational Titles

State Substance Abuse Prevention Coordinators

ALABAMA

Prevention Coordinator
Department of Mental Health
200 Interstate Park Avenue
Montgomery, Alabama 36193-5001

ALASKA

State Coordinator
State Office of Alcoholism and Drug
  Abuse
P.O. Box H-05F
Juneau, Alaska 99811-0607

ARIZONA

Prevention Program Representative
Office of Community Behavioral Health
  Services
411 North 24th Street
Phoenix, Arizona 85008

ARKANSAS

Prevention Coordinator
Director of Governor's Partnership in
  Substance Abuse Prevention
P.O. Box 1437
Little Rock, Arkansas 72203-1437

CALIFORNIA

State Prevention Coordinator
Department of Alcohol and Drug
  Programs
111 Capitol Mall
Sacramento, California 95814

COLORADO

Prevention Program Director
Alcohol and Drug Abuse Division
Department of Health
4210 East 11th Avenue
Denver, Colorado 80220

CONNECTICUT

Prevention Coordinator
Alcohol and Drug Abuse Commission
Prevention Division
999 Asylum Avenue
Hartford, Connecticut 06105

DELAWARE

Division of Alcoholism, Drug Abuse,
  and Mental Health
Director of Training
1901 North DuPont Highway
New Castle, Delaware 19720

DISTRICT OF COLUMBIA

Prevention Coordinator
Office of Health Planning and
  Development
1600 L Street NW, Suite 715
Washington, DC 20036

FLORIDA

Prevention Coordinator
Department of Health and Rehabilitative
  Services
1317 Winewood Boulevard
Tallahassee, Florida 32399-0700

GEORGIA

Prevention Coordinator
Division of Mental Health and Substance
  Abuse Prevention Resource Center
878 Peachtree Street NE, Suite 319
Atlanta, Georgia 30309

HAWAII

Alcohol and Drug Abuse Division
Department of Health
Prevention Program Specialist
P.O. Box 3378
Honolulu, Hawaii 96801-9984

IDAHO

State Prevention Coordinator
Substance Abuse Program
Department of Health and Welfare
450 West State
Boise, Idaho 83720

ILLINOIS

Prevention Coordinator
Division of Prevention
100 West Randolph, Suite 600
Chicago, Illinois 60601

INDIANA

Director, Prevention and Planning
Department of Mental Health
117 East Washington Street
Indianapolis, Indiana 46204

IOWA

Prevention Coordinator
Bureau of Prevention and Training
Division of Substance Abuse and Health
  Promotion
Department of Public Health
Lucas State Office Building
Des Moines, Iowa 50319

KANSAS

Alcohol and Drug Abuse Services
Program Development Director
300 SW Oakley
Topeka, Kansas 66606

KENTUCKY

Prevention Coordinator
Division of Substance Abuse
275 East Main Street
Frankfort, Kentucky 40621

LOUISIANA

Prevention Coordinator
Division of Alcohol and Drug Abuse
1201 Capitol Access Road
P.O. Box 3868
Baton Rouge, Louisiana 70802

MAINE

Prevention Coordinator
Office of Alcoholism and Drug Abuse
  Prevention
Department of Human Services
State House Station #11
Augusta, Maine 04333

MARYLAND

Prevention Coordinator
Alcohol and Drug Abuse
  Administration's Prevention Services
201 West Preston Street
Baltimore, Maryland 21201

MASSACHUSETTS

State Prevention Coordinator
Division of Substance Abuse Services
Department of Public Health
150 Tremont Street
Boston, Massachusetts 02111

MICHIGAN

Prevention Coordinator
Office of Substance Abuse Services
2150 Apollo Drive
P.O. Box 30206
Lansing, Michigan 48909

MINNESOTA

Prevention Coordinator
Chemical Dependency Program Division
Department of Human Services
444 Lafayette Road
St. Paul, Minnesota 55155-3823

MISSISSIPPI

Prevention Coordinator
Division of Alcohol and Drug Abuse
1101 Robert E. Lee Building
239 North Lamar Street
Jackson, Mississippi 39201

MISSOURI

Prevention Coordinator
Division of Alcohol and Drug Abuse
P.O. Box 687
Jefferson City, Missouri 65102

MONTANA

Prevention Coordinator
Department of Institutions
1539 11th Avenue
Helena, Montana 59620

NEBRASKA

Prevention Coordinator
Division on Alcoholism and Drug Abuse
Department of Public Institutions
P.O. Box 94728
Lincoln, Nebraska 68509-4728

NEVADA

Prevention Coordinator
Department of Human Resources
505 East King Street
Carson City, Nevada 89710

NEW HAMPSHIRE

Prevention Coordinator
Office of Alcohol and Drug Abuse
  Prevention
Six Hazen Drive
Concord, New Hampshire 03301

NEW JERSEY

Prevention Coordinator
Department of Health
Division of Alcoholism and Drug Abuse
Trenton, New Jersey 08620-0362

NEW MEXICO

State Prevention Coordinator
Substance Abuse Bureau
1190 St. Francis Drive
Santa Fe, New Mexico 87503

NEW YORK

State Division of Alcoholism and
  Alcohol Abuse
Deputy Director for Prevention and
  Intervention
194 Washington Avenue
Albany, New York 12210

NORTH CAROLINA

Prevention Coordinator
Department of Human Resources
Division of Mental Health and Substance
  Abuse Services
Albermarle, North Carolina 27611

NORTH DAKOTA

Prevention Coordinator
Division of Alcoholism and Drug Abuse
Department of Human Services
1839 East Capitol Avenue
Bismarck, North Dakota 58501

OHIO

Prevention Coordinator
Department of Health
Department of Alcohol and Drug
  Addiction
170 North High Street
Columbus, Ohio 43215

OKLAHOMA

Director of Prevention Services
Department of Mental Health and
  Substance Abuse Services
P.O. Box 53277
Oklahoma City, Oklahoma 73152-3277

OREGON

Prevention Manager
Office of Alcohol and Drug Abuse
  Programs
1178 Chemeketa Street NE
Salem, Oregon 97310

PENNSYLVANIA

Prevention Coordinator
Division of Prevention and Intervention
  Services
P.O. Box 90
Health and Welfare Building
Harrisburg, Pennsylvania 17108

RHODE ISLAND

Prevention Coordinator
Division of Substance Abuse
P.O. Box 20363
Cranston, Rhode Island 02920

SOUTH CAROLINA

Prevention Coordinator
Director of Programs and Services
700 Forest Drive, Suite 300
Columbia, South Carolina 25204

SOUTH DAKOTA

Prevention Coordinator
Department of Human Services
Division of Alcohol and Drug Abuse
523 East Capitol
Pierre, South Dakota 57501

TENNESSEE

Prevention Coordinator
Division of Alcohol and Drug Abuse
  Services
706 Church Street
Nashville, Tennessee 37219

TEXAS

Statewide Prevention Coordinator
Commission on Alcohol and Drug
  Abuse
1705 Guadalupe Street
Austin, Texas 78701-1214

UTAH

Prevention Representative
Alcohol and Drug Abuse Clinic
50 North Medical Drive
P.O. Box 2500
Salt Lake City, Utah 84132

VERMONT

Prevention Unit
Office of Alcohol and Drug Abuse
  Programs
Chief Substance Abuse Prevention
103 South Main Street
Waterbury, Vermont 05676

VIRGINIA

Substance Abuse Prevention Coordinator
Office of Prevention, Promotion, and
  Library Services
P.O. Box 1797
Richmond, Virginia 23214

WASHINGTON

Prevention/Early Intervention
  Administrator
Division of Alcohol and Substance
  Abuse
Olympia, Washington 98504

WEST VIRGINIA

Prevention Coordinator
Division on Alcoholism and Drug Abuse
Department of Health and Human
  Resources
State Capitol Complex
Charleston, West Virginia 25305

WISCONSIN

Office of Alcohol and Other Drug
  Abuse
Prevention Specialist
One West Wilson Street
Madison, Wisconsin 53707

WYOMING

Prevention Coordinator
Division of Community Programs
Office of Substance Abuse
Cheyenne, Wyoming 82002

✚ THERAPEUTIC RECREATION

Therapeutic recreation is a specialized allied health field within the recreation profession. Associated with the leisure aspects of medical treatment, therapeutic recreation attempts to physically and socially rehabilitate patients who have chronic physical, psychological, and social handicaps. It involves recreation services that give the patient an opportunity to participate in recreational, leisure and group activities specifically designed to aid in recovery from or adjustment to illness, disability, or a specific social problem. There are two career opportunities in therapeutic recreation: the *therapeutic recreation specialist* and the *therapeutic recreation assistant.*

Therapeutic Recreation Specialist

Also known as a *recreational therapist,* the therapeutic recreation specialist plans, organizes, directs, and counsels medically approved recreation programs. The specialist encourages patients to develop recreational interests and skills and to participate in physical and social activities so that they may better cope with or recover from their illnesses or disabilities. Activities include sports, trips, dramatics, arts and crafts, discussion groups, nature study, and hobbies, and they are administered in accordance with patients' needs, capabilities, and interests. As part of a rehabilitation treatment team, the therapeutic recreation specialist observes and reports on patients' physical, mental, and social progress. This information is then incorporated into the planning of future therapies.

The specialist works in nonmedical as well as medical settings. In the former he or she may work for community recreation agencies to integrate the handicapped into the total community recreation program. Or the specialist may work for schools for the blind, homes for the elderly, orphanages, juvenile detention homes, or prisons. In medical facilities the specialist works in hospitals and rehabilitation centers and is concerned with among others, the mentally ill, the mentally retarded, and the physically handicapped.

A bachelor's degree, preferably in therapeutic recreation, or recreation with an option in therapeutic recreation, is the minimum level of education for professional status in therapeutic recreation. Programs in therapeutic recreation include classroom as well as a supervised clinical field experience. For executive positions in administration, research, and teaching or in the conducting of training programs a graduate degree is required.

High school students who are interested in a career in therapeutic recreation should become involved with physical education, public speaking, sports, dramatics, music, clubs, and other activities, all of which will help develop skills in basic recreational leadership. Interested students might work as volunteers or paid employees in playgrounds, camps, hospitals, or public and community facilities to gain experience in working with people. Recommended high school courses include physical education, biology, and behavioral sciences.

Credentials for the therapeutic recreation specialist are available from the National Council for Therapeutic Recreation Certification for applicants who meet the academic and experience requirements. Prerequisites for certification include 1) minimum of a bachelor's degree in therapeutic recreation or recreation with an option in therapeutic recreation, or 2) minimum of a bachelor's degree in rehabilitation, psychology, sociology, art or music education, dance, drama, early childhood education or related fields plus five years full time paid experience in a therapeutic recreation program; plus 18 semester hours of approved upper division or graduate level therapeutic recreation courses.

A few states currently require therapeutic recreation specialists to meet either certification or licensure criteria. For information on state requirements, write to the state licensing division, located in the state capital.

Salaries for therapeutic specialists vary according to geographic location, education, years of experience, and place of employment. A 1991 American Therapeutic Recreation Association survey found average salaries ranged from $25,600 to $31,100 a year.

For further information on career opportunities and certification requirements, contact the National Therapeutic Recreation Society, c/o National Recreation and Park Association, 2775 South Quincy Street, Suite 300, Arlington, Virginia 22206-2204 and the National Council for Therapeutic Recreation Certification, 49 South Main Street, Suite 001, Spring Valley, New York 10977.

Following is a list, supplied by the American Therapeutic Recreation Association, of programs in therapeutic recreation.

SOURCES:

American Therapeutic Recreation Association
National Council for Therapeutic Recreation Certification
National Therapeutic Recreation Society
Occupational Outlook Handbook

Therapeutic Recreation Specialist Programs

ALABAMA

Therapeutic Recreation Program
University of South Alabama
307 University Boulevard
Mobile, Alabama 36688

ARIZONA

Therapeutic Recreation Program
Arizona State University
Dept. of Leisure Studies
Tempe, Arizona 85287-2302

Therapeutic Recreation Program
Northern Arizona University
Box 6012
Flagstaff, Arizona 86011

ARKANSAS

Therapeutic Recreation Program
Arkansas Tech University
Russelville, Arkansas 72801

Therapeutic Recreation Program
Henderson State College
P.O. Box 7503
Arkadelphia, Arkansas 71923

CALIFORNIA

Therapeutic Recreation Program
Cal Poly State University-Pomona
Horticulture Department
3801 West Temple Avenue
Pomona, California 91768

Therapeutic Recreation Program
Cal Poly State University-San Luis
  Obispo
Recreation Administration
San Luis Obispo, California 93407

Therapeutic Recreation Program
California State University-Chico
Dept. of Recreation & Park Admin.
Chico, California 95929-0560

Therapeutic Recreation Program
California State University-Hayward
Dept. of Recreation
Hayward, California 94542

Therapeutic Recreation Program
California State University-Fresno
Dept. of Recreation Admin.
Fresno, California 93740-0103

Therapeutic Recreation Program
California State University-Long Beach
Dept. of Recreation
1250 Bellflower Boulevard
Long Beach, California 90840-7581

Therapeutic Recreation Program
California State University-Northridge
Dept. of Recreation
18111 Nordhoff Street
Northridge, California 91330

Therapeutic Recreation Program
California State University-Sacramento
Dept. of Recreation
6000 "J" Street
Sacramento, California 95819-6110

Therapeutic Recreation Program
San Diego State University
Dept. of Recreation
5900 Campanile Drive
San Diego, California 92182-0368

Therapeutic Recreation Program
San Francisco State University
Dept. of Recreation
1600 Holloway Avenue
San Francisco, California 94132

Therapeutic Recreation Program
San Jose State University
Recreation & Leisure Studies
One Washington Square
San Jose, California 95192-0060

Therapeutic Recreation Program
Whittier College
Physical Ed & Recreation
Whittier, California 90608

COLORADO

Therapeutic Recreation Program
Mesa College
Dept. of PE, Recreation & Leisure
Grand Junction, Colorado 81502

Therapeutic Recreation Program
University of Northern Colorado
Recreation Program
Greeley, Colorado 80639

CONNECTICUT

Therapeutic Recreation Program
Mitchell College
Dept. of PE & Recreation
New London, Connecticut 06320

Therapeutic Recreation Program
Southern Connecticut State University
Dept. or Recreation & Leisure
New Haven, Connecticut 06515

Therapeutic Recreation Program
University of Connecticut
Recreational Educational
Storrs, Connecticut 06269-1110

DISTRICT OF COLUMBIA

Therapeutic Recreation Program
Gallaudet University
Dept. of PE & Recreation
800 Florida Avenue NE
Washington, DC 20002-3695

Therapeutic Recreation Program
Howard University
Sixth & Girard Streets NW
Washington, DC 20059

FLORIDA

Therapeutic Recreation Program
Eckerd College
P.O. Box 12560
St. Petersburg, Florida 33733

Therapeutic Recreation Program
Florida State University
Leisure Svs & Studies
Tallahassee, Florida 32306

Therapeutic Recreation Program
Florida International University
Parks & Recreation Mgmt
Miami, Florida 33199

Therapeutic Recreation Program
University of Florida
Dept. of Recreation
Gainesville, Florida 32611-2034

GEORGIA

Therapeutic Recreation Program
Georgia Southern University
Dept. of Recreation/Leisure Studies
Statesboro, Georgia 30460-8077

Therapeutic Recreation Program
University of Georgia
Dept. of Recreation & Leisure Study
Athens, Georgia 30602

IDAHO

Therapeutic Recreation Program
University of Idaho
Moscow, Idaho 83843

ILLINOIS

Therapeutic Recreation Program
Aurora University
Recreation Admin. Dept.
Aurora, Illinois 60506

Therapeutic Recreation Program
Chicago State University
Dept. of Leisure Science
95th & King Drive
Chicago, Illinois 60628

Therapeutic Recreation Program
College of St. Francis
Dept. of Recreation & Leisure
Joliet, Illinois 60435

Therapeutic Recreation Program
Southern Illinois University
Dept. of Recreation
Champaign, Illinois 61820

Therapeutic Recreation Program
Western Illinois University
Dept. of Recreation & Tourism
Macomb, Illinois 61455

INDIANA

Therapeutic Recreation Program
Indiana State University
Dept. of Recreation Mgmt.
Terre Haute, Indiana 47809

Therapeutic Recreation Program
Indiana University
Dept. of Recreation Admin.
Bloomington, Indiana 47405

Therapeutic Recreation Program
Purdue University
Recreation Studies
West Lafayette, Indiana 47907

IOWA

Therapeutic Recreation Program
Iowa State University
Leisure Studies Curriculum
Ames, Iowa 50011

Therapeutic Recreation Program
University of Iowa
Dept. of Leisure Studies
Iowa City, Iowa 52242

Therapeutic Recreation Program
University of Northern Iowa
Leisure Services Division
Cedar Falls, Iowa 50614-0161

KANSAS

Therapeutic Recreation Program
Emporia State University
Dept. of HPER. & Athletics
1200 Commercial
Emporia, Kansas 66801

Therapeutic Recreation Program
Kansas State University
College of Agriculture
Manhatten, Kansas 66506

Therapeutic Recreation Program
Pittsburgh State University
Dept. of HPER.
Pittsburg, Kansas 66762

Therapeutic Recreation Program
University of Kansas
Dept. of HPER.
Lawrence, Kansas 66045

KENTUCKY

Therapeutic Recreation Program
Eastern Kentucky University
Dept. of Rec. & Park Admin.
Richmond, Kentucky 40475

Therapeutic Recreation Program
Murray State University
Murray, Kentucky 42071

Therapeutic Recreation Program
University of Kentucky
Curriculum in Rec. & Leisure Studies
Lexington, Kentucky 40506-0219

Therapeutic Recreation Program
Western Kentucky University
Dept. of PE & Rec.
Bowling Green, Kentucky 42101

LOUISIANA

Therapeutic Recreation Program
Grambling State University
Grambling, Louisiana 71245

Therapeutic Recreation Program
Southern University
Dept. of Leisure & Rec. Services
P.O. Box 9752
Baton Rouge, Louisiana 70813

MAINE

Therapeutic Recreation Program
University of Southern Maine
Dept. of Rec. & Leisure Studies
Portland, Maine 04103

MARYLAND

Therapeutic Recreation Program
University of Maryland
Dept. of Rec.
College Park, Maryland 20742

MASSACHUSETTS

Therapeutic Recreation Program
Boston University
School of Education
Boston, Massachusetts 02215

Therapeutic Recreation Program
Northeastern University
Health, Sport, & Leisure Studies
360 Huntington Avenue
Boston, Massachusetts 02115

Therapeutic Recreation Program
Springfield College
Recreation & Leisure Studies
263 Alden Street
Springfield, Massachusetts 01109

MICHIGAN

Therapeutic Recreation Program
Central Michigan University
Dept. of Rec. & Park Admin.
Mount Pleasant, Michigan 48859

Therapeutic Recreation Program
Eastern Michigan University
Recreation Division
Ypsilanti, Michigan 48197

Therapeutic Recreation Program
Grand Valley State University
Allendale, Michigan 49401

Therapeutic Recreation Program
Lake Superior State College
Sault Sainte Marie, Michigan 49783

Therapeutic Recreation Program
Michigan State University
Dept. of Park & Rec. Resources
East Lansing, Michigan 48824-1222

Therapeutic Recreation Program
Wayne State University
Dept. of Rec. & Park Services
Detroit, Michigan 48202

MINNESOTA

Therapeutic Recreation Program
Mankato State University
Dept. of Rec. Park & Leisure Serv.
213 Highland North
Mankato, Minnesota 56002

Therapeutic Recreation Program
St. Cloud State University
St. Cloud, Minnesota 56301

Therapeutic Recreation Program
University of Minnesota-Minneapolis
1900 University Avenue SE
Minneapolis, Minnesota 55455

Therapeutic Recreation Program
Winona State University
Eighth & Sanborn
Winona, Minnesota 55987

MISSISSIPPI

Therapeutic Recreation Program
Jackson State University
Jackson, Mississippi 39217

Therapeutic Recreation Program
University of Southern Mississippi
School of Human Performance & Rec.
Hattiesburg, Mississippi 39406-5142

MISSOURI

Therapeutic Recreation Program
Central Missouri State University
Rec. & Tourism Program
Warrensburg, Missouri 64093

Therapeutic Recreation Program
Missouri Western State College
Dept. of Leisure Management
4525 Downs Drive
St. Joseph, Missouri 64507

Therapeutic Recreation Program
Northeast Missouri State University
Dept. of Recreation
Kirksville, Missouri 63501

Therapeutic Recreation Program
Northwest Missouri State University
Maryville, Missouri 64468

Therapeutic Recreation Program
Southeast Missouri State University
Dept. of Recreation
Cape Girardeau, Missouri 63701

Therapeutic Recreation Program
Southwest Missouri State University
Recreation & Leisure Studies
901 South National
Springfield, Missouri 65201

Therapeutic Recreation Program
University of Missouri
Dept. of Rec. & Park Admin.
Columbia, Missouri 65211

NEBRASKA

Therapeutic Recreation Program
University of Nebraska at Omaha
Rec. & Leisure Studies Program
Omaha, Nebraska 68182-0216

Therapeutic Recreation Program
Nebraska Wesleyan University
50th & St. Paul
Lincoln, Nebraska 68504

Therapeutic Recreation Program
University of Nebraska-Lincoln
Lincoln, Nebraska 68588

NEW HAMPSHIRE

Therapeutic Recreation Program
University of New Hampshire
Leisure Mgmt. & Tourism
Durham, New Hampshire 03824

NEW JERSEY

Therapeutic Recreation Program
Kean College
Urban & Outdoor Rec. Div.
Morris Avenue
Union, New Jersey 07083

Therapeutic Recreation Program
Montclair State College
Dept. Per. & Leisure Studies
Upper Montclair, New Jersey 07043

NEW MEXICO

Therapeutic Recreation Program
University of New Mexico
Albuquerque, New Mexico 87131

NEW YORK

Therapeutic Recreation Program
Ithaca College
Dept. of Rec. & Leisure Studies
Ithaca, New York 14850

Therapeutic Recreation Program
Lehman College
250 Bedford Park Boulevard West
Bronx, New York 10468-1589

Therapeutic Recreation Program
Mohawk Valley Community College
Recreation Leadership Program
1101 Sherman Drive
Utica, New York 13501

Therapeutic Recreation Program
New York University
Dept. of Recreation
New York, New York 10003

Therapeutic Recreation Program
St. Joseph's College
Recreation Dept.
Patchogue, New York 11772

Therapeutic Recreation Program
State University of New York
Dept. of Recreation & Leisure
Brockport, New York 14420

Therapeutic Recreation Program
State University of New York
P.O. Box 2000
Cortland, New York 13045

Therapeutic Recreation Program
Utica College of Syracuse
1500 Burrstone Road
Utica, New York 13502

NORTH CAROLINA

Therapeutic Recreation Program
Catawaba College
HPER Dept.
Salisbury, North Carolina 28144

Therapeutic Recreation Program
East Carolina University
Leisure Systems Studies
Greenville, North Carolina 27858-4353

Therapeutic Recreation Program
Mars Hill College
Dept. of Recreation & Leisure
Mars Hill, North Carolina 28754

Therapeutic Recreation Program
Mount Olive College
Dept. of Recreation & Leisure
Mount Olive, North Carolina 28365

Therapeutic Recreation Program
North Carolina Central University
Dept. of Physical Ed. & Recreation
Durham, North Carolina 27707

Therapeutic Recreation Program
University of North Carolina-Greensboro
Recreation & Leisure Studies
Greensboro, North Carolina 27412

Therapeutic Recreation Program
University of North Carolina-Chapel Hill
Curriculum in Leisure Studies
Chapel Hill, North Carolina 27599

Therapeutic Recreation Program
University of North Carolina-
Wilmington
HPER, Recreation & Park Mgmt.
601 South College Road
Wilmington, North Carolina 28403-3297

Therapeutic Recreation Program
Western Carolina University
Recreation Management Program
Cullowhee, North Carolina 28723

NORTH DAKOTA

Therapeutic Recreation Program
North Dakota State University-Fargo
Leisure Studies
Fargo, North Dakota 58105

Therapeutic Recreation Program
University of North Dakota
Division of Recreation
Grand Forks, North Dakota 58202

OHIO

Therapeutic Recreation Program
Ashland College
Recreational & Adaptive PE
King Road
Ashland, Ohio 44805

Therapeutic Recreation Program
Bowling Green State University
School of HPER
200 Eppler South
Bowling Green, Ohio 43403

Therapeutic Recreation Program
Central State University
Recreation Dept. of HPER
Wilberforce, Ohio 45394

Therapeutic Recreation Program
Kent State University
School of PERD
Kent, Ohio 44242

Therapeutic Recreation Program
Ohio University
HPER-Rec Studies
Athens, Ohio 45701

Therapeutic Recreation Program
University of Toledo
2801 West Bancroft Street
Toledo, Ohio 43606

OKLAHOMA

Therapeutic Recreation Program
Oklahoma State University
Dept. of Leisure Sciences
Stillwater, Oklahoma 74078

Therapeutic Recreation Program
University of Oklahoma
Rec. Admin.
Norman, Oklahoma 73019

Therapeutic Recreation Program
University of Tulsa
HPER
600 South College
Tulsa, Oklahoma 74104

OREGON

Therapeutic Recreation Program
University of Oregon
Leisure Studies & Services
Eugene, Oregon 97403

PENNSYLVANIA

Therapeutic Recreation Program
Butler County Community College
Park & Rec. Management
P.O. Box 1203
Butler, Pennsylvania 16003-1203

Therapeutic Recreation Program
East Stroudsburg University
Dept. of RLS
East Stroudsburg, Pennsylvania 18301

Therapeutic Recreation Program
Lincoln University
HPER
Lincoln, Pennsylvania 19352

Therapeutic Recreation Program
Penn State University
Dept. of Leisure Studies
University Park, Pennsylvania 16802

Therapeutic Recreation Program
Slippery Rock University
Environmental Education
Slippery Rock, Pennsylvania 16057

Therapeutic Recreation Program
Temple University
Broad & Columbia
Philadelphia, Pennsylvania 19122

Therapeutic Recreation Program
Villa Maria College
Community Rec./Rec. & LS
2551 West Eighth Street
Erie, Pennsylvania 16505

Therapeutic Recreation Program
York College of Pennsylvania
Recreation Curriculum
Country Club Road
York, Pennsylvania 17403-3426

SOUTH CAROLINA

Therapeutic Recreation Program
Benedict College
Recreation Dept.
Harden & Blanding Streets
Columbia, South Carolina 29204

Therapeutic Recreation Program
Clemson University
Parks, Rec., & Tourism Mgmt.
Clemson, South Carolina 29634-1005

SOUTH DAKOTA

Therapeutic Recreation Program
South Dakota State University
Dept. of HPER
Brookings, South Dakota 57007

Therapeutic Recreation Program
HPER
University of South Dakota
Vermillion, South Dakota 57069

TENNESSEE

Therapeutic Recreation Program
Memphis State University
HPER Department
Memphis, Tennessee 38152

Therapeutic Recreation Program
Middle Tennessee State University
Rec. & Leisure Studies
Murfreesboro, Tennessee 37132

Therapeutic Recreation Program
University of Tennessee
Dept. of HLS
1914 Andy Holt Avenue
Knoxville, Tennessee 37996-2700

TEXAS

Therapeutic Recreation Program
Texas Women's University
P.O. Box 23717
Denton, Texas 76204

Therapeutic Recreation Program
University of North Texas
Dept. of Kines., Health, & Rec.
Denton, Texas 76203

UTAH

Therapeutic Recreation Program
Brigham Young University
Dept. of Rec. Management
Provo, Utah 84602

Therapeutic Recreation Program
University of Utah
Dept. of Rec. & Leisure
Salt Lake City, Utah 84112

VERMONT

Therapeutic Recreation Program
Green Mountain College
Dept. of RLS
Poultney, Vermont 05764

VIRGINIA

Therapeutic Recreation Program
Ferrum College
Ferrum, Virginia 24088

Therapeutic Recreation Program
George Mason University
4400 University Drive
Fairfax, Virginia 22030-4444

Therapeutic Recreation Program
Longwood College
Farmville, Virginia 23901

Therapeutic Recreation Program
Old Dominion University
Dept. of HPER
Norfolk, Virginia 23529-0196

Therapeutic Recreation Program
Radford University
Dept. of RLS
Radford, Virginia 24142

Therapeutic Recreation Program
Shenandoah College & Conserv.
Dept. of PE & Rec.
Winchester, Virginia 22601

Therapeutic Recreation Program
Virginia Commonwealth University
923 West Franklin Street
Richmond, Virginia 23284-2015

Therapeutic Recreation Program
Virginia Polytechnic Institute
Rec. Program
Blacksburg, Virginia 24061

WASHINGTON

Therapeutic Recreation Program
Central Washington University
Ellensburg, Washington 98926

Therapeutic Recreation Program
Eastern Washington University
Rec. & Leisure Services
Cheney, Washington 99004

Therapeutic Recreation Program
Pacific Lutheran University
School of PE
Tacoma, Washington 98447

Therapeutic Recreation Program
Pierce College
9401 Farwest Drive SW
Tacoma, Washington 98498

Therapeutic Recreation Program
Washington State University
PE, Sport & Leisure Studies
Pullman, Washington 99164

Therapeutic Recreation Program
Western Washington University
Recreation & Parks
Bellingham, Washington 98225

WEST VIRGINIA

Therapeutic Recreation Program
Marshall University
Park Resource & Leisure Services
Huntington, West Virginia 25755

Therapeutic Recreation Program
Shepherd College
Rec. & Leisure Services
Shepherdstown, West Virginia 25443

Therapeutic Recreation Program
West Virginia State College
Dept. of HPERS
Box 434
Institute, West Virginia 25112

Therapeutic Recreation Program
West Virginia University
Forestry, Rec., & Parks Mgmt.
Morgantown, West Virginia 26506

WISCONSIN

Therapeutic Recreation Program
University of Wisconsin
P.O. Box 413
Milwaukee, Wisconsin 53201

Therapeutic Recreation Program
University of Wisconsin-Madison
Madison, Wisconsin 53706

Therapeutic Recreation Program
University of Wisconsin-LaCrosse
LaCrosse, Wisconsin 54601

Therapeutic Recreation Assistant

The *therapeutic recreation assistant* assists the therapeutic recreation specialist in carrying out recreation rehabilitation programs in hospitals and communities. The assistant usually has limited responsibilities in organizing and directing programs and more often specializes in particular activities such as athletics, dramatics, music or arts and crafts.

For training, the assistant must graduate from an associate degree program in therapeutic recreation or recreation with an option in therapeutic recreation from a community college or university.

Credentials are available to those individuals who meet the National Council for Therapeutic Recreation Certification's prerequisites. Applicants should have either 1) an associates degree in therapeutic recreation or recreation with an option in therapeutic recreation, or 2) an associates degree in recreation plus one year full-time paid experience in a therapeutic recreation setting, or 3) an associate degree from an accredited school which includes a minimum of 12 semester units or 18 quarter units from two of the following areas: adapted physical education, related biological/physical sciences, human services, psychology, sociology, special education, or creative arts; and 6 semester units or 8 quarter units of therapeutic recreation content coursework; and one year full-time paid experience in a therapeutic recreation setting, or 4) completion of a National Therapeutic Recreation Society approved 750-hour training program for therapeutic recreation paraprofessionals, or 5) four years full-time paid experience in a therapeutic recreation setting.

Salaries for therapeutic recreation assistants vary by geographic location and size and type of facility.

For more information on therapeutic recreation careers, write to the National Therapeutic Recreation Society, c/o National Recreation and Park Association, 2775 South Quincy Street, Suite 300, Arlington, Virginia 22206-2204.

Information on certification requirements can be obtained through the National Council for Therapeutic Recreation Certification, 49 South Main Street, Suite #001, Spring Valley, New York 10977.

For training programs contact community colleges and universities in your area or write to the National Therapeutic Recreation Society at the above address.

SOURCES:

National Council for Therapeutic Recreation Certification
Dictionary of Occupational Titles

✚ VISION CARE

There are many specialized fields in the medical practice of vision care, including optometry, ophthalmology, orthoptics, and opticianry. The optometrist is a doctor of optometry who examines eyes and related structures, detects visual abnormalities, and prescribes either corrective lenses or orthoptic procedures to preserve or restore maximum vision, or refers the patient to an ophthalmologist. The ophthalmologist is a medical physician who specializes in the diagnosis and treatment of all eye diseases and abnormal eye conditions. The ophthalmologist also prescribes drugs, corrective lenses, and other treatments. Both the optometrist and the ophthalmologist are professionally licensed medical practitioners and have graduated from schools of optometry and medicine, respectively.

Orthoptics is the clinical science of ocular motility, and orthoptists use visual training aids in the treatment of crossed eyes and other eye disorders. Opticianry is the science of optics; and opticians translate, fill, and adjust ophthalmic and optometric prescriptions, products, and accessories. The optician may be employed either as a dispensing optician, an ophthalmic laboratory technician, or as both.

Discussed below are the allied health careers in vision care of the *paraoptometric, (optometric assistant, optometric technician),* the *ophthalmic medical assistant,* the *orthoptist,* the *dispensing optician,* and the *ophthalmic laboratory technician.*

Paraoptometric: Optometric Assistant, Optometric Technician

The paraoptometric serves as a technical aide, under the direct supervision of an optometrist, and may be classified as either an *optometric assistant* or as a more highly trained *optometric technician.* The functions of a paraoptometric vary, but usually include several responsibilities in one or more of three general work categories: office, technical, and ophthalmic duties.

Office duties include scheduling appointments, record keeping, recording patients' case histories, preparing patients for examinations, and recording examination results. Technical duties consist of assisting the optometrist with eye testing procedures such as determining angle and width of visual field, measuring corneal curvature, and measuring intraocular pressure. The paraoptometric may also assist patients with vision training and eye coordination exercises if they suffer from focusing defects. If the optometrist dispenses corrective lenses, then the paraoptometric may also assist in facial measurement and frame selection, or in the fitting of contact lenses. The paraoptometric often provides instruction to patients on lens care procedures.

In some circumstances the paraoptometric, if sufficiently trained, may be engaged in ophthalmic duties in a laboratory, where she or he modifies conventional glasses or contact lenses, keeps an inventory of ophthalmic materials, and cleans and cares for the laboratory instruments.

In a small optometrist's practice, the paraoptometric may perform all of the above duties, whereas in a larger practice there may be specialization in either vision training, chairside assistance, office management, or laboratory or contact lens work. Most paraoptometrics are employed by optometrists in their private practices, while the remainder work in health clinics and vision care centers.

The paraoptometric may work with patients of all ages, from young children with vision or reading problems to the elderly who may require special therapeutic devices to improve declining vision.

Although most are trained on-the-job in an optometrist's office, the optometric assistant may, as an alternative, receive formal training in a one-year certificate program offered by a community college or vocational-technical school. The optometric technician, on the other hand, must complete a two-year associate degree program to gain more comprehensive training in the technical aspects of optometry. Optometric technician programs are offered at community and junior colleges, vocational-technical institutes, and through several schools of optometry.

High school graduation or its equivalent is required for acceptance into an academic or an on-the-job training program, and recommended high school subjects include courses in English, mathematics and office procedures.

Registration as a paraoptometric assistant and technician is available to those individuals who meet specific educational and/or experience requirements and successfully pass the American Optometric Association's registration examination.

Depending upon the size and the type of the optometrist's practice, geographic location, and level of education, the average paraoptometric earns from $10,000 to $20,000 or more per year.

Following is a list, supplied by the American Optometric Association, of schools that offer educational programs in paraoptometrics. Those interested in on-the-job training as an optometric assistant should contact their local or state optometric society or refer to the yellow pages of the telephone directory for potential employers who may have entry-level positions.

For additional information on registration or career opportunities as a paraoptometric, contact the American Optometric Association, 243 North Lindbergh Boulevard, St. Louis, Missouri 63141-7881.

SOURCE:

American Optometric Association

Paraoptometric Programs

ALABAMA

Paraoptometric Program
Community College of the Air Force
Allied Health Department
Maxwell, Alabama 36112

COLORADO

Paraoptometric Program
Colorado Mountain College
901 South Highway 24
Leadville, Colorado 80461

FLORIDA

Paraoptometric Program
Erwin Voc-Tech Area Center
2010 East Hillsborough Avenue
Tampa, Florida 33610

Paraoptometric Program
McFatter Voc-Tech Center
6500 Nova Drive
Davie, Florida 33317

Paraoptometric Program
Miami-Dade Community College
Vision Care Technology
950 NW 20th Street
Miami, Florida 33127

Paraoptometric Program
Traviss Technical Center
Health Occupations Education
3225 Winter Lake Road
Lakeland, Florida 33803-9709

INDIANA

Paraoptometric Program
Indiana University
School of Optometry
800 East Atwater
Bloomington, Indiana 47405

IOWA

Paraoptometric Program
North Iowa Area Community College
Health Programs Department
500 College Drive
Mason City, Iowa 50401

MICHIGAN

Paraoptometric Program
Ferris State University
College of Optometry
Big Rapids, Michigan 49307

MINNESOTA

Paraoptometric Program
St. Cloud Technical College
1540 Northway Drive
St. Cloud, Minnesota 56303

Paraoptometric Program
Southwestern Voc-Tech Institute
Highway 212 West
Granite Falls, Minnesota 56241

NEBRASKA

Paraoptometric Program
Mid-Plains Community College
Interstate 80 at Highway 83
North Platte, Nebraska 69101

OHIO

Paraoptometric Program
Owens Technical College
Oregon Road
Toledo, Ohio 43699

PUERTO RICO

Paraoptometric Program
National College Business/Technology
Allied Health Department
P.O. Box 143
Manati, Puerto Rico 00701

SOUTH CAROLINA

Paraoptometric Program
Greenville Technical College
P.O. Box 5616
Greenville, South Carolina 29606

TEXAS

Paraoptometric Program
Sheppard Air Force Base
School of the Health Care Sciences
Department of the Air Force
Sheppard AFB, Texas 76311

WASHINGTON

Paraoptometric Program
Spokane Community College
North 1810 Greene Street
Health Science Building
Spokane, Washington 99207

WISCONSIN

Paraoptometric Program
Lakeshore Technical College
1290 North Avenue
Cleveland, Wisconsin 53105

Paraoptometric Program
Madison Area Technical College
3550 Anderson Street
Madison, Wisconsin 53704

Ophthalmic Medical Assistant

The *ophthalmic medical assistant* aids and is supervised by the ophthalmologist in the diagnosis and treatment of medical and surgical eye problems. The ophthalmic medical assistant collects data necessary for the ophthalmologist to make diagnoses, and assists him or her in the care of patients.

The ophthalmic assistant performs a large number of routine technical procedures involving vision measurement tests and direct patient care. The assistant records medical histories, measures patients' visual acuity, eye movement, field of vision, color vision, intraocular pressure, corneal curvature, and also measures the power of corrective lenses. In direct patient care, the ophthalmic assistant changes eye dressings and administers eye drops. The assistant may also make adjustments and minor repairs to ophthalmic instruments and corrective lenses.

Ophthalmic medical assistants work primarily for ophthalmologists in their private practices, but they are also employed by hospitals, clinics, and university research and training centers.

Certification by the Joint Commission on Allied Health Personnel in Ophthalmology is awarded at one of three proficiency levels: assistant, technician, and technologist. Certification at each level is granted after meeting specific educational and experience requirements, sponsorship by an ophthalmologist, a current CPR (cardiopulmonary resuscitation) certificate and successful passing of a certification examination. As an example, candidates for the assistant (beginning) level must have one year of work experience and successfully complete an approved training program or an approved home study course. Different educational guidelines and amount of work experience apply with higher levels of certification.

A high school diploma or the equivalent is required to enter training in ophthalmic medical assisting. Training may be acquired through an educational program, accredited by the American Medical Association's Committee on Allied Health Education and Accreditation, which combines both academic and clinical experience. A home study course approved by the American Academy of Ophthalmology or the Canadian Ophthalmological Society is also available.

Salaries for ophthalmic medical assistants vary because of geographic location, type of employee, level of certification, and amount of work experience.

For further information on education, training, or certification as an ophthalmic medical assistant, interested persons should write to and ask for specific information from the Joint Commission on Allied Health Personnel in Ophthalmology, 2025 Woodlane Drive, St. Paul, Minnesota 55125-2995. Information on specific program requirements, length of programs, and fees should be directed to the Program Director at the schools in question.

Following is a list of training programs provided by the Joint Commission on Allied Health Personnel in Ophthalmology. The programs are accredited by the Committee on Allied Health Education and Accreditation of the American Medical Association, the Canadian Medical Association, and approved by the Joint Review Committee for Ophthalmic Medical Personnel. Home Study Courses for Ophthalmic Medical Assistants are approved by the Joint Review Committee for Ophthalmic Medical Personnel and are also listed below.

KEY:

(1)   Programs accredited by the AMA's Committee on Allied Health
        Education and Accreditation
(2)   Programs accredited by the Canadian Medical Association
(3)   Programs approved by the Joint Review Committee for Ophthalmic
        Medical Personnel
(a)   Programs for the ophthalmic medical assistant
(b)   Programs for the ophthalmic medical technician or technologist
(c)   Home Study Course

SOURCE:

Joint Commission on Allied Health Personnel in Ophthalmology

Ophthalmic Medical Assistant Programs

ARIZONA

Ophthalmic Assistant Program (3a)
Pima Medical Institute
3350 East Grant Road
Tucson, Arizona 85716

CALIFORNIA

Home Study Course for Ophthalmic
  Medical Assistants (3c)
American Academy of Ophthalmology
Box 7424
San Francisco, California 94120-7424

Ophthalmic Assistant Program (3a)
Jules Stein Eye Institute
100 Stein Plaza
Los Angeles, California 90024-1771

Ophthalmic Assistant Program (3a)
Naval School of Health Sciences
Ocular Technician School
San Diego, California 92134-6000

DISTRICT OF COLUMBIA

Ophthalmic Medical Personnel
  Program (1b,3a,)
Georgetown University Medical Center
Dept. of Ophthalmology
3800 Reservoir Road NW
Washington, DC 20007

FLORIDA

Ophthalmic Technologist Program (1b)
University of Florida
Dept. of Ophthalmology
College of Medicine
Gainesville, Florida 32610

ILLINOIS

Ophthalmic Assistant Program (3a)
The Eye Center Carbondale/Marion
1200 West De Young
Marion, Illinois 62959

Ophthalmic Technician Program (1b)
Triton College
2000 North Fifth Avenue
River Grove, Illinois 60171

LOUISIANA

Ophthalmic Assistant Program (3a)
Tulane University Medical Center
Dept. of Ophthalmology
1430 Tulane Avenue
New Orleans, Louisiana 70112

MASSACHUSETTS

Ophthalmic Medical Personnel
  Program (1b,3a)
Boston University Medical Center
80 East Concord Street
Boston, Massachusetts 02118

MICHIGAN

Ophthalmic Technology Program (1b)
Detroit Institute of Ophthalmology
15415 East Jefferson Avenue
Grosse Pointe Park, Michigan 48230

MINNESOTA

Ophthalmic Technology Program (1b)
St. Paul Ramsey Medical Center
640 Jackson Street
St. Paul, Minnesota 55101

NEW JERSEY

Ophthalmic Assistant Program (3a)
New Jersey Medical School
Dept. of Ophthalmology
90 Bergen Street
Newark, New Jersey 07103-2499

NEW YORK

Ophthalmic Assistant Program (3a)
CMEOA, Inc. with Manhattan Eye, Ear
  and Throat Hospital
46 West 86th Street
New York, New York 10024

Ophthalmic Technologist Program (1b)
New York Eye & Ear Infirmary
310 East 14th Street
New York, New York 10003

NORTH CAROLINA

Ophthalmic Technician Program (1b)
Duke University
Box 3802
Duke University Eye Center
Durham, North Carolina 27710

PUERTO RICO

Ophthalmic Technician Program (1b)
University of Puerto Rico
College of Health Related Professions
Dept. of Ophthalmology
P.O. Box 5067
San Juan, Puerto Rico 00936

TEXAS

Ophthalmic Assistant Program (3a)
Academy of Health Sciences
Medicine and Surgery Division
Ft. Sam Houston, Texas 78234-6100

VIRGINIA

Ophthalmic Technologist Program (1b)
Old Dominion University/Eastern VA
  Medical School
600 Gresham Drive
Norfolk, Virginia 23507

WEST VIRGINIA

Ophthalmic Assistant Program (3a)
Carver Career and Technical Education
  Center
4799 Midland Drive
Charleston, West Virginia 25306

Ophthalmic Assistant Program (3a)
West Virginia University
Dept. of Ophthalmology
Health Sciences Center North
Morgantown, West Virginia 26506

CANADA

Home Study Course for Ophthalmic
  Assistants (3,a,c)
Centennial College
Box 631, Station A
Scarborough, Ontario
Canada M1K 5E9

Ophthalmic Medical Technologist
  Program (2b)
5850 University Avenue
Halifax, Nova Scotia
Canada B3J 3G9

Home Study Course for Ophthalmic
  Medical Assistants (3c)
Southern Alberta Institute of Technology
1301 16th Avenue NW
Calgary, Alberta
Canada T2M 0L4

Ophthalmic Medical Technician
  Program(2b)
Stanton Yellowknife Hospital
Dept. of Ophthalmology
Box 10
Yellowknife, NWT
Canada X1A 2N1

Orthoptist

Under the supervision of an ophthalmologist the *orthoptist* is an eye muscle specialist who diagnoses and treats defects in eye coordination. The orthoptist performs diagnostic tests for visual acuity, binocular cooperation, and focusing ability, in both children and adults, and then instructs patients in the proper use of their eyes in corrective eye exercises.

Most orthoptists work for one or more ophthalmologists in their private practice or they are employed by clinics, hospitals, or medical schools. Some orthoptists do research, while others teach.

After completing 24 months of orthoptic training, students are eligible to take an exam administered by the American Orthoptic Council. With a passing score, students are then eligible to take the oral/practical section of the exam and if successfully completed, students are then awarded a certificate in orthoptics.

Following is a list of accredited training programs supplied by the American Orthoptic Council. For more information on career opportunities, training prerequisites, and certification requirements in orthoptics, interested persons should contact the American Orthoptic Council, 3914 Nakoma Road, Madison, Wisconsin 53711.

SOURCE:

American Orthoptic Council

Orthoptist Programs

FLORIDA

Orthoptist Program
University of Florida
Shands Hospital
Gainesville, Florida 32610

IOWA

Orthoptist Program
University of Iowa Hospitals
Dept. of Ophthalmology
Iowa City, Iowa 52242

MARYLAND

Orthoptist Program
Johns Hopkins Hospital
Wilmer Institute
Baltimore, Maryland 21205

MICHIGAN

Orthoptist Program
University of Michigan
W.K. Kellogg Eye Center
1000 Wall Street
Ann Arbor, Michigan 48105

MINNESOTA

Orthoptist Program
University of Minnesota
Dept. of Ophthalmology
516 Delaware Street SE
Minneapolis, Minnesota 55455

NEW YORK

Orthoptist Program
New York Eye & Ear Infirmary
Allied Health School in Ophthalmology
  Orthoptics
310 East 14th Street
New York, New York 10003

TEXAS

Orthoptist Program
University of Texas Med School at
  Houston
6411 Fannin
Houston, Texas 77030-1697

WISCONSIN

Orthoptist Program
University of Wisconsin Hospital
2880 University Avenue
Madison, Wisconsin 53705

CANADA

Orthoptist Program
IWK Hospital for Children
5850 University Avenue
P.O. Box 3070
Halifax, Nova Scotia
Canada B3J 3G9

Orthoptist Program
Hospital for Sick Children
555 University Avenue
Toronto, Ontario
Canada M5G 1X8

Orthoptist Program
University Hospital
Dept. of Ophthalmology
Royal University Hospital
Saskatoon, Saskatchewan
Canada S7N 4J9

Dispensing Optician

Also known as an *ophthalmic dispenser,* the dispensing optician supplies, adapts, and fits eyeglasses and/or contact lenses prescribed by ophthalmologists and optometrists. The dispensing optician does not examine eyes or prescribe corrective lenses.

Upon receipt of the prescription for eyeglasses, the dispensing optician measures the client's facial contours and assists the client in lens and frame selection. The dispenser then either writes a work order for an ophthalmic laboratory to grind the lenses, or does the grinding himself. After the lenses are ground and inserted into the frames, the dispensing optician adjusts the frames and fits them properly and comfortably onto the client's face. The dispensing optician also provides follow up care, in the event eyeglass frame readjustment or repair is needed.

In the fitting of contact lenses, which requires considerably more expertise, the dispensing optician measures the curvature of the client's corneas (the front transparent part of the eye over which the contact lenses will fit) with a special instrument, and then prepares the appropriate specifications for the contact lens manufacturer. The optician instructs the client on how to insert, remove, and care for the contact lenses.

Most dispensing opticians are employed in retail optical shops, while the remainder may own their own shops, own a franchise from a large optical chain, work for ophthalmologists or optometrists, or are employed by ophthalmic goods manufacturers or wholesalers. A dispensing optician may be employed to only supply corrective lenses, or may be trained as an ophthalmic laboratory technician, a contact lens fitter, or ocularist, (one who makes and fits artificial eyes).

The two methods of becoming trained as a dispensing optician are on-the-job training apprenticeships and formal optician educational programs. These are offered by community colleges, vocational-technical schools, and the Armed Forces. Apprenticeships last two to four years, and include training in math, drafting, psychology, physiology, business law, accounting, and mechanical optics. Formal dispensing programs offered by schools are twenty-four months in length and award associate degrees upon graduation.

Currently, twenty-one states require that their practicing dispensing opticians be licensed. Licensure information is available from the state's licensing division, located in the state capitol. Certification examinations are available in dispensing opticianry and contact lens-fitting, from the American Board of Opticianry/National Contact Lens Examiners, 10341 Democracy Lane, Fairfax, Virginia 122030-8010.

Recommended high school courses for those students interested in a career in opticianry include physics, algebra, geometry, anatomy, and mechanical drawing.

Earnings for dispensing opticians vary with skill, specialty, and geographic location. According to a 1991 survey by the Opticians Association of America, entry level apprentices averaged $12,800 and entry level licensed certified opticians averaged $21,000 a year. Earnings for dispensing opticians who run their own business ranged from $25,000 to $50,000 or more a year.

Following is a list, supplied by the Opticians Association of America, of accredited educational programs in ophthalmic dispensing. Persons interested in further information on career opportunities in opticianry should contact the Opticians Association of America, 10341 Democracy Lane, P.O. Box 10110, Fairfax, Virginia 22030-2521. Persons interested in potential dispensing opticianry apprenticeships in their area should contact the state licensing board, their state opticianry association, or employer if currently employed in the opticianry field.

SOURCES:

American Board of Opticianry/National Contact Lens Examiners
Opticians Association of America
Occupational Outlook Handbook

Ophthalmic Dispensing Program

ARIZONA

Ophthalmic Dispensing Program
Pima Community College
2202 West Anklam Road
Tucson, Arizona 85709-0001

FLORIDA

Ophthalmic Dispensing Program
Hillsborough Community College
P.O. Box 30030
Tampa, Florida 33630

Ophthalmic Dispensing Program
Miami-Dade Community College
950 NW 20th Street
Miami, Florida 33127

GEORGIA

Ophthalmic Dispensing Program
Dekalb Technical Institute
495 North Indian Creek Drive
Clarkston, Georgia 30021

MASSACHUSETTS

Ophthalmic Dispensing Program
Newbury College
129 Fisher Avenue
Brookline, Massachusetts 02146-5796

MICHIGAN

Ophthalmic Dispensing Program
Ferris State University
Big Rapids, Michigan 49307

NORTH CAROLINA

Ophthalmic Dispensing Program
Durham Technical Community College
1637 Lawason Street
Durham, North Carolina 27703

NEW JERSEY

Ophthalmic Dispensing Program
Camden County College
P.O. Box 200
Blackwood, New Jersey 08012

Ophthalmic Dispensing Program
Essex County College
303 University Avenue
Newark, New Jersey 07102

NEW YORK

Ophthalmic Dispensing Program
Erie Community College
6205 Main Street
Williamsville, New York 14221-7095

Ophthalmic Dispensing Program
Interboro Institute
450 West 56th Street
New York, New York 10019

Ophthalmic Dispensing Program
Mater Dei College
Riverside Drive
Ogdensburg, New York 13669

Ophthalmic Dispensing Program
New York City Technical College
300 Jay Street
Brooklyn, New York 11201

OHIO

Ophthalmic Dispensing Program
Cuyahoga Community College
2900 Community College Avenue
Cleveland, Ohio 44115

TEXAS

Ophthalmic Dispensing Program
El Paso Community College
P.O. Box 20500
El Paso, Texas 79998

VIRGINIA

Ophthalmic Dispensing Program
J. Sargeant Reynolds Community
 College
P.O. Box C-32040
Richmond, Virginia 23261

Ophthalmic Dispensing Program
Naval Ophthalmic Support & Training
 Activity
Thomas Nelson Community College
Dept. of Navy/NOSTRA
Yorktown, Virginia 23691-5071

WASHINGTON

Ophthalmic Dispensing Program
Seattle Central Community College
1701 Broadway
Seattle, Washington 98122

Ophthalmic Laboratory Technician

Also called an *optical mechanic,* the ophthalmic laboratory technician grinds and polishes eyeglass lenses according to the specifications of a prescription, and then inserts the lenses into frames. The technician may also be trained to become a contact lens fitter and/or a dispensing optician.

Formal training programs for the ophthalmic laboratory technician, one year in length, are offered by community colleges and vocational technical schools. Further information on training in the ophthalmic laboratory may be obtained from the Opticians Association of America, 10341 Democracy Lane, P.O. Box 10110, Fairfax, Virginia 22030.

According to data from the *Occupational Outlook Handbook,* the annual salary for most ophthalmic laboratory technicians in 1991 ranged from $12,000 to $17,000.

Following is a list, supplied by the Opticians Association of America, of Ophthalmic Laboratory Technology programs. Persons interested in further information on career opportunities in opticianry should contact the Opticians Association of America, 10341 Democracy Lane, P.O. Box 10110, Fairfax, Virginia 22030-2521.

SOURCES:

National Academy of Opticianry
Opticians Association of America
Occupational Outlook Handbook

Ophthalmic Laboratory Technology Programs

FLORIDA

Ophthalmic Laboratory Technology
  Program
Pinellas Technical Education Centers
901 34th Street South
St. Petersburg, Florida 33711

MINNESOTA

Ophthalmic Laboratory Technology
  Program
Anoka Technical College
1335 West Main Street
Anoka, Minnesota 55303

Ophthalmic Laboratory Technology
  Program
Eveleth Technical College
Highway 53
Eveleth, Minnesota 55734

NEW YORK

Ophthalmic Laboratory Technology
  Program
National Technical Institute for the Deaf
Rochester Institute of Technology
One Lomb Memorial Drive, #1255
Rochester, New York 14623-0887

PUERTO RICO

Ophthalmic Laboratory Technology
  Program
International Institute of Technology
Avenue Ponce de Leon, #703
Hato Rey, Puerto Rico 00917

VIRGINIA

Ophthalmic Laboratory Technology
  Program
Naval Ophthalmic Support & Training
  Activity
Dept. of Navy/NOSTRA
Yorktown, Virginia 23691-5071

✚ OTHER CAREERS WITHIN THE HEALTHCARE FACILITY

In hospitals and other healthcare facilities there are many clerical and staff positions that do not require specific health-related education or training. For example, in many hospital administrative, and physical plant departments there are jobs and careers at all levels - from clerk and secretary, to technician and engineer, to administrative assistant and unit manager that require no formal medical or health education. Thus in finance, business, communications, information management, human resources, public relations, patient admissions, purchasing, housekeeping, volunteer services, central services, and security and maintenance, a general educational background ranging from a high school education to vocational training to a bachelor's degree in social sciences or business may very well be sufficient training for certain job responsibilities.

For information on career opportunities in these fields, interested students should talk with Directors of Human Resources at area healthcare facilities, instructors at postsecondary institutions and with individuals currently employed in the healthcare field.

One other way to learn more about careers in healthcare administration is through membership in professional organizations. Members, through newsletters and other publications, are kept abreast of healthcare issues and can share ideas and expertise with other professionals in their field. Often these organizations offer student and affiliate memberships. The American Hospital Association offers several personal membership groups to professionals in the health fields of volunteer services, healthcare education and training, social work, hospital engineering, hospital risk management, marketing, personnel administration, information management, patient representation, ambulatory care, central service, and materials management. For information on the Personal Membership Groups, write to The American Hospital Association, 840 North Lake Shore Drive, Chicago, Illinois 60611.

539

Central Service Technician

Working in a hospital's Central Service Department, the *central Service technician's* primary responsibility is the cleaning and sterilizing of medical supplies, instruments, and equipment, according to prescribed procedures and techniques. Usually working under minimal supervision of the director of central service, who is usually a registered nurse, the technician receives or collects contaminated surgical instruments, gloves, containers, treatment trays, syringes, and other supplies and equipment from operating rooms, patient wards, emergency units, outpatient departments, and laboratories. He or she either disinfects these items with antiseptic solutions or gases, or sterilizes them in steam autoclaves or in similar equipment. The technician then stores the items or distributes them to their appropriate hospital unit or department.

The central service technician also assembles, labels, and seals sterile and nonsterile treatment and dressing trays or packs including blood transfusion sets, surgical trays, intravenous infusion sets, and obstetrical packs.

The minimum educational requirement for central service technicians is a high school diploma or the equivalent. Some employers may offer a three to six month on-the-job training program. Other educational programs are offered by community and vocational-technical colleges. In order to become a certified central service technician, applicants must have been employed one year in a central supply department or successfully complete courses in central service technology offered by some vocational-technical schools.

For additional information on career opportunities in central service technology, interested persons should contact the Personnel Director of their local hospital or the American Society for Healthcare Central Service Personnel of the American Hospital Association, 804 North Lake Shore Drive, Chicago, Illinois 60611.

SOURCE:

Dictionary of Occupational Titles
American Society for Healthcare Central Service Personnel of the American Hospital Association

---

Hospital Admitting Officer

In a hospital the *admitting officer* arranges the admission and discharge of patients in accordance with physicians' requests, hospital policies, and the availability of facilities in the hospital. She or he interviews the patient or the patient's relatives for biographical data and financial data and explains hospital services, charges, insurance coverages, and payment procedures. The admitting officer also notifies the appropriate ward and hospital department of the patient's admittance. Other duties may include the supervising and the training of assistant admitting officers and admitting clerks in a large healthcare facility. In a small healthcare facility, the admitting officer may work alone in the admitting office but also carry out certain duties in the credit department.

A bachelor's degree plus some on-the-job training is the usual educational requirement for the position of admitting officer. One to two years experience working in a healthcare facility or social agency is also required by some hospitals for employment.

Salaries for admitting officers vary depending upon experience and the size and location of the facility.

For additional information on career opportunities and training as an admitting officer, an assistant admitting officer, or as an admitting clerk, interested persons should contact the Personnel Director of their local hospital.

SOURCES:

Dictionary of Occupational Titles
Occupational Outlook Handbook

Ward Clerk

The *ward clerk* assists the unit's nursing staff by performing a variety of clerical tasks that ensure the efficient operation of the nursing unit. The ward clerk provides services both for the patients and also for the management of the hospital. These services can be divided into four categories: reception, communication, clerical, and safety.

Receptionist duties include receiving new patients, directing visitors, and providing patient information to physicians, nurses, and other medical staff upon request. Communication duties include answering the phone, answering patient requests on the intercom system, and delivering mail and messages for patients. With a certain degree of knowledge of medical terminology the ward clerk also can operate hospital communication systems and help to coordinate the activities of medical personnel on the ward. The ward clerk's clerical duties include transcribing physicians' orders, copying and compiling data on patients' charts, and scheduling tests and other appointments for patients. She or he also maintains essential records for the operation of the nursing unit such as recording hours worked and absenteeism of unit personnel, filing records and reports, verifying stock inventory, and requesting additional supplies and equipment when shortages occur. Finally, the clerk's responsibilities for ward safety include helping keep work areas clean, eliminating potential accident hazards, and making emergency code calls when required.

Training requirements for the position of ward clerk vary amongst hospitals. Some hospitals tend to employ candidates who have graduated from a formal educational course in ward clerk skills, while others may only require knowledge of medical terminology and data entry skills. Some on-the-job training may also be offered.

Recommended high school courses for students who are looking into a career as a ward clerk include English, secretarial skills, and mathematics.

Persons interested in career opportunities and training as a ward clerk should contact the Personnel Director of their local hospital.

SOURCES:

Dictionary of Occupational Titles
Occupational Outlook Handbook

Further Reading

Alperin, Stanley, *Careers in Nursing*, Ballinger Publishing Company, 1981.

American Medical Association, *Allied Health Education Directory*.

Anderson, Lynn, *Exploring Careers in Library Science*, The Rosen Publishing Group, 1985.

Ashley, Martin, *Massage a Career at Your Fingertips*, Station Hill Press, 1992.

Bacotti, Joseph L., *Opportunities in Opticianry*, VGM Career Horizons, 1983.

Basta, Nicholas, *Opportunities in Engineering Careers*, VGM Career Horizons, 1990.

Baxter, Neal, *Opportunities in Counseling and Development*, National Textbook Company, 1990.

Bioengineering Education Directory, Quest Publishing Company.

Brown, Margaret F., *Careers in Occupational Therapy*, The Rosen Publishing Group, 1989.

Caldwell, Carol Coles, *Opportunities in Nutrition Careers*, VGM Career Horizons, 1992.

Cardoza, Anne de Sola, *Opportunities in Homecare Services Careers*, VGM Career Horizons, 1993.

Centron, Marvin J., and Marcia Appel, *Jobs of the Future*, McGraw-Hill Book Company, 1984.

Davis, Audrey B., *Medicine and its Technology*, Greenwood Press, 1981.

Doucet, Lorraine D., *Medical Technology Review*, J.B. Lippencott Company, 1981.

Farr, J. Michael, *50 Fastest Growing Jobs*, Jist Works, Inc., 1991.

Field, Shelly, *100 Best Careers for the Year 2000*, Prentice Hall, 1992.

Frederickson, Keville, *Opportunities in Nursing Careers*, VGM Career Horizons, 1989,

Gordon, Susan and Kristin Hohenadel, *Careers Without College: Healthcare*, Peterson's, 1992.

Harkavy, Michael, *101 Careers A Guide to the Fastest-Growing Opportunities*, John Wiley & Sons, Inc., 1990.

Heitzmann, Ray, Ph.D., *Opportunities in Sports Medicine Careers*, VGM Career Horizons, 1991.

Helm, Kathleen and Peggy Sullivan, *Opportunities in Library and Information Science*, VGM Career Horizons, 1986.

High Technology Careers: A Guide for Counselors, The Center for Occupational Research and Development, 1984.

Hollis, Joseph and Richard Wantz, *Counselor Preparation: Programs, Personnel, Trends*, Accelerated Development, Inc.

Kane, June Kozak, *Exploring Careers in Dietetics and Nutrition*, The Rosen Publishing Group, 1987.

Kendall, Bonnie, *Opportunities in Dental Care Careers*, VGM Career Horizons, 1991.

Kinsinger, *Education for Health Technicians*, American Association of Junior Colleges.

Kitchell, Frank M., O.D., *Opportunities in Optometry*, VGM Career Horizons, 1982.

Kleiman, Carol, *100 Best Jobs for the 1990's and Beyond*, Dearborn Financial Publishing, Inc., 1992.

Lederman, Ellen, *Health Career Planning A Realistic Guide*, Human Sciences Press, 1988.

Peterson's Guide to Graduate Programs in Engineering and Applied Sciences, Peterson's Guides.

Petras, Kathryn, and Ross Petras, *Jobs '93*, Simon & Shuster, 1993.

Pickett, George E., M.D., and Terry W. Pickett, *Opportunities in Public Health Careers*, VGM Career Horizons, 1988.

Savage, Kathleen M., and Annette Novallo, eds. *Professional Careers Sourcebook*, Gale Research Inc., 1992.

Savage, Kathleen M., and Karen Hill, eds. *Vocational Careers Sourcebook*, Gale Research Inc., 1992.

Schmolling, Paul, William R. Burger, and Merrill Youkeles, *Careers in Mental Health: A Guide to Helping Occupations*, 1986.

Sigel, Lois S., *New Careers in Hospitals*, The Rosen Publishing Group, 1990.

Sigel, Lois Savitch, *Exploring Careers in Public and Community Health*, The Rosen Publishing Group, 1984.

Snelling, Robert O. and Anne M. Snelling, *Jobs! What They Are...Where They Are... What They Pay*, Simon and Schuster, 1992.

Swanson, Barbara M., *Careers in Health Care*, VGM Career Horizons, 1992.

U.S. Department of Labor, *Dictionary of Occupational Titles*.

U.S. Department of Labor, *Occupational Outlook Handbook*.

Vacc, Nicholas and Larry Loesch, *Counseling as a profession*, Accelerated Development, Inc.

Appendix A: State Departments of Public Health

ALABAMA

Department of Public Health
434 Monroe Street
Montgomery, Alabama 36130-1701

ALASKA

Department of Health & Social Services
P.O. Box H
Juneau, Alaska 99811-0610

ARIZONA

Department of Health Services
1740 West Adams Street
Phoenix, Arizona 85007

ARKANSAS

Department of Health
4815 West Markham Street
Little Rock, Arkansas 72201

CALIFORNIA

Department of Health Services
714 "P" Street
Sacramento, California 95814

COLORADO

Colorado Department of Health
4300 Cherry Creek Drive South
Denver, Colorado 80222-1530

CONNECTICUT

Department of Health Services
150 Washington Street
Hartford, Connecticut 06106

DELAWARE

Department of Health & Social Services
P.O. Box 637
Dover, Delaware 19903

DISTRICT OF COLUMBIA

Department of Human Services
1660 "L" Street NW
Washington, DC 20036

FLORIDA

Department of Health
1323 Winewood Boulevard
Tallahassee, Florida 32399-0700

GEORGIA

Division of Public Health
878 Peachtree Street NE, Suite 201
Atlanta, Georgia 30309

HAWAII

Department of Health
1250 Punchbowl Street
P.O. Box 3378
Honolulu, Hawaii 96801

IDAHO

Department of Health & Welfare
450 West State Street
Boise, Idaho 83720

ILLINOIS

Department of Public Health
535 West Jefferson Street
Springfield, Illinois 62761

INDIANA

State Board of Health
1330 West Michigan Street
Indianapolis, Indiana 46206-1964

IOWA

Department of Public Health
Lucas State Office Building
Des Moines, Iowa 50319-0075

KANSAS

Department of Health and Environment
900 SW Jackson
Topeka, Kansas 66612-1290

KENTUCKY

Cabinet for Human Resources
275 East Main Street
Frankfort, Kentucky 40621

LOUISIANA

Department of Health & Human
Resources
325 Loyola Avenue
P.O. Box 60630
New Orleans, Louisiana 70160

MAINE

Department of Human Services
Statehouse Station #11
Augusta, Maine 04333

MARYLAND

Department of Health & Mental Hygiene
201 West Preston Street
Baltimore, Maryland 21201

MASSACHUSETTS

Executive Office of Human Services
150 Tremont Street
Boston, Massachusetts 02111

MICHIGAN

Department of Public Health
P.O. Box 30195
Lansing, Michigan 48909

MINNESOTA

Minnesota Department of Health
717 Delaware Street SE
Minneapolis, Minnesota 55440

MISSISSIPPI

State Department of Health
P.O. Box 1700
Jackson, Mississippi 39215-1700

MISSOURI

Department of Health
P.O. Box 570
1738 East Elm Street
Jefferson, Missouri 65102

MONTANA

Department of Health & Environmental
Sciences
Cogswell Building
Helena, Montana 59620

NEBRASKA

Department of Health
301 Centennial Mall South
Lincoln, Nebraska 68509

NEVADA

Division of Health
505 East King Street
Carson City, Nevada 89710

NEW HAMPSHIRE

Department of Health & Human
Services
Six Hazen Drive
Concord, New Hampshire 03301-6527

NEW JERSEY

Department of Health
Health & Agriculture Building
Trenton, New Jersey 08625

NEW MEXICO

Department of Health
1190 St. Francis Drive
Santa Fe, New Mexico 87503

NEW YORK

Department of Health
Corning Tower Building
Albany, New York 12237

NORTH CAROLINA

Department of Env Hlth & Natural Res
P.O. Box 27687
Raleigh, North Carolina 27611-7687

NORTH DAKOTA

State Department of Health
State Capital, Judicial Wing, 2nd Floor
Bismarck, North Dakota 58505

OHIO

Department of Health
246 North High Street
Columbus, Ohio 43266-0588

OKLAHOMA

State Department of Health
P.O. Box 53551
Oklahoma City, Oklahoma 73152

OREGON

Health Division
800 NE Oregon Street, #21
Portland, Oregon 97232

PENNSYLVANIA

Department of Health
P.O. Box 90
Harrisburg, Pennsylvania 17108

PUERTO RICO

Puerto Rico Department of Health
Building A, Call Box 70184
San Juan, Puerto Rico 00936

RHODE ISLAND

Department of Health
Cannon Building
Three Capitol Hill
Providence, Rhode Island 02908-5097

SOUTH CAROLINA

Dept. of Health & Environmental
Control
2600 Bull Street
Columbia, South Carolina 29201

SOUTH DAKOTA

State Department of Health
523 East Capitol
Pierre, South Dakota 57501-3182

TENNESSEE

Department of Health & Environment
344 Cordell Hull Building
Nashville, Tennessee 37219

TEXAS

Department of Health
1100 West 49th Street
Austin, Texas 78756

UTAH

Department of Health
P.O. Box 16700
Salt Lake City, Utah 84116-0700

VERMONT

Department of Health
60 Main Street
P.O. Box 70
Burlington, Vermont 05402

VIRGINIA

State Health Department
109 Governor Street
P.O. Box 2448
Richmond, Virginia 23218

WASHINGTON

Dept. of Social & Health Services
Mail Stop ET-21
Olympia, Washington 98504

WEST VIRGINIA

Department of Health
1900 Kanawha Boulevard, #519
Charleston, West Virginia 25305

WISCONSIN

Division of Health
One West Wilson Street
P.O. Box 309
Madison, Wisconsin 53701-0309

WYOMING

Department of Health
117 Hathaway Building
Cheyenne, Wyoming 82002

Appendix B: List of Associations

American Academy of Physician
  Assistants
950 North Washington Street
Alexandria, Virginia 22314-1552

American Art Therapy Association
1202 Allanson Road
Mundelein, Illinois 60060

American Association for Medical
  Transcription
P.O. Box 576187
Modesto, California 95357

American Association for Music
  Therapy
P.O. Box 80012
Valley Forge, Pennsylvania 19484

American Association for Respiratory
  Care
11030 Ables Lane
Dallas, Texas 75229

American Association of Blood Banks
8101 Glenbrook Road
Bethesda, Maryland 20814-2749

American Association of Dental
  Examiners
211 East Chicago Avenue
Chicago, Illinois 60611

American Association of Legal Nurse
  Consultants
P.O. Box 3616
Phoenix, Arizona 85030-3616

American Association of Medical
  Assistants
20 North Wacker Drive, Suite 1575
Chicago, Illinois 60606

American Association of Nurse
  Anesthetists
216 West Higgins Road
Park Ridge, Illinois 60068

American Association of Occupational
  Health Nurses
50 Lenox Pointe
Atlanta, Georgia 30324

American Association of Surgeon
  Assistants
1730 North Lynn Street, Suite 502
Arlington, Virginia 22209

American Athletic Trainers Association
  and Certification Board
660 West Duarte Road
Arcadia, California 91007

American Board for Certification in
  Orthotics and Prosthetics
1650 King Street, Suite 500
Alexandria, Virginia 22314-2747

American Board of Industrial Hygiene
4600 West Saginaw, Suite 101
Lansing, Michigan 48917-2737

American Board of Opticianry/National
  Contact Lens Examiners
10341 Democracy Lane
Fairfax, Virginia 22030-8010

American Board of Registration of
  Electroencephalographic Technologist's
P.O. Box 11434
Norfolk, Virginia 23517

American College of Cardiology
9111 Old Georgetown Road
Bethesda, Maryland 20814-1699

American College of Health Executives
840 North Lake Shore Drive
Chicago, Illinois 60611

American College of Nurse-Midwives
1522 K Street NW
Washington, DC 20005

American College of Obstetrics and
 Gynecologists
409 Twelfth Street SW
Washington, DC 20024-2191

American Counseling Association
5999 Stevenson Avenue
Alexandria, Virginia 22304-3300

American Counseling Association
5999 Stevenson Avenue
Alexandria, Virginia 22304-3300

American Counseling Association
5999 Stevenson Avenue
Alexandria, Virginia 22304-3300

American Dance Therapy Association
2000 Centura Plaza, Suite 108
Columbia, Maryland 21044

American Dental Assistants Association
919 North Michigan Avenue
Chicago, Illinois 60611-1682

American Dental Association
211 East Chicago Avenue
Chicago, Illinois 60611

American Dental Hygienists' Association
 for Oral Health
444 North Michigan Avenue, Suite 3400
Chicago, Illinois 60611

American Dietetic Association
216 West Jackson, Suite 800
Chicago, Illinois 60606

American Foundation for the Blind
15 West 16th Street
New York, New York 10011

American Fund for Dental Health
211 East Chicago Avenue
Chicago, Illinois 60611

American Health Information
 Management Association
919 North Michigan Avenue, Suite 1400
Chicago, Illinois 60611-1683

American Industrial Hygiene Foundation
2700 Prosperity Avenue, Suite 250
Fairfax, Virginia 22031

American Kinesiotherapy Association
P.O. Box 611
Wright Brothers Station
Dayton, Ohio 45409-0611

American Library Association
50 East Huron Street
Chicago, Illinois 60611

American Massage Therapy Association
820 Davis Street, Suite 100
Evanston, Illinois 60201-4444

American Medical Association
515 North State Street
Chicago, Illinois 60610

American Medical Record Association
875 North Michigan Avenue, Suite 1850
Chicago, Illinois 60611

American Medical Technologists
710 Higgins Road
Park Ridge, Illinois 60068

American Medical Writer's Association
9650 Rockville Pike
Bethesda, Maryland 20814

American Nurses' Association
9 Jay Gould Court
P.O. Box 2244
Waldorf, Maryland 20602

American Occupational Therapy
  Association
1383 Piccard Drive
P.O. Box 1725
Rockville, Maryland 20849-1725

American Optometric Association
243 North Lindbergh Avenue
St. Louis, Missouri 63141-7881

American Orthoptic Council
3914 Nakoma Road
Madison, Wisconsin 53711

American Physical Therapy Association
1111 North Fairfax Street
Alexandria, Virginia 22314

American Psychiatric Association
1400 "K" Street NW
Washington, DC 20005

American Public Health Association
1015 15th Street NW
Washington, DC 20005

American Registry of Diagnostic
  Medical Sonographers
2368 Victory Parkway, Suite 510
Cincinnati, Ohio 45206

American Registry of Radiologic
  Technologists
1255 Northland Drive
Mendota Heights, Minnesota 55120

American School Health Association
7263 State Route 43
P.O. Box 708
Kent, Ohio 44240-0708

American Society for Healthcare Central
  Service Personnel of the American
  Hospital Association
840 North Lake Shore Drive
Chicago, Illinois 60611

American Society of Clinical
  Pathologists
2100 West Harrison Street
Chicago, Illinois 60612-3798

American Society of Cytology
1015 Chestnut Street, Suite 1518
Philadelphia, Pennsylvania 19107

American Society of
  Electroneurodiagnostic Technologists
204 West Seventh
Carroll, Iowa 51401

American Society of Radiologic
  Technologists
15000 Central Avenue, SE
Albuquerque, New Mexico 87123-3909

American Society of Safety Engineers
1800 East Oakton Street
Des Plaines, Illinois 60018-2187

American Therapeutic Recreation
  Association
P.O. Box 15215
Hattiesburg, Mississippi 39404-5215

American Veterinary Medical
  Association
1930 North Meacham Road, Suite 100
Schaumburg, Illinois 60173-4360

Association for Education and
  Rehabilitation of the Blind and
Visually Impaired
206 North Washington Street, Suite 320
Alexandria, Virginia 22314

Association for the Advancement of
Health Education
1900 Association Drive
Reston, Virginia 22091

Association for the Advancement of
Medical Instrumentation
3330 Washington Boulevard, Suite 400
Arlington, Virginia 22201-4598

Association of Medical Illustrators
1931 North Meacham Road, Suite 100
Schaumburg, Illinois 60173-4360

Association of Physician Assistants
950 North Washington Street
Alexandria, Virginia 22314

Association of Schools of Public Health
1015 15th Street NW, Suite 404
Washington, DC 20005

Association of Surgical Technologists
7108-CS. Alton Way
Englewood, Colorado 80112

Association of University Programs in
Health Administration
1911 North Fort Myer Drive, Suite 503
Arlington, Virginia 22209

Biological Photographic Association
115 Stoneridge Drive
Chapel Hill, North Carolina 27514

Biomedical Engineering Society
P.O. Box 2399
Culver City, California 90231

Broadcast Education Association
1771 "N" Street NW
Washington, DC 20036

Cardiovascular Credentialing
International
P.O. Box 611
Wright Brothers Station
Dayton, Ohio 45409-0611

Centers for Disease Control - National
AIDS Information Clearinghouse
P.O. Box 6003
Rockville, Maryland 20850

Commission on Graduates of Foreign
Nursing Schools
3600 Market Street, Suite 400
Philadelphia, Pennsylvania 19104-2651

Council on Education for Public Health
1015 Fifteenth Street NW, Suite 403
Washington, DC 20005

Dental Assisting National Board
216 East Ontario Street
Chicago, Illinois 60611

Dietary Managers Association
One Pierce Place, Suite 1220W
Itasca, Illinois 60143-3111

Emergency Nurses Association
230 East Ohio Street, Suite 600
Chicago, Illinois 60611-3297

Foundation for Hospice and Home Care
519 "C" Street NE
Washington, DC 20002-5809

Health Sciences Communications
Association
6728 Old McLean Village Drive
McLean, Virginia 22101

Institute of Food Technologists
221 North LaSalle Street
Chicago, Illinois 60601

Institute of Laboratory Animal
Resources
2101 Constitution Avenue, NW
Washington, DC 20418

International Association for Healthcare
Security and Safety
P.O. Box 637
Lombard, Illinois 60148

International Society for Clinical
Laboratory Technology
818 Olive Street, Suite 918
St. Louis, Missouri 63101-1598

Joint Commission on Allied Health
Personnel in Ophthalmology
2025 Woodlane Drive
St. Paul, Minnesota 55125-2995

Joint Review Committee for Respiratory
Therapy Education
1701 West Euless Boulevard, Suite 300
Euless, Texas 76040

Joint Review Committee on Educational
Programs in Nuclear Medicine
Technology
1144 West 3300 South
Salt Lake City, Utah 84119-3330

Junior Engineering Technical Society
1420 King Street, Suite 405
Alexandria, Virginia 22314-2715

Medical Library Association
Six North Michigan Avenue, Suite 300
Chicago, Illinois 60602-4805

National Association for Drama Therapy
19 Edwards Street
New Haven, Connecticut 06511

National Association for Music Therapy
8455 Colesville Road, Suite 930
Silver Spring, Maryland 20910

National Association for Poetry Therapy
225 Williams Street
Huron, Ohio 44839

National Association of Alcoholism and
Drug Abuse Counselors
3717 Columbia Pike, Suite 300
Arlington, Virginia 22204-4254

National Association of Childbirth
Assistants
P.O. Box 12037
Santa Rosa, California 95123

National Association of Dental
Laboratories
3801 Mt. Vernon Avenue
Alexandria, Virginia 22305-2491

National Association of Emergency
Medical Technicians
9140 Ward Parkway
Kansas City, Missouri 64114

National Association of Social Workers
750 First Street NE, Suite 700
Washington, DC 20002-4241

National Athletic Trainers Association
P.O. Box 911721
Dallas, Texas 75391-1721

National Board for Respiratory Care
8310 Nieman Road
Lenexa, Kansas 66214

National Council for Therapeutic
Recreation Certification
49 South Main Street, Suite 001
Spring Valley, New York 10977

National Environmental Health
Association
720 South Colorado Boulevard
Suite 970
South Tower
Denver, Colorado 80222

National Executive Housekeepers
Association
1001 Eastwind Drive, Suite 301
Westerville, Ohio 43081

National Federation of Licensed
Practical Nurses
P.O. Box 18088
Raleigh, North Carolina 27619

National Institute for Occupational
  Safety and Health
Robert A. Taft Laboratories
4676 Columbia Parkway
Cincinnati, Ohio 45226-1998

National League for Nursing
350 Hudson Street
New York, New York 10014

National Mental Health Association
1021 Prince Street
Alexandria, Virginia 22314-2971

National Registry of Emergency
  Medical Technicians
P.O. Box 29233
Columbus, Ohio 43229

National Rehabilitation Counseling
  Association
633 South Washington Street
Alexandria, Virginia 22314

National Society for Patient
  Representation and Consumer Affairs
840 North Lake Shore Drive
Chicago, Illinois 60611

National Therapeutic Recreation Society
2775 South Quincy Street, Suite 300
Arlington, Virginia 22206-2204

National Commission on Certification of
  Physician Assistants
2845 Henderson Mill Road NE
Atlanta, Georgia 30341

Nurses Association of the American
  College of Obstetrics and
Gynecologists
409 Twelfth Street SW
Washington, DC 20024-2191

Oncology Nursing Society
501 Holiday Drive
Pittsburgh, Pennsylvania 15220-2749

Optician's Association of America
10341 Democracy Lane
P.O. Box 10110
Fairfax, Virginia 22030

Society of Diagnostic Medical
  Sonographers
12770 Coit Road, Suite 508
Dallas, Texas 75251

Society of Vascular Technology
1101 Connecticut Avenue NW
Suite 700
Washington, DC 20036-4303